THE C
Part II

ETHIOPIA
TRANSFORMATION AND CONFLICT

*The History of the Ethiopian People's
Revolutionary Party*

Kiflu Tadesse

University Press of America,® Inc.
Lanham • New York • Oxford

Copyright © 1998
University Press of America,® Inc.
4720 Boston Way
Lanham, Maryland 20706

12 Hid's Copse Rd.
Cummor Hill, Oxford OX2 9JJ

All rights reserved
Printed in the United States of America
British Library Cataloging in Publication Information Available

Library of Congress Cataloging-in-Publication Data

ISBN 0-7618-1097-8 (cloth: alk. ppr.)
ISBN 0-7618-1098-6 (pbk: alk. ppr.)

∞™ The paper used in this publication meet the minimum
requirements of American National Standard for information
Sciences—Permanence of Paper for Printed Library Materials,
ANSI Z39.48—1984

To the victims of the Red Terror, may thy name, dream and aspiration live forever!

To the survivors of the Red Terror, the conscience of our *Generation*, you meant no harm to anyone, but prosperity to our Motherland and joy to our destitute brothers and sisters. Glory be to you! You are the victims of history and blessed be your tender heart!

Blessed be the Ethiopian mothers who had to face boundless anguish, agony and misery!

Contents

List of Acronyms xiii
Preface xv
        Notes to Preface xxii
Acknowledgement xxiii
Introduction xxv
        Notes to Introduction xli

1

        Post Land Reform Struggle 1

        Southern Ethiopia - September 1975 to February 1976   1
            Keffa 1
            Sidamo 4
            Arsi 6
        The Struggle in the North 6
            Unrest in Wello and Shoa 10
                  Proclamation No. 71 10
        Conditions in the Urban Areas 12
            Workers' Discontent - Labor Movement
                  in 1975/76........ 14
                Labor Movement goes Underground 18
                Formation of the Ethiopian
                Workers Revolutionary Union 22
            The Provisional Office for Mass
                Organizations Affairs and Labor 24
            Other Underground Mass Organizations 28
            Underground Mass Organizations and the EPRP 29

        Part II

            EPRP's Organizational Activities 30
            The Central Committee 31
            Organs of the Party and the League 34
            EPRP's Drive for Further Merger 36

The "Red Flag"	37
The GA group	41
The Bellissuma Group	43
The Haji Kutta Group	44
The Afar Liberation Front	45
Hizbawi Ametse	45
Notes to Chapter I	46

2 Transformation of the State Apparatus — 53

The Provisional Office for Mass Organizations Affairs	53
POMOA and the Initial Phase of the Formation of a Police State	56
POMOA and the *Abyot Medrek* (Forum)	56
POMOA and *Yewuyeyet Kebeb*	58
POMOA and the National Democratic Revolution Program	61
Response of the EPRP to the Call for the United Front	62
POMOA and Mass Organizations	65
Political Significance of the Formation of POMOA	68
EPRP's Organizational Activities	70
The EPRP and the MEISON	70
EPRP's Infiltration of the MEISON	75
EPRP's Financial Difficulties	77
Problems and Difficulties - EPRP Leadership	80
The Youth League	83
The Ethiopian People's Revolutionary Army - the Rural Armed Wing	87
Expansion of EPRA	90
Preparations to launch an Armed Struggle in Sidamo	92
Notes to Chapter 2	94

Table of Contents

3

Transition from Peaceful -Violent Form of Struggle 101

POMOA and the Unrest in Harer 101
The Crisis Within the Derge 102
    Alienation of Derge Members
        and Its Effect . . . 103
    EPRP's Role in the Crisis Within the Derge . 107
Repressive Institutions Empowered 109
EPRP Selected as the Main Target 113
    The EPRP and the Impending Crisis 117
    The June 1976 EPRP CC Meeting . 118
    The Second Plenum of the EPRP CC 119
Notes to Chapter 3. 126

4

**The Declaration of the War of
    Annihilation and Its Effects** 129

Political Significance of the War of Annihilation 131
Legal and Juridical Implications of War of Annihilation 132
War of Annihilation - Phase One 133
    Political Isolation 133
    Psychological Warfare 134
    Physical Annihilation 135
EPRP's Reaction -August 1976 CC Meeting 136
    The September 1976 EPRP CC Meeting . . . 139
    Addis Abeba Interzone Jeopardized 140
    Resisting the War of Annihilation 143
        Workers Resistance 144
        The 3rd ELAMA Congress 145
        All Ethiopian Workers
        Trade Union (AEWTU) . . 147
EPRP's Urban Defense Wing (UDW) 148
    Initial Military Operations 154
Notes to Chapter 4 159

5

The Turning Point - the Triumph of Violence over Moderation 163

Struggle within the Derge 163
The EPRP CC - Organizational Activities 170
    The Politbureau (PB) Paper 173
    The Third EPRP CC Plenum 176
    Formation of a Faction - Phase One 180
        Takeover of EPRP Activities in Shoa 182
    The February 1977 EPRP CC Meeting 185
    The War of Annihilation - Phase Two 188
        The Regime and the Youth 189
        Mass Confession 192
        Mass Terror 193
        The 1st Search/Destroy Campaign . 194
        EPRP's Preparations 195
        The 2nd Search/Destroy
            Campaign in Action 197
            The Campaign and its
            Effects on MEISON 201
        The 2nd Search/Destroy Campaign 201
    Profile of the EPRP CC 204
    EPRP Leadership's Plight 206
Notes to Chapter 5 209

6

The Ethio-Somali Conflict 215

The Origins of the Conflict 216
    The Unfolding Conflict 218
Derge and Ethiopian Nationalism 221
Derge and the Mass Organizations 223
International Significance of the Conflict 225
Soviet Involvement was more than Military 228
The EPRP and the Ethio-Somali Conflict 229
    EPRP's Effort to Form a Front 231
    Impact of the Ethio-Somali Conflict on EPRP 235

Table of Contents

POMOA "Withers" Away 237
State Power Transformation 245
Continuation of the Conflict in Eritrea 248
    The Derge Retaliates 248
    EPRP and Its Role in the Conflict in Eritrea. ... 249
        EPRP Structure in Eritrea 249
        EPRP Resumed Contact with
                Eritrean Fronts ... 252
        EPRA Activities Among the
            Ethiopian Army in Eritrea 254
        Crisis in the EPRP in Eritrea 257
        EPLF Imprisons EPRP Members .. 259
Notes to Chapter 6 260

7

The War of Annihilation is Stepped Up 269

The Third Search and Destroy Campaign 271
The Fourth Search and Destroy Campaign 273
    Other Victims 276
    The Dead were also Penalized 279
"Youth Associations" - New Torture Chambers 282
Retaliation - EPRP Defense Activities 284
The Prisons 287
    Prison Codes of Communication 290
    Activities in Prisons 291
        Ward No. 7 292
            Osman... 293
            Belayneh... 294
            Kassu Kumma... 296
Notes to Chapter 7 302

8

EPRP Organizational Activities 307

EPRP's Foreign Relations 310
EPRP - Plagued by Factional Activities 312
    Lieutenant Abebe Jemma and the Faction ... 316

The Generation, II

   May Day and the Faction 316
   Members of the Faction in the Movie Theaters 318
   Other Factional Activities 318
   Liquidation from Within - Party Zone Two . 319
   Liquidation from Within - ELAMA Zone Two 320
   The Addis Abeba IZ Fell in Danger 322
   Differing Perspective 326
 EPRA and Urban EPRP Structure Lost Communication 328
 EPRP's Organizational Condition in 1977/1978 332
   The Sidamo IZ 336
   EPRP Activities in Harerghe 340
   EPRP Activities in Keffa 342
 Youth League Activities 343
 EPRP's Political Activities Abroad 346
   Regional Committee in North America 347
   EPRP Committees in Europe,
      Middle East and Africa 348
   Problems of the EPRP Structure Abroad ... 349
   Political Differences and
      Organizational Problems 349
 Notes to Chapter 8 357

9

The Ethiopian People's Revolutionary Army 365

The Life of a Guerrilla Army 365
Military Operations 370
The Rectification Movement 375
   EPRA Documents - The Constitution 377
   EPRA by-laws 379
The EPRP CC Group in Assimba 384
The EPRP and the TPLF 389
Predicament of the EPRA in Tigrai 399
The Strategic Retreat 404
Political Significance of the Defeat of the EPRA 407
Notes to Chapter 9 408

x

Table of Contents

10
Party and Military Activities in Begemidir 417

    EPRP Structure in Begemidir 420
    The Ethiopian Patriotic Democratic
        Organization (EPDO) 424
    Begemidir- The Restructuring of the EPRA 425
        Army of Region One 426
        Army of Region Two 428
        Army of Region Three 430
        Army of Region Four 434
        Relationship Between Regional
           EPRA and Local EPRP 437
    The Fourth EPRP CC Plenum 441
        Rank and File Revolt in the "Liberated" Area 448
        Crisis in Region One 451
        Problems of Region Three 452
        Region Two Army - Challenges 456
    Notes to Chapter 10 463

Epilogue 469
    Notes to Epilogue 469
Postscript 491
Glossary of Amharic words 497
Bibliography 499
Index 507

List of Acronyms

AEPA	All Ethiopian Peasant Association
AEWTU	All Ethiopian Workers Trade Union
ALF	Afar Liberation Front
AMC	Agricultural Marketing Corporation
AZ	Addis Zemen
CADU	Chilalo Agricultural Development Unit
CC	Central Committee
CELU	Confederation of Ethiopian Labor Union
CIA	Central Intelligence Agency
CID	Central Investigation Department
CoCos	Commanders Committees
COPWE	Commission to Organize the Workers Party of Ethiopia
CPC	Communist Party of China
CPSU	Communist Party of the Soviet Union
Derge	The military committee formed in June 1974
DF	Democratic Front
ECHEAT	Ethiopian Oppressed Masses Unity Struggle
EDU	Ethiopian Democratic Union
EFLNA	Eritrean Forces for Liberation in North America
ELF	Eritrean Liberation Front
EMALEDEH	Union of Ethiopian Marxist-Leninist Organizations
ENLF	Ethiopian National Liberation Front
EPA	Ethiopian Peasants' Association
EPDM	Ethiopian People's Democratic Movement
EPID	Extension and Project Implementation Department
EPLF	Eritrean People's Liberation Front
EPLO	Ethiopian People's Liberation Organization
EPPDO	The Ethiopian People's Patriotic Democratic Organization
EPRA	Ethiopian People's Revolutionary Army
EPRDF	Ethiopian People's Revolutionary Democratic Front
EPRP	Ethiopian People's Revolutionary Party
ESUNA	Ethiopian Students Union in North America

ETA	Ethiopian Teachers Association
ETU	Ethiopian Trade Union
FC	Foreign Affairs Committee
ICM	International Communist Movement
IZ	Inter-zone
MALRED	Marxist-Leninist Revolutionary Organization
MC	Military Commission
MITU	Manufacturing Industrial Trade Union
MOC	Mass Organizations Committee
MP	Military Police
MPLA	Mozambique Popular Liberation Army
NATRACOR	National Transport Corporation
NCO	Non-Commissioned Officers'
NDR	National Democratic Revolution
NRCC	National Revolutionary Campaign Council
OAU	Organization of African Unity
OC	Operations Committee
OLF	Oromo Liberation Front
OPDO	Oromo People's Democratic Organization
OSO	Oppressed Soldiers Organization
PA	Peasant Associations
PB	Politburo
PDRE	People's Democratic Republic of Ethiopia
PMAC	Provisional Military Administration Council
POC	Provisional Organizing Committee
POMOA	Provisional Organization for Mass Organizations Affairs
POW	Prisoners of War
PPG	Provisional People's Government
PRO	Public Relations Office
RC	Regional Committees
RF	Red Flag
RM	Rectification Movement
RRC	Relief and Rehabilitation Center
SALF	Somali Abo Liberation Front
SNM	Somali National Movement
SSDF	Somali Salvation Democratic Front
TPLF	Tigrai People's Liberation Front
UDW	Urban Defense Wing
WCC	Women's Coordinating Committee
WPE	Workers Party of Ethiopia
WSLF	Western Somalia Liberation Front
YL	Youth League

Preface

Man is largely a social construct, and to deny a man the social meaning of his death is to kill him twice, first in the flesh, then in the spirit. The purpose of history cannot be to teach lessons or impose a moral lecture on the reader. But history can have a cleansing effect. (The Rwanda Crisis - History of a Genocide, Gerard Prunier)

It has been about nine years since the actual writing of *The Generation* began. The process of writing a book could be compared with pregnancy. The baby grows in the mother's womb while a book takes shape in the mind of an author. Unlike the baby, who weighs a few pounds, the ideas that eventually take the shape of a book have no definite weight, but all the same, an author feels that he walks around with a heavy weight upon him. Unlike pregnancy, the process of producing a book may take years; in my case it took about nine years. Besides, the 'labor' to compose a book begins when the first sentence is written. From there on, every sentence, paragraph and chapter is an outcome of "labor", sometimes an intense one. During pregnancy, the mother could be provided with some medical support, while the author has no recourse except himself and his sources of information.

The newly born baby will have a mother that would take care of him/her; however, when after several years of laboring the book is "born", it stands by itself with little or no support and has to be nurtured while it still is under "labor". I do not know what a mother feels after giving birth, but an author might feel that he has lost his treasure. Even though I know that this work could be of some contribution, I felt that I was robbed of the secrets that I was supposed to keep for myself and parts of my soul left me along with the book.

Be that as it may, this is the second and the last volume of a two-part sequel, *The Generation*. The first part covers the formative stage of the Ethiopian People's Revolutionary Party (EPRP) - from the late 1960s to 1975. The second part deals with one of the most turbulent periods of Ethiopian history, that is, from 1975 to 1980. This was a period when some of the economic measures enacted earlier took effect and major societal transformation took place. During this period, the revolutionary movement of the early seventies degenerated into one of the most barbaric rule Ethiopia had ever witnessed. The second volume delineates the course that the revolutionary movement followed and provides background information on the conflict that unfolded. By 1980, the revolutionary movement that began in 1974 had subsided and the Derge had emerged as an unchallenged force. The opposition, including the EPRP, had been so weakened that it no more posed a threat to Mengistu's rule.

When the first volume of *The Generation* came out in 1993, the first draft of the second volume was already completed and for the last several months, the author had to rework the draft, get in touch with individuals who would be good sources of information and embellish the content of the book. As was indicated in the first volume, the second volume is also

> [A]bout a generation of Ethiopians who embarked on an arduous struggle to transform its country . . . It was a generation of activists who came together because of altruistic aims and goals. It was a generation that was visionary, idealist and perceptive and consisted of the most enlightened and brightest citizens.[1]

The second volume is also about the Ethiopian revolutionary movement, the dynamics of the struggle and alliance of forces that unfolded in the course of the movement. It is about a struggle that engulfed the entire country and knocked at the door of every citizen. The book provides insight about the gradual degeneration of the revolutionary movement. It describes the meteoric rise of the EPRP to prominence and its gradual disintegration due to external and internal factors. The book provides the details of how the revolutionary movement degenerated and fell under the control of few individuals. It furnishes information about government policies and acts that intensified the nationalist struggle and directly or indirectly assisted the nationalist movements in dominating the Ethiopian political scene. The book also pays attention on the role of the two super powers, the Soviet Union and the USA, and the new alliance of international forces that emerged in the late seventies.

Even though sketchy and sometimes superficial, some writers have attempted to provide a glimpse of the history of the 1974 movement. So far, very few insiders, be it on the Derge's side or that of the opposition, have offered their own historical analysis or interpretation of events. Unless this is done, the events that affected the course of the Ethiopian history and the lives of millions of her citizens will be relegated to oblivion.

Preface

The early 1980s, when writing the history of the Ethiopian People's Revolutionary Party was embarked upon, was a period when the members of the organization had become disappointed as a result of the deterioration of the political condition of Ethiopia and the course of events within the EPRP itself. Many EPRP members and sympathizers had become disillusioned not only about the turn of events; some even had begun doubting the *raison d'etre* of the EPRP and it's ideological and political tenets. Many had tended to forget the dialectical interrelationship between defeat and victory. So, the author levied upon himself the obligation of sharing whatever he knew about the history of the EPRP. When writing was commenced, it was not the general public that the author had in mind, but EPRP members and sympathizers, hence, the need to provide EPRP's history in its details.

In the course of writing the book and when Ethiopia plunged into deep crisis, it became more than evident that an insider's view of the history of the EPRP was of paramount importance. The crisis resulted from the concerted campaign of the military regime, right elements and nationalist forces against the entire generation of activists. The campaign was so virulent and lethal that the EPRP was portrayed as an evil force that was the primary cause of the ills of the country. The victims of the campaign are many, including former EPRP members. Some doubted and still doubt that the struggle and the sacrifice paid was in vain, hence the necessity to provide an insider's perspective.

Furthermore, this book reminisces the story of those who had fallen victim to repression and the survivors of the repression, the dearest sons and daughters of Ethiopia. It is also presented for the parents, and particularly, the mothers who lost their beloved ones. Therefore, writing this book is also the author's way of conveying his sympathy to all those who had been hurt, to those bright and energetic Ethiopian sons and daughters who paid with their lives, to see a brighter future, a prosperous and a conflict-free country. To those whose untimely "departure" Ethiopia still misses. May they know that history did not forget them!

History is a convex mirror where the specter of the past overshadows the present, where unaddressed issues of "antiquity" haunt the memories of the present. This book examines the origins of some of the major political issues that still dominate the Ethiopian political scene, among them, the issue regarding the national conflict, its origin and subsequent evolution. The role and position of the EPRP regarding the national conflict are discussed and it seems the Derge opted for an entirely different alternative which probably led to the current quandary. When the EPRP raised those issues in the mid and late seventies, many did indeed heed to its leadership, with a large number of Ethiopians remaining indifferent. When the conflict became intensified and reached an unprecedented level in the early 1990s, many awoke from their slumber, the way Edgar Alan Poe's character - Rip Van Winkle - awoke from his sleep of twenty years, to find out that the world and his surrounding had changed.

Writing the history of the later day EPRP is an exacting endeavor both from its technical standpoint and the complexities of the issues to be covered. As the period recedes, so does memory and accounting events in their totality becomes more and more difficult. Lack of appropriate documents that would have helped to validate some of the stated facts made the effort more difficult. The history of the Ethiopian revolutionary movement is partly like a wave of emotion where ideas and actions, violence and human lives and idealists and hirelings were embodied into one. When writing on those events, an insider can in no way be indifferent, but has to go through a labyrinth of emotional feelings. Extricating oneself from those subjective feelings is a difficult quest which needed an uninterrupted internal struggle.

It is true that the EPRP of the earlier period had supporters as well as avowed enemies. As was indicated earlier, the later group might dwell on the weaknesses, shortcomings and mistakes of the EPRP. Presentation of the facts and events the way they were made were issues that the author debated upon. Finally, it was resolved to present the history in its entirety not only to be true to those who had been victimized, but also that the coming generation would learn both from our strength and vulnerabilities, achievements and mistakes and success and blunders. It will be the duty of the present day reader to scan through the events and incidents described in the book in their true historical settings. It should also be realized that EPRP's history is part of Ethiopia's history and those who want to present their alternatives should first ask themselves whether they would overcome their civic responsibilities or settle past scores.

Some of the events covered in this book are controversial, and as a participant of the movement, it was very difficult to remain neutral. However, the author had tried to be fair. Whenever circumstances required it, he had furnished documents. It was done so not only for the sake of the books' readability, but also to be fair to those silent 'voices' who cannot provide their own version of the events. After saying that, it is imperative to add that the author himself, who was a victim of the mindless repression, was

Preface

not neutral regarding some events, such as, the process known as the "Red Terror". He had gone to great length to describe its emergence and evolution. The author does not claim to know the history of the EPRP in its entirety and, therefore, what is contained in this book is only a slice of the big pie. Even though the author had made efforts to obtain some information from the appropriate sources, the book has limitations regarding EPRP activities abroad and relationship with foreign governments and organizations. Hopefully, those that have the documents and information will provide us with their insight and when they and others furnish their side of the story, it may be possible to see a bigger picture.

Due to its organizational importance, its large membership and because of the author's familiarity, EPRP activities in major cities, such as, Addis Abeba, are focused upon. The August 1975 Extended Conference of the EPRP was an important event, hence the need to refer back to the decisions enacted during this gathering. The EPRP program was among the documents that the Conference promulgated.

As a symbolic gesture, only a very small fraction of EPRP members and incidents related to individual activists are mentioned in the book. Describing the later part of the struggle, the manner in which leading activists of the EPRP operated under the barrel of a gun, and how they endured the vicissitude of life were mentioned whenever the situation warranted them. This is done in order to show the intensity of the struggle and its effect on decision making process. Incidents that may seem trivial nowadays, but that had significant bearings during the turbulent days of the late seventies are mentioned in order to indicate their influence on the decision making process. The author has written about the strength and frailties of the participants of the movement. He has provided some insight into the course of the thought processes of the activists under the most repressive of conditions and, along that line, he had shed a very small part of his personal experience. Unless it it important and is part of the narration process, he has refrained to discuss his role in the struggle. Whenever possible, he had made subtle digression to demonstrate peasant life style, traditional holidays, such as 'buhe', the 'meskel' celebration among the Gurages, peasant superstition, such as, the 'wefe' concept, the '*Bet Baria*' of Welkaite, etc.

In line with the first part of *The Generation*, effort is made "to portray events, incidents, decisions and activities realistically. Detailed analysis and interpretations of the activities are not provided (except some insignificant details here and there), only the account of the history itself."[2] In order to do that, placing oneself several years back in the setting where the incidents took place was mandatory. An objective account was provided and whenever there were doubts regarding certain incidents, repeated efforts to verify their authenticity was made.

The outcome of the Rectification Movements (RMs) conducted in the EPRA in 1977 and the EPRP structure abroad in 1979/80 are included in this work. In the course of both RMs, conflicts, problems and EPRP's difficulties were raised and discussed. Sifting through a large collection of documents and conducting discussions and interviews with participants of the movements, the author had tried to shade light on some of the relevant issues.

The section that deals with the labor movement was completed before 1984. As was indicated above, the first draft of this volume was ready by 1993 and in order to prepare it, the author had to resort to the tapes he prepared in 1984, the interview he conducted with Zeru Kehishen in 1987 and the number of interviews he conducted from 1988 to 1996, with leading and knowledgeable EPRP members and others. Besides, various EPRP publications, internal memoranda, student journals, letters and correspondences, official and government newspapers and periodicals, several books and other materials had been consulted. In the introduction, a synopsis of the history of the struggle discussed in part one of *The Generation* is provided.

The author had conducted discussion with a large number of the participants of the movement. He had also held few group meetings to discuss certain aspects of the movement. Since the last months of 1994, the author provided copies of the draft to a large number of former and current EPRP members whom he considered are knowledgeable. A good number of them had responded positively and their critique and commentaries are included in the book. There were some participants of the struggle that he would have liked to reach to, but due to technical and other problems, he was unable to do so.

The style of writing that the author pursued is in line with that of the first part of *The Generation* which tried to depict the revolutionary movement in its complexity and entirety. To express the human aspect of the movement, incidents and events are given proper places. As we all know, a revolutionary movement is a process where love/hatred, human stoicism/frailties, vileness/purity, conceitedness/modesty, cruelty/kindness etc., are expressed in their ultimate forms. Of course, this is besides the economic and political reforms that usually accompany a movement.

Preface

When the author embarked upon writing the history of the EPRP, he was aware of the difficulties ahead. In a situation where the ideology of the left is despised, so to say the least, to write the history of the EPRP needed a sober decision. In a country where a relatively large number of people were affected, at least indirectly, by some of the policies that the EPRP advocated, such as, the "land to the tiller", writing EPRP's history in ones name needed some degree of determination. Furthermore, either directly or indirectly, the book will address issues related to former adversaries of the EPRP. It is assumed that they will take up the challenge responsibly and come up with their side of the story and, if they do that, it we will be possible to see a much broader picture of the revolutionary movement.

In conclusion, in writing this book, the author had no 'ax to grind and no scores to settle', but he had to overcome a historical obligation that the victims of the repression had bequeathed upon those who had remained behind. *The Generation* is published partly on their behest. May their souls rest in peace!

Notes to Preface

1. Kiflu Tadesse, <u>The Generation</u>, Part I, Independent Publishers, 1993, page 1.

2. Ibid., page 4.

Acknowledgement

Towards the preparation of this book, among the steps that I undertook was to gather relevant documents and periodicals, conduct group and individual discussions and interviews. Hundreds collaborated. Many of them had taken part in the struggle in different capacities. In this group are included former leaders and active participants of the EPRP and the YL party zonal structures in Addis Abeba, Harerghe, Gonder, Shoa, Eritrea, Keffa, Sidamo, Gamu Goffa, Illubabor, Europe, the USA, Sudan, etc., and leaders and active members of the various levels of the EPRA command. Had it not been for the enthusiastic cooperation of these participants of the Ethiopian revolutionary struggle, that is, the real actors of the history itself, it would be impossible to present the book in its present format. Either their names or their abbreviations, or the code names of a good number of them are mentioned in different parts of the book, particularly in the bibliography and the Notes. There are some who had rendered important contribution in writing the book and do not want their identity to be disclosed. I express my deepest gratitude to all of you. It is my strong belief that you also have contributed your share in reconstructing the history of the valiant *Generation*.

As part of the preparation process, I had to show a certain section of the book or the entire manuscript to those that I believed would provide me commentaries. Almost all of them had responded and they have furnished me with penetrating observations and remarks. In this category fall SD, Yared Tebebu, M., Debebe, Girma T., GKY, GA, Mohabaw, AKB, GM, Girmai Tesfa Giorgis, TT, Girum (code name), Wubalem, AM, Getachew Begashaw, Doctor Mesfin Araya, Zeru Kehishen, FA, GA, Colonel Alemayehu Asfaw, Giday Zeratsion, Aregawi Berhe, Kassu Kumma, Hailu Mengesha, Abebe Tessema, Annette C. Sheckler and those who did not want their names to be disclosed. My gratitude also goes to Kebedetch Tekleab who designed the cover. I would like to express my appreciation and I thank all of you very much. Your spirited support provided me an additional confidence in writing the book.

Last, but not least, I would like to express my indebtedness to Charlie Johns, my brother Dr. Mesfin Tadesse and DHM who helped me in the editorial work and provided me with insightful observations, remarks and critiques.

Kiflu Tadesse, Washington D.C., December 1997

Introduction

In *The Generation* Part I, the formation of the modern state of Ethiopia and the emergence of the radical generation involved in the formation of the Ethiopian Peoples Liberation Organization (EPLO) were discussed. The process of forming the EPLO took more than two years. Until 1974, there were four EPLO group committees in existence in Ethiopia, Eastern Europe, Western Europe and the Middle East and North America. The majority of the members of the groups that merged to form the EPLO belonged to the generation of pioneer activists who had matured during the course of the student movement in Ethiopia. Most had some university education, only dropping out to pursue political activities. They represented various nationalities and tended to come out of lower-middle class family backgrounds. They were like-minded activists who came together because of their affinity to the cause. The starting point in their framework of analysis was an evaluation of the then prevailing political situation in Ethiopia. It was agreed that the primary and immediate objective of the revolution was the implementation of the slogan 'land to the tiller'. The broad objective was to change the social relations of production in the countryside. The welfare of the urban proletariat was to be promoted by special legislation, for example, by setting minimum wage standards. The economy was to be freed from external dependence and imperialist domination.

The main social forces that were to carry out the revolution would be the greatest beneficiaries, that is, the landless peasantry, the middle peasantry, the urban proletariat, and the petty bourgeoisie. The primary task of the democratic government would be to transform the social relations of production from their obsolete feudal form to a new form that was defined as 'bourgeois democratic'. Another issue on which consensus had to be reached concerned the main form of the struggle against the *ancien* regime. It was generally agreed that in the absence of the most elementary human and political rights in Ethiopia and the regime's propensity to treat any form of political activity as a criminal offence, it was deemed necessary to combat violence with violence.

A critical issue upon which consensus was also reached was the unconditional right to self-determination for nations, nationalities and peoples. The programmatic and political significance of the issue for the purpose of launching an armed struggle had a dimension of practical consequences. It was expected that the armed struggle would commence in remote border areas inhabited by members of the oppressed nationalities.

The discussion among EPLO members also took into account the peculiarities of the Eritrean struggle for independence. The groups that formed the EPLO took position concerning the multi ethnicity of Eritrea. The EPLO acknowledged that while a sense of Eritrean nationalism had emerged through the shared history of the region since the late 19th century, Eritrea comprised a number of separate nationalities which claimed the right to self-determination.

The groups that formed the EPLO also discussed the issue of the Ogaden, the bone of contention between Ethiopia and Somalia. The radicals decided that the inhabitants of the Ogaden had the right to determine for themselves whether they wanted to form their own state, join Somalia or remain in Ethiopia. Any attempt by the two states to forcefully influence the choice was to be condemned.

Another agreement that emanated from the analysis of the Ethiopian situation and the nature of the struggle involved was the type of organization necessary to wage the struggle. While the EPLO was conceived as a front, it was thought of as an umbrella organization under which various other groups of varying political orientation would organize. In practice, this goal was not fully realized. Throughout this period, recruitment focused on the Ethiopian left, among like-minded radicals who normally would have comprised the Marxist Leninist core of the front. In April 1972, the founding Congress of the EPLO was held in West Berlin. The reports of both the Provisional Organizing Committee (POC) and the various groups that formed the EPLO were approved. The Eritrean issue was discussed and the decision to recognize all liberation factions was confirmed. The second major item on the agenda was the program of the organization. General agreement had already been reached on what was known as the 'minimum program'. There was little for the Congress to do other than to decide the order of priority of the nine points of the program.

Agreement was also reached on the ultimate goal of the revolution, the maximum program, which was to establish socialism in Ethiopia. The Congress reaffirmed that a revolutionary situation existed in Ethiopia and decided that preparations must be made to begin the armed struggle. It was agreed that the First Congress enter into the history of the organization as the gathering of the First Communist Party of Ethiopia, a concealed core of the EPLO. One topic on the agenda that was long debated concerned the International Communist Movement (ICM). Revisionism, dogmatism and a third phenomenon characterized as "left in form and right in essence" were singled out as the main dangers within the ICM.

The concluding agenda of the Congress was the election of the leadership. It was agreed that nine leaders were needed to carry out the tasks given the size of the organization. At the end of 1972, the EPLO made arrangements for volunteers to be trained by the Palestinian Liberation Organization.

Introduction

MEISON (an acronym in Amharic for 'All Ethiopia Socialist movement') was another left group that was formed in 1968. The majority of those who formed MEISON were intellectuals who resided in Western Europe. In 1968,

> [T]he founders of the group were looking for a nucleus of like-minded militants who would control ESUE [Ethiopian Students Union in Europe]...to promote the group's political strategy and also to serve as a recruitment agency for a future political organization....Two groups of leaders were formed to carry out activities inside and outside Ethiopia.[1]

While the EPLO was making efforts to get organized, a revolutionary movement began in 1974 and the first stage of this process covered the period from the end of December 1973, when the first sign of revolt was signaled by the mutinous army in the southern part of the country, until the fall of the government known as the Aklilu Cabinet in February 1974. Concessions were made and some of the demands of the movement were fulfilled. The struggle continued and in order to stop and contain the further spread of the rebellion, a certain section of the ruling class had to be sacrificed, the Aklilu Cabinet was replaced by the more traditionalist group led by Endalkatchew Mekonnen.

The second period covered about three months while Endalkatchew was the Prime Minister. The students, teachers and taxi drivers continued with their protests. The more radical section of the army continued siding with the opposition. Workers in different industries went on strikes. Women held a demonstration demanding equal pay for equal work, while the three-day strike of postal workers paralyzed Ethiopian mail delivery. The role of the Ethiopian workers at this stage of the movement became more pronounced when the Ethiopian working class, led by its more radical wing of labor leaders, staged a four-day strike in March 1974. Mammoth demonstrations were held expressing the dissatisfaction of the unfair treatment of Muslims. The city of Addis Abeba was in a turmoil and the unrest spread to other cities.

In Jimma, a provincial city west of the capital, the people revolted and, in due course, a people's council was formed. In March, the revolt spread to such remote areas as Arba Minch and Bale, where fierce fighting took place between the police and the population. On March 28, a peaceful demonstration was conducted in Mekele demanding the resignation of the new Prime Minister. In Meki, about 130 km south-west of Addis Abeba, peasants revolted to reclaim their land. Workers in Awasa refused to work.

During the course of the second stage, issues related to democratic and human rights became one of the most important priorities. The army was split into moderates and extremists. After the government promised a raise in their salary, the majority of the soldiers went back to their barracks and demanded that the people give the government a respite. The situation, however, was such that around the end of this stage, former officials were rounded up and put in prison by the army. After each passing day, the demands of the people continued multiplying. The ruling group which then had economic power, was, until this time, dwarfed by the role of the Emperor. Power was in the hands of the monarch, who was also overcome by age. Emperor Haile Selassie was not in a position to make quick political decisions, as was the case some years before.

The New Cabinet could neither control nor address the demands of the revolutionary movement. On the other hand, it could not resort to a full scale repression in the absence of a mechanism to control the repressive apparatus. A full-fledged revolutionary situation was created in the country where the ruling group could no longer rule as before and the people would no longer be ruled in the old ways. Using this newly created situation, the military stepped in and the third stage of the revolutionary movement began. The third stage was the beginning of an end to the old ruling group which was stripped off its political power.

The participants of the movement can be categorized into three groups. The first group was made up of mass and professional organizations such as students, labor unions, teachers' associations, etc., and the second group was civil servants. The third group was the unorganized population.

While the movement was underway, two groups emerged, one within the military and the second, the left groupings in the country. Both groups presented themselves as contending forces and became the focus of the struggle. The military group was the former "Non-Commissioned Officers' (NCO) Committee", transformed into a political power known as the Derge which was formed on June 28, 1974. On July 1, General Aman Andom, who was not a Derge member, was appointed Chief of Staff. He became the minister of Defense in the civilian government of Lij Michael Imru who was hand-picked by the Derge. Aman Andom became the head of state in September 1974 when the Provisional Military Administration Council (PMAC) was formed. In due course, the vice-chairperson, Major Mengistu Haile Mariam, emerged as a leading figure of the Derge.

The other contending force was the left which had emerged in the late 1960s and had attained a certain degree of success to offer some political, ideological, and organizational guidance. At the wake of the revolutionary movement, there were at least twelve minuscule groups whose estimated membership was no more than eight hundred. Among the most important of these groups was the EPLO whose members included teachers, students, civil servants and some military officers. The left groupings coordinated the activities of the various mass organizations, which at the time had no contact amongst themselves. By introducing the question of political power and the demand for the formation of a provisional government, the left transformed

Introduction

the whole course of the movement. When the EPLO leadership took over responsibilities in June of 1974, the situation was such that it had to perform simultaneous tasks including party-building, the merger of the various left groups, publishing the organ of the party on a regular basis, making preparations for the armed struggle, and giving direction to the on-going struggle. It can be said that the EPLO CC was in a continuous session and a formal CC meeting was held at least once a week. Because of the absence of some important institutions, such as the Secretariat, the CC was overburdened. The main political task of the EPLO by mid-1974, as perceived by its leadership was to guide and to accelerate the unfolding political struggle along the lines set by the organization's ten point programme. The method chosen was to focus upon and to intensify the contradictions that gave rise to the struggle, first and foremost, class contradictions.

Beginning in June 1974, the majority of the Ethiopian left was regrouped under one organization, the EPLO. It was reorganized around a definite political program, had one center of leadership, and also began publishing its own newsletter. Of the twelve groups that took an active part during the 1974 movement, seven of them came under the umbrella of the EPLO. Five of the groups merged during the initial period of the formation. During this period and later on, a number of smaller circles and groups joined the EPLO. *Democracia*, EPLO's organ, became the center of attraction and continued to mobilize a wider number of participants around itself. The new structure, which was to be known as the zone system gave greater latitude for the expansion of the organization without causing any major strain on its overall structure. It also allowed defined jurisdiction and geographical territory for any of the committees to be formed. It created the mechanism for a wider degree of participation in the organization. Most of all, the new format laid down the basis for defined relations between higher and lower echelons of the organization. According to the new format, next to the Congress, the highest organ still remained the CC, followed by Inter-zonal and then zonal committees. Next to the zonal committees came Regional and Sub-regional committees, respectively. The lowest organizational bodies remained the basic committees, or institutional committees, as they sometimes were called. These were organized on the basis of localities or institutions.

The first organizational structure was the Addis Abeba IZ. Zonal committees were formed in Jimma, Bahir Dar/Gojam, Harer, Arsi, Wello, Tigrai and Sidamo. Organizational committees were formed in some parts of Shoa. Actual organizational activities of the Youth League began sometime in mid-1974, when its foundations were laid down. A provisional youth league committee was formed in July 1974 and the committee's assignment was to set up the structure of the League.

The Generation, II

One of the primary tasks of the CC in June 1974 was to prepare the ground to publish the organ, *Democracia* which became one of the most widely read papers both among its supporters and its enemies, primarily because of the content and the presentation of issues.

The EPLO central committee formed a committee of three to set up links with organized labor and to conduct political work within the Confederation of Ethiopian Labor Union (CELU) and in a brief period of time, the Workers Committee was able to recruit some additional EPLO members in the CELU office. Not long after, the committee was able to identify a group of radicalized workers who were critical of CELU's leadership and had regrouped themselves in a loosely formed labor opposition group.

Questions related to the political system (the first point of the program), land, democracy, an independent economy and the national question were recurring issues raised in *Democracia* in order to give the struggle an anti-feudalist and anti-imperialist direction. *Democracia* also made efforts to guide the new regime, which did not have any political or organizational experience. Of the two main sets of contradictions identified in the ten point EPLO program - feudalism and imperialism - the former was singled out as the most important at the time. The autocracy, the cornerstone of the feudal structure, became the main target of the EPLO, while public attention was still focused on the change of personalities in the government.

The radical left had made the monarchy a prime political issue that could not be evaded. Every issue of *Democracia* hammered on this question, pointing out that it was the Emperor who had appointed all the corrupt officials, therefore, no one was more responsible than him for the crimes and exploitation perpetuated against the people. The attack on the monarchy was a fairly straight forward and a relatively easy task. However, the possibility of a military coup in Ethiopia was in the minds of the Ethiopian left for quite sometime.

The EPLO leadership and the majority of the left were convinced that military intervention would spell disaster for the revolutionary cause in Ethiopia. The task of unraveling the nature of the emerging military regime was much more complex and difficult than the struggle against the failing autocracy. In these circumstances, a headlong attack on the military committee was deemed inadvisable. Rather, it was decided to adopt a two-pronged approach designed to radicalize the soldiers especially against the autocracy, and at the same time, expose their motives and explain the effect if they failed to respond.

While trying to persuade the Derge to take a more radical direction, at the same time, the EPLO felt the need to explain the role and the metamorphosis of a military regime. To forestall the emergence of a military dictatorship, the issue of popular participation in the revolution was raised.

Introduction

Much effort and an intensive campaign was conducted. The radical campaign succeeded in turning the popular movement against the autocracy. As the Derge began to strip piecemeal the Emperor of his powers, the issue of state power assumed greater urgency and the EPLO put increased emphasis on the demand for a Provisional Peoples Government (PPG). What was initially conceived of as a tactical slogan designed to illustrate an alternative base for a future regime, now attained new significance when many understood it as the formula for a transitional government.

The new regime nationalized all imperial institutions and finally dethroned the Emperor by allying itself with the strong anti-autocracy struggle and sentiment. On September 12, 1974, in just one stroke, the military regime dethroned the Emperor, disbanded the Parliament, suspended the constitution, established a military government and curbed democratic rights. This infringement on the basic democratic rights of the people was one of the major blows to the struggle that started in February 1974. The worst fear of the left had come true and a dangerous and deceptive military regime, able to combine reform and repression had taken power. The survival of the left became so precarious that it was feared it would fall prey at its infancy.

The relationship of the Derge to the Ethiopian labor movement turned sour following the curtailment of democratic rights and labor's right to strike. A CELU congress held in September 1974 came up with proposals rejecting the idea of the military as a caretaker government. The next day, while the congress was in session, members of CELU's executive council were summoned to the Derge's headquarters where attempts were made to intimidate them into withdrawing the offensive resolutions. When participants of the congress refused to do so, the military regime arrested three of CELU's officials. That action of the Derge further aggravated the situation and the participants of the congress resolved to call a strike if the officials were not released. In the Addis Abeba area, none of the unions went out on strike, except for the Meta Beer Factory, the leader of whom was arrested along with the CELU officials.

The ambitious soldier politicians were alerted to the necessity of controlling organized labor and, in the meantime, became determined to leave the ineffective CELU vice-president in power.

More serious manifestations of opposition were witnessed from some elements within the ranks of the military. These elements were opposed to the seizure of power by the military and demanded the recall and reelection of the Derge's members. The Derge took steps to neutralize these elements when it killed most of the radical soldiers in September/October 1974 .

All throughout this period, the Eritrean issue had remained unresolved and General Aman Andom traveled to Eritrea and proposed a number of suggestions, including the lifting of the State of Emergency. He was able to appease a certain section of the Eritrean society thereby alienating the rebels. However, he was unable to break the intransigence of the rebel organizations, which had Eritrean independence as their main agenda. Besides, his mediation effort was not well received.

On November 18, 1974, the media headlined an address by Major Mengistu Haile Mariam, the leader of an emerging hard line faction within the Derge, which repeated almost verbatim the propaganda line used by the imperial regime regarding Eritrea. He denounced what he called a handful of rebels in the north who were in the service of foreign powers and rejected the offer of peace. On 23 November, Aman was dismissed from all his posts. That night, Mengistu dispatched a force headed by his adjutant Colonel Daniel Asfaw, to the General's residence. When he learned that he was surrounded, General Aman Andom fought back and finally, shot and killed himself. The night that General Aman died, a massacre of fifty-nine prisoners, mostly officials of the *ancien* regime and members of the royal family was carried out. A week later, the selection of General Teferi Bente to replace Aman Andom as chairman of the PMAC was announced. The hurried appointment of General Teferi was intended to deflect the rumor that Mengistu was wielding power.

Following the death of Aman, the Eritrean question took a dramatic turn in the military, political and economic spheres. The peaceful and political approach to resolve the issue was discontinued. The Derge followed the footsteps of the previous regime and strangled peaceful Eritrean youth in the streets of Asmera.

The conflict in Eritrea became one of the issues that established EPLO's relationship with the Derge. The EPLO popularized the Eritrean question among the population that it was able to reach. Even though the left had made some breakthrough within a certain section of the society, the national issue still remained taboo. The EPLO had begun to explain the essence of the conflict in Eritrea and it was introducing a new and fresh approach to resolving the issue. The war, however, escalated.

Even though the left supported the struggle in Eritrea, the majority of the Ethiopian radicals did not accept the inevitability of Eritrean independence. They believed that the recognition of the right to self-determination and the expediency of the formation of an independent state were two separate issues. They were still hopeful that, in the proper circumstances, class solidarity would prevail over nationalism and Eritreans would choose to remain with Ethiopia.

The EPLO leadership was compelled to consider this issue anew toward the end of November 1974. The organization went beyond the recognition of the right to self-determination and demanded that it be resolved according to the demands and wishes of the people. *Democracia* proposed a referendum to ascertain the wishes of the people of Eritrea, and

Introduction

envisaged various arrangements involving autonomy, including federation. If the people wished it, *Democracia* stated that secession should be accepted. It was concluded that the Eritrean question should be resolved only peacefully and democratically. *Democracia* further demanded that the repression, arrest and torture of Eritreans should stop. *Democracia* went to great lengths to explain that it did not support disintegration, but the right to self-determination. In recognizing this right, radicals opposed suppression, not unity. To recognize the right to secede, pointed out *Democracia*, is not to support it. With insight that proved prophetic, *Democracia* warned that by making it impossible for the progressive forces to organize, the military regime was diverting the revolution from class lines to nationalism. This allowed the ruling classes of some nationalities to claim popular support and *Democracia* foresaw the degeneration of the revolution into a series of nationalist wars.

Near the end of 1974, the journal *Labader* (the Proletariat) was launched to provide a medium of communication with labor. Labader addressed the workers and was distributed mainly in working class neighborhoods.

Red Star, the internal journal of the EPLO, appeared at this time. It was designed as a medium of communication for party members and addressed theoretical, organizational and political issues.

Youth involvement and activities increased with the launching of the student campaign (Zemetcha) by the regime. According to a government statement, the purpose of the campaign was to spread the message of 'Ethiopia Tikdem' to the countryside, to promote literacy, agricultural development, public health, land reform, preservation of national heritage, and to gather information about the life of the peasantry. Students and teachers were to take part, while the normal process of education was to be interrupted. The campaign had obvious political implications, which were not missed by the emerging opposition. The Zemetcha initially met with a hostile reception from student and teacher organizations which insisted that rural development was not feasible without land reform.

The intention to send students to the rural areas before the enactment of major policy changes was considered a sinister move. Initially, the EPLO regarded the Zemetcha as a major obstacle to the organizational process that was underway. Sensing the impending dispersal of the students, the EPLO leadership made two decisions. The first was concerning the formation of groups to prepare manuals on central theoretical issues. The second step was regarding the formation of a provisional zematch committee to coordinate the activities of the EPLO and the Youth League structures and to form as many local "zematch committees" before they were dispersed to the various parts of the country.

What became known as the Zemetcha was officially launched on 21

The Generation, II

December, 1974. A more detailed guide for the student campaign was issued. A few weeks later, the students began moving to their assigned places and about sixty thousand university and high school students, both boys and girls, were deployed.

In a move designed to regain the initiative, which also demonstrated that the leaders of the new regime were developing political skills, the Derge issued a policy declaration on Ethiopian Socialism a day before launching the Zemetcha. Concurrent to this policy, the Derge moved further ahead of the radical opposition by announcing a series of nationalization measures on the first day of 1975. All banks, financial and savings institutions and all thirteen insurance companies were nationalized and were assigned to the upgraded National Resources Development Ministry. A month later, another sweeping measure was enacted. Seventy-two manufacturing enterprises were nationalized and the major share holding of another twenty-nine passed into the hands of the regime. Following the nationalization of industries, an idea began floating around the Derge concerning the status of labor and whether it was necessary to maintain CELU.

It should be remembered that in the early seventies, the EPLO, believing that peaceful means had been exhausted, had already embarked on the preparation for the commencement of an armed struggle. However, the breakout of the 1974 movement indicated that the avenue for conducting the struggle peacefully was open. Recognizing the new direction of the struggle, the EPLO had to embark in the peaceful struggle, without abandoning the armed means as a last resort. It was decided that the nucleus of the army should move closer to the Tigrayan border and, in the mean time, the organization inside the country would make preparations to create easy access to the area.

The area chosen as the initial guerrilla base was Adi Erob, a remote mountainous region in Tigrai province. All throughout its stay in the EPLF territory, no contact could be established with the army. This was partly due to the dispersal of EPLO members in some Tigrayan cities, as a result of arrest of some leading members. Following the incident, a further effort to establish a viable branch in Tigrai proved difficult. Left with no alternative, the EPLO had to begin all over and some Tigrigna speaking members residing in other parts of the country were sent to the area.

The nucleus of the army, which had stayed over a year in Eritrea, arrived in Agame, Tigrai, around December 1974. Soon after, almost one-half of the members of the nucleus defected.

An urban military wing was organized under a Defense Committee, during the last quarter of 1974. Initially, its main function was to acquire arms and finance for the organization and to protect party meetings, officials and property.

The 1974 movement continued advancing and hardly an issue of

Introduction

Democracia appeared without a mention of land reform. The Derge was pressured to make more concessions and on March 4, 1975, all rural land was nationalized and proclaimed the collective property of the Ethiopian people.[2] "No person or business organization or any other organization shall hold rural land in private ownership,"[3] stated the Proclamation. The land reform bill not only undermined the economic basis of the old order, but became the harbinger of new forms of social relations to production. The EPLO's response to the land reform proclamation was formulated at an urgently called meeting of the central committee. The central committee discussed a wide range of issues related to the land reform and the jist of it came out in *Democracia*. The land reform was conceived of as a powerful blow against feudalism, the first target of the revolutionary movement. Besides, it diluted one of the major demands of the south. It nullified the economic aspect of the national question, without addressing the political. These measures had outstripped the radical agenda and outdated the economic content of the EPLO program. To continue a revolutionary struggle where some of the major economic demands had in some way been addressed was one of the major problems that the Ethiopian radicals and the EPLO, in particular, faced.

The majority of the Ethiopian Left was at a crossroad and one of the options was to follow the MEISON, one of the important groups that took part in the 1974 movement. It decided to join the unrestructured and bureaucratic state apparatus. This option was never considered by the majority of the radicals who supported the EPLO for it meant joining the unreformed state structure, the oppressor of students, workers and national minorities.

As we are going to witness in Chapter I, following the proclamation of land reform in 1975, in most of the Southern provinces, fierce revolutionary struggles began taking shape with the peasants on one side and the former ruling class and the state machinery on the other. The most fierce of these struggles took place in Sidamo, Illubabor and Keffa provinces. Hundreds and thousands of lives were lost. Not long after the land reform was enacted, the zematch youth met head on with some of the major weaknesses and omissions of the reform. These were related to the democratic rights of peasants and zematch students. In many of the localities, the zemetcha students stood on the side of the peasantry and made efforts to resolve some of its problems. Only two months after the land reform Proclamation, the military government vowed that the zemetcha students would be the targets of the 'Ethiopia Tikdem' sword.

Democracia argued that the Derge suppressed the rebellion of feudal landlords while collaborating with those that still controlled the local state apparatus. The Derge was accused of suppressing the people who were struggling to implement the proclamation. At the same time, it rescued and preserved the old state apparatus, thereby giving the privileged sector an opportunity to dilute the very reform that it had enacted.

In the urban areas, immediately following the September 1974 strike, CELU's truncated leadership faced a formidable challenge from dissident branch leaders seeking to take control of the organization and make it worthy of its name. Their target was the vice-president, who had sabotaged the September 1974 general strike. CELU's last Congress had resolved to meet in January 1975 to decide on the future of its leadership. When the time arrived, delegates of the various unions in Addis Abeba and the vicinity came to the CELU office to attend the Congress. When it became clear that a National Congress could not be held, leaders of about 100 unions in Addis Abeba and the adjacent industrial area and representing the great majority, held a separate meeting and elected a nine-man provisional leadership for the Addis Abeba area and vicinity. It was headed by Marcos Hagos.

Some weeks after the proclamation of the land reform, the provisional leadership of the Addis Abeba and vicinity unions demanded a permit to hold a National Congress which would comprise the unions in Addis Abeba and vicinity, Harer, Eritrea, Gojjam and other provinces. The Derge refused to do that and expressed its support for the vice-president. The underground labor meeting which was interrupted for some time was resumed. In one of those meetings, it was agreed to take over CELU and form a provisional national leadership of Ethiopian labor. That idea was passed over to the branches in Asmera and other areas which mandated the unions in the Addis Abeba and vicinity to act on their behalf as well.

In March 1975, a meeting of the unions in Addis Abeba and the vicinity was called as planned. The participants of the unions in Addis Abeba and the vicinity arrived and the congress was opened. The meeting went ahead with its deliberations and elected a nine-man provisional leadership of the CELU. (As was indicated above, the Addis Abeba and vicinity unions had elected their own provisional leadership earlier.) While the meeting was underway, the military regime summoned the new leadership to its office and accused it of trying to create discord between the military regime and the workers and vowed that it would take measures if the labor leaders did not refrain from such activities.

While CELU's case was in a limbo, the Derge proclaimed May Day as a public holiday. Using May Day as a pretext, trade unions in Addis Abeba unanimously decided that they would not take part in the celebration unless their existence was recognized and their demands met. The Derge became embarrassed when it learned about the decision of the workers and sent three delegates to negotiate with the representatives of the workers. At the May Day celebration, hundreds of thousands of workers took part in the demonstration carrying placards that demanded for an "independent CELU", "democratic rights", and also stating that "the vice-president cannot represent

Introduction

CELU", etc.

Soon after the May Day celebration, the Provisional Leadership of CELU demanded that the Derge grant permission to conduct the National Congress. The Derge failed to respect the promise it had made earlier and, thus, the struggle of the Ethiopian labor movement under the military regime evolved as a struggle of the workers for an independent trade union. After realizing that the peaceful options were exhausted, the clandestine meeting of labor activists decided to take over CELU's leadership. On May 18, about 66 labor activists took control of CELU's office and prohibited the vice-president and his followers from entering the building. On May 21, the congress was called and it brought CELU under control. On the same day, the meeting was dispersed and the military regime issued a statement condemning CELU. CELU office was closed.

As soon as CELU was banned, a very large number of labor activists were pulled into the underground activity and a national strike committee was formed. As local committees were being formed and a strike became imminent, the military regime gave in and on May 31, it called a meeting of the representatives of the workers. The Derge gave in and all of the demands of the workers were met. The Ethiopian labor movement won the day and for the first time in its history, CELU began operating with little government interference. The Congress elected a thirteen-man provisional leadership and forwarded about thirty-two demands to the regime. Among these were the promulgation of a new labor law, minimum wage, and issues concerning the question of democracy. The Congress then decided to convene in three months time to review the outcome.

The second confrontation between labor and the regime took place when transport workers dismissed the owners of the various transport organizations and took the institutions under control. To diffuse the situation and partly to appease the workers without addressing their main demands, the military regime decreed the Urban Land Proclamation on July 26, 1975. The Urban Land Proclamation decreed that "... all urban lands shall be the property of the Government....No person, family or organization shall hold urban land in private ownership....No compensation shall be paid in respect of urban lands...." Rents were lowered, and quasi-government institutions called kebeles were formed.

Other areas of conflict were the teachers' union where the first friction between teachers and the military regime was over the newly proclaimed curriculum of education. The teachers were instructed to teach the spirit of the new policy known as "Ethiopian Socialism". Many of the teachers did not understand it and refused to collaborate. Instead, they demanded for teachers' seminar that would discuss the issue freely and openly. They also demanded that censorship be lifted. To discuss this and other issues, the teachers' unions national political committee, headquartered in Addis

Abeba, held it's first meeting in May 1975 and was attended by teacher delegates from around the country.

Another confrontation between the regime and the teachers was over the new educational policy that was drafted by the Ministry of Education under the direction of the Derge.[4] The teachers had voiced a similar protest in early 1974 when the policy known as the "Sector Review" was to be put into effect. The Ethiopian Teachers Association at its meeting held in Assela, Arsi, in June 1975, raised its objection about the improper selection of provincial representatives to the curriculum board.

In August 1975, the union held its congress in Jimma and by then, had undergone a fundamental personnel change. The Congress passed resolutions that were critical of the military regime. The resolutions, which were to be printed at the headquarters of the Addis Abeba branch, were confiscated by the military regime. The duplicating machines were also confiscated, the office closed and those considered ring-leaders were arrested.

Within the ranks of the Ethiopian radicals there arose differences when the group that took over MEISON's leadership in 1975 believed that "it was possible to form an alliance with the Derge that represented the left wing of the petty-bourgeoisie and could struggle for democracy." Before MEISON reached this conclusion, "around December and January 1974/75, genuine progressives had established a working relation and cooperation with the left-wing of the Derge," wrote *Sefiw Hizbe Dimtse*, MEISON's publication.[5] To reach that conclusion, the MEISON had to overcome its internal problems.

The internal struggle within MEISON was not public in 1974/75 and unaware of the new policies of MEISON, the EPLO Central Committee had decided to create some kind of an understanding and a common political and ideological front with MEISON. A bi-level contact was established. The proclamation of the land reform act finally breached the relationship, albeit an uneasy one, between the EPLO and MEISON.

While giving guidance to the struggle, the EPLO CC was making efforts to keep the organization abreast of the demands of the time and between March and August 1975, at least four CC meetings were conducted. One of the meetings was devoted entirely to the response of the EPLO to the land reform proclamation, while the rest focused on the preparation of the First Extended Conference. A meeting of the broad membership was deemed necessary to update the organization's program, to evaluate its performance, to amend its constitution and regulations, to assess the political situation in Ethiopia and the international situation and, finally, to expand the membership of the CC itself. Among the CC members themselves, a number of questions related to the constitution of the organization were being raised. These included the question of party democracy, the role of a

Introduction

general secretary, the numerical strength of the CC and the relation between the army nucleus and the party.

The Conference was opened during the third week of August 1975. The first item on the agenda of the Conference was the assessment of the current political situation in Ethiopia. The conclusion reached at came out as the program of the EPRP. The second item on the agenda discussed was the international situation, which the Conference assessed was conducive to revolutionary struggle. Concerning the international communist movement, the same dangers mentioned at the First Congress of the EPLO were seen as persistent; revisionism from the Soviet Union and dogmatism from China. The third item concerned the status of the organization. The Conference reviewed all that had taken place since the leadership shifted its center to Addis Abeba. The merger with other groups, the expansion of EPLO networks beyond the capabilities of the leadership, other problems of leadership, the formation of the various structures, and the problems encountered in coordination, inefficiency, communication, recruitments, etc., were discussed. Some of these problems were dealt with by changes in the constitution and the creation of new departments. More constitutional changes were made to promote party democracy. Among these changes was the elimination of the post of Secretary General.

All positions in the party were made elective, although the implementation of this rule was delayed until conditions permitted it. [6] Further changes were made regarding the holding of congresses to prevent their manipulation by the leadership.

The constitution also stipulated that the party structure in the army could hold its own Congress. The introduction of safety mechanisms to prohibit abuse of the constitution was deemed important. More detailed clauses were added to ensure that the Congress was called every three years.[7] Concerning the CC itself, a number of clauses were introduced that limited the power of the executive bodies.[8]

A major issue discussed was the expansion of the number of the leadership. Finally, the Conference delegated the CC to choose its members according to the criteria agreed upon. The Conference had to choose a new name for the party. The Ethiopian Peoples Liberation Organization, the name adopted by the First Congress in 1972, was little known and never used outside the organization. The Ethiopian Peoples Revolutionary Party (EPRP) became the choice of the Conference.

Immediately following the Conference, the first CC Plenum was held. By open ballot, the plenum elected a politburo and the secretary of the CC.

The date for the public declaration of the party was fixed at this meeting for August 26, 1975 which went down as the official birth date of the EPRP. Following the public declaration of the EPRP, the public was introduced to new values, understanding and new thinking regarding the process of organization. Until this time, very little was known of formation of an organization. The EPRP's political program was one of the first that a relatively large sector of the society had ever seen.

Notes to Introduction

1. Kiflu Tadesse, The Generation, Part I, Independent Publishers, 1993, page 73.

2. Proclamation No.31, Chapter II, No.3/1.

3. Ibid., No.3/2.

4. Hall, Marlyn Ann, The Ethiopian Revolution: Group Interaction and Civil - Military Relations, (dissertation), George Washington University, 1977, page 290.

5. Sefiw Hizbe Dimtse, No 50, page 10.

6. EPRP Constitution, Clause 6, By-laws, Clause 22.

7. EPRP Constitution, Clause 8.

8. EPRP By-laws, Clauses, 11, 12, 13, 16.

1

Post Land Reform Struggle

Part I

Southern Ethiopia - September 1975 to February 1976

In the last quarter of 1975, peasant assertiveness gained momentum, with zematch (campaign) students giving guidance and leadership to the struggle. Mass organizations became much more involved in the struggle while the military regime devised means to control them. The opposition, with the EPRP in the lead, gained momentum following the public declaration of the EPRP and the formation of underground mass organizations.

After mid-1975, the peasants' struggle in northern and southern Ethiopia took a different form. The struggle in the south continued as an extension to transform the land reform movement into an agrarian revolution.[1] The peasantry continued to form independent peasant associations and to arm themselves. To do so, the peasantry had to disarm members of the former ruling class. In some instances, such as in Sidamo and in some parts of Shoa, the disarming process was accompanied by confiscation and looting of properties, including hotels, flour mills, etc. Because of their narrow perception of class relationships, the peasantry believed that they had the full support of the state; former land owners dwelling in the urban areas became their targets and their rage was focused on the local gentry as well.

Keffa

One of the provinces where tumultuous unrest took place during the 1974 revolutionary movement was Keffa. Peasant revolt, workers strike and students demonstrations in 1974 finally resulted in the formation of what was known as the "People's Committee" that took over the administration of the capital city, Jimma. From that period, Keffa and in particular the capital

Jimma, was volatile.[2]

In the last quarter of 1975, in Keffa province, a confrontation between the people and the supporters of the regime took place following an effort to form a women's organization. Around mid-September 1975, the regime arrested some teacher activists following the convocation of the 18th Congress of the Ethiopian Teachers Association (ETA) held in Jimma. The ETA branch of Keffa province organized it. Among those arrested was Kebbebew, one of the inspiring leaders of the 1974 Jimma uprising and a secretary of the EPRP zonal committee in Keffa. Representing his zone, he had attended the Extended Conference of the EPRP held in August 1975.

In Jimma, in the third week of September 1975, when a demonstration demanding the release of the teachers was taking place, police opened fire and more than fifteen hundred people were rounded up and arrested. After a few days of interrogation, most of the detainees were released. However, about twenty teachers and zematch students remained behind bars. Some of them, including Kebbebew, never left prison.

With the crisis escalating, the military regime appointed military officers to the five districts of the Keffa province. However, the tension that had been building up did not abate; indeed, it continued to intensify. In Limu aweraja, the military regime dealt a blow to the opposition when it executed Haji Aba Foggi, representative of the Ministry of Land Reform of the area and a member of the EPRP, and zematch Wendirad Bekele. All of the zematch students of the Limu area were also arrested. This repression was a preemptive move against the Limu peasants, who by this time were making preparations to voice their grievances.

In Agaro, Gimbi and Mizan Teferi, in Keffa province, some zematch students were killed and more than fifty of them were transferred to Jimma.[3] While the repression against the peasants and the townspeople continued, the regime attempted to lure in those landlords who had taken up arms and had gone to the hills. One of the measures that the regime took was to give the landlords two and a half hectares of coffee growing land.[4]

The political situation in Keffa remained volatile, despite the repression conducted the previous year.[5] In April 1976, carpenters and masons went out to the streets demanding jobs. Following the nationalization of urban houses a year earlier, activities related to construction of houses had come to a standstill and the sector that depended on such activities was hard hit.

In Jimma, during the third week of April 1976, another major confrontation took place between the regime and the peasantry. Around 80,000 peasants gathered near a small town called Yebu, in memory of the repression conducted the previous year by Derge member Major Ali Musa and Major Lemissa (who later defected and joined the EDU). At the peasant gathering, members of the local government were chased away and the peasants conducted free discussions on issues concerning their conditions. The military force that came to disperse the crowd sympathized with the peasants and refused to collaborate with members of the local government.

The military regime regarded that sympathy as an ominous sign. Also, during that week, the peasants of Limu, Bonga and other areas disarmed some local landlords. Throughout the month of April 1976, the people continued asserting its rights. The unrest in Jimma was galvanized on May Day of 1976, when the city, guided by EPRP members and other activists, celebrated the event of its free will. When the Derge realized that conditions were getting out of control, it sent Major Getachew Shibeshi who arrived in Jimma on May Day and began giving back the guns to their former owners.

The situation remained tense during the first two weeks of May. In the midst of this turmoil, in the second week of May, a demonstration opposing the seminar organized by the Provisional Office for Mass Organizations Affairs (POMOA) was held.[6] POMOA, which had no support in the Jimma area, had opened its office sometime earlier and Demeke Harege Weyene, a MEISON member, was put in charge.[7] The seminar was organized for workers, peasants and teachers. Workers, many of whom were regrouped around the Ethiopian Workers Revolutionary Union (ELAMA),[8] boycotted the seminar and continued agitating against it. As a result, the seminar could not continue as scheduled.

In the third week of May 1976, the government ordered that people come out in support of its newly decreed policy regarding the war in Eritrea. That policy was known as the May Peace Initiative.[9] Upon decreeing the policy, the Derge had simultaneously launched a military campaign known as the "Raza Project" which had been under preparation since March 1976.[10] The Derge's call for support of its May Peace Initiative was not heeded and few people conducted demonstration in its support. The people's defiance triggered government retaliation and both the military regime and POMOA began conducting a massive hunt for those "culprits" who had induced the people into the opposition camp. Hundreds of workers, teachers and youth were arrested. More than one hundred twenty-five activists were summarily executed, including almost all of the leading activists of ELAMA.[11] Among those who were executed were veteran activist and secretary of the EPRP zonal committee Kebbebew G/Tsadik; the well-rounded intellectual and leading party member of the EPRP, Wondewossen Seyoum; Tsegaye, one of the leaders of the Teachers' Union in Keffa, and Hameza, an ELAMA activist, who had led the strike called by CELU in September 1975. Others executed included Hassen Abadir, Abdi Abadir, Boga Abajobir, Daniel Mengesha, Yohannes Teferra, Sultan Ibrahim, Fekadu, Debela Haji Nur and many others. Major Getachew Shibeshi threw some of the corpses in the Gibbe desert. Some of the prisoners were sent to Addis Abeba for further interrogation.[12]

On their way back to Addis Abeba, the Derge representatives committed similar atrocities in the small towns of Hoseena, Welkite and Welisso. Hundreds of youth activists were summarily executed and thousands of prisoners were sent to Addis Abeba, filling the prisons with young people, teachers and workers from all parts of the country. Because of this massive repression, the EPRP structure of the Jimma area was literally decimated. Although some efforts were made to recover, the EPRP was unable to mend the damage inflicted for quite sometime. In one stroke, the regime quelled the struggle that had been taking place for more than two years.

The repression conducted in Keffa resulted from the coordinated effort of the military regime and POMOA. While the military regime took charge of the repressive measures, POMOA marked who the targets should be and singled out the institutions upon which to focus. Unlike the preceding years when the regime conducted random repression and missed its targets, the regime was quite effective in the repression of early 1976 because of POMOA's collaboration. This collaboration of the regime and POMOA was regarded as a division of labor "between the mental and the physical."[13] The EPRP was aware that it was the "target of the...anti-progressive campaign" and "the new strategy of the 'selected officers' and the banda intellectuals is to hit the periphery first, before they hit the center. This is an attempt to nip the movement in its bud," commented *Democracia*.[14]

Prior to POMOA's formation, the Derge could not visualize the opposition beyond a few outspoken individuals. POMOA, which was capable of envisaging an entire structure of activists, taught the regime to look for structure and to realize that arresting a few ring leaders would not ease situations. To quiet the unrest, POMOA showed the military regime that it had to dismantle the entire structure of the opposition. The massacre and repression in Jimma was the prototype strategy that was needed to annihilate the opposition, including the EPRP. In the years to come, that approach was to be repeated in the various parts of the country.

Immediately following the massacre in Jimma, the EPRP CC passed a death sentence on the POMOA representative, Demeke Harege Weyene and Major Getachew Shebeshi, who were directly involved in the massacre.[15] Beginning around May 1976, EPRP squads looked for both individuals. Because of his elusive life style, the Major could not be tracked down, but Demeke was killed two or three months later.[16] Following his death, the Derge conducted a massive campaign and arrested hundreds of people.

Sidamo

The unrest unleashed following the declaration of the Land Reform Proclamation took place in the Sidamo province as well. The 27th battalion, stationed in Sidamo took matters into its own hand. Beginning in September 1975, prompted by an anti-government leaflet, the infamous military contingent mentioned above arrested teachers, zematch students and other government employees in the Hagere Mariam and Burji *weredas* and wreaked havoc among the Gujji and Derasa people. In the mopping up operation, more than one hundred seventy people, including prominent peasant leaders were killed; hundreds were imprisoned and more than seven thousand cattle were confiscated.[17] Following this incident, peasants of the Hagere Mariam area fled to the bushes. Some houses were set on fire and havoc reigned in the town. The atrocities of the 27th Battalion became so glaringly obvious and politically damaging that the military regime could not remain silent. To ward-off the escalating crisis, the military regime arrested and passed death sentence on the military officers who were behind the massacre. However, the regime was unable to redress the damage inflicted and some months later, about three hundred Gujji peasants, led by Hajji Kutta, left for Somalia for military training. The group, along with the Somali army, would return to Ethiopia a year or so later.[18]

At the end of April 1976, peasants in some parts of Sidamo disarmed some former landlords. In the capital Yirgalem, about 40,000 peasants surrounded the city, disarmed some former landlords and put ninety-eight of them in prison. Among those dispossessed, however, were also middle and lower commodity producers.

While the crisis was still unfolding, the military regime intervened re-arming the former landlords and freeing the prisoners, while arresting peasants, teachers and zematches.[19] The EPRP was accused of instigating peasant actions.

It is true that some of the deeds were instigated by zematch students, some of whom were members or supporters of the EPRP. However, the EPRP dissociated itself from such acts stating,

> "the confiscation of properties in some small towns, such as, Nazareth, Debreziet, Awassa, Welkite, etc., had very grave consequences... properties of the middle and small producers were also confiscated. This was a mistake. Let alone now, even for years to come, not only small producers, but the national bourgeoisie should not be the target of the revolution."[20]

Throughout 1976, the relationship between the military regime and the zematch students continued to worsen. As a result, a special circular dispatched to local government officials ordered the confinement of many zematch students to their camps. The circular, sent out by the vice-chairman of the Derge, Major Atnafu Abate, in July 1975, allowed government officials to discipline and, if need be, to arrest zematch students.[21] By December 1975, either because of difficulties related to the campaign program itself and/or local government pressure, some zematch students found it difficult to stay in the camps and they left either for the cities or to some neighboring countries. To alleviate the tension, on December 18, 1975, the regime declared a general amnesty to those zematch students who were willing to return to their camps and complete their program.[22] However, the amnesty could not ease the situation.

The zemetcha program had an adverse effect on students who were promoted to the eleventh grade. These students were not allowed to attend classes, find work, or take part in the student campaign, and, thus, they remained idle.[23] The zemetcha program deployed students who were eleventh graders and above and it had been decided that the next batch of zemetcha students would consist of those who were promoted to the eleventh grade.

Arsi

Arsi, a key province in the beginnings of the 1974 revolutionary struggle, had remained a volatile area. The struggle in the rural parts of Arsi intensified following the declaration of land reform in 1975. In the course of this struggle, a "Revolutionary Popular Committee" was formed.

One of the areas where intense conflict took place was the Arba Gugu aweraja. That conflict turned for the worse after the assassination of a leader of a peasant association. The peasants arrested a person whom they thought had committed the crime and handed him over to the administrator of the area.[24] The administrator released the alleged killer on bail and that action galvanized the conflict. The peasants, along with zematch students arrested the administrator, the police officers and the judges. Hoping to be vindicated, they took their "prisoners" to Assela, the capital of Arsi. However, Derge official released all of the "prisoners", thereby aggravating the condition of the peasants in Arba Gugu.[25]

The Struggle in the North

Partially because of the land tenure system in northern Ethiopia, the Land Reform Proclamation of 1975 had little impact on the day to day life of the majority of the peasantry of the north, and the struggle that erupted in 1976 had little or no relationship to the land decree. The main incident that triggered peasant discontent and rebellion was the regime's effort to mobilize the peasantry for the war front in Eritrea. The rebellion became more pronounced when the military regime engaged itself in peasant mobilization for the "Raza Project".

As indicated above, the preparation for the "Raza Project" began around March 1976. Raza is the name of a bird species found in the northern part of Ethiopia. The birds are famous for devouring locusts continuously and excreting uninterruptedly. Hence, labeling the project as "Raza" had a derogatory connotation.

To take part in the "Raza Project", peasants from Wello, Begemedir and Tigrai were assembled in March 1976. From the Begemedir province, three people were chosen from each wereda to attend the meeting held in Addis Abeba.

While organizing the "Raza Project", the military regime proclaimed the May Peace Initiative. In that proclamation, it was outlined that the Eritrean problem would be resolved on the basis of regional autonomy.[26] The May Peace Initiative called on Eritreans residing abroad to return to Ethiopia, however, the decree failed to lift the state of emergency in Eritrea.[27] The "Peace Initiative" was a diplomatic move of the regime intended to appease both domestic and international public opinion. Violence, expressed through the "Raza" campaign, still characterized the essence of the policies of the regime.[28]

Furthermore, regarding the struggle in Eritrea, the new policy outlined in the NDR program declared that "...an urgent as well as a historic duty of Ethiopian revolutionary forces, particularly the revolutionary force in Eritrea is to be united and foil the plots of the reactionary group...."[29] According to the Derge and POMOA, the reactionary group was the ELF.

In April and May 1976, government statements and the Abyot Medrek in the government owned newspaper focused on the struggle in Eritrea.[30] Various articles written under assumed names prepared the populace for the impending campaign. The rebel organizations were portrayed as forces who were objectively allied with the enemies of Ethiopia and that issue became the recurring theme of the media.

By this time, Eritrea, which had more than 167 small and medium-sized industries, was gripped in an economic crisis. Some of the medium sized industries that could employ thousands of permanent and seasonal employees, particularly those in the outlying areas, were either shut down or they were operating at a very low capacity. As indicated in a World Bank report, the condition in Eritrea had a staggering effect on the economy of Ethiopia.

Manufacturing production has declined steadily over the last three years, and at the end of 1975/76, it was 6.0% lower than in 1972/73....The major reason for production declines has been the situation in Eritrea, where transportation and security difficulties have affected both productive capacity and accessibility of markets, and which accounted for approximately 30% of manufacturing output in normal times....Other factors accounting for the decrease in production included management changes following nationalization, difficulties over raw material and spare part supplies, and labor disputes.[31]

A sizable part of the Eritrean countryside had fallen under the control of the rebel organizations. In September 1975, the American military base in Asmera, known as the Kagnew station, was attacked by Eritrean rebels and a number of Americans and Ethiopians were held hostages. There also were a few casualties.

Some days before the proclamation of the "Raza Project", *Democracia* disclosed the preparations and alerted opposition forces of the impending crisis. A crusade against the project began. Enumerating the possible consequences of the campaign, one of the *Democracia* issues predicted about the massive death of peasants, the destruction of property and the negative effect of the campaign on the unfolding class struggle in the north and particularly in Eritrea.[32] *Democracia's* commentary was in line with the decision of the August 1975 EPRP Conference which had concluded that the national issue could not be resolved militarily.[33] Another *Democracia* issue which came out to elaborate some of the decisions of the Conference had declared that the war in Eritrea had to stop and negotiation between the rebel groups and the regime had to start.[34]

EPRP's call fell on very receptive ears. The zematch students who by this time were struggle-tempered, became the forerunners in the crusade against the "Raza Project". Partly because of the agitation conducted by the EPRP in collaboration with the zematch students, in the Begemidir province, the turn out of peasants supporting the project became very low. Moreover, it was around this time that the EPRP Zonal Committee of the Begemidir area began publishing the "*Peasantry*", one of the first publications of the EPRP exclusively devoted to the peasantry.

Throughout April and May 1976, demonstrations opposing the military campaign in Eritrea were conducted in many parts of Ethiopia. During the May Day celebration of 1976, all throughout Ethiopia, the war in Eritrea became the main focus of agitation and "Stop the Genocide" became the rallying slogan. The Ethiopian People's Revolutionary Army (EPRA) conducted similar agitation against the project and, in Tigrai, in May, it took part in a military engagement, siding with the ELF.

From its inception, the "Raza Project" was ill-advised. The project was launched in May and June, when the peasantry was getting ready for the next farming season. In Gojjam, the peasants demanded a postponement of the date, but the regime refused to budge. As a result, very few showed up at the rally held in Bahir Dar. The project was doomed to failure long before it could get a foothold.

In Tigrai, particularly in Mekele and Maichew, hundreds of people were arrested for campaigning against the project. In Adewa, prisons became so overcrowded that some had to be released in order to provide space for the next batch of detainees.[35] The regime threatened to bombard Tigrayan villages unless the people participated in the "project". These threats produced the mobilization of more than two thousand five-hundred people from the Tembein *awaraja* (district) alone.[36]

In Wello, the regime rounded up peasants who had congregated to celebrate May Day. They were then taken to the campaign center in Adigrat, Tigrai. According to an internal memorandum of the regime, each hamlet in Wello was obliged to send one person. To select that person, villagers cast ballots. In some cases, children or disabled persons were selected. In the Alboko wereda of Wello, peasant huts were burnt to ashes when they refused to join the campaign. Peasants who attended weekly markets were rounded up and then taken to the battlefield, and that act forced many peasants to stay away from those locations where weekly markets were held.

Despite the protest and resistance in different parts of Ethiopia, the military regime was able to assemble thousands of peasants and lead them to the war front. No sooner did the peasant campaigners arrive in the battle zone when Eritrean rebels opened an offensive and inflicted colossal damage; the most devastating damage befell Wello peasants who were sandwiched between government military forces in the rear and rebel forces in the front.

The military regime's inability to peacefully resolve the Eritrean problem and the failure of the ill-advised "Raza Project" alienated not only Eritreans, but many of the peasants in the northern part of Ethiopia. It also became a blessing in disguise for the newly formed organization known as the Ethio pian Democratic Union (EDU). The EDU conducted intense political work amongst the peasantry. It armed its followers and long before it took over power, the EDU began appointing "administrators" to certain areas.

While the "Raza Project" was still under way, failure became imminent and the military regime began focusing on the May Peace Initiative, the gist of which was contained in the National Democratic Revolution (NDR) program.[37] Failure of the "Raza Project" notwithstanding, European countries, including the Soviet Union, continued to pressure Eritrean groups to negotiate with the Derge and resolve the conflict peacefully. POMOA and the regime conducted negotiations with the EPLF, but could not come to an agreement.

Despite efforts both on the military and diplomatic fronts, the Eritrean question remained one of the major unresolved problems of the country. It also became one of the major rallying demands of the Ethiopian youth, which expressed its dissent in the demonstrations it conducted, discussions it held, and underground papers it distributed.

In many parts of the country, the opposition, including the EPRP, continued popularizing the Eritrean question. In November 1974, the EPRP had come up with a new slogan regarding the conflict in Eritrea.[38] The EPRP advocated that the Eritrean issue should be resolved peacefully and democratically. Consequently, in many of the demonstrations, gatherings and meetings, the Eritrean issue remained one of the central points of agitation and it became one of the issues that put the EPRP at logger heads with the military regime. As a result, thousands of EPRP members and sympathizers became imprisoned and hundreds died carrying the banner of democracy.

Resolving the Eritrean problem remained a thorny issue even within and around the Derge itself. On July 13, 1976, partly because of a difference of approach to the resolution of the Eritrean issue, Mengistu single-handedly executed seventeen people including Derge member Major Sisay Habte, and General Getachew Nadew, Administrator of Eritrea. Derge member Major Kiros Alemayehu was also arrested and sometime later, it was reported that he committed suicide.

Unrest in Wello and Shoa

Beginning in September 1975, all over the country fierce fighting took place between the military regime and some members of the former ruling group. One of the most troublesome areas was the Wello province where some members of the ruling group had revolted and gone out to the hills. To quell the situation and suppress the "bandits", the regime took a number of steps, including the mobilization of the urban people. In October 1975, the regime claimed victory following a final show down at a place called Kutta Berr.

A relatively strong resistance against the military regime was underway in the Shoa province. As mentioned in *The Generation* Part I,[39] that resistance was short-lived. In September/October 1975, the leading figure of the group, Merid Birru, along with his followers, was killed. In February 1976, other notables, including Major General Kebede Worku and Kegnazmatch Mekonnen Wessenu were executed. The former governor of Gojjam province, Dejazmatch Tsehai Inkosellasie, was ambushed and killed by government forces.

In a move designed to influence the course that the Ethiopian Orthodox church was pursuing, the Derge removed the Ethiopian Patriarch Tewefelos and arrested him sometime later. He was first arrested in 1975 and kept under surveillance in a house by the Ministry of Foreign Affairs. The Patriarch escaped from his "house arrest" and headed to St. Gabriel Church, by the Old Airport area. After he arrived there, he instructed the person in charge to keep his presence secret. Not long afterward, the church was surrounded and the Patriarch was apprehended again.[40] During his stay under detention, the Patriarch did not mingle with other prisoners, but he was a lonely person. He was executed in mid-1977 and his whereabouts remained unknown until 1991, when his remains were found in the former compound of the Derge Intelligence Office.

Playing the carrot and stick game, the Derge granted amnesty to some landlords and their followers, while taking measures on other notables who had fled to the hills. "Reconciliation Committees" were making efforts to reconcile the Derge with dissident landlords; some members of these committees were ambushed while traveling in the western part of the Begemidir province and the leading figure of the group was killed. When some of the landlords surrendered, the Derge declared that they had been "baptized" in the "Ethiopian Tikdem" philosophy. Furthermore, in one of its conflicting gestures, the Derge struck more concessions to the members of the former ruling group when it promulgated Proclamation No. 71.

Proclamation No. 71

The land reform bill of February 1975 known as Proclamation No. 31

had enumerated the tasks and functions of peasant associations. However, it failed to recognize their rights and legal personalities. The relationship of the associations to the local state power was not spelt out and there was no provision that defined the accountability of the peasants' associations. Proclamation No. 31 of 1975 did not elaborate how the peasants could safeguard the gains of the struggle. Could they rely on the police force? If not, where were they supposed to obtain arms? Such was the condition until December 1975 when Proclamation No. 71 which dealt with the "... consolidation of peasant associations" was promulgated. The Proclamation recognized the legal personality of the peasants' associations and discussed the formation of service and producer cooperatives.[41] The most important aspect of the proclamation, however, was the provision that allowed the formation of peasant military contingents.

Proclamation No. 71 was the focus of *Democracia* No. 28, published during the last months of 1975. *Democracia* at length discussed the implications of the law and pointed out that the so called 'administrative and development committees' formed at the level of weredas, awarajas and provinces were controlled not by peasants, but by members of the local government. At the level of the wereda and awaraja, of the eleven members of the 'administrative and development committee', only three of them belonged to the peasants' associations. The rest were members of various government institutions. The chairpersons of the committees were the administrators of the weredas and awarajas. At the level of the province, not even a single peasant was represented in the "administrative and development committee" and its eleven members came from the various governmental institutions, including the police. According to the Proclamation, the committee formed at the level of the province was to have the prerogative of making final decisions. In line with the August EPRP Conference, *Democracia* argued that the new law deprived the peasants of the right to form independent associations, to exercise their rights and to safeguard their interests. It placed them under the control of the bureaucracy. The EPRP Conference of 1975 had set the tone of the struggle when it resolved that the peasantry had to be organized and armed in order to safeguard the gains of the struggle.

During the last months of 1975, independent peasant militia groups had emerged in many parts of the country. In some areas, they were known as 'the red Kafirs'. The EPRP program had advocated the formation of such groups[42] and some of them were formed by zematch students.

Proclamation No. 71 recognized the formation of peasants' military contingents. However, the criteria for membership remained vague and ambiguous. Explaining the significance of the Proclamation, *Democracia* asserted that it legalized the Derge's control of peasant defense units. The duties of these contingents were compared with those of the 'neche lebash'-- auxiliary peasant military contingents in the service of the Haile Selassie regime. *Democracia* concluded that Proclamation No.71 laid the groundwork to bring the peasantry under the direct control of the Derge and local governments, both politically and militarily. *Democracia* also argued that the Proclamation tightened the grip of the rising state bourgeois group over the peasantry. Furthermore, the Proclamation was regarded as a major document that legalized the linkage between the regime and the peasantry. It created conditions for the formation of a new peasant group that would be interested and involved in the activities of the state controlled by the Derge.

According to *Democracia*, the new law was considered regressive in comparison with Proclamation No. 31 of the land reform.

Conditions in the Urban Areas

Two years after the 1974 movement began, and a year after the Land Reform Proclamation, the economic condition in the urban areas remained grim. "Real GDP growth was 0.1% in 1974/75 and 2.7% in 1975/76, according to preliminary data. The average annual growth rate since 1972/73 has been only 1.4%. Given a population growth rate of about 2.5%, real output per head has been falling."[43] A *Democracia* issue of May 1976 stated that some of the major causes of the 1974 movement remained unresolved. Unemployment, high cost of living, scarcity of basic commodities and low income were pestering the urban dweller. *Democracia* attributed the low yield of the peasants' economy to the mobilization of peasants to the war fronts. Because of the mobilization, land was left fallow during farming seasons. Besides, the peasantry was unwilling to take its products to the markets, afraid that it would be rounded up. The World Bank report, however, concluded,

> [O]n the available evidence, the shortfall in marketed grain supplies was not caused by production shortfalls, but by a certain amount of dislocation in the marketing system and by increased stock holdings by farmers. One factor said to have influenced the rise in grain prices was a substantial increase in prices of manufactured consumer goods in many rural areas....[44]

Scarcity of products was also attributed to hoarding by some merchants in order to raise the price later on. Besides, "manufacturing investment had been declining in real terms since the early 1970s, with nominal investment in 1975/76 reaching about half the 1970/71 level."[45] The unrealistic price control policy that the regime tried to impose on the merchants, sometime during this period was mentioned as an additional factor for the disappearance of products from the markets. The confused economic policy of the regime and the unstable political condition of the country had their own toll, too.

The economic conditions of Ethiopia continued getting worse. Because of the new law that prohibited cutting trees, charcoal and similar products became scarce. The cost of teff (cereal) and other grains went up. In mid-1976, the price of many products had sky-rocketed; the cost of a kilogram of coffee had gone up by more than 100%, pepper by more than 400%, and the price of sugar had gone up too, when compared to the pre-1974 days. *Democracia* attributed the scarcity of sugar to exporting of more than 20% of the production.[46] Both as a warning and as a means to resolve the problem, the military regime executed some merchants who were accused of hoarding pepper and other essential items. Along with them, innocent citizens were also executed.

Shortage of industrial products was caused by scarcity of raw material, the high cost of industrial machines, lack of parts and transportation, and sabotage by businessmen who were engaged in the distribution network. Some commodities had either become scarce or were disappearing from the market. Because of shortage of parts, many factories were operating at low capacity. In mid-1976, "...cost of food had gone up by 30%, cost of medicine by 40%, home utensils by 45%, cost of clothing by 20%. In other words, the purchasing power of the worker had gone down by about 40-45%...," concluded *Democracia*.[47] The military regime had also decided to freeze workers' wages for two years.[48] This may be due to the government's overall deficit which had increased from "birr 45 million in 1973/74 to birr 314 million in 1975/76." The increases in expenditure were caused by "military and security outlays".[49]

Construction activities had come to a standstill and, as a result, unemployment remained a major concern. The Urban Housing Proclamation, which affected landlords, had also permanently dislocated a good number of masons, carpenters, etc. Many of them joined the army of the unemployed. Low moral of workers resulting from labor/management relationship was another major reason for low productivity. The regime's policy on the national question was an additional factor for the worsening economic conditions of the country. Because of the war in Eritrea, many factories were closed and imported items remained at the docks of Massawa and Asseb for quite a long time. Problems at Massawa and Asseb were cited as one of the reasons why medicine either disappeared from the markets or their prices went up. A transportation problem, caused by the failure to resolve the Afar issue, did play the major role in creating shortage of imported commodities. The major Asseb-Addis Abeba highway passes through the Afar region. Until it was able to skillfully rally the Afar Liberation Front to its side, the military regime was engaged in a fierce struggle with the Afar people.[50]

In the Humera commercial farms, in the Begemidir province, intense conflict between labor and farm owners continued mounting. Labor demanded the confiscation of commercial land and other properties. The military regime, which lacked the necessary political and technical readiness, refused to submit to the demands of labor. In the ensuing conflict, many of the laborers left for the Sudan and not long after, crisis fell on the plantations themselves and many of them were shut down.

As crises continued to multiply, the regime began pointing fingers.

However, *Democracia* reasoned that the discontent of the people was not imposed by few intellectuals or "anarchists", but it was rather a reflection of deep rooted economic and political crisis. If that condition was not alleviated, Ethiopia will face a colossal famine and many will perish, concluded a 1976 *Democracia* issue.[51] Furthermore, *Democracia* inquired how the 250 million dollars that the regime borrowed from the domestic banks and the 100 million dollar loans it received from the International Monetary Fund was spent.[52]

Workers' Discontent - Labor Movement in 1975/76

The relationship between the regime and labor had remained tense following the attempted strike in September 1974. Labor called the strike protesting the abolition of democratic rights, particularly labor's right to strike.[53]

The Confederation of Ethiopian Labor Union (CELU) had scheduled a Congress to be held in September 1975, sometime after the military regime had closed down the Addis Abeba branch of the Teachers' Union. The Derge did so following the resolution of the 18th Congress of the Ethiopian Teacher's Association that was held in Jimma. When informed about the Labor Congress, the Derge told CELU's leadership that it would not allow the meeting to be held. Aware of such previous experiences, it was the Workers' Congress held in May 1975 that set the date of the September meeting and the delegates for the Congress did not require confirmation. When the regime was informed about the arrangement and could do little to cancel the date of the Congress, the Derge's leaders inquired about the issues to be discussed and instructed CELU's leadership to focus only on those that were related to labor. Derge leaders ordered the labor leadership to cancel those points of the agenda that would discuss the Ethiopian situation. When the CELU leadership refused to concede, the military regime suggested that its security personnel would be present at the Congress. CELU leadership agreed on condition that their presence would be made public.

The CELU Congress was held from September 16-19, 1975. A great majority of the participants were new and radical activists of the working class, an outcome of the struggle of the preceding year. Following the triumph of the labor struggle in May 1975, many new unions were formed and some of the existing ones were reorganized.[54] Many unions had conducted meetings and ousted their former leaders and among the newly elected leaders were activists who were part of the labor struggle of the preceding year. The change in the composition of the union leadership was reflected in the Congress that was dominated by the new and radical labor leaders. The more moderate labor leaders, such as, Marcos Hagos, had to play a balancing role.

The Congress was held three months after the workers' struggle came out triumphant and the memory of that victory was still fresh amongst the participants, many of whom were still overconfident of their prowess. The Congress was held immediately after the EPRP declared itself public and almost all of the members of the EPRP worker's committee had been told to stay away from their work places in order to ward off any danger of arrest. The Congress was held for three consecutive days amidst an increasing tension among workers, partially caused by the unresolved problems of the transport workers unions. Some newly formed unions, like the University Workers Union, had been banned.[55] None of the demands forwarded by the Labor Congress held in May 1975 were met. The Provisional Leadership of CELU had presented the decisions of the May Congress to the regime and in August 1975, CELU's leadership inquired about the outcome. It was informed that the military regime had declined to address any of them.

In the opening speech, Marcos Hagos disclosed the names and ranks of the security officers who had come to follow up the activities of the Congress. The Congress then proceeded with its deliberations and in conclusion, demanded that the ban on the teachers' union be lifted and all of those arrested be released. Among other things, the Congress demanded for the promulgation of democratic rights, which included the right to strike. "Deprived of democratic rights," argued CELU resolution, "many unions are weakened and those that want to be organized are not allowed to do so...." Furthermore, the meeting concluded and forecasted that, "the class struggle is weakened and it is giving way to the nationalist struggle .... "[56] The CELU Congress expressed its concern regarding the activities of the police force and the various organs of local administration in weakening the zemetcha program and it provided incidents that took place in Bale, Illubabor and Shoa. The Congress demanded that the detained zematch students be released and a coordinating committee from the various mass organizations be formed to oversee the activities of the zemetcha program.[57]

The CELU Congress expressed its strong reservation about the effort that was underway to form a state sponsored political party. It expressed its strong doubts about the 'price control' regulation of the Derge which the Labor Congress believed was the cause of price hikes and the disappearance of some industrial products.[58] The Congress demanded that labor and other mass organizations be involved not only in 'price controlling', but also in market controlling activities. The Congress demanded that the government ease tax on essential items like medicine and stationery. It also demanded that fees paid for hospitals and clinics be reduced. The Congress passed resolutions demanding the promulgation of a minimum wage. It demanded that the so-called 'messiahs of change' be recalled. These were military officers who had been assigned in many of the factories and ministries. After discussing the case of seasonal employees, the Congress demanded that they become permanent. It was the practice of many institutions to retain employees as seasonal or temporary even after they had served for a number of years. The Congress passed resolutions on the women issue and the unemployed. The Congress renewed the same demands raised at the May 1975 Congress and resolved that labor would go out on a strike if,

> "1. the regime takes any measure on the provisional leadership of CELU as a consequence of the resolutions of the Congress; 2. bans CELU, 3. takes any punitive measure against those who distribute the resolution of the Congress."[59]

Without specifying a date for the strike, the congress mandated the leadership to form a strike committee that did not include members of the CELU's leadership. Sometime before the strike was called, the CELU leadership formed a two-layered strike committee. The purpose of the second strike committee was to take over leadership in case of any danger that might befall on the first one. The strike committee was composed of SI, representing the Akaki area, GT from the Transport Workers' Union, Wondiferaw from the Union of Gas Stations, Said from the Mercato area, Yirefu Bedane of the Gulele area, Shymeye, President of the Hilton Workers' Union, a representative of the workers of the Chilalo Agricultural Development Unit (CADU) and Kiflu Tadesse from the CELU office as a coordinator.

To coordinate the strike at the union level, a number of regional and local strike committees were formed. Anticipating a prolonged strike, duplicating machines, typewriters, papers and some cash were transferred from the CELU office to an undisclosed location.[60]

The decisions of the CELU Congress disconcerted the military regime. To thwart labor intransigence, the Derge decided to confiscate the papers carrying the resolutions of the Congress and assigned security personnel at the provincial bus terminal. As a result, many labor leaders were arrested. Seven union members of the Ethiopian Airlines were killed and about nineteen wounded while in the act of printing and distributing CELU's resolution. Among those killed were Gessese Hailu, Zenebe Sineshaw, Alemayehu Tessema, Gebre Kirstos Tewatchew, Moges Yemane and Abebe Fentaye.[61] These and similar incidents precipitated the crisis and CELU was forced to call a premature strike. The strike took place on September 29 and many of the unions in the Addis Abeba area took part, though some of the unions joined the strike a few hours later. The delay was a result of the confusion caused by the pamphlet announcing the strike. In order not to implicate CELU's leadership, the call came out on a pamphlet that did not bear CELU's heading. Those unions who doubted the authenticity of the pamphlet had to overcome their reluctance before joining the strike.

While the strike was underway, a bomb blasted and damaged the main office of the Telecommunications. A bank in Mojjo, a small town south of Addis Abeba, was robbed. The two incidents, which were ascribed as acts of sabotage by "terrorist" forces had negative bearings on the strike. An old Eritrean named Grazematch Asmerom was dubbed as the possible suspect for the bombings and he was arrested. Grazematch Asmerom was accused of "Arab connections" and labor leaders, particularly Marcos Hagos, who were arrested during this event, were interrogated and tortured to disclose how much "petro-dollar" they had been paid by Libya.[62] Grazematch Asmerom had an office not far from the Telecommunications headquarters. Other employees of Grazematch Asmerom were also arrested. One of them, Engineer Beedemariam, died as a result of torture and [63] Grazematch Asmerom lost his hearing.

The underground press pointed fingers at a paratrooper called Araya Fanta, as the perpetrator of the bank robbery in Mojjo. Araya Fanta, who was believed to be a government agent, was the individual who in 1974 fomented disagreement between the officers of the Airborne and the Air Force, thereby causing a serious rift within the military opposition.[64] The individual was also sent to the Awsa area of Sultan Ali Mirah, for intelligence activities.[65] The bombing of a government building and the bank robbery created suspicion among workers and many chose to return to work.

The reaction of the military regime was also swift. On September 30, 1975, the regime declared a state of emergency for the Addis Abeba area. It was decreed unlawful to assemble and demonstrate, to stop or to slow down work, to utter any unlawful words in public, to write and distribute unlawful articles, etc.[66] Government security personnel were entitled to search, arrest, imprison and enter the compound of anyone without acquiring any warrant.[67] It was also decreed that no more than two people should be seen together. A dawn to dusk curfew was imposed for a few days. A month or so later, the *Ethiopian Herald* stated, "Ethiopian nights have become peaceful and silence is 'truly' golden."[68]

Gun-mounted jeeps roamed the streets of Addis Abeba. Because of the swift repressive measures of the military regime, the strike could last only for about four days. In some areas outside of Addis Abeba, the arrest of some union leaders long before the strike was initiated left the struggle without leadership.[69] The regime's brutal and swift acts as well as the unions' lack of adequate preparation and other mistakes contributed to the failure of the strike. The regime's propaganda blitz was also a factor in weakening the workers' resolve. Besides, supportive letters from the newly formed kebele institutions condemning the strike were broadcast over radio and television.

The turn out for the strike was successful in the industrial areas of Akaki and Nefas Silk. In the Akaki area, workers went to the nearest forest during the day time, in order not to be dragged to their work places. The workers also clashed with soldiers. After the failure of the strike, six workers of the Akaki area were executed in front of an assembly of workers.[70] A worker of the Lazaradis factory in Nefas Silk was killed.[71] More than 500 labor activists, among whom were Marcos Hagos, Ali Hussien, and other leading activists, such as, Gebre Michael, Tedla Fentaye, Girma Woldesenbet, Mariye Teferi, Tadesse Kidane Mariam, Samuel Bekele and many others were arrested. Samuel Alemayehu, the newly elected EPRP

CC member and the Secretary of the Addis Abeba IZ was also imprisoned. Neither the Derge nor MEISON had any knowledge of his role in the EPRP. He was arrested for his association with labor activists.[72] A number of other leading worker activists and EPRP members, including Germatchew Lemma and Kiflu Tadesse, who were included in the most wanted list of the government were forced to go underground. As a result of this massive repression, CELU became a defunct institution, even though the office was not closed.

Major Getachew Shibeshi executed many workers of the Awash area because of their role in the strike. Some of the workers were taken to Asebe Teferi, in Harer, only to be executed. Following the nationalization of commercial farms in 1975, crisis had emerged in many of the institutions and workers employed in many of these enterprises had been facing enormous difficulties. In some cases, the regime became unable to pay their salaries. This was true of the Monterari state farm in Awash.[73] When they demanded payment, the Ministry of National Resources, which was in charge of the state farms, expelled eight hundred eighty five workers. The workers then marched to Nazreth to present their grievances. Similar workers' unrest was witnessed at the Nura Hera commercial farms where more than eighteen hundred workers were employed as cotton pickers. As a result of the conflict between management and labor, worker leaders were arrested. The workers then went on strike demanding the release of their leaders. The crisis could not be resolved peacefully. Finally, police opened fire at an assembly of workers and killed about ten and wounded about the same number.[74]

Labor Movement goes Underground

After the CELU strike failed, the labor movement found itself in total disarray. Almost all of the leading activists of CELU were placed in prison, and an intense man-hunt was underway to find those who had escaped arrest. In the midst of this crisis, a few of the leading activists that had escaped arrest established contact amongst themselves and they gathered together to determine the course of the struggle. Their first move was to form a committee, then known as a "Resurrection Committee". The name "resurrection" indicated a desire to call another strike. The founding members of this committee came from the Gulele and the Mercato areas regional strike committees. Among the first members of the committee were Yirefu Bedane, President of the Glass factory in Gulele, Wendifraw, President of the Gas Station Workers' Union, AB of the Mercato area Tailors' union, GT of the Legesse Feleke Transportation Union, and Kiflu Tadesse of the EPRP workers' committee.

In its first meetings, the committee discussed ways and means to instill workers' awareness so that they would care about their arrested leaders, visit them in the prisons, and help their families, thereby keeping the spirit of the strike alive. The newly formed "resurrection" committee passed its decisions to those that it was able to reach to and that strategy was so effective that it enabled the "Resurrection Committee" to mobilize a sizeable number of workers within a few weeks. The publication of a paper titled the *"Resurrection Committee"* enabled the committee to regroup and reorganize the scattered labor activists. Soon, a second leadership group and other regional committees were formed. The second committee included the secretary of CELU, Tessema Deressa, Teshager Berhane of the Commercial Bank, Haile Abaye of the Telecommunications, Fikru of the Ethiopian Airlines and others.

In December 1975, three months after the strike and while the labor leaders were still in prison, the military regime proclaimed a new 'Labor Law'. According to the Proclamation, twenty became the minimum number required to form a union in an establishment. The previous Code had fifty as the minimum number required. The new Proclamation dissolved both the local unions and CELU. Labor unions had to be formed anew and re-registered.[75] The Labor Code contained provisions where workers could have formal contracts of employment. It stipulated minimum conditions of labor, but no minimum wage, and it set the guidelines for settlement of disputes and arbitration.

The new Labor Law became the focus of the underground publications and both *Democracia* and *Labader* came up with lengthy articles. Both publications focused on the political and organizational aspect of the new Labor Law. *Labader* No. 20 discussed the implications of some of the provisions and stated that the new Labor Code did not provide answers to the grievances of labor. It did not address issues like minimum wage, health benefits and others.[76] According to *Labader,* the law curtailed workers rights and in a very subtle and refined manner denied the right to strike and the right to have an independent union. *Labader* discussed these and other worker related issues and labeled the new labor law a "Code of Slavery". The starting point both for *Labader* and *Democracia* was the EPRP 1975 Conference which, among other things, had resolved that workers were entitled pension benefits, that they had to take part in the administration of the nationalized factories and commercial farms. Their right to strike had to be respected and that the unions should be consulted before taking any action on any of the workers.[77]

Democracia No 30 focused on the class implications of the Labor Law and the role of the regime vis-a-vis the different sectors of the society. *Democracia* compared the issues covered in the new Labor Code to the demands of the CELU Congress of September 1975, and concluded that the Code did not even mention some of the benefits that workers were entitled to have under a capitalist system.[78]

Discussing the implications of the Labor Code, *Democracia* stated,

> As far as we are concerned, their origin, (the Derge) and what they think does not make much of a difference. What we focus upon is what they

practice and whom they serve. Their practice shows us that they are anti-labor and procapitalist, they advocate reform, not revolutionary struggle. In order to stay in power, they commit any crime. For the sake of their own interest, they betray the peoples' struggle...."[79]

Democracia also tried to clarify the confusion created as a result of the alliance of the military regime with some left groups, including the MEISON.[80] *Democracia* concluded that the Proclamation had paved the avenue for the Derge "to share power with the different sectors of the capitalist group, that is, the comprador, nationalist and the upper echelon of the petty bourgeoisie...."[81] According to *Democracia*, the Proclamation entrusted these groups with juridical power, a status that was considered an important step toward the formation of the new capitalist group within the state apparatus. Earlier on, the EPRP had asserted that the upper echelon of the petty bourgeoisie was the beneficiary of the nationalized industries.[82]

Beside the broader political and legal implications, the new Labor Code allowed the convocation of meetings to elect new union leaders while hundreds of labor activists were still in prison. That point did not go unnoticed and the "Resurrection Committee" came up with a slogan that read "no election unless our leaders are released" and began conducting an intensive campaign against the Derge's decision. That slogan was echoed by EPRP and other publications that a very significant sector of the working class embraced the idea and the Derge's drive for a new election faltered. Besides, the "Resurrection Committee's" organizational activities bear fruit among factory workers and in a brief while, many subcommittees were formed in Addis Abeba, Dire Dawa, Jimma, Wello, and Gojjam/Bahir Dar. Furthermore, the underground existence of the "Resurrection Committee" indicated the course that the workers' struggle was to follow. The "Resurrection Committee" became a "pilot project" for other underground organizations that flourished in the subsequent years of struggle.

Drawing lessons from the workers' struggle and initiative, the EPRP was able to find a form of organization that addressed the demands of the day. Initially, it was the EPRP workers' committee that concluded that the September 1975 strike could not be resurrected, but the organization formed for that purpose had to be maintained. In line with this, the EPRP workers' committee believed that the objectives of the "Resurrection Committee" had to be redefined and that its organizational format had to be changed. Accordingly, the short term objective of the organization would be to rally workers around issues related to the arrest of labor leaders, while the final objective would be to struggle for broader labor issues, among them, the right to strike and the right to form free and independent trade unions. For a final say on the need to recognize and endorse the formation of an underground labor movement, the EPRP workers' committee passed its proposals to the EPRP PB.[83]

The EPRP PB, which initially could not conceptualize the organization of workers separate from the party, rejected the proposal to form an underground labor organization. The EPRP workers' committee, in a very convincing manner presented a written follow up proposal. It explained that whether the EPRP endorsed the proposal or not, the underground workers' organization already existed and what the party had to do was to recognize the existence of that organization and give it a permanent feature. On the second attempt, the PB realized the need for such an organization and not only did it support the proposal, but it also generalized the concept and gave a guideline regarding the formation of underground organizations of labor, teachers and women.

The PB decision which came out in *Democracia*, discussed the dangers that the mass organizations faced. It pointed out that labor, teacher, and youth organizations had been rendered defunct and many activists were arrested. *Democracia* attributed these repressive policies to the fascist officer group within the Derge.[84] Discussing the tasks of progressives, *Democracia* stated,

> "in the urban areas, (we have) to reorganize and consolidate those mass organizations that the military regime had dismantled; that is, to make sure that the union leaders are released and that they resumed their tasks. If it is impossible to organize legally, we have to resort to clandestinity. At the present moment, it is very difficult to conduct any 'legal' struggle."[85]

Democracia also suggested that similar steps should be taken among teachers, students and women and the establishment of underground mass organizations was considered an important step to consolidate the EPRP.

The PB's decision regarding the formation of underground mass organizations had far reaching repercussions in the struggle ahead and it constituted one of the most important organizational decisions that the leadership undertook. To follow up the underground activities, the EPRP Mass Organizations Committee (MOC), composed of a CC member, the Secretary of the IZ, EPRP members from the organization of women, labor, and the Youth League (YL) was entrusted with the responsibility. The MOC was assigned to coordinate the activities among the different sectors of the mass organizations.

A few days before the EPRP PB made decisions on the above discussed issue, a controversy developed between the Addis Abeba IZ and the EPRP workers' committee. The IZ demanded that all worker members of the EPRP should fall under its structure. The EPRP workers' committee, which recruited most of the labor activists, wanted to maintain contact with them in order to follow up activities among workers. The conflict between the Addis Abeba IZ and the workers' committee was resolved after the PB clarified that worker party members could have dual membership in both the EPRP and the underground mass organizations. It was also made clear that the tasks of the two institutions, even though sometimes overlapping, were complementary.

Worker activists who had been taking active part in the underground struggle for more than six months were allowed to join the EPRP in October 1975. Many of them were linked to the Addis Abeba IZ. The new drive was based on the decision of the August 1975 Conference, rectifying the rigid and elitist approach of recruitment among workers.[86] According to the new regulation, any worker who accepted the program of the party, stayed on probation for a couple of months and conducted organizational and political activity was entitled to join the EPRP.

Joining rank within the EPRP structure was one thing, however, adapting to its mode of activities was another. When the workers joined the EPRP in large numbers, the organization still did not have a different study guide or approach that was suitable to them. Some workers complained about the study sessions which they regarded as complex and abstract. There were cases where efforts were made to convince workers about the origin of religion from an atheist point of view. Holding discussion on the national question was another sensitive area. Workers study sessions remained difficult and controversial until a guideline emerged sometime later.

Many EPRP members knew little about the history of the labor movement and thus, they were of little help to the workers. On the other hand, the disinterest of worker activists in EPRP activities other than the struggle in the working class compounded the problem. These and similar problems lingered even after the workers joined the party structure.

Formation of the Ethiopian Workers Revolutionary Union (ELAMA)

After abandoning the effort to call a strike, the "Resurrection Committee" focused on ways to sustain the workers struggle. One of the decisions of the provisional leadership of the "Resurrection Committee" was to give the organization a permanent feature and transform it into an underground labor organization. That organization was to be called the Ethiopian Workers Revolutionary Union, commonly known by its Amharic acronym, the ELAMA. It was formed sometime in December 1975 and it had its own provisional minimum and maximum programs. The minimum program included struggling for the release of labor leaders arrested in September 1975 and caring for their families. The final objective of the organization was to struggle for democratic rights, the formation of an independent CELU, the protection of workers' welfare and interests, the involvement of workers in factory administration and the promulgation of a progressive Labor Code.[87]

While making efforts to organize itself, the ELAMA conducted agitation against the new Labor Code and the election of new leaders. Three months after its formation, ELAMA decided to call a congress and formalize the discussions it had made in the interim. These included the discussions on the provisional program, the constitution and the internal regulations of ELAMA. The agenda items of the Congress were discussed by the membership. Delegates representation was commensurate with the size of the various committees that comprised the ELAMA. The Congress was held in the residence of Daro Negash, former President of the Berhanena Selam Printing Press Labor Union. Daro Negash, a dedicated woman fighter and a member of the underground organization, was a mother of eight children. She was summarily executed during the 1977 search and destroy campaign conducted by the regime in collaboration with MEISON. When she was executed, she was nine months pregnant and just about to give birth.[88]

Daro Negash's residence was located in the Kebena area, a very secluded area in the eastern part of Addis Abeba. Her residence could accommodate a large group. The first ELAMA Congress, which was held overnight, stayed for about 14 hours.[89] It was attended by about 27 representatives, most of whom were from the Addis Abeba and vicinity factories, and some from the Dire Dawa and Arsi areas. All of the participants of the Congress were worker activists and leaders who had little or no exposure to modern education, excepting three: Said, who represented the Mercato area trade unions: YD of the Sewing and Thread union, and Kiflu Tadesse.

The First Congress ratified ELAMA's program and constitution. It conducted discussions on the new Labor Code and repudiated it, calling for a promulgation of a new one. When discussing the immediate tasks of ELAMA, the Congress affirmed that no election should be conducted while most of the labor leaders were still imprisoned. The Congress also decided that the organization should be known as the "Ethiopian Workers Revolutionary Union". It would have a symbol and a publication to be known as the "*Voice of the ELAMA*". Finally, the Congress elected a nine-man leadership committee and a secretary.[90]

The leaflets containing the resolution of the ELAMA Congress were distributed among workers and the campaign for the release of labor activists was intensified. Through the coordination of ELAMA, by January and February 1976, almost all of the unions of the Addis Abeba area signed petitions demanding the release of their leaders. Because of the immense pressure, the labor leaders were released unconditionally on March 20, 1976; for the second time, the Ethiopian labor movement emerged triumphant; the first time was in May 1975.[91]

As soon as the leaders were released, the struggle, once more, gathered momentum. This time, workers discontent was expressed during the 1976 May Day celebration and the main demand of labor became the formation of an independent labor union. On the previous May Day, labor discontent had focused on former CELU's leadership who had refused to call a congress.

During the preparation for the May Day celebration, the regime and CELU came up with two different programs and approaches. When it was found out that the two approaches were incompatible, labor decided to go its way, except the compromise regarding the participation of youth in the demonstration. Representatives of the regime had demanded that the youth be excluded from the event.

When it allowed the celebration of the 1976 May Day, the Derge had envisaged that the people would still support the various measures that it had enacted. However, the support that the military regime had enjoyed a year earlier was fast waning and the May Day celebration reflected the conflict between labor and the regime.

Hundreds of thousands of workers took part in the demonstration and major demands of the society were addressed. When the regime realized that the people did not come out in its support, it resorted to violence. In the Addis Abeba area alone, many workers were killed, hundreds were wounded and arrested. The same scenario was repeated in Harer, Keffa, Sidamo, Gonder,[92] Gojjam and other provinces. The 1976 May Day celebration witnessed the growing assertiveness of labor in Ethiopian politics. However, labor's resolve had yet to be tested.

The formation of ELAMA was seen as a milestone in the struggle of labor against the military regime, particularly when hundreds of labor activists and leaders were languishing in prison. In that endeavor, ELAMA served as a new center to which leading activists could refer. It became an invisible spirit, having no office to be traced and no official leaders to be focused on. The sustenance of ELAMA's activities also served as a testing rod for the underground existence of mass organizations.

While labor activists were devising means to uphold their cause, the military regime came up with the idea of forming an institution that would handle the problems among labor and other sectors of the society.

The Provisional Office for Mass Organizations Affairs (POMOA) and Labor

POMOA was one of the major institutions that the Derge created after it realized the difficulties in handling the activities of the various mass organizations, including labor.[93] When POMOA took over the political and ideological role of the state, the labor movement was just coming out of the crisis resulting from the September 1975 strike. CELU had just begun legal activities in the wake of the release of its leaders. Beginning in February 1976, until the replacement of CELU by the All-Ethiopian Workers' Trade Union (AEWTU) in 1977, POMOA handled labor issues, operating on behalf of the military regime.

The first showdown between labor and POMOA took place in March 1977 when POMOA made efforts to control the unions through the discussion "clubs",[94] fora created in government institutions, factories, etc. The second showdown took shape when POMOA directly involved itself in the election processes within the workers' unions. As indicated above, the new Labor Code had stipulated that labor unions had to be re-registered and new leaders had to be elected. While many of the leaders were still in prison, some unions that had the backing of POMOA or were newly formed and had no part in the labor movement had elected new leaders. Following the release of the labor leaders in March, POMOA continued pressuring the unions to conduct elections.

The hasty drive for the election of new leaders was perceived as a deliberate attempt designed to remove from the election process active and defiant labor leaders, particularly those that had just been released and those that had been campaigning for the release of their leaders. The leaders were released when the ninety-day election and re-registration period was about to expire. The election process was speeded up and in a very short span of time, that is, by mid-March 1976, more than 655 unions were re-registered.[95]

According to the new Labor Code, workers were organized "according to their economic activity", that is, workers who were engaged in the same industrial production would be organized under one union. Accordingly, nine Industrial Unions would be formed. These included manufacturing; agriculture, forestry and fishing; construction; wholesale and retail trade; financing and insurance; social services; electricity, gas and water; mining and quarrying; transport, storage and communications Industrial Unions. The National Trade Union would be composed of the nine Industrial Unions. The new Labor Law had replaced the former organizational set up, which had recognized CELU as a confederation of individual trade unions.

Sometime in May 1976, a meeting was called at the Ministry of Community Development in order to discuss the electoral process and the formation of one of the new industrial unions, the Manufacturing Industrial Union. Most of the leaders who attended the meeting walked out declaring that they could not form the Industrial Union until all the unions elected their leaders. Some union leaders, led by the Akaki Indo-textile labor leader, T'am Yalew Eshete, responded to POMOA's call. T'am Yalew Eshete, who later became a CC member of the Workers' Party of Ethiopia (WPE), tried to form the Manufacturing Industrial Union along with about 50 union leaders. Because of this hasty drive, more than 200 unions of the manufacturing industries were left aside.

The boycott conducted by the labor opposition was so effective that the Ministry of Community Development was forced to postpone the meetings and wait until the election process was over and all of the unions had elected their leaders.

After ascertaining that the union elections were over, the meetings that would form the various industrial unions resumed. The first to conduct its meeting was the above mentioned Manufacturing Industrial Workers' Union. It was composed of more than 250 trade unions. The meeting that was attended by about four hundred worker representatives was held during the first week of June 1976. A confrontation took place when POMOA members made efforts to conduct the meeting. Workers resisted the move and elected Shiferaw Tessema as Chairman, Asfaw Demisse as Secretary, and a nominating committee of about five workers, all of whom were ELAMA members. When it failed to conduct the meeting, POMOA devised a number of other electoral procedures that would allow it to manipulate the proceedings of the meeting. Aware of POMOA's intentions, active labor leaders exposed the attempt. When POMOA found out that it could not affect the proceedings of the meeting, it devised other means of disrupting it and begin the whole process all over again. While the meeting was in session, the chairman and the secretary of the meeting were detained, using the expulsion of T'am Yalew Eshete from the meeting as an excuse. The meeting had expelled T'am Yalew Eshete for forming an Industrial Union when over two-thirds of the unions were not ready to do so. Following the above-mentioned incident, a Derge member announced to the participants that he had adjourned the meeting, only a day after it had begun.

About eleven long time labor activists, including Shiferaw Tessema, Yaregal Demisse, Asfaw Demisse, Tedla Fentaye, Gezahegne Teferra and Ali Hussien of the Indo Textiles, Daro Negash and others were arrested. Some of them were picked up from their work places while others were taken from the meeting hall and they were accused of infiltrating the gathering. It turned out that the "infiltrators" were worker representatives who did not carry their ID cards. Two employees of the Ministry of Community Development who were accused of collaborating with the labor opposition were also arrested.[96] The election process was disrupted and tension continued to mount among workers. Some of those arrested were released a few days later, while Tedla Fentaye, Gezahegne Teferra, Yaregal Demisse, Ali Hussien and others stayed behind bars for more than five years.

The election process remained suspended until a seminar organized by POMOA was conducted. In the midst of this tension, in June 1976, the underground labor organization, ELAMA, held its Second Congress in the Gulele area, in the compound of Ras Mesfin Sileshi. The Second Congress was attended by about nineteen representatives of the various ELAMA zones. One of the main issues of the agenda was related to the ongoing labor struggle. In its deliberations, the Congress reiterated its previous decision regarding the coordination of legal and underground activities. From September 1975 until the release of labor leaders in March 1976, the labor struggle had remained illegal. The Congress affirmed that conducive conditions had been created to conduct legal activities following the release of labor leaders. The ELAMA Congress also encouraged workers to take part in the seminars to be conducted by POMOA. Perceiving that the seminar was designed to weed out the "culprits" the regime was looking for, the Congress advised that active labor leaders should keep low profiles. The ELAMA decision came out opposed to the ideas espoused by some radical labor activists who were agitating for a boycott of the seminars to be conducted by POMOA. Following discussions on the program and constitution of the ELAMA, the Congress decided to make the underground organization public. POMOA held seminars for the unions that would form the different Industrial Unions; most of them were conducted peacefully. Confident that it had attained its objectives, POMOA decided to conduct the elections for the various Industrial Unions and assigned its members to function as nominating committee members. In some of these meetings, leading members of the groups that constituted POMOA took direct roles in the election process. In the meeting of the Service Industry - a meeting that was held on the Addis Abeba University campus - Negede Gobeze, Negist Adane and Sennay Likke were in charge of the seminar. Of the nine Industrial Unions, about five of them resented POMOA's incursions into their affairs; these unions took matters in their own hands and elected their own nominating committees.

Labor activists, understanding that POMOA would devise other obstacles unless it had a say in the nomination process, nominated two individuals for each post, and made sure that one of the nominees had the backing of POMOA. By July 1976, four Industrial Unions elected their union officers. In almost all of the cases, however, POMOA and the military regime lost the elections and they were unable to get any foothold in the labor leadership. It was then that POMOA concluded that labor was highly impregnated by "anarchists" and decided to get rid of the "unnecessary elements" before it ventured in another round of an election process. The entire election process for the Industrial Unions was called off for an indefinite period and that process *marked the beginning of the intensive repression, that is, declaration of the war of annihilation which was proclaimed in September 1976.*[97] As we are going to see in the coming pages, one of the first targets of the war of annihilation were leading worker activists and leaders.

While the election process was underway, around mid-1976, tension continued building up among the workers of the main Post Office. The workers had called a strike because of the prohibition against forming a union. Telecommunication workers also threatened to call a strike. The immediate factor that triggered telecommunications workers reaction was the decision to lay off more than 300 temporary employees.

As tension continued building, the issue of a national strike was raised and discussed at the meeting of the ELAMA IZ of Addis Abeba. The leadership argued that conditions were not ripe to call a strike and instead, recommended factory slowdowns in order to prepare the ground for the strike. In the mean time, unions were asked to pass petitions putting forth the same questions that CELU had raised. It was believed that such a process would popularize labor demands and indicate how much backing the demands had. Hundreds of unions discussed, signed and passed the petitions

to the regime. However, the Derge did not give them any attention.
In Assela, the Arsi province, a confrontation took place between labor and the Derge. In April 1976, CADU laborers demanded the dismissal of officials, some of whom were affiliated with POMOA. When the regime failed them, they took matters into their hands and dismissed the officials and elected new ones. The regime responded fast, and around mid-May 1976, as many as 50 workers, peasants, students, etc., were arrested. Some of them fled the area.

Other Underground Mass Organizations

The military regime began confronting and harassing the Teachers' Union following the resolutions and demands of the 18th Congress held in Jimma.[98] The Derge arrested some leaders and closed the main office of the Teachers' Union in Addis Abeba. That move galvanized the teachers' resistance. At the beginning of the second week of November 1975, more than sixteen thousand teachers from all-over Ethiopia went on strike. The regime did not respond to the teachers' demands. Instead, it continued arresting those who participated in the strike and those that it suspected to be behind the movement. In the meantime, the regime nationalized about 820 private schools that were attended by about 150,000 students.

It was during this crisis, in November 1975, that the underground teachers' association was formed. Given the relatively large number of teacher EPRP members, forming the underground teachers' union was not as difficult a task as that of labor. Under the guidance of the center, networks of underground teachers' association were formed in many parts of the country. The underground organization had a publication known as the "*Voice of Teachers*". Among the leading members of the group were, Yohannes Berhane, Berhanu Ijjigu, Kifle, BK, T. and Tesfaye Abebe.

A provisional committee to form the underground Oppressed Soldiers Organization was also formed during the last months of 1975. Among the founding members of the organization were Captain Amha Abebe and Sergent Wolde Medhin Abraha. The group began publishing the "*Voice of the Oppressed Soldiers*". Forming such an organization was a difficult task mainly due to the arrest and execution of many activists from the Engineering Corps, Army Aviation Corps, and around the Derge itself. When the provisional organizing committee was formed, it had very few committees in the military camps.

Some effort was made to organize an underground women's organization and in 1975, some ground work was laid down. However, due to an internal problem of the legally existing Women's Coordinating Committee, little headway was made toward consolidating the underground organization.[99] The Coordinating Committee for women put out a publication called "*Rise Up*" (*Tenesh*).

Underground Mass Organizations and the EPRP

The formation of underground mass organizations demonstrated the different avenues and forms of struggle that the people could resort to when deprived of legal and peaceful means. The formation of underground mass organizations was one of the main factors that made the EPRP what it was in the later days of the struggle. As a result of the political and organizational activities conducted during the previous year and the public declaration of the existence of the EPRP, its influence among the different sectors of the society began spreading. Moreover, the political might that the EPRP enjoyed was complemented by an organizational support following the formation of underground mass organizations. These organizations served as effective instruments to advance EPRP's cause and at the same time, they served as vehicles to further isolate the military regime. They also became important instruments and conveyor belts for the recruitment of tested and committed fighters. The EPRP was able to spread its policies among the different sectors of the society, including the advanced section of the Ethiopian working class. Following the formation of underground organizations, many individuals who had differing class backgrounds joined the EPRP and the class composition of the EPRP began to undergo some change. The EPRP became transformed into a formidable political force that one had to reckon with, either positively or negatively. Before the formation of these organizations, the EPRP had been an elite party of several hundred revolutionary intellectuals and youth activists.

The infusion of new blood into the EPRP structure had some effect on the organization itself. The EPRP had to adjust to the needs of the new influx of members and it had to change its modes of operations. It had to adjust its recruitment, study, organizational and other activities. Because of the influx of a large number of recruits, the rigorous discipline of the party was compromised and many members of the EPRP, who were little known elsewhere, had to be exposed to the newly recruited members of the underground mass organizations. These and other similar developments had an adverse effect on the EPRP, altering its highly secretive and elusive nature.

Part II

EPRP's Organizational Activities

The August 1975 EPRP Conference played a vital role in redefining EPRP's courses of actions.[100] When redefining the targets of the struggle, the gradual transformation of the state and the role of the state power (the Derge) within the overall feudal system had to be clarified. In order to do this, the objectives, the demands and the emphasis of the struggle had to be examined. In the program endorsed by the August Conference, both the short and long term goals and objectives of the EPRP were enumerated. Some aspects of the program would be implemented "when the people's dictatorship under the leadership of the proletariat is formed", stated the program. Even though the main targets of the struggle remained the same, that is, the abolition of feudalism and imperialism, the class configuration of the struggle was modified when the state bourgeoisie, although still weak, was considered to be one of the enemies of the revolution.[101] The correlation between the land reform and the national question was discussed and it was recognized that in southern Ethiopia the national problem was diluted while it had exacerbated in the northern region since the Derge had seized power.[102]

The August Conference had resolved that in the final analysis armed struggle was the primary form of resolving the class conflict. However, it was concluded that the party will struggle democratically and peacefully if "democratic rights are upheld".

The EPRP program, which came out in the midst of a revolutionary encounter had to deal with issues related to the ongoing struggle. By the last quarter of 1975, the land proclamation had destroyed the "material foundations of the *ancien* regime and carried economic transformation far beyond anything envisaged by the radicals."[103] These measures had outstripped the economic agenda of the radicals. It was pressing, therefore, to reorient the struggle by focusing on fundamental issues the regime had not, and was not likely to resolve.

By focusing on the role of the state, democracy became the cardinal issue and the peoples' right to organize and to arm themselves was the major demand. The absence of democracy was considered as a dire threat to the very survival of the left and to implement the economic reforms of the revolution as well. "Politics and economics cannot be separated" became the staple slogan of that period. Other slogans were "no genuine agrarian revolution without democracy", "let independent trade unions thrive" and "no nationalization without workers control".

The Central Committee

Following the enlargement of the EPRP Central Committee (CC) by the 1975 August Conference, new CC members with new thoughts and ideas became part of the leadership's decision making process.[104] The formation of the PB and the Secretariat enabled the CC to extricate itself from administrative functions. Following the delegation of administrative tasks to different committees, the CC became a decision making body, in the true sense of the term. Until this time, it was the CC that handled almost all activities, including administration. Nevertheless, because of new and additional assignments and the expansion of the organizational network itself, the formation of the PB and the Secretariat did not save some of the members of the EPRP CC from an over-concentration of tasks and responsibilities. On the average, one Central Committee member was still assigned to three committees while some were involved in as many as six.

A CC headquarters was established in the center of Addis Abeba, in the Gulele area, close to the former Medhani Alem school. The house, which was rented out under Engineer Osman Mohammed's name was one of the places where some CC members resided.

Until the house was passed on to the Defense Committee in August 1976, of the seven CC meetings conducted in 1975/76, three of them took place at the headquarters. The PB met at least every ten days, and two-thirds of the meetings were conducted in the headquarters. The Secretariat handled most of its activities from the headquarters and many of the needed files of the Central Committee were kept there. Besides organizational activities, the headquarters allowed some of the CC members to know each other more closely. Prior to this arrangement, some CC members met only during meetings or other occasions that were related to organizational activities.

The number of CC members residing in the house could vary from two to four at any given time. Among those that resided in the headquarters on a permanent basis were Berhane Meskel, Tesfaye Debessai and Kiflu Tadesse, all of them fugitives. One of the problems that they quite often faced, particularly during the initial period was how to procure a constant supply of food. It was agreed that only very few EPRP members, that is, those who had assignments with the Secretariat could come to the house. Even though the residents of the headquarters could get some help from these members on an irregular basis, many were the times that the fugitives had to leave their residence just for the sake of shopping. Most often, Kiflu, who had to go out for other organizational activities, handled the matter. Afraid of arousing the suspicion of the residents of the area, quite often, the CC members had to be confined to the house, with little or no food at hand and many were the times that they could eat only once a day. Engineer Osman, under whose name the house was registered was supposed to provide whatever was necessary for the household. However, he was a busy person and was unable to satisfy the demands.[105]

For security purposes, to assist the CC members and at the same time to avoid any conspicuous activities in the EPRP headquarters, Engineer Osman Mohammed hired a guard who called himself Shigute. He was a very secretive person who provided very little information about his past and himself.

According to a later day conversation, some of the activities conducted in the EPRP headquarters used to puzzle Shigute and at times, he would be astonished by what he saw. In a three-bedroom house that could rent for about four hundred Ethiopian birr, what Shigute saw was two or three poorly dressed individuals (the CC members) who stayed home most of the time. Whenever they had to go outside, they had to leave the house well camouflaged or they were driven in a car. Shigute also observed that they had friendly relationship with his immediate boss, Engineer Osman Mohammed. During the first few months of Shigute's stay in the headquarters, no one knew with certainty what had been going on in his mind. However, it was noticeable that he eventually began opening up and became protective and involved. Sitting outside and watching guard, Shigute would knock at the main door to inform his "bosses" inside the house to keep their voice low, or he would look around the compound for pieces of paper that he thought might compromise his "bosses". He used to either destroy or give the pieces of paper to the CC members. Shigute performed his duties properly until some months later when it was discovered that he was one of the workers of the Awash area who escaped the massive massacre conducted as a result of workers involvement in the September 1975 CELU strike. Originally, Shigute was from Kembatta, one of the main national groups in the southwestern part of Shoa. Like his new "bosses", the EPRP CC members, Shigute was a fugitive of the regime and it was his intention to keep himself anonymous.

Shigute became more involved and eventually became a member of the household. One of the members of the household, Yosef Adane, was assigned to conduct political discussion sessions with him and teach him how to read and write. A few months later, Shigute was passed on to the EPRP structure of the area. A year or so later, Shigute went to his 'natural' place and was employed in the Brick factory of the Gulele area and became one of the active ELAMA members. By that time, Engineer Osman Mohammed was a manager at the Brick factory.

From August 1975 to August 1976, that is, following the 1975 Extended Conference, Central Committee meetings were held at forty-five days intervals. In a period of one year, eight CC meetings were conducted. One of them was the first plenum. Such an arrangement was a major departure from the experience of the previous period when CC meetings were held almost on a continuous basis. Most of the meetings were held over night and almost all of them were attended by all of the CC members who resided in Addis Abeba, except those in the army and the foreign committee. By this time, more than ninety percent of the CC members lived in Addis Abeba. Tesfaye Debessai, who had to leave for Tigrai on assignments, could attend only four of the meetings.

The first CC meeting during this period was the plenum conducted during the last days of August 1975. It was on this plenum that important institutions of the EPRP, such as, the PB were formed.[106] The second CC meeting was held around the end of October 1975, in the EPRP headquarters. The state of emergency that was declared after the September labor strike was still in effect. The main issues of the agenda of the meeting were the merger of the EPRP with the "Red Flag" group and the condition of the nucleus of the army (EPRA). Regarding the "RF" group, the CC endorsed the proceedings for the merger and the various decisions made by the PB. The group was allowed to merge with the EPRP.

Regarding the EPRA, the military commission presented proposals to expand the army to some parts of the country. After some deliberations, the CC reached upon a consensus on the proposal and mandated the military commission to work out the details, in conjunction with the EPRA leadership and the party structures of the concerned areas. The meeting also mandated the Military Commission to compile the investigation regarding those who had defected from the nucleus of the army the previous year.[107] Some members of the army had defected in 1975 and they had asked for an amnesty from the regime. In order to implement and discuss the decisions of the August Conference and at the same time to conduct some kind of an orientation course in the EPRA, Tesfaye Debessai was given a mandate. He left for Tigrai to the nucleus of the army during the last months of 1975. Zeru Kehishen had been to the army in September of the same year and he had met some members of the army leadership and had discussed the outcome of the August Conference.

In December 1975, another CC meeting was held in the Asmera Road area, in the residence of Y.H/M, an EPRP member who had left Ethiopia on business related assignment. The main issues of the agenda were, relations between the Eritrean organizations, the prevalent Ethiopian situation and other organizational matters. The CC decided to establish a better relationship with the ELF and with this in mind, the EPRP delegation was mandated to negotiate with the leadership of the ELF and create conditions for cooperation.

The CC meeting also decided to form a cadre school in the Addis Abeba area. The purpose of the school was to conduct cadre training courses for members at different levels of awareness. This duty was delegated to the political department of the EPRP which was also assigned to prepare articles on a number of political and ideological questions.

The EPRP PB also held several meetings during this period and among the important decisions it made were the ratification of the proposal regarding the formation of underground organizations and the role of the EPRP members in the newly created discussion "clubs".[108] The PB also prepared a manual on organization. In the manual, the relationship between the Youth League and the EPRP, the duties and rights of the various committees and members were elaborately spelt out. Another major decision that the PB passed was the formation of a Democratic Front (DF). The PB assessed EPRP's efforts to form a United Front, began as early as 1972 and concluded that it had not materialized due to circumstances beyond the control of the EPRP.[109]

The PB concluded that the vast majority of the population remained beyond the reach of any of the Ethiopian organizations, the EPRP included. It was also concluded that a significant part of these sectors could not be rallied under EPRP's minimum political program; hence, the need for a much broader political program to mobilize these sectors. Still making efforts to form a United Front, the PB decided to form a DF in tandem. The DF was supposed to be an additional force that would be included in the United Front. The proposal was submitted to the CC and it was approved.

In order to initiate the project, a provisional leadership was formed of individuals who had broad followings and differing national backgrounds, including Marcos Hagos, EC, GT and others. The group conducted meetings where Tesfaye Debessai took some part. One of the tasks of the DF provisional leadership was to draft the provisional program, which it did. The provisional program of the DF was approved by the EPRP CC. Sometime later, organizing the DF was initiated. It was the intention of the EPRP to build the organization from top to bottom, however, practice showed that such an approach was, to say the least, very difficult. So, building the Democratic Front had to begin from the lowest echelon and DF committees were formed at the level of kebeles.

Organs of the Party and the League

From September 1975 until February 1976, over a period of about six months, some 15 *Labader* and about the same number of *Democracia* issues were printed. The Volume II Series of *Democracia*, which began coming out in February 1975, was printed in thirty numbered series and in three special editions. Because of the need to conduct intense agitation among workers, the number of *Labader* issues increased from the previous period. The Youth League and ELAMA had begun putting out their publications too.

Beginning in September 1975, *Democracia* was printed in four additional languages of Ethiopia. Besides the Amharic editions, *Democracia* was translated into the Oromiffa, Tigrigna, Welliata and Sidama languages. Production activities increased ten folds when compared to the previous year and the number of copies increased from a few hundreds to thousands and tens of thousands.[110] Typing and production of *Democracia* in the Welliata and Sidama languages were done by the production unit of the Sidamo zonal committee.

Most of the *Democracia* and *Labader* issues were devoted to the unfolding political issues of the time. Few of the issues were either prepared by the CC itself, or the different zonal committees. The special issues on Keffa and Sidamo, which discussed unfolding events in the two provinces, were prepared by their respective zonal committees. Both issues focused on the alliance of the local state power and the disgruntled members of the ruling class in their struggle against the peasantry, the workers, teachers, and zematch students.[111]

The publication of a new English-Amharic dictionary which contained new political, scientific and philosophical concepts was of some importance not only to the development of the underground literature, but to the Amharic language as well. Over the years, thousands of new words were added and new thoughts and concepts were expressed using the Amharic language. The dictionary was prepared by some university teachers.

The EPRP production committees which almost every day produced thousands of copies of the various publications had little or no time for rest and reflection. All of the members of a production unit lived together and for safety purposes, only the secretary of the committee knew the address of the unit. The rest of them came to the location blindfolded. When and if they had to go out, they were transported lying down on the floor of the vehicle.

Monotony and lack of direct and active participation in the ongoing struggle were some of the problems confronting members of production units. To alleviate the anxiety and to involve themselves in the struggle, members of a production unit formed their own party committee. As was evident, the production units of the EPRP were the treasured assets of the party and they were on the government's "most wanted" list as well. A small fault of the production units had very wide ramifications and it would bring about serious organizational and political crisis. Despite or maybe because of excessive precautionary measures, one of the units fell prey during the first quarter of 1976 and almost all of the members of the unit, along with one of the latest duplicating machines, a stockpile of papers and few hand guns were caught red-handed.

The production unit operated in a three-bedroom house located in an area known as the Asmera Road. The windows and doors of the house remained closed most of the time and the house looked vacant and desolate. The only time that the compound became active was when vehicles arrived either to fetch materials or take away the printed ones. An individual who wanted to occupy the house decided to force out the inhabitants, whom he thought were a bunch of youngsters. The decree on Urban Land and Housing had entrusted the kebeles to rent out houses and the individual mobilized kebele officials who, one fine morning, forced themselves into the house and landed upon the production unit of the EPRP. About three EPRP members were apprehended and they were imprisoned for a number of years. The government claimed victory and its moves inflicted a severe set back and a serious blow to the EPRP. However, production in the other units was stepped up, in order to minimize the political impact on the EPRP and to divert attention from those who were arrested.

Following this incident, a series of precautionary measures were introduced. It became a rule to assign some members as "guards" to production units. The "guards", who could easily mingle with the inhabitants of the area, became important sources of information for the units. Production units had to be decentralized in order to meet deadlines and shoulder work load of the various publications, to overcome security problems, to facilitate distribution and to deploy large manpower. In line with this, production units were formed under each zonal committee and each of the units was assigned to produce one or more of the publications. The Addis Abeba IZ which had confiscated about twenty duplicating machines from a government office was able to provide the machines to the various units. For emergency and other purposes, the IZ still kept some production units under its control.

Even though special efforts were made to upgrade the production capacity of the EPRP, because of the emergence of new publications and the increase in the number of copies to be printed, the production units were still unable to meet with the deadline. Because of the rapidly changing political condition, if an issue was delayed for more than two days, it meant that it would lose its significance and importance. Propaganda papers were given priority and some papers, like the internal journal, "Red Star", which was more of a theoretical nature, were delayed. The delay created tension between the Addis Abeba IZ which set the priorities for the production of the publications and the Political Department of the CC and particularly the "*Red Star*" committee and the ELAMA IZ.

Typewriters were allotted to each of the production units so that they handled both typing and production of the publications. The new arrangement solved a number of organizational, security, distribution and production problems. Because of the new adjustments, the regime was unable to locate the production units, despite its incessant efforts.

Due to the intensity of the struggle, the number of EPRP publications increased; obtaining materials for production and transporting them became other areas of concern. To meet with the new demands, stationery stores were opened in Addis Abeba and other provincial cities.

EPRP's Drive for Further Merger

The need for a further merger with other groups was necessitated by new political developments in 1975/76 that were perceived to undermine the EPRP and enhance the Derge's standing. One of these developments was the alliance of the regime with some prominent radical groupings, under the Provisional Office for Mass Organizations Affairs (POMOA). The MEISON, the Sennay Likke group and other prominent radicals began working with the military regime, thereby giving it a certain degree of legitimacy and acceptance, both domestically and internationally.

The regrouping of the radical force around the regime caused an alarm among leading EPRP members and it became necessary to look for other radical groups who until then had remained independent. It was believed that the new alliance would allow the military regime to stay in power much longer.

The Derge's moves were taken quite seriously and the EPRP made efforts to merge with six more groups. These were, the Ethiopian Communist Party, commonly known by its publication, the *Red Flag*; the GA group of the Illubabor area; the group behind the publication known as the People's Revolt, *(Hizbawi Ametse)*; some Oromos regrouped around the publication *Belissuma;* and an Oromo peasant group of the Gujji area, in the Sidamo province, headed by Haji Kutta. For a reason entirely different from those mentioned above, negotiation was initiated with the TPLF.[112]

The "Red Flag"

Contact with the "Red Flag" (RF) group was established around the end of August 1975 when Getachew Maru brought the case to the attention of the EPRP PB. Getachew Maru reported that he met Getahun Sisay (Gurmu), an activist whom he believed was a member of the former Abyot group. It was reported that Getahun Sisay's contact with the Abyot group had been severed in 1974 when most of the Abyot leadership was imprisoned. [113]Getahun had also informed Getachew that he had formed his own group when he was left on his own.

The successful merger with the Abyot group in mind, the EPRP leadership gave the permission to merge with the new group. Such was the confidence in the previous merger that Getachew was allowed to handle the case singlehandedly. (In the serious merger negotiations conducted earlier, it was a norm to involve at least two leading EPRP members). The "Red Flag" group was represented by Getahun.

Following the negotiation, agreement was reached on the political program of the EPRP and its assessment of the prevalent political situation. The only serious reservation that Getahun raised was regarding the Provisional People's Government (PPG) slogan. When the tactical significance of the slogan to rally a larger following was explained, the "RF" group expressed its acquiescence. In the course of the negotiation, Getachew asked if a person by the name Assefa Endeshaw belonged to the "RF" group and if the group had any association with those that published "*Spartacus*". The reply to both questions was negative. Right or wrong, it was believed that Assefa Endeshaw and the Sennay Likke group were behind "*Spartacus*" which had conducted an anti-*Democracia* campaign as early as 1974.

In the course of the negotiation, the "*Red Flag*" group 'disclosed' that it had a big truck which it used to conduct business with, that is, had a good financial standing and was behind the newly published book titled, "*Introduction to Socialism*". The group's 'activities' impressed the EPRP leadership and the small pieces of information invigorated the drive for the merger. While the negotiation process was underway, as a condition of the merger with the EPRP, the "Red Flag" group demanded to be represented in the EPRP Central Committee. It was informed that the case would be presented at the next EPRP CC meeting. The Red Flag also demanded to be represented in the Addis Abeba IZ, the Harer and the Wello Zonal committees. The EPRP PB agreed to all of the demands.

EPRP CC members were informed of the development regarding the merger process. After the whole process was over and agreement had been reached, the "Red Flag" group indicated that it would like to clarify a small deception that it had committed earlier. It disclosed that Assefa Endeshaw and "*Spartacus*" belonged to the "RF" group. Asked why he misinformed the EPRP in the first place, Getahun Sisay expressed his fear that the merger process would not go through if that information was disclosed. Despite the deception, the EPRP PB agreed to finalize the merger process. At about the same time that the negotiation process was over, the EPRP CC was to hold a meeting. Getachew Maru, anxious about the merger process, demanded that a member of the "Red Flag" representative attend the CC meeting instead of waiting for another two months. The PB could not decide on the matter on its own and instead, it agreed to present the merger case as a number one issue of the CC agenda. If the EPRP CC ratified the proposal, it meant that it would let the "RF" member attend the ongoing CC meeting. In its October meeting, the EPRP CC discussed and ratified the merger process, including the demand for a representation of an "RF" member in the EPRP Central Committee. The PB then asked the CC if the representative, who was waiting outside, could attend the meeting. Some CC members, among them Berhane Meskel, accused the PB of blackmail. They argued that it was wrong to inform the "RF" representative about the meeting before the CC made the final decision. Members of the PB, and particularly Getachew Maru, explained the underlying reasons for such an arrangement. The Central Committee instructed the PB that such an act should not be repeated. It also allowed Getahun Sisay to attend the meeting.

The EPRP leadership informed the members of the organization about the merger process with the "RF" group. While the integration of the "RF" group into the EPRP structure was underway, information about the properties that the group allegedly possessed, such as, the truck and the large sum of money it declared that it had, were found to be exaggerated. The "Red Flag" group had also claimed that it owned a store where stationery was sold. However, it was found that this was a newly started business with little merchandize on the shelves. Despite these ominous signs, the EPRP leadership went ahead and made efforts to finalize the agreed upon decisions.

Mid-way in the process of integration, the EPRP leadership faced a stiff resistance from the party structures in Addis Abeba, Harer and Wello. All of them refused to let "RF" members join their committees. The Addis Abeba IZ argued that the "RF" individual assigned to join it was not competent enough to take part in any of the leading EPRP committees. The

IZ refused to accept the individual even as a party member. The EPRP leadership tried to impose the agreed upon decision, but the Addis Abeba IZ became more adamant and could not be persuaded. The Harer zonal committee also refused to let the "Red Flag" member join it. The zonal committee suspected that the individual was an agent. The EPRP leadership, which already had developed some misgivings about the entire merger process was unable to enforce its decisions in light of such an allegation. A few months later, the Harer zonal committee was to be proven correct when the individual to be planted in the EPRP was appointed as one of the leading POMOA representatives of the Harer area. The individual eventually became one of the active participants in the search and destroy campaigns against the EPRP in the Harer province.[114]

The Wello zonal committee also refused to implement the decisions of the EPRP CC accusing the "Red Flag" as an anti-EPRP group. The zonal committee also questioned "Red Flag's" motive for the merger. It believed that the group wanted to break up the EPRP from within. To demonstrate its assertions, the zonal committee brought forth several incidents that were regarded as anti-EPRP acts. The Wello EPRP zonal committee was able to get information about "RF" committee through EPRP moles that had joined the group prior to the merger process. The zonal committee also brought forth other evidences proving "Red Flag's" effort to infiltrate the EPRP. The zonal committee expressed strong reservations about Assefa Endeshaw, who it believed was the ideologue and leading figure of the "Red Flag" group and categorically refused to admit him as a member.

Getachew Maru was sent to the Wello zonal committee to discuss the merger process. After some persuasion, the Wello zonal committee agreed to take some of the "Red Flag" members in its structure. However, a month or so later, the problems resurfaced and Getachew went back to Dessie/Wello, for the second time, to finalize the process. The Wello zonal committee presented him with more evidence regarding the anti-EPRP activities of the "Red Flag" group, even after the conclusion of the merger agreement. The zonal committee also presented some anti-EPRP pamphlets that the "Red Flag" was distributing. The zonal committee refused to take the rest of the members into its structure. Getachew made efforts to persuade the members of the zonal committee. However, members of the zonal committee resented his approach, which they regarded as high-handed and demanded that Getachew should not be sent as a delegate anymore.

A few "Red Flag" members who were little known, or of whom there were no reservations became part of the EPRP structure. Two of them were assigned as members of the internal journal of the EPRP and of the finance committee under the EPRP Central Committee. The first one was a former student activist, while the later was Major Shitaye, who later was identified as a leading member of the Sennay Likke group.[115] One of the members of the "Red Flag" group, Semu Negus, was in charge of an EPRP stationary store. Late in 1977, after the EPRP severed relationship with the "Red Flag", the individual was appointed as the Chairman of the Abyot Tebeka of Kefetegna 1, kebele 10 (the Atkelte Tera), Addis Abeba. Along with other members of the kebeles of the area, he turned out to be a notorious killer who hunted down EPRP members.

A few months following the merger process, the Addis Abeba IZ criticized the EPRP Central Committee about the way it had handled the entire process. The IZ argued that it would have provided information about the "RF" group had it been consulted before hand. The CC accepted the criticism and explained that it was side-tracked by the Derge's adroit political moves to mobilize the political groupings of the country to its side. The CC also criticized itself for letting the whole case be handled by only one of its members.

While the merger process with the "Red Flag" group was underway, the details of the October EPRP CC meeting, held in the presence of Getahun Sisay, were disclosed to the Derge security department. That case was reported back to the security department of the EPRP CC, by EPRP members around the Derge. According to that feedback, the Derge security department, particularly the Sennay Likke group, knew about the existence of the few months old EPRP headquarters and its location. They knew that Berhane Meskel was in Addis Abeba. The most striking revelation, however, was that Derge security officers obtained adequate information about a newly acquired EPRP vehicle. They knew the tag number, the color and the make of the car. The vehicle was known only to one or two EPRP CC members, and Tesfaye Debessai had used the car to transport Getahun Sisay. Most of the information that the Derge obtained was accurate in the details. The EPRP leadership, a victim of its mistakes, reviewed all of the demands that the "Red Flag" group had made. It found out that the "Red Flag" had made efforts to place its members on vulnerable and important EPRP committees. The EPRP leadership then decided to take a damage controlling step and until situations clarified, Getahun Sisay, the suspect, was sent to the EPRA, Tigrai where he was kept under close surveillance. Embarrassing and startling information stopped coming and the immediate danger facing the EPRP leadership was averted. As a result of these and other complications, the merger process with the "Red Flag" group was left half-finished. Some members of the "Red Flag" were still left out of the EPRP structure, while others had joined it. Those who did not join the EPRP structure continued pestering their comrades for abandoning them. The EPRP leadership, which had already realized its mistakes, could not push ahead and implement the agreements made with the "Red Flag" group. At the same time, for security and other considerations, it was unable to cancel the whole arrangement. In the mean time, the "Red Flag" group demanded that Getahun Sisay return from his "assignment".

Thus stood the situation until April 1976 when the military regime came out with its call for the formation of a front. The EPRP CC deliberated on the Derge's call for the formation of a front and passed its draft resolution to the Addis Abeba party and Youth League structures for discussion before a final decision was reached.[116] While the draft resolution was under discussion, "Red Flag" members who joined the EPRP structure, in collaboration with those who stayed out, made the internal draft resolution public. It was not known if members of the "RF" group were aware of the fact that the EPRP CC sent the proposal to its members for discussion before a final decision was made. The "Red Flag" group accused the EPRP Central Committee of conspiring to work with the Derge, without the knowledge of EPRP members.

Following this incident, the EPRP was unable to take any more threats and the Central Committee terminated the membership of all former members of the "Red Flag" group. The EPRP's response to the Derge's call for the formation of the front and the way the "Red Flag" handled the case became points of discussion for the semi-legal youth associations formed at the level of kebeles. The "RF" had intended to win the support of the youth by "exposing" the EPRP leadership. As a result of its miscalculations, the "Red Flag" became more isolated and lost whatever following it had.

A few months later, the "Red Flag" publicized a list of names that it suspected were leading EPRP activists and members of the Central Committee. The group did this to retaliate for similar mistakes committed by an EPRP Youth League committee in the Debreziet area, Shoa province. This event took place around the end of 1976. By this time, the military regime had declared the war of annihilation on the EPRP and many members of the organization were being hunted down. The sullen relationship of the "Red Flag" group and the EPRP further complicated Getahun Sisay's predicament and he was placed under arrest. At this time, Getahun was not aware of the sudden turn of events. Neither did he know the charges against him. Getahun was suspected of infiltrating the EPRP and it was feared that he might give himself up to the Derge and compromise the EPRP.

The EPRP leadership discussed what measures it had to take against "Red Flag" members and decided to ignore the whole case. With the "Red Flag" case in mind, the EPRP CC passed a decision not to retaliate on any group that claimed to be inclined more to the left on issues raised by EPRP itself.

The GA group

The GA was a group that espoused the EPRP's political line long before it was incorporated into the structure. The group conducted its activities in the Illubabor province, mainly in Mettu, Gore and Gambella. Leading figures were GKY, GA and Tarekegne. The first two, who were then fourth year law students at the Haile Selassie 1st University, discontinued their studies in 1973 and became engaged in revolutionary activities. GA was a dynamic and action-oriented radical who enjoyed support among high-school activists.

The youth in Illubabor was not active in the struggle of Ethiopian students until 1975 when its demand to form a student organization was rejected by the regime. Following the arrival of zematch students in the area, the level of activity among the youth in Illubabor gained momentum and many became radicalized. The zematch students became centers of attraction. The town's people, peasants and students would file complaints with the zematches, believing that they were government representatives.

The merger process of the EPRP and the GA group was conducted by Germatchew Lemma of the EPRP, and GKY and GA from the group. The EPRP program was discussed and an agreement was reached with no or little help from the EPRP CC. The group then took over EPRP activities in the Illubabor area. When the merger took place in 1975, the group had about 80 to 100 members. It had about four circles in the Buno Bedele area, nine in Mettu and a few circles in Gore and Gambella. Most of the members were youth activists and teachers. Of the members who joined the EPRP, about one-third were placed in the party structure while the rest became members of the Youth League.[117] Lieutenant Seyoum Demisse, a military analyst at the Ministry of Defense in Addis Abeba was among the members of the group that joined the EPRP. Lt. Seyoum had been an outstanding student of the Menelik high-school and a highly respected and talented intelligence officer. The officer had access to very sensitive military information, and in 1977, he established direct access to Mengistu Haile Mariam himself. In the years to come, Lieutenant Seyoum Demisse would be an invaluable source of information for EPRP.[118]

Following the completion of the merger process, the GA group was in the process of restructuring the local EPRP organization when its entire activity was disrupted. The crisis was triggered by a massive student and teachers anti-government and anti-MEISON protest. Dissatisfaction with the MEISON was building up for quite some time and it was heightened following MEISON's alliance with the military regime. Dr. Kedir Mohammed, a leading MEISON member, was the POMOA representative of the area. The administrator of the province, Hussien Ismail, was also considered a MEISON affiliate.

To spread its influence, the MEISON had opened up a book store in Mettu and had acquired a semi-legal status. The book store became the immediate target of the youth and in a march organized to protest against the regime, the book shop was burnt down. Hostility toward the MEISON continued to rise and some of its members were forced to leave the town. Both GA and GKY, who were considered leaders of the EPRP in the area, but in fact could count only three months after they joined the organization, were arrested in February 1976 along with fifty-four other people. They were sent to the Central Investigation Department in Addis Abeba. As a result of the crisis, EPRP activity in the area was weakened. Both GA and GKY remained in prison until July 1977.

Twenty-seven of those arrested were youth, labor and teacher activists, while the rest were accused of reactionary politics. Among the last mentioned was an 85-year old Kagnazmatch, nicknamed, "Kegnu"- the "rightist". "Kegnu" was one of the first detainees to be interrogated. When the interrogating officer asked him why he was arrested, "Kegnu" was annoyed that he should be asked the very question that he wanted answered. When the officer explained about the arms that were found in his house, "Kegnu" could not contain his anger. "Kegnu" explained that he obtained them during the war of resistance against the Italians and that he did not disarm innocent citizens. "Kegnu" was alluding about the Derge's decision to disarm citizens which began in November 1975. "Kegnu" went into great details and described his role and exploits during the war of resistance. The officer, who appeared to sympathize with "Kegnu", abruptly discontinued the interrogation and to demonstrate the flimsiness of some of the cases, called his staff and repeated the interrogation all over again.

Some days later, the Central Investigation Department (CID) branch informed "Kegnu" that he was free and could go home. "Kegnu" refused to leave the prison compound until the government returned his arms and his confiscated land, and gave him some means of transportation to Illubabor. Later on, for quite some time, in the premises of the Security Branch, one would refer as "an Illubabor case", to signify its flimsiness.[119]

The Bellissuma Group

Another minuscule group that the EPRP began to negotiate with was the Oromo group organized around the publication known as *Bellissuma*. The case was presented by Getachew Maru. Learning from its past error, the EPRP leadership involved the Addis IZ in the negotiation process. When the EPRP leadership inquired about Bellissuma, contradictory information came from Getachew and the Addis Abeba IZ. It was learned that Bellissuma was a minuscule Oromo group, many of whose members viewed the Oromo question as colonial and regarded the EPRP as a "Neftegna" organization. Neft means arms and Neftegna is someone who carries arms. Over the years, the word Neftegna had come to denote landlords in Southern Ethiopia. Most of the peasants of Southern Ethiopia were disarmed.

BC, a university activist, and Getachew Maru, on behalf of Bellissuma and the EPRP, respectively, conducted the negotiation. The EPRP did not encourage the merger of the two groups, instead, it decided to maintain the relationship and influence the political line of the group while helping it to stand on its feet. With this in mind, in the months that followed the negotiation process, the EPRP provided the Bellissuma group with some financial support and also produced and distributed its publications. As time went by, some leading EPRP members questioned the wisdom of helping an organization which, in the final analysis, the EPRP might not be able to control. Despite that reservation, contact with the group was maintained. In the course of the struggle, some members of the "Bellissuma" broke away from the group and along with others, formed the group known by its publication, "*Mukukula*". It was a group composed of young Oromo activists, some of whom belonged to the EPRP Youth League or sympathized with the EPRP. The group had a little known organization called the Oromo Peoples Liberation Organization.

In its drive to mobilize the radicals, the Derge was making efforts to lure in Oromo intellectuals and sometime during this period, an official newspaper, known as *Berissa*, appeared in Oromiffa. It employed the Geez script. Some Oromo and other intellectuals debated whether Latin or Geez Script would be more effective to express opinions in Oromiffa. Haile Fida, whose study was published in the early seventies, also suggested Latin as the script for Oromiffa.

The Haji Kutta Group

Haji Kutta was a leader of a section of the Gujji Oromo who live in Sidamo. Sometime in 1975, he was approached by members of the EPRP who took part in the student campaign. Among them was Nuredin Mohammed, code named Tewil, who later became a member of the EPRP CC sub-secretariat. Haji was a relatively young, bright and democratically inclined Oromo peasant who was involved in the study programs of the zematch students. In the course of the struggle, Haji was made a member of the Democratic Front that the EPRP was organizing.

Ever since he established contact with the EPRP, Haji had insisted that the organization should arm him and his followers in order to begin an armed struggle. The EPRP, which still believed that it had to pursue the peaceful form of struggle, was unable to provide the arms that Haji demanded. Instead, the EPRP explained the need to form a wider organizational network. For Haji, the organizational and political support was a given factor and he persistently claimed that he had hundreds of supporters who were ready to follow his lead. He remained undisuaded and persisted in asserting that an armed struggle should begin. When he knew that the EPRP could not meet his expectations, Haji suggested that arms could be obtained from the Somali government. The EPRP, which was aware of the irredentist plan of the Somali regime, had adequate knowledge of how that regime had impeded the Bale uprising of the 1960s and how it mishandled Oromo nationalist leaders who had gone to Somalia for assistance.[120] The EPRP told Haji about the strings that the Somali regime would attach to the aid.[121]

While the discussion with Haji was still underway, a Derge military contingent that was assigned in the Sidamo area conducted a massive massacre in various parts of the province and began looking for Haji,[122] who along with about three hundred of his followers had left for Somalia. The EPRP then lost contact with Haji. Efforts were made to reestablish contact through the leader of the Bale uprising, Wakko Guttu. However, a few months later, Wakko himself disappeared. Nothing was heard about Haji until his group returned to the area, along with the Somali army, sometime in 1977.

The Afar Liberation Front

The Afar people inhabit the Red Sea coast and the area along the highway leading to the then main port of Ethiopia, Asseb. The chieftain, Sultan Ali Mirah, was closely associated with the former ruling class of Ethiopia and owned a good share of the Tendaho plantation, property of the British owned Mitchell Cotts Company.

Negotiation to form a united front with the organization known as the Afar Liberation Front (ALF) was underway sometime in the mid-seventies. By this time, the EPRP had reached agreement with the ALF on major political and programmatic questions. However, the Afar Liberation Front abandoned the negotiation and allied with the Derge upon the declaration of the National Democratic Revolution Program (NDR) in April 1976. The NDR program had declared an autonomous Afar region and, in due course, some ALF members were assigned to important government posts in the Afar area.

During the mid-seventies, the Afar people had initiated armed confrontation with the regime and had attacked zematch students. As part of a general plan to quell this simmering dissatisfaction, the military regime was devising ways and means to bring the conflict to an end. Ali Mirah who had fled the country was believed to be behind the military activities.

Hizbawi Ametse

Around April 1976, the EPRP established a relationship with the group that published "*Hizbawi Ametse*" (People's Revolt). The group was composed of loosely clustered veteran activists and intellectuals, probably not exceeding twenty in number. Many of them, having studied in the United States, were placed in important government posts. Some of them became members of the POMOA. Among the leading figures of the group were Kebede Woubishet, DR, Mellese Ayalew, TK and HK. TK and Zeru Kehishen conducted the negotiation on behalf of the group and the EPRP, respectively. Even though no agreement could be reached on some of the major political issues of the period, both the Hizbawi Ametse group and the EPRP agreed to collaborate and exchange information. The EPRP published and distributed the group's publication.

Notes to Chapter I

1. Kiflu Tadesse, The Generation, Part I, Independent Publishers, 1993, Chapter VII.

2. Kiflu Tadesse, op.ccit., pages 213-214.

3. Democracia, Volume II, Special Edition.

4. Ibid., page 7.

5. Kiflu Tadesse, op.cit., Chapter VII.

6. See details Chapter II.

7. Demeke Harege Weyene was in the EPRP camp the previous year.

8. See details on page, 22.

9. Democracia, Volume III, No. 2 page 5.

10. Details are given elsewhere.

11. Interview with Ali, November 1994. Ali is a survivor of the execution in Jimma. In 1976, he was in prison after he and others were rounded up from the Agaro area.

12. Major Getachew Shebeshi who later became Brigadier General, committed suicide following the take over of power by the EPRDF, in 1991.

13. Democracia, Volume III, No.2, page 5.

14. Ibid., page 10.

15. See details in Chapter IV.

16. The above passages were based partly on Democracia, Volume III, No. 5.

17. Democracia, Volume II, Special Edition; Sefiw Hizbe Dimtse; No. 32, page 2.

18. See details at the end of Chapter I.

19. Democracia, Volume III, No. 5, page 8.

20. Democracia, Volume III, No. 3, page 8.

21. Democracia, Volume II, No. 22, page 2

22. Kiflu Tadesse, op. cit., page 216.
23. Democracia, Volume II, No. 19.
24. Democracia, Volume II, No. 22, page 2.
25. Arba Gugu is one of the areas where intense conflict took place following the take over of power by the EPRDF in 1991. Because of the conflict, many citizens, particularly Amharas, were victimized.
26. NDR program, Cl. No. 5.
27. Addis Zemen, May 18, page 7.
28. Democracia, Volume III, No. 34, page 2.
29. NDR program, preamble.
30. Addis Zemen, Abyot Medrek, April and May, 1976.
31. Economic Memorandum on Ethiopia, World Bank, September 23, 1977, page 31.
32. Democracia, Volume III, No. 4, page 6.
33. EPRP program, No. IV/1.
34. Democracia, Vol. II, No. 13, page 2.
35. Ibid., page 2.
36. Ibid., page 3.
37. Addis Zemen, May 18, 1976.
38. Kiflu Tadesse, op. cit., Chapters I and VI.
39. Ibid., page 209.
40. Interview with Tedla Fentaye, 1994. Tedla was one of the prisoners.
41. Proclamation No. 71, December 1975, Chapter II, Article 4.
42. EPRP program, No. III/1.
43. Economic Memorandum in Ethiopia, World Bank, September 23, 1977, page 13.
44. Ibid., page 16.
45. Economic Memorandum in Ethiopia, World Bank, April 22, 1977.
46. Democracia, Volume III, No.3, page 4.

47. Ibid., page 4.

48. Democracia, Volume III, No. 7, page 2.

49. Economic Memorandum in Ethiopia, World Bank, April 22, 1977, pages 20 and 21.

50. See details on page 44.

51. The cited section is based partly on Democracia, Volume III, No.3.

52. Ibid., page 5.

53. Kiflu Tadesse, op.cit., pages 161-162.

54. Ibid., pages 222-223.

55. Labader, No. 10, page 22.

56. CELU Resolution, September 1968, obtained from Teglatchen, No.2, October 1975 (1968), page 54.

57. Ibid., page 62.

58. Ibid., page 70-71.

59. Ibid., page 85.

60. When the strike failed after a few days, everything was returned back to the office unnoticed.

61. Addis Zemen, September 16, 1975.
In September 1975, Daniel gave the order to kill the airline workers. The individual was reputed to have killed innocent civilians, even without the knowledge of the Derge itself. He approved the killing of some youth in the Sebeta area, and ordered the execution of students and teachers who were picked up from the prisons of Tigrai and Wello. The teachers and students were burnt alive by Major Tamrat Babile on the Asmera-Addis Abeba highway.

62. Interview with Tedla Fentaye, 1994. Tedla, an employee of CELU, was one of the activists arrested. Tedla met and discussed with the Grazematch in the prison that was located at the former Bodyguard headquarters, near the Janhoy Meda. It was there where many labor leaders were detained. Grazematch did not know how and why he was chosen as the scapegoat.

63. The Derge did not disclose the death of Engineer Beedemariam to his immediate family even a year after his death. Interview with Tedla Fentaye, 1994.

64. As Labader later wrote, Araya Fanta had some role in convincing Colonel Alem Zewde to return from his self-imposed exile. The Colonel was the

chairperson of the committee that was formed in 1974 by the Endalkatchew regime to curb the opposition within the military. He was executed by the Derge in November 1974, along with other notables of the former regime.

65. Labader, No.12, page 2.

66. Emergency Declaration, September 30, 1975 Article 3.

67. Ibid., Cl. 5/a & b; page 6.

68. Ethiopian Herald, November 9, 1975.

69. Labader, No. 10, page 1.

70. Labader, No. 12, page 2.

71. Ibid., page 2.

72. After Samuel's arrest, Fikre Zergaw, the representative of the zone three committee became the secretary of the Addis Abeba IZ.

73. Labader, No. 26, page 1.

74. Ibid., page 3.

75. Negarit Gazeta, 35/11, Labor Proclamation, No. 64 of December 1975, Part II, No. 12.

76. Labader, No. 20, December 18, 1976.

77. EPRP Program, No.V/1.

78. Democracia, Volume II, No. 30, page 5.

79. Ibid., page 7.

80. See details in Chapter II.

81. Democracia, Volume II, No. 30, page 9.

82. 1975 EPRP program/preamble.

83. Two of the members of the workers committee, Germatchew and Kiflu had gone underground and TF was arrested and instead, Alemayehu Tilahun, an EPRP member who studied in the Soviet Union joined the workers committee. Alemayehu fell victim during the 1977 search and destroy campaign organized by the MEISON. Zeru Kehishen, another CC member also joined the workers committee around the last months of 1975. Because of the difficulty of disguising himself, Germatchew had to be confined to a house. To escape the boredom and lack of immobility, he used to exercise quite often. He used to stay in an efficiency in the midst of the city, in the area known as

Teklehaimanot. Most of the committee meetings were conducted where he resided.

84. Democracia, Volume II, No. 22, page 4.

85. Ibid., page 4.

86. Kiflu Tadesse, op.cit., pages 237-238.

87. ELAMA, Minimum Program, pages 4-5.

88. Right after Daro's execution, the inhabitants of the Arat Kilo area, where the killing took place, went out on a demonstration. To exonerate itself from the crime, the Derge arrested and executed the killer, Girma Kebede.

89. Just before the ELAMA Congress was to begin, one of the participants observed that the vehicle that used to transport the participants to the meeting place had a similar tag, like those used by the Ethiopian security personnel. The EPRP used to pass to its members the tags of vehicles that were being used by the regime's security personnel. Alarmed by the incident, an extra precaution was taken and a special watch group was formed. It was learnt later that the security office randomly selected and used tag numbers that were already assigned to individuals.

90. In the following years, a number of other worker related underground publications were printed. Among these publications was "The Akaki Proletariat" which conducted agitation in one of the major industrial zones.

91. Kiflu Tadesse, op.cit., Chapter VII.

92. In Gonder, a few thousand people took part in the May Day demonstration. Police arrested some demonstrators. The participants of the demonstration then went to the police station and demanded that the individuals be released. In the midst of this conflict, the police opened fire and wounded some. Among those wounded was a hearing impaired individual who still was carrying his banner. (Interview Mohabaw and Berhane, June 1994)

93. See details about POMOA, Chapter II.

94. See details in Chapter II.

95. Addis Zemen, March 9, 1976.

96. Addis Zemen, June 10, 1976.

97. See details in Chapter IV.

98. Kiflu Tadesse, op.cit., Chapter VII.

Post Land Reform 51

99. An article written by the Women's Coordinating Committee used to be published in the Addis Zemen as late as December 1975.

100. Kiflu Tadesse, op. Cit., Chapter VII.

101. EPLO program, No. 1.

102. Ibid., page 5.

103. Kiflu Tadesse, op. cit., page 209.

104. Kiflu Tadesse, op.cit., Chapter VII.

105. More on Engineer Osman in Chapter VII.

106. See details, Kiflu Tadesse, op. cit., pages 244-245.

107. Kiflu Tadesse, op.cit., Chapter VII.

108. See details in Chapter II.

109. See details at the end of Chapter I.

110. Democracia, Special Edition, August 2, 1976.

111. Democracia, Volume II, Special Edition, December 1975; and Democracia, Volume II, Special Edition 2, January 1976.

112. See details in Chapter II.

113. See details about the Abyot group, Kiflu Tadesse, op.cit., Chapter V.

114. Details given in Chapter III.

115. About the fate of Colonel Shitaye and the whole of the Sennay Likke group, see details in Chapter VI.

116. See details in Chapter II.

117. Interview with GA and GKY, 1989 and 1990.

118. For fear of being exposed, Seyoum did not join the EPRP party structure, or the Oppressed Soldiers Organization, but he was handled on a single contact by the security department of the IZ. However, after two years or so, Seyoum felt left alone and demanded to join the party structure in order to take part in organizational activities.
    The Addis Abeba IZ considered his demands and assigned members, including a zonal committee member, SKM, to study and discuss party policies with him. Probably, the surveillance conducted on one of those assigned EPRP members, who at the time was either residing, or frequented the residence of Seyoum, enabled Derge security personnel to

come to his residence. Seyoum was killed in the shoot out that followed.
119. Interview with GKY, 1989.
120. Kiflu Tadesse, op.cit., Chapter I.
121. See details Chapter VI.
122. Ibid., Chapter VII.

2

Transformation of the State Apparatus

From the time it came to power in 1974, the Derge had undertaken swift economic reforms. However, the livelihood of the people, particularly that of the urban populace remained unresolved. Major economic reforms enacted, the struggle hinged on issues of democracy and the EPRP CC was forced to conduct an uphill battle. Politics cannot be separated from economics became one of the major slogans of the radical generation and issues of democracy became the main rallying cry of the period. Independent peasant associations and the right to be armed became the rallying slogans of the peasantry. Intense struggles took place in some parts of Ethiopia. In the urban areas, the Derge continued undermining the legally existing teachers and labor organizations, which resorted to a clandestine form of struggle. When the Derge found out that it could not restrain that struggle, it came up with an ingenuous solution; it formed the Provisional Office for Mass Organizations Affairs (POMOA).

The Provisional Office for Mass Organizations Affairs

The Derge had been contemplating the formation of a party as early as December 1974. In its Proclamation of Ethiopian Socialism, it had decreed that a party would be formed.[1] When the Derge realized that it would be premature to form a political party, it resorted to a lesser form of an organizing body. The effort to form an official party was postponed. Initially, in September 1975, the Derge formed the People's Organizing Political Committee (POC). Derge members constituted the majority of this committee. However, a few months later, both the name and the composition of the committee were changed; the institution became the Provisional Office for Mass Organizations Affairs (POMOA).

In order to form POMOA, some Derge members approached a number of intellectuals belonging to the various political groups in the country. Senior Derge officers, including Mengistu Haile Mariam, conducted interviews with the candidates and discussed issues, including the PPG, the national question, the nature of the Derge and Socialism. Following the completion of the interview, a number of intellectuals including Mellese Ayalew, one of the founding members of the Ethiopian students union in the USA, Drs. Negede Gobeze and Haile Fida, MEISON leading figures who did their higher studies in Addis Abeba University and France, Dr. Eshetu Chole, an economist from Syracuse University in the USA, Yonas Admassu, a linguist and a poet, Dr. Sennay Likke, a chemical engineer who studied in the USA, Dr. Negist Adane, a pediatrician who conducted her studies in Moscow, Dr. Alemu Abebe, a veterinarian who studied in Moscow, Andargatchew Aseged, a leading MEISON member, Asefa Medhane, Fekre Merid, a leading MEISON member who did his higher studies in France, and Mesfin Kassu, a MEISON member and former activist of the students union in Ethiopia, were selected. Of the fifteen members of POMOA, seven were leading MEISON members. Haile Fida and Mesfin Kassu, both MEISON members, were made chairperson and general secretary of POMOA, respectively. POMOA had a publication known as *Abeyotawi Ethiopia* (Revolutionary Ethiopia).

As the name itself indicates, the circumstances that dictated the formation of POMOA were the unruly condition of the mass organizations and the need to bring them under the Derge's control. Following the usurpation of power by the military regime, CELU had called two strikes. The Ethiopian Teachers' Association (ETA) had passed resolutions critical of the regime and it had also called a strike. Besides, the regime had found it difficult to control the youth, in particular zematch students.

According to the Decree that formed POMOA,[2] some of the major tasks of the institution were,

> 1. to prepare a guideline that would allow the practice of democratic rights;...3. to ensure that the National Democratic Revolution program is implemented correctly, 4. to assist in the formation of the People's Democratic Republic, 5. to bring the bureaucracy under the control of the people, etc.

When the Derge began conducting the selection process, the EPRP became very apprehensive and stated, "(the regime) had opened discussion with some progressives and opportunists who claim to be progressives. Without giving the broad masses the chance to get organized, the Derge is attempting to form a committee composed of individuals who are neither elected nor have anyone's mandate."[3] Discussing the political activities of the newly formed institution, the POMOA, the same *Democracia* issue stated,

> its first task was to sugar-coat the activities of the regime, in order to be able to weaken the opposition and to bring the masses under control...its second task is to lump the opposition, both on the left and the right aisle, together and conduct agitation as if they belonged to the same category.[4]

The creation of POMOA was also regarded as a step toward the formation of a state party, and that move, the notion of which was alive as late as the first months of 1976, remained a major concern of the EPRP. *Democracia* Nos 26 and 29 discussed the formation of the one-party system and its relationship to the issue of fascism. *Democracia* No. 29, titled "One party or many parties?" discussed the dangers of the formation of a one-party system and the possible class composition of such a party. *Democracia* concluded that "the party would organize the backward section of the population and would be aligned with imperialist forces".[5]

Democracia No. 26 discussed the universal characteristics of fascism comparing them to the conditions in Ethiopia. Fascism's overtly anti-democratic stance and its inclination to form a one-party state was also mentioned. *Democracia* discussed some of the outstanding features of fascism, like its 'socialistic' overtone and its propensity to enact some reforms, when dictated by circumstances. *Democracia* also discussed fascism's ideology, arguing that it was based on national chauvinism and its proclivity to make a scapegoat of a religious group or a certain section of the population, for the problems of the country. Fascism exaggerated history to suit its purposes and the names of renown Ethiopian patriots were used for propaganda purposes, stated *Democracia*. *Democracia* further asserted that the Derge was intending to form some kind of a bureaucratic party from above.[6] Predicting the social base of such a party *Democracia* stated, "higher government officials, provincial, *awaraja*, and wereda government administrators, managers of production and distribution corporations, military and police higher officials, the comprador bourgeoisie, power hungry national chauvinists and those feudal landlords whom the government alleged were newly baptized in socialism" would be the leading figures of the party.[7] In conclusion, the paper demanded an unconditional right to organize.[8]

Sometime before it struck an alliance with the Derge, MEISON had introduced a theory which envisaged the Derge as an institution that had both left and right wings. That theory was made public following the Land Reform Proclamation of 1975.[9] MEISON could not see the Derge in its totality, but viewed it as two sections of one piece where one of its wings had leftist inclination and the other rightist.[10] Based on this theory, MEISON adopted a strategy of collaborating with what it called the left wing of the Derge, whose main figure was Mengistu Haile Mariam, while calling for the prosecution of the right wing and anti-people Derge members.[11]

The formation of POMOA was to prove an ingenious move of the Derge to win over some radical individuals and groups by giving them some place in the state apparatus, without, however, addressing the question of political power and democracy.

POMOA and the Initial Phase of the Formation of a Police State

POMOA had a budget of more than seven million Ethiopian birr a year. Leading members of the institution were paid close to one thousand Ethiopian birr a month, a sum of money then befitting that of a ministerial or equivalent position in the government of Haile Selassie.[12] When it commenced its activities, POMOA became an important institution; it carried out the political and ideological tasks of the regime from 1975 until the culmination of the "Red Terror" in 1978. A year or so after its formation, POMOA formed branch committees in almost all provinces, awerajas and weredas of Ethiopia. Of the fourteen provincial POMOA committees, MEISON controlled more than eleven. Some important institutions, such as the Addis Abeba and Harer branches of POMOA were chaired by such prominent MEISON members as Kebede Mengesha and Abdulahi Yusuf. POMOA branches in Illubabor, Wellega and Sidamo were chaired by Dr. Kedir Mohammed, Hailu Gerbaba and Eshetu Ararso, respectively, all MEISON leaders. In subsequent years, POMOA served as the transition institution and laid the groundwork toward the formation of the highly centralized state that came into being in early 1977. The radical circles that regrouped around POMOA were the precursors of the official state party, to be known as the Ethiopian Workers Party.

As indicated above, POMOA/MEISON took over the political and ideological role of the state until the Derge was able to train its own people and create its own institutions. The media was instrumental in this process and the first projects which POMOA embarked upon were known as the Abyot Medrek and the discussion "clubs" (*Yewuyeyit kebeb* - in Amharic).

POMOA and the *Abyot Medrek* (Forum)

During the fourth week of January 1976, the *Addis Zemen* newspaper devoted a section of its columns for what it called the Abyot Medrek. The columns were allotted for free discussion on contemporary and controversial issues. The Abyot Medrek provided an opportunity for the opposition groups and individuals to write articles in government controlled newspapers. The editor, the late Berhanu Zerihun, supported by POMOA/MEISON, was the main personality behind the project. In the duration of a few months, an average of three to four articles were printed every day and at least one of them expressed the opinions of the opposition. A variety of issues were raised and discussed, but the most important question debated in these columns was the question of political democracy with some emphasis placed on the issue of the formation of the PPG which constituted one of the important clauses of the EPRP program.[13] A *Democracia* issue that came out to herald the convocation of the EPRP Conference held in August 1975 had called that "the military junta had to be replaced by a PPG." As a precursor toward the formation of the PPG, it was suggested that, initially, "a popular revolutionary council" had to be formed.[14]

One of the first printed articles on the Abyot Forum was that of Ewnetu Ferede, a pen name that expressed the MEISON line. On their own initiative, EPRP members utilized the columns quite effectively. In due time, the political department of the EPRP became involved in the process and contributed articles elaborating the program of the organization. Among those who frequently contributed to the columns were Marta Wallelign, Bezabeh Belatchew (Berhane Meskel Redda) and Hamatcho Mahagano, pen names of activists in the EPRP camp; Ewnetu Ferede (pen name) and Yemane Araya from the MEISON camp.

Most of the articles written by those in the EPRP camp advocated the unconditional granting of democratic rights, "democracy yale gedeb", while those in the MEISON camp advocated conditional rights, "democracy *begedeb*". An article by Marta Wallelign posed a rhetorical question to elaborate upon who was advocating 'limited democracy' and she stated, "it was (perpetrated by) the so-called progressive bureaucrats who were entrusted to run the state apparatus. They coined the slogan in order to stay in power as long as they could."[15] An April 1976 *Democracia* issue that was titled "When we say Democracy; When they say Democracy" was devoted to the divergent interpretations of the issue of democracy.[16] *Democracia* had been demanding the promulgation of unconditional democratic rights.

In his article of February 27, 1976, Bezabeh argued that "the basis for the difference and conflict [that is, between the Derge and the opposition] revolved around the issue of who should lead the revolutionary struggle...a consensus to work together could be reached when an agreement is made on the character of the provisional government."[17] Bezabeh then went into a detailed analysis of how such a government was to be formed and what its tasks should be. That article generated a heated debate and those in the MEISON camp wrote a number of articles counter-arguing the thesis that Bezabeh presented. One of the articles stated, "to call for the replacement of the Derge by another provisional government is a reactionary step".[18]

Ewnetu Ferede, who supported the granting of 'limited democracy' (democracy *begedeb*), argued that precaution had to be taken regarding the declaration of democratic rights. He believed that the people had to be "politicized" before democracy could be granted.[19] Explaining the necessary steps to be taken Ewenetu stated,

>...[G]et rid of all reactionaries, conduct political studies and form revolutionary guards in the mass organizations. The members of these committees (that is, revolutionary guards) should be politically conscious supporters of the revolution....If the bureaucracy is weakened and replaced by genuine supporters of the revolution, then the media can open its doors to revolutionary literature....[20]

The above quoted passage contained POMOA's policy regarding the formation of the *Abyot Tebeka* groups which came into being around the end of 1976.[21] In his March 1976 article Ewnetu Ferede wrote,

> ...[T]he burning issue of the day is the granting of democratic rights and independence to those genuine revolutionaries. Make the broad masses more conscious and arm them. Arrest all reactionaries and those that breed confusion. If the above suggestions are not implemented, one should not be a prophet to predict that the revolution would be in danger."[22]

When Ewnetu referred to genuine revolutionaries, what he had in mind were those groups that were clustered around the Derge. Those that breed confusion were those grouped around the EPRP.

While the discussion on the Abyot Medrek columns in *Addis Zemen* was underway, confusion began spreading amongst EPRP members and sympathizers. Some of the articles that were printed in the *Addis Zemen* were regarded as the official lines of the EPRP. But the leadership declared, "*Democracia* is the only organ of the party and any view expressed elsewhere does not necessarily reflect the position of the organization."[23] In order to avoid more confusion, the EPRP leadership imposed some restrictions on itself. Like the general membership, any CC member was entitled and even encouraged to write on any issue that he thought was important. It was also decided that the leadership would not censor any of the articles which the members, including CC members wrote. However, to find out whether any relevant information was not compromised, EPRP CC members were required to present their articles to the departments that they belonged to. This self-limitation was intended to sensitize CC members who had access to critical information of the organization.

After the initiation of the Abyot Medrek columns, *Addis Zemen* became a scarce commodity and an hour or so after its publication, not a single copy would be found in the market. The black market price of the paper rose to more than 400% and a 10 cents (Eth.) newspaper was sold for 50 cents. However, about two months after the newspaper began publishing articles of the opposition, the MEISON and those groups close to the Derge began complaining and accusing the editor of partiality. They believed that the *Abyot Medrek* had become an instrument of the opposition. Soon, articles that were critical of the regime stopped being printed in the newspaper and one of POMOA's major experiments faltered. The newspaper also went back to its normal course of activities and the Abyot Forum became dominated by the groups around the Derge.

POMOA and *Yewuyeyet Kebeb*

During the first months of 1976, POMOA/MEISON came up with the idea of forming discussion "clubs", called *Yewuyeyet kebeb* in Amharic, (an idea probably copied from the Ziad Barre regime of Somalia), in the various government institutions, kebeles, factories, etc., and the regime decreed their formation in April 1976. The discussion "clubs" were fora the leadership of which was supposedly elected. The official purpose for their formation was the involvement of the people in the political struggle.[24] However, in a society where democratic right was not respected, the "clubs" could only be media through which the government disseminated its policies, followed up the activities of dissidents and members of the opposition.

Although participation in the activities of the discussion "clubs" was not mandatory, initially, almost every member of each institution attended the meetings to avoid surveillance. The discussions, which were conducted at least once a week, focused on political and other issues.

When the policy regarding the formation of the "discussion clubs" was made public, the EPRP PB decided that the party should influence the proceedings of the "clubs" and some EPRP members were instructed to stand for elections in the "club's" leadership. The rest of the EPRP members in the institutions were expected to maintain low profiles and remain clandestine. Besides the political advantages, it was believed that EPRP participation would allow the opposition to control the leadership post of the "clubs" and make spying on employees of the institutions very difficult.

Not long after the formation of the discussion "clubs", its members began discussing topics of their choice, rather than those sent down by POMOA. They discussed either important issues of the day, or issues that had direct relevance to their daily needs. An article that came out on the *Addis Zemen Abyot Medrek* of June 4 enumerated the complaints raised at the discussion "clubs". These included the demand for a raise in salary, the dismissal of certain administrators from certain institutions, the rejection of POMOA's guidance of the "clubs", the need for workers control of factories, etc. The author of the article, who seemed to have had adequate knowledge of the proceedings of the discussion "clubs" argued that the anarchists (that is, referring to the EPRP) were making efforts to sidetrack the discussions for their own political end.[25] "Anarchist" sabotage was an oft mentioned and discussed issue of the media and publications of groups allied with the Derge.

Even though the Decree regarding the formation of the "clubs" had allowed that discussions could be conducted on a wide range of issues, POMOA/MEISON became alarmed when sensitive issues began surfacing. POMOA did not like the new direction that the fora were taking and it declared that the "clubs" had to refrain from what it called "spontaneous actions". POMOA published a statement clarifying the misconception regarding the role of the "clubs".[26] Subsequently, on May 29, 1976, the Derge put out a statement which declared that, "...many of the "clubs" had ignored the guideline (sent by POMOA) and are focusing on their own personal demands, instead of political discussions." The regime then warned them to refrain from anti-revolutionary activities. Or else, declared the statement, "the military regime has the duty to carry out its historical responsibilities."[27]

A few months after their formation, the "clubs", the very creations of POMOA/MEISON became its targets. Anarchists, that is, EPRP members, were singled out as the instigators. It was true that some EPRP members and sympathizers had some influence in the proceedings of the "clubs" and some of them had been elected as chairpersons. However, the demands raised during the discussions were not new, neither were they fabricated by "anarchists", but had been voiced from the beginning of the 1974 movement. CELU and the Ethiopian Teachers' Association had gone out on strikes raising the same demands.

Another area of conflict between POMOA and the members of the various discussion "clubs" was accountability. When the idea of the formation of the "discussion clubs" was first initiated, it was designed that they would fall under the auspices of POMOA. However, labor considered such an arrangement a threat to its independent existence and resisted POMOA's encroachment. Labor unions did not and could not object to the formation of the clubs, even though their relation with the regime remained strained. However, they asserted that the "clubs" should be accountable only to CELU. When labor's resistance became pronounced, *Addis Zemen* blamed "anarchists" for labor's intransigence.[28] When many unions continued to object POMOA's intrusions, POMOA began designing other approaches.[29] Until then, discussion guidelines were published in the *Addis Zemen* and that newspaper became the official organ of the political "education" process. Commenting on the new approach *Democracia* stated, "after allowing the formation of the "clubs", (POMOA) tries to control them by sending topics of discussion...."[30]

To counter POMOA's moves and also partly deceived by the seemingly "democratic" condition, almost every institution of the country began printing its own semi-legal publications. Some of the pamphlets were so daring that they quoted and referred to underground papers, such as *Democracia*. However, the individuals, EPRP members included, who were behind the publications, eventually became targets of Derge surveillance.

In their few months of existence, the discussions that the "club's" conducted enabled government supporters to acquaint themselves with Marxist terminologies, without believing in the doctrine itself. To be sure, one of the first steps that POMOA undertook was to form a school for the training of political cadres in Addis Abeba, in the Gulele area, in the compound of General Wingate high-school. Sometime later, it was renamed as the Yekatit Cadre School and it was moved to the former residence of the Crown Prince. The political indoctrination in the Cadre School centered on major theoretical questions in philosophy and political economy. A special physical training course was given to selected individuals. The Cadre School also served as a recruiting ground for groups who comprised

POMOA.

In a year's time, the Cadre School "trained" thousands of cadres and sent them to government institutions, kebeles, workers' unions, etc. The "trainees" were also sent to different parts of the country, to operate as POMOA branch representatives. The task of those who were assigned to the various institutions was to guide and conduct political sessions and at the same time to follow and report on the activities of anti-government individuals.

Most of the cadres, and particularly those who were in charge, were paid the salary of a university graduate. They were given free housing, travel allowance and petty-cash. Some were provided with government vehicles. Corporal F. was an EPRP infiltrator of the POMOA in the Asmera area. Before he joined the cadre institution, he was paid no more than 150 birr a month, but after he joined the POMOA, his salary increased to 500 birr. He was given free housing and a daily allowance whenever he had to do some traveling.[31]

Besides its role in training political "activists", the cadre training institution opened up an avenue to a host of careerist and ambitious individuals and, as a result, a large group that had a vested interest in the existence of the military regime was created.

In order to cope with the situation, the EPRP CC decided to produce booklets on a wide range of political and economic issues. As was indicated elsewhere, it also decided to open up a cadre training school in the Addis Abeba area. Both tasks were assigned to the political department of the CC. For a number of reasons, including the weaknesses of the political department and the leadership's inability to enforce its decisions, the EPRP was able to come up with some theoretical works only in 1977, during which time it was in a deep crisis.[32]

As demonstrated elsewhere, when the effort to control the "clubs" through political means became difficult, the Derge and POMOA began transforming them into important instruments of repression. Initially, the "clubs" became institutions through which the regime identified its potential enemies. The placement of cadres in different institutions facilitated that effort and the government reached many corners of the society in a single stride. Although the cadres continued explaining the policies of the Derge, in due course, their tasks were redefined when they began serving as important arms of the state apparatus. In a brief while, the Ethiopian state became "politicized" and was transformed into a police state, unprecedented in the history of Ethiopia.

POMOA and the National Democratic Revolution Program

In April 1976, the military regime officially declared the formation of

POMOA, an institution a few months old by then. The military regime also made public the program of what it called the National Democratic Revolution. The program, which was drafted by POMOA, addressed major political and economic questions. The program stipulated that its objectives were "to gain victory over feudalism, bureaucratic capitalism and imperialism and...lay the foundation to build a people's democratic republic."[33] Furthermore, the program stated that success would be guaranteed when

> Anti-imperialist and anti-feudalist forces...are organized ...and united in a broad front. Victory is assured when a proletarian party is organized, strengthened and assumes full leadership of the front....Finally, an assembly, which will assume state power will be established.

MEISON's publication, *Sefiw Hizbe*, believed that the NDR program of the Derge would resolve Ethiopia's contemporary problems.[34]

Even though some of the points of the NDR program were discussed in detail, how and under whose auspices the program would be implemented was not elaborated. In other words, the program did not clarify whether the military regime would stay in power or would be replaced. The NDR program, however, mentioned that a "proletarian party" would take over power in the final analysis. In its publication *Sefiw Hizbe*, MEISON clarified that it was not the Derge that would be able to accomplish the NDR program, but the proletariat.[35] MEISON's paper suggested that "progressives" should intensify the struggle to form the "proletarian party". From this it was understood that the NDR program would enable the groups around the Derge to transform themselves into a decision making institution, after snatching power out of the hands of the Derge.

Be that as it may, the promulgation of the NDR program enabled the Derge to attain international support and acceptance amongst radicals and left circles all over the world, including the then Soviet Union.

On one of the points of the NDR program, it was declared that a broad United Front of all progressives should be formed. However, it was not specified who those progressives were and the qualifications for 'progressiveness' were not spelled out.

Response of the EPRP to the Call for the United Front

Some days before the declaration of the NDR program and the Derge's call for the formation of a front, the EPRP PB held a meeting in an apartment complex in the Ras Mekkonen Bridge area, Addis Abeba. The meeting was attended by all PB members, except Tesfaye Debessai. The main agenda of the meeting was the formation of a front with the Derge. Getachew Maru presented the agenda; he argued that a new political development necessitated a change of policy toward the regime and that the EPRP should strike an alliance with the Derge. According to Getachew, the new development included the formation of the Abyot forum and the "discussion clubs". The other PB members inquired whether he could provide enough details to warrant a policy change. Getachew then referred to hints in the *Addis Zemen* newspaper about a need to form a front. He also mentioned an *Addis Zemen* editorial of March 17, 1976 that mentions the necessity for a front. After mentioning the existence of two crystallized and consolidated progressive political groups, MEISON and the EPRP, the editorial appealed that they should strike a compromise and form some kind of a front.[36]

Getachew's arguments could not convince the rest of the PB members and despite the lengthy discussion, they failed to reach on an agreement. Three divergent views were expressed. While Getachew advocated forging some kind of an alliance with the Derge, Zeru Kehishen opposed the idea altogether, AW and Kiflu Tadesse wanted to see a major policy change regarding the issue of democracy, as a condition to establishing a working relationship with the Derge. Getachew could not provide additional evidence, if he had any. When it realized that no agreement could be reached, the PB decided to pass on the issue to the CC. Before the CC meeting was held, the National Democratic Revolution program of the Derge was proclaimed and the regime called for the formation of a front. It is still not known whether Getachew had any advance knowledge about the content of the new Proclamation. The other PB members did not.

The EPRP CC meeting was held in the residence of an EPRP member, Dr. William Hastings Morton, a British by birth and a professor at the Addis Abeba University.[37] He was a very close friend and comrade of Yohannes Berhane, an EPRP CC member and a lecturer in the Geology Department of the University. The main agenda of the CC meeting was related to EPRP's response to the Derge's call for the formation of a front and two divergent points of views came to the fore. The first one was presented by Berhane Meskel who whole-heartedly embraced the Derge's call for the formation of a front. He argued that the EPRP should make a historical compromise and form a front with the Derge. His premise for such a conclusion was the analysis of the Ethiopian condition. According to him, the Somali regime was threatening the territorial integrity of Ethiopia on the eastern part of the country; on the west, rightist forces, such as, the EDU were making efforts to undermine the revolutionary struggle. The economic condition of the country was deteriorating and the country was disintegrating, and according to Berhane Meskel, there would be no revolution without a country; hence the need to compromise and form a front with the Derge to save the situation.

The second point of view which was totally opposed to the first was advocated by Zeru Kehishen. Both points of views, of course, had their supporters. Zeru dismissed some of Berhane's arguments as utterly exaggerated. He argued that it was wrong and a betrayal of the cause to form a front with a government that had drenched its hands in the people's blood.

Zeru argued that to cooperate with an undemocratic regime was a defeat to democracy itself. It also was a betrayal of the struggle that was being waged in the various parts of the country. Zeru argued that the EPRP could not be a partner to the execution of progressives and democrats, and that such an alliance was treason and a self-defeat for the EPRP.

Getachew was conspicuously silent during the discussion, even though he had raised the issue at the PB meeting a few days earlier. The majority of the CC members were uncomfortable with the positions of both Berhane Meskel and Zeru. They did not appreciate the highly exaggerated thesis presented by Berhane Meskel. At the same time, they could see that the EPRP should change its policy toward the regime, provided a conducive political situation was created.

The majority of the CC members, with Yohannes Berhane and AW in the lead, presented a third alternative. This alternative was based on the standing policy of the EPRP forwarded by the First Congress, in which it was resolved to form a united front with all anti-feudal and anti-imperialist forces. A similar decision was passed by the EPRP Conference of 1975. The Conference had resolved that the front will be organized around what it called a minimum platform, that is, a program acceptable to all of the participants.[38]

The third alternative, with some modifications, laid the ground for an agreement. According to the third alternative, the EPRP had to accept the Derge's call for the formation of a front, provided that democratic rights were promulgated, the drive for the "Raza Project" was stopped, the repression against the Ethiopian people was halted, progressive and revolutionary political prisoners were released and that the Derge made its positions on these points public. It was argued that the EPRP would be ready to resume negotiations if the Derge accepted and implemented the above conditions.[39] According to the EPRP CC, the front to be formed should embrace all political forces of the country, including less known groups such as the Oromo Liberation Front (OLF), the Bellissuma, Tigrai People's Liberation Front (TPLF), ALF, Ethiopian National Liberation Front (ENLF) and the various mass organizations. The program of the front had to be ratified by those concerned and the process should be concluded with the knowledge and participation of the Ethiopian people.

Realizing the magnitude and the possible political implications of its decision, the CC sent its draft resolution for discussion to the members of the Addis Abeba party and Youth League structures. At the insistence of Berhane Meskel, the CC also formed a committee from amongst itself, to oversee the proper execution of the decision. This included the incorporation of the proposals that were supposed to come from the members, and printing and distributing of the special *Democracia* issue. Under normal circumstances, such technical activities were handled either by the PB or the Secretariat. The reports from the members were compiled and incorporated into the resolution of the CC, and the *Democracia* issue that discussed the formation of a front came out a week after the CC meeting took place and the EPRP made its position public.

Neither the Derge nor POMOA responded to the EPRP. An authoritative article[40] in the MEISON controlled journal, *"Addis Fana"* argued that "the EPRP responded fast because it did not understand the processes regarding the formation of a front."[41] The article indicated that Ethiopia was not ready to form a front. Formation of such a front at that time was tantamount to forming a provisional government through a back door, argued the article.[42] The Derge's and POMOA's silence startled the EPRP. It was not clear what POMOA wanted to achieve by declaring the need for a front and not following up the process of front formation. It also was not clear whether the Derge understood that a front was an institution that would be formed to bring opposing forces closer together.

Partly in response to the call for the formation of a front and as a result of the confusion created by the declaration of the NDR program, protest demonstrations began to take place in several parts of the country. One of these was the demonstration conducted by the employees of the National Theater in Addis Abeba who were being organized into a union. Following much haggling with their administration, they were given a green light to form the union. According to the new Labor Law, all, but government employees were entitled to form unions, provided their number reached 20.

While the National Theater employees were waiting for their certificate of registration, the Derge intervened and told them that they could not form a union. Angered by the reversal of the previous decision, the employees went on a demonstration after acquiring the permit to do so.

The peaceful demonstration was dispersed after the participants had marched a few kilometers. In the scuffling that ensued, two employees were killed and a few more were injured. Those who had thought that democratic rights had been proclaimed were disappointed.

POMOA and Mass Organizations

One of the major problems for POMOA was how to handle the various professional and mass organizations, including those of labor, teachers and the youth (regarding the labor movement, see details in Chapter I).

The Ethiopian Teachers' Association had remained without leadership since August 1975. After the teachers strike in November 1975, several teacher activists and union officers were arrested and some went underground.[43] When POMOA took charge, one of the four sectors that it focused on was the teachers' group. POMOA's four main targets, according to a WAZ League publication were, the Ethiopian Teachers Association, CELU, the Women's Committee and the Youth. These groups were labeled as the four "dens" of the EPRP.[44]

POMOA opened up an intensive campaign against the Teachers' Association. In articles appearing in the *Addis Zemen* newspaper in the first months of 1976, POMOA made repeated suggestions to cleanse the Teachers' Association of "anarchists". With the intention of controlling the teachers' movement, POMOA conducted seminars for a large number of teachers. However, POMOA was still unable to control the unions or get a foothold within the teachers' movement. In July and August 1976, POMOA stepped up its campaign against what it labeled as "anarchism" in the school system.

In the struggle to control the mass organizations, among the first to fall prey was the Women's Coordinating Committee which was formed a year or so earlier and had organized the March 8, 1976 celebrations of the International Women's Day. The committee had also composed some songs that were directly related to the issue of women. The committee which was striving to form a national women's association, was banned and replaced by a POMOA-sponsored committee. Some days before it was dissolved, the former Women's Coordinating Committee had expelled some activists belonging to the political groups allied with the Derge.

Important institutions that POMOA wanted to control were the Kebeles which were formed following the proclamation of urban housing in 1975. Throughout Ethiopia, 1791 Kebele associations were formed. Two hundred ninety-one of them were from the ten weredas of the Addis Abeba area.[45] The Kebeles were economic, political and quasi-military institutions that collected rents and "donations" on behalf of the government. In 1975, from the Tekle Haimanot area in Addis Abeba alone, they collected close to two million birr, in a period of some six months.[46]

The Kebeles were institutions that could reach the urban population quite easily and they were engaged in retailing some basic household items. Until the last months of 1975, the Kebeles remained outside the influence of both the regime and the opposition, even though they had sent out petitions condemning the September 1975 labor strike. A few months after their formation, attracted by the enormous amount of money that they handled, a special interest group began forming around kebeles.[47] Until it was revoked sometime later, the Urban Housing Proclamation had allowed the Kebeles to utilize the money obtained from houses rented for not more than 100 birr per month. It was this revenue that attracted some of the elected officials who made efforts to use their newly acquired position for their own personal ends. Bribery, nepotism and favoritism became rampant and some of the elected officials became arrogant and dictatorial.

Despite the inherent problems of the Kebeles, they became one of the battle grounds of the regime and the opposition in the first months of 1976. The regime made efforts to make the Kebeles extensions of the state apparatus and it assigned individuals to each of them to oversee their activities.[48] In May 1976, the regime ordered the Kebeles to mobilize the urban population against the Eritrean rebels and in support of the May Peace Initiative.[49]

The regime took the upper hand to control the Kebeles with the appointment of one of MEISON's leading figures, Daniel Tadesse, as minister of Urban Housing and Development. The Ministry was responsible for everything that had to do with housing, Kebele finance and other activities. By 1976, the Ministry was in charge of more than 45 million birr and for the brief period that it was in commission, it declared that it "spent" about 35 million birr.[50]

The EPRP and the Youth League organization on the other hand, wanted to influence kebele activities, a task that could be accomplished when popular individuals were elected to Kebele posts and when the kebeles themselves became popular institutions accountable to the inhabitants rather than extensions of the state apparatus.

When the military regime called off the student zemetcha in July 1976, a well politicized and tempered young group returned to the urban areas and focused on the Kebeles, thereby creating favorable conditions for the EPRP and its Youth League organization. Many young professional activists became engaged in kebele activities. They reorganized Kebele youth associations in a way that would enable them to reach a wider sector of the Kebele inhabitants. In due course, the youth associations served as fora for political discussions. The Kebeles also facilitated recruitment of members and the EPRP made efforts to utilize that opportunity.

A major show down between the opposition and the regime, represented by POMOA, took place at the second round of elections for Kebele associations in August 1976. POMOA and the Ministry of Urban Housing and Development drafted new laws and regulations to govern the Kebeles. Special criteria were set, determining which nominees should run for Kebele offices. During the first election of 1975, the Urban Housing Proclamation deprived former renters of the right to vote for a period of one year. At the second election of 1976, POMOA introduced a number of other new criteria, among which was the one that made zematch students who had voluntarily abandoned their campaign locations, ineligible for election. This was a deliberate arrangement intended to void from the election process a very large segment of the youth that was not supportive of the regime.

In July and August 1976, POMOA intensified its agitation against what it labeled as anarchist influence in the kebeles.[51] The timing of the campaign was also associated with the election of new officials. The Derge, uncomfortable with the activities in the Kebeles, had circulated an internal memorandum prohibiting the convocation of meetings and the election of new officials in those Kebeles where it was comfortable with the previously elected ones.[52]

To oversee the election proceedings, officials from governmental institutions were sent to the Kebeles. Candidates for the various Kebele positions were vetted by members of POMOA and the Ministry of Urban Housing and Development. As a result, MEISON was able to have some of its members and sympathizers elected to the kebele administration. In those areas where youth activity was strong, both in the capital city and in the provinces, the EPRP was able to have its members or supporters elected.

Despite the restrictions and the bureaucratic haggling, the second round of elections for Kebele offices was not concluded to the satisfaction of POMOA. Even after repeated attempts, POMOA failed to make the Kebeles extensions of the state apparatus. When it realized its failure, POMOA opened up a campaign against the Kebele institutions themselves. POMOA portrayed them as institutions dominated by run away landlords and their EPRP "sons". The EPRP was accused of "disruption" and "sabotage" of kebele activities, intimidation and harassment of kebele officials.

POMOA continued looking for other measures to bring the kebeles under control. A new measure was presented in an authoritative article in the *Addis Zemen* newspaper of July 1976. The article discussed the promulgation of a new law that "gives the kebeles more power and broadens their activities." Furthermore, "the Ministry of Public Housing and Development had indicated that this will be accomplished in the near future," concluded the article.[53] The new Decree discussed in the above article came out in October 1976. That Decree not only empowered the kebeles but also militarized them, allowing the formation of paramilitary groups known as *Abyot Tebekas*. In the years to come, the *Abyot Tebeka* group would become one of the most deadly instruments of repression in the hands of the Derge.[54]

As a result of the intense struggle for kebele offices, a large number of youth activists became exposed and vulnerable to government surveillance. The semi-legal youth associations intended to promote discussions became fora through which government agents would identify potential "enemies".

Political Significance of the Formation of POMOA

In their capacity as junior partners of the regime, those groups that controlled POMOA assumed a pervasive role within the state apparatus. In many provinces, POMOA branch offices acted as the alternative source of political power, thereby diminishing the authority of the local power. However, POMOA's power became omnipotent following the formation of the paramilitary force known as the *Abyot Tebeka*. In some areas, the *Abyot Tebeka* groups were placed under the direct control of POMOA branches. Quite often, the chairman of the Abyot Tebeka committee was nominated by POMOA or one of the groups close to the Derge.[55]

The formation of POMOA allowed MEISON and the Sennay Likke group to place their people in important government posts. Many of the pro-west individuals, who a few months earlier had been appointed to important government posts were demoted. Fifty-five individuals, including some prominent MEISON members, were appointed to important ministries. Sennay's group paid special attention to the military and in particular to individuals around the Derge. The MEISON was less active among the military; its focus was the civilian state apparatus. Daniel Tadesse, a MEISON leader, was made the minister of Public Housing.[56] Dr. Alemu Abebe was made mayor of Addis Abeba, Desta Tadesse, permanent secretary of the Ministry of Culture, Dr. Mekonnen Jotte, administrator of the Shoa province, Teffera Wonde, minister of Health, Terefe Wolde Tsadik, minister of Education, Yayehyirad Kitaw, Commissioner for the Commission of Higher Education, and many others were appointed to important government posts.

Because of the role of these and other political appointees, some of the activities of the state apparatus were redefined. The state apparatus became "baptized" and many of its employees, who had no prior knowledge of, or sympathy with the ideology of the Left began professing "Marxism". The state, which only a few years back had conducted an anti-socialist campaign became the "guardian" and proponent of the "socialist" ideology. Gone were the old Derge statements that accused the opposition "as rumor mongers who wanted to side track the course of the struggle," "divisive elements who wanted to divide the country," or "wolves in sheep clothing," etc. Eclecticism and banal propaganda became things of the past. Selected themes and topics, rather than incoherent and eclectic ideas were used to campaign against the opposition. *Because of POMOA/MEISON's involvement, the main differences that separated the radicals themselves became the concern of the state power and apparatus.*

The alliance of MEISON and other groups with the Derge also became a threshold for the Ethio-Soviet relationship. The Soviets wholeheartedly supported the Derge and regarded it as progressive. They provided it political and moral support. In the Soviet lexicon, the Derge and its members were termed radical democrats. The opposition was either ignored or condemned. The Soviets began campaigning against the EPRP. Soviet authors, such as Georgi Galpirin, labeled EPRP members as "extremists and pro-Maoists" and accused them of posing danger to the country.[57] Articles condemning the EPRP appeared in such publications of the Left as *L'Humanite* (Communist Party of France), *L'Unita* (Communist Party of Italy), *Unsere Zeit* (Communist Party of Germany). As indicated in *The Generation*, Part I, the Yemen government, a Soviet satellite state, distanced itself from the EPRP and Eritrean opposition groups. The Palestinian organizations, like the PDFLP, stopped supporting the EPRP.[58]

In the Soviet Union and other East European countries, anti-Derge political activities became prohibited. Suspected EPRP members studying in East European countries were persecuted. Some had to leave for western countries in search of domiciles. Ethiopian student unions that had been formed long before the Derge came to power were banned and, instead, Derge support groups were formed. Among those that encountered difficulties were seven Ethiopians who arrived in Hungary for a few months of training. All of them were affiliated with the EPRP. After they arrived in

Budapest, a MEISON member and the brother of Hailu Gerbaba, the POMOA representative in Wellega, began checking on their activities. A few weeks later, the Hungarian authorities confiscated their passports for fear that they might emigrate to Austria and seek political asylum. Towards the completion of their training, the Hungarian government began preparations to send the seven Ethiopians back home. However, the Ethiopians, who were in contact with the EPRP structure abroad, devised other means.[59]

EPRP's Organizational Activities

During 1976, two contradictory but interrelated phenomena began taking shape within the camps of the EPRP. Thousands of EPRP members and supporters were put into prison and hundreds were executed. EPRP structures in Jimma, Harer, Welliso, Welkite and other places were dismantled. At this time, the EPRP had not yet concluded that the peaceful form of struggle had been consummated. On the contrary, however, and as a result of the political and organizational activities of the previous years, EPRP's membership and followers increased by a large number. New structures were formed in Eritrea, Gamu Gofa, Bale and in many parts of Shoa. Impressive organizational work was conducted in the Begemidir area. Through the effort of the various levels of the party and Youth League structures, and in particular the Begemedir party interzonal committee, organizational activity was conducted among the peasantry of the Libo aweraja.[60]

Due to an intensive political agitation, denigrating and defaming it as a *"Neftegna"* organization, the EPRP was unable to gain any foothold in Wellega, the home base of MEISON and other Oromo nationalists. MEISON member and POMOA branch representative, Hailu Gerbaba, made sure that a non-Oromo outsider, such as a teacher or a government employee, could conduct no political activity in the area. Anyone with a political opinion was suspected, and, if that person did not belong to the MEISON group, he was victimized. Despite the difficulties, the EPRP made a number of efforts to conduct organizational activities in Wellega. Through Oromo EPRP members, a more concerted effort was made sometime in 1977, however, no substantial organizational work could be conducted.

As was discussed earlier, the formation of POMOA transformed MEISON's status when it became part of the state apparatus. Accordingly, EPRP's relation with the MIESON also underwent some changes.

The EPRP and the MEISON

Before the unfolding of the 1974 movement, the main difference separating the MEISON and the EPLO/EPRP was the assessment of the

Ethiopian situation and the immediate tasks of Ethiopian progressives. The EPLO/EPRP believed that the objective and subjective condition for a revolutionary struggle was present. The MEISON agreed that the objective condition to struggle was present. However, it argued that the subjective condition was lagging. Consequently, "before a revolutionary people's struggle starts, the people should conduct political struggles...." argued those in the MEISON camp.[61] The EPLO/EPRP asserted that the revolutionary struggle had began and what was missing was an organization that would lead the struggle.

Based on the assessment of the Ethiopian situation, the EPLO/EPRP began preparation to initiate an armed struggle. The MEISON, on the other hand vehemently opposed such a move. The MEISON argued, "[T]o arouse a people whose political consciousness is yet undeveloped, would not only result in repression, but will also create a reaction and force the people to give up the struggle."[62] The EPLO/EPRP agreed that political work was essential, but it could be done most effectively in conjunction with a revolutionary war and the organization proceeded to organize its armed nucleus. The discussion between the two groups was irrefutably concluded in favor of the EPLO/EPRP when the 1974 revolutionary movement erupted and the Ethiopian people rose up in unison.

For a period of some months in 1974, the MEISON group in Ethiopia and the EPLO/EPRP advocated the same political line and shared the same objectives. During this period, both the MEISON group inside the country and the EPLO/EPRP were very critical of the military regime. However, that condition was changed upon arrival in Ethiopia of leading MEISON activists, among them, Haile Fida, Negede Gobeze and Andargatchew Aseged. The MEISON then experienced an internal struggle over "the nature of the 1974 movement, the question of political power, positions regarding the Derge, relation with left oriented groups,...".[63] Finally, former MEISON positions were reversed and the leadership was changed.[64] It was also concluded that it was possible to form an alliance with the Derge.

As was indicated elsewhere, unaware of the new policies of MEISON, the EPLO CC decided to create some kind of an understanding and a common political and ideological front with MEISON. With this in mind, a bi-level contact was established after the arrival of the MEISON leadership from abroad.[65] Contact between the two groups was maintained until the proclamation of the land reform act in February 1975 when the MEISON made its new position known.

> Haile Fida had not shown up for two of his appointments, and when he did, he informed Tesfaye Debessai about the new "theory" of "Critique-support". Haile stated that the MEISON had decided to support the Derge while continuing to be critical. Tesfaye then asked how it was possible to criticize a government which legally forbid criticism? How could it be possible to criticize a government in the absence of freedom of speech? Whatever Haile replied, the answer satisfied neither Tesfaye

nor the EPLO Central Committee.⁶⁶

Before MEISON decided to ally with the Derge in the first months of 1975, it had concluded that it was impossible to work with the EPRP. This was because no agreement could be reached on the "...assessment of the Ethiopian situation, alliance of classes, and the nature of the Derge...," stated *Sefiw Hizbe Dimtse*. The paper further indicated that the EPRP was making efforts to form some kind of an anti-Derge front to take over power, while MEISON was struggling to empower the broad masses.⁶⁷

Furthermore, MEISON made a major policy change regarding multinational and nationalist organizations. Regarding the EPRP, *Sefiw Hizbe Dimtse* stated, "...our organization had been conducting criticism of the EPRP from May 1975, and as of September (1975), it began exposing the organization's (EPRP) counter-revolutionary nature."⁶⁸ MEISON took that position some months before allying with the Derge. At that time, the Derge itself did not declare that the EPRP was a counter-revolutionary organization.

Following MEISON's decision to ally with the Derge, events took their own course. *The differences that grew into enmity between the two political organizations stemmed from their analyses of the Ethiopian situation and their different approaches to the military regime. All other differences were corollaries.* According to the MEISON, an alliance with the military regime was an imperative which would advance the cause of the revolutionary struggle. "If it [the MEISON] had not taken that step, the revolution would be defeated",⁶⁹ commented *Sefiw Hizbe Dimtse*. Since the first month of 1976, MEISON was taking a leading role in POMOA.

As early as November 1975, after expressing its anxiety over the new relationship of the Derge with MEISON, the EPRP predicted that the Derge's standing among Ethiopian intellectuals would be enhanced. The role of the ruling junta in the Derge that was led by Mengistu Haile Mariam would be concealed. The Derge's image would be bolstered and it would have a better place among the international community, isolating the opposition force at the same time.⁷⁰ The alliance of the MEISON with the Derge was one of the events that the EPRP dreaded most. EPLO/EPRP members were quite aware of the danger of military regimes. This was based on their readings on the history of popular struggles in the Third World where

> [T]he military was likely to intervene and to seize power...when the foundations of existing regimes were crumbling....The military sometimes exploited the contradictions that gave rise to the revolutionary movement, and courted popular support by adopting a radical program. Inevitably, the Left challenged their right to rule. Unfailingly, however, they soon turned against the revolutionary movement, especially the Left, and suppressed it."⁷¹

EPRP's position regarding the Derge came out in its December 1975 *Democracia* issue and later in *Democracia* No 30, in which the New Labor Law was discussed. The title of the December issue, "Imperialism, feudalism and fascism are one and three at the same time" indicated how the EPRP viewed the regime. The title was a Christian parable taken from the belief of the three natures of God. In line with the EPRP program of 1975, the paper stated that imperialism and feudalism were the twin enemies of the people and that "the fascists [the Derge] had developed a complex relationship with them."[72] During this period, the US military base in Ethiopia was still functioning and the pact signed by the US and Ethiopian governments still remained in effect.

According to the EPRP, the regime was safeguarding the interests of "bureaucratic, comprador and petty bourgeois classes...even though it throws bits and pieces here and there to appease the people."[73] *Democracia* concluded that feudalism and the Derge were enemies of the people and the EPRP would not form any kind of alliance with them. MEISON asserted that the contradiction between the people and the Derge was secondary and categorically rejected EPRP's position.[74]

Intense political struggle took place between the two groups and when their relationship continued deteriorating, the MEISON labeled the EPRP as an enemy. According to *Sefiw Hizbe Dimtse*,

> ...[T]he enemies of the Ethiopian revolution are making all kinds of efforts to reverse the tide of the struggle....EDU feudalists with the help of imperialism and some Arabian countries, after forming a front with the ELF are encircling the revolution. The EPRP has also allied with them.[75]

In the last months of 1975, following the alliance of MEISON with the regime, three-fourths of the articles of *Sefiw Hizbe Dimtse* focused on the EPRP. MEISON's organ became preoccupied with exposing what it labeled as "petty-bourgeois" groups. Besides the *Sefiw Hizbe Dimtse*, the media, which gradually fell under the control of POMOA/MEISON, focused on the EPRP and played an effective role to weaken the opposition.

One of the first measures that the EPRP took during this time was to characterize the political role of MEISON. Earlier on, some of those who allied with the Derge were characterized as "opportunist intellectuals".[76] However, that characterization failed to express the actual feeling of the opposition. When the EPRP CC deliberated on the issue again, it recognized that the positions adopted by MEISON and other radical groups did not emanate from opportunism, but they were acts of betrayal. The CC then characterized them as banda intellectuals. *"Banda"* is an Italian word introduced to Ethiopia during the Italian occupation. Ethiopians who collaborated with the Italian government and caused heavy damage to their country and people were called *"bandas"*. The *"bandas"* provided information, conducted surveillance and served as employees of the Italian government. Characterizing MEISON as such had a bearing on the Ethiopian psyche and culture of the pre-Mengistu period, when loyalty and faithfulness were considered a virtue and betrayal a vice. A traitor is disrespected and ostracized and such a characterization was intelligible to the average Ethiopian. At the same time, that portrayal might have had an adverse effect on the further deteriorating relationship of the MEISON and the EPRP. Despite such characterization, the EPRP CC maintained that the struggle should continue to focus on the military regime, which still held political power.

Another point of difference between the EPRP and MEISON, visible during the last months of 1975, was the struggle in Eritrea. MEISON adopted a new position regarding Eritrea and concluded that the new alliance of forces, following the fall of the *ancien* regime, had forced the Eritrean fronts to ally with the enemies of the Ethiopian people.[77] MEISON's new policy might have enhanced the determination of the regime to resolve the Eritrean issue through violent means. During this period, MEISON was working with the Derge. MEISON also tried to categorize the Eritrean fronts into a right and a left wing.[78] The EPRP on the other hand continued struggling for the cessation of hostilities and the resolution of the Eritrean issue peacefully and politically. The EPRP continued demanding for the resumption of dialogue between the regime and the rebel organizations.[79] In the mean time, EPRP members went out to the streets of major cities condemning the repression perpetrated against civilians in Eritrea.

There were differences between the EPRP and MEISON on a number of other political issues, including the PPG slogan which *Sefiw Hizbe Dimtse* No. 35 discussed. Some of the questions raised by MEISON were challenging enough that the EPRP leadership was hard pressed by its members to clarify the issues. Both the Youth League and EPRP publications put out articles discussing the PPG and other issues. In this debate, MEISON accused the EPRP of trying to overthrow the military regime and forming a PPG in its place.[80] MEISON declared that it stood for "an armed, politically conscious and organized struggle." The EPRP was not opposed to the above quoted slogan as such and in its brief few years of struggle, if anything, it believed that it had attempted to politicize, organize and arm itself and the people. According to the EPRP, the difference between the two groups lay beyond the slogan. The issue was not whether it was imperative to organize and politicize the people, but how to do it in the absence of democratic rights. Besides, when the above slogan was coined around the end of 1975, MEISON had already become a junior partner of the government. Describing the implication of the above slogan *Democracia* concluded, "the slogan implied that the people needed a caretaker government (the Derge) until it became politically conscious and organized."[81] The *Abeyotawi Wetat*, organ of the EPRP Youth League dismissed the slogan as an attempt to blur and confuse the new role of MEISON within the state apparatus.[82]

In *Sefiw Hizbe Dimtse* No. 50, MEISON elaborated its final objective. It argued that some people and groups accuse MEISON "for not having a clear policy on the question of power." *Sefiw Hizbe Dimtse* elaborated, "...revolutionary and counter-revolutionary forces will demarcate their role both within the Derge and the military. That is why the people have to be more conscious, get organized and armed."[83] What the publication tried to express was that MEISON, along with some Derge members, would come out triumphant in the struggle for political power.

Even though the EPRP and MEISON conducted intense political struggles amongst themselves, initially, the average citizen was unable to understand their differences. The non-partisan intellectual regarded the difference between the two groups as semantic. To clarify the confusion caused by the alliance of MEISON with the Derge, it became imperative for the EPRP to provide explanation and analysis of some of the dividing political issues. One of the media that EPRP members used was the legal journal known as "Gohe" (Dawn).[84] The other major fora of discussion were the semi-legal youth associations formed on the basis of localities. The associations were formed by zematch students for the purpose of community service. However, in the following years, they were transformed into vehicles of political discussion.[85]

EPRP's Infiltration of the MEISON

Infiltration of groups had been discouraged after the EPRP recognized its negative impact during the first merger process of 1974, when it was found that many of the groups were infiltrating each other. The problem was resolved in time and the EPRP CC decided that political differences alone could not be used as the criteria to infiltrate another group. As a result, the EPRP refrained from infiltrating, even when it had ample opportunities to do so. EPRP Members who had access to such groups as the TPLF made suggestions to infiltrate it. However, in 1976/77, the EPRP did not consider the TPLF an enemy organization. MEISON itself was not infiltrated until it was known that it had allied with the Derge. That being said, which group to infiltrate remained an issue unaddressed until the EPRP leadership decided that any group or organization that collaborated with the Derge and became part in the drive to suppress the opposition movement would be infiltrated. Before considering any infiltration, the EPRP had to ascertain that the group to be infiltrated belonged to the enemy camp.

The main purpose of the infiltration scheme in 1976 was to enable the EPRP to obtain information about the activities of the infiltrated groups and the regime, to acquire information about their new policies and their major political and military moves, to know important personalities of the groups and their positions on certain major issues, etc. Also, infiltrators provided the EPRP with their analysis of political developments from the vantage position of the state apparatus.

In this endeavor, the first task of the EPRP was to find members who were very clear and firm in their political beliefs and understood the issues dividing the various groups. These members were then briefed about their new tasks as infiltrators and how they should behave in the new environment. The MEISON, which was desperately looking for recruits, was the major target. The cadre training school, the Yekatit Cadre School, where large groups of individuals were trained, provided the opportunity for recruitment.

After providing them with some training and when there arose a chance for infiltration, EPRP members made themselves available for recruitment. Some of the recruited EPRP members were placed in important MEISON structures, such as, the Addis Abeba MEISON youth IZ. There also were infiltrators in some of the special committees of the MEISON. Once placed in the structure, among the tasks that the infiltrators performed was making the institutions that they infiltrated inefficient and one of the methods employed was to "recruit" more EPRP members.

One of the areas that the EPRP successfully infiltrated was the POMOA branch of Asmera. The opportunity for recruitment came up when officers who had been to Eastern Europe for political training returned home and took over political leadership of the army in Eritrea. Some of the officers belonged to one of the groups that formed the POMOA. Among these officers were, Major Betsuamlak, from the army; Captain Yemane, from the Air Force; P.O. Damte, Navy; Captain Kassai, Air Force. The committee consisted of eight members. One of its first tasks was to initiate cadre training school in the Asmera area. The training center was opened in the headquarters of the Second Division. The POMOA branch demanded that the various army units select and send political trainees.

Using the newly created opportunity, ten EPRP members, including four military officers attended the course. Among them were Corporal F. and Captain Negash Zergaw. Captain Negash was a radical activist from the police force and a close friend of Captain Amha Abebe, a leading figure of the 1974 Jimma uprising.[86] Captain Negash Zergaw was the head of the education and public relations office of the Police Force in Asmera. He also was a member of the Asmera EPRP zonal committee, while Corporal F. was a member of the sub-zone.

Some of the EPRP members who participated in the seminars, such as, Captain Negash, won acceptance because of their relative political clarity. One of the issues discussed during the training session was the theory of the New Democratic Revolution, which most of the organizers of the seminar, who had their cadre training in East European countries, had little or no knowledge of. The East European communist parties, including the Communist Party of the Soviet Union (CPSU), regarded the NDR a Maoist theory. Instead, they advocated the non-capitalist path of development as an alternative form of societal transformation.

After the three months course at the cadre school, the EPRP members were recruited by the various political groups around the Derge. Captain Negash Zergaw joined the Waz League, while Corporal F. joined MEISON. In the Waz League and the MEISON structures, Captain Negash and Corporal F. became members of the POMOA branch offices and were in charge of the Asmera area.

Once placed in the structure of the MEISON and the Waz League, both Captain Negash and Corporal F. were able to know the activities of these groups. Whatever information was obtained was immediately passed on to the EPRP. Suspected EPRP members were notified before they were arrested. Besides, the infiltrators used their position to approach and recruit members for the EPRP. Sometime around April 1976, both infiltrators were sent to Addis Abeba for higher political training and when they returned, both were assigned as members of the main POMOA branch committee in the Asmera area. At the election for the leadership of the POMOA branch, Captain Negash Zergaw replaced Major Betsuamlak and became the secretary of the Asmera POMOA committee.[87]

Among the pioneer EPRP members who infiltrated the MEISON of the Addis Abeba area were Dereje I, Dereje II and Y (all of them code names). There were others like A., Gebre Selassie (Abdi), Bisrat and others.[88] The last two infiltrated the Marxist-Leninist Revolutionary League (MALRED), one of the groups that belonged to POMOA.[89]

Dereje was the code name of two EPRP members, who will still remain anonymous. During their stay in the MEISON structure, they provided the EPRP with information, some of which saved the lives of hundreds of suspected EPRP members and sympathizers. Dereje I was so innovative and active that he could obtain information about houses to be raided, members to be arrested, house to house search programs, the whereabouts of important MEISON leaders, etc. Dereje I obtained highly kept secrets of the regime that even the Security Department of the EPRP was unable to obtain.

Unless told to do so, infiltrators never disclosed their EPRP membership. Because of their public allegiance to POMOA or one of the groups near the Derge, many of them were alienated from their former friends, comrades and family members. They were regarded with disdain and contempt, but they had to bear that inconvenience in order to serve their organization.

EPRP's Financial Difficulties

By 1976, the EPRP was still constrained by financial problems. Its expenses had multiplied. Administrative and production costs had increased. The number of publications and materials to be published had grown. The number of professional activists that depended on the organization for their livelihood and activities had increased. The EPRA depended on the party both for its existence and its organizational activities. Many members had gone underground and the EPRP had begun renting houses. Membership contributions, the main source of EPRP revenue, had dwindled. Furthermore, the EPRP needed revenue to buy arms and vehicles to conduct its activities.

It was believed that the EPRP would partially solve its problems by means of a bank operation in Waldia, in the first months of 1976 (discussed below). The failure of that bank operation exacerbated the situation. The EPRP was in no position to handle the expenses that the ever expanding activities required. The financial crisis reached such a magnitude that it could not be ignored any more and the PB disclosed the matter to the general EPRP membership. The PB explained the dismal financial condition of the organization and appealed to the members to look for financial sources. Many members were caught by surprise. Youth League members, who knew little about the organizations' financial status, thought it to be well off. The PB's plea was turned into a campaign. Both party and Youth League members became involved in procuring money and the task became the duty of every committee and member of the organization.

Days after the appeal, a number of either League or party members who had access to government financial sources took away whatever cash they could lay their hands on and went underground. Such incidents took place in Harer, Jimma, Sidamo and Addis Abeba. In the Harer province, in one incident alone, the EPRP obtained as much as 150,000 Ethiopian birr. In mid-1976, more than three hundred thousand birr was drafted from different banks in Addis Abeba.

The overzealous EPRP youth began collecting contributions from all kinds of sources. Some youth activists were carried away by the process that they began selling valuables (like gold rings, earrings, jewelry, etc.) that belonged to their parents. Before long, the youth activists were ordered to stop such practices. A few months after the appeal, the financial problem of the EPRP was alleviated and the organization found some breathing space.

During these financial difficulties, EPRP members continued to demand explanations on a wide number of issues and the EPRP leadership conducted discussions with the various levels of the party structure, including the Provisional Youth League leadership. The leadership explained new policies, discussed current political conditions and responded to questions forwarded by the different committees. It also obtained some feedback on new policies and conditions of the organization. CC members met with either interzonal or zonal committee members at approximately forty-five days interval. The interzonal and zonal committees performed similar activities with committees under their jurisdiction. The same procedure was followed by the Youth League and the ELAMA structures.

Criticism and self-criticism sessions, which were held on a regular basis became important parts of inner party discipline. In two incidents, the Addis Abeba IZ had some misgivings about mistakes that it believed were committed by two EPRP CC members. The IZ forwarded its criticisms to the

PB which arranged a session attended by the IZ, the concerned CC members and two observers from the EPRP CC. Complaints and explanations were heard and criticism and self-criticism were exchanged.

It was in 1976 that the effort to expand and reach the various sectors of the society bore some fruit. Underground organizations sprouted; they were geared to the demands of different sections of the population. Among these was the ethnic-based organization known as the Gurage National Democratic Movement, better known by its publication, the *Amared*, (meaning "Get Armed"). An effort to form the ethnic-based Kembatta and Haddiya underground mass organization was also underway. One of the founding members, Abiyu Airsamo, a national from the area, later joined the factional group known as the "Anja", which was formed within the EPRP.[90]

The *Amared* attained sympathy and support of the Gurage people and it popularized the programs of the EPRP among the Gurages. If there was any large national group that had embraced or sympathized with the EPRP, it was the Gurages. EPRP activity was facilitated by zematches and Gurage EPRP and Youth League members who were members of *Amared*. They had made an untiring effort to realize their objectives. Among the founding members of *Amared* were KM, Nuredin Mohammed, Fikru and Haile Wolde. Many of the Gurage people sympathized with the EPRP, but not for any nationalistic reasons. The Gurages, who were supposed to benefit from the Land Proclamation Act of 1975, had been disappointed in the course of its implementation. As in the other southern parts of Ethiopia, an intense struggle had erupted between the local state apparatus and the peasantry following the land reform proclamation. As indicated elsewhere, the balance of the struggle was tipped in favor of local landlords following the enactment of Proclamation No. 71. The Proclamation, which was decreed in December 1975, provided additional laws regarding the organization and consolidation of peasant associations.[91] Discussing the impact of the Proclamation on the Gurage peasantry, *Amared* stated, "only wereda administrators, police officers and other government officials take part in the decision making process of the committee formed by the new Proclamation." *Amared* further stated,

> To cite an example, the decisions passed by the kebele associations of the Cheha, Isja, Inemore, etc., could not be implemented....The peasants are disarmed and they are left helpless....Whenever they forward their grievances, repression is the response. Some of the students that sided with the people are either arrested or killed...production had decreased, business transactions had slowed down too. Some areas are already famine stricken, ...[92]

The degree to which the EPRP had been popularized amongst the Gurage nationality was witnessed at the Meskel national holiday celebrated in 1977. One of the important holidays of the Gurage people, particularly for the Christians, is Meskel (the finding of the True Cross) which has religious as well as social meanings. The holiday is deeply rooted in the history of the Gurage people. Many Gurages who reside in Addis Abeba and elsewhere return each year to their areas to celebrate the holiday. Weddings, engagements, business transactions, such as buying cattle or building houses, are conducted during this holiday season. During the celebration held in 1977, the holiday itself became politicized. A good number of the songs, speeches, etc., carried strong pro-EPRP sentiments or a condemnation of the regime.

Late in 1977, a very large number of Ethiopian youth of diverse nationality went to the Gurage area seeking refuge from the massive repression. The Gurage people not only gave them sanctuary, but also provided them with food and clothing during their stay in the Gibbe desert. The military regime made repeated efforts to get at the young activists and it conducted several house to house search and campaigns. More than once, the Gurage people, defending the youth, became engaged in armed confrontation with the regime and never gave in, until the youth themselves decided to leave the area. [93]

Problems and Difficulties - EPRP Leadership

The EPRP Central Committee members were not immune to the massive repression conducted and, by August 1976, almost all members of the leadership had to go underground. As a result, physical contact among the members of the leadership became less frequent and some of the tasks had to be conducted over the phone. To accomplish some assignments, some CC members had to stay together for more than forty-eight hours, thereby violating basic security precautions.

Around July 1976, Yosef Adane was arrested and later executed. Yosef was one of the hard-core EPRP CC members who had been part of the leadership since 1974. He was one of the CC members who made the EPRP what it was in the later days of the struggle. With his wide connections, Yosef was an important source of information. Yosef's financial standing was of an immense advantage to the EPRP, particularly in the initial period when the organization had no alternative to fall back on. Before he was executed, Yosef was severely tortured.[94]

Beginning in mid-1974 and for a period of a year and a half, the EPRP leadership had upheld a homogeneous approach toward the contentious issues of the period. There was no major political difference amongst leading members of the EPRP regarding the ongoing struggle. However, as of the beginning of 1976, serious differences on issues came to the fore. The main difference, as was discussed elsewhere, was on the nature of and the approach toward the military regime.

A leaflet titled "The Mass Line" and presumed to have been written by Berhane Meskel in 1977 stated, "the small difference grew into a political one at the beginning of 1976...", that is, after the April 1976 CC meeting. Elsewhere, the article stated, "...the dictatorial clique has unilaterally invalidated the decision passed by the whole party and Youth League membership on the question of forming a united front with the Derge."[95]

The above quoted statement was referring to the decision made by the CC at its meeting held in April 1976. Some CC members had begun contemplating collaboration with the Derge, and that tendency manifested itself at PB and CC meetings held in March and April 1976. As discussed above, a compromise solution was reached and the CC issued a statement declaring that the EPRP would begin negotiation with the Derge provided that certain conditions were met.[96] EPRP's response was ignored and the political struggle continued to intensify.

The political developments and the repression following the Derge's call for the formation of a front were viewed quite differently even within the EPRP CC itself. Two opposed views emerged at a CC meeting held at the beginning of June 1976. Events were interpreted in two diametrically opposed ways. The first point of view, supported by the majority of CC members was that the Derge's call for the formation of a front was a deliberate effort to win over domestic and international opinion and at the same time, isolate the opposition, including the EPRP. To corroborate the assertion, the repressions and massacre conducted on the first months of 1976, in many parts of the country, including Jimma, Welliso and Welkite were mentioned. The second point of view was entertained by Berhane Meskel. He argued that the repression was provoked by the EPRP and the blame rested squarely on the shoulder of the party and particularly on the PB which followed up the day to day activities of the EPRP. He also accused the PB for making little or no effort to popularize the call for the formation of a front. Divergent opinions were also expressed regarding the repression at the May Day celebration of 1976. Many of the CC members labeled the incident as a massive repression. However, Berhane Meskel considered it a provocation on the part of the EPRP. Thus, the rift within the leadership continued to widen. Because of these and other differences, the EPRP leadership lost its cohesiveness which was one of its major assets.

In spite of the creeping leadership problem, assisted by the fast tempo of the revolutionary movement, the EPRP was able to mobilize a large section of the population. The EPRP was, however, unable to transform that into an equivalent form of organizational networks. The problem was caused by the uneven development of the people's political readiness and the organizational incapacity of the EPRP to embrace a large membership. Even then, dictated by the conducive political condition, the EPRP continued expanding, despite some adverse effects. With the expansion of the EPRP network and the recruitment of new members, its clandestine nature was compromised and the organization became more and more vulnerable to danger. Despite these and other shortcomings, many EPRP members and sympathizers began to believe that the EPRP was an infallible and invincible organization.

Lack of political clarity on issues, such as, the nature of the transitional government, that is, the PPG, fascism, the state and the role of the state bourgeoisie, the land question, the Ethiopian economy, the international communist movement, the direction of the Ethiopian revolutionary struggle, etc., became areas of concern. EPRP's political and ideological problems became more accentuated following the formation of POMOA. POMOA had substituted the crude and eclectic propaganda of the Derge into a subtle form of ideological struggle that targeted the minds of EPRP members and followers. As was indicated earlier, the state itself became a proponent of the left ideology.

Due to inexperience and in some cases incompetence, organizational errors were repeatedly committed. Many continued clinging to the old-styles of operation. Despite new recruitment guides, some members still clung to the old guidelines. In order to overcome some of the problems, an organizational rectification campaign, coordinated by the political department of the Central Committee was conducted in 1975/76. In the internal paper of the EPRP, *Red Star*, articles elaborating issues of organization were printed. EPRP members in many parts of the country took part in the process and following the conclusion of the rectification movement, reports were compiled and sent to the leadership.

Following the formation of underground organizations, such as the ELAMA, the Teachers Association, etc., a number of structural and other organizational problems surfaced. Some of these problems were related to the status of the underground organizations vis a vis the EPRP, their relative independence and structural relationship to the EPRP. These issues were raised at the August 1976 Plenum of the EPRP CC and it was decided that the underground mass organizations, including the Youth League (YL), were independent institutions that had accepted the political program of the EPRP. The Plenum recognized that these organizations had their own leadership, constitution and by-laws that governed them and a network of structures running from top to bottom. It was asserted that final decisions regarding the affairs of the mass organizations should come from the various echelons of leadership of the organizations themselves.

The Plenum also resolved that EPRP's role would be to provide political leadership conducted through EPRP members who, at the same time, were members of the underground mass organizations. In order to facilitate EPRP organizational activities and to give better guidance, party members were assigned to the underground mass organizations. These members were supposed to be politically mature and should have an ability to lead. The party members had the same status and voting right as the other members of the underground mass organization committees. Persuasion was the method employed and the EPRP provided assistance in those areas where it could.

The August CC Plenum also decided that every level of the EPRP party structure should have a horizontal relationship to its counterpart committee of the mass organizations. Members of the party committees served as the liaisons between the EPRP and the mass organization committees found at each level. In the cases of the ELAMA and the Youth League higher committees, instead of single contacts, special party committees consisting of party and mass organization members served as liaisons. Besides linking the party to the ELAMA or the YL, the task of these committees included overseeing the activities of the mass organizations and consulting the EPRP on issues pertaining to the labor and youth movements.

Through the links or contact persons, the party committee could pass on guidelines to the mass organization committee that was found at its level. The mass organization committee would then discuss the issue and, after making the necessary amendments, might pass it onto the structure below it. If the mass organization committee did not agree on the guidelines sent by the party committee, it had the right to reject it. In that case, the issue would pass on to the next higher party and mass organization committees, until it reached the EPRP CC.[97] However, such occurrences were rare.

The Youth League

The role of the Ethiopian youth in the revolutionary process was so important that there was no political group in the country that did not make efforts to have its own youth branch. Ethiopian youth of the 1960s and '70s was characterized by its defiance of authority, unflinching commitment to the struggle, selfless devotion to what it believed in, and above all, its relatively sophisticated political cognizance. The youth was also characterized by its incessant quest for a better understanding of its surroundings and the world at large.

The EPRP won the sympathy of the youth after it articulated its demands and innermost feelings during the student Zemetcha. The EPRP shared the hardships, anguish, frustrations and misery of the zematch students. It also shared their exuberance in their day to day struggles, acclaimed their modest achievements, and above all, made efforts to give guidance to their struggle. Reciprocally, winning the soul of the Ethiopian youth meant life and vibrancy to the EPRP, which was still toddling.

The student Zemetcha program, launched in 1975 had mobilized close to sixty thousand participants. The purpose of the campaign was to spread the Derge's message, to promote literacy, agricultural development, public health, land reform, the preservation of the national heritage and to gather information about the life of the peasantry.[98] In many parts of Ethiopia, the zematch students had been in the forefront coordinating the peasant struggle. When the crisis in many of these areas continued mounting, many of the zematch students evacuated their camps. To persuade the Zemetch students, the Zemetcha headquarters assembled zematch representatives of thirteen administrative regions and assigned them as coordinators of the campaign.

The assembled Zematch students, instead, voiced some of the major demands of the peasantry, including the right to form independent peasant associations.

According to statistics provided by the government, the official death toll of participants who took part in the campaign was one hundred twenty. Some died of natural death, while others died en route to their homes after escaping from the camps. Still, others became victims of the repression. Thousands of zematch students were imprisoned and thousands evacuated their camps before it was officially called off. The Zemetcha program ended on July 19, 1976.[99] Sometime before the project was canceled, a special government circular had turned many zemetcha camps into detention centers.

Earlier, a *Democracia* issue had stated,

> ...[T]he campaign was a failure because no advance preparation or study was conducted. To waste the people's money, time and energy for a failed project is a criminal act. All those who administer, execute and cooperate with such a crime will be held responsible. To commit a mistake is not a crime, however, not to admit ones mistake and to let it remain unaddressed to is a serious crime.[100]

The *Democracia* issue quoted above had a direct bearing on the evacuation process. Even though *Democracia* tried to reflect the pathetic condition of the student zematches, its message increased the tempo of evacuation when many responded to the call. The evacuation itself stirred serious misunderstanding and differences among certain quarters of the EPRP. Provincial party structures that heavily relied on the zematch EPRP and League members sent their stern objections to what *Democracia* did to the struggle in their areas. The Sidamo and the Begemidir zonal committees were among those that expressed their dissatisfaction. The EPRP leadership made some efforts to redress the mistake, but it could not stop the tide. The zematch students had begun massive evacuations from their camps.

Sometime before the cancellation of the project, the Youth League had attempted to organize the youth under an underground Zematch Association. The ostensible purpose of such an organization was to coordinate the activities of the zematch students. Furthermore, the Youth League publications described that step as a preemptive move to counter "the efforts that the banda intellectuals" were making. MEISON and the groups that were allied with the Derge were making efforts to create their own youth organizations. When the Derge canceled the zemetcha program, the need to form a zematch organization ended. As mentioned above, the Youth League also made attempts to form urban youth associations, whose apparent function was to give service to the city. These semi-legal institutions played an important role in the activities of the Youth League and, until they were outlawed, they became media for political education.

By 1976, the EPRP Youth League, which had established itself in many parts of the country, had created its own independent channels of communication. It had grown from an organization of a few hundreds to thousands, from a few committees in Addis Abeba and some major cities, to hundreds of committees throughout the country. By the first quarter of 1976, thousands and tens of thousands of youth activists had been radicalized and tempered in the struggle that followed the proclamation of the student zemetcha. Except for Eritrea and Gamu Gofa, the Youth League had formed different levels of committees in all parts of Ethiopia and had begun publishing its own paper. However, due to lack of writing skills, the *Abeyotawi Wetat* remained an ineffective means of communication. One of the engagements of the youth which was popularized in 1976 was the Graffiti work, commonly known as "kebe" (wall painting and writing).

As indicated above, as the Youth League organization expanded, it faced a number of problems. Despite its organizational achievements, the Youth League was plagued by some internal problems. The sullen relationship between the various levels of EPRP party and Youth League committees discussed in *Generation* Part I still persisted. The Youth League, which began building an organization from bottom up, was still led by a provisional leadership.

Besides the internal problems, the Youth League faced enormous difficulties as a result of the onslaught of the regime and POMOA. In the repressions conducted in Harer, Jimma, Welliso, Welkite, Shashemene, etc., it was the youth, particularly EPRP youth activists who were severely victimized. By mid-1976, Ethiopian youth constituted a large section of the prison population. In those areas where intensive repression was conducted, the League structures were dismantled. The Youth League suffered a very heavy blow in the Wello province too. In mid-1976, at the instigation of POMOA branch representative Ayalew Kebede (who had defected from the EPRA in 1975 and joined the MALRED), the whole EPRP youth structure in Dessie and Komboltcha fell into the hands of the regime. Twice, Ayalew Kebede was able to plant government agents in the League structure, inflicting a severe blow to an organization groping and trying to stand on its feet. In one of the incidents, more than 200 Youth League members were arrested.

Another problem that the YL was confronted with was related to organizing women. The Women's Coordinating Committee (WCC) which was entrusted with organizing women had remained ineffective for quite a while. In order to consolidate the WCC, the YL, which was also engaged in organizing young female activists, was instructed to hand over the female members under its structure. After it began the transfer, the YL saw the ineffectiveness of the WCC and filed complaints. When the YL leadership found out that its complaints were unaddressed, it refused to hand over the female members under its structures.

In order to solve these and other problems, the Provisional Youth League leadership assessed the nature of the problems confronting it and decided to convene a founding congress, two years after the formation of the

Youth League. That proposal was endorsed by the EPRP Central Committee. The League leadership launched its preparation which included sending the draft constitution, internal regulations and other agenda of the Congress, to the general membership of the YL. As part of the preparation for the Congress, the various branches of the YL organization were asked to send in names that they thought might be considered as nominees for the League leadership.

The First Youth League Congress that lasted four days was held at the beginning of September 1976. It was held at the outskirts of Addis Abeba, on the road to Sebeta, in the residence of a peasant member who was recruited by zematch students. The Congress was held when the political crisis in the country had become acute and the EPRP was singled out as the focus of repression. For the sake of caution, party defense squads were assigned for the duration of the YL Congress. The League Congress was attended by 42-45 delegates, elected proportional to the membership of the League branches. Except for Gamu Gofa and Eritrea, members from the YL branches of the provinces attended the Congress.

The agenda items of the Youth League Congress consisted of a review of the current Ethiopian political condition, presented by the EPRP CC members Yohannes Berhane and Getachew Maru; organizational reports of the YL provisional leadership and the various zonal committees; organizational problems of the League, particularly relationship between the League and the party, the constitution, internal regulation, by-laws, and symbol of the League; election of the Youth League leadership; and public declaration of the existence of the League.

Even though it was difficult to keep track of the number of YL members, due to the ongoing repression, by September 1976 it was reported that the Youth League had about 10,000 members. In just a matter of days, this figure would change drastically. As a result of the repression, a figure that was confirmed the previous week could be off by a margin of hundreds or even a thousand the following week.

In its four days of deliberation, the Youth League Congress ratified its major documents, including the constitution and internal regulations of the organization. The constitution defined the age limit to become a Youth League member. It was decided that anyone who was between 15 and 25 years old could be a member.[101] According to the statute of the League, final power rested on a congress which was to be conducted every three years. The YL National Congress could also be called whenever one-third of the membership demanded its convocation and that idea was supported by one-half of the numbers.[102]

One of the main agenda items raised and discussed at the Congress was the relationship between the League and the EPRP. The question which had remained unresolved, particularly in the provinces, was that of the relative independence of the League structure from the EPRP. Some EPRP zonal committees regarded the Youth League branch as part of the party structure.

Some even regarded it a branch without an entity of its own. The decisions of the August 1976 CC plenum were discussed with the participants of the Congress.[103]

The Congress elected its CC, Standing Committee and Secretary. Most of the members of the provisional leadership were elected to the Youth League Central Committee and Aklilu Hiruy was elected Secretary of the organization. Most of the elected YL CC members were former leaders of the high-school student movement. A special nomination procedure, then known as a "quota" system was employed as part of the election process. This was done in order to include individuals who did not attend the Congress and who were from areas outside of Addis Abeba. Later in its struggle, the League learned that some of those who were elected as a result of the "quota" system lacked the qualities of leadership. Among the CC members elected were, Aklilu Hiruy, Tito Hiruy, Sirak Teferra, BB, Gezatchew Teferra, Tibebe (code name), Ferenju (code name), Alemayehu Egzeru, Gezahegne "Gonderew", TM and GZ.

After four days of deliberation, the League Congress was successfully completed and it strengthened the resolve of the members. The Congress was considered a milestone in the history of the Ethiopian youth movement and the Youth League became one of the first formidable underground forces.

The Youth League First Congress was conducted peacefully. However, the peasant who had provided his residence for the Congress lost his life a few days later. One of the squad members, assigned as a security guard, was arrested. He provided all the information he knew about the EPRP and guided Derge security personnel to the residence where the Congress had been held. Government military forces came after dusk, when everybody was at home and demolished the house with long range mortars. The whole family of the peasant was killed. Some of the arms obtained at the Sendafa operation were also destroyed.[104]

It was during the last months of 1976 that the Youth League, having conducted its first congress in September 1976, made itself public. [105] The Constitution, which was ratified at the Congress stated, "the Ethiopian People's Revolutionary Youth League is an organization that had accepted the ideology, political and organizational lines and both the minimum and maximum program of the EPRP."[106] The League also declared that any youth (who is between the ages of 15 and 25) and who accepted the program, the final objective of the League, the internal regulations and who is willing to take part in one of its committees could be a member.[107]

The Ethiopian People's Revolutionary Army - the Rural Armed Wing

The decision to form an army was made in 1972, at the First Congress of the EPLO/EPRP. Training was initiated in 1973 and the first batch of trainees were sent to the Middle East during the same period. After the completion of the training, the nucleus of the EPRA left for Ethiopia, via the hinterlands of Eritrea where it was forced to stay for over a year.[108] It was decided that the nucleus of the EPRA operated in Tigrai. In the years that followed, the EPRA branched out to Wello and Begemidir provinces. Furthermore, the EPRP CC made decisions to initiate armed struggle in Sidamo, Harer and Shoa provinces. Preparation to commence armed struggle in these provinces was initiated in 1975/76 and indigenous members were sent to Tigrai for military training.[109]

When the nucleus of the army arrived in Tigrai, during the last months of 1974, the EPRP structure in Tigrai still did not recuperate from the crisis that befell it. As noted in *The Generation*, "When the EPLO was trying to establish a viable structure in Tigrai, ...the dispersal of the members in some Tigrayan cities...had made conditions more difficult"[110] The EPRP structure in Tigrai remained disorganized and weak all through that year, making communication with the nucleus of the army and the EPRP leadership difficult. That condition forced the nucleus of the army to act on its own. The army's problems were compounded when the EPRP CC members Berhane Meskel and Tesfaye Debessai departed for Addis Abeba to prepare for and attend the party gathering. Berhane Meskel was in charge of the army and Tesfaye had gone there on organizational assignments.

As of April 1975, the CC became engaged in preparing the documents of the August conference and its attention was diverted to other areas of activity. Consequently, the problems of the nucleus of the army remained unattended and it had its most difficult period between March and September 1975. By this period, the army nucleus had grown to about thirty men and besides what they carried, the EPLF had given the group more armaments.

Contact with the nucleus of the army was reestablished in September 1975, following the conclusion of the August 1975 Conference of the EPRP. Zeru Kehishen was sent to the area to convey the messages of the CC and discuss the decisions of the Conference. During the discussions, it was revealed that the leadership of the nucleus of the army had been given a special guideline instructing it not to engage itself in military activities. The guideline, which confined the nucleus to a certain area and away from the villages was given by Berhane Meskel, at a meeting where Tesfaye Debessai was also present. According to the guideline, the EPRA would not engage itself in combat, save for self-defense purposes. At a later CC meeting in Addis Abeba, when Tesfaye asked where such guideline came from, Berhane Meskel referred to a decision of the CC meeting held abroad, in April 1974. As a consequence of this guideline, the army nucleus had remained inactive and in a state of limbo for quite sometime. The TPLF, which began operations around this period, had carried out daring military activities, including a bank operation in Axum, and was able to solve some of its immediate financial needs.

Sometime before the arrival of Zeru Kehishen, the EPRA leadership called a meeting of its members to discuss the steps it had to take. The EPRA, left on its own, felt isolated, abandoned and despondent. Some of the members questioned whether the EPRP CC was still interested in the armed struggle. TPLF's agitation regarding EPRA's inactivity further aggravated that condition.

A provisional program was prepared and EPRA members decided to conduct military and propaganda activities. Until this time, the nucleus of the army operated according to the guideline set in 1974 and did not know how to operate under the changed political condition. It did not know under what name to conduct its activities and what program to use. Because of the need to pursue the peaceful form of struggle, the EPRP still did not reveal that it had an armed wing.

To overcome the difficulties and seeking assistance, the nucleus of the army sent a three-man delegation to the EPLF. When the members of the delegation heard the news regarding the public declaration of the EPRP in 1975, they canceled their program and returned to Tigrai where they found the new program of the EPRP.

As was indicated above, Zeru Kehishen was sent to Tigrai in September 1975, sometime before the public declaration of the EPRP. He conducted discussions with some members of the leadership of the EPRA who complained about the attention that the EPRP CC gave to the army. EPRA leadership and some other members felt that the EPRP CC did not give the armed struggle primacy, and some members of the army demanded Berhane Meskel's return to the EPRA. Like the rest of the organization, the EPRA also had severe financial difficulties. EPRA's operation in Sabba, Tigrai, was to alleviate that problem.

Sometime before the decisions of the EPRP CC, allowing more mobility instead of confinement to certain areas were discussed and the guideline mentioned above was disregarded, the nucleus of the army conducted few operations. According to the new guideline of the CC, the nucleus of the army could conduct hit and run operations on some selected government posts. However, it was made clear that the military activities should in no way be related to the EPRP, which still believed that the peaceful form of struggle was not consummated. The complaints and the demands of the EPRA were passed on to the CC and to assist political and organizational activities, some more active members, including Berhane Iyasu, a veteran activist, joined the EPRA.[111]

At the end of 1975, Tesfaye Debessai was sent with an assignment both to the EPRA and the Eritrean fronts. On his first trip, Tesfaye could accomplish only the assignments related to the EPRA. The EPRA conducted a mini-rectification campaign and some of the harsh rules and regulations of the EPRA[112] were scrapped.

Expansion of EPRA

The EPRA, which was operating only in the Tigrai province was restructured during the last months of 1975. Some of the units were sent out to the Wello and Begemidir provinces. A third of the EPRA units were left in Tigrai, while others were supposed to be placed in an adjacent area, bordering the Tigrai, Wello and Begemidir provinces. According to the master plan, the task of the last detachment was to play a supportive role and link up all of the forces in the three provinces. The three commands of the EPRA in Wello, Begemidir and Tigrai would form a big Y, where the three arms represented the three commands in the three provinces and the point where they met would be the area where the fourth detachment operated.

Prior to the arrival of the EPRA in this Begemidir area, the party structure had conducted some organizational activities and had deployed some professional EPRP members amongst the peasantry. It had made some headway among the peasantry and recruited some peasant leaders in Tselemt, including the legendary figure Abba Takele and his brother Aba Alemu. Aba Takele was an organizer, a warrior and an enlightened peasant leader whose vision and values were uncommon in his peasant surroundings. Since Abba Takele and his elder brother had involved almost all members of their families and relatives in the activities of the EPRP, they practically had no one to attend to their land.[113]

The party structure in Begemidir was involved in the study of areas where the EPRA would conduct military activities. With this in mind, some members of the zonal committee and Iskender Demisse (code named Germai),[114] toured the western part of the Begemidir province, in the last months of 1975. By this time, the zonal committee had deployed some members in the area. When Iskender began touring and studying the political and military conditions of the area, the EDU had already begun a low level military operation. Because of EDU's activities and other military considerations, Iskender concluded that the EPRA could not initiate an armed struggle in the western part of Begemidir. He returned to the Begemidir province some months later and conducted a similar study in Tselemt, thus preparing the ground for the commencement of an armed struggle in Begemidir.[115]

As the detachments were about to be deployed, tension between the military regime and the peasantry was mounting due to the "Raza Project". That condition facilitated the activities of an EPRA unit that began operating on the northern tip of the Begemidir province, close to the Tigrai border. For a year or so, the entire force of the EPRA in Begemidir consisted of three platoons, "gantas", and carried manual rifles. The "gantas" gradually moved to the area known as Tselemt, where government presence was minimal. Some months later, the EPRA group in Begemidir was able to move to different parts in the northern and western parts of the province.[116]

The three detachments sent to Wello were supposed to operate in the northern part of the province, from where they could easily retreat to Tigrai in case of any adversity. The units were also given an additional assignment of procuring financial support. In response to the call of the EPRP leadership for such support, the Wello zonal party committee proposed to raid a bank in Waldia, a small town in Wello. The party committee was then instructed to conduct a detailed study. The committee later informed the EPRP leadership that it had conducted the study and indicated that there was over half-a-million Ethiopian birr in the Waldia bank. Based on this preliminary information and with the hope of obtaining more en route, in April 1976, Tesfaye Debessai, along with the command of the EPRA decided that the unit would begin its movement south. However, members of the Wello party committee, who were supposed to provide the units with more information, failed to appear at the designated meeting places. The unit continued its movement hoping to get some feedback on its way. It crossed four awerajas, a distance of about one hundred fifty miles, before it reached Waldia, where the bank was located. Long before it reached its destination, the government had become aware of the movements of the units and the news about the bank operation was in circulation even in Addis Abeba.

At the instigation of the local military command and police, which at this time was conducting a military campaign against revolting former landlords, the peasantry tried to surround EPRA units. The units did all they could to avoid the confrontation. For the peasantry, retreat was viewed as a sign of weakness and it continued to pursue the units. After exchanging some fire, the units retreated one more time, but they were surrounded again while taking a break. The units had traveled a long distance, most of the time without having anything to eat, and thus many were exhausted.

When they realized their predicament, some members of the unit, including the commander, Teferi Berhane, died fighting. Some were taken prisoners. Fewer than ten managed to return to Assimba. Few escaped and went either to Tigrai or Addis Abeba. Among them was Berhane Iyasu. Thus, the unit that was sent to the Wello area fell victim. Among those who were captured and imprisoned was Woubishet Retta, the political commissar of the group. Both he and Teferi Berhane were among the few founding members of the EPRP and the EPRA as well. Before they joined the EPRA, both Woubishet and Teferi had pursued higher studies in journalism and engineering in the Soviet Union, after completing studies at the Polytechnic Institute of Bahir Dar in Ethiopia.

According to the discussions that the leadership conducted following the above mentioned incident, it was found that the *a priori* feasibility studies conducted by the zonal committee were insufficient. The units had to traverse hundreds of miles in a hostile territory where the EPRP had conducted little or no political work. The units moved deep into an "enemy territory" where they had no rear to retreat to. Such a mission contradicted the basic tenets of guerrilla warfare.

The decision to send the units to raid the Waldia bank was a disaster which had very far reaching ramifications in subsequent developments. Among other things, it necessitated the appraisal of the struggle for land reform in a new perspective. The effect of the 1975 land proclamation on the peasantry had to be reassessed.

The arrested EPRA members were taken to Addis Abeba and while in prison, they were approached by MEISON members, including Negede Gobeze.[117] They were asked to denounce the EPRP publicly, in return for clemency. After repeated effort, all, but one or two refused to collaborate. When the war of annihilation was decreed in September 1976, Woubishet Retta and the other EPRA members were among the first to be executed publicly.[118]

Preparations to launch an Armed Struggle in Sidamo

When the EPRP made preparations to begin an armed struggle in the Sidamo province, it selected that area because of the prevalent contradiction between the peasantry and the landlord group, its diverse national composition, its terrain and its proximity to Kenya, which could be used as a rear area. Sidamo also offered a relatively well organized EPRP party structure.

Since the proclamation of land reform in 1975, the Sidamo peasantry was engaged in an intense struggle which revolved around the formation of independent peasant associations, the right to get armed and the disarming of some landlords. The Sidamo area had witnessed a number of massive peasant uprisings, the first of which took place in June 1975.[119]

The preliminary study regarding the commencement of the armed struggle and most of the initiative regarding the study came from the Sidamo zonal committee which also carried the responsibilities of conducting the day to day activities.

The initiative of the zonal committee and the study it presented were approved by the EPRP CC. The EPRP bought some armaments and obtained others from different sources. Besides, the EPRP raided the Sendafa police camp and sent some of the arms it obtained to Sidamo. However, en route to the area, a portion of these fell into the hands of the government.

In September 1976, after the completion of the preparation for an armed struggle, one of the Sidamo armed units was sent to the location where the struggle was to commence. The second unit, consisting of the leadership, Berhane Iyasu and YA among them, was to follow suit. However, a small incident disrupted the entire process. Some police officers came to the house where the leadership group was staying. They were looking for a zematch student who had evacuated his camp. The leadership group was absolutely unprepared for the incident and when the members of the group saw the police entering the hut, they tried to hide themselves. They jumped into a barn and startled the cows, thereby arousing the suspicion of the police officers who, by this time had entered the hut. When the officers began moving in the direction of the barn, members of the leadership opened fire, killed some of the officers and escaped. They ran to a nearby forest where they were surrounded. Berhane Iyasu, who had survived the tragedy in Wello, and another member were victimized. AY escaped. He was able to walk down to the provincial bus terminal, eluded the hot pursuit and returned to Addis Abeba safely.

Because of the incident, government vigilance was stepped up. Communication was lost with the unit that had already gone to the Sidamo hinterland, and it could get no guidance and leadership. Left on its own, it had to rely on itself for all of its needs, which included feeding itself. Not long afterwards, some members of the unit fell into the hands of the government and the attempt to form an armed nucleus in the Sidamo area was thus suspended. In a later day assessment of the preparation, the inadequate training and unpreparedness of the unit, problems of communication and the hasty dispatch of the unit without a leading body were cited as some of the causes for the failure. Another major obstacle was the terrain selected to initiate the armed struggle. The above and other errors and weaknesses were taken into consideration when preparing the second attempt of an armed struggle that would take place a year or so later. In order to make up for the errors, some indigenous EPRP members were sent to Assimba for further military training. They returned some time later and became involved in the second preparation to initiate armed struggle in Sidamo.

In the attempt to begin armed struggles both in Wello and Sidamo, it was the peasantry that was rallied against EPRA units. Leading EPRP members continued pondering over the fate of an armed struggle where land reform was promulgated. They wondered about the impact of the reform on the armed struggle. With the land to the tiller slogan partially fulfilled, how was the peasantry to be mobilized for the armed struggle? Having the economic aspect of the land issue resolved, at least juridically, was it possible to rally the peasantry on political questions alone? How is the armed struggle in Ethiopia to be different from those countries wherein it proceeded in the classical way? What was the solution for the particular Ethiopian condition? If conducting an armed struggle was difficult, how would the party survive? These and other issues became recurring themes of discussion among leading members of the organization. For a few months to come, no answer was forthcoming and the doubt lingered. At the same time, the political climate of the country became more volatile and conducting peaceful political struggle became much more difficult.

Notes to Chapter 2

1. Kiflu Tadesse, The Generation, Part I, Independent Publishers, 1993, Chapter VI.
2. Addis Zemen, April, 1976.
3. Democracia, Volume III, No. 2, page 6.
4. Ibid., page 6.
5. Democracia, Volume II, No. 29.
6. Ibid., page 5.
7. Democracia, Volume II, No. 29, page 3.
8. Ibid., page 6.
9. Sefiw Hizbe Dimtse, No. 32, pages 1-3.
10. Sefiw Hizbe Dimtse, No. 32, 33, 50.
11. Ibid., page 1.
12. Democracia, Volume III, No. 11, page 4. The average salary of a university graduate was about five-hundred birr.
13. EPRP Program I.
14. Democracia, Vol. II, No. 13, page 2.
15. Addis Zemen, April 4, 1976, page 9.
16. Democracia, Volume III, No. 2.
17. Addis Zemen, February 27, 1975.
18. Addis Zemen, March 20, 1976, page 5.
19. Addis Zemen, February 20, 1976.
20. Ibid., page 2.
21. See details Chapter III.
22. Addis Zemen, March 25, 1976.
23. Democracia, Volume III, No.2, page 1.
24. Addis Zemen, April 9, 1976, page 7.

State Transformation

25. Addis Zemen, June 4, 1976, pages, 2,5,7.
26. Addis Zemen, May 27, 1976, page 6.
27. Addis Zemen, May 30, 1976, page 8.
28. Addis Zemen, June 4, 1976, page 2.
29. See discussion in this Chapter, POMOA and the Mass Organizations.
30. Democracia, Volume II, No.2, page 7.
31. Interview with Corporal F., August 1990. F. was a POMOA member in Asmera, 1976-1977.
32. See details Chapter VIII.
33. Addis Zemen, April 21, 1976, 'Ethiopian National Democratic Revolution Program, Part I, page 3.
34. Sefiw Hizbe Dimtse, No. 40, May 19, 1976.
35. Ibid., pages 5-6.
36. Addis Zemen, March 17, 1976, Editorial. At the August Plenum of the EPRP CC in August 1976, Berhane Meskel revealed that he had called the Editor of the Addis Zemen Newspaper and suggested that he wrote an Editorial on the formation of a front. Even though Berhane Meskel argued that he had informed Getachew about the case, however, Getachew did not disclose this piece of information to the members of the PB.
37. See details about Morton Chapter V.
38. Democracia, Vol. II, No.13, page 3.
39. See details Chapter III, regarding the controversy that the issue aroused.
40. Democracia, Volume II, Special Edition.
41. The article was produced in response to the report submitted to the Derge by Lieutenant Amha Abebe and Lieutenant Tamrat Wolde Mariam. The report titled, "Unity and differences between the clandestine parties", discussed the dividing issues of the EPRP and the MEISON.
42. Addis Fana, May 8, 1977, page 39.
43. See details Chapter I.
44. Waz League, Volume I, No. II.
45. Addis Zemen, July 27, 1976, page 7.

46. Addis Zemen, February 6, 1976.
47. Addis Zemen, July 1976.
48. Addis Zemen, July 1976.
49. See details Chapter I.
50. Addis Zemen, July 23, 1976, page 1.
51. Addis Zemen, July and August, 1976.
52. Democracia, Volume III, No 6, page 2 and No. 7, page 3.
53. Addis Zemen, September 10, 1976, page 2.
54. See details Chapter III.
55. See details Abyot Tebeka, Chapter III.
56. See details about the Ministry, Chapter V.
57. Georgi Galpirin, Population Resources Economy, Progress Publishers, 1981, page 21.
58. Kiflu Tadesse, op.cit., page 233.
59. When they reached Rome, an Italian police officer who had the list of the defectors approached them and provided them safe sanctuary. Soon afterward, they were approached by the EPRP representative of the area and escorted to a shelter. In March 1977, some members of the group arrived in EPRA's base area, Assimba, via Sudan. Interview, Debebe, (code name), 1993. He was one of the members of the group.
60. See detail, Chapter IX.
61. Teglatchen, No. 4, 1973, page 51.
62. See details, Kiflu Tadesse, op. cit., pp. 79-81.
63. Ibid., pp. 225-229.
64. Sefiw Hizbe Dimtse, No. 50, page 8, January 1977.
65. Kiflu Tadesse, op. cit., page 227.
66. Ibid., page 227.
67. Sefiw Hizbe Dimtse, No. 50, page 4.
68. Ibid., page 4.

69. Ibid., page 10.

70. Democracia, Volume II, No. 23, page 9.

71. Kiflu Tadesse, op. cit., page 122.

72. Democracia, Volume II, No. 23, page 2.

73. Ibid., page 2.

74. Sefiw Hizbe Dimtse, No. 33, pages 5-6.

75. Ibid., page 10.

76. Ibid., page 9.

77. Ibid., page 7.

78. Sefiw Hizbe Dimtse, No. 32, page 1.

79. For more details regarding the struggle in Eritrea, see Chapters I and VI.

80. Sefiw Hizbe Dimtse, Nos. 31-35, 50.

81. Democracia, Volume IV, No. 8, page 5.

82. Abeyotawi Wetat, No. 4.

83. Sefiw Hizbe Dimtse, No. 50.

84. Kiflu Tadesse, op.cit., page 229.

85. See details page 282.

86. Kiflu Tadesse, op.cit., Chapters IV, V, VII.

87. See details Chapter VI.

88. See details Chapter VI.

89. During the "Red Terror" campaign of 1977/78, Dereje II was assigned as a member of one of the Derge's assassination groups, the tasks of which was to drive around town and stop and interrogate suspects. On one of its tours, the vehicle carrying the assassination squad suddenly stopped by GA and GKY, who were just released from prison following their arrest in 1976. Both of them were getting ready to leave for the EPRA and were returning home after picking up blank ID cards. Dereje II, who knew both activists at the University campus, felt that they would fall in danger. He let the other members of the assassination squad conduct the search while he examined their ID cards. Dereje II found that they were blank and became annoyed. That incident would have cost the two EPRP members their lives, however, Dereje pretended that everything was in order and told his colleagues to let

them go free.

Both GA and GKY knowing that they were caught red-handed, were very much surprised when they were freed. However, what surprised them more was that their case was reported to the EPRP long before they themselves reported on it.

90. See details in Chapter V.

91. See details in Chapter I.

92. Amared, No. 4., page 1.

93. Among active EPRP members of the Sebat bet Gurage who fell victim during the Red Terror were, Woldeab Denebu, Endale Nisre, Asfaw Gegbesa, Desalegne Tewaji and Kerwari K. Mariam. (Information obtained from T. H/Selassie)

94. See details about Yosef, Kiflu Tadesse, op.cit., Chapter V.

95. "The Mass Line", October 1979, page 2. (An unsigned article which is believed to have been written by Berhane Meskel Redda)

96. Ibid., October 1979, page 4.

97. EPRP Constitution CH. II/A 4.

98. For details regarding the zemetcha, see Kiflu Tadesse, op. cit., pp 179-182.

99. Addis Zemen, July 19, 1976, page 3.

100. Democracia, Volume II, No. 25, page 1.

101. Ethiopian People's Revolutionary YL Constitution, Chapter II, Article I.

102. Ibid., Chapter II, Nos. 8 and 9.

103. See details page 118.

104. See details about Sendafa operation in Chapter VI.

105. Abeyotawi Wetat, Volume I, No. 10,

106. EPRYL Constitution, Chapter I, No. 2.

107. Ibid., Chapter II, No.1.

108. Kiflu Tadesse, op.cit., page 191.

109. See details Chapters, II, V and VIII.

110. Ibid., page 192.

111. Berhane Iyasu was a veteran student movement activist and one of the founding members of the EPRP. See details Kiflu Tadesse, op. cit., Chapter VII.

112. AM, Interview, November 1994.

113. When crisis befell the EPRA in 1979-80 and some of its members began resigning and abandoning the struggle, Abba Takele tried to stop the tide. Unable to do so, he surrendered to the regime and died fighting the TPLF.

114. Iskender had attended the Ist Extended Conference of the EPRP, representing the EPRA.

115. While in the process of deploying EPRA units in the Wello province, some members of the Command - Jiggsa, Tsegaye Gebre Medhin, Woubishet Retta and Tesfaye Debessai - were encircled by the peasants of the Maichew area, Tigrai. Jiggsa told one of the leaders of the peasants that they were EPRP forces deployed in the vicinity. When he also informed the peasant that they had a relationship with Ras Mengesha Seyoum, the leader of the EDU, the peasant leader allowed them to leave the area and asked them to pass on his name to the EDU leader. Interview, AM, November, 1994.

116. See details Chapter IX.

117. Abyot, Volume II, No.5, page 9.

118. More on EPRA prisoners in Chapter VII.

119. Kiflu Tadesse, op. cit., Chapter VII.

3

Transition from Peaceful to Violent Form of Struggle

Beginning around mid-June 1976, it became clear that the regime was getting ready for an all out war against its opponents. To be sure, since October 1974 and in particular December 1974 when the Derge slaughtered about sixty officials of the former government, the military regime had conducted repressive measures against different sectors of the society. During this period, hundreds were killed and thousands were imprisoned. However, despite variations in the political conditions around the country, the peaceful form of struggle that began in 1974 was still in process. That condition was to change in September 1976 when the military regime declared the war of annihilation. *The declaration of the war of annihilation was preceded by an intensive repression in April, May and June 1976 and this period constitutes the transition from the peaceful to the violent form of struggle.* As was indicated elsewhere, after the repression in Jimma in May 1976, the next locus of systematic repression was the Harer area.

POMOA and the Unrest in Harer

At the beginning of 1976, worker unrest increased in the Dire Dawa area, Harer province. Many workers of the beef factory, Chandris, were laid off. Workers of the Dire Dawa Cotton Factory were also in conflict with the regime. Reacting to the crisis, the Harer ELAMA zonal committee suggested that a national strike be called and it asked for the consent and coordination of the national ELAMA leadership. In July 1976, the *Voice of ELAMA* stated, "we have learnt much from our past mistakes. Unless we conduct a thorough political and agitation work, we should never indulge ourselves in isolated strikes."[1] Apparently, the statement was a response made by the ELAMA leadership and the Addis Abeba ELAMA IZ to the demand of the Harer ELAMA zonal committee. The Harer ELAMA zonal committee grudgingly accepted the decision. However, before the zone committee could do anything, the repression intensified and many of the labor leaders from the Cotton Factory in Dire Dawa, Cement Factory, Railway Station, Commercial Bank, etc., were either arrested or fled the area.

The repression, which began sometime in May 1976 continued until September 1976 and spread to many sectors of the society. Initially, the Harer youth fell victim as a result of a crisis that followed a show performed in the Dire Dawa area. The show, which took place at a locality known as Gende Kore depicted the triumph of the struggle. Some Derge members who attended the show became dissatisfied and ordered the arrest of the organizers. In protest to this, the people went out on a demonstration, but the arrest continued and hundreds and thousands of labor, teacher and youth activists were rounded up from the various kebeles and were kept in prison. Many fled to neighboring countries and to the countryside.

The Harer POMOA, chaired by Abdulahi Yusuf, a veteran MEISON member, was in charge of the repression. Abdulahi was a one time official of the Ethiopian students' union in Europe. He was assisted by Lieutenant Girma and Denbi Dissasa. Abdulahi took the lead to exterminate youth and labor activists. He also sent some of the prisoners to the Addis Abeba branch of POMOA and specifically to Kebede Mengesha, for further investigation.

The struggle in Harer and particularly in Dire Dawa was weakened. Leading members of the EPRP zonal and sub-zonal committees and other activists were arrested. Some of them were executed at a later period. The tragic part was that it had taken the Ethiopian people's struggle fifteen to twenty years to produce these activists.[2]

The repression conducted in Harer was very much similar to that in the Jimma area. In both places, it was aimed not at individuals, but at an organizational structure. Abdulahi made sure that not only the "culprits", but the entire structure was also dismantled and he accomplished a very systematic and thorough "job". As in Jimma, the EPRP structure was crippled. In the indiscriminate repression, Abdulahi inflicted heavy damage on the EPRP, which still was engaged in peaceful political struggle.[3]

The repression in Harer in June and July of 1976 heralded the transition to the violent form of struggle. In the months and years to come, similar scenarios were to be repeated in different parts of the country. The violent approach that the regime adopted against the opposition was not an isolated incident, but a process that was tied up with the development taking place within the ruling group, the Derge.

The Crisis Within the Derge

Only two years after the formation of the Derge, the majority of its membership was relegated to a nonentity status, and power was concentrated in the hands of a few officers. Among these officers, olonel Mengistu Haile Mariam stood tall. He continued amassing power and was able to win the power struggle, at least temporarily. Mengistu had become so powerful that he was able to singlehandedly execute an influential Derge member, Captain Sisay Habte. Besides his personal traits, an important ingredient which gave Mengistu an advantage over the other officers was the advice and political support of POMOA and the groups around it. POMOA had been courting Mengistu since 1975. It was he who read the NDR program of 1976 over the radio and TV, unlike previous times when Derge statements were read out by official announcers.

Because of Mengistu's continuous change of group allegiance, winning him over to the side of one of the groups was a difficult process and POMOA members did all they could to recruit him to their respective group. In this process, Mengistu would pick one of the important personalities of POMOA to chauffeur him around for a week or so, and would seek advice from him/her in the meantime. If it was MEISON's turn, it would be pandemonium for the group; its members would walk around with their chins up and speak loudly about their victory and the correctness of their "theory". When Mengistu all of a sudden changed the saddle and picked up Sennay Likke, that would be the doomsday for the MEISON and everything was back to square one, and then all kinds of efforts would be made to get back his attention.[4]

Finally, it became evident that the groups in POMOA were able to win over Mengistu. This event signaled the formation of a new political power which consisted of Mengistu, the MEISON and the Sennay Likke groups. In alliance and with the assistance of POMOA and other officers, including Colonel Daniel Asfaw, an officer in charge of the contingent around the Derge, and Colonel Teka Tulu, the Derge security chief, Mengistu gradually wielded absolute power and began making decisions either on his own or in consultation with POMOA. *The formation of the new political power of Colonel Mengistu Haile Mariam and POMOA constituted an important ingredient in the process toward the transition from the peaceful form of struggle to the violent one.* It was this new political power that produced the new policy of the war of annihilation and the institutions that carried out the repression. The formation of the Mengistu/POMOA alliance also accelerated the tempo of the crisis both within the Derge and in the country as well.

Alienation of Derge Members and Its Effect

The alienation of Derge members from the political process might have begun as early as December 1974 when Mengistu played an active role in executing General Aman Mikael Andom. From that time on, Mengistu was making major decisions on his own, including executing an important Derge member, as was indicated earlier. Mengistu's arbitrary steps had created such fear among a large number of Derge members that the issue was raised at a Derge meeting held in July 1976.

The alienation of Derge members was further accentuated after the alliance of Mengistu with the political groups clustered around POMOA. Many of the Derge members, including its leading officers, realized that they had been pushed to the periphery, that their role was atomized and they were replaced by the new "political elites". Among those who felt left out was Lieutenant Alemayehu Haile, head of the Organization Department of the Derge, whose job was taken over by POMOA.

Many Derge members had also lost control of the state apparatus following the appointment of MEISON members to important and key government posts. POMOA, which was assuming a perfidious political role and was involving itself in the domains of the Derge members, was regarded with suspicion and fear. A POMOA article that appeared in *Addis Fana* had testified, "some, including Derge members, regard the coordination between the Derge and POMOA with great suspicion."[5]

As the alienation process within the Derge continued and the crisis in the country deepened, the military regime was left with two options. The first was to make major concessions and grant democratic rights and bring the people into the political process. This included sharing political power with opposition forces, multinational, as well as nationalist forces. The second option was to let things take their own course and intensify the repression. The Mengistu clique opted to pursue the second alternative. However, the resentment about the formation of the Mengistu/POMOA political power block was so strong that most of the Derge members were easily instigated when some of the disgruntled officers began the anti-Mengistu opposition. Consequently, at the end of June 1976, the Derge found itself in the midst of an intense power struggle. The animosity and bitterness toward POMOA and the groups around it were also heightened.

Reaction to the alienation within the Derge took two distinct shapes and directions. Open defiance, advocated by a minority of the Derge members was one of the forms through which anti-Mengistu opposition was expressed. However, the majority of the Derge members, under the leadership of the influential officers Lieutenant Alemayehu Haile, Captain Moges Wolde Mikael, General Teferi Bente, etc., chose the path of reforming the Derge from within. Mengistu was their target and both groups wanted to either get rid of him or diminish his power.

Open defiance was expressed by Derge members Lieutenant Seleshi and Beewketu Kassa who joined the revolting military groups of the Debreziet area. The Airborne, which involved the units in Asmera and Debreziet, mutinied in July 1976. The Air-borne was led by Colonel Alemayehu Asfaw. The incident that triggered the revolt was a unilateral decision of the Derge which ordered all members of the armed forces to wear the same kind of military cap. The Airborne, which had a distinctive purple beret, refused to give up its cap. In fact, during the tenth anniversary of the Airborne, in 1976, members in Debreziet and Asmera wore their purple cap, in defiance of the Derge's instruction. For the Airborne, the purple beret signified an accomplishment of the difficult military training.

Even though the dissatisfaction centered around this seemingly minor issue, the main cause for the revolt of the Airborne lay elsewhere. Sometime earlier, Airborne units had decided that the Derge should relinquish power to a popularly elected government. The Derge, however, did not budge in, but decided to rotate units from Addis Abeba to Asmera and vice-versa. According to the commander of the Airborne, Colonel Alemayehu Asfaw, when he and his other colleagues knew about the Derge's decision, they decided to overthrow the Derge and came up with a plan.[6] Three companies of the Airborne were to initiate the mutiny and the Air force would join in due course. One of the companies would storm the Derge's office, the former palace. The layout of the compound was provided to the Airborne by Lieutenant Seleshi, a Derge member. The second company would take over the headquarter of the Fourth division and the last one would bring the radio station under control. Because of lack of transportation, the rebels failed to implement their plan and they were sent to Asmera, Mendefera, where they continued coordinating the anti-Derge rebellion. Wary of their activities, the Derge summoned the commanders of the Airborne to Addis Abeba. Sensing danger, the commanders disregarded the order. When officer Fanta Belay of the Air force sent a message to Colonel Alemayehu Asfaw informing him that he should not come to Addis Abeba, the commanders of the Airborne decided to abandon their camp. Fanta Belay who later became a general was executed when the coup he and his colleagues attempted in 1989 was aborted.

Finally, forty-two paratroopers left their camp under cover of darkness and after acquiring a safe passage through the ELF held territory, marched some distance and joined the EPRA in Assimba. The role of the former members of the Airborne was of critical importance to the EPRA. Colonel Alemayehu Asfaw, a graduate of the Royal Military Academy, Sundhurst, and Staff College, Camberly, Great Britain was the first high-ranking officer to join the EPRA. A few months later, Colonel Alemayehu Asfaw became a member of the EPRA leadership. As valiant fighters and loyal members of the EPRA, most of the former members of the Airborne served as commanders of the various contingents. A good number of them lost their lives in the struggle.[7]

A different predicament awaited the remaining members of the Airborne group in Debreziet. To "forward" their grievances and implement their decisions, they demanded that Mengistu Haile Mariam come and address their meeting. The meeting was a ruse: the units made preparations to arrest Mengistu. Unlike the Air-force, which had been disarmed sometime earlier, the Airborne was well armed. A few hours before the arrival of Mengistu, he was informed of the plot and he declined the request. The Airborne compound was then surrounded. When they realized the danger, members of the Airborne fled from the Debreziet area and some of them joined the EPRP. Among those who joined the EPRP was one of the leaders of the group, Lieutenant Merid.[8] Officers Beewketu Kassa and Seleshi went underground. However, they were hunted down and killed in the Gojjam province.

In the final analysis, the break up of the Airborne signaled one of the most serious military disasters of the Derge. The revolt of the Airborne was a spontaneous act of the members themselves. No political group, including the EPRP, had any hand in the process.

The second group of opposition within the Derge, opting for reforming the institution from within, elected a fifteen-man committee after the July 1976 Derge meeting. Mengistu and Atnafu were not included in this committee. The task of the committee was to study the reasons for the unpopularity of the Derge, despite the economic reforms it had enacted. All through this period, unrest had become part of the fabric of the society and open defiance against the military regime was manifested in various ways. One of these was the spontaneous outburst of support exhibited toward civilian soccer teams whenever they had matches with teams from the army. (Among the prominent soccer teams of the country were those that belonged to the army or the police.) Following the matches, the exuberant crowd would go home chanting revolutionary songs, especially if a civilian team won the game.[9]

The committee that the Derge formed at its July meeting was assigned to come up with proposals regarding the formation of a civilian government and with means of resolving the internal crisis of the Derge.[10] The document that was prepared for the occasion was reported to have been found in the possession of Lt. Alemayehu Haile, following his execution in January 1977.[11]

The document had five subtitles: a. the origin of the Ethiopian revolution, b. the 1974 revolutionary movement, c. the achievements and shortcomings of the revolution, d. prevalent Ethiopian political condition and, e. what ought to be done. The document was very critical of POMOA and argued that the formation of that institution could not be considered as a substitute to the regrouping of the progressive forces of the country.[12] Furthermore, discussing the EPRP, it stated,

> the struggle between the left forces of the country at this time is between the EPRP and the Derge in the main. This is because ...the EPRP wants the formation of a popular people's government and that position had attained acceptance among the people....Its propaganda had spread throughout the country...."[13] The document then suggested, "a united front has to be formed and it has to take over power immediately.[14]

Among the forces that would be included in the front was the EPRP, because the organization "had expressed its readiness to form a front with the Derge." This point was in reference to EPRP's response to the call for the

formation of a front in April 1976.
As indicated above, some of the Derge's leading officers differed from the Mengistu/POMOA clique on how to handle the opposition. Mengistu and POMOA had opted for a forcible resolution of the conflict as a viable option, while the majority of the Derge members had not reached that conclusion yet. Some Derge members were adamantly opposed to a policy of confrontation as a method to resolve the conflicts facing the country.
The Derge's internal crisis was exacerbated by other incidents that took place within the army. In June 1976, the Air Force went on strike and forwarded popular demands. Most of the demands which came out in a leaflet titled the "*Voice of the Air-force*" had been aired in January 1975. One of the demands that the leaflet put forward was the redressing of the mistreatment of noncommissioned officers by their superiors.[15] During the June strike, members of the Air-force demanded the right to form "discussion clubs" in the various military units. When it learned of the strike in the Air Force, the military regime deployed the newly formed Nebelbal (Flame) force and surrounded the compound of the Air Force. A number of Derge officers, Mengistu among them, warned them to end the strike.[16]
In the Asseb area some officers mutinied demanding the formation of a popular government. However, the rebellion was quashed easily. Mutiny was in the making among the seventeenth battalion in Gofa Sefer, Addis Abeba, and a contingent in Nazareth. However, the Derge aborted the revolt while in its infancy. Earlier, the contingent in Nazareth had recalled its representative to the Derge, Tesfaye Gebre Kidan. However, the Derge refused to accept the demand. Because of lack of coordination, these and other rebellion in the various sectors of the army were easily aborted.

EPRP's Role in the Crisis Within the Derge

The crisis within the Derge had been anticipated by leading EPRP activists. The crisis was partly attributed to the incapacity of the regime to create a social base in spite of the number of decrees that it had promulgated. As early as December 1975, *Democracia* argued that the Derge remained vulnerable due to lack of a solid social base.[17] A *Democracia* issue at the beginning of 1976 argued that the Derge did not only take sides, but also was making efforts to establish a social base out of the national capitalist, the upper petty-bourgeois, and the state-bourgeois groups. It was doing this at the expense of the people, thereby depriving itself of the social base it needed for its survival, argued *Democracia*.[18]
Sometime around the beginning of 1976, the EPRP had formed a party committee around the Derge. It consisted of the Secretary, Captain Amha Abebe, Sergeant Major Wolde Medhin Abraha, Captain Moges Wolde Mikael and others. The party committee and particularly Captain Moges Wolde Mikael informed the EPRP leadership about the crisis within the Derge and the emerging anti-Mengistu resentment and demanded guidance.

When the EPRP leadership learned about the actual dissension within the Derge, it supported the reform movement. Even though it was perceived that the internal Derge situation that had created Mengistu would repeat itself as long as fundamental issues of democracy were not addressed, the EPRP leadership anticipated that the reform movement would somehow slow down the drive for the massive repression that was underway. It was conjectured that the internal adjustments and structural changes that the reform movement would promulgate would weaken Mengistu's role within the Derge. Besides, the Derge's internal structural changes would give the EPRP more access to the Derge and provide it a chance to influence the decision making process. The EPRP would also get some breathing time and space, in order to get ready for the impending crisis, which the EPRP believed was bound to come sooner or later. The EPRP would also be able to send as many of its members to the EPRA, get more funds and arms, and reorganize its structures.

As was indicated above, the EPRP leadership supported the reform movement within the Derge and Tesfaye Debessai and another CC member were assigned to explain the decisions of the EPRP leadership. The two EPRP CC members conducted a number of meetings with either the EPRP party committee by the Derge, or with Captain Moges or Captain Amha separately and discussed EPRP's suggestions.

The EPRP leadership suggested structural changes that would allow the majority of Derge members to take part in the decision making process. Furthermore, it was suggested that the Derge should have its own constitution and internal regulations, by which every member of the institution would abide. The Derge should have its own collective leadership, which could be set up in the form of a Central Committee, politburo and secretariat. The rules and regulations and the structural changes of the Derge should be designed in such a way that they would minimize the abuse of power by individuals.

Captain Moges, the newly elected chairperson of the Derge assembly, presented the EPRP party committee's suggestions at a Derge meeting and they were accepted with minor modifications. It was understood that the suggested structural change would deprive the Mengistu/POMOA alliance of the immense power it had accumulated and that power would pass over to the collective leadership of the Derge.

In the course of the struggle within the Derge, Mengistu was assigned as the chairperson of the civilian cabinet of ministers whose office was located away from the Derge office, near the Sidst Kilo. This was a deliberate effort designed to minimize Mengistu's influence, power and contacts around the Derge. It also was a move designed to enable other Derge members to control the security and military force that was in charge of the office of the Derge. The Derge military contingent, which at the time numbered in the hundreds, was under the direct auspices of Mengistu's confidant, Colonel Daniel Asfaw. The Derge meeting also decided to get rid of some of the ardent followers of Mengistu, such as, Colonel Teka Tulu. Neither Mengistu nor POMOA overtly objected to the reform movement. They rather picked on Captain Moges Wolde Mikael and Lieutenant Alemayehu Haile, who they thought to be opposed to their policy, and began a smear campaign against them. Both officers were labeled as EPRP moles within the Derge. Despite the contacts and acquaintances he had with some EPRP members and his sympathy toward the organization, Lieutenant Alemayehu Haile was not an EPRP member.

In order to divert the Derge's attention, to regain the power that was slipping out of their hands, and to pressure Captain Moges Wolde Mikael and his colleagues, Mengistu and POMOA intensified the anti-EPRP campaign, both within and outside the Derge. In July or thereabouts of 1976, Mengistu informed Captain Moges and other influential Derge members about the formation of his clandestine group, which was to be known by its publication, the *Abeyotawi Seded* (Revolutionary Flame). Mengistu invited important Derge members, like Captain Moges Wolde Mikael, General Teferi Bente, Lt. Alemayehu Haile, etc., to join his party. The officers, who had been blackmailed as EPRP agents could only accept the offer. For Moges, refusal would have been tantamount to admitting EPRP membership, so he had to accept the invitation. Besides, Moges also wanted to watch Mengistu's activities quite closely.

Initially, *Abeyotawi Seded* was composed of military officers, both from within and around the Derge. Among the important founding members of the Seded were Captain Fekre Selassie Wege Deresse, Sgt. Legesse Asfaw, Colonel Teka Tulu, Major Getachew Shibeshi, Corporal Mengistu Gemetchu, Corporal Gezahegne Worke, Corporal Germa Ayele and Corporal Begashaw Atalaye. Through the use of this new group, Mengistu, probably in close consultation with Sennay Likke, had intended to control the "unruly" Derge members, to counter the restructuring process that was already underway and regain the power that was slipping out of his hand. In the years to come, the formation of the *Seded* group was to prove another ingenious move of Mengistu to stay in power for more than seventeen years. *Seded*, a predecessor of the state party, the Workers Party of Ethiopia, would assume an increasingly important role in the ongoing struggle.

Furthermore, it was at one of the first meetings of the Seded where Captain Moges also took part, that Mengistu suggested the declaration of the war of annihilation against the EPRP. Some of the members of the new group, such as, Captain Moges, who opposed Mengistu's proposal, were blackmailed to a point that they were unable to oppose the idea openly. What Moges could do was report the matter to the EPRP.

Repressive Institutions Empowered

The cycle of violence that the Mengistu/POMOA alliance initiated would have been incomplete had it not been for the formation of new institutions that were geared and meant for the repression of people's voices. One of the establishments formed during this period was the *Abyot Tebeka* (Revolutionay Guard). When Mengistu emerged as the dominant figure, a special security force, whose task was to follow up the activities of the opposition and particularly the progressive sector of the society was formed.[19] Besides, as part of the intensification of the repression, the military regime formed a special military group known as the Nebelbal (Raging Fire). The Nebelbal was formed to counter the guerilla movement in the north and to be used as a special military group to safeguard the safety of the Derge itself. Unlike the rest of the armed forces which fell under the authority of the Ministry of Defense, the Nebelbal, trained by the Israelis and armed by the Chinese, was directly controlled by the Derge.

One of the most significant developments during the last quarter of 1976, however, was the empowerment of the kebeles. Even though the preparation for the formation of the Abyot Tebeka began earlier, the decree that legalized the institution, Proclamation No. 104, came out in October 1976.

> This second Proclamation gave the kebeles extensive: administrative, judicial and economic power, as well as the assumption of municipal functions. Furthermore, ...they (the kebeles) took *actions to control crime and counter-revolutionary activities*, [emphasis added] to supervise schools, to control the flourishing black market....[20]

The Proclamation introduced a pyramidal structure in which the kebeles were to be the base units. Above them came the Higher Kebeles or Kefetegnas, institutions that were to oversee the activities of 10 or so kebeles per jurisdiction. As a result, the new policy brought kebele activities under the supervision of fewer institutions and individuals as well. The new arrangement circumvented the shortage of 'qualified' manpower, while creating a controlling mechanism at the same time. The new arrangement required only one/tenth of the manpower that was previously utilized to control the kebeles. The MEISON, which during this period had stretched itself beyond its limit, was unable to provide committed people of its own to all of the kebeles, even if its personnel could get elected. The new arrangement proved to be one of the most ingenious devices of the MEISON. Daniel Tadesse, the Minister of Public Housing and Development was the leading person behind the policy.

The procedure for the election of the chairpersons of the higher Kefetegnas was arranged in such a way that POMOA was able to have its members or sympathizers elected to as many posts as possible. Unlike kebele meetings where the residents took some part and a certain degree of popular participation was mandatory, the Kefetegnas were formed by the executive committees of the kebeles, thereby providing POMOA the access and capacity to control the process. Consequently, in almost all of the elections conducted, either MEISON members or strong supporters of the regime were elected.

After assuming their posts, one of the first measures that the chairpersons of the Kefetegnas undertook was to make sure that the kebeles were run by individuals that at least complied with the policy of the Mengistu/POMOA alliance. If not, they were weeded out. In due courses, the Kefetegnas proved to be one of the most important mechanisms through which MEISON was able to wield power and control kebele activities.

The Proclamation mentioned above also included a declaration of the formation of city councils, which were to elect the Mayors of the cities.[21] When Proclamation No. 104 of October 1976 was decreed, a new kebele election was also conducted. One of the official criteria to be nominated was to support the National Democratic Revolution Program.[22] Besides, the individual could be nominated if he had taken part in the rally organized to celebrate the date that the Derge officially took over power, and the rally to condemn the attempt on Mengistu's life.[23] The nominee should also be one who had not evacuated the zemetcha camps.

Proclamation No. 104 also decreed the formation of the paramilitary group known as the *Abyot Tebeka*, an institution probably copied from the Cuban experience. A number of articles were also published elaborating the role and importance of *Abyot Tebeka* institutions.[24] The *Abyot Tebeka* was formed in government institutions, kebeles, factories, etc. Under each *Abyot Tebeka* committee came an armed detachment. The chairperson of the Abyot Tebeka committee became an *ex-officio* member of the kebele executive committee. Structurally, the kebele and the *Abyot Tebeka* committees were supposed to be different institutions, however, in due course of time and in practice, the *Abyot Tebeka* chairperson became the commanding figure of both.

The creation of the *Abyot Tebeka* signified the transformation of POMOA, and in particular the MEISON, into organizations that could lead and control urban paramilitary contingents. Initially, POMOA was responsible only for the political and organizational activities of the state.

Through the *Abyot Tebeka*, thousands of people were deployed in the service of the regime. A great majority of them neither had prior knowledge of the judicial system, nor adequate military training. Members of the *Abyot Tebeka* were recruited at the level of institutions or kebeles and, in many cases, they were composed of the declasse. To elucidate this, the *Abyot Tebeka* members of Kefetegna One, Kebele Four, in the area formerly known as Webe Bereha, and Kebele 29, in the provincial bus terminal area in Addis Abeba can be cited as examples. The members of the *Abyot Tebeka* group in Kebele Four were composed of individuals who used to perform all kinds of odd jobs, including cab washing. This was a group suspected of a number of holdups in the Afentcho Ber area where the group did its car washing. It was the Chairman Ergete Medebew who brought this group to a kebele meeting and lined them up by the podium in front of the residents. He then asked the consent of the residents to hire them as guards. The residents, who felt cornered and blackmailed, consented. It was this group of kebele guards who later was baptized into the *Abyot Tebeka* of Kebele Four.

Most of the *Abyot Tebeka* members of Kebele 29 were porters, pickpockets, etc., who did all kinds of odd jobs at the provincial bus terminal. Under the chairmanship of Fekadu, a former truck driver, the group was entrusted the responsibility of "safeguarding" the revolution. Kebele 29 was one of the kebeles that had committed innumerable crimes. The atrocities of Kebele 29 and Fekadu were made public after the EPRDF took over power in 1991.

POMOA had felt the need of involving the declasse group, at least, as early as April 1976, when the NDR program stated, "the lumpen proletariat is ready to stand on the side of the revolution...it is possible that it can become an instrument of reactionary forces. Therefore, the revolution should handle the lumpen proletariat with care and caution."[25] It can be concluded that the NDR program laid down the theoretical justification regarding the role to be assigned to the "lumpen proletariat". The October 1976 Proclamation finalized and at the same time legalized that process. The Proclamation ushered the involvement of the "lumpen proletariat" in the ongoing struggle. This was a period when the military regime was besieged on all corners and it was in dire need of support. Consequently, the "lumpen proletariat" would be one of the groups that would bail out the military regime from the deep crisis that it had placed itself in.

According to the October Proclamation, the main purpose of the *Abyot Tebeka* was to "safeguard" the revolutionary struggle. Article 10-e gave the *Abyot Tebeka* an immense power stating, "by the decision of the Ministry of Interior, it (the *Abyot Tebeka*) will perform the necessary defense and security measures." According to Proclamation No. 2, 1975, Article 6, the necessary "defense and security measures" were to be interpreted according to the group that controlled the *Abyot Tebeka*. According to MEISON, as was witnessed in the subsequent years, "necessary defense and security" measures entailed annihilating the EPRP and anyone that sympathized with it. When the *Abyot Tebeka* group fell into the hands of the other political groups, such as, the WAZ League and SEDED, "the necessary defense and security measures" meant getting rid of MEISON. The process continued thus, and eventually, the "necessary defense and security" measures meant an all out war against all dissenting groups and individuals, including the MEISON, WAZ League, etc.[26]

During the turbulent months of the late 1970's, it was neither the Ethiopian army nor the state security that played a pivotal role in defending the military regime, but the *Abyot Tebeka* group which was entrusted with the responsibility of implementing the policy of the war of annihilation. The declasse group was one of the forces that played a crucial role in suppressing the opposition movement of Ethiopia. Besides, in the course of the struggle, the Abyot Tebeka became involved in drafting tens of thousands of citizens for the war machine of the regime.[27]

The *Abyot Tebeka* not only became one of the deadliest institutions against the opposition, but also an omnipotent force controlling the lives of the residents of the kebeles. On the pretext of "safeguarding the revolution", a member of the *Abyot Tebeka* group could go into anyone's residence, day or night, arrest and torture anyone who was suspect, anyone who did not comply with the sexual and other whims of the group, or anyone who was not ready for bribery. The whole kebele was at the mercy of this group and innumerable atrocities were committed that only the Ethiopian people themselves could account for.

The *Abyot Tebeka* was also an institution through which some corrupt officials made profit by selling arms and ammunition in the black market. It was a common practice for members of the group to fire one or two bullets at night; in the morning they would inform their superiors that they had waged a fierce battle against "anarchists" and ask for a replenishment of ammunition.

EPRP Selected as the Main Target

Even though the military regime had resorted to violence only a few months after it took power, both the scope and the magnitude of the repression increased after the declaration of the NDR program in April 1976. The formation of POMOA and its involvement in the political process brought about a change in both the tempo and the span of the peaceful form of struggle. The involvement of POMOA on the side of the regime short-circuited the peaceful process and laid the ground for the commencement and intensification of the violent form of struggle, even when the great majority of the Derge members themselves were not ready to venture into such a choice.

The EPRP, which had embarked on the peaceful form of struggle since 1974, continued voicing its opposition regarding some major policies of the regime and, as a result, it became one of the main targets of the repression.[28] Even though the EPRP waged a peaceful form of struggle, it did not abandon the armed struggle. As early as 1974, it had anticipated that the peaceful form of struggle was only a transitional phenomenon that would soon dissipate. An August 1974 *Democracia* issue stated,

> ...[T]he military regime cannot fulfill the demands of democracy...a group that does not practice an internal democracy of its own, cannot fulfill the wishes of the people...the only solution it has is violence.[29]

Besides, following the appraisal of the Ethiopian political condition, the extended conference of the EPRP, held in August 1975 had concluded that Ethiopia's conflicts would in the final analysis be resolved only through armed means.[30] That assertion became a reality around June 1976 when the nature of violence underwent a serious change.

The sporadic aspect of the repression that had begun as early as September 1974 was replaced by a more systematic annihilation effort. Violence became an important policy of resolving the conflicts between the regime and the opposition forces in the country and the targets were set. Unlike the previous period, the violence was not limited to a single act, but became a process of systematic elimination of any dissent. Dissenting and expressing ones grievances were considered state crimes and anyone who raised his/her voice was labeled an anarchist or a reactionary, irrespective of his/her political affiliation.

The EPRP was singled out as the point of focus and Mengistu made efforts to drag the regime into the process of violence. A *Democracia* issue of that period stated, "the fabrications and accusations of Mengistu and the banda intellectuals are focused at the EPRP" and "Major Mengistu Haile Mariam, at a meeting he called, about three weeks back, [around the end of June 1976] presented EPRP's crimes."[31] The EPRP was accused of counter-revolutionary activities and economic sabotage. Mengistu also declared that he had obtained an evidence that proved the relationship of the EPRP with the EDU, the Somali government and the Eritrean organizations. Mengistu then suggested that the Derge had to open a campaign against the EPRP and give it a mortal blow.[32] *Democracia* argued that POMOA branch representatives constituted the main instigators for the anti-EPRP campaign in the various parts of the country. Describing their motives *Democracia* stated,

> when it was declared that there is no money to alleviate the famine and when workers were denied any kind of raise, the banda intellectuals, who were given a budget of many million birr, had been complaining about the role that the EPRP played to undermine their control of the people.[33]

At the beginning of July 1976, the military regime promulgated a new criminal law replacing Article No 9 of the Criminal Code. The aim of the new law was "to crush revolutionaries and revolutionary organizations, and to retard the progress of the struggle," stated *Democracia*.[34] Mengistu had also passed to its security office the names of 150 EPRP members and sympathizers who were to be executed.[35]

Mengistu's public comments regarding his new policy became a point of focus. *Democracia* reported on the speeches that he delivered at a Congress of the Service Industry Union and at a meeting of managers held around the third week of June 1976. He declared that he was ready to give a lesson in extermination.[36]

An August 1976 *Democracia* issue refuted all the allegations and accusations made against the EPRP. Replying to the serious charges regarding economic sabotage, the EPRP denied that it had taken any role. In a rhetorical manner, the EPRP explained the reasons for Ethiopia's economic problems.

The EPRP, like the "selected officers" and the banda intellectuals did not share power with higher state and industry officials...the EPRP did not use the country's money for the purchase of arms. The EPRP did not force the peasants to go out on a campaign during a farming season...the EPRP did not conduct military campaigns and execute small and mid-level businessmen . . . the EPRP did not spend the country's money on agents and banda intellectuals. On the other hand, the government of the "selected officers" had committed all of the above crimes and hence, it is not the EPRP but the regime that should be held accountable for the economic disaster.[37]

Besides the propaganda campaign that the Derge conducted, its Security branch made efforts to infiltrate the EPRP leadership. A Derge infiltrator, having laid low for quite some time, became very anxious and wanted to go up the ladder of the EPRP structure. After some hesitation, Kiflu Teferra, a member of the EPRP CC security department was assigned to contact the Derge agent. The CC member did not disclose his identity and the fact that he belonged to the EPRP leadership. Meetings were held. Dissatisfied with his new contact person, the infiltrator demanded to go up further. In his few days of investigation, Kiflu Teferra watched the behavior of the infiltrator. Because of his haste to get to the EPRP CC, the Derge's security branch violated basic infiltration rule, that is, patience. The impatient attitude of the agent made him suspect and the information that he provided, although correct sometimes, was found suspicious. It was at this juncture, during the last days of July or the first week of August 1976 that Captain Moges Wolde Mikael informed the EPRP leadership about the Derge's security network within the EPRP. Captain Moges had overheard some Derge security officers bragging about their new success at reaching the EPRP leadership.

Captain Moges, who was not informed about the new infiltrator, brought forth details that confirmed EPRP's suspicions. The EPRP then took the necessary steps to protect itself. Those individuals who had recruited the agent were suspended until further investigation. In the midst of this crisis, in July 1976, the EPRP celebrated the first anniversary of the declaration of its program; major Ethiopian towns and cities were flooded with wall posters, banners, leaflets, etc. It was also around this time that the Youth League devised the new propaganda method of writing and distributing major slogans on small pieces of paper. Besides its effectiveness, the new system did not require much preparation. Besides the EPRP, the other targets of the regime included the Ethiopian Democratic Union (EDU) and the ELF. Why were the EDU and the ELF targeted? Most of the contradictions and conflicts that had been simmering for more than two years erupted from September 1976 to January 1977. Members of the former ruling class, organized under the EDU, opened up a military campaign against the military regime.

A few months after the land reform proclamation, some members of the former ruling group were able to come out of their lethargy and attain international prominence when leading figures of this group formed the EDU. Among the leaders of this group were Ras Mengesha Seyoum, General Nega Tegegne and General Iyasu Mengesha. General Jafar Nimiere, former president of the Sudan, supported the group's effort to get organized and mediated between the leading individuals.[38]

The EDU held it's first meeting in Saudi Arabia and the immediate task of the organization was to give guidance to the scattered groups of former landlords who had revolted and fled to the hills. Consequently, the EDU was able to mobilize the gentry in the Begemidir, Wello and Gojjam provinces. The first encounter between the military regime and the EDU took place in September 1976 at Kokit, a small town in the Chilga district *(aweraja)*, Begemidir Province. The EDU force advanced deep into the northwestern part of the country and brought Humera and Metema, two important Ethiopian border towns, under control. In the ensuing conflict, a Derge battalion disintegrated. Some of the Derge's leading officers joined the EDU. In a brief while, the EDU advanced and controlled most of the northwestern part of the Begemidir province. The Derge acted quickly, deploying a mechanized force stationed in Jijjiga, to the Begemidir province.[39] Not long afterward, the Derge brought the situation under control. Right or wrong, according to a leading figure of the group, the discontinuation of the supply of arms and ammunition was regarded as one of the possible causes of the defeat of the EDU.[40]

An EDU detachment, known as EDU-Terenafit and led by Ras Mengesha, crossed over from the Sudan to Tigrai and launched an armed campaign. Not long afterward, it faced the TPLF, which had adopted an anti-feudal policy and wanted to have an exclusive control of the Tigrai area. Fierce and incessant battles were conducted between the two groups and hundreds of fighters and peasants fell victim. The armed conflict that began in 1976 lasted until 1978 when the EDU-Terenafit was defeated and was forced to retreat from the area.

The EDU also took part in an operation organized by the ELF. The operation took place in Omhager, a small town along the Sudan/Eritrean border. The Derge defended against the advance of the EDU and the ELF and it inflicted serious blows on both groups. The EDU, which based its leadership and command mainly in the Sudan, had an international support, including that from the Sudanese and Saudi Arabian governments.

The other target of the war of annihilation was the ELF. As was indicated elsewhere, the NDR program had singled out the ELF as a group that was espousing reactionary politics. However, both the ELF and the EPLF confronted the Derge. In September 1976, both organizations opened up offensives against the Derge military posts in Barka, Sahel and Keren. Many of the small Eritrean towns were besieged and they were left on their own. In January 1977, the EPLF controlled Karora, a strategic military post in the northern tip of Eritrea. Omhager also fell under the control of the

ELF. The newly formed and very much feared military division known as the Nebelbal was routed by the EPLF in the Keren area. By the beginning of 1977, both rebel groups had placed themselves in an offensive posture and ready to take over major cities. Confidence in the rebel's success was so high that many Eritreans believed that an independent Eritrea was on the horizon. Many Eritreans who used to reside in Ethiopia left for Eritrea, selling or disposing of their properties. Once more, many of them would become disappointed when the war continued and the Derge went on the offensive. A good number of them ended up in exile.

The EPRP and the Impending Crisis

In June 1976, an EPRP delegate went to Eritrea to conduct negotiation with the Eritrean organizations, particularly with the EPLF. Besides the overall importance of the Eritrean struggle to Ethiopia and vice versa, the Eritrean organizations remained important assets for the continuation of the armed struggle, providing a rear and an arms inlet for the EPRA. The mission of the delegation, led by Tesfaye Debessai, was part of the preparation to step up the armed phase of the struggle.

An EPLF mini-delegation greeted the EPRP group at the Eritrea-Tigrai border and escorted it to the meeting place. The meeting had an informal tone and EPLF activists, who did not belong to the formal leadership, were allowed to take part. Among the main issues raised during the discussion between the delegation of the two organizations were whether Eritrea was an Ethiopian colony, the vanguard role of the EPLF in the Eritrean struggle, the role of the EPRP in the struggle, etc.[41] In the course of the discussion, the EPLF leadership demanded that the EPRP mellow down the anti-EPLF activities of the Ethiopian Students Union in North America (ESUNA). The EPLF believed that the EPRP itself was conducting a campaign against it. The EPRP delegate informed its counterpart that it could try to influence the ESUNA, but could not promise that it would stop its activities. The EPLF, which believed that ESUNA was an extension of the EPRP, could not buy the arguments.[42] After a few days of discussion, the delegates of the two organizations produced a communique which is discussed elsewhere in this chapter.

During this trip, the relationship between the EPRP and the ELF, which had been discontinued for more than two years, was reestablished.[43] Despite the sour relationship of the two organizations, the EPRA and an ELF group by the Tigrai border had established a good working relationship as early as 1975. On its own initiative, the ELF force had provided some arms to the EPRA and had conducted training sessions for some EPRA members. The EPRA had also taken part in some of the military operations of the ELF. One of these was the "Raza Project". When negotiation was commenced, the ELF, unlike the EPLF, did not demand that the EPRP delegates recognize Eritrea as a colony of Ethiopia. The ELF also agreed to cooperate with the

EPRP, both in the rural and urban areas, and contact was established with an ELF Fedayeen, that is, urban guerilla unit, in Addis Abeba.

On its way back to the Tigrayan hinterlands, the EPRP delegate was approached by some EPLF members who had an interest in forming some kind of a revolutionary party within the EPLF. A lengthy discussion was conducted between Tesfaye Debessai and one of the leaders of the group, Iyob Berhe, a veteran student activist and pioneer EPLF member. He did his studies in the Soviet Union. Tesfaye conducted discussions on how such a party could be formed. However, he warned Iyob about the implications and dangers of forming an underground organization in a military establishment like the EPLF. Not long afterward, Iyob was removed from his post of the Southern Front and his whereabouts is still unknown. It is rumored that he was executed by the EPLF toward the end of the 1970's, along with other dissident Eritreans.

The June 1976 EPRP CC Meeting

The EPRP CC conducted a meeting in June 1976. The previous CC meeting was held in April of the same year. The main agenda item of the CC meeting was the deteriorating political condition in the country and what ought to be done. After appraising the Ethiopian situation, the CC concluded that the peaceful form of struggle was almost over. Left with no other choice, the EPRP had to resort to the armed struggle, as the main form of struggle.

The CC meeting also decided to restructure the organization and as part of this process, it decided to shift the leadership center. This meant that the members of the EPRP CC, the majority of whom resided in Addis Abeba, had to move out to a more safe area. It was also suggested that the urban activities of the EPRP should be coordinated and directed by some kind of a provisional committee. The June EPRP CC decided that it would make a final decision on this and other related questions in its Second Plenum, which was to be held a month or so later. In the mean time, it formed a committee to finalize the proposals. AW, a member of the leadership who had poor health, was told to go underground and was assigned to the Foreign Committee abroad.

In the days following the June CC meeting and as part of the preparation for the transition from one form of struggle to another, the appraisal of the EPRP CC was discussed with the various party and Youth League committees throughout the country and *Democracia* issues began focusing on the changing situations. Official signals regarding the changing political condition and form of struggle were hinted when *Democracia* stated,

> [T]he EPRP had done and will do its best so that the struggle will still assume a peaceful form. However, if the "select officers" regime blocks the peaceful course, it does not mean that the struggle will stop, or be

weakened. As a vanguard party of the proletariat, the EPRP would fulfill its historical responsibility by adopting a form of struggle that is commensurate with the prevailing condition.[44]

The Second Plenum of the EPRP CC

Ordinary EPRP CC meetings were held at least every forty five days. According to the EPRP constitution, a Plenum had to be held every six months and, before it could be convened, every effort should be made so that all of the members of the CC were contacted. A meeting would be designated a Plenum only when over two-thirds of the members of the CC attend it. The convocation of the 2nd Plenum was delayed due to the efforts to get in touch with CC members in the army and abroad, and with Tesfaye Debessai who was with the army.

The Second Plenum of the EPRP CC was held in August 1976, just a month and few days after the June CC meeting. It was one of the important gatherings of the EPRP leadership, and it was attended by all CC members save one who was abroad. It was held in the organization's headquarters rented under Kiflu Teferra's name. Kiflu Teferra, a fugitive by then, was on the governments hit list. The Plenum was an uninterrupted meeting that lasted for over 40 hours.

The main agenda items of the Second Plenum consisted of appraisal of the activities of the CC, the PB, and individual CC members; the communique signed between the EPRP delegate and the EPLF; assessment of the Ethiopian political condition; restructuring of the EPRP; the condition of the EPRA; immediate organizational security steps to be taken; co-optation of some more members to the CC, etc.

The first issue of the agenda was the appraisal of the performance of the EPRP in its few years of struggle. *This was the first and the last appraisal of the activities of the EPRP leadership, conducted by the participants themselves.*[45]

While appraising EPRP's contribution to the struggle, the 2nd Plenum commended the political and organizational achievements of the organization. Organizational success was expressed through the large following that the EPRP was able to rally in just a matter of a few years or so. Furthermore, the Plenum assessed that the EPRP had established itself as an important political force due to its political activities. EPRP's success was regarded as an outcome of its correct political and organizational line and the role that its members played in the activities of the organization. The 2nd Plenum commended EPRP's contribution to the struggle, despite the very difficult conditions created as a result of the reforms that the Derge enacted. The adoption of new concepts regarding the underground mass organizations was appraised as concurrent steps to meet the demands of the time.

The Plenum also appraised the mistakes and shortcomings that the

EPRP CC committed. That appraisal was conducted on two levels. The first one was on the EPRP CC itself, while the second one was in regard to the PB. With regards to the CC, among the major points of self-criticism were the engagements of CC members in day to day organizational affairs and their neglect of major questions of ideology. The CC believed that it had shown weaknesses in ideological debates of major political and ideological ramifications. In its two years of activities, not even once did the CC convene a meeting to discuss issues concerning the ideology of the EPRP. During almost all of the meetings held, discussions focused on either organizational issues or the political direction of the struggle. The neglect of ideological questions had serious political consequences in the course of the struggle. The CC also criticized itself for failing to read reports and follow up EPRP activities in the provinces. The problem was caused partly by lack of a secured place for EPRP's files and the underground existence of many EPRP CC members.

After examining the positive role that the PB played in providing day to day leadership and implementing CC decisions, it was criticized for the mistakes it committed. One of them was the error it committed during the merger with the "Red Flag" group. It was also criticized for failing to present analysis of unfolding events in a written form well before EPRP CC meetings were convened. The Plenum also criticized the PB for failing to present agenda issues for CC meetings well before they were convened. Criticism was also conducted on the various departments of the EPRP CC; the Political Department, the Military Commission, etc. The Military Commission was asked to present a report explaining why the armed unit that went into the Wello area had failed.

The Plenum then conducted self-criticism and criticism sessions on individual CC members. Mistakes, shortcomings and negative tendencies were criticized. One of the major weaknesses and shortcoming that was raised was the over-concentration of tasks in the hands of some CC members. The CC then decided that a CC member should not belong to more than three committees or departments. However, due to shortage of manpower, in the years ahead, that decision could only be partially implemented.

As was indicated earlier, the EPRP delegation headed by Tesfaye Debessai, after conducting a meeting with the EPLF leadership, including Esayeyas Afeworki, had signed a communique. Some of the points raised in the communique run contrary to EPRP's positions.

The EPRP believed that the Eritrean question should be categorized within the framework of the national question. However, the communique asserted that the Eritrean question was not a national one, but failed to clarify what it was. The communique also asserted that the Eritrean revolution will not only bring national independence, but it was also considered a national democratic struggle whose aim was to safeguard the interests of the Eritrean working class and peasantry.[46] Tesfaye was asked to explain about the spirit and the content of the communique and how he reached the above-mentioned conclusions. He explained that the EPLF refuted EPRP's position that Eritrea did not constitute one nation or nationality, but many who speak different languages and profess different religions, and that the struggle was the joint effort of all those that inhabited Eritrea. According to the EPLF, Eritrea is not a nation or nationality, but a country that was colonized by Ethiopia. Following a lengthy discussion, the delegation led by Tesfaye accepted the fact that the struggle in Eritrea could not be categorized as a struggle of only one group of people or nationality and the EPRP delegation agreed that it should not be viewed within the framework of the national question. However, to label that struggle anti-colonial was a conclusion that the EPRP itself had not reached at, and the EPRP delegation could not accept EPLF's arguments. Besides, the EPRP delegation explained that the question was an academic one that did not have a direct bearing on the resolution of the problem in Eritrea. Be it colonial or national, the EPRP had acknowledged the unconditional rights of nations to self-determination, explained the delegation.

After exchanging their points of views, the EPLF leadership wanted to sign some kind of a communique right on the spot, but the EPRP delegation insisted that it had to report the outcome of the discussion to the EPRP CC. The EPLF delegation became so furious and wanted to break up the negotiation process. It was then that the EPRP delegation gave in and signed the controversial communique. It did so in order to keep up the relationship of the two organizations, explained Tesfaye.[47] After listening to Tesfaye Debessai's explanation, the Plenum declared the communique void and passed its decisions to its members, who had also been demanding for an explanation. The CC also decided that it would not give in on an issue that the organization did not believe in and severely criticized the delegation for overreaching its mandate and compromising EPRP's political positions.

Both the EPRP and the EPLF delegation had agreed to distribute the communique. However, the Plenum annulled that decision and the EPRP could not accept the agreement.

After analyzing the events and political developments in the country during the last few months of 1976, very much in line with the June CC meeting, the Plenum recognized the fact that the peaceful development of the political struggle was almost over. It also recognized that the EPRP would adopt the armed struggle as the main form of struggle. The main thesis regarding the new political development was outlined in some of the *Democracia* issues of the period and in one of which, it was stated,

> Before launching an armed struggle, the broad masses had to learn from their own experience that the condition for the peaceful development of the struggle is over. It is also our obligation to present the necessary assessments and show the international progressive forces that the only alternative left is the armed struggle....The EPRP had made and will still make efforts for the continuation of the peaceful political struggle,

> however, if the 'select officers' regime impedes that path, it doesn't mean that the struggle will be weakened or will come to a halt...(but) it will force us to adopt another form of struggle....[48]

Even though the Plenum recognized the end of the peaceful form of struggle, it also realized that the Ethiopian people and the international community had not reached that conclusion yet, and so the EPRP refrained from declaring the switch to the armed struggle as the main form of struggle. Furthermore, the conflict and power struggle between Mengistu and the majority of the Derge members remained unresolved, thereby making conditions more complicated. The continuation of the peaceful form of struggle, even if temporarily, depended upon whether Mengistu or the majority of the Derge members won the struggle within the Derge.

The Second Plenum decided that intensive political and organizational activities should be conducted among the Ethiopian army. With this in mind, the Oppressed Soldiers Organization (OSO) was reorganized. Berhanu Ijjigu, one of the most capable organizers of the party and other EPRP members were assigned to take part in the reorganization process. The OSO also assumed an important status when it established a direct link with the Addis Abeba IZ. As part of the drive to win over the military, a decision was passed encouraging EPRP members to join the Ethiopian army whenever conditions allowed. In the years to come, a good number of EPRP members joined the Ethiopian army.

When discussing the issue of political work in the Ethiopian army, Berhane Meskel linked it to an insurrection and suggested that the party had to prepare itself for such an event. He did not elaborate what he had in mind and his suggestion was not taken quite seriously. For some CC members, his suggestion seemed quite contradictory to what he had been advocating since April 1976. Berhane strongly advocated that the EPRP should establish some form of an alliance with the Derge. At another CC meeting held in August of the same year, Berhane withdrew his suggestion regarding the insurrection.

In line with the assessment of the Ethiopian political situation, the EPRP had to reorganize itself. The June CC meeting had recommended that the EPRP leadership center had to move to another location and the committee that was assigned to come up with the proposals argued that a provisional body should take over the tasks of the leadership in the urban centers. Tesfaye Debessai, who did not attend the June CC meeting, asked what the status of the new provisional leadership would be, *vis-a-vis* the EPRP constitution. The June CC meeting had overlooked the constitutional aspect of the issue and apparently, the newly proposed institution, that is, the so-called provisional leadership, had no status in the constitution. The idea was dropped altogether and instead, the Plenum decided that only six CC members should stay around and provide leadership for activities in the urban centers, and that the remaining members of the leadership would be assigned to the different parts of the country.

Transition from peaceful to violent form 123

As part of the restructuring process, the tasks of certain committees were combined and some committees were eliminated. For organizational purposes, the whole of Ethiopia was divided into six regions and all of the zonal committees would fall under six interzonal committees. The six interzonal committees were: the Harer; the Sidamo area, which brought together the Gamu Gofa, Bale and the Sidamo zonal committees; the IZ in the north, which regrouped the Tigrai, Wello and the zonal committee in Eritrea; the Begemidir and Gojjam IZ; the Shoa and the Addis Abeba IZs.

It was anticipated that communication between the EPRP leadership and the various IZs would be discontinued for a long period and under such conditions, the IZs had to function and make decisions on their own. Except for the Addis Abeba and the Shoa area committees, all of the other IZs would be autonomous with one CC member assigned to each of them. His task would be to facilitate the decision making process of the IZ. In the form of an internal regulation, the Plenum outlined the duties and functions of the CC members to be assigned to the different IZ committees. The internal regulation was prepared in such a way that the assigned EPRP CC members would make decisions on behalf of the leadership, when the situation demanded it. However, provisions that would limit the role of the CC members were also incorporated into the by-law. The purpose of such provisions was to minimize the danger of stifling the initiative of the IZs.

Melaku Marcos, a veteran activist, even though not a CC member, was entrusted the responsibility of the Sidamo area. Samuel Alemayehu was assigned to the Harer area, ZB and Fikre Zergaw, who were newly coopted alternate CC members, were assigned to the Begemidir and Tigrai areas, respectively.

When new assignments were allotted to the different committees around the CC, the Plenum was unable to abide by its own decisions, which had stipulated that a CC member could not be assigned to more than three departments and that only six CC members would stay in the Addis Abeba area. Contrary to that decision, except those assigned to the different IZs and the army, all of the CC members were assigned as members of one or another CC department and most of them were forced to stay in the urban areas. The Plenum realized that it was entrapped by the new arrangement and could not come out of the vicious circle. Hoping to take some measures in due course, it left the decision unamended.

To overcome difficulties in case of crisis, it was decided that every important committee of the EPRP, such as, the IZ, the Zone, etc., should have "shadow" committees. These were committees that would be activated only when the main committees, say the IZs, became unable to operate, or the members fell in the hands of the government. According to the decision of the Second Plenum, the members of the "shadow" committee would be introduced to each other in advance and they would be told about their future activities. However, that decision of the Plenum was altered when members of the IZs and zonal committees argued that such a step would bring about unnecessary acquaintances of members long before the committees themselves were activated and the arrangement would cause a security danger to the EPRP. It was suggested that members of the "shadow" committees could be informed about their future tasks and could remain prepared, without however being introduced to each other. One of the members of the committee could keep the message and decode it when necessary. The EPRP CC accepted the amendment.

The Plenum discussed the condition of the EPRA, and a number of problems related to manpower, leadership, finance, arms, etc., were raised and discussed. The basis for the discussion was the complaint that the EPRA leadership had made regarding the attention given to the army.

The Plenum also discussed the problems and weaknesses of the EPRA. It was pointed out that the EPRA did not engage in activities that would make it self-sufficient, either in terms of arms and finance. Throughout its existence, the EPRA depended on the urban party structure, when it should have been the other way around. To alleviate the problems of the EPRA, it was decided to send whatever finance and other necessary materials that were available.

As part of the preparation for the upcoming difficult times and also to solve EPRA's problems, the Plenum decided to send many EPRP members to the EPRA. Many members who were exposed and who had placed themselves as security risks began departing.

One of the decisions made at the Second Plenum was the co-optation of new CC members. According to the EPRP constitution, the CC could co-opt additional CC members without, however, exceeding one-third of the original number of the CC itself.[49] This was a provision that would safeguard the composition of the CC that the previous Congresses or Conferences had elected. It was based on the understanding that CC members elected by a more representative body, in this case, the First EPRP Congress held in 1972, should always be in a clear majority.

So, according to the EPRP Constitution, until the next congress, the EPRP CC was entitled to co-opt only seven more members. After discussing the Ethiopian political condition and the tasks of the EPRP, the Plenum decided that it had to enlarge the CC and it co-opted four more alternate CC members, leaving the other three openings for future emergency needs. The co-opted members were, ZB, Fikre Zergaw, MGE and E. ZB was a former leading member of the byot group, who played an important role in organizing the party in the Begemidir and Gojjam areas. Fikre was a former Addis Abeba IZ secretary who had left for the EPRA. MGE was one of the founding members of the nucleus of the EPRA. The reason why MGE had to be co-opted was to empower the EPRA leadership by raising the number of CC members in the army. MGE's co-optation was also an indirect response to the demand of the EPRA leadership. Samuel Alemayehu was made a full CC member.

Because of the clandestine nature of the EPRP and the fact that even

CC members had no knowledge of who constituted the EPRP, co-optation was not an easy task. In the absence of any other alternative, the EPRP CC set certain criteria, and it then considered a number of nominees and discussed each of them. Often, very few or sometimes one or two CC members, other than the nominating member were acquainted with the nominee.

Finally, as a result of the impending crisis, it was anticipated that there would be a disruption of communications, and for quite some time, convening another CC meeting would be difficult. That condition would leave the EPRP without leadership when it would be needed very badly. In order to meet with the problem halfway, the Second Plenum mandated the PB to take over leadership until the situation improved. Morever, the Second Plenum instructed the PB to create conditions and bring the leadership together. It also ordered the PB to discuss its decisions with all CC members that it could possibly reach.

While the Plenum was in session, one thing led to another and Berhane Meskel mentioned that it was he who had called the Editor of the *Addis Zemen* newspaper and instructed him to write an Editorial on the formation of a front.[50] Getachew Maru had presented that Editorial at the PB meeting of March 1976, as evidence of the Derge's willingness to form a front. When Berhane mentioned the case, he was asked why he didn't inform the CC about his role. Berhane replied that he had informed his PB contact man, Getachew Maru. When Getachew denied any knowledge of the case, Berhane accused him of lying. Berhane became so furious that the two exchanged some name callings. That incident left many of the CC members baffled, suspicious and angry. It left a scar that had some bearings in the events that were to take place a few months later.[51]

Notes to Chapter 3

1. Voice of ELAMA, August 1976, page 2.

2. See details in Chapter VIII.

3. Sometime in 1977, Abdulahi Yusuf was accused of indirectly helping the Somali "aggression", by disarming those whom he considered were "neftegnas". POMOA conducted an investigation regarding the allegations and prepared a report. Sometime later, Abdulahi was found dead. It was believed that he was assassinated by a Derge squad.

4. Interview, Y., MEISON infiltrator, 1988.

5. Addis Fana, April, 1977, page 41.

6. Interview, March 1997, Colonel Alemayehu Asfaw, Commander of the Airborne, 1975-76.

7. Among them were Hebistu, Taye Tola and Wendemagne.

8. See details in Chapter IV.

9. This situation was discussed in the Addis Zemen newspaper of May 28, 1977.

10. EPRP Politburo Document, 1976, page 3.

11. See details in Chapter IV.

12. Document prepared for the reform movement in the Derge. Quoted from Addis Fana, June 1977, page 28.

13. Ibid., page 29.

14. Ibid., page 30.

15. Voice of the Air force, December 27, 1975 page 1.

16. Democracia, Volume III, No. 6, page 4.

17. Democracia, Volume II, No. 23, page 5.

18. Democracia, Volume III, No. 2, page 2.

19. Ibid., page 7.

20. Abera Yemane Ab, The Defeat of the Ethiopian Revolution and the Role of the Soviet Union, Proceedings of the 2nd International Conference on the Horn of Africa, page 92. Abera Yemane Ab was a leading MEISON member and an official of the Ministry of Public Housing.

Transition from peaceful to violent form 127

21. See details 238.
22. Addis Zemen, October 22, 1976, page 1.
23. See details in Chapter IV.
24. Addis Zemen, December 19, 1976.
25. NDR program.
26. See details in Chapter VI.
27. See details in Chapter VI.
28. "It was the understanding of the [EPRP] leadership that most of its members would join the newly formed nucleus of the army in the rural areas. As the unfolding events changed the political course, the third CC meeting decided to shift its center to the urban areas of Ethiopia, in order to place itself in the midst of the intense struggle. The majority of the Central Committee members had to be involved in the political and organizational struggle,. . ." Kiflu Tadesse, The Generation, Part I, Independent Publishers, 1993, pg. 134.
29. Democracia, Volume I, No. 6
30. Preamble of EPRP 1975 program.
31. Democracia, Volume III, No. 7, page 2.
32. Ibid., page 2.
33. Ibid., page 2.
34. Democracia, Volume III, No. 7, page 3.
35. Democracia, Volume III, No. 2, page 2.
36. Democracia, Volume III, No. 6, page 3.
37. Democracia, Volume III, No. 7, page 2.
36. Interview, Major General Nega Tegegne, founding member of the EDU, April 1984, Sudan.
39. The removal of that mechanized force might have facilitated the advance of the Somali force to occupy a large chunk of the eastern part of Ethiopia in 1977.
40. Interview, Major General Nega Tegegne, founding member of the EDU, April 1984, Sudan.
41. See details page120.

42. Interview with MGE, April 1991, a member of the EPRP delegation.

43. Kiflu Tadesse, The Generation, Part I, Independent Publishers, 1993, Chapter VI.

44. Democracia, Volume III, No. 6, page 3.

45. More details on the EPRP CC, Chapters V, VIII.

46. EPRP/EPLF Communique, 1976.

47. The author's recollection of Tesfaye's Testimony at the 2nd Plenum, 1976.

48. Democracia, Volume III, No. 6, page, 3.

49. 1975 EPRP Constitution, Ch. III, A 9.

50. This was in reference to the Addis Zemen Editorial of March 17, 1976, mentioned in Chapter II. The Editorial came out sometime before the Derge declared its NDR program.

51. See details in Chapter V.

4

The Declaration of the War of Annihilation and Its Effects

Following the formation of POMOA, two contradictory phenomena began taking shape. The first was the formation of the new political power of Mengistu and POMOA while the second one was the emergence of an internal Derge opposition to the rule of the Mengistu/POMOA alliance. In the midst of this political crisis and power struggle, the Mengistu/POMOA alliance introduced a major shift of policy that *de facto* and *de jure* kindled a wave of violence that would last until the overthrow of the military regime in 1991. Initially, that policy was known as the war of annihilation. However, in the course of the struggle, it assumed different names. In November 1977, it was labeled as the "Red Terror".

During the last days of August 1976, the Mengistu/POMOA alliance began preparing the new policy of the war of annihilation. Mengistu presented to the Derge his plan of annihilation, which included a massive repression against the three main opposition forces, the EPRP, EDU and ELF and anyone who was suspected of having any connection with them. The war of annihilation was in effect a war against the progressive forces of the country, the very catalysts of change, the nationalist struggle and members of the former ruling groups.[1] The immediate brunt and the target of the repression were the progressive sectors, which included the militant Ethiopian youth, who had been a formidable force of change; teacher-activists, who had been prominent in the struggle for change; the militant and class conscious worker activists, who had been the very inspiration of the struggle.

Earlier, when the news about Mengistu's final move was known, the EPRP tried to block it, using the connections and influence it had in the Derge, but failed to do so. It was believed that once Mengistu Haile Mariam committed the state apparatus to an anti-EPRP campaign, it would be difficult to bring it to a stop; for once the bureaucracy starts its campaign, it will keep grinding it on. The EPRP would become the official scapegoat for the ills of the society.

The declaration of the war of annihilation was preceded by the 1974 Special Penal Code which introduced the "ex post facto application of the law"[2] and opened up the door for arbitrariness. *The declaration of the war* of annihilation in September 1976 was the beginning of the "Red Terror," a campaign that resulted in the massacre of tens of thousands of Ethiopians. The Derge endorsed Mengistu's proposals and promulgated a decree to that effect. The Derge statement "condemned the so-called Ethiopian People's Revolutionary Party as an agent of subversion and counter-revolution."[3] The EPRP was accused of all types of crimes, including economic sabotage, creating discord between the "toiling masses and the military", sabotaging power supply lines, etc. Furthermore, it was stated that the EPRP was allied with the imperialist camp, "had [the EPRP] opposed the Provisional Military Government's decision to execute 60 officials of the former feudal regime...."[4]

The decree of the war of annihilation was the work of Mengistu, a few other Derge members and POMOA/MEISON. The rest of the Derge members were coerced into the process. The Decree of the war of annihilation allowed that any EPRP member would be executed on sight. Any members of the security force, including the newly formed kebele guards and the Abyot Tebeka institutions were given the license to take measures against anyone that they thought was an EPRP member. Anyone who was suspected of EPRP connections was liable to be arrested and tortured.

A day before the declaration of the war of annihilation, *Addis Zemen* published an article which condemned and characterized the EPRP as a "fascist" organization. The purpose of the article was to prepare the public for the impending crisis. The article was based on a resolution of the Ethiopian Students Union in Europe, one of the student factions controlled by MEISON.[5] In September 1976, the publication titled *Abeyotawit Ethiopia*, the organ of POMOA/MEISON, argued that the difference with the EPRP was not based on differing political lines, but a conflict between progressives and reactionaries,[6] the EPRP being considered reactionary.

The War of Annihilation against the EPRP, the EDU and the ELF was made public on September 11, 1976. The EPLF, which POMOA/MEISON considered progressive, was not mentioned. During this period, POMOA/MEISON was making efforts to widen the wedge between the two rival Eritrean organizations. With that in mind, POMOA arranged some kind of a negotiation with the EPLF and sometime around mid-1976, Haile Fida and the Derge's Political Affairs Committee chairperson, Captain Sisay Habte, had been to Eritrea to negotiate with the EPLF.

Right after the declaration of the war of annihilation, throughout Ethiopia, there were state sponsored and organized demonstrations in its support. The EPRP and the other political organizations mentioned elsewhere were condemned. Before these events, the EPRP had not been mentioned publicly; however, following the declaration of the war of annihilation, that name became a recurring theme of the media and was known to every Ethiopian household.

Denouncing the EDU, the ELF and the EPRP at public gatherings became a ritual. In one such incident, an elderly traditional chief of the Ebenat Aweraja in Begemidir, denounced the EDU and the EPRP and left out the

ELF while concluding his speech at a gathering of peasants. While the gathering was about to disperse, one of his advisors whispered some words in his ears. The old man became nervous and called on the peasants to wait until he uttered his last word. He then told them that one of the groups that had to be condemned had been left out and after he denounced the ELF, he told the crowd to disperse. When such denunciations were conducted, it was a usual practice to raise the left hand. The peasantry, however, used to raise the right hand. The peasantry of northern Ethiopia associates the left side with the devil and raising that hand is considered a bad omen.

Some Ethiopianists claim that the war of annihilation was declared after the assassination attempt on Mengistu.[7] The proponents of such claims would not have reached such a wrong conclusion had they observed when the war was declared and when the attempt on Mengistu was made. The decree regarding the war of annihilation, which was under preparation for some months, was made public on Ethiopian New Year, September 11, 1976, while the attempt on Mengistu was made on the 23rd of the same month. Others, including MEISON, state that the "Red Terror" campaign took place between November 1977 and May 1978.[8] During this period, MEISON had gone underground and apparently, such timing is intended to exonerate the MEISON of the atrocities of the "Red Terror".

The "Red Terror" was the climax of a process of violence unleashed following the declaration of the war of annihilation in September 1976.

Political Significance of the War of Annihilation

Strategically, for the Mengistu/POMOA alliance, the war of annihilation meant the elimination of any and all opposition and control of the mass organizations, including kebeles and discussion "clubs", control of the urban populace and finally, absolute control of power. In the immediate tactical sense, the war of annihilation was a design meant to side-track the internal restructuring and reorganization process of the Derge Discussing why it was declared at the time, *Democracia* argued that it was an indirect result of EPRP's popularity and the dwindling influence of the Mengistu/POMOA alliance. That condition had created concern and consternation.[9] Promulgation of the new policy regarding the war of annihilation was also perceived as a reaction to dissatisfaction and the gradual spread of opposition in the various parts of the army, the very social base of the regime.[10]

For more than two years, the political direction of the regime had remained unpredictable despite the various economic measures it had enacted. The declaration of the war of annihilation, however, unveiled the Derge's targets and how they were to be dealt with. The main enemies of the regime were the EPRP and those organizations mentioned in the declaration. *This event also signified a definite shift of policy and meant a declaration of war on those classes and sections of the population where the EPRP had an organizational foot-hold and political support.* These included workers, poor peasants, the lower stratum of government employees, the youth, teachers, etc., forces which had brought about and given leadership to the 1974 revolutionary movement, at least in the initial stage.[11] The war of annihilation became the culmination of the process that began in September 1974 when the military regime curbed democratic rights. It also meant that the peaceful form of struggle that began in the wake of the 1974 revolutionary movement had to give way to the armed struggle as the main form. Two years after the regime came to power, the intensity of the struggle, the polarization of and the resistance to the military regime increased. That condition indicated that the form of struggle was bound to change *and the declaration of the war of annihilation became the specific form through which the transition from the peaceful to the violent form of struggle took shape.*

Legal and Juridical Implications of the War of Annihilation

Since it came to power, the military regime had conducted a number of illegal and arbitrary actions. One of these was the execution of sixty former government officials and the head of state, General Aman Michael Andom, in December 1974. Furthermore, "[T]wo days before the November 1974 massacre, special criminal codes No. 8 and No. 10 were enacted. Opposing "Ethiopia Tikdem", undermining the authority of the Head of State, engaging in labor strikes, distributing pamphlets, etc.," were defined as new forms of crimes.[12] Since that period, the regime had committed a number of offenses against the populace, under the pretext of guarding the victories of the revolution. In these series of events, the declaration of the war of annihilation constituted the abrogation of any form of decent rule and paved the way for total arbitrariness. It undermined what was left of the judicial system when it allowed individuals to take measures against anyone they suspected. The whole country fell under the mercy of groups and individuals, such as the *Abyot Tebeka* members.

Until the declaration of the decree of the war of annihilation, the regime eliminated its enemies either in a very subtle way, or fabricated stories to justify its actions. The regime did not have the courage to publicly declare the execution of progressive activists for their role in the struggle. However, the Derge was able to do that after POMOA laid down the ideological and political justifications for its actions. As a result, in September 1976, it became a routine task of the regime to hunt down individuals who were opposed to its policies.

A major difficulty that the Mengistu/POMOA alliance faced was the fact that their targets were forces whose exact numerical strength or exact identity was unknown. This was due to the clandestine nature and activities of the organizations. For the Derge, the "enemy" was an elusive object that was difficult to target. As a result, certain categories of the society, particularly those sectors mentioned above, and any force that did not comply with the policies of the Mengistu/POMOA alliance had to be regarded with suspicion.

The War of Annihilation can be categorized into two periods. The first phase began in September 1976 and came to an end in February 1977 and the second began in early February 1977.

During the first phase, besides the main objective as mentioned above, the war of annihilation was also used as a ploy to side-track the struggle within the Derge itself. In February 1977, Mengistu came out triumphant and the struggle within the Derge was resolved in his favor. Consequently, during the second phase, the annihilation campaign became an end in itself.

War of Annihilation - Phase One

During the first phase of the war of annihilation, the Mengistu/POMOA alliance was in a defensive posture due to the struggle within the Derge. Even though Mengistu still controlled a certain part of the state apparatus, such as, the Derge security department and the contingents around the Derge office, power was slipping out of his hand. In this regard, one of the unruly yet very important institutions was the Ministry of Information, whose minister became an ally to the anti-Mengistu faction. Following the formation of POMOA, the ministry had been placed under its supervision. However, when the crisis within the Derge continued gathering momentum, the Mengistu/POMOA alliance became unable to dictate its policies and political lines to the ministry. That situation remained unaltered until Mengistu took over power in February 1977 and the minister, Tesfaye Tadesse, was arrested. He stayed in prison for quite some time.

The initial stage of the war of annihilation consisted of three component parts, political isolation, psychological warfare and physical annihilation. The most important and the final objective of the war was physical annihilation.

Political Isolation

One of the major goals of the war of annihilation was to isolate the target organizations and particularly the EPRP from the society and the leadership from the rank and file members. This process was initiated after the formation of POMOA and the media and other institutions were effectively used. As was indicated above, what was new during this period was that the EPRP was singled out as the main "culprit" and its name, which had remained a taboo, was made public. Through the media and the public gatherings, not only was the EPRP portrayed as an evil force causing misery to Ethiopia, but also one that should be done away with. The EPRP was portrayed as a force in league with "the landlord class in the Sidamo, Bale, Wello, Tigrai and Begemidir provinces."[13] It was portrayed as a mercenary group in league with external forces. It was argued, "on some major questions of the revolution, the disgruntled petty-bourgeois individuals grouped around the EPRP leadership had sided with feudal and imperialist forces."[14] The EPRP was also portrayed as the cause for the dismal economic condition of the country. It was portrayed as a destructive force, working hand and glove with what the regime labeled as secessionist groups. "The EPRP and the secessionist group that calls itself the Eritrean Liberation Front are two sides of the same coin ...all those reactionary and imperialist forces that provide support to the ELF, directly or indirectly had concluded a military, financial, and political pact with the EPRP."[15]

Some months earlier, POMOA had characterized the EPRP as an anarchist force and the Derge appropriated that designation beginning around September 1976. Labeling the EPRP as such had a purpose; it would discredit and portray the organization as an anti-socialist force that did not understand the stages of the revolutionary struggle.[16] It also meant that the EPRP did not and could not represent the working class and other classes that had an interest in Socialism. The EPRP was also accused of fourteen counts of "crimes," most of which were related to the struggle of the working class. The EPRP was accused of "12. declaring that there is no private property under socialism" and that it "had mobilized the lumpen-proletariat to confiscate even bars, small kiosks, barber shops, etc."[17] The purpose of such allegations was to create fear and suspicion among the affected sectors.

In September 1976, the Derge produced statements almost every other day. Most of the statements, which were the works of POMOA, had departed from the Derge's previous eclectic and demagogic characterizations. Instead, they appealed to the political and ideological demands and instincts of the day.

As part of the political isolation process, the EPRP was accused of economic "sabotage" in a Derge statement of September 17, 1976. The malfunctioning of state farms, the unreaped harvest and the breakdown of tractors in the Chebo and other Gurage areas were labeled as economic sabotage by the EPRP.

The EPRP was also accused of letting the zematch female students engage in prostitution in order to finance itself.[18] A *Democracia* issue sarcastically commented that the EPRP would not be surprised if the Mengistu/POMOA alliance made the EPRP responsible for the famine in Wello, Kelafo and Ogaden.[19]

Psychological Warfare

During the first phase of the war of annihilation, the 'nerve warfare' was limited to getting "confession" from alleged former EPRP members, who declared their change of fidelity. As of October 1976, the "confessions" were made public. The alleged EPRP members "confessed" that they had been following a wrong political line, either hoodwinked or misled by the EPRP leadership. It was disclosed that when they realized their mistakes, they had sided with the Derge.

The ultimate objective of such "confessions" was to initiate others so that they also followed suit and joined those groups that were working with the military regime. It was a tactic designed to cause massive desertion from the EPRP camp. The psychological warfare, which was crude in its presentations, had little impact during the first phase of the war of annihilation. However, during the second phase, it took a form of "mass confession" that had a very debilitating effect on the EPRP.

Physical Annihilation

The months following the declaration of the war of annihilation were one of the most trying periods for the EPRP. To be a member of the EPRP or to be suspected as one was a crime punishable by death. Anyone, anywhere and anytime could kill a person he thought of being an EPRP member. Almost all members and supporters of the EPRP had to carry that heavy burden on their shoulders. The most vulnerable were those who had been imprisoned earlier. Following the declaration of the war of annihilation, thousands more of EPRP members and supporters were thrown into prisons. Many more went underground. Thousands were executed. "In September alone, more than 120 youths were executed..., [in Addis Abeba] among them were fourteen and fifteen-year-old kids."[20] Most of the activists were arrested between July and September, a very sizeable number of them between September 19-24, 1976. Only a fraction of the number arrested and executed was made public.

Protest demonstrations made in opposition to the declaration of the war of annihilation were the pretexts for the massive arrests. The alleged crimes of some of the youth were the paintings of slogans found on walls (graffiti works). Many of them were picked up from their residences by kebele officials. The repression in the Kebena and the Afencho Ber areas of Addis Abeba proved to be the most disastrous. In one of these incidents, one family lost all of its children and all of them were EPRP affiliated.[21] *Democracia* stated that it would retaliate for the death of its members and expressed its condolences to the parents.

In October 1976, the Derge made public announcements about the execution of more EPRP members.[22] On November 3, the Derge announced that it had executed 23 "anarchists". On November 18, another 27 people were executed. Executed during this period were members of the Addis Abeba Interzone, who had been arrested at the beginning of September 1976. Yosef Adane, an EPRP CC member, arrested in August 1976, was also executed. Both the IZ and the CC members were tortured beyond human imagination and disfigured beyond recognition. Their eyes were pulled out, and they were forced to feed on their own flesh. Other EPRP members executed were members of the EPRA, who were taken prisoners of war in Wello a few months earlier. The commissar Woubishet Retta and Zerea Beruk, and other activists like Mulugeta Siltan and Yetbarek Hiskias, former activists in the USA, were also executed.

The repression and execution took place in various parts of the country.

In Gonder, on December 7, 1976, more than fifty youth, workers and others were executed at public gatherings called by the local state power. The intention of the officials for gathering the people was to condemn the EDU, which was making efforts to control some parts of the Begemidir province. However, the event turned into an anti-Derge platform and the POMOA branch representative asked the Administrator, Colonel Emiru Wonde, to open fire on the participants. Colonel Emiru refused to do so and made a speech chastising the regime. Bypassing the Administrator, the POMOA branch representative, in collaboration with Captain Melaku Teferra, the Derge representative of the area, made a decision to open fire on the peaceful protesters, killing many of them. In the history of Gonder, December 7, the bloody Sunday, is remembered as the day when the people turned their face away from the regime.

In Dire Dawa, a demonstration was held to demand the promulgation of democratic rights and the release of prisoners arrested since May 1976. Hundreds of people were rounded up and were thrown into prison. As a result, the EPRP structure in Dire Dawa underwent a severe crisis.[23] When the families of those who were arrested demanded that their sons and daughters be released, the Derge transferred them to Harer. Sixty-six activists suspected of EPRP connections were to be arrested in the Harer city; however, the local party structure obtained the information and was able to save some of them. Among those arrested during this period were members of the EPRP leadership in Harer. Alemayehu Ayalew and Kifle Alemu were later executed. Alemayehu, the father of two children, was a graduate of the Haile Selassie Ist University and a high-school teacher. Other EPRP members who were arrested during this period and executed sometime later were Simet Birru, Getachew Indayelalu, Mulu Deneke, Negash Mussa, Solomon Haile, Mekedem Haile, Afeworque, Tezerra, Degu Haile Selassie and others.[24]

EPRP's Reaction -August 1976 CC Meeting

The declaration of the War of Annihilation brought forth a major change in how the EPRP viewed the struggle. EPRP's reaction fell into two categories. The first was related to a major shift of policy regarding the form of struggle, while the second was related to the immediate response to the declaration of the war of annihilation.

Right after the August Plenum,[25] the PB held meetings and discussed the deteriorating political condition in the country. It reached a conclusion and about two weeks later, that is, at the end of August 1976, it presented proposals to a CC meeting. In its analysis of the deteriorating political situation, the PB singled out the Mengistu/POMOA alliance as the cause and perpetrator of the violence and as the force that was behind the preparation for the massive repression. From the reports acquired from the EPRP party committee by the Derge, the PB had learned that the Mengistu/POMOA alliance was threatening and cajoling the Derge to implement that policy, despite the

The War of Annihilation 137

fact that there was less enthusiasm among the rank and file Derge members.[26]

Those who were spearheading the struggle within the Derge, such as Captain Moges, believed that the new policy advocated by the Mengistu/POMOA alliance was designed to side-track the restructuring of the Derge. The leaders of the movement within the Derge were blackmailed so much that they were in no position to raise any objection to Mengistu's moves. However, Captain Moges Wolde Mikael believed that the new policy of the war of annihilation would be watered down when the Derge's structural changes were put in effect and Mengistu's power was curtailed.

Sometime before the proposal to declare the war of annihilation was presented to the Derge, Captain Moges had seriously suggested that the EPRP get rid of Mengistu. He informed the organization that Mengistu was making preparations to move out of the Fourth Division headquarters to the compound of the Derge's office, the former Palace. Moges believed that the relocation would make Mengistu's movements very difficult to track. Giving weight to that report and the recommendations of the EPRP party committee by the Derge, the PB concluded that those elements that were advocating and jostling the Derge to unleash the war of annihilation should not be given the chance to do so. History, usually governed by social, political and economic laws, can also be affected by the role that individuals play. In the Ethiopian case, Mengistu's role was considered detrimental to the struggle at large and to the EPRP in particular. Leading EPRP members considered it imperative to eliminate him.

The PB also concluded that the EPRP had to take measures against the other perpetrators of the policy of the war of annihilation. It was conjectured that if they were removed from the political scene, the EPRP would get respite and temporary relief and the colossal danger hovering over thousands of EPRP members and the rest of the progressive sectors of the society would ease at least for a while. The PB called its approach as an offensive-defense. According to that approach, the EPRP should be able to engage itself in an active defense, in contrast to a passive defense.

Following the presentation of the PB's proposal, at the August CC meeting, Berhane Meskel and Getachew Maru expressed their opposition right away. Getachew, as a member of the PB had agreed on the proposal, but at the CC meeting he denied ever doing so. The rest of the PB members were very surprised, but thinking that it might have been a misunderstanding, did not dwell on it.

An intense discussion was conducted on the PB's proposal and the main opponent, Berhane Meskel, argued that to eliminate Mengistu, the head of a state, would be tantamount to putschism. He also argued that both Mengistu and the leading policy makers of the war of annihilation were making political decisions, and hence, deciding to eliminate them would be wrong and a terrorist action. Other CC members argued that the Mengistu/POMOA alliance wanted to open a war of annihilation on almost all progressive sectors of the society despite the resistance and reluctance of other Derge members.

Mengistu and his clique were trying to redirect the whole course of the struggle into a quagmire. Removing them from the decision making process would be an important step for the struggle and the EPRP.

While the debate was underway, Getachew Maru brought forth a piece of information which indicated Mengistu's willingness to negotiate with the EPRP. Asked where he obtained his information, he replied that it was provided by his brother, who was a Derge member. For a period of several months, Captain Moges Wolde Mikael and the EPRP party committee responsible for activities around the Derge had been the main sources of information for the EPRP and Getachew's source of information had not been known to the EPRP leadership until this moment.

After the new revelation, the EPRP CC was confronted with two contradictory pieces of information, further polarizing the discussion. Some of the CC members, particularly members of the PB, thought that the injection of the information was a deliberate move intended to side-track the CC. However, a good number of the CC members wanted to probe the authenticity of the new piece of information.

The CC meeting further discussed the PB's proposal and cast a vote. The proposal to eliminate Mengistu, leading figures who had originated and drafted the decree of the war of annihilation, and those who had provided the names of suspects to be executed, carried through by a slight majority.

Casting votes was a rare occasion in the proceedings of the EPRP CC. The actual practice was to discuss and hammer out issues until a consensus was reached. Even when there were sharp differences, as during the discussion of the call made by the Derge for the formation of a front, in April 1976, some kind of a compromise would be devised rather than voting on the issue. The cleavage amongst the EPRP CC members at the August 1976 CC meeting was an unfamiliar phenomenon. It was a depressing event for many of the CC members, save Berhane Meskel, who believed that he had rallied some supporters.

After the vote was cast, the winning side of the CC group, reasoning that such an important issue could not be decided by a simple majority vote, withdrew its votes. It also suggested that the issue should remain open and be discussed at another CC meeting. By so doing, the winning CC group created conditions so that the other CC members obtain an opportunity to clarify their doubts regarding the piece of information that Getachew provided, that is, to scrutinize their merits and demerits. A good number of the CC members still remained very skeptical about the information Getachew provided and after deliberating on the issue for quite a while, it was decided to verify its authenticity. In order to do so, two or three CC members were assigned to meet Getachew's brother first and then Mengistu. However, before they arranged a meeting with Mengistu, they were instructed to inform the CC about their findings.

In the midst of this confusion, the Mengistu/POMOA alliance declared the war of annihilation. As a result, the CC members assigned to meet

Mengistu could not even get in touch with Getachew's brother. Until today, the whole incident and arrangement remains shrouded in mystery. The most disheartening incident, however, was the arrest of one of the CC members, E., who was entrusted to get in touch with Mengistu. Before the controversial piece of information was revealed, the PB had decided that all members of the leadership, including E., should go underground.

While probing and verifying the new piece of information mentioned above, the CC had also decided to continue the reorganization of the urban armed units. The preparation included training and arming of the units.

The September 1976 EPRP CC Meeting

Right after the Derge declared the war of annihilation, the PB met and discussed the unfolding political developments. After reaching a consensus, the PB presented its proposals to a CC meeting held in September 1976. Through a majority vote, the CC meeting recognized that the peaceful form of struggle had given way to the armed struggle as the main form and decided to come out publicly and explain the changed conditions. A *Democracia* issue of the second week of September 1976 stated,

> [U]nderstanding the nature and the last ditch efforts that the fascists will make and understanding that in the final analysis the decisive role would be played by a force supported by the people, it has been quite a while since the EPRA was formed and engaged in an armed struggle. In order to counter the anti-EPRP campaign, the organization will pay more attention to this wing....[27]

Recognizing the primacy of the armed struggle had meant paying more attention to the EPRA, "the main form of organization, that can be used for the protracted and decisive struggle" and other preparations related to it.[28]

The other major point discussed at this CC meeting was the tactic to be employed to counter the Mengistu/POMOA offensive. The issue, first raised at the August CC meeting, remained the main topic. It was related to the adoption of an offensive-defense measure against those elements behind the decree of the war of annihilation.

The CC spelled out that it would take measures against leading figures who had perpetrated, drafted, and coerced the Derge into the implementation of the war of annihilation. Neither the Derge, as an institution, and its members in general, nor the political organizations and their general membership would be targets of the EPRP. The CC made it clear that it did not intend to engage in the offensive-defense struggle against the Derge and the MEISON or the Sennay Likke group in general, but would retaliate against those who perpetrated and were behind the war of annihilation. The CC believed that these individuals, many of whom were not Derge members, were the ones pushing the military regime into the political abyss. They were the ones who had accelerated the tempo of violence and forced the state apparatus into conflict with a significant section of the population.

The gist of the decision adopted by the CC, with some additional clarifications was printed in an October *Democracia* issue:

> We are not interested in taking measures against anyone who has differing or even opposed view from us....We will take measures against those individuals whose duty is to compile and forward the list of names of progressives for execution. Those individuals who sniff around and expose progressives, those who, for their own personnel ends go beyond the call of duty and present names of suspected EPRP members for the inhuman measures of the fascists....[29]

The CC's decision was not new. As early as August 1975, the EPRP Conference had decided that it would pass judgement on those who perpetrate violence on the people.[30]

Besides the above enumerated measures, it was decided that the defense activities of the EPRP would still include procuring arms and money. Government institutions remained the main targets. If any targets other than government institutions had to be considered, these would be reviewed by the Military Commission and the measures to be taken had to be decided on the specific merits of the institutions.[31]

The majority of the CC members approved the proposal presented by the PB except Berhane Meskel and Getachew Maru. With a wide margin of votes, the CC gave the permission to go ahead and take the measure against Mengistu and those individuals who were behind the war of annihilation. Berhane Meskel, who still opposed the decision, argued that to kill or eliminate a head of state like Mengistu was tantamount to putschism.

Furthermore, the CC reiterated the mandate that the Second Plenum had already given the PB. In the event of a crisis - that is, if the CC could not meet - the PB was mandated to make necessary political and organizational decisions in the name of the EPRP.

At this September CC meeting, Getachew, a member of the PB, caused consternation when he denied that he had supported the decision presented by the PB. Before the meeting, the PB believed that it had reached a consensus on the proposal to be presented, but the scene at the August 1976 CC meeting was repeated. Many of the CC members were baffled and they recommended that the PB sort out its problems before it came to a CC meeting. The discussions of the PB meeting had been recorded and it was proven that Getachew's statements conflicted with the record.

Addis Abeba Interzone Jeopardized

A week or so after the declaration of the war of annihilation, the entire membership of the second Addis Abeba IZ fell in the hands of the regime. The first Addis Abeba IZ functioned from around July 1974 until September 1975. It was replaced when most of its members were either given other assignments, or became victims of the repression. The second Addis Abeba IZ, which was formed around October 1975, fell in danger in September 1976. The third IZ was formed around the end of September, or the beginning of October 1976 (see Details below). The fourth IZ was formed around July or August 1977 and the fifth IZ was formed in January/February 1978.

The second IZ, composed of a relatively younger group of activists, came into existence when the EPRP was fast growing and expanding. It was a period when the various EPRP structures were engaged in the most intense organizational and political activities. With the entire organization, and the IZ in particular, preoccupied with day to day activities, the youthfulness of the members of the IZ was of some value. The IZ handled enormous activities that were unfolding with every passing day. Even though it was under an unbelievable pressure, the IZ followed up the production of the various publications. The IZ members, who were young and energetic, had to be tempered in the course of the struggle.

In September 1976, a number of problems began cropping up in the IZ and the first one was related to one of its members, Abiyu Airsamo. At a discussion held at the IZ meeting, he stood opposed to the decisions of the 1976 September CC meeting and raised objections to the measures to be taken against Mengistu and leading POMOA members.

Raising a differing point of view in itself did not cause the problem; two members of the CC had also expressed objection to that decision. The problem arose when Abiyu refused to implement the decisions of both the CC and the IZ. As part of the offensive-defense tactic of the EPRP, the CC had passed instructions to distribute arms. In line with this, the Addis Abeba IZ passed arms to the zonal committees under its jurisdiction. Abiyu Airsamo, who was the Secretary of the zone in the Akaki area, zone-five, failed to hand over the arms. Abiyu did not disclose his acts to the IZ until the Youth League structure of zone-five reported that no arms had reached them.

The Addis Abeba IZ, furious about the breach of discipline, demanded that Abiyu return the arms, and in the mean time, suspended him from its committee. The IZ passed its decision to the PB. According to the internal regulations of the EPRP, a committee could suspend a member but only a higher body had the prerogative of *removing* him from that committee.[32] Abiyu never returned the arms; a few months later, the arms were sent to the military group of the clandestine faction within the EPRP (more on this elsewhere). In the brief history of the EPRP, this breach of discipline was the first of its kind.

While Abiyu's case remained unresolved, the entire IZ committee fell victim in September 1976. The IZ had held a meeting in the Kolfe area, in Addis Abeba and one of its vehicles was parked not far from the meeting place. After the meeting was over and the members were about to disperse, a corporal dressed in civilian clothing blocked the road so that the vehicle could not move away.

Believing that it was a routine matter, the IZ members began negotiating for passage. However, the individual did what he could to delay the departure of both the vehicle and the members. It was not known what really motivated the corporal. However, it was conjectured that when he saw some strangers leaving their vehicle and heading for a house, he had become suspicious. Because he did not see which house they entered, he had decided to report the matter and block the vehicle until a government force could arrive. A good hour or so was wasted negotiating with him, and before they knew what was happening, the IZ members were surrounded and arrested with important party documents, the minutes of their meeting, and some arms.

The IZ members, being armed, could have forced their way out, but failed to do so, probably due to lack of psychological preparedness. Among the IZ members who fell victim was the virtually unknown yet a very dedicated member, Teka Amare. He was the representative of zone-3 committee. He was a veteran activist of the student movement, a long time party member and founding member of the zone. Elias W/Mariam was also arrested during this time.

The IZ members were then taken to the fourth police station, and later transferred to the Central Investigation Department (CID). Despite the gruesome interrogation process, the IZ members refused to budge and collaborate with the regime. Some of them passed away during the torture process. The torture was so severe that IZ member and veteran activist, Berhanu Ijjigu, gave in and agreed to lead security personnel to his residence, which was also the headquarters of the propaganda department of the EPRP CC. Some CC members either paid occasional visits or passed a night there.

On the day security personnel came to Berhanu Ijjigu's residence, the other residents of the house were in a process of evacuation; some had been relocated, but others remained behind. Derge officers surrounded and entered the house, leaving some of their officers in the vehicle and by the entrance. They encountered Kiflu Teferra, who had gone to the house that morning, Mezgebnesh Abiyu (Berhanu's wife), Yohannes Berhane and Melaku Marcos. The officers handcuffed all, except Mezgebnesh, whom they did not consider a threat. They then began searching the house.

One of the officers was overwhelmed when he found some cash in one of the rooms and kept himself busy stashing away the fortune that had fallen into his hands. Kiflu Teferra, whose hands were tied to his back, grasped the gun that was hidden just above his behind and, turning his face around, opened fire and hit the guard by the gate. Mezgebnesh untied his hands and Kiflu grabbed an automatic rifle lying close by. Unaware of what had taken place, the other officer, along with Berhanu Ijjigu came to the scene. The officer was gunned down. The last to come to the scene and to be hit was the officer who had been stashing money in his socks. After they untied each other, all of the EPRP members, including the IZ member Berhanu Ijjigu, managed to escape.

The arrest of the IZ members took place when coordinating the activities of the various structures of the Addis Abeba area was considered essential to withstand the forthcoming crisis. Besides, the IZ members had invaluable information, including the locations where cash and arms were hidden. They controlled EPRP's bank accounts and were the contact persons of valuable EPRP members placed in special government posts. They also were the guardians of IZ documents. These and other information were not known either to the EPRP CC or members of the zonal committees. However, through prior arrangements and the assistance of Berhanu Ijjigu, it was possible to retrieve some of the information.

Until the formation of a new IZ, some CC members had to take over some of the tasks of the IZ and they had to be involved in its day to day activities. Such an arrangement definitely had a toll. The CC members, particularly Tesfaye Debessai, had to expose themselves to more danger when staying away from it was the prudent choice.

The third IZ, which came into being at the end of September or the beginning of October 1976 was formed according to the new EPRP constitution which stipulated that IZ members had to be elected by the zones that constituted them. Accordingly, the zone committees elected and sent their representatives to join the IZ. Using its constitutional prerogative and to facilitate the political activities of the committee, the EPRP CC assigned Germatchew Lemma as an additional IZ member. Germatchew Lemma was a law student at the Haile Selassie Ist University and a former president of the University student union.

To explain EPRP's policies and as part of the new structural arrangement, Zeru Kehishen was assigned to take part in policy making IZ meetings. In order to alleviate the problems that the new IZ was facing, Tesfaye Debessai, who was the formal CC contact man, allotted a good part of his time, both to explain policies and discuss organizational activities.

The IZ formed its first Secretariat and elected Germatchew as its chairperson. In a brief while, the IZ was able to handle most of the activities, which included production and distribution of the various publications, giving leadership to the structure under its jurisdiction, handling of the different mass organizations, etc. Besides the enormous tasks it shouldered, the IZ was also entrusted to handle the newly formed military structure of the organization.

Members of the IZ were: Berhanu from zone-two, Berhanu Ijjigu, Berhane from zone-one, "Jarso", from zone-four, "Asfaw", from zone-three and Germatchew. Because of the unresolved case of Abiyu Airsamo, zone five remained unrepresented for some time. Abiyu, who was suspended from the IZ, but remained a member of zone five committee, still refused to collaborate in transferring the members of zone-five and the property of the zone.

Resisting the War of Annihilation

One of the first measures that the EPRP enacted to withstand the impending crisis was to hold committee meetings less frequently. Furthermore, two approaches were devised to combat the crisis. The first was the offensive-defense tactic discussed above, while the second entailed drawing the populace into the struggle so that the EPRP would not be singled out, isolated and victimized. That lesson was drawn from the massive repression conducted in Jimma and Harer. Some months earlier, *Democracia* had noted the Derge's new tactic and commented, "the new strategy of the *selected officers* and the banda intellectuals is to hit the periphery of the rank of the progressives first and deal a mortal blow at the center in the end."[33]

Members of the CC went to the various sections of the EPRP, including the YL and the ELAMA structures, to discuss the Ethiopian situation and the policy changes. During these discussions, members of the leadership demanded that the party and Youth League structures come up with ideas to combat the repression. In response to the call, the youth and party committees decided to organize mini-demonstrations at the level of kebeles and conduct "practical work", that is, wall paintings, etc. The ELAMA decided to call a strike.

A member of the "Oppressed Soldiers Organization" who was assigned as one of the guards at the Radio Station in Addis Abeba, reported that he could make it possible for the EPRP to read messages or its program on Radio Ethiopia. The PB was not opposed to the idea as such, but declined to use the opportunity, for fear that it would be misunderstood as a sign that the EPRP was taking power.

Workers Resistance

The working class was one of the sectors directly affected by the declaration of the war of annihilation. Thousands of its activists became the prime targets of the ongoing repression. The Mengistu/POMOA alliance, facing stiff resistance in forming government controlled Industrial Unions, had a direct interest in pacifying that struggle. As was indicated earlier, one of the main reasons for the promulgation of the war of annihilation was the cleansing of the working class of "anarchists" or undesirable elements. [34]

Of the first batch of forty-seven activists to be publicly executed following the declaration of the war of annihilation, over half were workers. Among them were CELU leaders, such as, the Chairperson, Marcos Hagos, the Secretary, Tessema Deressa, other members of the CELU leadership and staff members, Getachew Amare, Ali Hussien, Tsegaye Alemayehu, Yilma Tiruneh, Alemayehu Tilahun, etc. The EPRP found the list and advised many of them to go underground. The regime arrested labor leaders from "the Pepsi, Coca-Cola and Garment factories, from the banks, the Ethiopian Airlines, Mosvold, Addis Tyres, etc."[35]

As a result of the witch hunt, almost all of the active CELU employees had to go underground, leaving that institution with some secretaries and other nonessential employees. Within a few days, hundreds of labor activists were imprisoned. The underground labor organization realized the level of the crisis and called for an ELAMA Congress.

The Third ELAMA Congress

When the third ELAMA Congress was called, CELU was nonfunctional and the labor movement had no legal leadership. As a result, the responsibility for resisting the repression fell squarely on the shoulders of ELAMA.

The Third ELAMA Congress was conducted in mid-September 1976, in the Addis Ketema area at a place known as Sebategna. It was held in a private school, courtesy of ELAMA members who also were kebele officials. In spite of the relatively secured condition, the Congress had to be guarded by defense squads. The Congress was held for half a day and it was attended by 17-19 representatives of the ELAMA structures of Addis Abeba and the Harer areas. Representation was according to the size of the zonal committees, except for some unions that were invited because of their strategic importance for the strike to be called. These included the Ethiopian Airlines and the Anbessa transport union.

After electing the chairperson, the Congress began hearing reports on the outcomes of the decisions made by the Addis Abeba ELAMA IZ in July 1976. In response to the demand of some members, particularly the branch in Harer, who wanted to call a strike as early as July, the Addis Abeba ELAMA IZ had opted for other alternatives. As a preparatory step for the strike, the ELAMA IZ had decided that workers should conduct production slow down and sign petitions to be sent to the regime.[36]

At the third ELAMA Congress, it was reported that hundreds of members of the labor unions had sent in their petitions to the regime. The theme common to almost all of the petitions was the issue of an independent labor union. After assessing the condition among the working class and the impending political crisis, the Congress realized that the labor struggle had already lost many of its leaders. If the situation continued unabated, many more would be arrested and there would be no one to either lead the struggle or call and coordinate the strike. Even though it realized the difficult conditions ahead, the Congress decided that it had no alternative but to call a strike. The Mengistu/POMOA alliance had left labor a choice of either struggling and, if possible, achieving some gains, or sitting idly and waiting for a silent death.

To reach an agreement on the strike was not difficult, but when to call it was a controversial issue. A number of possible dates were suggested, but in the absence of a better alternative, it was agreed to call the strike on September 22, the beginning of the third week of the month.[37]

After it learned about the decisions of the ELAMA Congress, the EPRP PB inquired about the readiness of the workers to go out on a strike. The report presented at the ELAMA Congress was made available to the PB which passed on the information to the party and Youth League structures instructing them to coordinate their activities with that of the labor movement.

The strike took place as scheduled; however, because of the massive repression and lack of competent leadership at the level of factories, as well as a number of other problems, it was sustained only for three or four days. In some cases, unions went back to work on the afternoon the strike was called. Until this time, all of the strikes were called by CELU, save that of September 1976 which was called by an underground labor organization. Whether ELAMA was accepted as an alternative to CELU remained an issue of concern.

The excessive politicization of the paper announcing the strike, that is, raising the question of the popular slogan, the Provisional People's Government (PPG), was harmful, as was also the exaggerated agitation conducted prior to the strike, and the failure of the attempt on the life of Mengistu.[38]

When it was known that the strike, the sabotage activities, and the attempt on Mengistu's life failed, citing phrases from some of the publications that discussed the gradual spreading of the crisis and the possibility of a popular uprising, Berhane Meskel began accusing the PB of trying to call some kind of an insurrection.

As was indicated above, the September labor strike was called by the ELAMA Congress which had no knowledge of the attempt on Mengistu's life. The date of the strike was selected after debating on a number of alternatives. ELAMA being an autonomous institution which had its own constitution and a set of regulations, the PB had no say in calling a strike or choosing the date of the strike, which was forced on the ELAMA itself. However, after the PB learned the decision of ELAMA, it had indeed instructed the youth to coordinate its activities with those of labor. Peaceful mini-demonstrations, organized by the YL took place in many of the kebeles. Furthermore, the attempt on Mengistu's life had no relationship whatsoever to either the strike or the demonstrations conducted by the youth The final attempt on Mengistu's life took place after six or seven aborted trials. The first unsuccessful attempt took place immediately after the declaration of the war of annihilation. Besides, in September 1976, it seemed that the reform movement within the Derge was gathering momentum, the Mengistu/POMOA alliance was losing the battle and leading EPRP activists were awaiting the results of the struggle within the Derge.

Failure notwithstanding, the direct participation of a certain section of the working class on the side of the opposition, particularly the EPRP, signified a major departure in the class composition of the struggle, which in the initial period had remained confined to the revolutionary intelligentsia and the youth. The involvement of the workers in the struggle was deemed so important that a *Democracia* issue of December 1976 categorically asserted that the EPRP was a proletarian party.[39]

The short-lived strike could not stop the massive repression against labor unions. The labor movement, which had resisted the military regime for more than three years and had remained resilient, fell into jeopardy and the event marked the beginning of the end of an independent labor movement in

Ethiopia. Even though severely repressed, labor had overcome the challenges it faced and had catapulted itself onto the political scene at least twice. Besides the massive repression of worker activists, the formation of the state controlled union, known as the All Ethiopian Workers Trade Union (AEWTU), in December 1976, constituted the *coup de grace* for the independent existence of the Ethiopian labor movement. The AEWTU was formed when many of the labor activists had either gone underground or were locked up in prisons.

All Ethiopian Workers Trade Union (AEWTU)

As was indicated in Chapter II, when POMOA failed to have its people elected to the leadership posts of the various unions, the meetings of some of the Industrial Unions were postponed for an indefinite period. The disrupted meetings, however, were initiated after the declaration of the war of annihilation and POMOA conducted seminars for two of them. Leading MEISON members, Negede Gobeze and Andargatchew Aseged among them, led the proceedings.

The first to hold its meeting was the Manufacturing Industrial Trade Union (MITU) which held its third meeting on October 2, 1976. As was discussed in Chapter II, MITU had two abortive meetings prior to this one. They were postponed when POMOA realized that its followers would not be elected to leadership posts. The October meeting of the MITU was held for six days and the main issue on the agenda remained the election of new leaders. According to the criteria set forth by POMOA, to qualify for the election, both for the nominating and the leadership committees, the candidate should have: taken part in the rally that was organized to oppose the attempt on the life of Mengistu,[40] participated in the celebration organized to commemorate September 12, the Derge's anniversary; and not taken part in the September 1976 labor strike. These criteria effectively barred the unions that did not support the regime.

The meeting of the Transports Industrial Union was held after the participants attended the seminar organized by POMOA. The Union proceeded to elect its own chairperson, but POMOA's representatives declared their intention to conduct the meeting. When POMOA's incursion was objected to by the participants, the representatives disclosed the above-mentioned criteria and disqualified almost all of the activists from taking part in the election for the nomination committee. After a heated debate, a compromise was reached in which the chairperson and the members of the nomination committee would be elected from the unions outside of Addis Abeba. Apparently, this was a deliberate move by POMOA intended to avoid the unions in the Addis Abeba area, which it felt were influenced by "anarchists".

The meeting proceeded with its deliberations and the nomination committee presented two nominees for each of the leadership slots. One of the nominees was supported by the opposition while the other one had POMOA's backing. Supporters of POMOA objected to the procedure, on the grounds that it would benefit the "anarchists".

The meeting was stalled and following a brief commotion, the nominating committee was forced to step down, and in its place, nominees from six of the unions that POMOA controlled began acting as the nominating committee. Resenting POMOA's forceful incursion, the participants of the meeting refused to take part in the election process. At this point, armed officers entered the meeting hall and forced the workers to conduct the election.[41]

The same pattern was repeated in those Industrial Unions where the election process was postponed until the declaration of the war of annihilation. By that time, many of the active leaders of the workers movement had been arrested or had gone underground. This was true of some of the elected officials of the Service Industries. All of the members of the Wholesale and Retail Industrial Union executive committee members were arrested. [42]

Following the preparatory steps mentioned above, that is, forming the various Industrial Unions, POMOA moved to the next stage of the formation of the National Union. POMOA, which had an inexhaustible source of ingenuity, held the meeting at Ambo, about 125 kms west of the capital city, Addis Abeba. The purpose of such an arrangement was to keep the participants of the meeting away from any external influence while the meeting was in session and to exert maximum influence on the outcome of the meeting.

In the election, POMOA emerged victorious, with Tewedros Bekele and Temesgen Madebo elected president and vice-president of the National Union. Tewedros was one of the individuals who had collaborated with the former vice-president of CELU, who in 1975 had been the target of the labor movement.[43] The meeting also ratified the new constitution of the National Union. The inauguration ceremony, which was held on January 10, 1977, was attended by Colonel Mengistu Haile Mariam.

Despite these and other measures that POMOA/MEISON undertook, the resistance to the newly formed National Union remained strong for quite some time. Besides the demand for an independent union, workers resisted the decisions to raise membership fees, recruitment of workers for the war front [44] and cancellation of payment for overtime work.

In the ensuing months, ELAMA continued to loose contacts and influence among the working class. The Derge made all efforts to keep the workers' movement under control. Among the steps it undertook was to provide AEWTU an annual budget of 600,000 Ethiopian birr.[45] The German Democratic Republic and the Soviet Union provided some assistance too. The only source of income of the independent CELU that existed from May to September 1976 was its membership contribution.

EPRP's Urban Defense Wing (UDW)

To resist the war of annihilation, the EPRP leadership regrouped and restructured its urban armed wing. Furthermore, as was indicated elsewhere, training and arming of the urban armed units was stepped up when the news about Mengistu's final move to declare the war of annihilation was ascertained. The urban armed units, which were formed as early as 1974, [46] remained ineffective for more than two years. Until mid-1976, the units were engaged in training themselves and conducting studies of future targets. However, following the massacre of activists in Jimma, as was indicated in Chapter II and III, the units were assigned to take action on Major Getachew Shibeshi and Demeke Harege Weyene, who were responsible for the massacre.

Around July 1976, when it became evident that the military regime was about to declare war on the EPRP, a number of decisions were made defining the tasks and the role of the urban armed wing in the overall ensemble of the Party structure. One of these decisions included the adoption of the offensive-defense tactic. As a result of this policy which implied a major policy reorientation, the urban military activities of the EPRP became one of the major preoccupation of the organization for a year or so. *Democracia* outlined that policy when it stated,

> ...In order to defend ourselves and resist the counter-revolutionary repression, and to give a lesson to those who still think that they can live in peace after arresting and executing people, to arouse and show the people that it is possible and probable to struggle till victory, we have formed the urban defense squads.[47]

The UDW was entrusted with some major activities that were considered extremely vital for the very survival of the EPRP which during this period was under difficult conditions. Even though some of the tasks had been outlined since the inception of the urban defense wing way back in 1974, because of the dramatic transformation of the political condition in the country from a peaceful to a violent one, the UDW began assuming a ubiquitous role. Furthermore, political conditions had deteriorated to such an extent that it was perceived that they could be improved only through armed means. Therefore, obtaining arms was deemed not only important, but it was also considered as one of the essential requirements for EPRP's survival.

All throughout its few years of existence, the EPRP was unable to get any substantial military assistance. It was believed that the EPRP had enough manpower to form many military contingents, however, it was unable to do so primarily because of lack of arms. The EPRP lacked the necessary armaments even for the rural struggle. It was also reasoned that urban armed activity was an important component for the continuation of the struggle even in the rural areas. [48] When the peaceful form of struggle gave way to the armed one in the last quarter of 1976, the entire weaponry that the EPRA had did not exceed one hundred automatic rifles.[49]

The effort to get arms from the Eritrean organizations failed due to the political strings attached to the assistance. The EPLF wanted the EPRP to recognize its assertion that Eritrea was an Ethiopian colony.[50] East European countries had begun warming up relationships with the Derge and were not willing to collaborate with the EPRP. As a result, the EPRP had to be self-reliant both in its military and political activities. Obtaining arms remained one of the major tasks of the UDW.

The second major task of the UDW was obtaining funds. Gone were the days when the EPRP could conduct its activities by membership contributions alone. Many of its members had already gone underground. The money obtained through other means was not sufficient to run the ever growing activities of the EPRP. Besides major organizational and political activities, the EPRP had to support financially thousands of its professional members. The third and major task of the UDW was to defend the EPRP, that is, its members and property.

Creating distability was part of the offensive-defense tactic. *Democracia* earlier on had stated, "...we will also foil their [the Derge] effort to stabilize in the urban areas,"[51] hence the establishment of the UDW.

In its brief existence of three years, the UDW had undergone three major structural changes. It had also assumed broader responsibilities.

Stage one of the activities of the UDW encompassed the period from its inception in 1974 until mid-1976. During the first period, the Wing had no relationship with the urban party structure. With only a single CC contact, it came directly under the EPRP CC. The Wing had a shadowy existence even to the general membership of the EPRP. During this period, the Wing's major military activities were safeguarding committee meetings and production units, training of members, conducting studies on certain government military facilities, etc. One of the main reasons why the EPRP defense wing kept a low profile during the initial stage was due to the nature of the ongoing peaceful form of struggle which the EPRP CC had decided to follow through. During this period, the structure of the urban defense establishment included the operational committee, that is, the leadership and its four committees organized on a zonal basis.

Stage two of the activities of the UDW began around June 1976 when the peaceful form of struggle was almost consummated and the military regime was on the verge of declaring the war of annihilation. Urban Armed Wing was the official name adopted and commensurate with the new situation, the Wing underwent certain changes. As indicated above, during the first stage, only one EPRP CC member was assigned to oversee the activities of the Wing. However, during the second period, a definite urban military hierarchy was formed. It included the Military Commission at the top, where Yosef Adane, Tesfaye Debessai and R. took part. Next in the hierarchy came the Rural and Urban Armed Wing leadership committee. Among the members of this committee were, Germatchew Lemma, Berhane Iyasu, MT, Lieutenant Merid and Captain Amha Abebe. The UDW committee was deemed so important that two CC members of the EPRP military commission were assigned to take part in its proceedings. One of them, Tesfaye Debessai, attended meetings when the situation demanded, while R. was a permanent member of the wing. Under the Urban Armed Wing (UAW) came the Operations Committee (OC) which was composed of the commanders of each unit. The lowest echelons of the UDW were the units themselves. The Operations Committee, which was composed of qualified and professional military activists, was the responsible body to follow up military actions.

The number of units under the UAW was few in the initial stage, however, as time went by, their number increased and their tasks expanded. The Operation Committee had its own center at the former EPRP CC headquarters, which still remained under Engineer Osman Mohammed's name, (see details Chapter II). The Operations Committee was also in charge of the arms under its control.

The task of the UAW committee was to implement and follow up EPRP CC decisions related to urban military activities. These included providing military leadership to the urban wing, conducting training and study sessions, leading operations, giving guidance to the various units under the UAW and looking after the well being of the members of the units.

During the second stage of the reorganization process, an important psychological preparation, aiming at militancy, was conducted among the members of the defense units. The psychological preparation included defending oneself. Besides, as of September 1976, many of the leading and underground EPRP members began carrying arms and that process became part of the psyche for an underground existence, at least in the urban centers. Because the EPRP was in no position to provide protection to its individual members, including CC members, arms, mostly revolvers, were provided depending on availability.

By June 1976, the UAW consisted of 25-30 members consisting of few units. Each unit was composed of the commander, the commissar and three or four members. Depending on the target, one or more units would be assigned to conduct an operation, coordinated by the commanders or the Operations Committee.

The third phase of the UAW began around December 1976 when two major developments took place. The first and probably the most important was the analysis that the PB came up with regarding the Ethiopian situation and the course of the struggle. The analysis paid serious attention to the effect of the land reform proclamation and the role that the three months old urban armed activities played during the course of the struggle. The PB paper contained some major policy reorientations and shifts.[52]

The other major change introduced during the third period was the restructuring of the entire urban military wing. The UAW which had remained an elite body of professional activists, was expanded to a point that in a few weeks time, almost all EPRP zonal committees, including those in the various parts of Ethiopia, formed their own military structures. The urban military structure became a permanent feature of the EPRP, the League and the ELAMA when they became not only political bodies, but military institutions as well. They began providing leadership to military related activities in their respective areas and hundreds of members became involved in the process. The new shift indicated the beginning of the militarization of the various EPRP political structures and, as the repression intensified, that process was accelerated. The changes introduced during the third phase remained unchanged throughout the existence of the UAW.

The ELAMA military structure was limited at the level of the Addis Abeba IZ. However, both the party and the Youth League had their military structures at zonal levels too.

The UAW, which was under the EPRP CC, was dissolved in December 1976 and the "Commanders Committees" (CoCos) were formed under each party zonal structure. These were in charge of the military activities of the zones. A zonal committee member was assigned to each of the CoCos. Along with the new restructuring process, the IZs and zonal committees were entrusted with the responsibilities of deciding the targets of operations, the political activities of the units, etc.

During phases one and two, the targets of operation had to be approved by the Military Commission of the EPRP CC. The zonal committees of the party, the League or the ELAMA, either by themselves or by the instigation of the military wings under their jurisdictions, would come up with possible targets. The EPRP used all sources of information to get to its targets.

During the third stage (after December 1976), the Addis Abeba IZ in conjunction with the Military Commission of the EPRP decided on possible targets. In the provinces, the zonal committees were given full responsibility for selecting their targets.

After reaching on a decision about a certain target, the Addis Abeba IZ forwarded its decision to the Military Commission, which then checked to see if it fell within the policies of the EPRP. In some cases, some zones erroneously identified EPRP members as possible targets. One such case was C., who as a precaution was not placed under the Addis Abeba IZ. The nature of his government activities had forced him to be regarded as anti-EPRP. To camouflage himself, C. had to pretend that he was executing the government's assignments promptly and properly. The YL reported that C. posed a threat and asked for an action to be taken against him. After reviewing the case, the IZ supported the YL's demand and passed its report to the Military Commission, but the latter told the IZ to disregard the matter.[53]

After mid-1977, when the EPRP CC was weakened and only a couple of its members were left in the Addis Abeba area, the IZ took over most of the decision making responsibilities. The remaining CC members reviewed the decisions of the IZ and collaborated when necessary.

During the third period, a special structural arrangement was introduced to make the military wings more effective. The units under the party, the League, and the ELAMA came together under one command, then known as the Unified Command. The Unified Command, which was operational only on special occasions was regarded as a special task force. It was formed at the level of the zones and it was composed of the Secretaries of the CoCos of the EPRP, the YL, and ELAMA structures. The new structure came into being during the first months of 1977 and it was operative during the major house to house searches conducted in March 1977.

While the UAW was being restructured, members of the Ethiopian Airborne joined the EPRP structure. This was after the break up of their unit following a revolt at the end of July 1976.[54] When that rebellion failed, almost all of the members of the units dispersed in all directions. Some of them were contacted by the EPRP affiliated Oppressed Soldiers Organization. Many of them joined the EPRP and brought about a qualitative change in the composition of the units of the UAW. Besides the human factor, the arms which were obtained from the members of the Airborne were of importance to the EPRP. Most of the arms were of the latest models, such as, M-14 automatic machine guns, of which the EPRP had few or none. Some of the arms were sent to the units that were about to begin operating in the Sidamo rural area.

Lieutenant Merid, a gifted, fearless and dedicated officer was among those who joined the EPRP. Merid's military ability was witnessed in the first encounter of an EPRP UAW unit that was coming back from an unaccomplished mission. The unit had been assigned to force the release of arrested members of the Addis Abeba IZ, (details discussed elsewhere). However, waiting for an opportune moment to conduct the operation, the unit stayed on past the curfew hour of midnight. On its way back to its headquarters, the squad was stopped by a heavily armed government military patrol. The patrol asked members of the EPRP squad why they violated the curfew. Lieutenant Merid replied that they were coming from a wedding. Still suspicious, members of the government unit told members of the EPRP squad to step out of their vehicle.

Pretending that he was obeying the orders and holding only one of his hands up, Merid unexpectedly opened fire, and all of the members of the EPRP unit escaped. However, four government officers were killed during the exchange of fire.

Merid also took a major part in the attempt to assassinate Mengistu Haile Mariam in September 1976. Following the attempt on Mengistu's life, security was stepped up and the paratroopers, including Merid became possible targets.

In September 1976, while walking in the mercato area, Merid, by coincidence, met one of his colleagues from the Asmera branch of the Airborne. They agreed to meet on another day. On the date of the appointment, while Merid was standing and waiting for his colleague, Major Mekonnen Seyoum, member of the police security department and Colonel Leulseged Fikre Mariam of the police investigation department, jumped out of their car and fell on Merid. Merid, who had his hands on his grenade, released the ring. The explosion killed Major Mekonnen Seyoum. Colonel Leul Seged was wounded and two other officers died on the scene. Lt. Merid, the hero of the Airborne unit also died and the EPRP lost one of its ablest military leaders.

Initial Military Operations

One of the first activities of the UAW was the Sendafa Operation, which was planned to procure arms from one of the government arsenals. Sendafa is a small town about forty km. north-east of Addis Abeba. The target of the operation was the Police Officers training center. The information regarding the training center was obtained through the EPRP party committee of the area and passed on to the EPRP military commission. Tesfaye Debessai contacted the EPRP members of the area in order to have first hand knowledge.

After obtaining the necessary information, the UAW prepared the plan of operation and discussed it with the concerned committees and individuals in the area. Most of the tasks of the Sendafa operation were executed by officer EPRP members of the training center itself. The officers, who directly or indirectly had access to the arsenal were also in charge of the training center. On the day of the operation, they assigned EPRP members as sentries and other important and key positions. The truck driver was an EPRP member too. Following these and other arrangements, the mission was successfully accomplished and the truck loaded with arms, left the center peacefully. Sometime later, members of the EPRP military units escorted it to its destination. Fifteen pistols, 100 automatic rifles, carbines, heavy machine guns and a large round of ammunition were obtained.

The operation took place during the first days of September 1976. It was a smooth operation except for a sergeant who refused to collaborate. The sergeant was disarmed and kept under guard until it was over. However, he made an attempt to escape and jeopardized his life.

After unloading the bounty of the operation in a house that belonged to an EPRP member, in Kefetegna-2, Kebele 4, on the very day or so, the arms were distributed to the various parts of the EPRP structure. During the next day or so, the military regime arrested some of the officers of the training center. One of the officers who had been a sentry on the day of the operation committed suicide declaring "Victory to the EPRP". Most of the EPRP members who had taken part on the operation had already gone underground.

Another operation was regarding Mengistu. The EPRP CC passed a death sentence only on three Derge members, Colonel Mengistu Haile Mariam, Major Getachew Shibeshi, for the massacre in the Jimma area, and Colonel Teka Tulu.[55] Regarding POMOA, decision was passed only on those who had designed and drafted the policy of the war of annihilation.

Beginning in August 1976, the UAW of the EPRP began studying Mengistu's movements. During those days, Mengistu resided at the 4th division headquarters and worked at the former palace. Because of Mengistu's preparation to relocate to the palace, an intense effort was made to neutralize him before he moved out of the Fourth Division headquarters. On his way from his residence to the Derge's office or vice versa, Mengistu never used the same route. The UAW had intended to ambush Mengistu's car when it reached either the gates of the 4th division headquarters or the Derge's office. However, because of security considerations, that idea was not pursued.

Mengistu's unpredictable movements and his inconsistent travel schedule, both from and to the Derge's office caused serious difficulties. At times, he could be an hour or so late, thereby causing security problems for the units who would be waiting for an ambush. After six or seven trials, ambushing as a means of reaching Mengistu was changed, and instead, an approach called "following a moving target" was adopted. According to the new approach, the units would follow Mengistu's vehicle when it left either the Fourth Division headquarters or the Derg'se office, until it reached the designated area of ambush. The vehicles following Mengistu and those waiting by the ambush corner would then open fire.

In order to expedite the operation and as means of communication, a number of signal systems were arranged. Right at the Derge's gate, an individual was placed to inform the next person in line about the arrival of the target. That message was then relayed from one to another, until it reached those who were waiting by the corners, at the end of the line. Using a number of signal techniques, including coded signs, such as, the movement of hands, flash lights, and car lights, it was possible to pass messages regarding the identity of the target car and on which side of the car Mengistu was sitting. One of the EPRP vehicles, using car light as its signal, moved in front of the vehicle carrying Mengistu and informed the others about the arrival of the target.

The ambush, which was arranged for September 23, 1976, at 6:30 p.m., was to take place by the National Stadium. As soon as Mengistu left the Derge's office, the car that signaled his arrival began to move. However, it was blocked by other cars and those waiting by the ambush area remained uninformed about Mengistu's arrival. The EPRP unit that had been following Mengistu's vehicle from behind opened fire when it reached the designated area and put Mengistu's entourage out of action, but those who were waiting at the ambush site failed to take any action.

By the time those who were following Mengistu reached him and opened fire, his vehicle was close to the gate of the headquarters of the Fourth Division. His driver maneuvered and speeded up and Mengistu ducked under his seat. He was able to survive with only a minor wound. According to Captain Moges Wolde Mikael, when Mengistu came out of his vehicle, he was in terrible shape and in shock, hiding under the seat and his pistol lying on the floor.

Before this operation took place, members of the UAW units had been criticized for repeatedly failing to take actions. Their last attempt was a desperate move.

In September 1976, a bank operation which had been planned well in advance took place. The EPRP had some members who worked in the bank and they provided the details about the transfer of money from the bank to other destinations. They also knew the time the money would be moved out of the bank, at what time it would reach its highest accumulation point, how many employees would be around and the specific location where the money was to be found.

The UAW made thorough and precise preparations of how many and what kinds of armaments to use, how many members to deploy, what kind of support to use and where to keep the money immediately after the operation. In case of a failure of the master plan, a contingency plan was also arranged.

Ten members took part in the operation. Some of them acted as traffic officers, making arrangements for escape. Some members of the units, dressed in military uniforms, entered the bank and overpowered the employees, some of whom had prior information about the operation. The operation took place just before 10 o'clock in the morning when the money was packed to be sent to another location. The operation was smoothly carried out and the money was given to the Addis Abeba IZ, that already had prepared the hiding places.

In a single operation, the EPRP obtained more than 1.2m Ethiopian birr, a sum of money that would help the organization keep up many of its activities. Not long after the operation, 200,000 birr was sent to the rural armed force, 200,000 birr was assigned to the different parts of the party and League structures, 200,000 birr was used to purchase arms and ammunition, mainly for urban needs. The rest of the money was hidden or deposited under different accounts. However, due to the ever mounting repression, when account holding EPRP members went underground, the accounts became frozen. The regime also recovered a certain portion of the cash at a house raid it conducted in the vicinity of the Bole Airport.

The targets of a "Mercato" operation in mid-September 1976 were high-level MEISON leaders. According to information provided by an EPRP member who infiltrated the MEISON, some leaders of the organization were supposed to have a meeting in the Mercato area. Among those who were supposed to attend the meeting was Mesfin Kassu, a leading member of POMOA and believed to be one of those who drafted the policy of the war of annihilation. He was believed to be one of the first persons to establish MEISON's contact with Mengistu. Sometime before the operation took place, Getachew Maru, who did not have any structural relationship with the units, contacted them and made efforts to stop the operation. The urban units informed him that they were executing CC decisions and proceeded as planned.

The meeting place was raided by EPRP units, but no important MEISON member attended the meeting. At a later date, the EPRP learnt through the infiltrators that MEISON had been informed about the danger and might have told its members to cancel the meeting. Who tipped the MEISON about the operation still remains unknown.

In the initial stage of the armed operations, not all efforts were successful and some of them were complete failures. They failed not because the targets resisted, but because of unforeseen circumstances or bad planning. One of those operations was on Teka Tulu, the Derge Security chief and Mengistu's right-hand man. He was directly involved in the repression of workers. Colonel Teka Tulu advocated the war of annihilation and took an active part in executing that policy. Teka, who also was considered an obstacle to the democratization process within the Derge, was dismissed from his post and pensioned. Later, by the effort of Mengistu, he was sent to the Soviet Union for political studies. Teka was one of the founding members of the Seded.

Teka resided in the Gulele area. By September 1976, EPRP UAW units had been tracking him for some time, but had failed, mainly because of his irregular schedule. Teka went to his home at odd hours and the units were forced to wait in ambush for a long period. In due course, the residents who lived by the ambush site grew suspicious of the irregular activities and the strangers. One evening, the unit encountered a large crowd whose number continued swelling.

The residents asked the EPRP unit members about their identity and when their suspicions were confirmed, they tried to capture them. The EPRP members refrained from shooting at the people and they ran, but the residents chased them and began throwing rocks. Then a member of the unit let off a grenade and scared the residents. The unit members escaped unharmed, however, following this incident, the Teka Tulu operation was canceled. Currently, the Colonel is under detention and awaiting trial for his role in the "Red Terror". He was detained following the takeover of power by the EPRDF government in 1991.

A few leading POMOA members were executed by EPRP or ELAMA squads. Among leading MEISON members killed during this period was Fikre Merid, a leading member of POMOA and believed to be one of those who drafted the policy of the war of annihilation. On the day he was killed, the EPRP unit was out on a different assignment when it encountered Fikre and made a decision on the spot. Members of the unit, who did not even prepare an escape route, ended up in a dead end alley while trying to escape. One of them, a former paratrooper, jumped over a wall and escaped, while the others were arrested on the spot. Among those arrested was the IZ member, Yetbarek Hiskias, who returned from the USA to join the struggle. He was the brother of the veteran activist, Tselote Hiskias.

As part of the resistance to the war of annihilation, the EPRP employed a number of other methods to deter people from assisting the regime in its crusade against the EPRP. The names of individuals engaged in anti-EPRP activities were mentioned in underground leaflets, or these people were contacted by close friends or relatives and asked to refrain from their activities. At times, written warnings were sent out to those who were taking part in the annihilation effort. There were times when "graffiti" paintings were drawn on the walls of the residence of these individuals. The system had deterred some of the individuals from becoming part of the war of annihilation.

Despite the precautions taken, some mistakes were committed by EPRP UAW units. In January 1977, units took measures against an individual believing that he was Tesfaye Tadesse, one of the most wanted individuals by the EPRP.[56] Tesfaye Tadesse was among the first individuals to put out a paper disclosing the identity of some EPRP members. Tesfaye and the other person resembled so much that, before the operation took place, an EPRP member who knew Tesfaye Tadesse testified that it was him. However, it was learned that he was an altogether different person.

Besides the EPRP, the ELAMA and the YL structures took part in the operations. The ELAMA units paid more attention to activities and individuals directly related to the cause of workers; the League was in charge of individuals at the level of kebeles. In the last months of 1976, ELAMA units undertook the operation on Tewedros Bekele, the handpicked chairman of the state controlled national labor organization. The units entered his office dressed in military uniform. Following this operation, a wall was built around the union office and a special security system was put in place. The ELAMA units were so effective and determined that they also took part in other EPRP related operations, such as, against one of the most notorious and sadistic head of the Special Security Branch, Major Teshome. He was directly responsible for the torture of EPRP members and in particular labor activists.

In brief, the formation of the Mengistu/POMOA political alliance meant the declaration of the war of annihilation and an end to the peaceful form of struggle that began in 1974. The period of transition from the peaceful to the violent form of struggle was one of the most difficult periods in the history of the EPRP. Besides the challenges that the EPRP faced as a result of the declaration of the war of annihilation, the most difficult task, however, was to determine and define the characteristic features and the political direction of the transition. Before the enactment of the 1975 land reform, particularly before the eruption of the revolutionary movement in 1974, it was believed and understood that the struggle was bound to follow the classical path, that is, it would be a protracted armed struggle that would be initiated and conducted from the rural areas. However, the 1974 movement and the reforms that the Derge enacted changed the Ethiopian political setting, the class alliance and the demands of the day.

The crisis within the Derge that began around June 1976 remained unresolved for about six months. Even after the declaration of the war of annihilation, the struggle continued gathering momentum and it seemed that the crisis would be resolved in favor of the reformists who were led by Moges and Alemahehu, however, the Mengistu/POMOA alliance made its last frantic and ferocious move.

Notes to Chapter 4

1. Addis Zemen, September 10, 1976.

2. Yacob Haile Mariam, The Destruction of the Rule of Law Under Military Dictatorship in Ethiopia, Proceedings of the 5th International Conference of the Horn of Africa, page 51. Regarding the Special Criminal Code, see Kiflu Tadesse, The Generation, Part I, Chapter VI.

3. Ethiopian Herald, 13 September 1976, page 1.

4. Ethiopian Herald, 13 September 1976.

5. Addis Zemen, September 10, 1976, page 1.

6. Abeyotawi Ethiopia, Year I, No. 10, September 1976.

7. Ethiopian Notes, North East African Studies, No. 1, 1979, page 7.

8. Abera Yemane Ab, The Defeat of the Ethiopian Revolution and the Role of the Soviet Union, Proceedings, 2nd International Conference on the Horn of Africa, page 93. Fred Halliday, Maxine Molyneux, The Ethiopian Revolution, Verso Editions, 1981, page 123.

9. EPRP PB paper, page 3.

10. Democracia, Volume III, No. 9, page 2.

11. Ibid., page 1.

12. Kiflu Tadesse, op. cit., page 190.

13. Derge Statement, September 18, 1976.

14. Derge Statement, September 18, 1976.

15. Derge Statement, Addis Zemen, November 4, 1976, page 6.

16. Derge Statement, September 11, 1976.

17. Ethiopian Herald, September 14, 1976, pages 5, 6.

18. Democracia, Volume III, No. 9, page 2.

19. Ibid., page 2.

20. Labader, Volume II, December 1976, page 2.

21. Democracia, Volume III, Special Edition, page 1.

22. Babile Tola, To Kill a Generation, pages 81-86.

23. Interview, GM, January 1995. GM was a member of the EPRP IZ in the Harer province. He was arrested during this period and stayed in prison for over two years.

24. Interview, AKB, January 1995. AKB was a member of the EPRP leadership in Harer.

25. See details in Chapter III.

26. Memorandum, Kiflu Tadesse and Zeru Kehishen, 1988, Amsterdam, Holland.

27. Democracia, Volume III, No. 9, page 3.

28. Democracia, Volume III, No. 11, page 4.

29. Ibid., page 5.

30. EPRP Program, A. II, 4.

31. In a later development, some irregularities regarding the confiscation of money had taken place. Some of these problems were rectified.

32. EPRP By-laws, A. 3, page 1.

33. Democracia, Volume III, No. 5, page 10.

34. See details in Chapter I.

35. Democracia, Volume III, No.9, page 2.

36. See details in Chapter II.

37. A number of dates were suggested as the possible days to call the strike. The second week of October 1976, which would have given ample time for preparation, was disregarded because it was pay day and by then, most of the activists would either go underground or would be imprisoned. The other date picked up was the last week of September, where two major holidays would occur at the same time, and most of the factories would be closed, making the strike ineffective.

38. Democracia, Volume III, No. 12.

39. Voice of ELAMA, December 19, 1976, page 2.

40. See details 154.

41. Labader, Volume II, December 1976, page 4.

42. Voice of ELAMA, December 10, 1976, page 3.

43. Kiflu Tadesse, op. cit., Chapters VI and VII.

44. See details in Chapter VI.
45. Report presented at the AEWTU Congress of May 1978, page 13.
46. Kiflu Tadesse, op. cit., Chapter VI.
47. Democracia, Volume III, No. 11, page 4.
48. See details Chapter V.
49. Interview, MGE, 1990.
50. See details in Chapter II.
51. Democracia, Volume III, No. 11, page 4.
52. See details in Chapter V.
53. Most of the information regarding the UAW was provided by the EPRP contact man to the Military Commission, R.
54. See details in Chapter III.
55. See details in Chapter III.
56. Kiflu Tadesse, op.cit., Chapter VI.

5

The Turning Point - the Triumph of Violence over Moderation

Struggle within the Derge

The struggle within the Derge for internal democracy initiated around June 1976 continued until January 1977. A Derge general meeting in December 1976 voted to make some structural changes. One of the main issues discussed at this meeting was the omnipotent power that Major Mengistu Haile Mariam had accumulated and specific instances of power abuse were cited. An outcome of this meeting was the document titled the 'Decree to Clarify the Duties and Responsibilities of the Derge and the Council of Ministers.' It was made public on December 29, 1976. The Decree introduced a new structure that vested power in the Congress of the entire Derge members. Under the Congress came a Central Committee that was elected by the Congress and a 17 man Standing Committee responsible to the Central Committee.

The Decree clearly specified the responsibilities of each institution. Major policy decisions, such as, declaration of war, conducting of foreign policy, making military, political and economic pacts, giving guidance to political parties, proclamation of decrees, ratification of death sentences, taking measures against Derge members, etc., became the sole prerogatives of the Congress.[1] The duties and responsibilities of the Derge CC, the Standing Committee, the chairpersons, etc., were also clearly spelled out. The new Decree, while giving most of the powers to the Congress and the Derge CC, at the same time, deprived the chairpersons of their power. The most obvious delimitation of power was that assigned to the vice-chairman, at the time, that of Mengistu Haile Mariam. According to the new arrangement, the vice-chairman's duty would be to chair the meeting of the Council of Ministers, a more or less advisory body that had a limited say in the affairs of the government.

The new Decree was a blow to the chairpersons, who until this period had exercised uncontrolled power. It also was a fatal blow to the Mengistu/POMOA alliance, which was left with little or no power. Even though the Decree had much wider political ramifications, it was the

Mengistu/POMOA alliance that was the target and the one to lose the most.

During the restructuring process, the Derge appointed a committee to study the excesses that POMOA had committed in its few months of existence. As a result of the investigation, it was decreed that POMOA would be accountable to the Standing Committee of the Derge, instead of the previous arrangement which placed it under Mengistu.[2] To limit POMOA's power, it was decreed that only the Standing Committee could decide and make public statements in the name of the government.[3] POMOA had been responsible for some of the statements made by the Derge.

In the course of the six months struggle within the Derge, two groups and a third amorphous body came into being. The first one consisted of the majority of the Derge members with Captain Moges Wolde Mikael and Lt. Alemayehu Haile as the leading figures. General Teferi Bente, the Chairperson and Colonel Hiruy Haile Selassie, the Derge's security chief also belonged to this group. Even though the group had a large following, it still did not control the state power and apparatus and was engaged in a process of allocating and defining power to the various institutions of the Derge itself.

The second group consisted of the Mengistu/POMOA alliance, which had very few supporters within the Derge. Its main support came from outside, that is, POMOA and the leadership of the Derge's operational and security forces. Even though minuscule, the Mengistu clique still controlled the special military contingent that was in charge of the Derge office. POMOA had direct access to the mass organizations, including the kebeles and the Abyot Tebeka groups.

The third group consisted of the amorphous and minuscule group of Atnafu, who supported the movement in the Derge but did not take an active part in the process. Overtly declaring himself a supporter of the movement, Major Atnafu Abate nevertheless tried to remain neutral during the whole process. Winning his support was a major preoccupation of the Moges group. He was so important to the democratization process of the Derge that in October 1976 Captain Moges, after talking with Atnafu asked the EPRP to conduct discussions with him. The EPRP assigned WG, an enlightened EPRP activist, to handle Major Atnafu. They conducted a number of meetings, some of them in the residence of Major Atnafu, in the Fourth Division headquarters.

The struggle within the Derge weakened the Mengistu/POMOA alliance to a point that by December 1976/January 1977, *de jure*, Mengistu had become just another Derge member, except that he had some loyalists who controlled important institutions. That condition cooled down the effect of the war of annihilation declared in September 1976. It imposed some limitations -- *de jure*, of course -- on the activities of the Mengistu/POMOA alliance.

It was the desire of many Derge members to get rid of the POMOA itself, even though there was no public statement to that effect. Colonel Hiruy, who was not an EPRP member, but had contact with the organization through EPRP members, was so bitter about POMOA and the MEISON that he made all efforts to lift the security provided to the members of these institutions.

Because of the reform enacted within the Derge, the Mengistu/POMOA alliance could not conduct the repression as intended. So, the offensive war cry that the group was making was transformed into an equally loud cry of defense. It was around this time that POMOA came up with its somewhat strange slogan, "arm us, do not let them wipe us out", {astatekun atascheresun}. This was strange because an organization should have been able to arm itself, if that was its need. POMOA also continued demanding that the newly formed Abyot Tebeka groups be armed.

When it knew that it was losing the political battle, the Mengistu/POMOA alliance became desperate. In December 1976, Mengistu made an arrangement to visit the USSR. Captain Moges Wolde Mikael, suspicious of the move, decided to accompany Mengistu to the USSR. For some inexplicable reasons, Mengistu postponed the trip. It was suspected that Moges's move might have caused the cancellation.

Following the structural changes within the Derge, the Mengistu/POMOA alliance became frantic and throughout December1976 and January 1977, it was rumored that the alliance was to make a coup. Mengistu's intentions were not kept secret, but became the talk of the town. The EPRP informed Captain Moges and other EPRP members in and around the Derge about the danger. In one of its last desperate efforts, the EPRP contacted General Teferi Bente, through his son, Ayneshet Teferi, an EPRP member. The General was informed about the danger, but he remained confident and declared that the condition was under control. Moges, who took the situation seriously, requested information from the Head of the Derge Security Department, Colonel Hiruy Haile Selassie. Until he lost his life in the Mengistu coup, Colonel Hiruy, who heavily relied on his formal security network, disregarded innumerable leads and informed his colleagues in the Derge that there was no danger whatsoever. At this time, the Mengistu/POMOA alliance was conducting its preparations outside the Derge's legal channels.

When it was found that many Derge members were not ready to believe the rumor regarding the coup, the EPRP suggested to Moges that the Derge should assign an officer who was not loyal to Mengistu as head of the military contingent of the Derge office. Until then, the Derge contingent had been led by a Mengistu confidant and a notorious killer, Colonel Daniel Asfaw. Because of legal and other constraints, the Derge failed to take that measure. The EPRP then suggested to Moges that the Derge should move its headquarters from the former palace to the compound of the Fourth Division. At this time, the Fourth Division headquarters was not controlled by the Mengistu clique. Because of the indecisiveness of Major Atnafu Abate and other Derge members, this suggestion did not materialize either. It was believed that, if the Derge was able to relocate its offices to the Fourth Division headquarters, it might have been able to consummate the restructuring process that it had begun. Captain Moges Wolde Mikael, who some days before the coup had already sensed its imminence and was in no position to stop it, asked the EPRP to provide him with hand grenades. Moges, who had a vast military arsenal under him, but was not in control of it had to demand arms for his own protection. The party provided him with some grenades. However, it was not known if he carried one when the coup took place in February 1977.

The struggle within the Derge had major impact on the EPRP as well. Since August/September 1976, the EPRP had concluded that the peaceful form of struggle had ended. However, when the power of the Mengistu/POMOA alliance slackened and a new political force began emerging, it created a seemingly relaxed political condition. Even though the EPRP leadership still believed that the peaceful form of struggle was over, the new development mentioned above and the continuation of the democratization process within the Derge diluted the leadership's resolve to vigorously follow through its decisions. The wait and see attitude derailed some of the decisions made at the August 1976 CC Plenum. It created some hope that the EPRP might get some breathing space and time to make more preparations in terms of restructuring the organization and obtaining arms and finance. Even though some leading EPRP members had left for the EPRA, more than five months following the decisions of the Plenum, many of the CC members and other leading activists still remained in Addis Abeba and they became witnesses to the Mengistu coup and the quagmire that took place in February 1977.

Days before the coup, an unusually high number of delegates from Eastern Europe and Vietnam began flocking to Ethiopia. Cuba began showing some interest, and in November 1976, the official Cuban newspaper, *Grandma*, began writing articles about Ethiopia. Cuba was one of those few countries that still supported the struggle in Eritrea. Fidel Castro visited Ethiopia in March 1977, a month or so after the Mengistu coup took place.

As early as October 1976, after condemning the assassination attempt on Mengistu, the USSR strengthened its ties with the Mengistu clique. After a series of negotiations, as was mentioned elsewhere, he was invited to visit the USSR. In the meantime, the USSR appointed one of its ablest Ambassadors, Anatoly Ratanov, a member of the Central Committee of the Communist Party of the Soviet Union. Earlier, he had been assigned to trouble spots such as Guinea Bissau. In January 1977, cultural agreements were signed with Rumania.

In November and December 1976, a close relationship was established with the German Democratic Republic. A few days after the coup, on February 11, 1977, the most ardent supporter of the Mengistu clique and a PB member of the Communist Party of the former East Germany, Mr. Lambert came to Ethiopia. In November 1976, East European countries began sending POMOA all kinds of printed materials.

Sometime before the Derge's Decree to restructure itself was made public, the Soviet news agency APN, which had adopted an analysis very much in line with that of the Mengistu/POMOA alliance began writing about the dangers that the Ethiopian revolution encountered. The situation in Ethiopia was compared to that of Chile, that is, with the coup that toppled the Allende government in 1973. The Soviet press had been condemning the EPRP. However, in mid 1976, it began accusing the EPRP for collaborating with feudalists and imperialists.[4]

The Mengistu/POMOA alliance became more and more desperate and it began preparations for the final show down. In January 1977, POMOA arranged a seminar for the kebeles and it was attended by a large number of participants. The kebele seminar decided that *Abyot Tebeka* groups had to be armed and the anti-EPRP struggle had to be intensified. The seminar also called for a mass rally to be held at the end of January 1977.

A few days before the coup, a MEISON squad, along with some members of the Waz League, opened fire at a university students gathering on the University campus killing some students.[5] These and other developments further aggravated the situation and the coup rumor continued spreading.

At the end of January 1977, the Chairperson of the Derge, General Teferi Bente, delivered a speech to the Ethiopian people. In his speech, he squarely focused on external enemies, the Sudan and Somalia, which he believed were supported by imperialist forces and were making efforts to sidetrack the course of the struggle in Ethiopia. The Chairperson declared that those who did not want to see a strong Ethiopia were preparing to invade it.[6] The approach, emphasis and political direction of the Chairperson's speech contradicted that of the Mengistu/POMOA alliance, which had been focusing on internal enemies as the main cause for the malice of the country. The Chairperson's views were, of course, supported by at least the leading members of the Derge, who took part in the restructuring process. The Chairperson made his political direction clear and called on all progressive, anti-feudal, anti-imperialist and anti-bureaucratic capitalist forces to form a United Front.[7]

The Chairman's speech, and in particular, his shift of emphasis surprised many Ethiopians. All throughout this period, the Derge had kept its internal struggle secret from the Ethiopian people and very few people knew about the direction of events. Neither the Derge nor leading figures of the movement explained the motives and the driving reasons for the restructuring of the Derge. *Furthermore, Derge reformists did not create conditions to promote their cause and they did not involve the people in the struggle. They did not publicize the abuse of power by some of their members and at the same time, they did not exonerate themselves from some of the crimes of Mengistu.*

A day after the Chairman made his speech, a massive rally was held in Addis Abeba. It was called by POMOA and organized by the kebeles. Addressing the rally, Chairman Teferi Bente one more time stated,

> ...[S]tanding at this podium, at this very time, I implore all progressives and intellectuals to form a party and a United Front. Unless this is done, our revolution will still remain in a great danger."[8]

His speech was brief, heartfelt and to the point. Both speeches of the Chairman showed a differing political direction from that of the Mengistu/POMOA alliance and did not mention the EPRP as an enemy. Implicitly, the call for the front was also addressed to the EPRP.

At the same rally mentioned above, representatives of the kebeles and the national labor union (AEWTU) delivered speeches too. The most important speech, however, was that of the POMOA/MEISON representative who gave a direct reply to the Chairman's speech. In a very clear and precise manner, the representative elaborated the Mengistu/POMOA alliance's political line, thereby declaring the EPRP as the main target. In a metaphorical way he declared, "in order to defend oneself from an enemy who is 10 km away, one must take a decisive measure against the enemy who is only five meters away."[9] Of the three main enemies, spelled out for annihilation, the speech focused on the EPRP as the main target.

The POMOA representative further declared that the sure and guaranteed way of success was to organize the *Abyot Tebeka* groups, both at the level of institutions and regions. In this same speech, the POMOA representative transmitted an important message when he declared, "...so that Ethiopia cannot be the second Chile, we should do what Chile did not do. Chile fell victim because it did not arm its people. At the same time, Allende neglected his enemies next door...." This was an indirect reference to those Derge members who were leading the restructuring process within the Derge. Before he was killed in the bloody coup of 1973, some supporters and important military officers of the Salvador Allende government had been killed and some had already changed allegiance.

The Mengistu coup took place on February 3, 1977, only a few days after the rally. Mengistu had asked that a meeting of leading Derge members should be called so that he could deliver a report about the student campaign known as the "development through cooperation". While the Derge members were assembled, Colonel Daniel Asfaw led a group of officers into the hall and arrested leading figures of the Derge opposition. They were then taken to the basement and executed. Among those slaughtered were General Teferi Bente, Captain Moges Wolde Mikael, Colonel Hiruy Haile Selassie, Colonel Asrat Desta, Captain Alemayehu Haile, Captain Teferra and Corporal Haile Belay. While the coup was in progress, leading MEISON members were awaiting the outcome at the POMOA headquarters.

Captain Yohannes Meseker, the head of the Derge's investigation department, committed suicide after killing two of the leading members of the coup, Sennay Likke and Colonel Daniel Asfaw. All throughout the crisis, Captain Yohannes knew the danger that the Mengistu clique posed and was constantly warning the Moges group to take action, however, his warning was ignored. Since the early days, Captain Yohannes Meseker never liked the political direction of the Derge. As an investigation officer, he had come across a number of cases that he found to be flimsy.

After the coup, Ayneshet Teferi, an EPRP member and the son of

General Teferi Bente, was arrested. Ayneshet was incarcerated in the former palace until he was sent for execution on Easter of 1977.

In January 1977, Atnafu was touring the southern part of Ethiopia, on the pretext of organizing peasant militia contingents. However, it was suspected that he was distancing himself from the crisis that was broiling within the Derge. When the coup took place, Major Atnafu Abate was in Wellega and he learned about it the way the rest of the Ethiopian people did. It was reported to the EPRP that he was distracted when he heard about the news and asked if he could get in touch with the armed wing of the EPRP, the EPRA. However, not long after, Mengistu ordered him to return to Addis Abeba.

Mengistu's move forced active officers, such as, Captain Amha Abebe, to go underground. Captain Amha's and Sergeant Major Wolde Medhin Abraha's pictures came out in the *Addis Zemen* newspaper and they formed part of the most wanted list of the government.

The day after the coup, at a rally called by the kebeles, Mengistu declared that the "revolution had moved from a defensive to an offensive posture". He also declared that the Moges-Alemayehu group "had him planned for lunch, but he had them for breakfast". This was to say that he moved faster than they did. As the other major statements read by Mengistu, it was known then that this speech was prepared by MEISON.

In order to take part at the rally celebrating the coup, peasants, many of whom were Oromos of the areas surrounding Addis Abeba, were mobilized. On their way to the rally, joyous and festive, they came chanting songs and eulogizing General Teferi Bente. When they reached the Abyot Square, they were informed that the General had been executed. They were stunned and shocked. Only a few days before, the Chairperson had appealed for their support against foreign aggressors. They had come from as far away as Sululta, about 10 miles away from Addis Abeba proper, heeding his appeal, but he was not there to address them. The peasants' return from the rally was a pitiful scene -- as painful as the coup itself. The peasants were heading home, with their heads down, their eyes staring at the ground, not uttering a single word to each other. They continued marching, puzzled, stunned, shocked and angry. They continued marching in groups of ten, twenty,...but all together. They kept on marching, silently and quietly. Their leader was executed, but no explanation was given; strange it seemed, indeed bizarre it was.

When all was over, Mengistu emerged as the unchallenged master of the Derge. In a single strike, he eliminated almost all of his rivals and controlled the Derge. Mengistu appointed his confidants, Colonel Teka Tulu, who had been sent to Moscow for political education, and Major Getachew Shibeshi, to head the Derge's security and operations departments, respectively. The rest of the Derge members succumbed to Mengistu's rule and, *de facto*, the Derge seized to exist; only the name and the facade remained.

The coup also signified that the conflict in Ethiopia could be resolved only by force. Besides, it paved the path for Soviet dominance of Ethiopian politics. A couple of days after the coup, almost all of the Eastern European countries expressed support for the Mengistu clique. The Soviet Union, which usually was slow to react to such events, was one of the first to give unconditional support to the Mengistu regime. This became an additional evidence that indicated that the Soviet Union, in some way or another, had been aware of what was taking place in Ethiopia.

The EPRP CC - Organizational Activities

The Ethiopian radical generation had avid interest in international affairs and in particular in events related to the International Communist Movement (ICM). One such event in 1976 was the death of Mao-tse-dung, one of the most inspiring leaders of the left. Mao-tse-tung passed away on the second week of September 1976. When he died, he was in his eighties. His death reinvigorated discussions when many EPRP activists made efforts to review some of the basic tenets of his theory.

In the early and mid-sixties, when the Ethiopian radicals were looking for solutions to many of the mind-boggling Ethiopian problems, it was in the works of Mao that they found some of the clues. Mao, who was respected and admired for the original approaches he used to solve his country's problems, gained the admiration and respect of the Ethiopian left. When in the early 1960's, he defied the paternalist approach of the Communist Party of the Soviet Union (CPSU) and the political line advocated by Khrushchev, Mao became more respected. However, many of the Ethiopian left were not sure of the wisdom of some of his later policies.[10]

Some years before he passed away, Mao's influence had already waned. Although he had addressed many of the questions that the Ethiopian radicals raised in the early and mid-sixties, he also had left as many questions unanswered. Many Ethiopian radicals wondered how the Chinese would claim that they had embarked in a socialist construction only a few years after the triumph of the so called New Democratic Revolution? How were the Chinese able to by-pass the New Democratic phase of the struggle only in a few years time and embark upon the socialist phase? When did the New Democratic Revolution end and the Socialist phase begin? What were the economic prerequisites of the New Democratic phase? They also wanted to know if China was a socialist country. When Mao drifted away from the CPSU and characterized the Soviet system as social-imperialist, many wondered what that characterization entailed and they wanted to know if he elaborated his thesis. Internal party struggle was an area of concern for the Ethiopian radicals and they pondered if Mao had provided solutions as to what form it should take. They also wondered why Mao stayed in power until his last days. Many had formed negative attitude about Mao's personality cult. They wondered if he ever succeeded in preparing a generation that would follow his cause and line?

These questions became more pertinent following the arrest of Mao's widow and other activists sometime after his death. The group had taken an active part in what was known as the "cultural revolution" and leading figures of the movement were arrested and sentenced to years of imprisonment.

Following Mao's death, the communist world, which already was divided into two major camps, continued to disintegrate. Former supporters of the Chinese line were divided into many factions. Some remained supporters of Mao while others supported "the three world theory" of Deng Tsio Peng. Among the victims of the crisis was ESUNA, one of the Ethiopian student's unions abroad, which split into more than three factions.[11]

Besides the condition in the International Communist Movement (ICM) in 1976, the political and economic conditions in Ethiopia had turned for the worse. The rebellion within the army, the Air-force and the Airborne had exacerbated the crisis within the military. Peasant rebellion had become a recurring event. Because of these and other developments, beginning around August 1976, a number of questions were asked by leading EPRP activists. What should the course of the Ethiopian revolutionary struggle be? With the crisis ever getting deeper, what would the fate of the regime be? Most of the economic programs of the radical left appropriated, how could one sustain the struggle? What path should the struggle follow? Was it feasible to rally the people on political platforms alone and triumph in the struggle? If not "land to the tiller", what should the economic agenda of the armed struggle in the rural areas be? A radical land reform enacted, how is the rural armed struggle to continue? With little or no international support, how does one obtain arms and finance to sustain the relatively large organizational network? Short of supporting and collaborating with the regime, how does one get international help? How is it possible to coordinate the struggle in Eritrea with that of the rest of the country? These and similar questions began haunting the minds of the activists.

That confusion and uncertainty were reflected at the Youth League Congress held in September 1976 when Yohannes Berhane and Getachew Maru, who attended the meeting representing the EPRP CC, presented differing points of views and conducted a heated discussion. During this period, the EPRP leadership did not come up with a comprehensive policy and assessment of the Ethiopian situation.

Besides general lack of clarity on the direction of the struggle, it was the radical land reform that became a recurring theme among leading EPRP activists. Due to the reform and other measures, it was felt that the struggle in Ethiopia could not follow the classical path espoused by many countries, the examples of which the Ethiopian left had endorsed. What form the struggle should assume and what new elements it should introduce remained points of discussion even after the declaration of the war of annihilation in September 1976.

Despite the political uncertainty and difficult conditions, EPRP publications continued coming out. Over a period of one year, from February

1976 to 1977, 25 regular and 2 special issues of *Democracia* were printed - an average of two *Democracia* issues per month.

Sometime before the violent resolution of the Derge's internal crisis in favor of Mengistu, the process of the struggle within the Derge itself created a dilemma. It was perceived that if Mengistu and his clique were removed from the state power, the group that would take over political power had either to follow Mengistu's path and fall into the same political abyss or grant democratic rights and create conditions for a broader participation of the people in the political process. Under such conditions, what role the EPRP should play remained in question. Furthermore, the political crisis continued spreading and, right or wrong, around the beginning of September 1976, many leading EPRP activists began contemplating the possibility of a popular uprising, and such ideas were expressed in some of the papers.

As was indicated above, a number of questions that called for some kind of explanation began to surface. The party and Youth League structures demanded a comprehensive analysis of the Ethiopian situation. With this in mind, in October 1976, the EPRP PB held at least three meetings and prepared what was to be known as the 'PB paper'. The PB meetings were attended by all of the members, including the newly elected member, Tselote Hiskias. He was elected to the PB replacing AW who was sent abroad. Tesfaye Debessai prepared the initial draft and presented it at one of the meetings. The PB then discussed the paper and after adding and deleting whatever was necessary, recommended that it be reworked and presented at another meeting. The same draft became the main agenda of an another PB meeting and the paper was read and discussed for the second time. In order to avoid the unpleasant incidents that took place at the August and September CC meetings,[12] each and every PB member was specifically asked if he had questions and amendments. Getachew was specifically asked if he was in agreement with the thesis presented in the paper. Getachew mentioned three points that he thought had to be included in the paper. He argued that more emphasis should be given to feudalism and imperialism. His notes were taken into consideration. He then argued that more emphasis should be given to the rural armed struggle. Getachew was then asked to rephrase his amendments and all of his points were included in the analysis. Finally, for the first time in its short history, the PB not only cast a vote, but all of the members were asked to spell out their support or opposition to the paper. The outcome of the meeting was recorded in the PB minutes. The PB paper was then approved unanimously.

Because of the difficulty of calling a CC meeting, the first edition of the PB paper was circulated to almost all of the CC members on individual basis. Sometime later, the same paper was distributed and discussed by the departments around the CC, leading activists of the organization, the Addis Abeba IZ, the zonal committees, the Youth League CC, IZ and zonal committees, party cells in the EPRA and the Foreign Committee.

Until January 1977, feedback was received regarding the 'PB paper', both from CC members and the party and League structures. Most of the information was favorably inclined toward the 'paper' and acclaimed it for its originality and the efforts it made to encompass Ethiopian reality. Some members expressed reservation, among them a party cell in the EPRA.[13]

The PB paper was then reworked to include some of the feedback. Due to the intense security problems, conducting even PB meetings was difficult, therefore, the final version of the PB paper had to be reviewed individually. After all of the members of the PB read the paper and expressed their consent, the final draft was sent for printing. The first edition came out in October or the beginning of November 1976 and it was passed down the structure through the Addis Abeba IZ. Only twenty or thirty copies of the first edition of the PB paper were printed. The first edition of the PB paper came out when the Derge was still in crisis and the Mengistu/POMOA alliance was fast losing its grip on political power. The paper expressed the prevalent political condition, attributing the declaration of the war of annihilation to the Mengistu/POMOA alliance. Besides, the paper also accused Derge members of cowardice.

The second and final edition of the PB paper came out in February 1977, following the resolution of the Derge crisis in favor of the Mengistu/POMOA alliance. It came out after two CC members, Getachew Maru and Berhane Meskel were stripped of their membership by the Third CC Plenum in November 1976.[14] The main thesis both in the first and the second versions were identical; however, the second edition reflected the changed political condition of the time, that is, the resolution of the internal Derge crisis and the ascendance to power of the Mengistu clique.

The Politbureau (PB) Paper

The paper begins with an introduction to the declaration of the war of annihilation against the EPRP and discusses the accusations that were labeled against the organization. It also discusses the motive for declaring the war.[15] It then states that the war of annihilation was declared when the EPRP did not fire even a single bullet, despite the massive repression directed against it.[16] The EPRP was still engaged in a peaceful political struggle[17] and it was pursuing the peaceful political path until it was forced to declare an armed struggle as the main form, argued the paper.[18]

Enumerating some of the major tasks awaiting the EPRP, the paper indicated that the organization should conduct a coordinated armed struggle both in the rural and urban areas. The EPRP should form anti-imperialist, anti-feudal and anti-fascist committees and build the Democratic Front. It should consolidate the mass organizations and at the same time form new ones. The various organizational structures should function autonomously so that they would be able to cope with the crisis.

The struggle should not lose its momentum, but "push the fascistic regime from one crisis to another", argued the 'paper'.[19] Once the Derge consolidated and stabilized itself, it was argued, it would "disguise its fascistic nature."[20] It was perceived that the stabilization of the Derge would make it difficult to withstand the crisis that was bound to follow. The military regime had made efforts to stabilize itself by promulgating some reforms, mostly with the deep seated aim of side-tracking the struggle. However, due to the momentum of the struggle unleashed in 1974 and the role of the opposition, the Derge remained unable to attain its desired objective.

The balance of power and the alliance of classes were also among the issues that the PB paper discussed. It was argued that the military regime was unable to resolve the root causes of the 1974 revolutionary movement, that it was in conflict with all classes, and that it was gripped in a deep internal crisis. Hence, it

> [I]s a regime that could come down any time...however this doesn't mean that the working class and the broad masses...would be able to take power. That needs enough preparation on our side. What we wanted to show and imply is that the regime did not have a social base that would allow it to withstand the pressure if pushed from within and without.[21]

When the second and revised edition of the PB paper came out, the intern al contradiction in the Derge had been resolved and Mengistu was in full control of the state power.

The thesis regarding the Derge's social base was not original; it had been discussed in a number of *Democracia* issues.[22]

The contradictions of the regime with the various classes of the country, an issue that had been raised repeatedly, was discussed extensively.[23] This was mentioned to demonstrate that Mengistu's regime was a weak one. [24] With an optimistic tone the paper then argued,

> ...[I]f we follow a correct strategy and tactic, if we follow the mass line, and if we are able to coordinate the struggle under... front...the objective situation would be dismal to the fascists and banda intellectuals and favorable to revolutionaries.[25]

The paper then concluded that it had become impossible to conduct peaceful political struggle and the armed struggle had to be intensified, instead. If the armed struggle is not intensified, "the regime would be able to single out and execute our party members, class conscious workers, and this will in turn retard the struggle...which will lose its steam and they (the regime) will get some breathing space. The workers will lose their confidence in the party,...and we will be unable to conduct political, organizational and agitation work," argued the paper.[26] If the armed struggle was not intensified, "they (the Derge) will mobilize their forces and land a severe blow on our rural army, which will then suffer from lack of ammunition and supplies."[27]

The paper also raised the point where the armed struggle should be conducted, stating that it should be conducted both in the rural and urban areas. Long before the PB paper came out, the urban armed activity of the

EPRP had assumed a much wider dimension and scale. However, the urban military activity of the EPRP had not been assessed and given a proper place within the strategy and tactics of the party. It was this PB paper, in its last section, that theorized and defined the urban armed struggle within the broad strategy of the EPRP.

In order to show why an armed struggle had to be conducted in the urban areas, the paper brought forth arguments of how and in what respects the Ethiopian revolutionary struggle was different from the struggle in Vietnam and China. Since these were the countries from which the organization derived most of its experience, explaining the deviation was important in itself. On the other hand, the paper wanted to indicate what it believed were marked differences and salient features of the Ethiopian struggle. The PB paper reasoned that surrounding the cities from the countryside was the main characteristics of the strategy of the struggle both in Vietnam and China. According to the PB paper, the land question, that is, the acute contradiction between feudal landlords and tenants was the main reason for following such a strategy. Despite the underlying differences of these countries and Ethiopia, the PB paper stated that the EPRP should still conduct rural armed struggle and consolidate its rural army, the EPRA. Citing shortage of arms as its main problem, the PB paper stated,

> "...[U]sing our armed groups in the urban areas and confiscating arms from the regime, we should be able to provide arms both to our urban and rural armies. The EPRA should also make efforts to arm itself."[28]

Furthermore, unlike in Vietnam or China, in Ethiopia, "the land reform had blurred the contradiction in the rural areas...but not in the urban. It [the Derge] was still unable to build political base in the urban areas."[29] The PB paper then argued that the Derge did not have the strong political base that the Kuomentang of China had. The Derge was also entangled in deep contradictions; therefore, "it is possible to wage an armed struggle in the urban areas as well, and if adequate preparation is made, in the final analysis, it is possible to conduct a popular uprising."[30]

When the 'PB paper' addressed the question of armed struggle in tandem with the issue of political power, not only did it acknowledge the existence of EPRP's urban armed structure, but also theorized the role of the urban armed movement vis-a-vis the Ethiopian revolutionary struggle. It was theorized that it was possible to conduct rural as well as urban armed struggle. It summarized the experience of the EPRP following the commencement of urban armed activities in September 1976.

The new approach discussed in the 'PB paper' was a major departure from the policy adopted at the First Congress of the EPRP. The Congress had stipulated that rural armed struggle was the main form of struggle. When the Congress made that decision in 1972, the primacy of the rural armed struggle was viewed in contradistinction with the peaceful form of struggle. Moreover, EPRP's armed struggle policy was based on the strategy of encircling the cities from the countryside. EPRP's urban military units, formed in the earlier days, were regarded as auxiliary defense units of limited scope.

The second major point of departure of the 'PB paper' was the fact that it argued the possibility of an armed popular uprising, or an insurrection. When the EPRP laid down its policy at the First Congress, it was clearly stipulated that the struggle would be protracted and the first task of the organization would be to liberate the countryside and form people's power in a significant portion of the country before an insurrection was launched. It was with this understanding that the nucleus of the EPRA was deployed in the Ethiopian hinterlands. However, the 1974 revolutionary movement changed the political scenario when the PPG, the slogan for the transition period, came to the fore and became an important feature of the struggle.

When the PPG was first raised, it was meant to be a tactical slogan to rally popular support. As time went by, particularly when the crisis deepened and the regime became less stable, the struggle in the various parts of the country continued to intensify. The crisis within the Ethiopian army sharpened. The opposition to the Derge continued gathering momentum and the PPG slogan assumed such a different meaning and connotation that it formed part of the EPRP program ratified by the Extended Conference held in August 1975.

> The previous program [of the First Congress] envisioned a protracted people's war and formation of a broad based people's government. The new program (ratified at the August Conference) perceived two stages in the formation of a people's government. When this new concept was introduced, the Conference did not and could not clarify how it was to be formed and its relationship to the protracted armed struggle."[31]

Furthermore, in 1975/76, the PPG slogan became one of the major points of discussion in the *Abyot* Forum of the *Addis Zemen* newspaper[32] when a number of articles came out indicating and suggesting how a Provisional Government should be formed. Gradually, the PPG slogan departed from its initial role and assumed a more strategic nature, being envisioned not only as a tactical slogan, but as part of the transition process and a solution to the political crisis in the country. Many were the times that the PPG was presented as an alternative form of transitional political power. Even though it was highly popularized, the slogan still remained shrouded with ambiguity and controversy.

The PB paper, which was not original as such, but a partial summation of the experience of the few years of struggle of the EPRP, presented some major issues that were different from the decisions of the First Congress.

The Third EPRP CC Plenum

The third EPRP CC Plenum was held in November 1976, in the house of a teacher EPRP member, in the former Mesfine Harer St., (now Belay

Zeleke Godana) Addis Abeba. It was held following the declaration of the war of annihilation and, because of the tense security condition, the meeting lasted only for a few hours. All through this period, a good number of EPRP members were being imprisoned or executed. Some of the EPRP structures had already been dismantled. Due to the switch from the peaceful to the armed form of struggle, the EPRP was still groping to adjust. The necessary psychological preparedness needed to engage in armed struggle was not formed yet among the membership. That being said, the EPRP faced an internal problem that originated in the CC itself.

In September 1976, right after the declaration of the war of annihilation, the EPRP CC had decided to take measures against Mengistu and leading POMOA members, and the PB passed that decision to the various levels of the party and YL structures. Anticipating the depth of the unfolding crisis and the difficulty of holding a CC meeting, the Second Plenum, held in August 1976, had mandated the PB to take the necessary measures to safeguard the EPRP.[33]

It was discovered later that as soon as the decision of the September 1976 CC meeting was passed to EPRP members, two CC members, Berhane Meskel and Getachew Maru began conducting a counter agitation wherever and whenever they could. They did this both within and outside the EPRP structure. Even though the CC was not aware of the formation of a faction within the EPRP at this time, the first breach of discipline was noticed when Berhane Meskel contacted the main defense unit of the EPRP in September 1976 just before the unit was about to go out on a mission. Berhane discussed his opposing views and tried to convince the units not to take any measures either on Mengistu or leading POMOA members. Berhane Meskel had no formal relationship with the members of the defense units that he contacted. Among those that he tried to convince were Berhane Iyasu, a member of the UAW and Yetbarek Hiskias, an IZ member. The two members reported the matter to the EPRP CC.

When it was realized that he had breached organizational discipline, Berhane Meskel was approached by members of the CC, first by Tesfaye Debessai, then by Kiflu Tadesse and Tselote Hiskias. They asked him to respect the Constitution, which entitled any CC member to hold any view on any issue, but to abide by a decision once it had been discussed and the leadership had reached a conclusion. He was also instructed to use proper channels, such as the internal journal, the *Red Star* to air his views.

According to EPRP's Constitution, a minority within any of the leadership echelons had the right to raise an issue at another meeting, even after decisions had been reached.[34]

Berhane Meskel continued his campaign and was able to influence "Berhane"(code name), an IZ member of the Addis Abeba area who participated in the IZ representing zone-1 committee, Tadesse a member of zone-1 committee and others. Berhane Meskel was residing with some of these individuals.

Getachew Maru, who served as the CC contact person to the YL organization, failed to communicate the decisions of the September EPRP CC meeting to the YL leadership. When the PB learned about Getachew's failure or inaction, it sent another CC member to explain the decisions of the September CC meeting. Getachew also began contacting his former comrades of the Abyot group, by which time he had severed his formal organizational relationship, to discuss his views. A leading member of the former Abyot group and a member of the EPRP CC provided the PB with detailed information on what Getachew was doing and the form of agitation that he was conducting. Had it not been for this leading Abyot member, who himself remained confused until he attended the November Plenum, Getachew's activities would have passed unnoticed.

As was indicated elsewhere, the relationship between Getachew and the other PB members had become sour following the incidents at the August and September CC meetings.[35] Following the encounter at the September CC meeting, the rest of the PB members had begun questioning Getachew's credibility. When he failed to convey the decisions of the September CC meeting to the YL leadership, the mistrust deepened. Information provided by the leading member of the Abyot group exasperated the situation further. When Getachew further failed to pass the decisions contained in the PB paper, which came out in October/November 1976, to the YL CC, it became 'the last straw that broke the camel's back.' Getachew's case was raised at a PB meeting held in October/November 1976.

Getachew's actions were viewed not only as violations of democratic centralism, but also as major breach of confidence. He was suspended from the PB until the CC reviewed his case at its next meeting. According to the internal regulation of the EPRP, the PB could only suspend one of its members. Final decisions rested with the EPRP CC.

The crisis in the PB incapacitated the leadership and it was with the intention of resolving the problems in the leadership that the EPRP CC Third Plenum was called. The Plenum was attended by all CC members, save those who were abroad, in the EPRA or in prison. The main issue of the agenda was the suspension of Getachew Maru from the PB. The charges against him were presented. The core argument for his suspension being breach of the EPRP's Constitution.

Following the PB's report, other CC members recounted more incidents. It was relayed that sometime in late September or early October 1976, Getachew had been discussing current issues with two CC members, Yohannes Berhane and Kiflu Teferra. One thing led to another and in the course of the discussion, Getachew had vowed that "they" would not sit by idle. The CC members, not taking these remarks seriously, had not shared them with other members of the leadership, until the case assumed a wider magnitude at the November CC Plenum. Getachew was asked whom he was referring to when he said that "they" would not sit idle. He was also asked about the implications of the vow. He failed to give an adequate reply. From later events, it was known that this was the period that the two CC members had formed a clandestine faction within the EPRP. [36] At this time, the EPRP CC still did not know the broader activities and engagements of Berhane Meskel and Getachew Maru, and it was not aware that they had formed their own group.

After deliberating on the issue, Getachew participating and defending himself, the November CC Plenum decided that he had violated organizational discipline and democratic centralism, which were believed to be the corner-stones of EPRP's Constitution. Getachew's violations were viewed in light of the severe repression that the EPRP was undergoing. This was a period when hundreds of EPRP members were victimized. Furthermore, the meeting took note of Getachew's threats and cast its vote. As part of the voting procedure, each CC member was asked to spell out his/her support or opposition to the decision. Except Berhane Meskel, the CC members agreed to strip Getachew Maru of his CC membership, though he retained his party membership.

The only issue that the PB presented was regarding Getachew; however, Samuel Alemayehu presented Berhane Meskel's case and demanded a review. Berhane Meskel was asked why he had arranged informal contacts with EPRP members and conducted an agitation against the September CC decisions. He was asked why he had made efforts to stop the defense units from performing their assignments. He was also asked why he had campaigned against the CC decisions to members of the IZ and the zones.

After deliberating on the cases presented, the Third Plenum decided that Berhane had violated the EPRP's Constitution and the CC unanimously voted to strip him of his CC membership, though he still retained his party membership. Berhane Meskel did not deny the charges, he argued that he was stripped of his CC membership because of his differing views and argued that he was being blackmailed. The Plenum upheld that he was entitled to holding differing views and that he could present his views through the proper organizational channels. Berhane Meskel argued that the PB would not allow his articles to reach the party structure. Both Berhane Meskel and Getachew were members of the editorial committee of the internal journal of the EPRP, the *Red Star*. The Plenum promised that the CC itself would make sure that his articles would be printed and passed on to the structure in a week's time. Berhane agreed to send in his article, but he never did. Not long afterward, he severed relationship with the EPRP and changed his location. The EPRP could never reach him after that. The third Plenum which took administrative and organizational measures to curb the crisis within the leadership, did not address the political ramifications of its decisions. It did not discuss the impact of its decision on the members of the organization. It should be remembered that both Berhane Meskel and Getachew Maru were recognized veteran activists and leaders.

The decision of the Plenum was then passed on to the various party and YL structures. In the Addis Abeba area, members of the CC went to the various committees to explain the case. An internal paper was also prepared to that effect. A CC member was specifically assigned to explain the decisions of the Plenum to some former members of the Abyot group.

Formation of a Faction - Phase One

The formation of the faction within the EPRP can be categorized into two phases. The first phase covers from September 1976 until April 1977, while the second phase began in May 1977 when some members of the faction started collaborating with the Derge.

The activities of Berhane Meskel and Getachew Maru, which were kept secret from the CC, began unfolding following the disclosure of the decisions of the third CC Plenum to the EPRP and the YL members. Some EPRP members opened up and explained that they had been contacted by the CC members. To relay their messages, the two CC members had been contacting former members of the Abyot group, the EPRP sub-Secretariat of the Shoa province, other members of the EPRP CC sub-Secretariat, members of the Shoa EPRP party committee, members of the Addis Abeba party zones and interzone, members of the zonal defense units, members of the Youth League CC and the main defense units of the EPRP. Some of these members were asked to provide their stories in writing.

KM, one of the founding members of the EPRP and a member of the Shoa sub-secretariat was at a comrade's residence when he met Berhane Meskel whom he had known as a student activist.

> After exchanging greetings, since I did not think that Berhane Meskel was in Addis Abeba, I asked him what he was doing here. He told me that he was a prisoner of the EPRP CC. I did not take him seriously; I thought that he was teasing. He then told me that he had differences with the CC and said that he could not understand why the EPRP does not work with the Derge and emphatically argued that the EPRP had to do so. This was a period when a large number of EPRP members were executed by the Mengistu clique and I was very shocked to hear those words from Berhane Meskel. He then asked me about conditions in Shoa. I reported my encounter with Berhane Meskel to the EPRP CC.[37]

Another revelation about the formation of the faction came from two leading members of the group itself; Getachew Assefa, a member of the Editorial Board of *Democracia* and "Berhane", a member of the IZ who represented the zone one committee. They informed the EPRP CC about the formation of a clandestine committee within the EPRP and disclosed that they had been conducting meetings in the presence of both CC members since September 1976. Until this confession was brought forth to the attention of the EPRP CC, in the first months of 1977, the extent of the factional activities within the EPRP remained unknown. According to the revelation, besides the two CC members, the other leading members of the faction were, Abiyu

Airsamo, a member of the EPRP zone-five committee in Addis Abeba and Endrias, a member of the political department of the EPRP. Almost all of them were very close friends of Getachew Maru.

When they learned about the expulsion of Berhane Meskel and Getachew Maru from the EPRP CC, Getachew Assefa and "Berhane" decided to reveal what they knew about the faction. According to the report provided by these two members, one of the factors that induced them to report the case to the EPRP leadership was their discovery of the two CC members' desire, particularly Berhane Meskel's, to form some kind of alliance with the Derge. In a written letter addressed to the leadership, "Berhane" (code name) of zone one explained that Berhane Meskel was regrouping an armed group in order to use it as a bargaining chip or a pressure group to force the Derge to negotiate with him. According to the revelation, Berhane Meskel preferred the rural areas of Shoa, both for the sake of expediency and relative security. Besides, Berhane Meskel believed that the Addis Abeba youth would join him in large numbers and enhance the prestige of his group if he had an armed unit.

Both "Berhane" of zone one and Getachew Assefa gave similar accounts about the factional activities. After conducting criticism and self-criticism sessions, they resumed their organizational activities. Getachew Assefa remained a member of the Editorial Board of *Democracia*. "Berhane", who previously had been suspended from the Addis Abeba IZ and zone committees,[38] was reinstated to both of them a few months later.[39] It was after these and other similar revelations that the CC learned about the formation of a faction within the EPRP. The most damaging act, as far as the EPRP leadership was concerned, was that of zone one defense committee. Berhane Meskel persuaded the secretary of the defense committee not to be engaged in the offensive-defense activities of the EPRP.

As was indicated earlier, the Addis Abeba IZ contact man for zone one, "Berhane" and the secretary of the defense committee of zone one, who then were members of the faction, were informing their respective committee members that they should not engage in the offensive-defensive activities of the EPRP, arguing that it was not the policy of the leadership. By this time, the Addis Abeba IZ had discussed the decisions of the September CC meeting and it had assigned its contact persons, including "Berhane" of zone one, to pass on the issue to the zones and sub-zones, however, "Berhane" failed to do so. When they felt that Berhane of zone one was conveying the wrong message, other members of the zonal committee began arguing to the contrary. Those who became confused remained neutral. When the zone committee reached an impasse, some of its members began inquiring about the policy of the EPRP CC from members of the YL zone one committee. It was then that the zone one party committee's case was brought to the attention of the YL leadership that passed it on to the PB. The PB then assigned Tesfaye Debessai and Tselote Hiskias to discuss the decisions of the September EPRP CC meeting and resolve the differences. In the course of this discussion, members of the CC also explained the breach of discipline committed by the IZ contact person and the Secretary of the defense committee. When it learnt that Berhane, the contact person for zone one committee did not pass its decisions, the IZ suspended him from its committee, but he remained a party member and was handled on the basis of a single contact.

The zone one committee, in a separate meeting of its own, suspended the defense secretary from the zone after discussing the breach of discipline. It also assigned another contact person. In retaliation, the secretary of the defense committee refused to hand over the units, the arms and the cash that still was in his possession, and used the structure under him and EPRP's property for activities related to the faction. From October 1976 until March 1977, the zone one defense structure which had a large number of youth members was totally incapacitated and could not take part in resisting the war of annihilation. During this period, EPRP members were victimized by the hundreds and thousands. After realizing the condition of the zone one defense structure, the Addis Abeba IZ formed a new structure in March 1977, in the midst of the most deadly house to house search.

Based on the above discussed events and other reports that came from different members of the EPRP, in March 1977, the EPRP CC decided to arrest both former CC members. At a pre-arranged meeting, Getachew was apprehended, but the CC was unable to reach Berhane Meskel who, by then, had made his independent preparations that included the formation of an armed group. In order to pursue his objective, he established contact with the EPRP party structure in the Shoa area.

Takeover of EPRP Activities in Shoa

In the first months of 1977, peasants revolted in many parts of the Shoa province. One of them was in Shoa Robbit, an area where the government owned a large farm, run by prisoners. The people in the town and the peasants revolted and after fining the wereda administrator 1000 birr, they discharged him from his post. The task of administering the wereda fell into the hands of the officials elected by the kebeles and peasant associations. Following the uprising, some kind of a people's government prevailed; peasants, the youth, teachers, employees of the EPID, Tobacco Monopoly and other workers of the area took part.

Partly responding to the crisis, the Derge appointed a host of political administrators, among them Dr. Mekonnen Jotte as the Administrator of the Shoa province and Assefa Gebre Mariam as the administrator of the most rebellious Aweraja, Yifatena Timuga.

In the first months of 1977, Dr. Mekonnen Jotte, accompanied by well armed and equipped soldiers, went to the Kobbo wereda, Shoa province, to quell the rebellion. He dismantled the newly formed "People's Administration", arrested some activists and conducted an intensive campaign against the EPRP. While the Administrator prepared to leave the area, the peasants of Rasa and Guba decided to ambush him and waited for over seven days and nights at a selected site. However, Dr. Mekonnen took another route and escaped the ambush.[40]

Shoa was one of the strategically located areas as far as the EPRP's organizational activities were concerned and it was one of the six major areas where the EPRP had intended to commence armed struggle. The EPRP had initiated armed struggle in Tigrai, Wello, Begemidir, and the Sidamo provinces. By 1976, it had already established itself in two of them.

The study regarding the locations in Shoa began as early as 1975. The hinterlands of Merhabete, a treacherous terrain in the Yefatena Temuga Aweraja, the area known as the "ring",- adjacent to Wello and the Dankale area -- Menz, Geshe and the Debre Sina areas were selected as possible sites to begin an armed struggle.

Besides their strategic significance, the armed activities to be initiated in the Shoa and Sidamo provinces were *also designed to create relatively safe areas where EPRP members and sympathizers from the cities of the central and southern parts of Ethiopia would retreat in case of major calamities.* The EPRA controlled areas in Tigrai and Begemidir were used as possible retreat areas from the cities in the northern parts of the country.

When the large search and destroy campaign was unleashed in Addis Abeba both in March and April 1977, it was to the rural areas of Shoa that the EPRP sent a good number of its leading activists for safety. Moreover, in September and October 1977, leading members and committees of the EPRP and the YL were instructed to reside in some Shoa urban and rural areas. Among the committees that moved to these areas was the Editorial Board of *Democracia.*

As part of the preparation to commence an armed struggle in the Shoa area, sometime in 1976, indigenous EPRP members were sent to the EPRA for military training. Because of the crisis in the EPRA,[41] the takeover of the areas studied to initiate the armed struggle in Shoa and the instability created as a result of the repression, EPRP's effort to initiate the armed activity was delayed and the trainees were forced to stay in the EPRA for an indefinite period.

By October or November 1976, the Berhane Meskel faction established contact with the EPRP party representatives of the Merhabete area. That contact was established with a clear purpose of taking over of the areas that the EPRP had been studying to conduct an armed struggle. The study had been going-on for quite some time and detailed studies, which both Berhane Meskel and Getachew Maru were familiar with, had been prepared.

After convincing the party committee of the Merhabete area, the Berhane Meskel group took over the studies. Around March 1977, Berhane Meskel organized a small armed group and went to Merhabete, to the specific location that the EPRP had studied. That takeover constituted a major set back to EPRP's activities and its efforts to create a retreat zone.

Furthermore, another major disaster befell the EPRP when Abiyu Airsamo, who was suspended from the Addis Abeba IZ, refused to pass over some members of the zone-five structure. Abiyu was the secretary and the contact person of the zone to the Addis Abeba IZ. Without the knowledge of the IZ or the EPRP leadership, Abiyu sent over 28 workers of the Akaki area to Merhabte, to join the Berhane Meskel group. The information regarding Abiyu Airsamo's activities came to the attention of the EPRP following the escape and return of four of the workers to Addis Abeba. They wrote a detailed report about the case. They reported that they were not informed that they were being sent to the group organized by the faction, but that they were joining the EPRA of the Shoa area that the faction named as "mini-Assimba". (Assimba was the base area of the EPRA in Tigrai). Be that as it may, when it was known that the Berhane Meskel group had taken over the site selected in the Merhabete district, the EPRP began paying more attention to other alternate sites.

Despite the crisis caused by the faction, at the beginning of 1977 the EPRP was able to regroup and lay down its structure in some parts of Shoa. It established itself in some of the important districts and towns, that is, Shoa Robbit, Debre Sina, Ataye, Debre Berhane, Selale, Welkite, Nazreth, Arbaya, Gemza Wereda, Cheffa Robbit, etc. The EPRP Shoa zonal committee was composed of the representatives of the various sub-zonal committees. The contact to the center was KM, a member of the Secretariat. He had been assigned there since 1975 and had a major role in organizing and consolidating the EPRP structure.

The party structure of the Shoa area, along with some other members, including those from the Airborne units, became engaged in the study to initiate an armed struggle. However, the effort came to a halt when one of the leading members of the committee, Kifle, went public and disclosed EPRP's clandestine activities. Besides, one of the members of the armed group defected and informed the regime about some of the plans, which included an operation on the police station in Ataye.[42] As a result, some EPRP members fell into the hands of the government. Those who survived the crisis were moved to different locations. The preparation to commence an armed struggle in the Shoa province was temporarily discontinued.

Peasant rebellions led by some former landlords were also taking place in other parts of Shoa, such as Mehal Medda, Muger, Menz, etc.[43] In one of them, the peasantry brought the surrounding area under its control and vowed to defend it to the last. EPRP members who had some role in these activities informed the EPRP leadership about the case[44] and demanded a more qualified political leadership. In response, some arms and additional members were sent to join the people against the regime. In the meantime, the EPRP group that had joined the peasant revolt was asked to conduct studies about the prospect of transforming the rebellion into a full-fledged armed struggle. Among leading members of the group sent to the area was the veteran activist MZ.

Realizing the severity of the crisis and its ramifications, the regime made some concessions to the people and averted the danger. Those peasants who had gone out to the hills went back to their homes. As a result, a group of about thirty EPRP members were left on their own. In order to save the peasantry from the Derge's retribution, the EPRP group moved away from the area and finally ended up in the Kesem desert, adjacent to Harer province. The more the group drifted away from the inhabited areas, the more it isolated itself from the people and getting basic supplies became more and more difficult. Finally, it was realized that it was difficult to initiate an armed struggle in that area and the EPRP group was withdrawn from the location.

The February 1977 EPRP CC Meeting

The February CC meeting took place soon after the Mengistu coup in February 1977. The meeting was conducted at the residence of EPRP members in the Tekle Haimanot area, in Addis Abeba. It was located in a large compound that was also shared by others. The residence happened to be one of those places where some party documents used to be kept or buried. In order not to arouse the suspicion of the people residing in the compound and because of the on-going repression, special precautions and arrangements, such as, the assignment of squads, were made. Like the previous gatherings, this was also an overnight meeting.

Sometime after the meeting began, the whole compound, approximately the size of a soccer field, was swamped with all kinds of pamphlets and the ground turned snow-white. The defense units in charge became annoyed and reported the matter to their contact person and the CC meeting was disrupted. It remained difficult for quite a while to figure out what had taken place and the CC members were told to be on the ready to leave the compound. Since the compound was shared by other residents, it was very difficult to predict their reaction should they see pamphlets scattered all over the place.

Both the units and the CC member in charge conducted an investigation and saw a dog with a piece of paper in its mouth. Thinking some foul play, they followed it and, to their surprise, they found out that it had dug out some of the party documents. Taking a mouthful of the pamphlets and scattering them around, the dog was trying to make its *boring* night more pleasant. In this *endeavor*, the dog was assisted by the wind, which scattered the leaflets to cover the whole compound. While the rest of the CC members were awaiting the result of the investigation, Yohannes Berhane returned and told the story with his witty and humorous tone. Perhaps he himself might have found a topic for one of the witty short stories that he used to write.

Hours were wasted before the situation was under control. Since calling another CC meeting was extremely difficult, the meeting was resumed.

The February CC meeting was attended by nine CC members. The main issues of the agenda included: the Eritrean question, relationship with the Eritrean organizations, foreign relations, reviewing the decisions of the

August Plenum and the EPRA.

It should be reiterated that after discarding the communiqué signed by the EPLF and the EPRP delegates in August 1976, the Second CC Plenum had formed a committee to study the Eritrean question. Accordingly, the committee prepared a paper and presented it to EPRP CC members who reviewed it in groups of twos and threes. It should be remembered that this was a period of intense repression and conducting a meeting where a large number of members took part was avoided. Adding or deleting whatever they had to, the CC members passed their feedback to the PB which prepared the final draft and sent it back to the CC members.

One of the first issues of the agenda of the February CC meeting was reviewing the paper regarding the question of Eritrea and formulating a new policy and approach to resolve the problem. The above mentioned paper, which became the basis for the agenda of the February CC meeting, reviewed the history and the struggle in Eritrea, with a special focus on the events of the last 100 years or so. It also discussed how the Eritrean struggle for independence began and enumerated certain basic principles that progressives of both oppressor and oppressed nationalities should adopt.

Based on historic, economic, cultural and political premises, the meeting resolved that the EPRP could view the Eritrean question only as a national one. It declined to accept the claim that Eritrea was an Ethiopian colony, thereby clarifying the confusion that was created as a result of the EPRP/EPLF communiqué signed in 1976.

The next important point that the paper addressed and the CC meeting ratified was EPRP's policy regarding the ongoing struggle in Eritrea. When the EPLO/EPRP was formed in the early seventies, the national question had constituted one of the major points of the program and the EPRP had supported the struggle in Eritrea and the right of Eritreans to self-determination. The national question had been one of the main issues discussed among the radical groups of the country and the EPRP had been one of the first groups that fought against what it believed to be injustice commited against Eritrean and other nationals.

Since November 1974, the EPRP had advocated peaceful and political resolution of the Eritrean question. This policy came out as opposed to the militaristic approach of the regime. Besides, in 1974, the EPRP called for a referendum in order to determine the will of the Eritrean populace.[45] However, at that time, both the fronts and the regime were not ready for such an option.

The new element that the paper presented at the February CC meeting introduced was the question of expediency, that is, the recognition of Eritrean independence. The paper discussed the wide support that the Eritrean struggle for national independence enjoyed and argued that the nationalist cause had overshadowed the class struggle. It was analyzed that the nationalist struggle in Eritrea had become an obstacle to forge an alliance of the oppressed peoples of Eritrea with the peoples in the other parts of Ethiopia. "Failure to resolve the national struggle in Eritrea peacefully had relegated the class struggle to a secondary level," it was stated.[46] Until this time, the struggle for democracy and economic welfare remained the dominant feature in the rest of Ethiopia. Unless the national aspect of the Eritrean problem was resolved, it was argued, the class question could not find a solution.[47] Recognizing Eritrean independence would create understanding and better relationship between the peoples of Eritrea and Ethiopia and [48] would create conditions for the cooperation of Eritrean and Ethiopian progressives and people and facilitate a *higher unity* based on mutual consent and understanding, it was argued.

In conclusion, the EPRP CC decided that progressives should accept the independence of Eritrea, in order to resolve the fratricidal war and establish solidarity with the Eritrean people. The human and economic cost of the war was an area of concern as well. Furthermore, ressolving the Eritrean issue would allow the Ethiopian people to focus on issues related to the class struggle. It was presumed that EPRP's new policy would gain it sympathy among Eritreans and the EPRP's political and organizational activities would be facilitated.

After agreeing, in principle, to support Eritrean independence and before making the decision public, the CC sent the draft to the party and Youth League structures for a final say on the issue. With some minor changes, EPRP's position regarding the Eritrean issue came out on the *Democracia* issue quoted above.

The other agenda item discussed in the February CC meeting was the mandate to be given to the EPRP delegation that was to conduct negotiation with the Eritrean organizations. A delegation that was to be headed by Tesfaye Debessai was formed; its main task was to follow up the negotiation that had begun the previous year. Unlike the previous negotiations where EPRP delegates had committed some errors due to lack of a clear mandate, and had caused some embarrassment to the EPRP, the February CC meeting gave detailed guidance on the agenda for negotiation.

One of the first questions that the EPRP delegation could discuss with its Eritrean counterparts with full confidence would be the position of the EPRP on the question of the on-going struggle in Eritrea and the issue of Eritrean independence. The other major point raised was how to approach the fronts, particularly the ELF. By 1976, it was known that an underground "communist" core was formed within the ELF and one of the problems was how the EPRP delegation should respond if that clandestine group wanted to conduct the discussion on behalf of the front. The EPRP CC had no knowledge about the composition and policy of the clandestine group and its relationship with the ELF itself. Unable to come up with a better alternative, the February CC instructed the EPRP delegation to conduct the negotiation only with the ELF. If approached by the clandestine group within the ELF, the EPRP delegation was instructed to limit itself to collecting documents and information.

In 1977, one of the major concerns of the EPRP remained obtaining arms. The February CC meeting discussed how to strengthen existing relationships with governments and organizations and establish new contacts with others. With this in mind, the relationship with the Somalia government was revived.[49] That contact had first been established in the early seventies. The relationship with the Chinese government was also given special attention. It was emphasized that the EPRP should continue providing adequate explanation and assessment of the Ethiopian situation in order to dispel the Chinese illusion regarding the nature of the Derge. The Chinese remained supportive of the military regime until the Derge established a warm and friendly relationship with the government of the former Soviet Union and signed a military pact.

The CC meeting reviewed the decisions of the August Plenum and discussed the process of sending more members and some necessary materials and finance to the EPRA. It also discussed the case of those CC members assigned to the different IZs and made some modifications consistent with the changes that the organization was under-going. The commencement of the armed struggle in the Sidamo area was another issue of discussion.[50]

The last point on the agenda was related to the EPRA. A number of problems, particularly those that were related to the combat readiness of the EPRA were raised and discussed. The report was presented by Fikre Zergaw, who was assigned as Secretary of the IZ in the Tigrai and Wello areas. After deliberating on the issue, the CC mandated the delegation to be headed by Tesfaye Debessai to conduct some kind of a rectification movement in the EPRA.

Before the CC meeting was adjourned, three CC members raised questions about the wisdom of conducting the urban and rural armed struggle on equal footing. The CC members, however, were not opposed to the idea of conducting armed struggle both in the urban and rural areas. The CC began deliberating on the issue, but did not go far enough due to lack of time. By then, it was already dawn, and the meeting had to disperse. The meeting decided to discuss the issue at its next meeting, which never took place.

The February 1977 meeting was the last gathering of the EPRP CC proper which had led the EPRP from its inception. When the CC meeting adjourned, most of the CC members did not know that this would be their last meeting. The CC had even decided that it would conduct another meeting to resolve some of the issues that were already raised. The CC, whose number had dwindled due to the repression and factional activities, was to lose some of its invaluable members in the months ahead.

The War of Annihilation - Phase Two

It was mentioned that the campaign and propaganda of the regime was specifically targeted at the EPRP leadership.

The first phase of the war of annihilation was more selective and the repression could not be intensified the way the originators had intended. This was primarily due to the struggle within the Derge and the gradual isolation of the Mengistu/POMOA alliance, the group behind the repression. The second phase of the war of annihilation took place under a changed political condition. Following the coup in February 1977, the Mengistu/POMOA alliance gained the upper hand and it controlled political power and the intensification of the war of annihilation became the number one agenda item of the alliance.

Phase II of the war of annihilation, even though similar to the first phase in its intents and goals, employed different approaches. An *Addis Zemen* newspaper editorial stated, "after 'exposing' and conducting criticism and self-criticism, the Welliso activists gave the names and pictures of anarchists to kebele officials. . .Addis Abeba student fighters should start the same process."[51] The editorial, written by the late Berhanu Zerihun, after enumerating the crimes of the EPRP, stated, "because of the danger its poses, the fascist group (meaning the EPRP), has to be nipped in the bud."[52]

The second phase of the war of annihilation had three more additional characteristics. These were, "mass confession", "mass terror" and search and destroy campaigns. Furthermore, during this phase, the Ethiopian army, the security, or the police force took very minimal or at best supportive roles in the repression. POMOA and particularly MEISON rallied the "discussion clubs", the kebeles and the Abyot Tebeka to conduct the repression.

During the second phase, the military regime came out with a number of public announcements geared to destroying the EPRP. Most of these statements focused on the youth and the working class. It was also proclaimed that the seventeen years old Evangelical Radio Station was nationalized. The Derge did this on the pretext of religious equality; however, the regime might have been attracted by the powerful wave length of the station. By nationalizing the station, the Derge abrogated the thirty-year agreement signed between the previous regime and the World Lutheran Church.

The Regime and the Youth

Since the declaration of the war of annihilation, one of the primary targets of POMOA and the regime had been the youth. Following the opening of schools in September 1976, intense political activities took place on the school grounds. These activities were further stepped up after the return of zematch students in July 1976. Schools became political grounds for rival groups on both sides of the political spectrum and both anti and pro-Derge campaign rhetoric was exchanged.

In February 1977, POMOA organized a two day seminar for about 1500 students. The seminar was conducted at the office of the National Council. By this time, schools had been transformed into arenas where the extermination campaign expressed itself more vividly. Radical students were singled out and they became the targets of the repression when, beginning around the end of January 1977, schools were frequently visited by armed "students" and members of the *Abyot Tebeka* who intruded in the activities of the schools.

Discussion "clubs", organized at the level of the various schools, were transformed into centres of mass "confession". According to the Decree which established the discussion "clubs", they were supposed to be outlets of free political discussions and students used them as vehicles to politicize themselves and raise their demands. Student Activitim was not without its price. Those students who for one reason or another did not support the regime were left with little or no alternative. If they stayed in school, they had to take part in the discussions organized by the "clubs" and thus be identified with the EPRP and become easy targets of the repression. On the other hand, if they avoided the discussion "clubs", their absence would give POMOA a free hand to mobilize a large following and coerce those that were opposed to its policies. Whether they took part in the discussions or not, it did not matter much; either way, the students felt that they were the losers. Consequently, after conducting a campaign and convincing the majority of the student body, students in the Addis Abeba area boycotted classes as of January 27, 1977. Many of the schools were closed and remained so for about a month. Around the third week of February 1977, the Ministry of Education ordered students to go back to their schools. It also declared, "... any unauthorized meeting is illegal...it is prohibited to carry any kind of weapon (including knives) to school."[53] When the statement released by the Ministry did not persuade students to go back to schools, kebeles were ordered to arrest any youth that they saw in the streets during school hours. However, with a vast number of unemployed citizens and zematches that had evacuated their camps, implementing that decision was not easy.

Unable to sustain the boycott for long, students went back to their schools and one of the main activities of POMOA became weeding out "reactionary" students. As a result, the arrest of activists from the school grounds continued and sometime in February 1977, in a statement titled "[B]eing young is no excuse for being reactionary", the regime declared that it will not sit by idle, while its sons are murdered by fascist youngsters. A Derge statement released on February 14, 1977, further accentuated the massive repression of students in the school compounds. After enumerating what it called an assault on "progressive" students, the statement declared,

> "...[the Derge] realizes that it has not only the right, but the duty to take revolutionary defensive measures against reactionary students and teachers...so, the Committees for Education and the kebele associations...in collaboration with the regime, should take appropriate measures."[54]

The so-called Committee for Education came into being in September 1976. In the Proclamation, it was decreed that schools would be governed by a committee composed of members from kebele or peasant associations, a teacher and a student each of whom was elected by his/her constituency and the Principal. It was also stated that the member of the committee should accept the NDR program of the Derge.[55] The committee was entrusted with the sole responsibility of guiding and administering the school. To enforce its decisions, "it [the committee] will collaborate with the kebele association in the area, or the *Abyot Tebeka* or the Peasant Association, or the Police."⁵⁶ This was in contrast to the EPRP program promulgated in August 1975 which stated that the rights of students to get organized, take part in the schools' adminstration, curriculum preparation and disciplinary activities would be respected.⁵⁷

In the first months of 1977, POMOA representatives, accompanied by Abyot Tebeka members of the different areas went to the various schools and held meetings and read out names of students labeled as "reactionaries". If the students were present at the meetings, they were arrested and sent to the newly formed kebele prisons. At the prisons, some of the students were tortured while others were executed. Only very few of them were released. A typical example would be the case of the Technical School of Addis Abeba where in the first months of 1977, student members of the MEISON unexpectedly called a meeting of the entire student body. MEISON members, accompanied by an *Abyot Tebeka* group arrived at the meeting hall. When the meeting commenced, a list of about one hundred student names was read out and they were asked to come out and stand by the podium. Only twenty-four did. The rest, aware of what was coming, had stayed away from school. Of the twenty-four arrested, twenty confessed and were released; four were executed.⁵⁸

To counter these and other government actions, students decided to cleanse the school grounds from what they believed were government informants. Supporters of the regime became identified with its violent policies and many, rightly or wrongly, were regarded as its agents, and were intimidated. With the aim of defending themselves, students harassed and beat those they thought to be government agents. Some students were victimized at the Teferi Mekonnen, Kokebe Tsebah, the Commercial School, General Wingate, Prince Mekonnen, Medhane Alem and Shemelis Habte schools.⁵⁹

As a result of the massive repression that ensued and afraid of its consequences, many students preferred to stay away from schools. The discussion clubs, many of which were led by the underground student organization affiliated to the YL, were weakened and MEISON took the upper hand. Consequently, among the main targets of the search and destroy campaign were those students who had been away from the schools for fear of repression. Those students numbered in the thousands. The names of most of these students were in the hands of POMOA. During the search and destroy campaign of March and April 1977, student informants rendered an incalculable service to the regime by identifying the student activists. A very large number of these students were arrested and subjected to torture or "mass confession", a new form of self-denunciation.

Mass Confession

During the first phase of the war of annihilation, the act of confession focused on individuals and was broadcast over the media. During the second phase, however, the confession assumed a mass nature when almost all of those institutions that came into existence following the formation of POMOA, such as the discussion "clubs" and the *Abyot Tebeka* were gradually transformed into instruments of terror. Under the direction of POMOA/MEISON, a broad campaign of "denouncing oneself", known in its Amharic, "yemagalete zemetcha" took place in many of the factories, schools and kebeles. For a period of a year or so, the whole country was gripped in a process of "mass confession" and "self-denunciation". During the initial stage of this campaign, the names of some of the activists were read over the media. However, in the course of the struggle, such incidents became routine and day to day events.

At a "self-confession" session, POMOA members would demand that "anarchists" voluntarily come to the podium. If no response was forthcoming, names of alleged "anarchists" would be read out and the public was encouraged to provide more names. That process was repeated until the names of all of those that were suspected of "anarchist" connections were provided and POMOA representatives felt that they had the situation under control.

The accused individuals were then told to come out to the podium and line-up in front of the audience. They were then asked to testify if they had any relationship with the EPRP. If so, they were asked to condemn the organization. In the initial phase of this process, that is, in the first months of 1977, very few admitted that they belonged to the EPRP; most denied that they had any relationship with the organization or its affiliate mass organizations. Many of them had no relationship with the EPRP and had nothing to "expose" or hide. Some of them became victims of the process either because of bad relationships with POMOA representatives or because of their outspoken character. A good number of these individuals became "exposed" when they presented their grievances during the discussions conducted at the "clubs". They did so not because they supported the EPRP, but because they thought that the military regime might solve some of their problems.

Coordinated by POMOA, the "mass confession" conducted in one of the institutions was then made public. This was done to provide lessons to other areas where such an activity did not take place. At the same time, it was done to instill fear in the minds of the citizens, as the Amharic saying indicates, "*Inen yayeh teketa*" (learn from my experience). As a result, in February and March 1977, one of the major engagements of the radio, the TV and the newspapers was broadcasting the "mass confessions" conducted in the various institutions.

In the second week of March 1977, "mass confession" was conducted in eight factories of the Akaki area. That activity was coordinated by Abyot Tebeka members. Among these factories was the Addis Tire, where a very large percentage of the workers had been highly radicalized and were taking active and leading roles in the workers struggle. Seventeen workers were arrested at the mass confession.[60] By this time, their leader, Achameleh Kebede, the former president of the union, was an underground activist. Similar "mass confessions" were conducted in many of the factories, among them were the Ethio-Cement Factory and Ethio-Metals. In order to avoid the repression, many workers stayed away from their work place, thereby increasing the rate of joblessness. In the case of the Addis Tire factory mentioned above, "of the three shifts of workers of the factory, only one third of them were effectively employed", stated *Democracia*.[61]

In the Shoa province of Welliso, in a number of government institutions, such as, the Malaria Eradication Center and elementary and high schools, a number of teachers and students were arrested, after alleged "mass confession".[62] Similar student "mass confessions" were conducted in Hosaena, Shoa province.[63]

During the "mass confession", efforts were made to involve ordinary citizens by coercing them to take some role in the process. In many parts of the country, the regime coerced parents to come out against their daughters and sons. When that approach failed to work, the regime fabricated stories to that effect. A case in point would be the incident in Dessie where it was reported that the parents of the Weizero Siheen High School students had asked the government to take actions against their sons and daughters. [64]

Mass Terror

The main objective of the "mass confession" was to imbue "mass terror" among the citizens and, during the first months of 1977, it became to be known as the "Red Terror". As was indicated in Chapter IV, the cornerstone for the "Red Terror" was laid down in September 1976. However, it had remained ineffective due to the struggle within the Derge.

The intensification of the war of annihilation in the first months of 1977 transformed the whole society into a mamooth police state and it seemed that the conflict would be resolved only through armed means. The center to coordinate the repression being POMOA/MEISON, the most important instruments of terror were the *Abyot Tebeka* committees formed both at the level of institutions and kebeles. At the beginning of 1977, POMOA/MEISON had all the necessary instruments of repression, save prisons, which were to be provided some time later.

In the first months of 1977, some of the *Abyot Tebeka* committees were not controlled by POMOA. When some of these institutions exhibited less vigor, Abyot Tebeka groups of adjacent or far away kebeles came to their areas to conduct the repression on their behalf.

Unlike the first phase, where the arrest was selective, in the second phase, in February 1977, the repression assumed a massive nature and became arbitrary and indiscriminate. Thousands of EPRP members, particularly from among the working class and the youth were arrested. In certain parts of the country, particularly in the provincial cities and small towns, POMOA representatives forced a certain section of the society to conduct parades, carrying placards that read "anarchists", counter-revolutionary, etc.

One of the specific forms through which the "mass terror" expressed itself was the program known as the search and destroy campaign.

The First Search and Destroy Campaign

The program of the search and destroy campaign originated at the POMOA office of the Addis Abeba branch, chaired by Kebede Mengesha, a a veteran student activist and a leading member of the MEISON.[65] Prior to this, in November 1976, the Derge had conducted a house to house search to confiscate arms. However, the first major search and destroy campaign in Addis Abeba was supposed to be launched at the end of February 1977. According to the program of MEISON, the campaign was to be conducted for 72 consecutive hours, blocking all the streets, leading in and out of Addis Abeba. It was also planned to halt all forms of activities, including movement, for the 72-hours period and Addis Abeba inhabitants were supposed to stay at home. It was planned that government units would conduct a house to house search and arrest or kill anyone that they thought was an EPRP member or sympathizer and finally destroy the EPRP in a single blow.

This plan in hand, POMOA called a seminar for about four hundred police officers who were supposed to take part in the program. The seminar was held for about three days and in the course of the discussion, the participants exhibited unwillingness and reluctance to take part in the campaign. They raised a number of technical problems, indicating the difficulty of conducting such a campaign. One of the major points raised was the difficulty of halting movement for 72 hours. They explained that there were areas that had to operate for 24 hours, such as, hospitals, hotels and stores. To express their opposition, the police officers also raised many loopholes in the plan. When POMOA realized that it could not use the police force in this campaign, it branded the police force as reactionary. It was true that the police force had harbored some grudge against POMOA, as a result of the loss of its Derge representative, Captain Alemayehu Haile, a leading member of the anti-Mengistu faction who was executed during the Mengistu coup. The EPRP, particularly the "Oppressed Soldiers Organization" had also established a network in the police force. Captain Amha Abebe, a leading EPRP member and the chairperson of the "OSO" was from the police force. When POMOA realized that it could not conduct the campaign as it had intended, it made certain adjustments.

EPRP's Preparations

When the details of the February 1977 search and destroy plans were known, the PB conducted an emergency meeting in the Mercato area. The decisions of the PB were then discussed with those CC members who at that time resided in Addis Abeba.

The PB meeting considered three options to resist the search and destroy campaign: remain totally inactive and await the outcome of the campaign, deploy EPRP defense units and resist the campaign, or open up offensive-defense operations.

During the house to house search conducted in November 1976, what EPRP and Youth League members did was to hide away incriminating evidence and take some precaution. The EPRP did not confront the force that went out on the campaign. Because of the nature of the campaign, whose focus was confiscating arms, the damage inflicted on the EPRP was minimal. However, during the second campaign, POMOA had vowed to arrest anyone that it suspected and, even if the EPRP remained inactive, POMOA/MEISON was resolved to inflict as much damage. Consequently, the first option, that is, remaining inactive was considered inappropriate for the new form of campaign that POMOA had organized. The second option, that is, deploying units was also disregarded, because of lack of personnel, know how and arms, and above all, the human cost it would inflict on the EPRP. The third option was selected as the most appropriate for the situation. It was decided to conduct sabotage activities against selected government properties without, however, involving human causalities. The aim of the plan was to divert the attention of the military force away from the search and destroy campaign, without confronting it. As was indicated earlier, when the plan to conduct the campaign for 72 consecutive hours did not materialize, EPRP's plans were also modified.

As part of a precautionary step, the PB decided to send many EPRP members out of Addis Abeba to the rural areas of the Shoa province. Consequently, over forty-five leading activists were temporarily sent out through the party structure. About the same number of activists were sent out by the Youth League structure. Some members, including Zeru and Tselote, went to the Tigrai area, and were able to reach the EPRA. Other members made their own arrangements. Only Kiflu Tadesse and Tesfaye Debessai remained in Addis Abeba, after arrangement was made in the residence of some diplomats. However, Tesfaye's diplomat hosts, very much afraid of *Abyot Tebeka* members, who they thought to be zealots and ignorant of international law regarding diplomatic immunity, could not keep Tesfaye beyond two days. The diplomats became much more worried after they realized that one of their housekeepers had been making efforts to know who Tesfaye was and what he was doing in the diplomat's residence.

It was during this period that the PB learned about the loss of some of the areas in the Shoa province that the EPRP had earlier on prepared for a retreat in the event of a calamity. As was discussed elsewhere, by the first months of 1977, some of those locations, regarded as EPRP retreat areas were taken over by the faction led by Berhane Meskel. Some of the party committees in these areas had severed contact with the EPRP leadership while others were found to be unreliable. This revelation, at this crucial hour was a severe blow to the EPRP.

To be able to withstand the campaign, the PB introduced some structural changes regarding the urban military units. The party, the YL and ELAMA structures were combined to form what was known as the unified command. By the beginning of 1977, each party zonal committee had between four to six units under its command and when combined with the Youth League and ELAMA structures of the same jurisdiction, that number could reach about eighteen. The unified command was assembled only for a joint operation demanding a larger force. Under other circumstances, the units remained under the zonal committees of their respective structures. By the beginning of 1977, in the Addis Abeba area alone, all combined, that is, the party, the Youth League and the ELAMA, there were between fifty to sixty units with two hundred twenty five to two hundred fifty members.

In March 1977, while getting ready to withstand the search and destroy campaign, the EPRP lost four of its invaluable leading members: Yohannes Berhane, a member of the CC and one of the leading members of the *Democracia* Editorial Board; Melaku Marcos, a veteran activist, a knowledgeable intellectual, Secretary of the Sidamo, Gamu Gofa, Bale and Arsi IZ, and a "CC" member without portfolio; Nega Ayele, an economist and a lecturer at the University of Addis Abeba and a member of the EPRP political department; Dr. William Hastings Morton, a British lecturer at the Addis Abeba University and a member of the EPRP. All of them were killed on their way to a safe retreat in the Langano area, Sidamo province.

When it was known that the search and destroy campaign was to unfold, Melaku, who had come to Addis Abeba to discuss the preparation to initiate a southern armed front of the EPRP, informed his close comrades that he could take them to the Sidamo area until conditions improved. With this in mind, arrangements were made and Dr. Morton came into the picture to provide means of transportation and to give the group a plausible disguise. On a Saturday morning, on the day that the campaign was expected to begin, the members named above and AY left for the south, via the Akaki road.

In order to avoid the check point at Akaki, three of them, Yohannes Berhane, AY and Melaku Marcos stepped out of the vehicle just before the city limits. As they walked through an alley, past a factory gate in the Kaliti area, two of them in front and AY following, they encountered Abyot Tebeka members from one of the factories. They tried to run away, but they were chased by the *Abyot Tebeka* members and a mob of workers that was just going out on a break. Yohannes and Melaku were killed on the spot. Yohannes and Melaku were irreplaceable EPRP members in their fields of engagements, Yohannes as a talented writer, and Melaku as an able organizer and leader. Besides, Melaku's loss had a debilitating effect on EPRP's activities in the Sidamo province.

AY who was following at some distance, walked away quietly and took the city bus to Addis Abeba. This was the second time that AY had escaped from a calamity. His first encounter was in 1976 in the Sidamo province when he escaped unharmed.[66]

Nega and Dr. Morton, who drove past the check point peacefully were waiting for the others when they heard gun shots and, sensing danger, cancelled the plan to drive to Langano. As they returned to Addis Abeba, members of the *Abyot Tebeka* opened fire and killed both of them.

Neither the regime nor the *Abyot Tebeka* members knew that they had eliminated some of the most valuable members of the EPRP. Unable to find any excuse for the shooting, the *Addis Zemen* newspaper reported, "Khalid Abdul Aziz, an individual whose identity is unknown, an Englishman, and another Ethiopian were killed after an exchange of gunshots that took place after the individuals refused to disclose their identity. The *Abyot Tebeka* members found them taking intelligence pictures of the Kaliti Shirt Factory."[67] Yohannes Berhane was carrying an ID card bearing the name Khalid. On the ID, it was shown that his "occupation" was photography.

Dr. Morton, who had developed a deep affection for Ethiopia, was buried in the country where he wanted to live and die.

The Search and Destroy Campaign in Action

Because of difficulties of execution, POMOA was unable to conduct the campaign for an uninterrupted period and made certain adjustments. The search and destroy campaign was launched on March 22, 1977. Abyot Tebeka members, the army, kebeles, POMOA and particularly the MEISON and the other groups around the Derge took part in the campaign. The Derge decreed a number of statements restricting public movements.[68] The campaign took three days.

There were indiscriminate arrests of youth, workers, and anyone suspected of EPRP connections. Thousands fell prey and the prisons were filled to capacity. Some EPRP defense units fell victim while on duty and the government claimed that it had confiscated thousands of arms.[69] Carrying arms was legal in some parts of Ethiopia and in 1976, it was believed that there were close to ten million rifles and pistols in the hands of the citizens.[70]

The defense activities of the EPRP were partially successful and as a result, it was possible to divert the attention of the army to other areas. Because of the extreme brutality of POMOA representative like Girma Kebede, in certain parts of the city residents went out on spontaneous demonstrations. Among those Girma executed was Daro Negash, a mother of eight children. When she was executed, she was nine months pregnant, ready to give birth. Daro was the president of the Berhanena Selam Printing Press workers' union and one of the founding members of the underground labor organization, the ELAMA. Daro had hosted the first Congress of ELAMA at her residence. At the time of her arrest, she still was operating legally.

As indicated elsewhere, one of the major targets of the Mengistu regime was the EPRP CC. Over a period of about fifteen months, from February 1977, the Derge made more than twenty exaggerated announcements stating that EPRP CC members had been killed. Apparently, that was also part of the psychological warfare. But it was also true that it was during this campaign that some of the most valuable and irreplaceable members of the EPRP were killed, including Tesfaye Debessai, secretary of the EPRP CC and Marcos Hagos, the veteran workers' leader, and chairperson of the national labor organization, CELU. Alemayehu Tilahun, a CELU activist also disappeared.

By the end of February 1977, many of the leading members of the EPRP had left Addis Abeba. Among those who stayed in Addis Abeba were Tesfaye Debessai and Kiflu Tadesse. Tesfaye was supposed to lead the delegation to negotiate with the Eritrean fronts and the arrangement for his departure was one of the reasons why he was delayed. When the information about the search and destroy campaign came to the attention of the EPRP, feeling guilty at the thought of leaving the entire Addis Abeba EPRP structure at such a time, Tesfaye and Kiflu Tadesse, each on his own, decided to stay behind and combat the crisis along with the rest of the members.

Kiflu Tadesse and Germatchew Lemma tried to persuade Tesfaye to temporarily leave Addis Abeba, however, without openly expressing disagreement, Tesfaye chose to stay in Addis Abeba. After learning about his decision, Germatchew summoned Tesfaye to come and stay with him, in a remote area in the northern part of Addis Abeba, in the residence of Berihun Mariye, an EPRP member. Either Berihun Mariye or his spouse were involved in kebele activities.

A day after the campaign began, Berihun Mariye warned Tesfaye and Germatchew that his residence would also be searched on the next morning and asked them to devise means of avoiding the crisis. The three discussed their options. Berihun Mariye argued that they all should go either to his or his spouse's office for the day and be back at dusk, when the streets would be cleared of the participants in the search and destroy campaign. At this time, the search and destroy campaign did not target offices. Berihun Mariye convinced Tesfaye, but Germatchew argued that they should go to the nearest forest and stay there until the group conducting the campaign had left. Tesfaye and Berihun Mariye tried to convince Germatchew, but failed to do so. It was Germatchew's resolve never to walk unarmed, so going to the city was not his choice. He was also aware of his conspicuous appearance and was afraid that he would be spotted quite easily. Germatchew was over six feet tall, lean, light-skinned, with chiseled features. When they found it difficult to convince one another, each decided to go his way.

Germatchew headed to the nearest forest, along with another EPRP member. While in the forest, he heard some voices and figured out that people were coming towards his direction. As part of the search and destroy campaign, the regime had also assigned some military units to watch the forest areas. While roaming in the forest, the military group had come across fresh footsteps and began following the lead. According to Germatchew, he figured out that the military personnel were following him at a distance of about 100m. However, even though very close, due to the dense forest, the group was unable to see Germatchew. Germatchew continued walking for over an hour until he reached an open space where he saw two huts at a distance.

He then recalled his father's advice that a hunter should track his prey not from behind or from the front, but from the side, so that the wind would not blow the human scent towards the prey. So, when he reached the open area, Germatchew made an abrupt 90 degrees turn and began walking parallel to the group, but in the opposite direction. Because of the dense trees and shrubs, neither Germatchew nor the group could see each other. A few minutes later, he heard a round of shots, but Germatchew continued walking. He walked for a distance of about fifteen miles and left the forest on the opposite side that he had entered it. He walked a few more miles and reached an EPRP location safe.

It was learned later that the military group had opened fire on the huts that Germatchew saw, thinking that the persons that they had been following had entered them. The hut caught fire and its owners, an old poor couple, were found dead.

Berihun Mariye and Tesfaye headed to Berihun Mariye's spouse office and, on the way, Tesfaye decided to pass-by the residence of Nuredin Mohammed, whom he met at the gate. Tesfaye then asked Nuredin if he had seen Kiflu, the other CC member who remained in Addis Abeba. When Nuredin informed him that Kiflu was inside, Tesfaye told him that he would return and headed for Berihun Mariye, who was waiting for him somewhere in the area. It still is not known why Tesfaye came to the house. However, it was guessed that he came there either to find out whether Kiflu had survived the campaign, or perhaps Tesfaye came there to stay. When he discovered that there was another CC member in the house, he might have changed his mind, not wanting to put two eggs in one basket.

It was realized later that the vehicle carrying Tesfaye passed through the Tekle Haimanot area, where leading members of the MEISON were conducting the search and destroy campaign.

Apparently, the squad identified Tesfaye Debessai and began following the vehicle. It was Tesfaye who on behalf of the EPRP used to conduct negotiations with the MEISON. That organization knew not only that Tesfaye was in Addis Abeba, but also knew some of the camouflages he used. Even though he was a fugitive, Tesfaye used to meet Haile Fida.

Unaware that they were being followed, Tesfaye and Berihun Mariye reached their destination, the Kidane Beyene building, near the Ambassador theater. Just before he entered Berihun Mariye's wife office, Tesfaye saw an individual he suspected to be a MEISON member and decided to leave the building right away. The MEISON squad, which had been following Berihun

Mariye's vehicle was by the gate when Tesfaye descended the stairs and reached the ground level. The squads then opened fire and instantly killed Berihun Mariye who was walking in front. Tesfaye, who was following behind, was hit on the head and ran upstairs. By the time he reached the sixth floor, his face was covered with blood and he had already begun to become delirious. He then found a window and jumped down from the sixth floor, dying instantly. The MEISON squad then called Negede Gobeze, who came to confirm the identity of the victim.[71] Berihun Mariye's spouse was detained and she stayed in prison for a while. It was she who recounted the story to Germatchew following her release. Because of the way he committed suicide, Tesfaye was nicknamed "Amoraw", the bird. In the years that followed, many imitated Tesfaye's lead and committing suicide became the preferred method to die than to fall in the hands of MEISON and Derge killers.

The death of Tesfaye Debessai was the single most serious blow that MEISON inflicted not only on the EPRP, but on the Ethiopian radical generation. Within the ranks of the EPRP, no one could replace or take over the role of Tesfaye. The EPRP would have been better-off with half of its CC members gone, instead of one Tesfaye, who was the ideologue, organizer, politician and father of the organization. Tesfaye, who did not care much to be public, was little known even among EPRP members. However, he was the most respected individual among those that knew him closely. Tesfaye did not talk much, but whenever he did, everyone listened to every word he uttered. He was simple, down to earth and modest and had a deep-seated democratic instinct. In his political thinking, he was not only complex, but he could also see far beyond anyone else. Even though no one said it aloud, some of the remaining CC members knew that the EPRP would not be the same after his death. The EPRP had lost its spirit. The EPRP lost its leader when it needed him most, when it needed someone as far-sighted as Tesfaye, to give guidance.

During this same campaign, it was in the same forest area of Entoto that other EPRP members stayed, among them DHM and his comrades. When they stayed in the forest for three days, they had to go to the nearest church to beg for food. Four youth activists who were found hiding in the forest area of Entoto were apprehended. The youth were living in a cave and a fifth person used to go to the city to obtain food items. The youngsters had been living in the forest for quite some time when all of them were rounded up. It was believed that the person who had been commuting to the city had informed on them.

Their arrest was broadcast over the radio and TV and all four of them were executed. Two of them were the sons of Officer Cherinet, a member of the Ethiopian army. When he knew that he had lost his sons, the officer became deranged and a few weeks later he was found dead. It was believed that he had committed suicide. About two months later, his spouse died of high-blood pressure after attending the gathering held in memory of Officer Cherinet. According to Ethiopian Tewahedo tradition, forty and eighty days after the death of a person, close relatives, family members and friends gather together to remember and pray for the deceased.[72]

Similar search and destroy campaigns were conducted in many parts of Ethiopia. In Gojjam, in the city of Bahir Dar, about one hundred thirty people who were suspected of EPRP connection were arrested.[73] Some of them fled the city. Among them were members of the Gojjam EPRP zonal committee. Some of the prisoners escaped after overpowering the guards. Those who remained behind were executed; it is believed that they were buried in the prison compound.[74]

The first search and destroy campaign inflicted a very serious blow to the EPRP, even though it did not finish it off the way POMOA had intended to. The EPRP lost some of its invaluable members, but it survived the crisis.

The Campaign and its Effects on MEISON

The Mengistu/POMOA alliance was the main force behind the war of annihilation. POMOA/MEISON took the major responsibility and the lions' share in providing the leadership, designing the approach and mobilizing of the personnel for the event. While the search and destroy campaign was in progress, conflict arose in three major areas of the government circle. The first was between the Mengistu Haile Mariam and the Atnafu Abate groups.

Atnafu, who had tried to remain neutral in the Derge's internal struggle, grudgingly accepted Mengistu's dominance following the February 1977 coup; but when the residents of Addis Abeba raised a furor against the search and destroy campaign of March 1977, Atnafu saw an opportunity to be in the lime light one more time. He opposed the campaign and when many Derge members followed his lead, the campaign was called-off. One more time, Atnafu emerged as a contending force against the dominance of Mengistu.

When the search and destroy campaign of March 1977 faltered, it opened up a soar wound and many Derge members who had been harboring dislike for the MEISON, used the opportunity to express their dissatisfaction. The animosity and fear of many Derge members towards the MEISON resurfaced and the role of that organization came into perspective. The search and destroy campaign, intended to finish off the EPRP, opened the path for the downfall and demise of the MEISON itself. From this time onward, MEISON's influence within and around the state apparatus dwindled. MEISON became a victim of its policies. In its desperation, it committed other miscalculations and eventually it was forced to go underground. More on this in Chapter VI.

The Second Search and Destroy Campaign

The second search and destroy campaign was conducted at the end of April or the beginning of May 1977. Among the distinctive differences of this campaign from the previous one was the absence of MEISON from the process. This was due to the conflict among the ruling circles themselves. The campaign was coordinated by the Waz league and the *Seded* groups. Even though Sennay Likke had been killed earlier on, his followers, Colonel Shitaye, a pilot from the Air-force and a graduate of the Addis Abeba University, Shewandagne Belete, a graduate of the University, etc., took a prominent role in the process.

Learning from the excesses of the previous search and destroy campaign, the regime made efforts to make the second campaign more orderly. The first noticeable change was in regard to the composition of the participants. The first search and destroy campaign, dominated by the MEISON, was assisted by Abyot Tebeka groups. The second campaign, however, was conducted by members of the Ethiopian army, in collaboration with the kebeles. Unlike during the first campaign, most of the participants of the second one did not have clear perspective about their assignments. Some of them were looking for arms. Others did not know how to identify EPRP members, as a result, the degree of arbitrariness was reduced.

Few days before the second campaign was launched, the security network of the Addis Abeba EPRP IZ, particularly Derje I,[75] the EPRP mole in the government, knew that it was coming and warned the organization to make the necessary preparations. However, members of the EPRP CC failed to get any information from their sources. Because of this conflicting situation, a discussion was conducted on whether a campaign was possible at that time. It was concluded that there might not be one, for the simple reason that Mengistu himself was in the USSR. It was argued that it would be difficult to deploy a large military force while he was away. The argument was strong and the reasons plausible and Dereje's information was not given enough weight. As a result, the EPRP was unprepared to withstand the second search and destroy campaign.

In the last days of April 1977, at six o'clock in the morning, almost all of EPRP's activists were caught by surprise when they found out that the entire Addis Abeba city was being searched. Regardless, even the most wanted members of the EPRP avoided the military groups by moving to areas that had already been searched. Besides, because of EPRP's influence in the Mercato area, or the absence of kebeles themselves, the degree of the crisis was minimized and evading the search and destroy group was not very difficult. Considering the lack of preparation for the crisis, the loss inflicted on the EPRP was not as severe as the previous one.

However, it was during this second campaign that EPRP members Kiflu Teferra, a CC member, Mulugeta Zena, a veteran activist and a member of the political department of the EPRP and Captain Amha Abebe, an influential activist around the military regime were killed.

While the second campaign was underway, a search squad came to the house of Dagnatchew Ayele, an EPRP member and the chairperson of the kebele. It was in Dagnatchew Ayele's residence that Captain Amha Abebe and Tebebe, both of them fugitives, were residing. Captain Amha was making preparations to leave for Sidamo where an EPRP armed group was under formation.

Forewarned about the arrival of the search group, Captain Amha Abebe and Tebebe hid above the ceiling in the special place designed for such occasions. Dagnatchew's place was searched and the Abyot Tebeka group left without finding any incriminating evidence.

A few moments later, a government counter-insurgence team arrived at Dagnatchew Ayele's residence. Dagnatchew Ayele who was the chairperson of the kebele was conducting the search campaign in his jurisdiction and he was not aware of the arrival of the team.

The government was tipped about Dagnatchew Ayele's house by a defecting EPRP member. The defector had informed the government about an arm cache that had been brought to this house in order to make another assassination attempt on Mengistu, who sometime within that period was expected to pass through the street leading to the Bole Airport. The house of the EPRP member was located not far from the Bole street.[76]

It is not certain whether the counter-insurgence team knew that Captain Amha Abebe was staying in the house. Anyhow, the informant began showing the security personnel the exact location where the arms were hidden, under the floor of the room. It was in this room that Captain Amha Abebe and Tebebe were hiding. The military officers then decided to take an immediate action on the owner of the house, Dagnatchew Ayele and another member of the household. Captain Amha Abebe who already was on the alert, reacted fast. He threw a grenade and Tebebe and him jumped down from the ceiling, from where they were hiding. According to Tebebe, the grenade killed all six officers[77] and a fragment hit Captain Amha Abebe.

When Captain Amha Abebe and Tebebe left the house, they faced a large number of military personnel who had surrounded the house and cordoned the area. Consequently, Captain Amha Abebe and Tebebe had to open fire to find passage. In the shoot out that followed, Captain Amha Abebe was hit on his shoulder while he was trying to protect Tebebe. As he was running, Captain Amha Abebe continued losing blood and became unable to walk any further. Left with no alternative, Captain Amha and Tebebe stopped a vehicle and forced the driver to give them a ride. The driver who disclosed his EPRP membership, was more than willing to collaborate. When he discovered about the identity of the driver, Captain Amha Abebe decided to get off of the vehicle, lest he might not jeopardize the life of another EPRP member. They ran for a while, but Captain Amha Abebe realized that he had little chance of survival. He then committed suicide. Thus, one of the most dedicated and fearless activists of the Ethiopian revolution passed away.

Tebebe ran for some distance and arrived at a wedding ceremony. He met a supportive group which took away his hand gun and hid it. His cloth which had been drenched in blood was changed and he was allowed to mingle with the crowd. The military personnel who were in close pursuit, came to the wedding ceremony and kept on looking for Tebebe. No one cooperated and Tebebe left the area the next morning. On the same day that the incident took place, Dagnatchew Ayele was arrested and executed. His corpse was thrown at the Abyot square.

Captain Amha Abebe had taken part in some major EPRP related activities and he was one of the few military officers who took an active role in the revolutionary movement since its beginning. Captain Amha Abebe was a veteran EPRP activist and one of the leaders of the Jimma uprising during the turbulent months of 1974. He also was a member of the mini-Derge (sub-committee of the Derge) of Jimma.[78] He had been sent to the Soviet Union to study about party formation.

Upon his return from the USSR, Captain Amha had been given an assignment in the Derge's office, where he served as one of the most valuable sources of information for the EPRP. Amha had also been a member of the EPRP party committee responsible for activities around the Derge. When the internal crisis within the Derge began, even as an outsider, he had been one of those officers who directed the course of the movement. Captain Amha Abebe had been a member of the leadership of the underground "Oppressed Soldiers Organization" and had taken part in the attempt to assassinate Mengistu Haile Mariam.

During the second campaign, Kiflu Teferra, along with Mulugeta Zena also went to the nearest forest, not far from the house where Captain Amha wanted to pass the day. They stayed in the forest for the whole day and when they heard gun shots from a nearby area, they returned to the house where they were residing. However, before they reached their house, they found out that the campaigners were still in the area and decided to go back. However, it was already too late; government security forces had spotted them. While trying to flee, both Kiflu Teferra and Mulugeta Zena were shot from behind.

Kiflu Teferra and Mulugeta Zena were veteran activists and founding members of the EPRP. Kiflu Teferra had taken part in the founding Congress of the EPRP held in 1972. As a member of the EPRP CC, Kiflu had served the organization under different capacities. The loss of Kiflu constituted another major blow to the leadership of the EPRP, whose [numerical] strength by this time had already dwindled.

As more and more CC members fell victim, no information was released to the members. As an expression of the dictum, 'you do not shed tears for a fallen comrade, but avenge for him' (*le tagaye yetagelewal inje ayaleksum*), EPRP members were not given the chance to grieve the death of their leaders, neither were they told that the EPRP had lost its core national leadership group.

Profile of the EPRP CC

The First EPRP CC, consisting of nine members, was formed in 1972, at the First Congress. Up until the Extended Conference of August 1975, the number of EPRP CC members was eight, following the resignation of one member in 1974.[79] That member later joined the MEISON. By the decision of the Extended Conference of 1975, seven more members were added and the CC was enlarged to fifteen. However, the Foreign Committee failed to inform one of those elected and the CC number was fourteen.[80]

As part of the merger agreement with the "*Red Flag*" group, another individual was added to the CC and the official number of the leadership reached sixteen. When four more members were added at the Second Plenum, the number reached 20. At the crown of the peaceful form of political struggle in 1976, defacto, the EPRP had 18 CC members, disregarding the one who remained uninformed and the representative of the "*Red Flag*" group.[81]

National composition -[82] Nine of the EPRP CC members, i.e., 50% of the total, were Amharic speaking individuals from different parts of Ethiopia, i.e., Shoa, Gojjam and Begemidir. Six (33%) were Tigrigna speakers, and two (11%) were Oromigna speakers. There was one Gurage CC member. All, but one of the CC members were male.

Educational background - All of the CC members had finished or reached a university level of education; all of them had finished at least the third year of university study. Thirteen of the eighteen CC members, 70% of them, had finished their undergraduate studies. Seven, that is, over 40% of the EPRP CC members were holders of masters degrees. Tesfaye Debessai had a Ph.D. and he was working for his second one in the wake of the 1974 revolutionary movement. Thirteen of the CC members had finished some years in the University College of Addis Abeba. Ten of the CC members had received either their first or their second degree abroad. Of this number, six (33%) did either their first or second degree studies in the USA; the rest did their studies in Europe. Over 50% of the CC members studied humanitarian science. There were a few engineers and geologists.

The average age of the EPRP CC was 30. In 1976, the youngest member was 26, the oldest 34.

Class background-- Two of the CC members were of poor and middle peasant background, and eleven of them, 61% of the total, were from low-income families whose average income did not exceed 300 Ethiopian birr per month, with an average family of six people. The rest were from middle class families, whose average income was about 600 Ethiopian birr, possibly with a family size of four.

Income--Until August 1976, about half of the CC members, that is, 50%, had their own source of income. Their average income was 600.00 birr (then $300.00) per month. The income of the highest paid member was 1200.00 birr. The rest of the CC members were professional revolutionaries who had either gone underground or semi-underground. By mid 1976, none of the CC members had their own house. About half of the CC members were living either in houses provided by the EPRP or with their comrades. Only two CC members had vehicles of their own. As underground members of the EPRP, the CC members, like other EPRP members, were provided an allowance of forty Ethiopian birr a month.

Struggle experience-- By 1976, the average period that the CC members had been in the struggle was about 10 years. The longest period that some of the CC members, like Berhane Meskel and Zeru Kehishen, stayed in the struggle was 12 years, and the least was seven. By 1976, almost all of the CC members had been involved in some kind of an underground struggle for at least six years.

The EPRP CC was composed of members of two generations of revolutionary activists. A good number of them were from the older generation of veteran activists, while some were of the younger generation. All of the CC members passed through the struggle of the student movement. One was involved in the activities of labor, while Tesfaye, a student of philosophy, had embraced Marxism on his own quest for a just system. During his search for the "right" philosophy, Tesfaye embraced and became a devoted student of the teachings of great philosophers from the utopian socialist St. Simon through Jean Jacques Rousseau, Immanuel Kant, etc., until he read the works of Karl Marx.

Marital status--25% of the CC members were either married or were living with female companions. The rest were single.

EPRP Leadership's Plight

By March 1977, the EPRP CC that was formed at the First Congress held in 1972, conducted about 51 CC meetings and three Plenums. During its stay abroad, from 1972 until 1974, the CC conducted three meetings. From June 1974 until August 1975, that is, for a period of fifteen months, it conducted about 37 meetings, an average of two CC meetings a month. From September 1975 until the declaration of the war of annihilation in September 1976, it conducted two Plenums and seven ordinary CC meetings; an average of a CC meeting every forty days. From the declaration of the War of Annihilation in September 1976 to February 1977, that is, over a period of six months, the EPRP CC conducted only two CC meetings - one Plenum and an ordinary one. According to the EPRP constitution, an ordinary CC meeting was supposed to be held every two months.

Beginning around September 1975, the CC held fewer meetings compared with the same period of the previous year. As was discussed in *The Generation*, Part I, (Chapters V and VI), from June 1974 to August 1975, the EPRP CC had assumed the role of the PB and the Secretariat. Following the formation of those institutions at the 1975 August Conference, the CC became relieved of some of the duties. However, some CC members were still overburdened by a variety of tasks.

Except those who were abroad or in the EPRA, all of the meetings were attended by all of the CC members. For a period of over three years, CC decisions were reached on consensual basis. Chairpersons were elected for every meeting.

During its existence of few years, that is, from September 1975 until the end of March 1977, the PB conducted about 48 meetings. In the first period, that is, from September 1975 until the declaration of the war of annihilation in September 1976, it conducted about 36 meetings; that is, an average of one every ten days. From September 1976 to March 1977, meetings were held less frequently - an average of one every fifteen days. As a matter of precaution, most of the meetings of the EPRP CC were held overnight.

The first PB of the EPRP ceased to exist as an institution as of March 1977 and did not hold any more meetings. By March 1977, four of the members of the institution were alive, and they were unable to come together. One was abroad, and two in the EPRA in Tigrai, while the fourth remained behind in the urban areas.

The EPRP CC, which was composed of eighteen members, can be placed into two categories of participants. The first group consisted of twelve CC members who had taken part in most of the CC or the PB meetings and proceedings, and in one way or another had influenced the course of the EPRP. Some of these CC members had taken part in almost all of the CC meetings, and all had attended a good number of them. This hard core EPRP CC group had been responsible for many of the leadership's decisions up until February 1977. Within this category fell Tesfaye Debessai, Berhane Meskel Redda, Yosef Adane, Kiflu Tadesse, Kiflu Teferra, AW, Zeru Kehishen, Yohannes Berhane, Getachew Maru, Samuel Alemahehu, Tselote Hiskias and AB. The second group consisted of six CC members who had attended few leadership meetings, or who had joined the leadership at a later date. Four of them, Iyasu Alemayehu, Tsegaye Gebre Medhin, ZB and Fikre Zergaw had taken part in fewer than three EPRP CC meetings and two, MGE and E. attended no CC meeting at all. They were co-opted to the CC at the Second Plenum, in 1976.

By March 1977, four of the core CC members, Tesfaye Debessai, Kiflu Teferra, Yohannes Berhane and Yosef Adane had been killed, three during the search and destroy campaign in March and April 1977. Getachew and Berhane Meskel had been expelled from the EPRP CC. Consequently, of the twelve core CC members, only six remained. Of this number, one was sent abroad while three joined the EPRA. Two of the members remained in the urban areas.

Because of death and dispersal, what constituted the core EPRP leadership that had been responsible for what the EPRP was in its beginning phase of the struggle was weakened to a point that the initial composition of the core group was changed. It was in February 1977 that the initial core leadership of the EPRP conducted its last meeting.

When the remaining leadership group resumed its activities a few months later in Tigrai, only three of the core CC members took part in the proceedings. The rest were those who had little or no role in the previous activities of the EPRP CC.

As was indicated above, the EPRP CC did not anticipate that it would face such a degree of crisis. Except for the assessment conducted at the Second Plenum, in 1976, the CC was unable to evaluate its achievements or failures. It also left many things unfinished, including the later policies of the EPRP. Above all, it left the EPRP vulnerable and exposed to serious organizational and political problems. It left the EPRP without a tested leadership that might pull the organization out from the very difficult situation.

The demise of the EPRP leadership and leading EPRP activists was a turning point in the Ethiopian revolutionary struggle. It may be asked why the EPRP CC did not create conditions that would enable the leadership to survive the crisis. It is not up to this book to give an adequate reply to the question. One fact, however, is certain: most members of the leadership and leading activists of that era did not consider themselves irreplaceable and consequently, they had to place themselves in the forefront of the struggle. The psyche of that generation was such that many of them did not attach any importance to themselves; they sincerely believed that what they had begun would be finished by those who remained behind. From organizational standpoint, the failure to shift the center of leadership to the rural areas, particularly to the EPRA, when it was known that the peaceful form of struggle had given way to the armed form had a bearing too. That issue was raised at the August Plenum of 1976 and the struggle within the Derge had diluted the belief and resolve that the armed phase of the struggle had attained the main form. Leading activists of the EPRP, including members of the leadership, probably unknowingly, were awaiting the results of the Derge internal restructuring process. Many believed that the EPRP would get some respite, if the peaceful process to restructure the Derge was consummated. Besides the wait and see attitude created as a result of the Derge's internal problems, the success of the rural armed struggle following the proclamation of the 1975 land reform, still remained one of the major worries of leading activists. EPRP's failure to sustain the armed struggle initiated in Wello and Sidamo had their own impact too.

Even though technical, another reason why the leadership was tied to the urban areas was the decision of the August Plenum which assigned members of the leadership to the various CC departments in the urban areas. The CC [83] had enormous tasks and could not afford dispersion of its members.

Notes to Chapter 5

1. Addis Zemen, December 30, 1976, pages 1 and 9.

2. Ibid., page 9, cl. 7/3.

3. Ibid., page 9, cl. 7/4.

4. Addis Zemen, January 16, 1977, page 8.

5. In an interview, in 1994, Negede Gobeze, one of the leading figures of the MEISON admitted that his organization had given the order to shoot in the "air". Tobia, July 1994, page 13.

6. Addis Zemen, January 31, 1977, page 6.

7. Ibid., page 6.

8. Addis Zemen, February 1, 1977, page 8.

9. Ibid., pages 7-9

10. Kiflu Tadesse, The Generation, Part I, Independent Publishers, 1993, Chapter III.

11. See details in Chapter IX.

12. See details in Chapter IV.

13. Discussion with Yared Tibebu, March 1996. He was a member of a party cell within the EPRA in Assimba.

14. See details page 176.

15. See details Chapter III.

16. It may not be accurate to state that the EPRP did not fire a single bullet. Even though it was not made public, sometime in May/June 1976, EPRP units had gunned down Demeke Harege Weyene, one of the main instigators of the repression in Jimma.

17. PB Paper, pages 2 and 18.

18. Ibid., page 3.

19. Ibid., page 4.

20. Ibid., page 18.

21. Ibid., page 6.

22. See Chapter II.

23. PB Paper, pages 7-14.

24. Ibid., page 14.

25. Ibid., page 15.

26. Ibid., page 19.

27. Ibid., page 21.

28. Ibid., pages 21-22.

29. Ibid., page 21.

30. Ibid., page 21.

31. Kiflu Tadesse, op. cit., 1993, page 241.

32. See details in Chapter I.

33. See details in Chapter III.

34. 1975 EPRP's Constitution, Ch. III.A 6.b.

35. See details in Chapter IV.

36. See details page 179.

37. Interview, KM, a former member of the Sub-secretariat, responsible for the Shao area, 1994. This was a verbatim report of KM to the CC in 1976.

38. See details pages 180-181.

39. Though unsuccessful, Berhane of zone one collaborated to apprehend Berhane Meskel. He also participated to track down some of the members of the faction that had inflicted severe blows to the EPRP. (Details given elsewhere.)

40. Interview Demelash, an EPRP member of the area, October 1988.

41. See details in Chapter IX.

42. Interview KM, 1994.

43. Democracia, Volume IV, No. 2, page 2.

44. During this period, the leadership consisted of a two-man CC team. See details in Chapter VIII.

45. Kiflu Tadesse, op. cit., Chapter VII.

46. Democracia, Vol. IV, No .9, page 3. Among the issues discussed in this Democracia was the decision of the February EPRP CC meeting regarding the Eritrean question.

47. This methodology constituted a text-book approach of the Marxist philosophy.

48. Democracia, Vol. IV, No. 9, page 4.

49. See details in Chapter VI.

50. See details in Chapter VI.

51. Addis Zemen, February 27, 1977, page 2.

52. Addis Zemen, February 21, 1977, page 2.

53. Addis Zemen, February 21, 1977, page 9.

54. Ibid., page 9.

55. Addis Zemen, September 26, 1976, Proclamation, Cl. 15.a, page 6.

56. Ibid., Cl. 10.3.

57. EPRP Program, No. VI.1.b.

58. From a letter sent to TT in 1977 by his friend who at the time had direct access to the Technical High School.

59. Addis Zemen, February 12, 1977, page 9.

60. Addis Zemen, March 10, 1977, page 1; Addis Fana, May 1977, page 13.

61. Democracia, Volume IV, No. 1, page 2.

62. Addis Zemen, March 19, 1977, page 3.

63. Ibid., page 1.

64. Addis Zemen, March 15, 1977, page 1. For more details see Addis Zemen issue of March and April 1977.

65. A fact reported to the EPRP CC in 1977. Also see Abyot, Volume VIII, No. 2, page 13.

66. See details in Chapter II.

67. Addis Zemen, March 12, 1977, page 1.

68. Addis Zemen, March 22, 1976, page 9.

69. Addis Zemen, March 31, 1977.

70. Paul H. Brietzke, Law, Development and the Ethiopian Revolution, Bucknell University Press, 1982, p.162.

71. On the same day that the search and destroy campaign was conducted, Achameleh, an ELAMA member, Berhanu, an IZ member and Kiflu Tadesse, had made an arrangement to pass the night in one of the rooms of the Augusta Shirt Factory where an ELAMA member was in charge. When the three of them were about to eat dinner, about eight o'clock in the evening, the news about Tesfaye's death was broadcast over the radio and it sent chill through their spines. When they left the place the next morning, they found their sandwitches still laying on the table.

72. According to the Tewahedo faith of the Ethiopian Orthodox religion, on the fortieth day of the death of a person, his soul becomes separated from his flesh.

73. Addis Zemen, May 25, 1977.

74. This information was provided by one of the escapees, T.

75. When it became evident that MEISON was disintegrating, the EPRP told some of the infiltrators to join the Seded. Dereje I, the most valuable infiltrator of the EPRP, was among those who shifted allegiance and was given an important post in the bureaucracy. In order to lure more defectors, the Seded appointed to important posts those individuals who had abandoned the MEISON.

76. The EPRP leadership still believed in the importance of eliminating Mengistu and a number of attempts were made to that end. He was to be ambushed on February 14, 1977, when returning from a graduation ceremony at the Genet Military Training School. Another ambush was organized while he was en route to the Indian embassy to pay his condolences on the death of the former Indian Prime Minister, Nehru. None of the attempts materialized and after several trials, the idea of ambushing Mengistu was abandoned.

77. Tebebe has survived the ordeal and the story regarding the incident was based partly on the interview he provided. Tebebe argues that all six officers were killed when the grenade went off. According to government sources, only five officers were killed. Tebebe interview, 1997.

78. These were committees composed of military officers. They were formed in most of the areas where there were large military groups and they were in charge of the activities among the military.

79. See details, Kiflu Tadesse, op., cit., Chapter V.

80. Ibid., page 243.

81. See details in Chapter I.

82. This issue had never been a concern of the radical generation. Besides, the parents of some of the CC members were from different ethnic groups, hence the difficulty to establish the national composition.

83. See details in Chapter II.

6

The Ethio-Somali Conflict

In the wake of the 1974 revolutionary movement, two distinct categories of struggle unfolded. The first and dominant form was the struggle for economic and political reform waged in almost every part of Ethiopia. Multi-national organizations focused on issues pertaining to the cross-section of the majority of the Ethiopian society and they played an important role in articulating their demands.

When the military regime enacted major economic reforms, it significantly diluted the struggle thereby forcing the multi-national opposition to wage an uphill battle. Carrying on a political struggle devoid of concrete economic demands was a challenge. The political struggle had to be conducted on a higher and more abstract level, not easily visible to a people just emerging from the twilight of feudalism.[1]

The second category of struggle, also witnessed in 1974, was the one waged along the ethnic line. Even though the national problem was also addressed by multi-national organizations, nationalist organizations made efforts to wage their own separate struggle, focusing on the demands of their national group in the main.

As indicated above, the Derge addressed some of the main economic issues of Ethiopia and, as a result, it was able to pacify the class struggle. However, it failed to address the political aspect of the national issue and, instead, resorted to armed confrontation and made efforts to resolve the problem militarily. As a result, it created fertile ground for the emergence of nationalist groups in different parts of Ethiopia and, in particular, in the southern and eastern parts.

Following the proclamation of land reform in 1975, the peasantry conducted an intense struggle against local landowners and the local state apparatus. The peasantry was disappointed when the Derge stood by the ruling group[2] and ruthlessly crushed peasant rebellion. The gain of the struggle was partially reversed. Alienated peasant groups were forced to look for other alternatives. Among these were some Oromos of the Gujji and Borena groups, who decided to wage an armed struggle against the military regime.

As was indicated in Chapter I, sometime in mid-1976, over three hundred Gujji peasants and a similar number of Borenas left for Somalia for military training and to acquire arms. Other Oromo groups of the Harer area also took similar steps. The OLF, which by then was a small organization, was able to get some following in the Harer and Arsi areas. When it became evident that the Oromo groups had returned to Ethiopia after a few months of training, *Democracia* stated, "in the south, the Oromo national movement is being stepped up...quite recently, two groups had come back to Ethiopia [from Somalia] by way of Kenya."[3]

It was not only Oromos, but also Somali armed groups, directly assisted and guided by the Somali regime were deployed in some parts of Ethiopia, particularly in the Harer province.

The Origins of the Conflict

Rebellion of Somali pastoralists had been sparked in the early sixties. Inflamed by the seditious propaganda of the newly formed Somali Republic, "the goal of the...rebellion...was to break away from Ethiopia in order to join their kinsmen in the newly independent Somali Republic."[4] One of the groups that emerged during this period was the Western Somalia Liberation Front (WSLF), which espoused the belief that the Ogaden, Bale and the Sidamo areas comprised part of the Somali republic.[5] A similar peasant uprising took place in Bale in the early sixties and lasted for about a decade. The immediate cause of the uprising was taxation.[6]

The Ogadeni (Somalis living in the Ogaden) issue became complicated when it was tied to the Somali regime's irredentist plan, which was based on the five Somali nation.[7] The issue in its present form was first raised in the 1950's when "the British foreign secretary, Ernest Bevin, suggested that the two Somali territories, as well as the Somali area of Ethiopia, also under British Administration at this time, should be joined together in a single Somali state."[8] Somali reunification was raised again following the independence of that nation in 1960. During this period, the plan entailed the unity of all the Somalis living in Kenya, Ethiopia, Djibouti and the Somalia republic itself.

When Djibouti was about to regain its independence, that issue created political tension both in Ethiopia and Somalia and the regimes of the two countries decided to affect the political process of that small country. Djibouti, formerly known as the French Somaliland, regained its independence from the French on June 27, 1977. Djibouti is inhabited by the Afar and the Issa, who had kins both in Ethiopia and Somalia. The Somali regime considered the inhabitants of Djibouti as part of the Greater Somali nation. This belief was affirmed at the meeting of the ruling Somalia Socialist party held from January 4 to 15, 1977. The meeting characterized Djibouti as "the missing Somalia territory."[9] That being the case, about ten years back, that is,

> ...[I]n the March 1967 referendum, expertly maneuvered by the French authorities, a majority of voters had rejected the independence which the

Somali section of the electorate had sought as a step towards unity with the Somalia Republic.[10]

For Ethiopia, the issue of Djibouti transcended politics, simply because that country handled about 60% of Ethiopia's import/export. Both the country and the great majority of the inhabitants of Djibouti relied on the port for their income as well. The other outlet for Ethiopia, the Asseb port, had been developed as a major port in the 1950's, primarily with aid from the former Yugoslavia and had operated at a low capacity until it was renovated and upgraded by the East Germans in the 1980s.

> By late 1977, ships were waiting an average of 45 days for a berth, sometimes up to 90 days, and an average of 30 vessels were waiting for berths; surcharges owing to port delays added US $9 (birr 18) per ton to the cost of imported grain. The 1978/79 harvest was affected because by June 1978, the deadline for applying fertilizer, 22,000 tons were still at Asseb.[11]

Due to the dismal political and economic condition of Ethiopia, and the crisis in which the Derge found itself, the Ethiopian regime was in no position to demand for the annexation of Djibouti. However, in order to indirectly affect the political process in Djibouti, the Derge granted autonomy to the Afar in Ethiopia.

The Ethio-Somali conflict of the seventies can be categorized into two phases. In the first phase, the Somali regime formed the necessary institutions and organizations to wage war against the Ethiopian regime. The Somali regime had been providing military training for refugees from Bale and Sidamo, even after the Bale uprising subsided in the late sixties. "Three camps were opened in 1975 to train those who were willing to struggle for national (Somali) unification."[12] During the first phase, the Western Somalia Liberation Front (WSLF) and the Somali Abo Liberation Front (SALF) were reorganized.

> The first to be set up was the WSLF, in January 1976, in...a village near Mogadishu. Carefully prepared by a committee appointed by Ziad Barre and packed by his supporters, the meeting was attended by him and several top officials ...SALF was formed [reorganized?] in mid-June 1976 at a meeting held near Koreoli, attended by representatives of the guerrilla units and leaders of the refugee community in Somalia.[13]

Unlike the early days, when it had some form of autonomy, the WSLF in 1977 was under the tight control of the Somali regime. Both WSLF and SALF claimed the southern, southeastern and southwestern parts of Ethiopia.

The WSLF was composed of Somalis, with the Somali regular army taking a major role. In the third-quarter of 1977 when KT and her five friends escaped the Derge's repression and reached Keldessa, a small area in the Harerge countryside, they were placed under the control of the WSLF. They were then taken to a Somali colonel who was heading the entire army. Almost all of the officers that the five Ethiopian refugees encountered were members of the Somali regular army.[14]

Besides forming the above mentioned organizations, the Somali regime established or renewed relations with other Ethiopian opposition forces. Even though there is no evidence at hand, it is not difficult to imagine the espionage network that the Somali regime had laid down in Ethiopia. In the Harer area, that network included children.[15]

The Somali government timed the escalation of the conflict when in the central parts of Ethiopia the political crisis was becoming more acute, and in the north, the Eritrean struggle was gathering momentum.[16] The Afar people had revolted. The northwestern part of Ethiopia had fallen under the control of the EDU and the main railway linking Ethiopia to the outside world had been disrupted. In the urban and rural areas, the EPRP was waging political and military activities. In short, Ethiopia was undergoing severe political and economic crisis. Because of strained relations with the West, which had been the main arms source, the Ethiopian military regime faced a serious arms shortage. Before Ethio-US relationship turned for the worse, "[A]s part of the anti-Communist offensive in East Africa, the US sent $200 million worth of military equipment in 1976."[17] Apparently, it was during this period that the Derge received its last F5-E jet-fighters.[18] The Derge was in need of more armaments and in April 1976, it sent Captain Sisay Habte and a leading MEISON member to Vietnam to acquire spare parts. In September 1977, Mengistu asked the US for spare parts for the F5-E jets, but his demand was not met.

The Unfolding Conflict

Sometime before the conflict escalated, that is, during the last months of 1976, the SALF deployed guerrilla units in the Sidamo and Bale provinces. The WSLF followed suit in the first months of 1977. The SALF traversed the southeastern and southern parts of Ethiopia, while WSLF operated in the eastern part of Ethiopia.

The guerrilla forces of the two organizations did not have a horizontal relationship, nor did they have contact with their representatives in Somalia. Instead, "they had contact with the Ministry of Defense in Mogadishu from whence they received instructions..." and "[T]he guerrilla forces in the field were under the overall command of the Minister of Defense of the Somali regime, General Mohammed Ali Samatar."[19] The headquarters of the WSLF regional command was in Hargesa, Somalia.

During the first stage, the Somali government did not publicize its motives, but portrayed the struggle as if it was waged between the Ethiopian regime and the Somalis and Oromos. The conflict, however, intensified in the second half of 1977 when low level guerrilla activities took place in many southern and eastern parts of Ethiopia. When the conflict intensified, peasant associations demanded arms. The Derge did not respond, instead, "a process of re-arming the local landlords who were dispossessed by the land reform of 1975 was initiated. This action severely eroded the confidence of the peasantry and drove thousands of peasants either to join the insurgents or to remain indifferent."[20]

As the conflict escalated, outlying Ethiopian towns were over-run by the insurgents.[21] About ten days before Djibouti's independence, the WSLF disrupted the railway line linking Dire Dawa and Djibouti and brought the towns along the railway line under control. Furthermore, a significant part of the Ogaden was also over-run. Towns like Gode, Warder, Kebri Dehar, Teferi Ber, Togowechale and Degehabur fell into the hands of the insurgents. Jijjiga also fell in the hands of the Somali-backed insurgents. The departure of the mechanized brigade of the Third Division, to counter the EDU in Begemidir sometime in 1976, might have been a factor for the insurgents success in Jijjiga.

When they realized that the Ethiopian army had abandoned most of the locations and was regrouping in Harer, the Somali-led insurgents and Somali army focused on the northern part of Dire Dawa. They controlled Aiysha and Dewale and inflicted damage on the Ethiopian army in Dire Dawa. The airport and the gas depot in Dire Dawa were attacked.[22] In heavy fighting, however, the Somali army was routed from Dire Dawa in mid-August 1977 and the remaining force retreated east.

The Ethiopian military regime was quick to retaliate, systematically eliminating the peasant rebellion in many southern and eastern parts of the country. The regime became engaged in an indiscriminate repression. Small towns such as Gara Mulleta, Aerer, Feki, Gursum, Hurso, Biyo Keraba, Fedis, Jarso, etc., were destroyed and the inhabitants were forced to leave their areas. Describing the state of affairs *Democracia* commented,

> ...[A]ccused of collaborating with the armed infiltrators, Somali youth and elders, living in Dire Dawa, Megala...are indiscriminately slaughtered. Many Somali workers employed at the Railroad, the Cotton company...etc., are killed. Some had escaped to Djibouti and had asked for asylum. Aderis, Kotus (Oromos), and many followers of the Muslim religion are labeled as followers of the insurgents and they are persecuted. Left with no choice, many followers of the Muslim religion have begun to camouflage themselves as Christians...because of the absence of any other alternative, many Oromos and Aderis had joined the WSLF. In the urban areas, such as, Jijjiga, many youths had joined the fronts. The peasants, who frequently come to the cities to sell firewood and charcoal had become suspects and prime targets of the regime and many have stopped coming to the cities altogether. Because of this, grain and fire wood became scarce and that factor aggravated the problem in the cities. The peasants were then accused of creating famine in the cities....Many small towns had been wiped out, and those inhabitants who escaped the scourge, had run away for their lives.[23]

It was not only the Ethiopian military regime, but also the Somali army and the Somali backed organizations that committed atrocities. In its brief activities in the Harer area, the Western Somali Liberation Front inflicted heavy blows to the Ethiopian army and at the same time, antagonized a significant number of the inhabitants of the area. To be a Christian Ethiopian was a crime as far as the Somali regime was concerned. Consequently, Ethiopians residing in the areas over-run by the Somali-led insurgents were rounded up and sent to Somalia where they languished in prisons for over a decade. Many lost their lives. "Unable to distinguish a foe from an ally, the atrocities perpetrated by the WSLF against the peasantry and the followers of the Christian religion will eventually render the organization politically bankrupt," commented *Democracia*.[24]

The military conflict that erupted in the Harer area had a devastating effect on the Ethiopian economy. Soft drink factories at Babile came to a stand still. The agricultural and cattle center in Bisidimo was destroyed. The Wabi Shebelle Agricultural Development Project with its large number of tractors and farm equipments was destroyed. Mining projects were shut down. A large number of citizens were forced to evacuate their village and congregate in Dire Dawa and Harer, increasing the pressure on the inhabitants of the cities, who were expected to provide food not only to the Ethiopian army, but to the refugees as well.[25]

All through the first phase, the Somali regime denied its involvement in the conflict and attributed the military activities to the WSLF. The second phase of the conflict began in the summer of 1977 when the Somali regime directly deployed its army and Air-force. During this period, the Derge proclaimed the program known as the National Revolutionary Development Campaign. The military confrontation that began on a small scale was intensified. In July 1977, tanks, MIG-fighters and other heavy military armaments were deployed. On the first week of September 1977, the railroad line linking Dire Dawa and Djibouti was disrupted again. The Ethiopian regime began reporting about the demolition of "tanks, MIG-fighters, etc.", of the Somali regime. It reported on the neutralization of members of the Somali army instead of "infiltrators". In September 1977, sometime after the escalation of the war, the Ethiopian and the Somali regimes broke off diplomatic relations.

In July 1977, an Organization of African Unity (OAU) Committee, at a meeting held in the capital city of Gabon, Libreville, once again asserted that all member countries should be confined to the border demarcation laid down when they attained independence.[26] As of September 1977, the US and Britain stood behind the Ziad Barre regime of Somalia and concluded an agreement to supply arms. During the last months of 1977, Fidel Castro sent to Ethiopia a large contingent of Cuban troops and an all out offensive of Ethio-Cuban forces was launched in January 1978.

The major blow against the Somali army was inflicted at Jijjiga in March 1978 when the Ethiopian army, with the assistance of the Soviets and Cubans, captured the strategic hill-top known as Kara-Mara. That defeat was the climax of the war. After the debacle, the Somali regular army was forced to withdraw its forces from the Ethiopian territory.

The human and economic toll of the conflict for Somalia and Ethiopia was extremely grave. In this conflict, Ethiopia lost some of its well-trained (mostly Harer Academy graduates) military personnel and the Somali army was decimated. Thousands died in the desert sun during their retreat.

In a discussion between the Soviets and the Americans, the American Secretary of State Cyrus Vance strongly demanded that the Ethiopian offensive should stop at the Ethio-Somali frontier. In March 1978, Ziad Barre announced a unilateral withdrawal of its forces from Ethiopian territory and the Ethiopian army controlled the last military post on the Somali frontier. Even though low level skirmishes continued, the Ethio-Somalia conflict was concluded in favor of the Ethiopian regime.

Derge and Ethiopian Nationalism

The military activities of the "infiltrators" and the invasion of the Somali regime was a blessing in disguise for the military regime of Ethiopia. It brought about major changes in the political, ideological, military, diplomatic and organizational fields. The first and major element that the Ethio-Somali conflict introduced was an "ideology" which served the Ethiopian military regime as an important instrument to stay in power. That "ideology" had helped the military regime regain the upper hand in the struggle not only in the Somali sphere of military engagement, but also in Eritrea and other urban and rural areas where opposition to the regime was spreading.

When it held power in June 1974, the military regime portrayed itself as a nationalist force with "Ethiopia Tikdem" as its motto. When that approach proved ineffective, in December 1975, the Derge resorted to Ethiopian Socialism, which again did not serve the intended purpose. Finally, the Derge adopted "Scientific Socialism" in its NDR program, that came out in April 1976. However, the Derge's rallying "ideology" was to be changed after the escalation of the Ethio-Somali conflict. From April until June 1977, one of the recurring themes in the speeches of Mengistu was the question of the "Motherland", and "Motherland or death" was coined as the rallying cry. In due course, however, the rallying slogan was changed to "Revolutionary Motherland or death". In one of his April speeches, Mengistu raised the same slogan against the EDU, which by then had begun controlling some parts of the northwestern Begemidir province. The EDU was assisted by the Sudanese regime of Jafar Nimieri. In the speech delivered at the inauguration ceremony of the Tatek Military Center, the same theme was used to rally the newly recruited groups. Commenting about the need to change the aphorism, an Editorial of the *Addis Zemen* stated, "many people are suggesting that we ignore the new vocabulary of *revolution*, Marxism-Leninism and socialism and instead focus on the territorial integrity of the country."[27] Ethiopian nationalism, which had its roots deep in the Axumite civilization, is a form of nationalism that had gone through a number of complex historical metamorphoses. Ethiopian nationalism was the binding ideology to rally against the two Italian invasions of the 1890s and 1930s.

In the speech delivered at the Tatek Military Training Center, the Ethiopian population was told to heed the call of the motherland and be part of the crusade. However, by mid-1977, the Derge had conducted numerous military campaigns and had disarmed a large segment of the population.[28] In the initial stage of the Ethio-Somali conflict, a *Democracia* issue commented,

> [A]fter disarming the people, to call them to be armed is a deliberate attempt to deceive them and it is a ploy . . . to masquerade the Derge's internal crisis and divert the people's attention to external problems."

Besides, it was a deliberate effort to weaken the class struggle and the revolution, concluded *Democracia*.

Following months of military, ideological and psychological preparation, in July 1977, Mengistu openly and formally began the campaign for the "Motherland". In a speech he delivered, he stated,

> ...[I]n the east, the north and the south, ...an open invasion has taken place. They are opening up war fronts in every corner of the country. My compatriots, after understanding the danger posed against your land, property, family and the country and its unity, and understanding the intention of the war, which is to denigrate and make you a second class citizen...in the name of the Derge, I call upon you to rise up (ketet) for the war.[29]

The Somali regime had intended to gain some territory from Ethiopia and weaken the military regime at the same time, however, it failed to do so and brought about the opposite result. The Ethio-Somali conflict that erupted in 1976/77 was the very element the Derge needed to stay in power. The Derge adopted a form of nationalism that enabled it to quiet down a sizable percentage of the Ethiopian population and stabilize itself in the meantime. Besides, the Ethio-Somali conflict was a pretext for the massive military involvement of the Soviet Union, on the side of the beleaguered military regime of Ethiopia.

Next to the 1975 land reform, Ethiopian nationalism was the single most important instrument that the Derge used to rally and coerce the population. Furthermore, it was a means used to alienate its opposition, particularly the left opposition. The rallying cry was effectively used to recapture the cities that had been taken over by Eritrean rebels, some Somali-supported Oromo groups, Somali national movements and the Somali regime. Along with the daring and adventurous moves that Mengistu had undertaken all throughout his stay in power, the adoption of Ethiopian nationalism gave him leverage to stay in power for over seventeen years.

Derge and the Mass Organizations

One of the main forces that had to carry the burdens of the war was the peasantry. With the formation of the state controlled All Ethiopian Peasants Association (AEPA) on September 17, 1977, the military regime obtained a mechanism that enabled it to rally the peasants to its side. Initially, one of the main tasks of the association was to recruit and mobilize peasants for the war front. Those who did not want to take part in the war emigrated to other areas. Consequently, the displacement of the peasant from his plot during the farming season, either by the regime or on his own accord to join the liberation movements, exacerbated the crisis in the rural areas. "There will be a shortage of harvest next year, and this will be followed up by famine," commented a 1977 *Democracia*.[30] Indeed, in the late 1970s and 1980s, there was severe famine in many parts of Ethiopia. Furthermore, the peasantry also made contributions, either in cash or in kind, to the militia contingents that were under formation. A new form of tax was also imposed on the peasantry[31] and the EPRP came out with a slogan opposing it.[32]

In the urban areas, the kebeles and the so called "mass organizations" mobilized the city dwellers to contribute money to the war efforts, and mothers were summoned to provide "voluntary" service to the new recruits. For over three months, mothers were deployed to feed the hundreds of thousands of trainees at the Tatek Training Camp. A family that did not contribute its share in this effort and did not take part in the demonstrations organized by the regime was accused of collaborating with the enemy and was deprived of the right to buy basic items, which were rationed and sold by the kebeles at that time.

Both during and after the war, the economic condition of Ethiopia deteriorated. The cost of cereals, such as teff, wheat, etc., increased. In the urban areas, corn replaced wheat in making bread. "The years since 1975 have seen an acceleration in price increases. The Addis Abeba retail price index, the main indicator, rose at an annual average rate of 5-6 percent during the early 1970's; during the three fiscal years ending in mid-1978, it rose nearly 20 percent p.a.," commented a World Bank report.[33]

> The economic condition of the country is pitiful. Because of shortage of bread, people stand in queue at the bakeries. Teff has disappeared from the markets and if at all, it is only possible to get some through middle men. The price has sky-rocketed. Oil has become as scarce as French perfume..., stated *Democracia*.[34]

Addressing the causes of the economic problems a World Bank report stated,

> ...First, taking Ethiopia as a whole, there was and is ample scope for increases in on-farm grain consumption....Secondly, much of the former marketed surplus was the landlord's share; it was marketed because land-

lords required the cash for their own consumption or for retention in the urban centers. Thirdly, many farmers were able to harvest their grain, but because of the shortage of draught oxen, ...were unable to thresh it. Fourthly, trucking capacity was short due to the security situation on the Addis/Asseb road....Fifth, there was some diversion of grain supplies to meet military requirements. Sixth, uncertainty on the part of private merchants reduced their willingness to purchase and hold grain stocks; doubtless many of them also withheld stocks from the market as a speculation.[35]

Because of insecurity, business was severely curtailed and businessmen, gripped between nascent nationalism and fear of government retaliation, had to lie low. Every form of extortion was used to get money out of the people and one of them was the auctions regularly conducted through the kebele or peasant associations. Real wages fell not only as a result of increase of price index, but also due to government surtax.

From 1974-76, birr 30 million was collected in the form of an income surtax for drought relief; in 1977/78, birr 75.2 million was collected in the form of voluntary contributions for the military emergency, and in early 1979, a call was made to collect a further birr 71 million for drought relief.[36]

When the price of teff went up double the ceiling price in Addis Abeba in late 1978, the government tried to reestablish some control over the grain market by requiring traders to sell a portion of their product according to prices set by the government. To follow these activities, the Agricultural Marketing Corporation (AMC), which was established in 1976 was put in charge. In due course, AMC would also be involved in grain retailing.

In May 1977, at the instigation of government supporters, the workers of the main Post Office decided to provide free service on Saturdays and Sundays in emulation of the Bolshevik sybotnik.[37] That experience later spread to other branches of industry and the regime, albeit in an indirect way, began coercing workers into longer hours. The voluntary free service was transformed into an obligation for quite some time. In a somewhat sarcastic way, the editorial of *Addis Zemen* remarked,

> [A]s if the workers, instigated by the anarchists, did not demand higher pay last year, ...(this year), many workers had responded to the call of the motherland to provide free service on Saturdays and Sundays....[38]

The voluntary service was designed to increase production without raising cost.

The nationalistic policy of the regime had forced workers to suppress their demands so that the demands of the "Motherland" could come first. It was considered trivial to raise ones own demands when the country was in great peril. Anyone who had the courage to voice his grievance was hushed down. Thus the struggle of workers and teachers came to a standstill.

By mid-1977, the Derge had systematically weakened the opposition and had controlled the leadership of many of the "mass organizations", giving it free reign to mobilize thousands of workers for the war front. The Derge's control of the AEWTU[39] facilitated that process and many factories lost hundreds and thousands of activists and experienced workers. Many of these were regarded with suspicion by the leaders of AEWTU. The deployment of worker activists to the war front proved an effective mechanism to wipe out the already weakened workers opposition, and ELAMA lost many of its members. *Some of the enlightened workers had already been executed or had gone underground following the declaration of the war of annihilation in September 1976. After the Mengistu coup of February 1977, many more worker activists had been victimized. It was the remaining worker leaders and activists who were the focus of the mobilization for the war front during the Ethio-Somali conflict.*

At the training camp, the fate awaiting workers was gruesome. When they learned that the Derge had begun deducting 15% of their salary as taxation to augment the war effort, they demanded that their full salary be paid to their families. When the regime failed to address their demands, some workers escaped from the training camp. Those who stayed behind were executed.[40] Discussing the sad state of affairs among the workers *Democracia* commented,

> [W]hile on the one hand the cost of goods has gone up two or three times higher, the worker is obliged to contribute his salary...his wife is engaged in food preparation for the trainees at the Sega Meda and his sons are being witch hunted.[41]

In conclusion, the Ethio-Somali conflict and the adoption of Ethiopian nationalism gave the supporters of the regime such a high degree of confidence that they were encouraged to round up hundreds of thousands of peasants, youth, etc., from local markets, streets and villages for the war front. As a result, lawlessness and arbitrariness were perfected to their limits.[42]

International Significance of the Conflict

The Ethio-Somali conflict created a new political alignment of forces in the Horn of Africa. The long time friend of the Somali regime, the Soviet Union, after considering a number of geo-political and other diplomatic concerns, changed gear in the midst of the unfolding war and began supporting the military regime of Ethiopia. The USSR had established a warm relationship with the Somali regime following the *coup d'etat* of the former Defense Minister, General Ziad Barre, in the early seventies. The General appointed himself the President of the country, dissolved the Somali parliament and declared Scientific Socialism as the guiding ideology of the state. When the conflict between the Somali and Ethiopian regimes began unfolding, the first reaction of the Soviets was to act as a mediating force and contain the crisis. The Soviet Union, which was on friendly terms with both regimes was caught in between and had to make a difficult decision. It wanted to be in good standing with both regimes, but their deteriorating relationship would not allow that.

To mediate between the regimes, Fidel Castro of Cuba became involved in the process. He proposed that Ethiopia, Djibouti, Yemen and the Somali Republic form some kind of a confederation. That plan did not work. In July 1977, the Soviets conducted a diplomatic maneuver among Somali and Ethiopian officials. To break the impasse, the Soviets implored the Derge to cede some of the territorial claims of the Somali regime. However, the delegation led by Colonel Berhanu Bayeh refused to give in.[43]

In September 1977, the Soviets stopped arms shipments to the Somali regime. In July of the same year, the West had promised to provide the Somalis with defensive weapons.

> ...[F]ollowing promises of large donations for military purchases by Saudi Arabia, conditional on a break off of links with the USSR and indications of US and western support, on November 13, (1977) Somalia broke off relations with Cuba, and renounced Soviet treaty of friendship, withdrawing all military facilities and expelling the 6000 Soviet personnel in the country.[44]

Sometime before the Soviets broke off relations with the Somali regime, Mengistu had criticized them for assisting the Somali regime. In September 1977, Kenya, which has a sizable Somali population under its jurisdiction, condemned the Somali regime's maneuvers.

One of the most interesting diplomatic maneuvers of the time was the pact signed between the Libyan and the Ethiopian regimes. The pact had an economic undertone. It will be remembered that Ethiopia's relations with many Arab countries had remained strained because of the alliance of the Haile Selassie regime and later the Derge with the Israelis. Most of them, including Libya, supported the Eritrean organizations. At the 10th anniversary of the founding of the Organization of African Unity (OAU), in 1974, the Libyan leader President Moomar Qadaffi had proposed that the headquarters of the OAU be moved out of Addis Abeba, which he believed to be an American and a Zionist capital.[45]

Both the Derge and the Libyan regimes were opposed to the Nimieri regime of the Sudan, albeit, for altogether different reasons. The Libyan regime desired to oust the Nimeri regime and install the opposition group known as the Ansar Movement, led by Al Mahdi. On the other hand, the Ethiopian regime disliked Jafar Nimieri's support for the Eritrean organizations and the EDU. To implement their objectives, both the Ethiopian and the Libyan regimes began training and arming followers of the Ansar movement and in 1977, they attempted an ill-conceived coup to oust the Nimeri regime. A few months earlier, the Sudanese regime had assisted the EDU in raiding Metema, an Ethiopian town on the Sudanese/Ethiopian border. It was the intention of the Sudanese regime to wipe out the followers of Sediq Al Mahdi who at the time had regrouped in Gendeweha, a small town in the Begemidir province.[46] Following the aborted coup, some members of the Ansar movement were forced to vegetate in a western Begemidir town known as the Negade Bahir. Their condition was so dismal that some of them sold their belongings for a living.

In the diplomatic arena of the international scene, one of the most significant impacts of the Ethio-Somali conflict was the creation of political and military conditions for Soviet hegemony in Africa. Until the mid-fifties, the only relations the former Soviet Union established in Africa were with some Communist Parties in the Sudan and South Africa. The Soviet view on Africa was changed at the Bandung Conference of Asian and African leaders in 1955, and at the 20th Party Congress of the CPSU in 1956, where Joseph Stalin and some of his political lines were criticized and repudiated.[47] Over the years, the Soviet Union established diplomatic relations with many of the independent African countries and very cautiously, cultivated friendly relationships with many of them.

Following the defeat of the United States in Vietnam in 1975, the image of the former Soviet Union was enhanced. The Soviet Union was an ally of the Vietnamese and had provided all forms of assistance to the freedom fighters. Encouraged by the fierce struggle for world hegemony, in the late sixties and early seventies, Soviet industry became heavily involved in massive production of military equipment, thereby encouraging the Soviet Union to adopt a more aggressive foreign policy. Beginning in the mid-1970's, the Soviets became heavily involved in a number of African states, including Somalia, Guinea-Bissau, Angola, Mozambique and Ethiopia.

At the beginning of 1977, a few months after he had taken full power, Mengistu visited the Soviet Union. The outcome of that visit proved to be one of the most significant developments in the history of Ethiopia, perhaps comparable to the 1945 agreement signed by Emperor Haile Selassie on the establishment of a US military base in Ethiopia. When Mengistu visited the Soviet Union, his first priority was aid. A massive military shipment arrived a few days after he returned to Ethiopia.

The Derge's relations with the US government had been strained and on February 26, 1977, President Carter announced the ending of military assistance to Ethiopia on the grounds of human rights abuse. In retaliation, the Derge closed down the Kagnew military base, the US Mapping Mission and other military establishments of the US government in Ethiopia in April 1977. The Derge also expelled all US military personnel, except the embassy staff. In May 1977, the Derge expelled the US and British military attaches. In this game of *'Russian' roulette*, in May 1977, Sudan, which had been assisting the Eritrean rebels and the EDU, expelled Soviet military experts. Some months earlier, in November 1976, the US government had lifted the arms embargo against the Nimieri regime of the Sudan.

Soviet Involvement was more than Military

The West had been the source of armaments for Ethiopia for quite a long time. However, following the involvement of the Soviets, the Ethiopian military arsenal was overhauled. As of July 1977, direct air communication was established between Moscow and Addis Abeba and the new arrangement facilitated the procurement of large supplies of armaments enabling the military regime to train and arm hundreds of thousands of recruits. The process of building the military under the guise of militia training had begun a year or so earlier. However, the Ethio-Somali conflict hastened the tempo, and in a brief time, the Derge was able to mobilize one of the largest armies in sub-Saharan Africa. The influx of the new peasant recruits also significantly changed the composition of the Ethiopian army.

The Ethio-Somali conflict gave the Mengistu regime an ideological weapon and the upper hand in the political and diplomatic spheres and helped the Derge wield a vast army. Moreover, the large Cuban contingent in Ethiopia was of tremendous assistance to the beleaguered regime of Mengistu. Besides the military support, Fidel Castro's Cuba had involved itself in Ethiopia in many ways. In 1978, twelve hundred children between the ages of nine and fourteen were sent to Cuba, ostensibly for a prolonged educational program.[48]

The massive military expenditure of the Soviets and other East European countries to Vietnam, Afghanistan, Mozambique, Ethiopia and other countries had an adverse effect on their own economy too. It drained their economy and it is believed that it was one of the factors for the turmoil that took place in East European countries in the 1980's.

The Soviets and their former East European allies assisted the Derge in laying down the network for a large security apparatus. This role was played mainly by the former East-German government, which had superior knowledge of intelligence activities. The East-Germans overhauled the Ethiopian security network. New devices for telephone tapping and listening, sophisticated photo cameras, etc. were introduced. Many Ethiopians were sent to East Germany and other East European countries for further training in intelligence and espionage.

Initially, Soviet involvement in Ethiopia proved a tremendous political, moral and diplomatic boost to the besieged regime of Mengistu. However, in the years to come, the role the Soviet Union played on the side of the most repressive regimes, like that of Mengistu, cast incalculable ideological and political damage not only on the Soviet Union itself, but on socialism as well. Because of the Soviet Union's involvement on the side of such regimes, socialism was associated with the atrocities committed in those countries. The so called 'socialist' system became synonymous with mass terror, arbitrariness, deceit, economic disaster, massive uprooting of people, famine, repression, etc. The Soviet involvement in Ethiopia also changed the alliance of forces in the area. The US became more involved with the Somali and the

Sudanese regimes and other opposition forces in Ethiopia. The US government continued cultivating good relations with rebel nationalist organizations, through proxy countries like the Sudan and Saudi Arabia. China distanced itself from the Derge when Soviet involvement became imminent. At a rally held to commemorate "Revolution Day" on September 12, 1977, Mengistu condemned China along with the Central Intelligence Agency (CIA) for supporting the EPRP.[49]

The EPRP and the Ethio-Somali Conflict

In the publications of the EPRP, resolving the national question had remained one of the major issues for the organization. The issue was also raised in the meetings conducted in many parts of the country and during the demonstrations held in different places. The struggle for changing the land tenure system was also considered as part and parcel of the national issue. When, in the first months of 1976, the military regime was organizing the "Raza Project", that is, the military campaign against the Eritrean rebels, *Democracia* had commented,

> ...[I]n order to sidetrack the peoples struggle, Adolf Hitler mobilized the Germans against the Jews...and millions of Jews were massacred...the present regime (the Derge) is getting ready to follow the same 'tactic'."[50] The paper then discussed the impact of the "Raza" campaign, which was launched in March 1976. The paper argued that the campaign might lead to a civil war, which would further aggravate the contradictions between the nationalities.

A year or so later, discussing the impact of the Derge's policy on inter-ethnic relationships, *Democracia* stated,

> [D]uring the last one or two months [February and March 1977], the regime had decided to follow a course that would lead the country to a catastrophe. It had decided to mobilize the Ethiopian people against Eritreans and intends to bring a final solution to the problem...(under such conditions) it is absurd to think that the revolution will continue, once the class struggle had been replaced by a civil war.[51]

Because of the failure of the regime to properly address the national issue, the recurring question of the day was the impending civil war.

In the unfolding struggle for the rights of nations and nationalities, the role the EPRP played can be categorized into two parts. During the first period, which extends from the formation of the organization in 1972 until mid 1977, the EPRP viewed the country's fast developing crisis *as partly* caused by the ethnic policies of the previous regime and the Derge. The EPRP conducted political campaigns against these policies. During the initial period of this phase, Eritrea was the main focus.[52]

Following the land proclamation of 1975, the national issue in southern

Ethiopia was diffused when its economic aspect was partially resolved.

> It (the proclamation) nullified the economic aspect of the national question without addressing the political. The land reform was directed not only against serfdom, but against national oppression. In one stroke, land reform addressed both the economic problems of the people and the economic aspect of the national question.[53]

The failure to address the political aspect of the national issue, particularly issues of democracy, continued to compound the problem. The 1975 EPRP Conference had noted that the Derge's repression against the people in areas where nationalist forces were conducting their struggle had exacerbated the hatred amongst Ethiopian peoples.[54] In line with the Conference, a *Democracia* issue stated, "...(the regime) is facing problems in the Bale province...to intensify the crisis, it is inciting the people to fight against each other. It is instigating a clash between the Boranas and the Merihan (Somali clan), and the Gujji. ..with the...."[55] Another *Democracia* issue stated,

> [T]he regime, having decreed the May 18 Peace initiative of 1976, not only failed to resolve the national issue militarily, but is creating other Eritreas in the south as well...in order to suppress the struggle of the Oromo people, it has deployed a massive military force and is making efforts to incite conflicts amongst the Oromos themselves.[56]

The EPRP knew that the Somali regime had territorial interest in Ethiopia and was training and arming insurgents. However, the EPRP still believed that the Oromo and Ogadeni movements in the south and south-eastern parts of Ethiopia were outcomes of national oppression and it strongly condemned the policies of the Ethiopian regimes, while advocating the equality of the various national groups of Ethiopia.

Even when the Derge was making efforts to blame either neighboring or Arab countries for the exacerbation of the national problem in Ethiopia and, at the same time, was making efforts to topple the Nimieri regime in Sudan, the EPRP, although aware of the external support that the movements enjoyed, believed that the root causes for the national unrest were internal. The EPRP was convinced that the Derge was making efforts to externalize the problems, instead of looking inward to find solutions.[57] Discussing the political impact of the Derge's policies, a 1977 *Democracia* issue forecast, "*the national contradiction, which [until 1977] was secondary vis-a-vis the class struggle will assume a primary role.*"[58] It was also stated that the high-handed policy of the regime was the main factor for galvanizing the national movements and relegating the class struggle to a secondary status.[59]

The EPRP, believing that the Derge's and in particular Mengistu's policy regarding the national issue would eventually dismember and disintegrate Ethiopia, suggested that progressives should struggle to create conditions for the peaceful resolution of the problems.[60] Even though the Derge was blamed for the mounting tension among the various national groups, the EPRP also severely criticized the WSLF for the atrocities it committed in the Harer area.[61] In this area, the Oromo group known by its publication *Oromia* was conducting an intensive campaign against the Ziad Barre regime, long before the later decided to involve its regular army in the conflict. During this early stage, the EPRP held the Derge responsible for exasperating the national conflict. In its indiscriminate repression, the Derge had alienated a large segment of the population, including nationalist forces. Consequently, the EPRP held the Derge responsible for the exacerbation of the conflict and the organization continued making efforts to establish a relationship with the WSLF and the Oromo groups in the south (see details below).

Following the direct involvement of the Somali regime in the conflict, the situation in the Harerge province began to worsen. The EPRP, which until this time had been blaming the Derge, had to reevaluate the new development. Until a consensus among EPRP members regarding the Somali regime's role was reached, the Harer zonal committee was instructed to conduct a campaign against any group that forcefully intervened in the affairs of the national movements. In the leaflets which the Harer EPRP zonal committee distributed, the role of the Ziad Barre regime was condemned and campaign was conducted against his policies.[62]

EPRP's Effort to Form a Front

One of the major organizational priorities of the EPRP during the initial phase of the Ethio-Somali conflict was the establishment of a relationship with Oromo organizations conducting military activities in the south and southeastern parts of the country. Describing that policy a *Democracia* issue had stated,

> [I]n order to hasten the downfall of the regime and bring a popular and democratic system and coordinate and advance the struggle, organized progressive forces are duty bound to form a front.[63]

After reiterating the need to form a front, another *Democracia* issue warned that victory will not be achieved as long as the struggle remained uncoordinated and it was not mobilized against the regime.[64]

The effort to form some kind of relationship with the armed movements was resumed in 1977 and it was decided to contact the Gujji Oromo movement in the Sidamo province. The leader of the movement, Haji Kutta, was a member of the EPRP affiliated Democratic Front. As was indicated in Chapter I, Haji Kutta and some three hundred of his followers had left for Somalia in 1976. His followers returned to Ethiopia in mid-1977.

When the news about the arrival of Haji Kutta's group became known, the Sidamo EPRP zonal committee took over the responsibilities to contact the group. To pursue the task, the committee selected four of its Oromo members, some of whom had worked with Haji himself. The team was instructed to join the Gujji group that had begun conducting military activities in some parts of Sidamo. The four-member EPRP team was adequately briefed regarding its tasks and objectives. Its first and major task was to create conditions so that the Gujji group would be incorporated into the broader EPRP network, and if that failed, it was advised to prepare the ground for the formation of a front. If the last option did not work, the EPRP team was advised to join the Gujji group and conduct political work among the members of the group and, when conditions allowed, agitate for the EPRP program. The EPRP team was given a broad mandate and it was instructed to be very cautious in its dealings with the Gujji group. The team left the Sidamo urban area in mid-1977 and reaching the hinterlands where the Gujji group was located, demanded to meet Haji Kutta. To the disappointment of the EPRP team, the leader was not to be found there, and his lieutenants were in charge. It was learned later that Haji Kutta had remained in Somalia and the Somali regime had grounded him for fear that he might be too independent and disobey instructions.

The arrival of the EPRP team was reported to the leadership of the Gujji group and all of a sudden, all members of the team were arrested. In their first encounter with the leadership of the Gujji group, the members of the EPRP team learned that the Gujji army was led by Somali officers, who had absolute power and were in full control. While under detention, they were searched and about two thousand birr and some study materials, written in Amharic, were among the materials found in their possession. Anticipating that the EPRP members would be on their own for quite some time, the zonal committee had provided them with some extra cash.

The Somali officers were alerted when they found the articles that were written in Amharic. They interrogated the members of the team and asked why they wanted to join the Gujji group. The explanation provided was not accepted and all of the members of the EPRP team were sentenced to death. The night before their scheduled execution, the EPRP team overpowered the guard on duty and all of the members escaped. On their way to the Sidamo urban areas, it was reported that they encountered a Derge militia group and two of them were killed while trying to escape. The remaining two reached the Sidamo zonal committee and reported the incident. The EPRP was aware of the Somali regime's irredentist plans and its involvement in the armed coflict in Ethiopia, however, the first hand information regarding the Somali regime's role among armed Oromo groups was an important factor in determining EPRP's political line regarding the unfolding Ethio-Somali conflict.

The Somali regime had exhibited some hospitality and cooperation toward Ethiopian activists who fled their country in the late 1960's and early 1970's and it was at this time that the EPRP established relations with the Somali regime. The EPRP discussed its program, which supported the right to self-determination and the peaceful resolution of the Ogadeni people's problem. The EPRP program categorically opposed forceful intervention by the Somali or the Ethiopian regimes in the affairs of the Ogadeni.[65] Initial contact with the Somali regime was made abroad, however, relationship was maintained both through the EPRP Foreign Committee and inside the country. The EPRP wanted the renewed Somali contact in order to forge relationship with those groups that had the Somali regime's backing. The EPRP openly declared its interests along that line. The EPRP also wanted to obtain from the Somalis some military and financial assistance for its armed activities both in the rural and urban areas. On the other hand, the Somali regime wanted to contact the EPRP in order to neutralize the organization and in the mean time, minimize the resistance to the grand plan of the Somali regime, that was yet to unfold. Cognizant of the intentions of the Somali regime, during the first meetings the EPRP contact person demanded that the Somali regime avoid any kind of forceful intervention in Ethiopia. The contact person also discussed the negative impact of such an intervention on the unfolding struggle of the Ethiopian people.

The Somali regime denied harboring any such plans and agreed to introduce the EPRP to the WSLF and SALF. To establish contact and to conduct meetings, appointments were set in the rural areas in Harer. Seifu, a member of the EPRP CC sub-secretariat was put in charge. However, both the representatives of the Somali regime and the members of the nationalist groups never showed up at the appointment places.[66] The Somali regime agreed to provide arms, but repeatedly failed to keep up its promises. Except for some token gestures of a very negligible financial assistance and few hand guns, the Somali regime did not assist the EPRP as expected. When in mid-1977 the Somali regime's grand intentions began unfolding and it continued to break the promises it had made and also when EPRP's approach to change Somali's course through organizational and diplomatic means could not bear fruit, it became quite evident that the Somali regime was buying time to fulfill its objectives. Thus, the EPRP had to change its policy and follow a different course.

The military involvement of the Somali regime in the conflict in southern and eastern Ethiopia became evident to the EPRP sometime before the actual armed aggression took place in July 1977. As was mentioned above, the EPRP had already observed that Somali officers were providing leadership to some of the Oromo groups. The EPRP had also observed first hand that the Somali regime had no interest in bringing closer together forces opposed to the military regime. Furthermore, it also had become clear that some of the so-called armed groups deployed in the southern and southeastern parts of Ethiopia were pawns of the Somali regime's expansionist policies.

The EPRP expressed its strong reservations about the policies of the Somali regime and severed relationship around the end of May or the beginning of June 1977. However, a low level contact was maintained through the EPRP foreign office.

The involvement of the Somali regime terribly complicated the political situation in Ethiopia when the struggle in the south, southwestern and southeastern parts of the country became transformed into an Ethio-Somali conflict. The struggle for the national rights of the Ogadenis and the Oromos became entangled with the Somali regime's policies and was gradually transformed into an issue related to the territorial aggrandizement of the Somali regime. The demands of the Ogadeni and the Oromos were subdued and they became tied to the irridentist plan of the Somali regime's Greater Somalia. The situation became so complex that one could not help antagonize the Ogadenis and the Oromos when condemning the Somali regime's policies. In the same token, one could not help embitter a certain section of the Ethiopian people who had rallied behind the banner of Ethiopian nationalism when condemning the violent policies of the Ethiopian regime.

The EPRP was at a crossroads and its members continued to demand a further clarification of the unfolding conflict. A paper published by the Anjas (a splinter group formed by Berhane Meskel) further complicated things. In one of their papers, the splinter group condemned the Somali regime while supporting the Ethiopian military regime's juridical right in the war.[67] Another paper of the faction which came out during this period and represented the youth faction, expressed the same opinion, albeit, in a very polemical manner.[68]

Before the EPRP made its new policy public, a *Democracia* issue declared that the organization resolutely opposed

> ...[T]he massacre conducted against the oppressed people....The aim and the effort to 'resolve' the national question by forceful means, by any state or group, is contrary to our policy and hence we will fight against it", stated the paper.[69]

The EPRP leadership in the urban centers had to take the lead in the discussion regarding the Ethio-Somali conflict and present a political position commensurate with the unfolding events. A paper that discussed the origins of the Ethio-Somali conflict was prepared. Analyzing the major causes and the class perspective of the conflict, it paid attention to the most recent struggle of the Somalis in the Ogaden and the Oromos of Bali. After describing the historical origin of the conflict, the paper, which was distributed only to EPRP members, discussed what ought to be done and what position the EPRP should adopt. Based on the study, discussions were conducted both in the party and the Youth League structures and the gist of the discussion and the political position of the EPRP was printed in *Democracia*, Volume IV, No. 9, May/June 1977.

The paper provided a historical analysis regarding the emergence of Somali and Oromo national movements in Ethiopia. In this fourteen page *Democracia* issue, EPRP's policy regarding the Ethio-Somali conflict and its position regarding the various forces in the conflict was expressed. The publication held the Derge as the primary force responsible for the spread of the war in different parts of the country. According to *Democracia*, the war was "an extension and expression of the dictatorial and contemptuous policies of the military regime."[70] The military regime failed to provide political and democratic solution to the national issue and as a result, national movements emerged, argued *Demcracia*. After reiterating the long standing EPRP's support for the struggle of the Oromo and Somali people, *Democracia* condemned the Derge's policy and the war that it unleashed against these people.

Democracia also did not spare the Somali regime, which made efforts to exploit the national contradictions in Ethiopia.[71] "The Somali regime's interference in the struggle of the Oromos will not only side track it, but the struggle itself will lose support and be defeated...[and in the end] the leadership [of the Oromo groups] will be held accountable."[72] Further, *Democracia* expressed stern opposition to the forceful involvement of the Somali regime in the struggle of the Somali people in Ethiopia. After enumerating acts of infringements of the Somali regime in the affairs of the Somali people in Ethiopia, *Democracia* warned that interference would eventually assist the military regime in suppressing the peoples struggle. Finally,

> [N]either the Derge nor the Somali regime will ascertain the rights of the Ogadeni and the Oromos, but the people themselves....The Somali regime's interference... *will create serious impediments to the Ethiopian revolutionary struggle*...Therefore, we will condemn and struggle against it." stated *Democracia*.[73]

The Impact of the Ethio-Somali Conflict on the EPRP

The opposition, with the EPRP in the lead, had been giving political and ideological guidance to the struggle that began in 1974. *Following the consecutive economic reforms of 1975, the Derge outstripped the economic agenda of the radical left. When it adopted Ethiopian nationalism in 1977, the Derge gained the upper hand in the ideological sphere as well.*

Combining coercion with an appeal to the nationalist instinct of the people, the Derge was able to dictate its policies. Those sectors of the population that were affected by the Derge's economic polices of 1975 supported the war which they regarded would abort the course of the revolutionary movement, stated *Democracia*.[74] The EPRP, which believed that the war was not to the advantage of the people of either Ethiopia or Somalia, was in no position to persuade the populace, which was unable to transcend the nationalism espoused and advocated by the Derge. The media portrayed the EPRP "as an organization that questions the very existence of Ethiopia and advocates its avowed enemies."[75] The same article also stated that the EPRP was an organization that would like to erase Ethiopia from the map of Africa. The EPRP was portrayed as an agent of the Somali regime. It was called a fifth column.[76]

Besides the anti-EPRP campaign of the Derge and the repression it conducted, the EPRP was unable to get an enthusiastic welcome from any of the nationalist movements. It was a tragedy that Oromo and Somali organizations in the Harer area lured the Ethiopian youth to their side and ruthlessly massacred a large number of them later. The Harer youth, who had been voicing protest against the ethnic policies of the regime, was caught between the Derge's "Red Terror" of 1977 and the Ethio-Somali conflict. When conditions in the urban areas became more and more repressive, youth activists went to the areas controlled by the Somali supported groups seeking shelter. Some of them were lured into the WSLF and a few from among them were sent back to the cities to persuade and bring their friends. Hundreds of youth who vehemently opposed the Derge and fought for the rights of the oppressed nationalities fell into the hands of Somali and Oromo nationalists. It is believed that from the Jijjiga area alone, over three hundred young activists had left for the WSLF, seeking shelter. The whereabouts of many of them were unknown. However, about forty of them were in prison in Hawayi (in Somali) until the end of the 1980s.[77] An Oromo activist who was collaborating with one of the Somali backed organizations confirmed the sad fate of many of the Jijjiga youths, after he himself joined the refuge population in the Sudan in 1980.[78] Many were executed.

The unsuspecting Ethiopian youth activists were executed mainly because of their national origin and their allegiance to the EPRP. Some of them were forced to take part in the military activities of the WSLF. Among them were twenty-four Hareri youth activists who went to Mogadishu for shelter.[79] When they refused to take part in military activities, all of them were placed under detention.

The EPRP had taught its young followers about the national oppression in Ethiopia and the repressive policies of the different regimes. However, it failed to point out the dangers posed by the narrow nationalist tendencies of the nationalist forces, or the effect of their propaganda in spreading discord among the various ethnic groups. Besides, the EPRP failed to present a comprehensive study of the direction of the nationalist struggle. As a result, the EPRP itself, which was making efforts to win the trust of the oppressed nationalities and advocated their rights, became their victim. Its supporters, the idealistic Ethiopian youth, who had little to do with the hundreds of years of national strife, was ill-prepared to face the danger posed by the nationalists.

Sometime before he fell victim, Tesfaye Debessai was of the opinion that the EPRP had made some progress in fighting national chauvinism and it should pay more attention to the dangers posed by narrow nationalism. Because of the ongoing repression of the regime against the various nationalities, Tesfaye's idea was accepted by some of the leading members of the EPRP, however, it was considered untimely. It was feared that it would alienate the nationalist organizations and create difficulties in forming a front.

As was indicated earlier, the Ethio-Somali conflict had resulted in a major realignment of forces in the Horn of Africa. In 1977, the two superpowers, the Soviet Union and the United States, changed their roles in Somalia and Ethiopia. When the Soviets abandoned the Somali regime and supported the Derge, that shift of allegiance created the misconception that the Derge and not the opposition was struggling for the "socialist" cause. The impact of this development was more noticeable in the arena of international relations as a consequence of which serious demands and pressure were exerted on the EPRP leadership. Both from within the organization and without, interpreting Soviet involvement in Ethiopia became imperative.

The Anjas (the faction) and the student movement abroad, particularly the one in the USA, had characterized the Soviet Union as social-imperialist. They became vocal and insisted that the EPRP characterize the Soviet Union as such. Since its founding congress in 1972, the EPRP had been undecided about the so called social-imperialist theory. Unable to reach a conclusion, the extended conference held in August 1975 had recommended that a study should be conducted on the issue. No breakthrough was made even when the Soviets became directly involved in Ethiopia in 1977. A few months after the involvement of the Soviets, a study on the nature of the Soviet Union was prepared by the political department of the EPRP and was presented to the urban leadership. The leadership then passed on the draft for discussion to the structures both inside and outside the country and suggested that an elaborate discussion be conducted.[80] A few months later, the draft, with some modifications, was approved by the general membership and the EPRP accepted the social-imperialist theory.[81]

Besides the above mentioned ideological aspect, Soviet involvement brought about some changes in the character and targets of the struggle, the alignment of forces and the main focus of the struggle in Ethiopia. The targets of the struggle had been imperialism, feudalism and bureaucratic capitalism even after the 1974 movement began. However, in mid 1977, the target of the struggle was changed when the Derge and Soviet involvement constituted the primary focus of the opposition.

POMOA "Withers" Away

The escalation of the Ethio-Somali conflict and the adoption of Ethiopian nationalism as the guiding ideology of the state allowed Mengistu Haile Mariam to become the champion of that cause and the guardian of Ethiopia's territorial integrity. The opposition, both in the urban and rural areas, was seriously weakened. Peasant uprisings were ruthlessly suppressed. The national movements, particularly those in the south, were dealt with a heavy blow. The advance of the struggle in Eritrea was halted and the Derge recaptured many of the cities.[82] Consequently, the military regime, which had a shaky base until mid-1977, began to stabilize, and this brought about a chain reaction. Until this time, the military regime's policies were dictated by events. However, since the last quarter of 1977 the Derge was able to dictate its own agenda and program.

Hundreds of Derge supporters, trained in the former Soviet block countries were assigned to important government posts. The would-be state party, the Seded, recruited a large following that it became self-reliant and began conducting ideological and political activities. This new reality made MEISON and other civilian political groups around the Derge dispensable.

Besides the organizational skill that the new military cadres acquired, spreading Ethiopian nationalism which is as old as Ethiopia itself, did not require modern elites. It is an ideology deeply ingrained in the psyche and emotions of a large section of the citizens.

With the advent of Ethiopian nationalism, the role of MEISON was relegated to the periphery. It was diminished so much that Mengistu had his speech on the "Call for the Motherland" written by others when MEISON grumbled about drafting it.[83]

The Derge's effort to control the mass organizations, the gradual weakening of the EPRP, and the diminishing threat it posed to the Derge were additional factors that made POMOA, and MEISON in particular, irrelevant as far as Mengistu was concerned. POMOA had helped the Derge weaken the opposition and bring the mass organizations under control. As was indicated elsewhere, MEISON's over-concentration of power was an issue of concern to Mengistu. Whatever the underlying reasons, *by mid-1977, POMOA had accomplished its historical mission and it had become evident that it was an institution that could easily be dispensed with.* Paradoxically, the diminishing role of the opposition hastened POMOA's demise, rather than consolidating it.

Ever since the formation of POMOA, MEISON and the WAZ League had been rivals competing for political and organizational influence. To recruit some following, the WAZ League used to focus on members of the military. According to information revealed later, WAZ League had also infiltrated the Seded.[84] MEISON, on the other hand, had placed its members in important government posts and was in control of the civilian wing of the state apparatus.[85] Beginning in September 1976, MEISON controlled the leadership of the various mass organizations. Its members controlled AEWTU, the *Abyot Tebeka* committees, the various kebele associations and more importantly, the Higher kebeles that controlled the kebeles. A year or so later, one of the most prominent members of MEISON, Daniel Tadesse, at a meeting held with some members of the European Economic Commission stated, "...efforts are being made to organize women. Following the formation of the General Urban Association (an institution that the kebeles would account to) it will take over the administration of the city."[86]

At the inauguration ceremony of the Addis Abeba General Council, about three months since he met the EEC members, Daniel Tadesse clearly spelled out,

> the urban associations that are being formed are the lower echelons of the popular government under formation....As of this hour, the Addis Abeba General Council, representing the people, has already taken over

the city's administration.

Daniel further noted that over 250 Women's organizations were formed, youth associations were in the process of formation, and, "...in the coming week, the Derge is going to arm all the *Abyot Tebeka* groups."[87] Prominent MEISON member, Dr. Alemu Abebe was elected Mayor of Addis Abeba. A contender for the mayorship, Gutta Sernessa, was executed by unknown snipers. The murder was attributed to the EPRP, which had no knowledge of it.

To many of MEISON's opponents, regrouped around the Derge, it had become evident that MEISON was preparing to take power gradually and peacefully, initially in the urban centers. These and similar developments and efforts of MEISON did not go unnoticed among their partners. That MEISON was controlling a huge chunk of the state apparatus, including the leadership of the newly formed mass organizations, was a serious concern to its rivals, including some Derge members. That concern was expressed in the resolution adopted by cadres of the Political School in December 1977.[88]

As early as December 1976, *Sefiw Hizbe Dimtse* itself stated,

> ...{Recently} some accusations are made against the MEISON that it does not want the alliance of the progressives, it does not want the union of the Marxist-Leninist groups to form a proletarian party, that it makes efforts to transform itself into a proletarian party....[89]

According to the Editorial of *Addis Zemen*,[90] that accusation became more serious following the formation of the "Union of Ethiopian Marxist-Leninist Organizations" (the EMALEDEH). This was in reference to the efforts made to reorganize the groups that had allied with the Derge which included MEISON, WAZ League (Sennay Likke's group), ECHAAT (Baro Tumsa's group), MALRED (Tesfaye Mekonnen's group) and Seded (Mengistu Haile Mariam's and Legesse Asfaw's group). *Sefiw Hizbe Dimtse* had also stated, "...we have formed a struggle alliance. We formed the alliance based on the analysis of the Ethiopian situation..."[91]

The "alliance", in its initial form, was formed in December 1976. However, it was reorganized in February/March 1977 when the various groups that formed POMOA published a manifesto and formed EMALEDEH. Ostensibly, the ultimate aim of the umbrella organization (EMALEDEH) was to see through the formation of a proletarian party and a united front. Three individuals from each political group took part in the leading body of EMALEDEH. Representing the Seded, Mengistu was one of the individuals who took part in the proceedings of EMALEDEH. An underground leaflet of the period had classified the process of unification in three stages. Be that as it may, in order to have broader power and more say in the newly formed alliance, the groups that formed the EMALEDEH became engaged in a massive recruitment drive. Aware of the new conditions, *Sefiw HizbeDimtse* stated,

> [A]ll those individuals who are making efforts to become members of the organizations are not necessarily revolutionaries. Imperialist agents, other reactionaries and infiltrators...would make efforts to join....[92]

Using the newly created opportunity, some EPRP members were "recruited" by MALRED, which was the smallest and least organized group. In its desperation, the group began recruiting anyone it laid its hands on. Of those EPRP members recruited by MALRED at this initial stage, three of them played prominent role. Two of the EPRP infiltrators were MALRED representatives of the Gonder and Bale provinces. Moreover, the MALRED group of Jimma was also infiltrated.[93]

In any event, relations among the various groups associated with the Derge turned for the worse after the first quarter of 1977. When the Ethio-Somali conflict began to unfold, MEISON and particularly its POMOA representative in Harer, Abdulahi Yusuf, attempted to organize and arm Oromo peasants. That move of the MEISON was resisted both locally and at the center in Addis Abeba. To investigate the accusation, POMOA formed a committee. At the same time, the Derge disarmed the peasants in Harer and armed some former land-owners. "This policy was intensified after the Somali successes in mid-1977, in response to the desperate need for more men to help hold onto Harer and Dire Dawa."[94]

As relations among the various groups around the Derge continued deteriorating, MEISON's control of the newly formed para-military institution, the *Abyot Tebekas*, heightened the crisis further. Until this time, MEISON's control of the Abyot Tebeka institution had allowed the organization to accumulate immense power and enhance its dominance. The entire *Abyot Tebeka* was directly responsible to the Ministry of Public Housing, headed by Daniel Tadesse. As MEISON's relations with the other groups deteriorated, *Seded* and WAZ League formed an alliance. Probably after getting a green light from Mengistu, the WAZ and *Seded* groups began demanding a share of power in some of the areas, such as, labor (where MEISON had the upper hand), various ministries, the Cadre School, the kebeles and peasant associations.[95] The other political groups demanded equal say in the activities of POMOA, which until the third month of 1977 had been dominated by MEISON.

As was indicated elsewhere, those who opposed MEISON's over-concentration of power voiced their protest using the crisis created by the search and destroy campaign of March 1977, organized and conducted by MEISON. While the campaign was still underway, Addis Abeba residents went out on a spontaneous demonstration to protest against the brutality of the leading figures of the campaign and the execution of some residents.[96] As a result, fingers were pointed at MEISON and as of this period, MEISON's authority began to diminish.

The major showdown among the various groups around the Derge took place during the formation of the militia at the Tatek military camp. The MEISON argued that the militia should be politicized so that it would not transform itself into a "white army",[97] and suggested the formation of a political structure within the army. It also suggested that the army should have a "revolutionary, instead of a bureaucratic leadership."[98] At the May Day Celebration of 1977, a POMOA representative stated,

> [W]e the oppressed and the revolutionary are engaged in a life and death struggle. In order to free from the rotten...bureaucracy, the revolutionary struggle needs a leadership that is composed of progressive officers, progressive forces, and class conscious members of the oppressed people.[99]

Despite these and other appeals, MEISON's ideas met stiff resistance, particularly from the Seded. MEISON's idea was rejected and its interference in the affairs of the army was considered a transgression. Sergeant Legesse Asfaw, one of the leading members of the Seded, began spearheading the anti-MEISON opposition within the military. The Sergeant had become more powerful following his election to head the Commission formed to politicize the Army and Police, in February 1977.[100]

To make matters worse, some members of the WAZ and *Seded*, rivals of MEISON, were assigned to important posts in the military training camps, thereby enabling them to influence conditions in the camps. MEISON, which was angered by the new turn of events, tried hard to bring about some adjustments, but to no avail.

Besides the issues mentioned above, differences continued simmering on a wide range of questions among those groups that formed POMOA. One of the areas of disagreement was Soviet involvement in Ethiopia. In its Conference of March 1977, MEISON had decided to conduct an intensive campaign regarding "democratic rights, self-reliance and national independence."[101] In its No. 53 issue, *Sefiw Hizbe Dimtse* stated that Ethiopia should be self-reliant even though the country might need assistance. Furthermore, *Sefiw Hizbe Dimtse* stated,

> ...[I]f we began to rely on foreign forces, not only will the revolution be short-lived, but it means that we are calling for that day when the country will be enslaved again."[102] In the conference held in March 1977, MEISON condemned Soviet involvement in Ethiopia. Discussion was conducted on how to characterize the Soviet system and it was suggested that the issue should be studied further.[103]

Until this period, MEISON had recognized the Soviet Union as a socialist country.

MEISON's concern for Ethiopian national independence could be one of the factors that forced it to adopt a more nationalistic line. However, MEISON might have had other immediate organizational concerns as well. A good number of the members of *Seded*, particularly those who had been trained in the Soviet Union and were less sophisticated both ideologically and politically, were favored by the Soviets. These military cadres were contending to take the political upper hand from the MEISON. Consequently, Soviet direct involvement in Ethiopian affairs meant an enhanced support to Seded at the expense of MEISON.

Differences that separated the various groups around the Derge included the issue of democracy. In mid-1977, MEISON demanded an unconditional right to organize, while the other groups argued that it should be conditional, that is, granted only to the "oppressed". When the same issue of democratic rights was discussed in the *Addis Zemen Abyot* forum a year earlier, MEISON had argued that it should be limited, that is, it should be conditional right, "*democracy begedeb*".[104] At that time, the EPRP demanded for an unconditional democratic right, "democracy yalegedeb". When MEISON reversed its position a year and a half later, it was understood that the group was confident of its wide organizational networks and its control of the leadership of the various mass organizations. During this period, that is, as of May 1977, the media characterized MEISON as a nationalist and arrogant organization.[105]

In July 1977, EMALEDEH published an action program that recognized only conditional democratic rights. MEISON and ECHAAT, which were campaigning for unconditional democratic rights, condemned that decision. When MEISON realized that the opposition led by Seded was stiffening, it formed a clandestine group within EMALEDEH itself, in collaboration with MALRED. The MALRED group, whose leading members had defected from the EPRP/EPRA in 1975, disclosed to the regime the formation of the secret group within the EMALEDEH. That disclosure could be one of the factors that brought about a stunning defeat for MEISON and forced it to go underground quite prematurely.[106] Another factor could be the Derge's decision taken at its meeting held in June 1977, "the final decision to move at the MEISON and its leader Haile Fida...."[107] It is not certain if the MEISON was aware of the Derge's decision, however, whatever the cause might be, the halcyon days of the MEISON came to an abrupt end.

The Derge attributed MEISON's dispersal to the change in the charter of POMOA, promulgated on the fourth week of August 1977. Earlier, in July 1977, the Derge had made some personnel changes, announced the formation of a Political School and appointed new officials.

Following MEISON's dispersal, it was officially broadcast over the public media:

> [S]ome progressives did not like the renewed charter of the POMOA that gave wider participation for the progressives and advanced the cause one step forward, ...because of this, either from the main or branch offices of POMOA, some members have disappeared....[108]

When the MEISON leadership went underground, many of its members became confused. At one stroke, many former MEISON members, including EPRP infiltrators, shifted positions and joined the other groups.

When MEISON left the Union and went underground, ECHAAT still remained a member of the EMALEDEH, even though it refused to change its position on the issue of democratic rights.

Some of MEISON's leaders left for Ambo and Kembatta, in the western and southwestern part of Shoa province, and northern Shoa where they thought they had solid organizational network. After arriving in the rural areas of Shoa, one of the groups was exposed by the people and many of the leading members of MEISON, including Haile Fida, Negist Adane, Terefe Wolde Tsadik, Desta Tadesse, etc., were arrested. Kebede Mengesha and Daniel Tadesse committed suicide. Leading members of MEISON in Illubabor, Wellega and the Sidamo provinces left for the rural areas too. The Wellega and the Illubabor groups, among whom were Dr. Kedir Mohammed, one of the founding members of MEISON and Hailu Gerbaba were arrested. Very few of the leading MEISON members survived the ordeal and that organization lost over thirty of its leading activists. Hundreds of other MEISON members residing in different parts of the country were arrested and sentenced to years of imprisonment.

Some MEISON members, such as the POMOA representative of Sidamo, Eshetu Ararso, made some efforts to initiate an armed struggle. In its "Critical Assessment", MEISON had indicated that "it had held discussions with national movements in Somalia . . . to initiate an armed struggle."[109] and Eshetu had conducted some interviews over the Somali radio to that effect. MEISON's effort proved a failure and Eshetu himself lost his life.

About twelve MEISON members, including Haile Fida, were sent to the prison at the headquarters of the Fourth Division. They were incarcerated along with the officials of the previous regime, to whose downfall the Ethiopian radicals had a major role. Members of the Engineer corps of the army arrested in September 1974 and other intellectuals were part of the prison population of the Fourth Division headquarters.

Sometime after they became acquainted with the rules and regulations of the ward that they belonged to, MEISON members demanded to be introduced to the prisoners so that they could present their views. Haile Fida presented MEISON's view regarding the Ethiopian political condition. Following his presentation, Fitawrari Abebe Seyoum, a former vice-Administrator of the Tigrai province asked,

> ...[W]hen a wife wants to run away from her husband, what she first does is to prepare a place where she will go and reside. Until she finds a place of refuge, she will submit and endure whatever hardship she has to face. All of you were placed in very important government posts. How was it possible that you were unable to find a place of refuge?

MEISON members confidently replied that they had armed, politicized and organized the Ethiopian people and that it would force the government to release them. The Fitawrari became annoyed and replied, "when we all were imprisoned, we thought that the country would break-up without the Emperor and our leadership. We also thought that the people would come to our rescue, but things did not turn out that way." The Fitawrari further reminded Haile that a country could only have one king and that man was Mengistu. As long as he was alive, explained the Fitawrari, Mengistu would not allow a contending "king".[110]

MEISON members continued expressing their confidence in the people. The Fitawrari reminded them that they were naive to think that Mengistu will release them so they could take away his power and also warned them that they might soon be killed. The entire MEISON group was executed on July 10, 1978. On that same day, Berhane Meskel who was captured in Merhabete and other leading members of the WAZ League were also executed.[111]

During the last months of 1977, a section of MEISON headed by the Mayor of Addis Abeba, Dr. Alemu Abebe, broke away from the organization and formed the group known by its publication "*Keye Fana*" (the Red Path). The group advocated collaborating with the Derge. In the years to come, Dr. Alemu Abebe, who had an interesting and close relationship with the Soviets,[112] became one of the leading members of the state party, the Ethiopian Workers Party.

Sometime before the imbroglio among the groups around the Derge occurred, MEISON had sent some of its leaders abroad. When the crisis surfaced, one of them, Negede Gobeze, returned to Ethiopia. According to his own personal account, Negede intended to negotiate the release of those arrested and to find out about the possibilities of collaborating with the regime.[113]

Some months after MEISON went underground, the other groups affiliated with the Derge were either suppressed or went underground one at a time. At the first meeting of the Commission to Organize the Workers Party of Ethiopia, Mengistu accused ECHAAT of coalescing with the Somali regime.[114] ECHAAT was a predominantly Oromo group and was led by Barro Tumsa. The group was forced to go underground. Some of its members and supporters, including the Reverend Gudina Tumsa, former land reform minister Zegeye Asfaw, POMOA representative Assefa Chabo and Tesfaye Habiso were arrested. Along with the ECHAAT group, a sizeable number of Oromos were arrested or went underground, thereby alienating an important Oromo segment that had lent its hands to the regime and played a very crucial role while the Derge was making efforts to stabilize itself. Barro Tumsa, the leading member of ECHAAT who probably had retained dual membership all throughout, joined the OLF.[115] It was believed that Barro and his followers were eliminated in the internal power struggle of the OLF. The next group in line was MALRED and most of the leadership of that group was arrested.

Of the five groups that constituted POMOA and later the EMALEDEH, only Seded, predecessor of the official state party, the Ethiopian Workers Party, survived. The WAZ League itself was accused of infiltrating the Seded, its partner.[116] Leading members of the WAZ, among whom were Major Seyoum and Tadele Mengesha were accused of plotting a *coup d'etat*, after infiltrating the Seded. It was believed that one of the leaders of the WAZ League had informed on their activities. Probably as a remuneration for his service, that former leader of the WAZ League was appointed a member of the politburo of the Ethiopian Workers Party. A number of other WAZ League members, among them Colonel Shitaye, Gulilat Gebre Mariam, Sirewe Mengiste, Major Berhanu Kebede, Captain Negash, Lieutenant Dinku, Major Getachew Agede, Major Wolde Meskel, Commander Negash and Master Technician Getachew were arrested and executed in September 1978.[117]

After the elimination of almost all of the groups around the Derge, in February 1979, the Voice of Unity (organ of EMALEDEH), endorsed the actions taken so far, declaring "...2. they would form the Party, not through the merger of organizations, but through the merger of sincere communist individuals...the latter (the groups) would wither away or die."[118] It was then that Mengistu raised the slogan, "EMALEDEH, from unity to merger", (Emaledeh kehibret wede wuhidet) and brought about the end of the independent existence of all political groupings.[119] That event marked the beginning of the formation of the state party, the Ethiopian Workers Party, which was to dominate the Ethiopian political scene for a period of over ten years. At a meeting of military commissars held in August 1979, Mengistu Haile Mariam was selected as the "Ma'eekel", the Center, that is, the embodiment of the Party to be newly formed.[120] Proclamation 174, which decreed the formation of the commission to form the Ethiopian Workers Party came out in December 1979.

State Power Transformation

While the political groups around the Derge bickered, Mengistu was wielding authority and transforming the state power. Following the formation of the National Revolutionary Campaign Council (NRCC) in 1977, "the army, the police and the militia" fell under the Council's direct control.[121] The Ethiopian military was restructured into five military zones known as "task forces" (*Gebre Hailotch*), and they had their own appointed military heads.[122] The stated objective of this arrangement was the defense of the country.[123] A unified power was instituted, instead of power sharing between the Derge and POMOA. From the last months of 1975 to mid-1977, POMOA was in charge of the ideological and political tasks of the state. Following the promulgation of the new Decree, the National Revolutionary Campaign Council was put in charge of the "ministries, government institutions and mass organizations."[124] That means the Revolutionary Council was made in charge of the political, ideological, economic and military function of the state, thereby allowing Mengistu, the chairperson of the Council, the chance to wield absolute power. The Decree brought POMOA under the total control of Mengistu, the chairperson of the Revolutionary Council.[125]

A similar scenario had taken place in Somalia in the early 1970s. The Ziad Barre regime had an institution similar to POMOA, known as the Public Relations Office (PRO); it had expanded to every facet of the state bureaucracy and mass organizations. "In 1972, the PRO, . . was renamed as the Political Office and was incorporated into the President's Office, thus putting it under Ziad Barre's personal control."[126]

The Decree for the National Revolutionary Campaign Council (NRCC) formally brought the various mass organizations under the umbrella of the state apparatus. *De Jure and de facto*, the independence of the mass organizations was curtailed when[127] they became extensions of the state apparatus. The process of undermining their independence, begun with the formation of POMOA, was completed.

The Proclamation for the NRCC officially recognized that the Ethiopian economy was a war economy. It stated about the interventionist nature of the state in the minutest details of the lives of the people, under the pretext of the defense of the Motherland. The ground for excessive state intervention in economic activities was justified by policy decisions that were undertaken in 1976 and 1977.

> Under a proclamation issued in December 1976, all private truckers in Ethiopia have been made associates of the National Transport Corporation (NATRACOR). They have not been nationalized, but are subject to NATRACOR coordination and control....[128]

All banks and financial institutions of the country had been placed under the National Bank of Ethiopia, the central bank. As a result, the regime was able to control private business through bank credit. Besides, the state also had the ability to regulate the issuance of import and export *licenses*. Since the end of 1975, no new entrant into private industry or commerce was permitted to operate in more than one line of activity or establish a branch; wholesalers were limited to a capital ceiling (excluding the value of buildings) of birr 300,000, retailers to birr 200,000 and industrial producers to birr 500,000.[129]

Following the proclamation of the NRCC, the interventionist nature of the state became so pervasive that a significant portion of the retail business was handled by the newly formed kebele cooperatives. That move further pauperized those individuals who were engaged in small retail businesses and at the same time, it gave the regime a means to control the inhabitants. It was common to prohibit coupons that were essential to buy necessary items to people who did not go out on state organized rallies or attend one of the 'rituals' of the state.[130] The accentuation of the interventionist nature of the state further paved the way for more arbitrariness. The Proclamation, coupled with the official repression, pushed lawlessness to its limit. A "ransom" of $250.00 birr was demanded in order to get back the corpse of a person executed by the regime.[131]

Mengistu, who earlier had some problems controlling his fellow Derge members, was able to bypass them and make decisions using the NRCC. The last remaining individual who could pose some resistance to Mengistu's dominance was Atnafu. In April 1977, at the ceremony for the formation of the militia, Atnafu condemned the EPRP, with which he had established contact some months earlier. In the months following the February 1977 Mengistu coup, Atnafu formed a group known as the *Abyotawi Seyef* (Revolutionary Sword), to counter the influence of Seded. Through the advice and persuasion of some individuals around him, Atnafu was made to see prison realities in Addis Abeba as the repression intensified. According to the individuals who accompanied him to the prisons, Atnafu was so appalled by prison conditions that he unilaterally and unconditionally released thousands of prisoners, the majority of whom were EPRP members.[132]

In November 1977, Major Atnafu Abate, one of the founding and influential members of the Derge and 46 other officers were executed. Their execution was decided at the third Derge meeting held in mid-November, 1977. According to the statement released, it was alleged that Atnafu had said,

> under the pretext of socialism and class struggle, the people is denied democracy, justice and peace. Many Ethiopians are running away from their country. That condition in the final analysis will deprive the country of its intellectuals. We have to find ways to release those imprisoned and to reconcile with others.[133]

The last sentence was understood to be in reference to the repression conducted against the EPRP.[134] Major Atnafu Abate was also accused of advocating mixed economy, allying with landlords, refusing to accept the socialist ideology, etc. He was accused of taking side with the EPRP and the EDU. He also was accused of establishing relationship with the Church and was sympathetic towards the West.

Some months before he was executed, it was rumored that Atnafu was to be Mengistu's next victim. Atnafu's predicament was also the topic of an issue of the *Voice of the Oppressed Soldiers*, a publication of the EPRP affiliated Oppressed Soldiers Organization.

The execution of Atnafu meant total and undisputed control of state power by Mengistu. It also meant, particularly after the formation of the National Revolutionary Campaign Council, that no individual among the Derge could claim any share of power. The Derge, which was elected by the various units of the army and which came to power during the turbulent years of the 1974 struggle was castigated into oblivion. Derge members began serving the NRCC in different capacities. Members of the NRCC were appointed by Mengistu and his cliques. Some of those appointed were Mengistu loyalists and his course mates at the Holeta Military Academy.[135] Many Derge members were appointed as chief administrators of provinces and to positions in the state apparatus depending upon the good will of Mengistu.

The third Derge meeting, which decided Atnafu's fate, also decided to intensify the 'Red Terror' against what it called the 'white terror' of the EPRP.[136]

Continuation of the Conflict in Eritrea

Following the failure of the "Raza Project", which was conducted in 1976,[137] the Eritrean rebel organizations intensified the offensive and captured a number of cities in the northern part of Eritrea, along the main highway and in the western part by the Sudanese border.

> The process began in the first week of January (1977) with the fall of Karora, a small post on the northern border. It was taken by the EPLF, whose forces then began to clear government troops from the towns of the Sahel by taking Nacfa and Afabet, then moved on to the Keren region to capture Elaberet and, by May, had entered Debarawa, a copper-mining town only 27 kms from Asmara. ELF units captured Om Hager in the west, in January, then entered Tessenei in May and Agordat in September.[138]

Important cities and military posts such as Dekemehari, Mendeferra, Adi Quala, Segeneiti, etc., fell into the hands of the rebels in mid-1977. In April 1977, the rebels inflicted some damage on the Ethiopian Oil Refinery in Asseb.

Of the two rival organizations, it was the EPLF that scored most of the victories. Concerning these activities John Markakis commented, "[I]n Eritrea at this time, the rebel advantage appeared decisive, yet it was primarily due to Ethiopia's political and military disarray. The nationalist movement itself had not healed the debilitating political and military division in its ranks, nor did the guerrilla army possess the organization and weaponry required for positional warfare and the defense of towns."[139]

The Derge Retaliates

In April 1978, not long after the war with the Somali regime was over, the Derge announced an offensive against the rebels in Eritrea. The advance of the rebel organizations was halted and the campaign known as the Northern Expedition was launched in mid-June of the same year. During Mengistu's visit to Cuba, Fidel Castro, former supporter of the Eritrean organizations, denounced them as secessionists. In the second week of June 1978, under the auspices of former East European countries, discussions were conducted between the military regime and the Eritrean fronts.

One of the Palestinian leaders, George Habash, made efforts to mediate between the Derge and the Eritrean forces, but without success. In June, a similar effort was made with the EPLF in Berlin, and the ELF was invited to Moscow.[140] The mediation was sponsored by former East European countries. However, no tangible result could be achieved. In the same month, both the ELF and the EPLF agreed to negotiate with the Derge without setting any pre-conditions.

In spite of the diplomatic maneuvering, the Derges' Eritrean offensive was launched as scheduled. In July, the Derge began a three-pronged northern drive that pushed out the rebels from their newly conquered areas. The siege at Massawa was over and in the same month, Tessenai, Dekemehari and Akordat fell in to the hands of the government. A decisive offensive took place when the Derge took over Keren at the end of November 1978. The fall of Keren was an immense moral boost to the regime and a blow to the fronts. The EPLF withdrew from the towns it had captured, save Nakfa in the Sahel.

The EPRP and Its Role in the Conflict in Eritrea

Ever since the student days of the late sixties and early seventies, the Eritrean issue had been one of the major problems that haunted the memory of the radical generation. It was one of the main issues that the EPRP addressed in its program. Since November 1974, the EPRP had advocated a peaceful resolution of the Eritrean problem. In line with that policy, the EPRP had conducted agitation and publicized the Eritrean question. At the same time, the EPRP had made efforts to create a better understanding and relationship with the rebel forces in Eritrea. The policy that the EPRP pursued regarding Eritrea had been one of the major points of difference with the military regime.[141]

EPRP Structure in Eritrea

The peaceful resolution of the Eritrean issue had remained one of the cardinal policy issues of the EPRP since it was founded in 1972. From that time on, one of the main foci of the EPRP was the struggle in Eritrea and "[F]or the first time in the history of the country, the Ethiopian left, including the EPLO, took to the streets of some major towns to raise their voices against the raging war in Eritrea."[142] EPRP publication exposed the Derge's policies and *Democracia* expressed its fear and argued that the Derge propaganda would create national hatred and contradictions that would pass on to future generations. Furthermore,

> [W]ith insight that proved prophetic, *Democracia* warned that by making it impossible for the progressive forces to organize, the military regime was diverting the revolution from class lines to nationalism. This allowed the ruling groups of the various nationalities to claim popular support and *Democracia* foresaw the degeneration of the revolution into a series of nationalist wars.[143]

Advocating the peaceful resolution of the Eritrean problem, the EPRP also made efforts to win over supporters in Eritrea, both among the Ethiopian military and the rest of the populace. To do that, as was discussed in the previous chapters, the EPRP laid a structure in Eritrea and presented itself as an alternative force. By presenting a policy and political direction diametrically opposed to the Derge and its predecessor, it was the EPRP's objective to indicate that there still was a multinational alternative, that is, the choice was not only between the Derge and nationalists forces. It was the EPRP's aim to show the Eritrean people that there was a multinational force that sympathized with the struggle of the Eritrean people and vehemently condemned the injustice conducted against them.

The EPRP structure in Eritrea assumed a definite shape sometime during the last months of 1976. During this period, the EPRP structure in many parts of the country was undergoing severe crisis. However, because of the struggle for Eritrean independence, government repression in Eritrea focused on Eritreans rather than members of other nationalities.

Using POMOA as its stepping stone, the EPRP had infiltrated higher echelons of the WAZ League and the MEISON in Eritrea. Among those who infiltrated the POMOA were Lt. Negash Zergaw, Corporal F., Captain Mekre Haile Selassie, Fantu, Getahun, Alemu and four other teachers. Lt. Negash became the chairperson of the POMOA branch in Eritrea, replacing Major Betsuamlak, a member of the WAZ League. Through their contacts in the government circles, EPRP members performed a number of activities.

In mid-1976, the EPRP stepped up its organizational activities in Eritrea and some EPRP members, TF and SD were sent to the area. The newly assigned members had legal covers to stay in Eritrea, thereby resolving one of the difficulties facing the EPRP.

One of the first measures that the newly assigned EPRP members took, along with others in the area was restructuring and streamlining EPRP's organizational activities. In September or October 1976, a zonal committee, consisting of, SD, TF, MA and Lt. Negash Zergaw was formed. As was indicated in the previous chapter, Lt. Negash was an active police officer, a graduate of the Aba Dina Police College and a student of Public Administration at the Addis Abeba University. He was an all-rounded officer, well read, with a deep understanding of political developments.

After forming the zonal committee, sub-zonal committees were formed on the basis of profession, unlike in the other parts of Ethiopia where structures were organized on the basis of regions. Teachers, the military and the youth had their own separate committees and in many of the major military camps, EPRP committees were formed. EPRP structures were laid down in Keren, Asmera, Adi Kaiyeh, Segeneiti, Mendefera, Dekemehari, etc., among the police, the Nebelebal and the army. By the end of 1976, the EPRP had formed committees and cells in many of the military institutions of Eritrea. The committees were composed of EPRP officer members who belonged to different contingents.

Directly above the cells or the basic committees formed at the level of contingents or schools came the regional committees composed of the secretaries of the basic committees. When various EPRP regional committees congregated, they formed the sub-zone; one of these committees which was in charge of EPRP activities in the military was composed of officers. It was the EPRP regional committee for the Asmera area where, Lt. Negash, a member of the zone, took part. The chairperson of the EPRP regional committee of the Asmera branch was Major Sisay, an army officer, who at that time was one of the commanders of the army in the Asmera area. Other members included a lieutenant and Corporal F.

The Keren area EPRP regional committee was chaired by Lt. Takele, an officer from the Gonder area. He was the commander of the 16th Battalion of the Nebelbal.

Another sub-zone was formed of representatives of the basic committees and it was composed of teachers from the Prince Mekonnen, Haile Selassie Ist, Point Four technical schools and others. Members of the sub-zone committee included SD, the contact person with the zone, MA, from Prince Mekonnen, Abebe, from Haile Selassie Ist and others. Similar committees existed in Keren, Dekemehari, Mendefera, etc. The EPRP zonal committee in Eritrea also had its own Youth League structure.

Among the major activities of the zone was propaganda work among the Ethiopian army. The EPRP zonal committee in Asmera produced a publication focusing on the demands and aspirations of the military. It came out at least twice a week and, in the initial phase, the circulation was two to three hundred copies. Gradually, the circulation increased and at its peak, it reached over two thousand. In the initial phase, because of technical incapacity, the EPRP zonal committee was assisted in producing the pamphlets. When the zone became organized and acquired some copying machines, a typewriter and a typist, it published unaided.

The publication of the zone, known as "*The Voice of the Oppressed Soldiers*" was effective because of the issues it raised and discussed. The publication was prepared by the sub-zone committee that was composed of military personnel. Most of the articles were based on the demands and grievances of the soldiers, which included relations between officers and non-commissioned officers, food rationing, mistreatment of the militia, etc. Before an article was written, it was a usual practice for the sub-zone to gather information from EPRP committees in the various military camps. In its program of 1975, the EPRP had a provision regarding what it termed the people's army, that is, the military force that the EPRP envisaged to form. The program had stated that the political rights of members of the peoples' army would be respected and low ranking officers would be protected from the abuses of high ranking officers.[144]

Furthermore, one of the main goals of the zone publication was to popularize the EPRP program regarding the Eritrean issue, that is, to educate about the need to resolve the Eritrean question peacefully and democratically. Along that line, the publication tried to explain what the Eritrean question constituted and the real causes of the struggle. Because of the accuracy of the information contained in the papers and the degree of intimacy with the issues, the zone publication shortly became very popular and gained acceptance among a certain section of the military in Eritrea.

The EPRP had about one hundred full fledged party members, about fifty Youth League members and thousands of members in the various mass organizations that were affiliated to the EPRP. Of these, over 90% were in the mass organization of the Oppressed Soldiers. One of the factors that helped expedite recruitment among the military was the decision of the Second Plenum of the EPRP CC recommending that EPRP members become recruited in the Ethiopian army.

It remained difficult for the EPRP zonal committee in Asmera to recruit Eritreans into its structure. It had no more than 30 Eritrean members. The rest were from other nationalities of the country.

Besides its regular activities, that is, recruitment, collecting memberhsip dues, conducting propaganda activities, etc., the EPRP structure in Eritrea was directly involved in procuring arms, military paraphernalia, etc., for the EPRA. To win over the Ethiopian military to the EPRP's cause and recruit military personnel was another major task of the EPRP structure in Eritrea. The zone performed a number of tasks along that line and it was successful in its efforts had it not been for the problems and obstacles it encountered from the EPLF.

EPRP Resumed Contact with Eritrean Fronts

The EPRP made its last contact with the EPLF around mid-1976 and a joint communique was signed. As was indicated elsewhere, the EPRP CC discarded the communique and during the first months of 1977, an EPRA delegation was sent to the EPLF to continue the negotiation that had already begun. When Esayeyas, the leader of the EPLF was informed of the arrival of the EPRP delegation, not only was he unwilling to conduct the negotiation, but also he did not even want to see the group in his surroundings. He felt that the EPRP was making efforts to establish good relationship with the EPLF, while accusing and attacking him through one of its affiliate student organizations. This was in reference to ESUNA which had been conducting a campaign against Esayeyas. He perceived ESUNA's acts as part of EPRP's general scheme to isolate his organization and himself from other international organizations.

At about the same time that the EPRP recognized Eritrean independence, ESUNA had rejected and condemned secessionism and listed a number of accusations against Esayeyas Afeworki. He had been informed about ESUNA's position and, as a result, he had developed some hostility toward the EPRP.[145] ESUNA was one of the student unions that supported the EPRP and it had produced a good number of activists, some of whom joined the EPRP.[146]

Finally, Esayeyas agreed to see the EPRP delegates and, during the meeting, the EPRP delegation made efforts to explain ESUNA's independence and its right to its own decisions.[147] Esayeyas could not accept the argument presented by the EPRA delegation. Following this incident, the already strained relationship of the EPRP and the EPLF worsened.

One of the missions of the EPRP/EPRA delegation was to attend the EPLF's first congress. The EPLF, formed in 1971/72, held its First National Congress in the Sahel from January 23-31, 1977. In the opening speech, EPLF representative explained the assistance that his organization had provided the EPRP and the efforts that the EPLF made to improve the worsening relationship between the EPRP and the TPLF. He then condemned the EPRP, which he believed to be trying to isolate the EPLF. He expressed unreserved support for the TPLF. At this juncture, it became obvious that the EPLF had tilted toward the TPLF, which unhesitatingly had accepted the premise that Eritrea was Ethiopia's colony.[148] Until this time, the EPLF had given the impression that it regarded both groups even-handedly. It had acted as a mediating force to resolve the conflict between the EPRP and the TPLF.

Representing the EPRP/EPRA, the army commander, MGE and Tsegaye Gebre Medhin attended the EPLF Congress. MGE delivered a speech on behalf of the EPRP. The speech, which expressed an overtly positive regard toward the EPLF, reflected the spirit of the communiqué signed by the EPLF and the EPRP delegates a year earlier.

While the Congress was still underway, a member of the Yemeni delegation expressed interest in holding a discussion with the EPRP and thus informed the EPLF. The EPLF, agreeing to the proposal, informed both the Yemeni and the EPRP delegates that EPLF members would be present at their meetings. The discussion achieved little and the Yemeni delegate devised means to meet with the EPRP delegates in private. Through a Yemeni intelligence officer who also attended the EPLF congress, secret arrangements were made and the Yemeni delegate held separate discussions with EPRP representatives. In the discussion that ensued, the Yemeni delegate expressed his serious reservations about the EPLF and asked the EPRP delegates what their response would be if the Derge would make another call for a formation of a front. The Yemen Democratic Republic had a very close relationship with the Soviet Union and most of the country's political appointees had been trained in some of the top cadre schools of that country.

Along with the strain produced by ESUNA's position on the struggle in Eritrea, the relationship between the EPLF and the EPRP deteriorated further over the issue of EPLF fighters who had defected to the EPRA. The fighters, who were not in agreement with the EPLF leadership, had gone to the EPRA seeking protection. The EPRA provided the EPLF members safe passage.

According to an agreement signed between the two organizations, if a fighter either from the EPRP or the EPLF defected and asked for protection, he would be provided an "asylum". However, the arms he brought with him would be returned to the concerned organization.[149]

Because of the strained relations between the EPRP and the EPLF, the EPRP Foreign Committee was unable to pass arms through the EPLF and had to resort to the ELF instead.

EPRA Activities Among the Ethiopian Army in Eritrea

The EPRP zonal committee in Eritrea paid special attention to propaganda and agitation work among the Ethiopian military. In its program of 1975, the EPRP had indicated that officers who refused to raise arms against the people and oppressed nationalities would be rewarded and compensated.[150]

After concluding an agreement with the EPLF, the EPRA stationed three of its members, among whom were DS and GM, in the rural areas of Dekemehari, at a place called Dirfo, to conduct political agitation among the Ethiopian army.[151] The main task of the team was to produce leaflets and propaganda papers meant for the Ethiopian army. The EPRA team used EPLF facilities and, at least every week, propaganda papers were loaded on donkeys for distribution among the Ethiopian army in urban centers. Furthermore, the EPRP branch in Asmera and the EPLF exchanged information on Derge military policies and strategies, troop movement and disposition.

As part of the agreement, the EPLF had consented to facilitate the activities of the EPRA and give safe passage to members of the Ethiopian army who voluntarily would give up and join the EPRA. In almost all the leaflets produced, it was made clear that anyone who wanted to defect might get safe passage to the EPRA through the EPLF. Partly due to the campaign, a large number of the members of the Ethiopian army gave themselves up to the EPLF, without putting up any meaningful resistance. Desertion occurred in areas such as Keren and Asmera. According to the EPLF, leaflets of all sorts were found in the pockets of many of the surrendering officers.

The portrayal of the EPLF as a progressive force both by the Derge and POMOA might have had a role in the desertions. Such a characterization of the EPLF remained unchanged until the military regime declared what it called the Northern Expedition at the beginning of 1978. In the preparation for the campaign, the regime revised its policy and labeled the EPLF as an enemy.[152]

The EPRP zonal committee in Eritrea also took a role in some of the operations conducted by the EPLF. One of the first areas of collaboration was the operation of the Sembel prison in Asmera. Among the prison population were two EPRP members, Gebre Egziabher Haile Mikael (code named Gayem) and Haile Mariam Woldu) who were arrested in Tigrai and sent to Eritrea.[153]

Sembel was one of the largest prisons in Asmera where many Eritreans suspected of collaborating with the fronts and particularly with the EPLF, were incarcerated. In July 1977, the EPLF conducted a successful operation and over 800 prisoners were set free. Some of those imprisoned for petty criminal offenses preferred to stay behind and serve their terms.

Sometime in mid-1977, the EPLF informed the EPRP about its plan to attack the Derge force in Keren. The EPRP group in Asmera requested that the EPLF provide safe passage to those who demanded to be escorted to the EPRA.

Keren was one of the most important military posts that fell in the hands of the EPLF in 1977. Keren had been one of the most fortified military posts built when Eritrea was under Italian rule, and one of the last bastions of the Italians before they were defeated by the Allied Forces led by the British General Platt. It took the allied force over two and a half months to dislodge the Italians from Keren.

At the beginning of July 1977, EPLF forces, in preparation to seize Keren, "constructed an extensive network of roads leading from (the) main bases in Senhit Province, built several bridges...constructed more than 100 kms of feeder roads around the city ....."[154] The EPLF then began surrounding Keren.

The operation took place on Sunday, July 5, 1977 and the engagement continued through Monday. On Tuesday, the 16th Battalion abandoned its post and demanded safe passage to the EPRA. The EPLF proceeded with its assault and the only formidable resistance it faced was that of the force in and around the army headquarters. While the battle was underway, *Democracia* commented, "the 16th Battalion has the desire to surrender and join the fighting forces. The morale of the military force in Keren is so low that it is unable to continue the fight."[155] On July 8, 1977, Keren fell. The EPLF routed the entrenched and fortified Ethiopian army in a matter of four or five days.

The above quoted *Democracia* optimistically stated that the members of the 16th Battalion were about to join the fighting forces, meaning the EPRA. It was expected that the unit would be provided with a safe passage along with its arms and equipment. Unfortunately, the EPLF did not keep its word. The battalion was disarmed and its members were considered Prisoners of War (POWs) and were escorted to the EPLF base area. When the breach of the agreement between the EPLF and the EPRP was known, the EPRP branch in Asmera demanded that the EPLF keep its word and hand over all of the members of the battalion and their arms. The EPLF refused to do so on the grounds that none of them had demanded to go to the EPRA. All of the officers of the battalion, including the commander and the EPRP member Lt. Takele himself, not only were they denied the right to join their organization, but also were forced to languish in EPLF prisons. It is even believed that the EPLF had eliminated the leadership of the battalion. Certainly, it has been over nineteen years since the incident took place and the whereabouts of the leading officers of the 16th Battalion are still unknown.

Sometime in mid-1977, the EPLF hit some of the sites of the Asmera military base with a very high degree of accuracy. The areas affected included key junctions, where different runways branched out, gas depots, electrical distribution networks, etc. The Derge was surprised and became suspicious when targets known only to a handful of military personnel were attacked. When the Derge began rounding up officers, nearly two thousand military personnel, some of them EPRP members, such as, Major Sisay, surrendered to the EPLF fully armed. As part of the agreement concluded between the EPLF and the EPRP, the officers were supposed to be escorted to the EPRA. However, not a single individual, including Major Sisay and other leading EPRP members were allowed to join the EPRA. EPRP representatives in Asmera demanded that those who surrendered be given safe passage to the EPRA. Once again, the EPLF replied that no one had demanded so. The whereabouts of the officers still remain unknown. It is believed that the EPLF eliminated the officers, including Major Sisay.

When the EPLF undertook an operation in Segeneiti sometime in the last quarter of 1977, many EPLF fighters were killed, including some of the leaders. Angered by the death of their leaders and as a sign of retribution, rank and file EPLF fighters executed many of the POWs right after the operation. Some of the EPRP zonal committee members who had gone underground and were staying at Ala, in the rural area of Dekemehari, where the killing took place, witnessed the executions of POW's.[156]

The EPRP structure in Eritrea made special efforts to place some of its officer members in the logistics departments of the Ethiopian army in order to procure supplies for the EPRA. Through the efforts of the officers, the EPRP was able to smuggle out close to 50,000 blankets, military fatigues, field jackets, boots, belts, etc. According to the agreement with the EPLF and because of lack of any other alternative, the EPRP zonal committee in Asmera passed all the materials to the EPRP/EPRA through the EPLF. Promising to pass it on, the EPLF kept everything for itself and not a single item reached the EPRA.

The manager of the Nyala hotel of Asmera, who was able to get hold of about fifty thousand birr of the hotel, contacted the EPLF and asked to get a safe passage to the EPRA, however, he never reached his destination and his whereabouts remain unknown.[157]

During a period of several months, the EPRP zonal committee handed over to the EPLF over three thousand arms, excluding those that the surrendering officers carried, thousands of ammunitions, sacks of dried Ethiopian bread, "dirkosh", large amount of medical supply, copying machines, etc. Through its members in the Point Four Technical School,[158] spare parts for radios, oscilloscopes, etc., and a radio transmitter that could cover a distance of about 100 kms were dispatched to the EPRA. Believing that agreements would be respected, the EPRP zone committee in Asmera handed over the equipments and arms to the EPLF. Neither the provisions nor arms reached their intended destination.

During this period, the EPRP was undergoing a severe crisis and there was little or no contact between the various EPRP centers, that is, between the structure in Addis Abeba, the EPRA, the zonal committee, etc. The EPRP zonal committee in Asmera could not get any response from its contact person TF in Dirfo, Eritrea. Wary and suspicious of some of the developments, the EPRP zonal committee in Asmera wanted to get in touch with the EPRA contact person in Dirfo. The EPLF representative fabricated excuses and made sure that the EPRP zonal committee in Asmera and the EPRA contact person never met. All throughout, the EPRP contact person in Dirfo was not informed about the zonal committee's activities. When the representative of the EPRP zonal committee insisted to meet TF and demanded for other arrangements, the EPLF representative informed him that the EPRA contact person was away from his post. However, until he left the area around the end of 1977, TF, the EPRP contact person in Dirfo, never left his place.

In the few months of cooperation, thousands of EPRP members and sympathizers were lost in the hands of the EPLF. A large number of these were officers whose input would have transformed the EPRA. The arms that the EPRP group in Asmera sent would have made the EPRA a formidable force. However, the EPLF made sure that neither the personnel nor the arms reached the EPRA. EPLF's actions were not without reason. The EPLF clearly understood that its nationalist objectives and EPRP's multi-national aims were incompatible and consequently, *in Eritrea, it was the EPLF, rather than the Derge that played the major role in weakening the EPRP. There could be a number of reasons to EPLF's hostility towards the EPRP, one of the major motivations being EPLF's fear of a strong multi-national organization that might be able to resolve the national issue. The EPLF was aware that such an organization would be a serious impediment to itself and other nationalist groups.*

Recruitment among Eritreans was another area of disagreement between the EPRP and the EPLF. In one of its first encounters with Berhane Meskel in 1971/72, the EPLF had openly protested that the EPRP should not recruit Eritreans. The EPRP CC had rejected EPLF's protest and had made it clear that it would recruit anyone who accepted EPRP's program. The EPRP had also made it clear that it did not have any recruitment restriction, based on nationality, color, race, etc. In spite of EPRP's policies, recruitment drives in Eritrea had to be very discreet and circumspect.

Because of lack of communication, naiveté and unsuspecting attitude towards the EPLF, the various levels of the EPRP leadership did little to abate the damage that the EPLF inflicted. By this time, the EPRP was in deep crisis, as was indicated earlier, communication between the different sections of the EPRP had been impeded to the extent that the left hand did not know what the right was doing. Besides, by 1977, the EPRP was not aware that the EPLF had categorized it as an enemy. The EPRP still believed that it would mend the differences it had with the EPLF. Furthermore, the EPRP had not assessed the course that nationalist forces would pursue.

Crisis in the EPRP in Eritrea

The EPRA team that was assigned to conduct political agitation among the Ethiopian troops quit its activities on its own and left for Assimba sometime during the fourth quarter of 1977. In its activity of a few months, the team learned that the EPRA could achieve little in its cooperation with the EPLF and asked that the EPRA revise its decision regarding the arrangement.

In mid-1977, sometime before the Derge was to launch its counter offensive against the Eritrean fronts, the repression against the EPRP was stepped up and its structure in Eritrea, which had no urban military units of its own, was dismantled. Besides its regular activities, the EPRP zonal committee in Eritrea served as the link between the EPRA and the center in Addis Abeba, while the Tigrai structure was gripped in crisis.[159] FT, who was stationed at Dirfo, was supposed to serve as the liaison between the EPRA and the Asmera EPRP structure. However, beginning in mid-1977, the EPLF made sure that the different sections of the EPRP did not communicate.

When he knew that EPRP's crisis had worsened, the EPLF contact person, code named Haile Leul, suddenly disappeared. The EPRP zonal committee was left on its own, amid intensive Derge repression. SD, secretary of the zonal committee resorted to the emergency contact person of the EPLF. This was a prior arrangement set up in case of unforeseen circumstances. To SD's surprise, it was revealed that the EPLF emergency contact person was Bereket Taeme who also belonged to the EPRP structure. It was then that SD realized that Bereket Taeme was a low level EPLF infiltrator.

The extent of EPLF's infiltration and its motives are difficult to discern; however, some of its immediate objectives were to follow EPRP activities in Eritrea and recruitment of Eritreans. As was indicated elsewhere, recruitment of Eritreans had remained one of the areas over which the EPLF and the EPRP had disagreed.

With the help of the EPLF emergency contact person, Bereket, SD left for Nefasit, a small town outside Asmera and contacted the EPLF. The EPLF representative did not like SD's unauthorized arrival and openly expressed his anger when he saw him in the area. Though too late, it was then that the EPRP structure in Eritrea sensed foul play and became suspicious. Anyhow, contact with the EPLF was reestablished, but the EPLF representative remained unwilling to facilitate communication between SD and FT, the EPRP-EPRA contact person who still remained in Dirfo.

As the EPRP crisis in Eritrea deepened, some of its leading members went underground and left for Ala, one of the recruitment centers of the EPLF. Among those who went there were SD, the secretary of the zone; Corporal F., a sub-zone member of the EPRP, Lieutenant Negash Zergaw, a member of the EPRP zonal committee, and one of the most influential EPRP members in the military. Negash had left behind his two-month old son and his spouse, who was imprisoned for over eight years.

The departure of the members of the Asmera zonal committee further weakened the contact between the EPRA and the EPRP structure in the other parts of the country. Until this time, even though loose and weak, it was through the EPRP zonal committee in Eritrea that the center in Addis Abeba made efforts to maintain contact with the EPRA. Direct contact had been severed since May 1977.

EPLF Imprisons EPRP Members

Members of the EPRP zonal committee in Asmera reached the EPLF controlled area and asked for safe passage to the EPRA in Tigrai. However, they were detained for over eleven months and a half. Their status, that is, whether they were prisoners or not was not disclosed and flimsy reasons were given for the delay. Whenever the EPRP members complained about the delay, the EPLF continued giving all kinds of excuses.

During their stay in the EPLF camp, the EPRP members provided day to day services, fetching water and logs, cooking food, etc., for the newly arrived Eritreans. Conditions remained thus until EPLF members discovered that the EPRP members had secretly sent over fifty thousand birr to the EPRA,[160] without the knowledge of the EPLF. Thereafter, the detainees were forbidden to read books and were subjected to intense interrogations by the EPLF security organization, the "Halwa Sawra". The security organization made efforts to extract information regarding EPRP organizational activities among Eritreans.

When the EPRP members became more vocal and asked to be sent to the EPRA, the EPLF representative told them that the EPRP had splintered into three factions and that he did not know to which one of the groups he had to send them to and, instead, decided to let them go to the Sudan. The EPRP members insisted to be sent to the EPRA in Assimba. The EPLF representative, who stated that he had no contact with the EPRA, escorted the detainees to a market place along the Eritrean-Tigrayan border. When they were parting, the EPRP group demanded the materials they had brought, which included about five hundred military fatigues, blankets, boots, arms, etc. The EPLF representative explained that the goods had been sent through another route and promised that they would arrive soon. The material never showed up, but the EPRP members did arrive safely in Assimba. Lieutenant Negash Zergaw, one of the most valuable members of the EPRP fell victim at the battle that took place between the EPRA and the TPLF, not long after his arrival in Assimba.[161]

The EPRP structure in Eritrea, though weakened, somehow survived the crisis through 1978, that is, until the Derge was about to launch its major offensive.

The EPRP was very vocal in popularizing the rights of Ethiopian nations/nationalities. Despite that position of the organization, no working relationship could be established with nationalist forces. Rather, EPRP members and followers became victims of these forces, particularly the EPLF. Hundreds of EPRP members and followers were lost in the hands of the EPLF. Furthermore, the EPLF cut EPRP's external and internal arms and other logistics supply.

Notes to Chapter 6

1. Kiflu Tadesse, The Generation, Part I, Independent Publishers, 1993, page 211.

2. Kiflu Tadesse, op.cit., Chapter VII.

3. Democracia, Volume IV, No. 7, page 1.

4. Kiflu Tadesse, op. cit., page 27.

5. Patrick Jilkes, The Dying Lion, St. Martin's Press, New York, page 216.

6. Ibid., pages 24, 81.

7. The Somali government had a long standing interest in the area known as the Ogaden and the northeastern part of Harer, formerly known as the 'Haud'. A Somali government sponsored guerilla activity was being conducted in the Harer and the Bali areas until it was forced to disband in the late 1960's.

8. Africa South of the Sahara, 1978-79, Europa Publications, 1978, page 849.

9. Addis Zemen, June 12, 1977, page 2.

10. Africa South of the Sahara, op. cit., page 849.

11. Economic Memorandum on Ethiopia, World Bank, April 22, 1980.

12. John Markakis, National and Class Conflict in the Horn, Cambridge University Press, 1987, page 224.

13. Ibid., page 225.

14. KT, Interview, 1993.

15. KT, Interview, 1993, reminiscence of a discussion with a Somali officer in Hargeisa, 1979/80.

16. See details on pages 6-9.

17. Harry Joiner, American Foreign Policy: The Kissinger Era, The Strode Publishers, 1977, page 198.

18. Andargatchew Tiruneh, The Ethiopian Revolution, Cambridge University Press, 1993, page 216.

19. John Markakis, op. cit., pages 225 and 226.

20. Proceedings, 2nd International Conference on the Horn of Africa, page 95.

21. Addis Zemen issues of June 1977.

22. EPRP report, Siefu Tena, page 2. Siefu was a member of the EPRP sub-secretariat that was in charge of the Harer area.

23. Democracia, Volume IV, No. 8, page 13.

24. Ibid., page 1.

25. EPRP report by Siefu, page 4.

26. Addis Zemen, July 12, 1977, page 1.

27. Addis Zemen, July 18, 1977, page 2.

28. Democracia, Volume IV, No. 4, page 2.

29. Mengistu's speech, Addis Zemen, July 24, 1977, page 8. At one of those public gatherings, Mengistu threw and broke three bottles in the midst of his speech. The bottles supposedly carried the "blood" of the three enemies of the Ethiopian people, Imperialism, Feudalism and Bureaucratic Capitalism.

30. Democracia, Volume IV, No. 4, page 3.

31. Ibid., pg. 3. The excise tax on many of the imported consumer goods had also increased; the price of gas also went up. (Addis Zemen, May 20, 1977, pg. 1)

32. Democracia, Volume IV, No. 7, page 3.

33. Economic Memorandum of Ethiopia, World Bank, Sept. 23, 1977, page 18.

34. Democracia, Volume IV, No. 7, page 3.

35. Economic Memorandum of Ethiopia, World Bank, Sept. 23, 1977, page 30.

36. Ibid., page 28.

37. Sybotta stands for Saturday in the Russian language. Some years following the take over of power by the Bolsheviks, workers of one factory decided to work on a Saturday, without any payment. That practice spread and was emulated by others. It was a tradition of the Soviets to work one free day every year.

38. Addis Zemen, May 29, 1977, page 2.

39. Addis Zemen, July 14, 27, and 30, 1977.

40. Democracia, Volume IV, No. 10, page 2-3.

41. Democracia, Volume IV, No. 7, page 3.

42. Democracia, Volume IV, No. 1, page 3, and Addis Zemen, August 7, 1977.

43. Dawit Wolde Giorgis, Red Tears, The Red Sea Press Inc., 1989, pp. 45-46.

44. Africa South of the Sahara, op.cit., page 852.

45. Speech of Qadaffi, at the 10th Anniversary of the OAU, from Ethiopia at Bay, John H. Spencer, page 323.

46. Giday Bahrisume, Amora, 1993, page 121.

47. Linghoffer, A.J., Soviet Perspectives on African Socialism, Associated University Press Inc., 1969, pages 44-45.

48. Addis Zemen, May 10, 1978.

49. Addis Zemen, September 12, 1977, pages 1-2.

50. Democracia, Special Issue, Volume III, No. 3, page 2.

51. Democracia, Volume III, Special Issue, page 2.

52. Kiflu Tadesse, op. cit., Chapters III, V and VI.

53. Ibid., page 209.

54. 1975 EPRP Program/Preamble.

55. Democracia, Volume IV, No. 2, page 2.

56. Democracia, Volume IV, No. 1 page 3.

57. Ibid., page, 3.

58. Democracia, Volume IV, No. 7, page 4.

59. Ibid., page 4.

60. Ibid., page 4.

61. Democracia, Volume IV, No.7 and 8, pages 1 and 13.

62. Interview, AKB, November 1994. AKB was a member of the EPRP zonal committee in Harer.

63. Democracia, Volume IV, No. 1, page, 4.

64. Democracia, Volume IV, No. 7, page 4.

65. EPRP program, 1975, A/2.

66. One of the most important individuals in this effort, Seifu, fell in the hands of the regime in August 1977. Seifu was also involved in procuring arms to the EPRP.

67. The Mass Line, a paper believed to be written by Berhane Meskel, pages 7-8.

68. The Bolshevik Youth, Volume I, No. 1, page 2.

69. Democracia, Volume IV, No. 7, page 5.

70. Democracia, Vol. IV, No. 9, page 2.

71. Ibid., page 6.

72. Ibid., page 10.

73. Ibid., page 11.

74. Ibid., page 13.

75. Addis Zemen, November 6, 1977, page 2.

76. The term fifth column was first applied to the supporters of the rebel forces in Madrid, during the Spanish Civil War of 1936. Four of the rebel columns, assisted by their comrades in Madrid, surrounded the city and attacked the regime. The label fifth column was attributed to those who operated from within the city.

77. KT, interview, 1993.

78. Discussion with Ali, 1980, Sudan. Ali was informed about the case by one of the participant of the repression.

79. KT, Interview, 1993.

80. An EPRP paper, Modern Revisionism and Social-Imperialism, page 1.

81. The paper on 'Modern Revisionism . . .' raised a number of questions and also affirmed that the Soviet leadership began revising the basic tenets of the socialist ideology, beginning at the 20th Congress in 1956. That process was accelerated following the conclusion of the 23rd Congress held in 1966. The Ccongress had adopted profit and incentive, rather than the socialist ideology as the guiding prin ciple of the system. (Ibid., page 9) In order to elaborate the point, the paper dis cussed the lop-sided relationship of the Soviets with the Indian government and concluded that the Soviets were exporting capital. (Ibid., page 10)

82. Details on page 248.

83. Y., MEISON infiltrator, Interview, 1988.

84. To be discussed on page 244.

85. See details, Chapter II.

86. Addis Zemen, May 21, 1977, page 3.

87. Daniel Tadesse's Speech, Addis Zemen, July 30, 1977, page 10.

88. Addis Zemen, December 24, 1977, page 9.

89. Sefiw Hizbe Dimtse, No. 48, page 2.

90. Addis Zemen, December 24, 1977, page 2.

91. Sefiw Hizbe Dimtse, No. 48, page 4.

92. Ibid., page 4.

93. Gebre Selassie (EPRP code name Abdi) was among those infiltrators assigned at the Tekle Haimanot area in Addis Abeba. When the "Red Terror" was in full swing in 1977/78, Gebre Selassie formed part of the team that conducted the investigation process. Late in 1977, when he felt that the EPRP was weakened and he could be of no service to the organization, he distanced himself from the MALRED and left for the EPRA. Gebre Selassie, who arrived in the USA in 1984, was found hung at the New York Central Park.

94. North-East African Studies, No.1, 1979; The PMAC, Origins and Structure, Part II, Pliny the middle aged, page 20.

95. Tesfaye Mekonnen, Yedress Lebaletariku, Netherlands, page 246.

96. See details pages 197-201.

97. The army that fought the Red Army of the Bolsheviks was known as the "white army".

98. Addis Zemen, May 1, 1977, page 7.

99. May Day POMOA representative speech, 1977.

100. Addis Zemen, No. 292, August 28, 1979.

101. MEISON's Assessment, page 28.

102. Sefiw Hizbe Dimtse, No. 53, page 2.

103. The information was provided by an EPRP infiltrator who attended the meeting held at one of the residence of MEISON's leaders.

104. See details, Chapter II.

105. Sefiw Hizbe Dimtse, No. 59, July 11, 1977.

106. In the book titled, "Yedress Lebaletariku", one of the leaders of MALRED provides a slightly different version of the whole story. Following the formation of EMALEDEH, he stated, MALRED opted for a broader alliance and discontinued collaborating with the MEISON. Furthermore, he stated that the MEISON was unhappy about that decision. Tesfaye Mekonnen, Yedress Lebaletariku, page 213.

107. North-East African Studies, Ethiopianist Notes, Pliny the middle aged, Part Two, 1979, page 13.

108. Statement by POMOA, Addis Zemen, August, 30, 1977, page 10.

109. MEISON's Critical Assessment, page 24.

110. Gezahegne Teferra, Interview, 1989. He was a prisoner at that time and a participant of the discussion.

111. See details about Berhane Meskele's group in Chapter VII.

112. Kiflu Tadesse, op.cit., Chapter III, page 107.

113. From the author's discussion with Negede Gobeze, 1985, Washington, DC. Negede arrived in Ethiopia as a Yemeni national, escorted by Yemeni security personnel. He was then taken to the Cuban embassy. When his arrival was known, Seded members began looking for him. At that time, Mengistu was in Cuba on a state visit. According to the account provided by Negede, Mengistu knew about the matter in advance and had given the green light. Whatever the case might be, the Cubans, who were embarrassed by the turn of events, as signed bodyguards to Negede and without accomplishing much, took him out of Ethiopia secretly, on a chartered plane.

114. Mengistu Haile Mariam, 1st COPWE Congress Report, June 16, 1980.

115. When Barro went underground, it is believed that his parents held a wake so that the regime could not follow his whereabouts. It was assumed that the idea was engineered by Barro himself.

116. Mengistu Haile Mariam, 1st COPWE Congress Report, June 16, 1980.

117. Tesfaye Mekonnen, op.cit., pages 482 and 491.

118. Voice of Unity, Volume II, No. 5, pages 14-15.

119. It is interesting to note that Fidel Castro "at first tried to form a single organization from the union of his own guerrilla movement, the students, and the existing communist party, but had to abandon this in favor of a new communist party structured on an individual basis." (Christopher Clapham, Transformation and continuity in revolutionary Ethiopia, Cambridge Univ. Press, 1988, pg. 69)

120. Addis Zemen, No. 292, August 28, 1979.

121. National Revolutionary Campaign Council Decree, Cl. 4-1.

122. Addis Zemen, July 24, 1977, page 1, Decree NRCC, Cl. 10.

123. Decree, Cl 4-1, August 31, 1977, page 4.

124. Ibid., Cl. 4-2.

125. Negarit Gazeta, POMOA, Organization and Improvement Proclamation, July 14, 1977.

126. John Markakis, op.cit., page 219.

127. Decree, NRCC, Cl. 5-1.

128. Economic Memorandum in Ethiopia, World Bank, Sept. 23, 1977, page 7.

129. Ibid., page 9.

130. Democracia, Volume IV, No.1, page 1.

131. Ibid., page 3.

132. Among those who were spared at this time were the two younger brothers of the author of this book. They had been imprisoned at the CID and were awaiting their fate.

133. Derge Statement, November 13, 1977.

134. Pliny the middle aged, op.cit., page 14.

135. Democracia, Volume IV, No. 2 page 2.

136. Ibid., page 13.

137. See Chapter I.

138. John Markakis, op. cit., page 141.

139. Ibid., pages 141-142.

140. John Markakis, op. cit., page 246.

141. Kiflu Tadesse, op.cit., Chapter VI.

142. Kiflu Tadesse, op. cit., page 172.

143. Ibid., page 174.

144. EPRP Program No. VII.4.

146. ESUNA had resolved that all progressive forces, including Eritreans, should form a front. When the EPRP delegation reached the EPLF area, Amde Tsion, a former member of the Eritrean students union in America, had also reached Eritrea and had informed Esayeyas about ESUNA's position on the national question and the Eritrean question in particular. ESUNA had also accused Esayeyas about the way he had handled the Menkeas and other problems. The Menkeas were members of a dissident movement within the EPLF and leading figures of this group were former members and activists of the Ethiopian

Student Movement.

146. From the late 1960's, ESUNA was engaged in a serious debate regarding the national issue. There were sharp differences among its members on how the national issue had to be addressed. When ESUNA split in the early 1970's, among the major causes were the divergent views on the national issue. That issue had been a recurring theme. In mid-1970, ESUNA became engaged in an intense debate with an Eritrean student group known as the EFLNA, which was affiliated with the EPLF. EFLNA supported the thesis that Eritrea was an Ethiopian colony.

148. A 1976 publication of ESUNA had stated, "[A]lthough ESUNA extends support to EPRP's endeavor to wage the New Democratic Revolution in Ethiopia, ESUNA is not a youth organization of the EPRP." Combat, Volume V, No. 2, October 1976, page 2.

148. See details in Chapter X.

149. Wedi Libbi, a code name of an EPLF fighter, who suspected that EPLF fight ers had found refuge in the EPRA, demanded their return. An EPLF force came close to the EPRP territory and tried to coerce the organization. Afraid of the consequences, the EPRP informed the EPLF that the individuals had left the area. In the meantime, the EPRP sent the fighters to the EPRA in the Begemidir area and later to the Sudan.

150. EPRP Program No. VII.5.

151. The place was an EPLF recruitment center, code named 02. Fessehaye, a graduate of the Building College of Addis Abeba, was in charge of the center.

152. The policy and the new approach was presented by Amanuel Gebre Yesus, code named Girmai, at a seminar conducted as part of the preparation to launch one of the major military campaigns.

153. Kiflu Tadesse, op. cit., Chapter VI.

154. Vanguard, EPLF Publication, August 1977.

155. Democracia, Volume IV, No .2, page 2. Mulugeta Zena, a leading EPRP activist wrote to the Regional Party Committee in America, ". . . recently, over four hundred soldiers of the Keren area have joined the EPRA." (Mulugeta Zena, Correspondence to the EPRP Regional Committee in America)

156. Interview, SD, 1990.

157. Interview, TF, 1990.

158. The Point Four used to be supplied by the International Labor Organization, and the Kagnew Military Station in Asmera.

159. See details page 328.

160. One of the officers who came along with the EPRP members had taken some cash from government treasury in Asmera and was intending to use it for himself. However, the EPRP members manipulated him and took away the cash and sent it to TF, who left for the EPRA right away. The officer then brought the case to the attention of the EPLF that made a frantic effort to get to TF, but it was already too late. TF was gone.

161. See details in Chapter IX.

7

The War of Annihilation is Stepped Up

Throughout 1977, the intense repression of 1976 was continued with full vigor and ruthlessness. Thousands of EPRP suspects were rounded up at factories, government institutions and kebeles. According to the preliminary findings, in Addis Abeba alone, 55,000 people had been killed during the Red Terror.[1] Similar atrocities were committed in Shoa: Nazareth, Debre-ziet, Ambo, Hosaena, Ataye, Kara Kore, Shoa Robbit, Chefa Robbit, etc.

> In February 1978 alone, in Nazareth (outside the Atse Gelawdios school, near the Gimb market and St. Mary church), I have seen the corpse of some twenty one teachers, students and other people I didn't know but who were alleged to be EPRP members.[2]

In just one incident in Mettu, Illubabor, sixty six EPRP members were arrested during the first week of January 1977.

In the Debre Berhane area, the entire EPRP structure fell victim when the Anjas (splinter group) began collaborating with the regime. Some of these people were members of important EPRP committees and they had some valuable information to offer. As a result, in December 1977 alone, more than thirty EPRP members were arrested. The bones of seventy people executed during this period were found during an excavation in mid-1992.[3] In Wello; in Dessie, Woldiya, Komboltcha and other towns, large number of EPRP members and sympathisers were victimized.

> In Woldiya, I have personally witnessed in 1978 (November 22, March 17, and December 20) the Red Terror - I have counted forty nine mutilated bodies thrown on the streets.[4] In Debre Marcos/Gojjam, thousands were imprisoned and in October 1977, in December 1977, and in June and August 1978, numerous batches of prisoners, no less than 25 [at any one time], were taken out and killed."[5]

In Bahir Dar/Gojjam, in 1978, hundreds of prisoners were executed. Many of these were teachers and students of the Pedagogy and the Bahir Dar Polytechnic Institute. In Harer and Dire Dawa and in Gonder hundreds were arrested and many of them perished. In Sidamo; in Walliata, Sidama, Gedio,

Negele Borena and other areas, thousands had fallen victim of the "Red Terror". According to a newly published book by Abdi Abdulahi, in Negele Borena alone, hundreds of activists perished during the "Red Terror".[6] In August 1977, more than twelve teachers, students and officers were taken to Wendo Genet and executed. In the last months of 1977, about twenty activists were executed. In December 1977, more than fifteen officers were executed at Agoba. In March 1978, about twenty five student activists were executed at a place called Warka. On August 17, 1978, the corpse of eight activists were thrown on the streets of Negele Borena. Again, on August 18, 1978, sixteen activists were taken out of prison, executed and their corpse were thrown at a place called Miesa. Along with the sixteen activists, officer Mesle Ayenu, who turned his face away while shooting at the activists, was also executed. Leading figures of the repression in Negele Borena included Tadesse Bogale, head of the intelligence office, Dawit Yacob, POMOA/MEISON member, officer Zerea Beruk Sori, Captain Arega, member of the EMALEDEH, Major Kefeyalew Adigeh, head of the police department of the area and officer Tesfaye Robele, interrogator.

After the Derge was deposed, mass graves were found in Addis Abeba, in places, such as, Kotebe, Kerchelle (where the former officials of the Haile Selassie regime were buried), and in Debre Ziet, Gonder, Jimma, Bahir Dar and Dessie. The digging was not over in 1997. The remains of the Emperor were found buried in an unmarked grave adjacent to the office of Mengistu Haile Mariam.[7]

During the "Red Terror", to expedite the repression, the Derge posted pictures of EPRP members or suspects all over Addis Abeba. Kebele guards, prostitutes, etc., were summoned to kebele offices to study the pictures and they were told to report back whenever they saw the individuals. The new move created difficulties for those EPRP members whose pictures were posted. They were forced to avoid the areas they had frequented most and had to stop meeting in bars.

As part of the evolution of the repression, the regime's ability to get more information about its adversary was stepped up when the splinter group from the EPRP began providing very accurate and precise information, the likes of which the Derge had not had before. The splinter group provided the Derge with names of EPRP members, houses where EPRP members resided or visited, the layout of EPRP structure in many areas, meeting places and EPRP organizational techniques.

Besides the regular military and security organs of the state, the Derge formed special "squads" that roamed the streets of major cities. In mid 1977, the Derge armed members of the *faction* and they also roamed areas where EPRP organizational activities were conducted. Some of the "Derge squads" assumed various names. The kebeles also organized their own "squads", with full mandates to take measures against anyone they suspected.[8]

The Third Search and Destroy Campaign

The first search and destroy campaign in Addis Abeba was conducted in March 1977 and the second in April/May 1977. The third campaign was launched in October 1977.

The search and destroy campaigns had undergone a profound change after the formation of the Addis Abeba Mayoral Council under the supervision of Dr. Alemu Abebe, a former member of the MEISON and a very close ally of the Soviets. The formation of the Council partly signified the culmination of the process of creating the institutions needed to pursue the "war of annihilation" to its logical conclusion. The Mayor was also in charge of the *Abyot Tebeka* institution and Higher Kebeles, and had access to the military.

The policy of "War of Annihilation" proclaimed in September 1976 underwent some changes. It was to be known as the Red Terror. The techniques for conducting the repression were refined and employed a number of methods. However, the goals remained the same.

The Red Terror aimed at the total elimination, be it physical or otherwise, of the opposition. However, the Red Terror's final aim was to cow down the society at large. The spirit of opposition and dissension had to be erased from the minds of the people once and for all. The Red Terror was nondiscriminatory and its targets ranged from the pioneer youth of ten to the seniors who were in their sixties and seventies. It aimed at both sexes. Class background was of no importance and members of the working class, the peasantry and the intelligentsia were targeted. Ones profession and whether in the long run one would be useful to the country was also immaterial; if he/she was suspected he/she had to be eliminated. It was not important to provide hard evidence. Suspicion alone was cause enough to inflict death. Anyone professing support for the regime was awarded the license to kill. It did not matter what kind of judgment was passed or whether it was passed on the right person or not. If some innocent people were killed in the process, the mistakes were either excused or justified. That was the exact message that Mengistu wanted to relay to the United Nations Secretary General at Libreville when he said, "when countries begin the revolutionary process, the West begins talking about violation of human rights."[9]

During the Mayoral Inauguration ceremony of 1977, Dr. Alemu Abebe promised that he would intensify the campaign of annihilation. In October 1977, the third search and destroy campaign was officially declared. In the third week of November 1977, the media announced the formation of some form of an alliance of the various mass organizations, to suppress what they labeled as "reactionaries and anarchists."[10]

Unlike previous campaigns, which were limited to a few days, the third campaign was designed as a continuous process, to stop only after it had achieved its goals. In the Addis Abeba area, the campaign had its focus particularly on those areas like the Mercato, Sebategna, Gulele, Kolfe and Tekle Haimanot. These were melting pots where a large number of youth from all over the country congregated looking for refuge from the repression. Some of the officials of the kebeles of these areas were either neutral or their leadership sympathized with the EPRP.

The campaign was conducted in the evenings and late at night, to assure the presence of the targets. The areas to be searched were sealed off. The special task force was empowered to arrest and, if need be, to kill anyone it thought to be anti-government.

In some areas of Addis Abeba, EPRP defense squads switched off main electric lines in order to foil the campaign. In the majority of these places, the inhabitants themselves turned off their lights and refused to turn them on when asked by the authorities. The pitch dark areas were difficult for government forces to go into.

In one instance, the search and destroy group was provided with light from vehicles brought in for the occasion.[11] In many areas, resistance groups known as the "*Oo-Oo-ta* Committees", composed of mothers, were formed. The purpose of these committees was to organize the residents so that they would scream, cry loud and produce a shrill sound. When government forces arrived, along with members of the political groups and the Anjas, they found the streets and houses unlighted. In addition to the shrill, high-pitched voice, pots and pans were banged against each other to produce disturbing noise. The forces deployed for the occasion could not conduct the campaign. The only place where one of the campaign groups was able to operate was a kebele in the Kolfe district. It was assisted by an Anja who had an intimate knowledge of the area. In the repression that followed, ten adults and one youth were killed. More than eighty mothers, fathers and children were arrested. The third search and destroy campaign was concluded without achieving its intended goals. *In this campaign, Ethiopian mothers went an extra mile to defend their children.* The mistreatment of many mothers by kebele officials and the forced labor at the Tatek Training Camp made them more sympathetic to the call of the youth. The mothers' activity was coordinated by the "the Organization of Oppressed Women", which was affiliated with the YL organization of the EPRP.

Ethiopian mothers began taking part in the struggle in the first week of September 1977, when some twenty mothers held a demonstration and went to the Derge's office demanding the release of their children and imploring that the repression was halted. Their demands were not heeded; they were reprimanded and told to disperse.

In Addis Abeba, a number of demonstrations composed mainly of mothers took place from September until November 1977. The mothers of the Bella area, those in the vicinity of the former Military Hospital, that is, Kebena, Tekle Haimanot, Gulele, in kebeles five to twenty-three, the Nefas Silk and Qerra, conducted demonstrations. Furthermore, many mothers became involved in EPRP organizational activities, such as, hiding documents and armaments, finding shelter for activists and providing information. These and similar incidents had a remarkable psychological effect on EPRP and YL members who wrongly or rightly concluded that their hard work and effort were showing some result. A *Democracia* issue of the time stated, "...the direct involvement of the oppressed women is an expression of the degree of maturity of our struggle. "[12] Among many EPRP members and particularly the youth, the main targets of the repression, there developed a sense of euphoria in their *temporary success*.

The new form of resistance and the involvement of mothers in the struggle induced the military regime into two public statements intended to win over the minds and souls of the people. One of the statements was titled "A Revolutionary People Does Not Hide Its Enemy Under Its Arm". After condemning the EPRP, it stated, "...they (anarchists), using the institution known as the "Family council" conduct anti-government propaganda. In some areas, they force you to turn off the lights...they also tell you to cry out loud, thereby creating mental anguish and disturbance.... "[13] The statement accused the EPRP of side-tracking the course of the struggle and it stated, "...the anarchists, holding the Ethiopian map on the one hand and bread on the other, ask you to make a choice."

The "Family Council" mentioned in the Derge statement was an institution that EPRP members had formed in order to involve the family in the struggle. Each household formed its "Family Council" and held meetings to discuss political and family-related issues. The "Family Councils" were designed to create understanding and harmony among the members of the family and particularly between the youth and their parents. After a pilot project, EPRP and YL members had been instructed to form "Family Councils" in their households. "Family Councils" had been formed as early as 1974 and they became more effective when the repression was at its peak in mid-1977.

The Fourth Search and Destroy Campaign

Until November 1977, localized protests, mainly of mothers, continued in some areas of Addis Abeba. The fourth search and destroy campaign began at the end of November 1977 and lasted for over a year. In each area, the campaign continued as long as EPRP influence could be seen. The first target was the structure in the Addis Abeba area, while those in the provinces followed.

The Fourth Search and destroy campaign was a combination of the various coercion methods and techniques employed since the war of annihilation was first launched in September 1976. As part of the psychological warfare, it was common practice to broadcast the arrest or death of EPRP "CC" members or leaders while they were at meetings. It was also a common practice for Derge death squads to roam the cities and arrest or kill suspects. The vehicles of these squads would stop behind those they suspected; if they became frightened, the suspects were told to get into the vehicles. Some ran away and were shot from the back. A few escaped.

During the last months of 1977, the repression was stepped up and the process known as "*Netsa Irmja*," (unrestricted action) was introduced. This was to be the climax of the "war of annihilation". The regime gave official license to its kebele and *Abyot Tebeka* loyalists to take any measure against anyone who was considered an enemy of the "revolution".[14] Describing the situation *Democracia* stated,

> ...[A]nyone can go into a private domain and take any action he wants to, anytime of the day....What makes the new process different is the fact that the regime has legalized the process and in order to shun responsibility, it made sure that its dirty job was carried out by AETU, the kebeles....[15]

Before this policy came out, the decision to kill was made by leading institutions or higher authorities. "*Netsa Irmja*" was not new to Ethiopia. It was a process that had been used by the fascists during the Italian occupation of Ethiopia in the late 1930s.

Beginning in November 1977, localized search and destroy campaigns were staged, coordinated either by the Mayor of Addis Abeba, Dr. Alemu Abebe himself, or on the independent initiative of kebeles and Higher kebeles. Without prior notice, a certain portion of the city would be sealed off and all kinds of movement would be curtailed. Any suspicious-looking individual and anyone without a document was arrested on the spot and sent for interrogation. Anyone who carried an identification card of a different kebele became a target. Some EPRP members, caught off-guard, managed to escape, while others were apprehended along with the arms they were carrying or leaflets they were about to distribute. Others were caught with some minor evidences of their involvement in the struggle, such as pieces of papers where they had scribbled notes.[16] One of the most zealous of the squads of the Addis Abeba area was known as "*Madebo*", named after the vice-president of the AEWTU who was assassinated in mid-1977. That squad was responsible for the death of a very large number of suspected EPRP members.

Cordoning of some of the main streets was one of the most common ways of conducting the search and destroy campaigns. Kebele officials would block either the entire kebele or some of the main streets of the kebele to conduct the campaign.

In one of those incidents, the author of this book fell in danger after leaving the house where he had passed the night, in a kebele in the "Sebategna" area. He was carrying an ID card of a different kebele. He saw two *Abyot Tebeka* members asking for identification cards and conducting body searches. The author, who was carrying a gun, had two choices: either to get caught red-handed or to defend himself. Luckily, the *Abyot Tebeka* members were distracted when they began searching the bodies of two ladies who happened to be in front of the author. Searching the body included fondling ladies' breasts. While the author was contemplating his course of action, one of the *Abyot Tebeka* members reproached him and told him to leave. He did not want the author of this book to observe how the "search" was conducted.

The repression among the working class was renewed when Lt. Legesse Asfaw gave the go ahead at the meeting of the Agriculture, Hunting, Forestry and Fishing National Trade Unions. A similar instruction was given at the seminar conducted for the Wholesale and Retail, Road and Construction, Electricity, Gas and Water, Mining and Quarrying National Unions. The seminar was conducted at the beginning of December 1977, at the National Council meeting Hall. In the repression that followed, hundreds of workers of the various factories were arrested and tortured.

The repression was further intensified in almost all government institutions, schools and "discussion" clubs. Employees who had been taking active roles in the discussions became the immediate targets. The repression was especially severe in those institutions where Derge members who belonged to the *Seded* group took part.

Invaluable EPRP members fell victim to the uninterrupted massive repression. Among them was Mekuria Tegegne, an active youth who had been elected to the YL CC in 1976. However, he joined the EPRP zone-5 party structure, in the Akaki area, sometime later. Mekuria, along with other members of the zone, such as, MF, were making efforts to reorganize the zone, after the zone secretary, Abiyu Airsamo, turned out to be an Anja and refused to hand over members of the zone. In order to reestablish contact with members, Mekuria had to go to Akaki frequently. On one of his trips, he was picked up by a "Labor" *Abyot Tebeka* group that had been tipped about his arrival. Mekuria was shoved around, beaten and asked to denounce the EPRP. He consented to do so and was taken to an assembly of workers. However, Mekuria conducted a pro-EPRP agitation. When it realized what Mekuria was up to, the *Abyot Tebeka* group disrupted the meeting, dragged him out and beat him until he once again agreed to denounce the EPRP. The same scenario was repeated at the next assembly of workers. The *Abyot Tebeka* members made three or four more attempts. When they realized the "incorrigible" character of Mekuria, they simply beat him to death.

A month or so later, his younger brother Ashenafi Tegegne, a member of the *Mercato* EPRP YL zonal committee was arrested while conducting a meeting in the Kolfe area. Three or four days later, Ashenafi and the other members of the committee, already tortured and dismembered, were taken to the place where they had been picked up. The father of Ashenafi, Ato Tegegne Bedane, who had no idea of what was taking place, was summoned and ordered to stand by and watch. Then, the four youth activists were told to lie down on a bed and they were shot to death. The shocked and distraught father was unable to shade tears; he brought forth his other children, who were under ten years old, lined them up and asked the killers to repeat the same act. Following this incident, Ato Tegegne Bedane had to be hospitalized for more than three months.

Aklilu Hiruy, Secretary of the YL CC, was not in the list of wanted people by the regime, but he was detained in the Tekle Haimanot area by a

MEISON squad that had been tipped about his whereabouts. While he was being escorted to the vehicle that was parked some distance away, Aklilu escaped, dashing down a hill. But an unarmed *Abyot Tebeka* member had been watching the entire episode from a distance. As Aklilu walked away, he was hit on the head and knocked out. Aklilu, re-arrested, was taken to the CID and languished there for some months.

Aklilu was one of those EPRP members who were tortured beyond human endurance. Often, he was left hanging from a pole for more than twenty-four hours with feet up and head down. Aklilu had a wealth of information at his disposal, but never revealed any of the secrets he knew and died with dignity. Aklilu had gained the confidence of the youth's leadership and his loss was a severe blow to the YL organization. He was an able organizer and a man of enormous patience who could handle the endless problems and differences among youth activists. Aklilu discontinued his studies in Switzerland in 1974 to join the revolutionary movement in Ethiopia.

Even though born from a well to do family, Aklilu and his four other brothers joined the struggle at an early age. Two of his younger brothers, Fikru Hiruy and Tito Hiruy, also fell victim during the "Red Rerror".

Other Victims

Seyoum Tsegaye was the only child for his parents. He was a resident of Dire Dawa. He was arrested sometime in 1978 and died while being tortured. When his mother learned about the death of her son, she lost her sanity.

Fayeza Mohammed was a Harari and a leading member of the EPRP affiliated women's underground organization in the Harer province. She was arrested during the peak season of the Red Terror. She endured severe torture and, in the end, she was executed. Her hands and head were severed and displayed on the streets of Dire Dawa.

The Woubishet family lost three of their sons, Minyelshewa, Yeshitela and Meshesha, during the "Red Terror." The elder brother, Minyelshewa, was a member of the YL zonal committee in Dire Dawa. Many EPRP members were killed at meetings set up by the Anjas or members who had decided to switch allegiance. Among those killed was Meheret Wolde Amlak, the founding member of the Addis Abeba University Workers Union. He was killed by a "labor" squad headed by a former Ethiopian Radio reporter, Aberra Lemma. Until perhaps the 1990's, Aberra Lemma was the chairperson of the so called Ethiopian Writers' Association. Aberra, was affiliated to one of the political groups associated with the Derge, and was a member of the Hotel and Service Industry Union.

Meheret was supposed to meet an ELAMA member in the Gedam Sefar area. As he was waiting, he was surrounded. He jumped over a fence and ran, but was shot from behind. His assailants sent his corpse to the Saint Peters Cemetery, in the Gulele area.

During the turbulent days of the "Red Terror", Colonel Berhane of K. 15 kebele 23 lost all four of his children in just a single night. When Sergeant Solomon knocked at the door of the Colonel, his four children, Moges Berhane, Girma Berhane, Teferra Berhane and Demisse Berhane were fast asleep. Moges was the youngest and he was only thirteen. The kebele chairman, Sergeant Solomon, dragged all four of them and took them away. A few days later, it was known that all of them were executed. The devastated mother of the children lost her mind and until today, she keeps on calling the names of her children and talks to them, assuming that they still were by her side.

In the Sebategna area, a Derge military contingent surrounded a house where some youth used to conduct activities. The youth activists were told to leave the house with their hands on their heads. One of them, a female activist, pulled a grenade out of her cap and threw it. The explosion killed some of the officers and a few youth activists escaped. One girl escaped after an old woman hid her behind an "*Akembalo*" (the lid of an oven used to bake Ethiopian bread, *injera*). The security officers were in and out of the kitchen several times, but were so nervous that they failed to spot the girl.

Indeed, it was a time of "Living Dangerously".[17] The entire generation of activists of this period, including the EPRP CC members, had to operate under the most difficult of circumstances. The author of this book was part of that large group that had to undergo the severe repression. In mid-June 1977, the regime focused on leading EPRP committees, tapping telephone conversations and keeping around-the-clock watch on certain houses. The author of this book had no place to live and no place to hide (thirteen of the houses of the EPRP were raided by the government, see details below). He went to one of the houses in the Sebategna area which was supposed to have been abandoned. Nuredin Mohammed and other members of the household also came to the house. Before they entered the compound, all of them checked to make sure that they had not been followed, but within an hour or so, twenty-three well-armed soldiers came and surrounded the house. One of the officers lightly knocked at the door and demanded that they open it. Nuredin's sister, a girl of about thirteen, peeped through a crack and saw soldiers standing around. She informed the adults of the danger and in the meantime, told the soldiers that she was coming to open the door. This gave the EPRP members time to escape. Using the prearranged exit, all of the members escaped, except for Nuredin's girl friend who was unable to climb the tall fences. Sometime later, it was learned that the regime had been conducting surveillance on suspected houses with binoculars or telescopic cameras.

Again in June 1977, the author of this book had several appointments in one of the most crowded quarters of the *Mercato* area, which was frequented by EPRP members. A large crowd congregated in the area and everyone minded only his business. Vehicles rarely came to the place. The author was going to his last appointment of the day, with a member of the Addis Abeba IZ, Mekonnen Belay. He noticed a white Peugeot parked at a distance of about twenty meters from the meeting spot. There were five passengers in the vehicle, all watching the spot where the author was to meet Mekonnen. As they saw the author, they jumped out of the vehicle, but he maneuvered his way through the crowded streets of the Sebategana and went down a creek some distance away and escaped. The presence of the vehicle in one of the most inaccessible parts of the city and the security officers' knowledge of the meeting spot, known only to Mekonnen and the author, still remains a mystery. Due to the internal problems of the EPRP and tapping of telephones, meeting places and times were arranged only by those concerned, and only by word of mouth.

On a June evening in 1977, in the area known as the Wube Bereha, kebele 4, around nine o'clock in the evening, as the author was returning from an appointment, he encountered two *Abyot Tebeka* members, with other kebele officials following at some distance. The *Abyot Tebeka* members were following a young man, who was on his way to his residence. The young man, aware that he was being followed, opened a gate and in a flash, went into one of the row of houses and disappeared. The *Abyot Tebeka* members became confused and could not figure out which of the doors he had unlocked and entered. When they turned around, they saw the author of this book and asked what he was doing in the area at that time of the night. He informed them that he had come to pay condolences to a friend who was residing in the neighborhood. They then asked him for an ID card. In order to buy time, the author gave them his work "ID" card, which was written in English. The guards could not read it and asked him for a kebele card. In the meantime, they began searching his body and touched the pistol that he was carrying. The author, contemplating means and ways of escape, saw an electric pole close by and acted quickly, jumping behind the pole for cover and opening fire before his assailants could react. One of the *Abyot Tebeka* members ran for his life after shooting a couple of times, the other one stayed behind and continued shooting at a range of three meters. The author continued returning the fire until the second foe also ran for his life. The author chased him to an intersection, about one hundred meters away, and then he went on his way.

The author felt that he had been wounded and would fall unconscious soon. He continued walking away from the compound he wanted to enter into, trying not to jeopardize those inside. Dizzy from the smoke of the gun powder, he remained delirious for a while. When that feeling faded away, he checked his body and found that he was hit on the thigh and was limping. By this time, it was past ten o'clock in the evening. To pass the night and get medical treatment, he had to go to the Sebategna area, crossing through three or four kebeles that were famous for their atrocities and he had to cover a distance of about four miles. There was no transportation and the streets were deserted, except the Abyot Tebeka members who were patrolling them. Left with no other choice, he decided to act drunk and mumble incomprehensible words at the *Abyot Tebeka* members that he encountered and he continued walking. Blood continued trickling down his thigh, into his shoes and on to the street. Luckily, he was able to reach his destination.

In August 1977, the author encountered another incident in the Shoa province in the town of Kara Kore, arriving right in the midst of a search and destroy campaign. He had gone there on EPRP related activities and was expecting to meet the contact man of the area. On that same day, the awaraja administrator, Assefa Gebre Mariam, along with his entourage, arrived at the town and began looking for "*Tsegure Lewite*", meaning, an alien to the area. The author, who knew that he fitted that description, joined the chorus of spectators walking along with the search and destroy groups. Given the circumstances, this was the best choice, because the inhabitants of Kara Kore did not know whether he had come along with the search and destroy groups, and consequently could not identify him as an alien. After accompanying the group for a while, when the opportunity arose, the author boarded a van that was heading toward the awaraja capital Ataye. There, the van stopped in front of a police station, which had already been alerted about "*Tsegure Lewites*". When the author left the van in Ataye, he could not meet his comrade at the designated place. Some of the police officers, standing by the station, looked at him with suspicion. He went toward them and in a very casual manner asked where he could find a place to eat and drink. They responded positively.

The Dead were also Penalized

Even though the fourth search and destroy campaign had certain similar characteristics with the preceding ones, it also had some very distinct additional features. In the previous stages of the repression, the psychological warfare focused on the propaganda aspect, while during the last months of 1977, it was pushed to its limits. The corpse of suspected EPRP members and others were thrown on the streets and allowed to rot. The corpses were thrown where the victim would be identified by his/her family, friends or relatives. They were left near schools, in front of their houses, near factory gates and at important intersections. The corpses of seventeen workers of the Anbesa Transport Corporation were thrown in front of the gate of the institution and left there for three days. In December 1977 alone, the corpses of more than three hundred suspected EPRP members were thrown on the streets. Many of them were mutilated beyond recognition. On the backs of some of the corpses, degrading insults and slogans, alleging counter-revolutionary activities were posted.

No one was allowed to touch the corpses. Mourning was forbidden, and mourners were condemned as counter revolutionaries. Often, parents were forced to take part in denunciations of their "counter-revolutionary" sons and daughters. The message of such activities was to instill terror in those who remained behind. Parents, brothers, sisters and comrades, who had not seen their beloved for a while, roamed the cities in search of their corpses. The Ethiopian mothers were the main losers of the repression. Many became victims of high blood pressure and diabetes and many developed heart diseases. Some died prematurely, while others became insane like Wateyo.

Wateyo was a grandmother of a teen-ager who was executed and thrown onto the streets of Kefetegna 11, Kebele 14 in Addis Abeba. During one of her visits to the prison, the grandmother, who usually fetched food for her imprisoned granddaughter, was told that she had been transferred to another prison. Wateyo tried to locate her granddaughter, but was unable to do so, until one of the guards told her where she could be found. She went to the place and found the body of her small granddaughter lying on the street, covered with dust. Wateyo lost her mind; she wandered around until, a month or so later, she was found in a church. Wateyo could not control herself and was unable even to bury her beloved granddaughter. Hopelessly insane, she was chained and confined to a house until she passed away in the early 1990s.

'Wieni' was a girl who probably was in her mid to late twenties and she resided in Higher 2, kebele 4. Her brother who used to support his parents, was a fugitive from the government for quite sometime. He communicated with his family on a regular basis. Then contact ceased and the worried parents inquired about him, but without success. When the regime began throwing corpses onto major streets of the city, Wieni continued visiting all of the sites, with the hope of seeing at least the remains of her brother. She continued inquiring about the sites where new corpses had been displayed and visited many other places. She encountered corpses laying face down or leaning against walls, many of them bullet ridden. Many of the corpses had been disfigured that it was difficult to identify them. Unable to find her brother and unable to stand the agony of continuously searching for him, Wieni left the country before her health turned for the worse. There were hundreds and thousands of Wienis who had been searching for their beloved ones. Very few were successful. Moreover, they were not as lucky as Wieni. They had to stay in the country and live with the anguish and memory of their beloved ones.

Weizero Yeshi Wolde Mariam lost all three of her immediate family members in just a few days. When the event took place, she was away for a few days to visit a sick relative. When she returned, she found out that her younger son had been taken away by members of kebele 29, Addis Abeba. He was executed and his corpse was thrown on the streets. Her husband died of high blood pressure the moment he was informed about his son. A few days later, her other son committed suicide.

Weizero Agedu Seweneh used to live in Gonder. During the "Red Terror" campaign, her son, Teferi Mengistu, was arrested. Like all mothers, Weizero Agedu never believed that her son could be considered a criminal. She was waiting for the day that he would be released. One morning, she found the corpse of her little son by the footsteps of her house. She was stunned and petrified and never recovered from the shock. She died a few years later, because of her grief. Thousands of Ethiopians were killed in the Gonder province and the remains of about fourteen hundred corpses were dug out and reburied at the Cemetery by Adebabai Jesus Church following the takeover of power by the EPRDF government.[18]

B. was only five years old during the period of the "Red Terror". One day, he came back from his preschool and found strangers inside his house. Alarmed, he looked for his mother, but she was not to be found. He waited for some time in the hope that a member of his family would show up, and the child fell asleep. When he woke up the next morning, he looked for his mother, but again, she was not to be found. A day, a week, a month, a year, a decade elapsed, none of the members of B.'s family appeared. Throughout this time, the kebele and some relatives took care of B. For more than ten years, B. remained unable to explain the entire incident until he became reunited with his family in the USA.

All of B.'s brothers and sisters, who resided in the Kazanchis area and who were involved in the struggle went underground after they were informed that they were to be arrested. Derge security forces came looking for them, but could find no one in the house. On that day, the mother was away from the house and when she returned, her neighbors waited for her by the street side and informed her that Derge security forces were waiting for them. The mother abandoned her entire belongings and a few days later, the entire family made an arrangement and left the country.

T. was a father and a guard, a resident of Kefetegna 2, kebele 9, Addis Abeba. His daughter was taken away by members of the *Abyot Tebeka* after she fetched him dinner. The father made desperate efforts to find his little daughter and visited those sites where corpses were displayed. However, he could not find a trace of her, until one day when he saw her shawl ("Gabi") covering a corpse that was lying by the former Cinema Empire.

The corpse of Adenew Gerito, Emiru Gebcherasha, Worku Agelo and Tenange were left lying by the doorsteps of their house located in Kefetegna 2, kebele 9, Addis Abeba. Three days later, the remainings of the corpse were picked up by the kebele officials who carried out the execution. Three of the victims were cousins. They were among the few educated Shakecho, a minority national group of the Illubabor area. Tenange was the girl friend of Worku Agelo. It is believed that a member of the *Anja* (the splinter group) and a close friend of Adenew had informed on them.[19]

The killer was Gesegese, who had admitted that he had killed eighty-four people.[20] Gesegese and his Kebele colleagues refused the request of one woman for her son's body which was left unattended, in the open air. When she visited the corpse the next morning, she found that half of it had been eaten by hyenas. On the third day or so, she found that the corpse was gone, except the jaws and some teeth. She then hid the remains of her son in her shawl and took them away for burial.[21]

Not all prisoners were "counter revolutionaries". Some were arrested because they owned a vehicle, a house or money which Derge officials or Abyot Tebeka members wanted to possess. Said Yusuf was a Somali from the Hargeisa area. He left Somalia for Jedda, Saudi Arabia, for fear of political persecution in his own country. During the peak season of the Red Terror, Said Yusuf arrived in Addis Abeba only to "chew" chat.[22] While he was staying in Addis Abeba, the *Abyot Tebeka* committee of Kefetegna 2, that was led by Mekonnen Teklu, arrested him and confiscated his belongings, including his cash. Furthermore, they destroyed his documents to cover up the crime. While in prison, Said learned the Amharic language and was able to communicate with the prisoners; he became a popular figure among them. A few years later, Mekonnen Teklu was arrested and was thrown into prison, and there, he met Said. About five years later, Said's uncle, who was involved in the formation of the Derge-supported Somali Salvation Front had him released. As soon as he left prison, Said became the representative of the Front and resided in one of the most expensive hotels of the country.[23]

It was also a common practice to arrest a member of a family when the person to be detained was not found. In one such incident, in the area known as the "Italian village", an eighty year-old lady was imprisoned for about two weeks. In another incident, a ten month-old child was taken to prison along with his mother whose husband had gone underground.[24]

Not only human beings, but dogs had also become victims of the "Red Terror". In 1977, kebele guards went around and poisoned a large number of dogs that barked and alerted people of the approach of Abyot Tebeka members who came at night.

"Youth Associations" - New Torture Chambers

The official kebele youth associations formed in July and August 1977 were to play an important role as institutions of coercion. They were also used to rally the youth behind the regime. In their few months of existence, one of the primary tasks of these associations was to curtail EPRP's influence. Young people were obliged to be registered in these associations. Initially, the YL structure could not decide whether its members should register. In August 1977, faced with a serious dilemma, the YL leadership presented the question to the EPRP CC members, who referred the case to the Addis Abeba IZ. While the matter was under discussion, some YL zonal committees told their members to join the associations.

Initially, the associations were used as stages of confessions of "sins" committed against the "revolution". In the course of the repression, the youth associations were transformed into centers of interrogation as the regime decided to detain and arrest the majority of the youth of each kebele. In many associations, the entire membership of the EPRP YL structure of the area was placed under one roof and very few escaped detention.

Kebele officials, members of the *Abyot Tebeka* and assigned cadres conducted the interrogation sessions and all forms of torture were used to extract information, twenty four hours a day.

Upon arrival, the prisoner would be taken to the torture chamber for interrogation. When he acted innocent or refused to collaborate, he would be subjected to torture, beginning with flogging. Before the torture began, the mouth of the prisoner was stuffed with a piece of cloth that had been drenched in blood, pus or vomit.

The methods of torture ranged from beating to the insertion of red-hot iron into the organs of women prisoners. Some of the torture techniques included letting a piece of cloth or paper that was soaked in gasoline burn on the body of the prisoner or on the breasts of women prisoners. Many of the women were raped several times a night. Many were the times that heavy weight was tied to the penis or testicles which were then squeezed.[25] Often, the prisoner was hung from the wrists or suspended upside down from a bar to which he/she is tied. That method of torture is known as the 'parrot perch' ("*Wefeyelala*").[26] Still hanged on a bar, the prisoner would be beaten and in many of the cases, he would be left suspended for a long period, most of the time, face down. During this process, the hands of the prisoners remain bound.

There were cases where the hair of the prisoner was put on fire and the burn remained unattended. To make it more painful, prisoners were tortured on the same spot repeatedly. The unattended wound then became highly infected and many were the cases where the body decomposed while the prisoner was still alive. Prisoners smuggled in antibiotic tablets, but the supply was no match for the demand of the prison population.

The nails of prisoners were plucked out. Some of them were pushed head down into a barrel that contained human excrements, pus and vomit.

Psychological torture was one of the methods used. The prisoners were forced to wake up late in the night and listen to the agony of their comrades and colleagues who were being tortured. The disfigured and bleeding prisoners were then brought to the room where the rest of the prisoners were assembled. Some of the prisoners were tortured so much that they had to be carried to the assembly room.[27] There were cases where the prisoners were forced to watch as a comrade was burned alive. Abate Achule, a prisoner of Kebele 29 was burned alive in front of his fellow prisoners. His body was left rotting for two days, in the corridors of the prison.[28]

Quite often, after intensive torture of one or two prisoners, the officials declared to the assembled prisoners that they had acquired information regarding those EPRP members who had not confessed, and demanded that they come to the fore. The torture and psychological warfare was so intense that many were unable to withstand it. When someone they respected gave in or they were told that he had provided some information, it was a severe blow to their morale.

Some of the youth collaborated to save their lives, and provided information about the EPRP structure. During this process, it became common to hear former EPRP members denounce their past and try to lure in others into the same cycle. Their shift of allegiance to the side of the "revolution" was publicized and the process, of course, had a snowball effect.

Once identified by one's comrades, it was difficult to play innocent.

So, Derge cadres, with the assistance of the Anjas in some cases, would sit down with the prisoners, one at a time, with a drawing of the EPRP structure to which the member belonged in their hands, and demand that they fill in the missing information and links. By repeating this process, the officials were able to get a fair picture of the local EPRP structures, the institutions where EPRP committees were found, membership numbers, their activities, etc. This was a sophisticated procedure that could only be done with the assistance of the intelligence of the former East European countries, who had knowledge of underground organizational structures in their own countries.

In the course of the prolonged torture process, a very large number of prisoners became paralyzed. Some lost their hearing, some their sight and yet others had permanent nerve damage. Many men became impotent and many women prisoners became sterile.

The whereabouts of many Ethiopians still remain unknown. When activists disappeared or in some cases left for the EPRA, or to some neighboring countries, they could not and did not inform their families. As a result, many families continue looking for their sons and daughters with the hope of finding them somewhere. Some mothers resolved to undergo a "*Subae*" until they knew about the whereabouts of their children. They slept on floors, wrapped their waists with belts made up of cords or resolved not to wash their hair until they hear about their beloved ones.

By combining a number of techniques of repression -- psychological warfare, "Red Terror", "*Netsa Irmja*", mass arrest, search and destroy campaigns, death squads, mass confession and mass terror, the Derge was able to inflict a very severe blow to the opposition, particularly the EPRP and its Youth League organization.

Retaliation - EPRP Defense Activities

The offensive-defense military tactic of the EPRP that was adopted in August 1976 remained in force throughout 1977. The defense structure of the EPRP that was put in place in August 1976 remained unchanged. The policy regarding EPRP's targets remained the same and anyone who informed, executed and went beyond the call of duty to entrap EPRP members was focused on. Getting finance and arms were still the top priorities of the EPRP even in 1977.

According to the counting done in mid-1976, the EPRP had more than two thousand five hundred full-fledged party members in Addis Abeba alone and about the same number scattered around the rest of the country.[29] The Youth League, which made itself public on March 8, 1977, had more than ten thousand members by then. Members of the various mass organizations affiliated with the EPRP numbered in tens of thousands. These figures, of course, do not include those in prison.

During its peak period, in May 1977, the self-defense squad members of the entire Addis Abeba structure numbered close to four-hundred fifty.[30] In all Ethiopia, there were five-hundred fifty to six hundred squad members.

Shortage of arms continued to be one of the major problems of the EPRP and the urban organizations made efforts to procure them. Following the Ethio-Somalia conflict in 1977, an arms black market flourished in Harer and the EPRP made efforts to arm itself. However, because of the repression of June 1976, the Harer structure was unable to fulfill EPRP's expectations.

The EPRP army, the EPRA, also made attempts to provide arms to the urban structure. In November 1977, two EPRA contingents moved to the Wello area, to accomplish two specific missions. One mission was to hand over arms to the Wello party structure, which in turn would pass them on to structures in other parts of the country. The second mission of the contingents was to provide passage to members of the EPRP who had reached the Wello area.[31]

Chairpersons and other members of the *Abyot Tebeka* committees who were behind the massive repression were the focus of EPRP self-defense squads. Individuals who had personal contact with Mengistu, and who were the architects of the repression became EPRP's targets. These included individuals placed in important posts, such as, Major Teshome, Colonel Leulseged Fikre Mariam and Colonel Mulugeta Eshete.[32] Because of their elusive movements or other factors, the EPRP was largely unable to track down some of those who had killed and arrested hundreds of EPRP members and sympathizers. Among them was the most notorious interrogator and torturer Sergeant Teshome Baye and the architect of the Red Terror, Dr. Alemu Abeba, the Mayor of Addis Abeba. Alemu had been pinned down by EPRP squads quite a number of times. However, the squads were unable to take action against him, lest they jeopardize the life of his ex-wife, who always accompanied him. She was six or seven months pregnant and Alemu used her as his shield.

The Derge had been conducting secret executions even from among those that either worked for it or belonged to one of the groups that were allied to it. Among these incidents was the attempt to get rid of the Defense Minster, Ato Ayalew Mandefro, who was lucky enough to escape unharmed. After his escape, Ato Ayalew approached Mengistu who denied any knowledge of the event. Among those that the regime or a certain faction within the government secretly executed were Tesfaye Tadesse, Abdulahi Yusuf, Gutta Sernessa, one of the candidates for the Addis Abeba mayorship and Lt. Gebeyaw Temesgen, one of the most prolific writers of the Derge.

By the first months of 1977, EPRP's defense activities spread to other parts of the country where there were relatively stable organizational structures. Among them were Gonder, Gojjam, certain part of Shoa, Harer, Sidamo and Wello. Due to the incessant repression and the inability of the local structures to handle such activities, no defense units were formed in the rest of the country.

In those areas where defense activities were conducted, they lifted the morale of members and sympathizers, at least temporarily. An action taken against a notorious member of an *Abyot Tebeka* or any person that was allied with the Mengistu group became an inspiration and an occasion to rejoice.

Besides their broader political ramifications, the urban defense military activities, in conjunction with other organizational activities, gave *temporary respite* to EPRP members and sympathizers, even during that period when the Red Terror was in full swing. Urban military activities were considered so important that, by a special instruction of the leadership in Assimba, the EPRA Political department was documenting each and every operation.

In mid-1977, most of the Ethiopian urban centers and Addis Abeba in particular, had become quite dangerous to conduct any meaningful political activity. In the Mercato area of Addis Abeba, the various levels of the leadership, that is, the CC team, the IZ, the secretariat, the YL CC, some zonal committee members and hundreds of activists conducted their activities, resided and spent their spare time. Mercato and the vicinity was a relatively safe place for a short period, mainly because of the density of the population and the regime's difficulty in conducting systematic repression. EPRP's influence on a number of kebeles of the area might also have had an impact for Mercato's relative safety.

With time, the intensity of the repression was stepped up and notorious killers began bringing the kebeles and the Higher Kebeles under their control. Among the most notorious of these were Ergete Medebew (Kefetegna 1), Kelbessa Bekema (K-9), Fekadu (kebele 29), Elias Nur (K-2), Endale Gossaye (K-4), Basazenew Bayissa (K-15), Tenker (K-5), Haji (K-2), Mulugeta Semru (Bahir Dar), Getachew and Belatchew (K-3), Dendir (Welliso), Gedlu Abebe (AEWTU), Tilaye Teshome (K-4, kebele 50), Alemayehu (K-13, kebele 06), Chief Tesfaye, etc.

Some months after it was initiated, a number of urban EPRP structures heavily relied on urban military activities. As a result, there were incidents where distribution of publications had to be done by armed units. There also were times when urban units conducted what they termed 'armed propaganda'. These were short propaganda speeches delivered by armed units of the EPRP at locations where a large crowd had congregated. By this time, areas that had been relatively safe for conducting political activities had turned into danger zones.

When the repression intensified, there were continuing demands to take more actions against kebele officials who the members felt to be detrimental to their survival. As the political condition of the country deteriorated and it became more and more difficult and risky to hold meetings, urban military activities assumed a pervasive role. The most courageous and dedicated members were assigned to take part in these activities and they became an endangered species. Because of their engagement in military activities and lack of safe meeting places, many of the units neglected political studies, even after the introduction of a political commissar system.[33] That situation eventually led to a deterioration of the morale of the armed units themselves. Some of them continued to question the wisdom of conducting urban and rural armed struggle on equal footing. However, they were told to wait until the leadership clarified its position.

Besides these political problems, the EPRP faced organizational difficulties as well. The various units required houses where they could keep their arms, conduct training and prepare for operations. Because of these activities, many of the EPRP houses were known to a fairly large number of members. Furthermore, the members themselves were exposed to each other, thereby making the EPRP vulnerable and placing it at the mercy of individuals. The regime's and the Anjas' focus on the members of the urban military wing, both militarily and psychologically, further aggravated the crisis among the members of the units.

Without the party's authorization, Democratic Front committees, organized at the level of kebeles began forming their own units. However, when it became known, they were told to discontinue their activities.

The Prisons

Penitentiaries are not new to Ethiopia. There were thousands of them even during the reign of Emperor Haile Selassie. According to one report, "[E]ach administrative unit, from the *wereda* to the province had two jails....It is reported that there were some 12,500 jails spread around the empire...at anyone time during the reign of the late Emperor."[34] One of the largest life sentence penitentiaries, the Alem Bekagne (meaning, I have had enough of the world), was built during the reign of Menelik. Following the take over of power by the military regime in 1974, the number of prisons and prisoners increased manifold.

> More than 25,000 peasant associations dot the countryside each with its own jail. Each one of more than 660 weredas (the smallest administrative unit), has at least two prisons. The 102 awerajas (districts) similarly have their jails and police station prisons. Besides these, each wereda, aweraja and provincial town has under it dozens of its own prisons. Thus in Addis Abeba alone there are more than 335 prisons, if one includes police stations, the 4th Army Camp, the Menelik Palace and Alem Bekagne.... Moreover, there are more than 4,770 kebele prisons in the country. The peasants' association, the kebele and the government-run prisons add up to 31,500 prisons.[35]

During the reign of Emperor Haile Selassie, the prison population consisted of mainly petty offenders and criminals. However, from 1975 on, the Ethiopian prisons were filled with political prisoners of all hues. The main prisons in Addis Abeba consisted of the Kerchele, a word derived from the Italian word for prison, 'carcere', Alem Bekagne, the Central Investigation Department (CID), the Military Police, the Fourth division Headquarters of the army and many temporary detention centers, such as, in the Police training camp at Kolfe, Sendafa, or in Gojjam, at the place known as Botar.

The Alem Bekagne is a prison for those sentenced for life. Initially, the compound was arranged in such a way that only the tops of trees and the sky could be seen from the prison grounds. New prisons were opened up in the former Palace and the headquarters of the Fourth Army division. There also were temporary prisons that were used for special occasions. The five hundred or so labor leaders arrested in September 1975 were sent to the compound of the former Crown Prince, the Maichew Military Camp and to the Military Police.

The kebele prisons were capable of accomodating twenty to two hundred people and the Higher Kebeles, between six to eight hundred a day.[36] During the peak seasons of the Red Terror, most of the prisons were full and some of them had been over-crowded. In 1977-78, in Addis Abeba alone, anywhere from thirty to one hundred thousand people might have been held prisoners at any given time.[37]

According to reports, hundreds and at times thousands of people were arrested every day and similar numbers were killed every day. The prison population fluctuated: a prison that had a population of five hundred one day could go as low as three hundred the next day and climb to six hundred the day after.

The Kerchelle, which had a prison population of about one-thousand five hundred in 1976,[38] jumped to eight thousand five hundred a year and a half later, when Gezahegne Teferra, one of the prisoners, was transferred from the Fourth division headquarters.[39] Kerchelle and Alem Bekagne accommodated prisoners who had been sentenced or whose interrogation was completed. It was reported that the prison cells in the Kerchelle were large sized barns and in the "good" old times, prisoners used to sleep on beds and later on mattresses. When the prison population increased, the prisoners had to sleep on the floor. The open space where they could stretch their legs was turned into sleeping space.

During the first months of the Derge rule, political prisoners were released, except for Eritrean prisoners and convicted criminals. Many of the Eritrean prisoners in the Kerchele were serving terms for their involvement or relationships with the rebel organizations. In 1976, the prison population of the CID included about forty Eritreans who had been rounded up from different parts of the country. These prisoners had no visitors nor anyone to serve them food. Many claimed that they had no idea why they had been arrested. One night, they were taken away and nothing was heard about them anymore. Other prisoners assumed that they had been executed.[40]

According to reports, during the peak period of the repression, each prison cell or "barn" in the Alem Bekagn was occupied by more than seven hundred people, and more than two hundred women prisoners were 'herded' together in a cell. It is not difficult to imagine the condition of "bath" and toilet facilities.

While the Red Terror was underway, the personnel of the prison system was also changed profoundly. The system was run by amateurs and criminal elements with no prior training or experience. This was true of the prisons in the Higher kebeles which were under the direct control of the *Abyot Tebeka* committees.

The CID, which was located in the northeast side of Addis Abeba, contained 12 cells, each about 16 sq. m., two reserved for women. There were eight toilet spaces and two shower facilities for the entire prison population which, at the peak of the "Red Terror" reached close to 1000 on any given day.[41]

Many of the prisons had very "hard working" and "diligent" employees who were available to take any kind of order any time of the day and night. Among them was Sergeant Teshome Baye who was one of the main investigators in the CID and directly responsible for the interrogation and torture of many detainees. He was given a house in the compound of the CID and he used to work round the clock, including Sundays and holidays. For many of those who survived the repression, the name Sergeant Teshome Baye brings anger and disgust. EPRP squads made attempts on his life, but did not succeed.

Each cell in the CID was originally intended for five to six people. When GKY was imprisoned in 1976, there were between twenty and twenty-three people in each cell. Sometime in 1975, when Kassu Kumma was sent to the CID, forty persons per cell had become the norm. There were prison cells that held more than sixty people. The prison cells were packed beyond their limits and had poor or no ventilation. The air that the prisoners breathed out would rise and condense on the ceiling and drop down as water on the prisoners. Because of the large population of prisoners and lack of space, execution was found to be the easiest and least laborious form of handling prisoners.

When Kassu was sent to his cell, he was startled to witness prisoners who stood by on their feet for hours on end. Because of lack of space, the prisoners had arranged shifts and some sat while others slept. Some of the prisoners were given preferential treatment, because they had been tortured so brutally that they were unable to stand, but could only sit or lie down.[42]

Among the first victims of the "Red Terror" were EPRA members who had been arrested in Wello and taken to Addis Abeba. When their names were called, just before they were to be sent to the "guillotine", they began singing the EPRA song known as the "*Lezemenat*" (For Centuries). They aroused the feeling of those imprisoned that the whole prison population joined them in the chorus. The EPRP members then shouted anti-Derge and pro-EPRP slogans.

Gebre, nick named the "Guragew", was a criminal who had been in the prison for nineteen years and he had not seen such a phenomenon in that time. Gebre knew that

[W]hen prisoners are called to be executed, they either began praying, crying or sobbing. Some wet their pants. Some of them prepared pants for such emergencies. I have never seen anyone singing and laughing before he goes to his death. Living is seeing, so they say.[43]

Prison Codes of Communication

Prisoners learned and invented codes and languages of their own. Usually, prisoners were uninformed even about the day or the date that they were to be executed. Over the years, prisoners observed some details that hinted about such events and, in the prison lexicon, a number of seemingly inconsequential acts signified important things. If prison gates were opened in the middle of the night, if dinner was served earlier than the schedule, if relatives were told not to bring in food, if the belongings and clothes of the prisoners were returned to the relatives, etc., that meant that there were prisoners to be executed.

Every prisoner at the Alem Bekagne was identified by and required to carry a file number which was commonly known as "oranta". Whenever the name of a prisoner was called and he was asked to carry his "oranta and gabi" (shawl), it signified execution. He or she was not expected to return. Few indeed came back.

In 1977, a small misunderstanding at the prison in the Fourth division headquarters of the army led to serious confusion. One of the members of the former ruling circle had a chronic illness and he had asked the commandant of the ward to make an arrangement with a doctor. Gezahegne Teferra who was the commandant of the ward, made the arrangement and one evening, an ambulance came to take the prisoner to a hospital. The prisoners did not see the ambulance, but heard the main gate open. They then heard the sounds of footsteps and were overtaken by apprehension. They anxiously awaited to know whose turn it was to be taken away.

The commandant of the ward, along with the prison guards knocked at the door of the sick prisoner and called him to come out. The prisoner became frantic and nervous and he asked Gezahegne to give him some time and began to chant a war song, "Zeraf, zeraf, born like a man, won't die like a woman...." Gezahegne then realized the misunderstanding and explained to the prisoner that an ambulance service was waiting for him. Maybe still suspicious, the prisoner refused to go out and told Gezahegne that he was feeling all right and declined to take any treatment.

Neither an ambulance service nor any kind of medical treatment was common in the prison system. There were no medical facilities for thousands of prisoners who were maimed, mutilated, had broken bones, or dehydrated. Officially, "there was a police assistant nurse...who is supposed to look after the health of prisoners."[44] Quite often, prisoners helped each other out and in some cases, they had no need for qualified health professionals, save for lack of medical equipment and medicine. There commonly were a number of imprisoned medical doctors or paramedical professionals. "In the middle of

November (1977), there were nine doctors at that one police station prison alone (CID), six of whom were medical doctors."[45] When conditions allowed, prisoners smuggled in medication.

Because of unattended wounds, many of the prison cells smelled offensive. This was part of the technique of the "Red Terror" and it was deliberately intended to break the inner strength of the prisoners.

Prisoners were not allowed to pursue the due process of law. They never stood trial, neither did they defend nor admit their crimes. In some cases, verdict was passed on through sealed envelopes which the prisoners labeled as the "Postal" decision. This was a system used only in some of the prisons, like in the Fourth division headquarters of the army. It was considered decent, when measured by the norm of the system prevailing during the peak season of the repression. During this period, prisoners would be picked up and sent to the death chamber and then buried in one of the forests in the outskirts of the cities or towns. Some attempted suicide. Tibebu, who was accused of taking part in the assassination attempt on Mengistu, knew that he would be executed in the final analysis. Unable to withstand the agony of waiting, he decided to take his life.

Activities in Prisons

Despite the uncertainty of life and the bleak future, some of the prisoners organized their cell mates into committees and conducted a number of activities. In the CID, where tension was always high, the prisoners engaged themselves in story telling exchanging jokes, and question and answer sessions related to the struggle. Even under the most congested and difficult conditions, they organized theaters and educational activities as well. Besides, the prisoners were not docile. They engaged in protest movements, including hunger strikes. One such act took place in October 1977. In the last quarter of 1977, as a sign of protest, the prisoners sent back the food that some of the parents had brought in and the Derge put out a statement condemning the act.[46] In most of the prison wards, since all prisoners were not supplied with food, whatever was brought in was shared by all of the prisoners. Some of the prisoners were from poor families and others had no relatives in Addis Abeba.

Among the prison population, there were some who were as big as life itself and made prison life easier to handle. Some of these prisoners were engaged in political activities. Some were councilors, while others acting as medical personnel, helped their inmates clean their wounds. They treated their comrades and colleagues with whatever medicine they could lay their hands on.

In the main prisons of Alem Bekagne and Kerchelle, where the most qualified and dignified Ethiopians gathered together, the prisoners were engaged in a number of activities besides entertaining themselves. Prisoners took roles in various activities, all in their own field of interest or profession. True to expectation, the prisoners opened up schools in the prisons. The first step along that direction was to initiate a first grade class both for the prisoners and the prison guards, the police officers. The initial attempt proved successful and when they tried to open a second grade class, the prisoners encountered resistance from the prison management. However, because of the involvement of police officers in the education system, the problem was solved. In due course of time, the prisoners opened up and began running an elementary school. When thousands of high school students and additional well-qualified teachers joined the prison population, the school system was enlarged to include a curriculum for high school. All of the prisoner students who sat for the first high school leaving examination, organized by the prisoners, passed with a grade that would allow them to enroll in the Universities. Some indeed joined the Addis Abeba University after they were released. Accounting, language and vocational training courses were also provided to prisoners.

The prisoners set up libraries and, in collaboration with some organizations, they brought in new books. In the initial phase, the library at the prison by the Fourth division headquarters was controlled by religious people and carried few books, most of which were religious.[47] When they were reorganized, books of all sorts, including revolutionary ones were made available and reading became one of the main engagements and past time activities of many of the prisoners.[48]

Ward No. 7

This was one of the wards in the CID where most of the suspected EPRP members were kept together. In the Ward, which was about 16 sq. meters, there were more than forty prisoners, among whom were the prominent and inspirational figures of the prison population, Teacher Belayneh G.Mariam and Engineer Osman Mohammed. There also were three Air-Force colonels who were exemplary in their day to day activities.

In Ward No. 7, the prisoners were fed only once a day and they were allowed "bath" facilities once a day. Prisoners of Ward No. 7 were regrouped in various committees that were engaged in playing theater, story telling, and they kept themselves busy all through the day.

The Ward was filled to its capacity, so sitting down was arranged by shifts. Among those who were "privileged" was ngineer Osman Mohammed, who had been incapacitated. Both he and Teacher Belayneh G.Mariam had been tortured for several months, at least twice a day. It was customary to hear their names called around midnight and at six o'clock in the morning every day. Every part of their bodies was lacerated and mutilated. They were repeatedly tortured on the same wounds. Whenever they returned from the torture chamber, they always acted jovial and no pain could be discerned on their faces, despite the fresh wounds and bruises. But their fellow prisoners felt their agony. Their moral strength was such that their tormentor, Sergeant Teshome Baye publicly spoke of their endurance and "stubborn" characters.

Osman and Belayneh were the inspirations of their prisoner friends and the sublimation of high moral standard and value.

Prisoners like Engineer Osman Mohammed, who were severely incapacitated, were not allowed to leave their cell, even if they could. Whenever they had to go for an interrogation or to use the "bath facility", they were taken after darkness fell. Their tormentors did not want them to be seen in public.

Osman...

Engineer Osman Mohammed had studied in the former USSR. When he completed his studies in the mid-sixties, he was advised by the Soviets to pursue post graduate study and he agreed. He studied in Odessa; the officials informed him that he could continue his study at Kiev, in the Ukraine. An appointment was set up with a Soviet official to discuss the matter further. To Engineer's surprise, he found out that he was to be recruited as a Soviet agent. The proposal for a higher degree had been a reward and a ploy at the same time.

When he realized the catch, Engineer Osman Mohammed changed his mind about pursing his studies. However, afraid that he would encounter difficulties, he kept the idea to himself and told his contact "man" that he would like to go to Germany for a vacation. In the meantime, he purchased a one way ticket to Ethiopia. Leaving most of his belongings in Kiev, he went to Germany and then via Germany, to Ethiopia. He never returned to the USSR.

Engineer Osman Mohammed was one of the least known of the radicals, but one of the most dedicated and selfless fighters of the EPRP. He was much older than most of the EPRP members, an asset and an inspiration to those who knew him. Engineer Osman was a 'walking' encyclopedia of Ethiopian economy and history. He knew the small details and nuances of everyday life that one cannot find in history books. He knew almost every event that was going on in the country. Engineer Osman Mohammed had such an abundant wealth of information that the Editorial Board of *Democracia* consulted him before an article on a subject related to economics was printed. Engineer, in an offhand way, would tell them the details of the market, the price of textiles, oil, etc., in the various markets of the country and by how much they went down or up.

With his extremely wide networks of friends and acquaintances, Osman Mohammed was an organization by himself. He had very close friends all the way from a shoe shine boy to some members of the Derge, and was a humorous and sociable person.

Walking or driving with Engineer was a difficult affair. He would stop anywhere and one would see a shoe shine boy coming toward him. Many of the shoe shine boys regarded him as their friend and they were quite at ease when they talked with him. Engineer Osman would spend hours with them and learn what the shoe shine boys were talking about. Engineer Osman Mohammed would again stop at one of the shops in the Mercato area and talk to one of his merchant friends and learn a few things about the condition of business and trade. He also used to hang out with some Derge members and officers, including Captain Fisseha Gedda and Major Nadew Zekarias. None of the Derge members suspected that he belonged to the EPRP. His acquaintance with these and other Derge members enabled him to know about some of the major activities of the state.

Engineer Osman Mohammed was a member of the finance committee of the EPRP CC where Colonel Shitaye also took part. Colonel Shitaye joined the finance committee following the merger agreement with the "Red Flag" group. When the merger agreement did not go through, Colonel Shitaye was dismissed from the finance committee. Sometime later, it was learned that Colonel Shitaye was a member of the Sennay Likke group, the WAZ League.[49]

Like any other person, Engineer Osman also had his own weaknesses. Probably because of his numerous activities and engagements, he had grown forgetful to the extent that the appointments he had set with his fiancee would slip his mind. In one of those incidents, his fiancee became furious and called his home, the headquarters of the EPRP CC. His fiancee might have not known Engineer Osman's involvement in the struggle and had no idea about his house either. The author of this book picked up the phone and heard the voice of an angry woman on the other end of the line. She asked if Engineer was home. She was told that he was not. She then instructed the receiver to tell Engineer to give her a call. She also reminded the receiver not to forget passing the message. Apparently, the woman might have thought that she was talking to a houseboy or a guard. The message was relayed to Engineer, but maybe because of other priorities, he did not call. The woman called again and asked if the "guard" had passed the message. He told her that he had done so. She then warned him, "if I find out this to be a lie, I know what I am going to do with you."

Engineer Osman Mohammed was arrested in connection with the house he rented out. The EPRP CC had moved out of the house and it had been passed over to the Urban Armed Wing, a member of which defected sometime earlier and informed the Derge intelligence about the house. Engineer Osman was then taken to the CID. Sometime later, he somehow injured his ankle while trying to escape from prison.

Belayneh...

Belayneh G.Mariam was a teacher at the former Sibiste Negash high school. He joined a study circle around 1973 and began conducting studies along with some high school activists. He was recruited by Alemayehu Egzeru, who later became a member of the EPRP YL CC. In 1974, Alemayehu introduced him to Getachew Assefa (Getachew Asfaw Wossen), a member of the *Democracia* Editorial Board.[50] The cell continued conducting theoretical studies until around April 1975 when Belayneh G.Mariam became a probationary member of the EPRP.

In 1975, the Addis IZ was consolidating its manpower to form another zone in the Akaki area. As part of this plan, Belayneh was transferred to the IZ and he formed the first party zone of the Akaki area along with others. His contact man from the Addis Abeba IZ was Abiyu Airsamo.[51] Belayneh's house served as the printing center of the zone five area.

Belayneh was committed to the struggle long before he joined any of the groups. When the author of this book met him in 1975, Belayneh was living in a workers' quarter of the Kaliti area. Even though he was paid a decent salary, he was leading the life of an average worker. He had very few belongings, among which were a black board, a wooden table and a bench. He did not have a mattress or bed, but slept on a rug. Belayneh used to take an active part in community related activities and he conducted literacy campaign for the workers of his area.

Belayneh G.Mariam was suspected and arrested while still a teacher. His case became more serious after the Derge knew that his house had been used to store some of the arms obtained in the EPRP raid on the Sendafa Training Center in September 1976.

Belayneh and Osman were among the few and rare "angels" who made prison life easier to endure. As members of Ward No. 7, they were engaged in many activities of the group. Activities in Ward No. 7 were proceeding quite normally until February 26, 1977 when the prison guards came and told the prisoners to close the door, which usually was kept open. This was an unusual signal which rang the bell of death. The order to close the door of the Ward came around five o'clock in the afternoon, in the midst of a theatrical performance. The prisoners knew who were to be called and the Ward was overwhelmed by an eerie silence. The smiling faces of the prisoners turned ashy, their erect heads stooped and their activities came to a stand still. Belayneh and Osman tried to keep up the spirits of their fellow prisoners and went on with their activities as if nothing was to happen.

Around eight in the evening, the prisoners heard the sound of a vehicle and the main gate of the prison was opened. From a distance, heavy footsteps of soldiers were heard. Passing by many of the wards, the soldiers reached Ward No. 7 where they stopped. Once again, an eerie silence fell over the Ward. The only sounds were the breathing and heart beat of the inmates themselves. The door was opened, and teacher Belayneh's name was called first. When they realized that their worst fear had come true, the prisoners began crying, shouting and sobbing, calling Belayneh's name. He stood up and told his comrades to give his shawl, "gabi", his only property, to his mother, and then he began shouting "Victory to the EPRP", "Victory to the people's struggle" and "Death to the Fascists". The soldiers could not let him continue to shout anti-Derge slogans. They dragged him out. Inmates of Ward No. 7 were left in a frenzy, realizing that their "spirit", the epitome of their courage, had been taken away.

A few moments later, the heavy footsteps were heard coming toward Ward No.7 again. The soldiers stopped by the door and asked Engineer Osman to come out. Osman, who had been crippled because of the incessant torture and mutilation, could only stand up with the help of inmate friends. While still sitting, Engineer began shouting, "Victory to the EPRP", "Death to the Fascists", but the soldiers did not let him finish his sentences. They grabbed him, broke his arms and took him away.

The sound of the heavy footsteps receded from Ward No. 7 and the doors of the other wards were opened and closed. Even though the story teller did not see what took place outside of his cell, he could imagine that other prisoners were also ordered to leave their wards. After the departure of Osman and Belayneh, the prisoners in Ward No. 7 thought that it was all over for the day. But that was not true. One more time, they heard those heavy footsteps coming toward their Ward. The door of the Ward was opened and Kassu was asked to come out. "When I heard my name called, I was so stupefied that I thought I was floating in the air. I never thought nor imagined that I was a candidate for execution. I could hear my inmates crying and calling my name, but I was so shocked and delirious that I did not know what I was doing."[52]

Kassu Kumma...

The story of Ward No. 7 was partly recounted by Kassu Kumma, a young activist who had survived the execution that took place in February 1977. He was arrested while he was spending a night at a friend's residence by Legehar (the railway station) in Addis Abeba. Around midnight, someone knocked at the door and ordered them to open up. The security personnel did not give Kassu and his friend time to dress and Kassu was caught naked. The security personnel came to the house led by an EPRP member who under severe torture had disclosed about Kassu and EPRP related activities. That member did not know whether Kassu was passing the night in the house. As soon as they entered the house, the security personnel began to search the place. Finding lime powder in a sack, they concluded that it was one of the materials that the EPRP used to paint wall slogans. The lime powder had nothing to do with the EPRP or Kassu; it belonged to the owner of the house who worked at a tennis-court where he used the powder to decorate and line up the tennis field. With the "hard evidence" in their hands, the security personnel dragged Kassu out of the house.

Kassu was taken to the CID, Ward No.7. On the day of his arrival, he saw some familiar EPRP members. Using body language, they signaled him not to disclose any information. Sometime later, one of them handed him a small piece of paper instructing him to keep quiet all the time. In the small note, Kassu was also instructed not to admit any of the accusations that the interrogators were to make against him.

On the day he arrived at the CID, Kassu was taken to the interrogation chamber of Sergeant Teshome Baye. Kassu did not know the charges against him. He also did not know how the Derge intelligence knew he would be at his friend's place on the night he was picked up. One of Sergeant Teshome's first questions was *how much he was paid to serve in a military squad of the EPRP. Kassu was also asked how much he was paid per person killed.* Kassu pleaded ignorant to all of the accusations labeled against him. He was then told to take off his shoes and when he did, the Sergeant saw holes in his socks. "The EPRP pays you eight-hundred birr a month, how come it does not buy you socks?" asked the Sergeant. Kassu did not have a reply to that question either.

Like the rest of the prisoners, Kassu was tortured, but he refused to give in. Usually, prisoners took extra precautions to avoid the agents who followed their activities. However a collaborator-prisoner saw Kassu talking to an EPRP member he had known previously and informed on him.

The Sergeant ordered his staff to tie Kassu's hand to his body and Kassu had to be undressed, fed and lifted up by his fellow prisoners, for about fifteen days. A few days before he was sent for execution, Kassu was called to the interrogation chamber and told to sign a paper. Kassu agreed to do so provided he could read the content. Kassu was then given the paper enumerating the crimes he was alleged to have committed.

It was written that he had killed people, and that he was paid one thousand birr by the EPRP. Kassu refused to sign and Sergeant Teshome Baye retorted, "whether you sign or not, you would still be 'fertilizer'." [53]

After they were told to leave their cells, Engineer Osman, Belayneh, Kassu and forty-five other prisoners were led to a truck. Before they reached the truck, they had to pass in between two columns of soldiers, lined up on two sides. The soldiers wore long overcoats and helmets and they carried electric wires in their hands. The moment a prisoner entered the *gauntlet,* he was tackled from behind and one soldier jumped and sat on his back. The others tried to break his arms and, stretching them behind his back, tied them up in such a way that the wire passed through the mouth, the neck and the legs, which were bent up.

The heavy electric wire was placed in the mouth in such a way that whenever the prisoners made any movement of their legs, hands or their body, the wire would not stretch, but would cut through their mouth and keep going deeper. In some cases, because the bones of the arms were broken, they tended to move to the fore, tightening the rope on both the neck and the mouth.

Thus bound, the prisoners were thrown on the truck in a pile, face down. Kassu slid to the side and landed on the floor, which was wet with urine, waste and blood of the dying prisoners. Minutes after they were thrown onto the truck, many of the prisoners had passed away either because of the weight on top of them or because of the way they were tied up. Kassu heard the voice of a former official of the Imperial Court nearby,[54] [probably Akale Worke H. Wolde, the younger brother of the former prime minister, Aklilu H. Wolde] sighing his last gasp and saying his last prayers. He prayed for his children, whom he thought would have no one to look after, again and again calling and praising Saint Gabriel, until his voice faded away and stopped altogether. The day the execution took place, Yekatit 19 (February 26) is dedicated to the Saint, according to the Tewahedo Christian religion.

When the vehicle began moving, Kassu could hear the disturbing voice of the dying men. Some were groaning, some crying, some gasping their last breathes and some calling for help, but many were silent. The vehicle continued moving and headed to a thickly wooded area. After traveling on an asphalt road for a while, the vehicle began moving on a rough country road. Pebbles continued hitting the bottom of the truck, and those who were still alive crawled for shelter behind the corpses of their "silent" fellow prisoners, mistaking the noise for gun shots.

Belayneh G.Mariam had been chewing the wire in his mouth and it broke apart. He untied his legs and arms and saw that two jeeps, with the executioners inside were following the truck. Belayneh G.Mariam then began looking for Engineer Osman Mohammed, flipping over a number of bodies. Most of his comrades were dead but those who were still conscious summoned him to untie them. Among them was Nega Haile Mikael whom Belayneh untied.[55] Belayneh then continued looking for Engineer Osman and finally found him, but it was too late. The hero of Ward 7 was dead.[56] Belayneh then turned to the other prisoners and untied seven of them. The rest, about forty of them, had already died.

On that February night, 590 suspected EPRP members were picked up from the various prisons and executed. Among those who were killed on this night were twenty workers of the Addis Abeba Cement Factory, who had been arrested on February 25, 1977.

Belayneh G.Mariam and the other seven prisoners broke the side window of the truck and jumped out when the truck slowed down at a turn and when the jeeps following the truck were out of sight. Belayneh let the others escape first and was the last person to jump out. The officers in the jeeps had become aware of some movement and had been watching attentively. When Belayneh G.Mariam jumped out of the truck, they opened fire at him and hit him in the leg. Kassu believes that three of the escapees were killed at this time. Like the rest of the escapees, Kassu jumped out of the truck and landed in a ditch. He stayed there for a while and not long afterward, he heard intermittent gun shots and the rattling of the leaves of the nearby shrubs.

Not far from where he was hiding, he heard two soldiers expressing their fear. They had thought that some force had come and helped the prisoners escape and were discussing how to respond to their superiors. After exchanging some thoughts, the officers advanced a few meters and stopped near a grader, which had been assigned for the occasion. The wind then blew the dust that the grader was unearthing, almost forcing Kassu to sneeze and jeopardize his life.

The truck stopped not far from the place where the prisoners had escaped. Kassu hid in the bush and watched the mass execution. According to Kassu, "the prisoners were taken to the hole that was dug for the occasion and the vehicles turned their light on them. The soldiers then opened fire intermittently, on one group at a time. Then, they turned off the lights of the vehicle and waited for a while, in order to ascertain that there was no movement. They then brought forth another group of prisoners and repeated the same process."[57] Kassu stayed there even after the soldiers had gone and saw a horde of hyenas come to the place and lick the ground, which was soaked with the blood of the victims.[58] Their task accomplished, to be safe, the soldiers walked by the side of the truck. They were unable to figure out what had happened.

Kassu lay down and waited for about two hours. When he left the ditch, he could hardly walk and had no idea where he was. He crossed a stream and then found a small lane, which led to a major highway. He heard roosters and realized that dawn was breaking. On the highway, he saw large vans of the Dairy Farm and figured out that he was in the Shola area, on the southeastern side of Addis Abeba. Hidden behind some shrubs, he observed the passers-by and saw some elderly people dressed in white. Then he recalled that the executions had been on a Saturday night and concluded that the people were going to a nearby church.

Not knowing what to do next, Kassu continued to observe. After a little while, he saw a young boy coming. Kassu was naked and he shivered in the morning chill. His head was shaven. He was bruised and had big cuts on his mouth and cheeks. There was blood stains all over his body.

Afraid that he might scare the young boy, Kassu decided not to call him. Instead, he slipped out of the bush and grabbed the boy by the arms and pulled him to the nearby shrubs. Kassu then told him that he had escaped when kebele guards were trying to arrest him and asked him for some clothing. The dumbfounded boy could utter not a single word, but he left and came back with some clothes. After helping Kassu Kumma dress up, the boy took him to the nearest tearoom. Since it was early in the morning, the tearoom was deserted. When the employees of the tea-room saw Kassu, they were unable to hide their shock and could hardly believe their eyes. The employees, as they had baked bread the previous night, had heard truck movement and figured out who Kassu was. They let him use their bath facility. When Kassu washed and cleaned the blood from his face, the fresh wounds came out even more glaringly. He was served tea, which he could not drink because of his swollen tongue. The employees then gave him some fifteen cents for the bus. Finding the bus stop crowded, Kassu stood as far away from the other people as possible and waited for the bus. No one came near him, but the crowd was gazing in his direction. Thinking that they were looking at him, Kassu tried not to pay attention, but the people continued to stare. Kassu then turned around and saw a picture of Mengistu Haile Mariam in a Nazi hat and Swastika. The poster had been placed at the bus stop the previous night.

Kassu boarded a bus. It was crowded and people were standing, but the seat beside Kassu remained vacant all through the journey. When the bus reached the Ministry of Communications, it was stopped by Police. Kassu thought that they were after him and decided to jump through the windshield and land on the street. He waited for a few seconds and realized that the door of the bus was not opening and no one was coming in. He saw many bikes passing by and figured out what it was. Still riding the bus, he saw one of the escapees, Hailu Gebre/Eghziabher, walking barefooted, among some people of the surrounding rural area.

Reaching the mercato area safely, Kassu Kuma went to a residence and met an EPRP member who was about to leave. Kassu was so disfigured that his comrade did not recognize him. Kassu grabbed him by the arm and identified himself. The individual was frightened; after calming him down, Kassu told him that he had been released from prison. He then asked for a cap, shoes and a turtle neck shirt, in order to hide the wounds and the bruises. Kassu then sent his comrade to his parents. When the individual arrived in the neighborhood, he saw a large tent in front of Kassu's house: Kassu's parents, who had been given their son's belonging the previous day, were mourning his death. The *comrade* came back and informed him what he had seen. He also helped Kassu establish contact with the EPRP.

On the fourth day after their escape, four of the prisoners, Kassu, Teacher Belayneh G.Mariam, Yilma (code name) and Fikru Yosef, code name (Yitbarek?) met at an EPRP shelter.[59] Belayneh, who wore only pants, walked more than seven miles and reached the mercato area, where he established contact with the EPRP. Since all personal belongings had been given to the families, most of those who survived the ordeal were left half-naked.

Until their wounds healed, Belayneh G.Mariam and Kassu were hired as guards. Belayneh resided near the headquarters of the CID and he did not feel comfortable in that area. During the second search and destroy campaign, disguised as a peasant, he left for the Akaki where he had previously resided. While crossing one of the kebeles, by the Bulbula river, he was detained one more time and sent to the CID. Sergeant Teshome Baye was awe-stricken when he encountered the person he had sent to the "guillotine". The case was reported to the Derge and Belayneh was kept under custody. Numerous attempts were made to persuade Belayneh to denounce the EPRP and collaborate with the Derge, but he refused to do so. Finally, he was executed like the rest of activists of the period.

The massive repression directed against the EPRP did incalculable damage to the organization. The best sons and daughters of the society died. Of course, the EPRP and its sympathizers were not idle while the Derge unleashed its repression. Despite the odds, many fell victim fighting against the "Red Terror".

During the "Red Terror", not only Mengistu Haile Mariam and his impassioned followers, but thousands of Abyot Tebeka members, kebele officials, government cadres, political appointees and members of the political groups around the Derge drenched their hands in the blood of Ethiopian children. In this 'theatrical performance' called the "Red Terror", Mengistu was the leading clown, but he was not alone. He had his replicas all over the country. These were over-zealous followers who heeded his appeal.

The genocide perpetrated during the period known as the "Red Terror" had an incalculable effect on the morale of the society. The "Red Terror" was not limited to physical elimination of the 'enemy', it is a process that disgraced the moral values of the society. A brother informed on his sister and vice versa, a husband on his wife, a wife on her husband, a son on his father and his mother, a friend on his friend, a comrade on his comrade, a neighbor on a neighbor, a grown up on a teen-ager and teen-ager on a grown up. At public gatherings called by the kebeles, the inhabitants were forced to endorse the execution of one of the residents. Parents were forced to sign the death warrant of their children and "collaborate" in their execution. Many were betrayed by their beloved ones and those they trusted. The breach of societal moral was so severe that it left a permanent wound in the souls of those Ethiopians who had undergone the ordeal. A comrade, a friend, a brother, a sister, a mother and even a grandmother was not to be trusted. Trust, which had been one of the important values and virtues of a society that still had strong feudal cultural traits was erased from the minds of many.

The loss of trust had a major effect on the attitude of the people who wanted to join in organized struggle. Specially in those areas like Addis Abeba, where the depth of the crisis was beyond any human imagination, people shunned away from any form of organized underground activity. The process not only cast a severe blow to the EPRP, but also demoralized the society to such a degree that the process of organization itself became synonymous with betrayal. Despite the worsening political situation of the later years of the Derge and the immense need to form a resistance movement, many chose to keep their innermost feelings to themselves, afraid that they may be betrayed again. Even today, that is, during the reign of the EPRDF government, lack of trust remains the main obstacle for a concerted and coordinated struggle.

In the Ethiopian history, the "Red Terror" was a period when the ugliest side of mankind became the dominant feature. The "Red Terror" was a campaign directed not only against the EPRP and its sympathizers, but also against humanity itself. A large segment of the Ethiopian population was victimized. In many cases, it was the parents, the mothers, fathers, brothers, sisters and relatives, that is, the ones who remained behind, who were forced to bear the anguish, for reasons that they were not aware of. Many of their victimized sons and daughters were liked and respected among their peers and did nothing unusal that would offend either them or their neighbors. Even though some of the parents were aware of the activities of their sons and daughters, they did not know the extent of their involvement in the struggle. They also did not know that conducting discussions and demonstrations and distributing pamphlets would be a crime of the highest level.

Notes to Chapter 7

1. This was just a preliminary finding of the execution during the "Red Terror", by a committee that the EPRDF government formed in 1991.

2. Babile Tola, To Kill a Generation, Free Ethiopia Press, 1989, page 179. The quotation was taken from a testimony of one of the prisoners in Shoa.

3. Negat, Part II, Video tape prepared by the EPRDF in 1991.

4. Babile Tola, op. cit., page 170. The quotation was taken from a testimony of one of the prisoners in Wello.

5. Ibid., page 167. The quotation was taken from a testimony of one of the prisoners in Gojjam.

6. Abdi Abdulahi, The Unfortunate Generation, Addis Abeba. It is not indicated when the book was published. Probably it was published in 1996. Abdi was a participant of the movement. The information regarding the atrocities in Negele Borena were based on Abdi's book, pp. 72-81.

7. Ethiopian TV, 1991.

8. Democracia, Volume IV, No. 10, page 7.

9. Guardian, London, July 6, 1977.

10. Addis Zemen, November 18, 1977.

11. Democracia, Volume IV, No.10, page 3.

12. Democracia, Volume IV, No.10, page 2.

13. Addis Zemen, October 20, 1977, page 6.

14. Derge Statement, Addis Zemen, October 24, 1977, page 9.

15. Democracia, Volume IV, No.10, page 4.

16. In September 1977, the author had planned to leave for the Sidamo province using public transportation. When he reached the bus terminal, he found out that kebele officials had sealed off the area and had forbidden all kinds of movement. That step was followed by a search and destroy campaign which continued for the whole day. Hundreds of soldiers, kebele officials, Abyot Tebeka members, some Anjas and defectors were deployed for the occasion and whoever was not a resident of the area, was a suspect.

    After making sure that there was no one among the Anjas who knew the author, he joined the by-standee who were watching the proceedings of the campaign, the "assesa". Many, including the officers, assumed that the by-standee had little or no relationship to the struggle and the author continued moving along with the crowd. By the end of the day, not a single person ventured to ask for his ID card, which was from Majete, a small town in northern Shoa.

Except for the magnitude and duration, the campaign was similar to the one that took place in Kara Kore.

17. This is a title of a film that depicted the massacre of the Indonesian left in the early 1960s.

18. A statement put out by the EPRDF government following the arrest of Major Melaku Tefera, in mid-May 1994. He was the architect of the "Red Terror" in Gonder.

19. SD interviewed the then maid of Adenew in 1996.

20. Ethiopian Review, September 1991, page 9.

21. Negat, Volume I, taped from Ethiopian TV, 1991.

22. Chat is a plant the leaves of which give a feeling of hallucination. See details, Kiflu Tadesse, The Generation, Part I, Independent Publishers, 1993, page 197.

23. This story was told by Y, a prisoner himself.

24. Democracia, Volume III, No. 11, page 4.

25. Ibid., page 5.

26. AI report, March 31, 1978.

27. For more information, see Babile Tola, To Kill a Generation, pages 150-153.

28. Ethiopian TV compilation, 1991, Mohammed, who gave the interview is a living witness.

29. This figure was provided by the Addis Abeba IZ. However, it was contested by other leading members of the organization who regarded the figure way below the actual number of EPRP members. By the time the counting was taken, hundreds of EPRP members had been thrown into prisons and the counting did not include incarcerated EPRP members.

30. Source, Addis Abeba IZ.

31. See details, page 329.

32. Most of those executed by EPRP squads were buried at the St. Joseph's cemetery, specially reserved for what the regime called "revolutionaries".

33. See details page 329.

34. AI Index, AFR/25/04/79, page 1.

35. Ibid., page 2.

36. Amnesty International, March 31, 1978, page 3.

37. Ibid., page 3.

38. Gebre KY, Interview, 1988.

39. Interview, Gezahegne Teferra, 1988.

40. Interview, Gebre KY, 1988. He shared the same prison with the Eritreans.

41. Amnesty International, March 31, 1978, page 5.

42. Interview, Kassu Kumma, 1990.

43. Interview, Gebre KY. From his discussion with Gebre the "Guragew".

44. AI reports, March 31, 1978, page 8.

45. Ibid., page 9.

46. Addis Zemen, October 20, 1977, page 7.

47. Interview, Gezahegne Teferra, 1988.

48. Other major activities included sports. Late in the 1980's, in the Kerchelle, three soccer teams of differing political allegiances were formed. The first team was called "Labader" and it had the support of EPRP affiliates, while the second, "Wezader," had the support of MEISON associates. The third was called "the Progressive Soldier" and it was affiliated with the WAZ League. Because of cleavage and tension, the names of the teams were changed and an effort was made to play down the political overtone of the soccer games.

49. Regarding the "Red Flag" group, see details in Chapter I.

50. In his confession to the Derge, Belayneh did not disclose Getachew's real name, but his code name, Ashenafi. Ifoyeta, June 1992, page 6.

51. Again, in the interrogation process while in prison, Belayneh did not disclose Abiyu's real name, but provided his code name, Girma. Ibid., page 6.

52. Interview, Kassu Kumma, 1990.

53. Interview, Kassu Kumma, 1990.

54. Kassu is not certain who that official was. An Amnesty International report claimed that the Minister for the Imperial Court disappeared from the prison in the Palace in July 1979. The Minister had undergone prostate surgery a few

days earlier. The Amnesty also reported, ". . .all 26 had been receiving food from their families since their arrests between 1974 and 1977. In July 1979, the prison guards suddenly refused to accept food or laundry from their relatives, without explanation." (AI 30 May 1991, page 37) Among those who disappeared were MEISON members.

55. Belayneh's confession to the Derge, Ifoyeta, June 1992, page 10.

56. Fikru Yosef jumped down from the truck and began running. On his way, he met two other survivors. As they ran, they were confronted by Abyot Tebeka members. Fikru jumped into a ditch and escaped, but one was caught. When Fikru left the ditch, he was covered with mud and stinking water. Apparently, the ditch Fikru jumped into was a sewage system. (Ifoyeta, June 1992)

57. Interview, Kassu Kumma, 1990.

58. Ifoyeta, April 1992, page 28. The article in this journal was prepared by one of the survivors, Fikru Yosef. He was seventeen years old at that time and a student at Mekonnen High School, Addis Abeba.

59. Fikru Yosef, one of the survivors, claims that he was sitting by Engineer Osman until he jumped out and escaped. He also stated that Teacher Belayneh had helped Engineer Osman jump from the truck. According to Fikru, Engineer Osman was incapacitated and he was unable to run for his life. He was then caught and executed like the rest of his fellow inmates. Four days later, Fikru met Alemayehu Egzeru, who took him to an EPRP shelter. After staying in the shelter for a few days, Fikru left for the EPRA. Currently, Fikru is one of the leading members of the EPRDF.

8

EPRP Organizational Activities

Soon after Mengistu took power in February 1977, the EPRP faced compounded problems both from outside the organization and from within. EPRP's problems can be categorized into five. First and foremost, the repression against the EPRP was among the harshest any political group had experienced. One of the main preoccupations of the military regime during this period was the total elimination of the EPRP and the Derge conducted an uninterrupted campaign that lasted for over a year. EPRP's second major problem was the challenges it faced from nationalist forces - the TPLF and the EPLF in the north and from the Somali regime backed insurgents in the east.[1] The third main problem was internal, that is, the challenges posed by factional activities which had significant political, ideological and organizational bearings. Factional activities also had serious impact on EPRP members moral and their determination to wage the struggle. As we are going to see in the coming pages, factional activities constituted an important ingredient in the repression against the EPRP. Furthermore, weaknesses, shortcomings, organizational and political errors and ideological limitations apparent since the founding of the EPRP in 1972 resurfaced in 1977 when the organization was pressured on all fronts. The fourth major problem was the complexity of the struggle following the Ethio-Somali conflict and the involvement of the Soviets in Ethiopian affairs. The fifth major problem that the EPRP encountered in 1977 was leadership crisis.

Some of the members of the EPRP leadership who left Addis Abeba temporarily were unable to return, and they were advised not to do so. As a result, the remaining EPRP leadership was split into two geographical areas. The majority, that is, eight, were with the EPRA in Assimba. This group of the leadership, many of whom were novices,[2] became so involved in the affairs of the EPRA that for over a year it paid little or no attention to the activities of the EPRP in the rest of the country.[3] This was a period when the EPRP needed strong leadership more than ever before. Two members of the CC who, as a matter of coincidence and unforeseen circumstances, remained in the urban areas, were entrusted with enormous tasks and responsibilities. From April 1977 until the beginning of September 1977, overseeing EPRP's activities was left to a two-man CC team composed of Samuel Alemayehu and Kiflu Tadesse.

Besides its numerical weakness, the two man CC team faced serious legal constraints. The two-man CC team had no status in EPRP's Constitution and no constitutional mandate to decide on policy related matters. Whatever decisions the two-man CC team made, they had to remain within the legal bounds and the broad frame-work of previous decisions of the EPRP leadership. Besides, respecting the EPRP constitution and By-laws was one of the serious issues raised during the criticism and self-criticism session of the Second Plenum in August 1976.

Whenever the two-man CC team had to make decisions beyond its constitutional mandate, it resorted both to the leadership in Assimba and the membership at large. Because of communication problems and the delay in reaching consensus, the EPRP, accustomed to quick action, lagged behind events. This was because the two-man CC team had to follow time-consuming procedures. This was witnessed when the EPRP was compelled to take positions on two major political questions of the time: the Ethio-Somali conflict and the nature of the Soviet Union. The two-man CC team prepared drafts and passed them onto the EPRP structures in the various parts of the country, the structure abroad, and the leadership in Assimba. Both issues were made public a few months later, after the involvement of a good number of the membership in the decision making process.

Even though there were demands by the membership to elaborate policies, the two-man CC team could not make its own decisions or alter policies that had been made previously. One example was the controversial policy contained in what was known as the 'PB paper'. The two-man CC team, which itself did not come to an agreement on the policies contained in the 'PB paper' in the first place, felt that it was beyond its prerogatives to make any alterations. It had to postpone the matter until such time that a regular CC meeting could be held. Consequently, questions forwarded by some members remained unaddressed.

There was an understanding that a CC meeting would be conducted soon and would address the issues raised. However, unfolding events in 1977 did not allow the leadership group in Assimba or in the urban centers to abandon their respective areas. Those in the urban areas were unable to leave the EPRP structure in different parts of the country by themselves, while those in Assimba were bogged down in the rectification movement of the EPRA.[4] The leadership was faced with such a predicament that the only alternative left was to follow day to day activities until conditions allowed for such a meeting to take place. The CC meeting did take place, but only two and a half years later, in June 1979. By then, the Ethiopian political setting and the EPRP had undergone profound change.

Communication between the leadership groups was made difficult by the crisis in the zonal committee in Tigrai at the end of May 1977. (To be discussed below). A member of the Addis Abeba zone three committee who shuttled between the two leadership groups two or three times was executed in a Tigrai town called Wikro in mid-1977. When communicating through

Tigrai became difficult, the only course left was to communicate through the EPRP zone in Asmera, which was not very effective either.[5]

In order to cope with the immense responsibilities and tasks, the two-man CC team had to spend most of its time together and conduct meetings almost every day. The two of them had to carry a work load that the whole CC could hardly have handled. Because of the enormous work load and the necessity of consulting on almost every issue of importance, Samuel and Kiflu had to live in close proximity.

The situation that the entire CC faced in the wake of the 1974 movement was repeated, except that in 1974 the leadership group was larger. Besides, in 1974, a very sizable number of leading members of the EPRP took part in the decision making process.[6] By 1977, however, many of those members had been executed and some had left for Assimba. The times had also changed. The earlier period was one of revolution, enthusiasm and optimism. In 1977, however, there was defeat and gloom. The earlier was a period of unity and cooperation, the later a period of dissension and fragmentation. In 1974, the *ancien* regime was dying and a new political power, the Derge, was just emerging. By mid-1977, however, the seasoned Derge was stabilizing itself. These were times where members, CC members included, counted their survival not in terms of years or months or even days, but hours. The repression was so severe that human lives desisted hourly. Meeting a comrade you had seen the previous day was cause for celebration.

Despite the difficult conditions and the bleak times ahead, the two-man CC team had to meet the challenge and act as though the EPRP leadership was still intact, in order to keep up the morale of the members.

Immediate problems facing the two-man CC team were, 1. the internal problem of the organization caused mainly by factional activities, 2. ideological and political problems and questions raised by members, 3. the immense political complications created by the Ethio-Somali conflict and the role and position of the EPRP in the complex political situation, 4. interpreting the involvement of the Soviets in Ethiopian politics, 5. problems related to the massive repression, intense psychological warfare and the defense and preservation of the EPRP, and 6. problems related to the constitutional constraints and leadership capabilities.

When it resumed its activities, the first and major task that the two-man CC team undertook was to figure out which committees to preserve, which to eliminate and which ones to combine. Samuel was assigned to be the contact person for the EPRP structures in the northern and eastern part of the country, which included Eritrea, Tigrai, Wello, Gojjam, Begemidir, the whole of Shoa and the Harer provinces. Because of Fikre Zergaw, a member of the CC who was assigned to follow up activities in the Wello and Tigrai areas, Samuel's duties in those two places were much lighter. Samuel was also assigned as the contact person for both the foreign committee and the EPRA. He was made the contact person of the political and security departments of the CC. Kiflu, on the other hand, was made the contact person for the Sidamo, Arsi,

Jimma and the Addis Abeba structures. He also joined the *Democracia* Editorial Board. Committees in charge of urban military activities were made accountable to the Addis Abeba and other IZs and zonal committees in different parts of the country.

In order to facilitate the activities of the two-man CC team, the four-man CC Sub-Secretariat, which had existed for more than two years was entrusted with broader responsibilities. At a later stage, the Sub-Secretariat became involved in the decision making process. Issues of wider ramifications and those related to the interpretations of existing policies of the EPRP were handled by the Two-man CC team. The Sub-Secretariat included Nuredin Mohammed, GT, KM and Mekonnen Bayesa.

Following the allotment of duties and responsibilities, the two-man CC team either delegated or entrusted power to leading EPRP members. Some members were assigned to important areas and departments. With this in mind, an IZ and a Military Commission with broad mandates were formed for the Sidamo area. The veteran activists Berhanu Ijjigu and A. were sent to the area. Along with Getachew Kumsa, Agere Addisu and other activists, the two leading veterans were assigned to lead the activities of the EPRP urban structure in Sidamo and speed up the formation of the nucleus of the rural armed group. A. was a former member of zone three committee In Addis Abeba and a member of the Urban Armed Wing until it was dismantled sometime later. Berhanu and A. served as the secretaries of the Sidamo IZ and the Military Commission, respectively. The Sidamo IZ was also in charge of the Gamu Goffa, Bale and Arsi areas.

EPRP's Foreign Relations

The Two-man CC team renewed relations with the Chinese government - relations established long before the EPRP held its First Congress in 1972. In 1975, the EPRP had decided to upgrade relations and was making efforts to contact the Chinese government through the embassy in Addis Abeba when an incident facilitated the case. Sometime in 1975/76, the military regime was negotiating with the Chinese government to procure some armaments and assigned Captain Moges Wolde Mikael and W., an EPRP member, to follow up the task. Performing the government's assignments, W,. at the same time, provided the EPRP with information regarding the negotiation of the military regime with the Chinese. Moreover, W. made efforts to influence the Chinese attitude toward the military regime. He aired critical remarks about the Derge and at times made favorable comments about the opposition, particularly the EPRP. He also expressed his personal consent on some of the issues that the Chinese raised, thereby paving the path for a better understanding. When conducting the government's assignments in 1975/76, W. did not disclose to the Chinese about his affiliation with the EPRP.

In mid-1977, when the two-man CC team took up responsibilities, one of its tasks was the continuation of the relationship with the Chinese government. It was decided that W. approached the Chinese government on behalf of the EPRP. Samuel Alemayehu was his CC liaison. The revelation of W.'s EPRP membership very much puzzled the Chinese, but it was a good beginning for the EPRP and W. remained the contact man inside the country for quite some time. In the course of the discussion, it was disclosed to the Chinese that Captain Moges was also an EPRP member. When the new contact with the Chinese was initiated in mid-1977, Moges was already executed by Mengistu Haile Mariam. The disclosure that Moges Wolde Mikael was an EPRP member gave additional weight to the relationship between the Chinese government and the EPRP.

The Chinese had been insisting that the EPRP forged some kind of an alliance with the Derge. The Chinese became more forceful in their insistence particularly following the land reform proclamation in 1975. In 1977, however, they realized the inevitability of Soviet involvement in Ethiopia and they stopped pressuring the organization. The issue was dropped silently and the EPRP did not harp on it.

All of the meetings of W. with his Chinese counterpart were conducted in the Chinese Embassy, on a one on one basis. W. was forewarned not to utter a single word, and body communication was used instead. Both W. and his Chinese counterpart would quietly take their seats in the prearranged room. When conducting negotiations, both sides wrote down their views on papers prepared for the occasions. Nothing was discussed orally.

In the course of the discussions, the Chinese official demanded that the EPRP condemn the system in the Soviet Union. He was informed that the EPRP had condemned Soviet involvement in Ethiopian affairs. As for the nature of the Soviet system, it was disclosed that the question was under study and the party would take a position when it was ready. The need to characterize the Soviet system had been raised as early as 1972, at the EPRP First Congress. The EPRP characterized the Soviet Union as Social-Imperialist[7] sometime in mid-1977 and informed the Chinese about the new policy. That disclosure assisted in improving Chinese-EPRP relationship.

The Chinese objected EPRP's policy regarding urban military activities. They based their disapproval on the Chinese experience of the 1920s when the Communist Party had led a series of unsuccessful insurrections and urban uprisings, and caused colossal damage to the Communist Party of China (CPC). The EPRP contact man, who frequently consulted his EPRP CC liaison, Samuel Alemayehu, discussed the differences and the salient features of the Chinese and the Ethiopian revolutionary struggle. In China, when the CPC pulled its forces to the rural areas, "land to the tiller" was the main rallying slogan, while in Ethiopia, the land issue had been diluted after the Land Reform Proclamation of 1975. The political assessment which led the EPRP to adopt urban armed activities was also discussed. However, even after a repeated effort, the Chinese could accept neither the assessment nor the conclusion that the EPRP had reached.

Despite Chinese reservations on some policies of the EPRP, relations with the Chinese government continued to warm up. In order to conduct the negotiation more freely, the leadership in Addis Abeba suggested that the EPRP Foreign Committee resume the contact. The Chinese heartily accepted the proposal and a few months later, a higher delegation composed of EPRP CC members was invited to China.

In one of the first meetings with EPRP delegates, the Chinese officials in Beijing raised their objection to the urban military activities of the EPRP. The EPRP delegation explained how the party had reached such a conclusion, but the Chinese could not be persuaded. Despite their reservations, the Chinese still continued relations with the EPRP. They provided some funds sometime in 1978 and gave military training to a few EPRA members in 1979.

Another EPRP delegation visited Beijing in 1979, after the Fourth Plenum of the EPRP CC had conducted an assessment of the EPRP and its role in the struggle.[8] The delegation informed the Chinese that the EPRP had criticized its policy on urban military activity and had dismissed X from the party. The delegation falsely portrayed X as the main proponent of the policy on urban military activities.[9] It seemed that the Chinese were convinced, because X had headed the previous delegation, which had disagreed with the Chinese over urban military activities.

During one of the earlier trips to China, the EPRP delegation had also visited the Kampuchian Khmer Rouge which had given the EPRP some assistance. At that time, the Khmer Rouge was still in power and the discussion with the EPRP was conducted in Phnom Penh. The EPRP delegation was startled by the eerie and ghostly silence that surrounded Phnom Penh. Lights were out in many of the apartments and very few people were to be seen on the streets.[10] Apparently, this was the period that the Khmer Rouge was deporting urban dwellers to the countryside for what it called a 'rehabilitation' process.

As part of the struggle on the diplomatic front, better relationship was forged with some center to left organizations in Europe. Some of them were minuscule groups. The Italian Socialist Party began collaborating with the EPRP, by providing assistance, such as, medicine and helping with some technical problems of the EPRP, etc.[11]

EPRP - Plagued by Factional Activities

The internal problems of the EPRP assumed a larger dimension when, as a result of factional activities, a certain section of both the party and the Youth League structures were decapitated. As of mid-March 1977, disruptive activities were stepped up when the *faction* preoccupied itself with getting arms and money from the EPRP. The EPRP targeted the regime, for its finances and arms, thereby taking all the risks that might fall on those who were conducting the military operations. Not all of the proceeds of the operations were appropriated by the EPRP. Some fell in the hands of the members of the *faction* due to the efforts of commanders who were members of the *faction*, or by units that had some relationship to it. To mention an example, in August 1977, the zone one party committee conducted a successful operation against a government construction site and obtained a large sum of money. The information regarding the site was obtained by an EPRP insider and the operation was well coordinated both from inside and outside. Following the operation, the commander led the members of the unit to the Amanuel Hospital area and asked them to give him both the money and the arms they were carrying. After he disarmed the unit, he told them that he was a member of the *faction* and took away the money. Before the members of the unit could report the incident to the Addis Abeba IZ, the EPRP member at the construction site reported that the cash he had assisted in expropriating had been returned to the government.

Medicine and clothing that the EPRP had accumulated for the EPRA in Tigrai fell into the hands of the *faction*. Some of the material was obtained through operations conducted by the urban units at the cost of lives. For purposes of safety, a certain portion of the accumulated item had been sent to the Shoa area. When part of the Shoa EPRP structure fell into the hands of the *faction*, the group took over almost everything, including the medicine and clothing. The main coordinator of these activities was Abiyu Airsamo.

The EPRP leadership, aware of the factional activities in Shoa, was informed about the day when the medicine was to be transported to the Merhabete area. By this time, at the beginning of March 1977, a small armed group of the *faction* had moved to Merhabete. An EPRP unit ambushed members of the *faction* while they were transporting the medicine and other properties expropriated from the EPRP. No life was lost; however, in the confusion that ensued, neither the EPRP nor the faction was able to retain any of the supplies.

Very generously estimated, the members of the faction, who were confined to the Addis Abeba and Shoa areas might number about one hundred, including those who had gone to Merhabete. In Addis Abeba, the Anja problem was confined to a certain group of the Z-1 party and Youth League structures. The working class organization, the ELAMA, was almost free of factional influence.

The *faction*, which began to reorganize itself as early as September 1976, became a major threat to the EPRP in the first months of 1977. From May 1977 to the end of August, the *faction* caused the EPRP damage that surpassed that caused by POMOA in its entire existence. Members of the *faction* were insiders who had adequate information in their hands, knew the patterns of operation and areas of activities of EPRP members. Above all, they knew some important EPRP members who were totally unknown to the regime and who were responsible for EPRP's activities at the lower echelons of the structure. They knew the strength and vulnerabilities of the EPRP and had some knowledge of the committees in their localities. When they realized the danger that the *faction* posed, the various zones and the IZ in the Addis

Abeba area insisted that some measures be taken against the group. The lower echelons of the EPRP structure, who bore the brunt of the problem were the ones who insisted most. As the internal problems of the EPRP continued to deepen, it became common to suspect anyone who dissented. Members who expressed discord and demanded explanations were intimidated. Afraid that they would be labeled, some members who had no relationship with the *faction* chose to keep their thoughts and ideas to themselves. Even though many EPRP members were aware what an intra-party struggle entailed, they were unable to integrate theory with practice. Since this was a period of severe repression where thousands were victimized on a daily basis, for many EPRP members closing their ranks rather than dissension was their priority. As the factional problem compounded, another major task of the two-man CC team was handling these internal problems of the EPRP.

As part of the response to the emerging general ideological and political crisis, which was manifested by the number of questions directed to the leadership, the two-man CC team, along with the political department and other leading members of the EPRP, produced a number of articles on a wide range of political issues. There were articles on the emergence of Fascism in general and the Ethiopian situation in particular, the International Communist Movement and the Soviet Union, social-imperialism, formation of a united front and EPRP's experience along that line, the origins of the Ethio-Somali conflict, etc. An effort was made to compile a book on the Ethiopian economy, but it remained incomplete. Some books were translated using EPRP's publishing house, the Kokeb Publishers, a legal business run by an EPRP member.

To address the internal problems of the EPRP, a seven page document titled "Intra-party struggle" was prepared by the two-man CC team and sent to EPRP structures around the country. The document summarized the discussions that had been going on among PB members and leading EPRP activists following the death of Mao-tse-Tung in September 1976. At that time, leading activists discussed the issues in general theoretical terms. However, the document titled the "Intra-party struggle" had to be more specific about the internal problems that had plagued the EPRP. The document set the tone for dealing with the internal problems of the EPRP.

The document described the experience of the International Communist Movement and, in particular, that of China. That issue was related to the existence of two lines in a proletarian party. It was affirmed that the proletarian and the bourgeois political lines always live side by side, even in a party that had espoused socialism. It was argued that the coexistence of these two ideologies formed the basis for differences within a proletarian party.[12] The two ideologies could coexist even after taking political power, argued "Intra-party Struggle".[13] According to the document, an intra-party struggle should be conducted on a continuous basis in order to raise the political awareness of the members and create a more homogeneous outlook.

In the section that discussed what the EPRP ought to do in order to overcome the problems that it was confronted with, three approaches were discussed. The first of these was termed the political method. "This is an approach where the members would conduct intensive ideological struggle through democratic discourse and persuasion. This is the main form of struggle that our party (the EPRP) should be engaged in."[14] The second approach, termed administrative, consisted of measures to be taken against those who did not abide by the basic political and organizational principles of the EPRP. Depending on the severity of the breach of discipline, the administrative measure might include demoting from a leadership post, denying the privilege of being a member, and demoting to probationary status, etc.[15]

The third approach was termed "organizational". Measures would be taken against individuals or groups who were engaged in an anti-EPRP activity, which included "confiscation of party property, publicizing the names of party members, engaging in the liquidation of the party, passing the names of EPRP members to the regime...,etc." The document stated that those who committed the above mentioned "crimes" had objectively allied with the regime and had opened war on the EPRP. "In order to guard the safety of the party and the members, the organization (the EPRP) will take appropriate measures against the individuals", provided that evidence "about the crimes that the individuals committed" was produced.[16] The last condition was attached because of the serious difference that arose between the two-man CC team and the Addis Abeba IZ. The IZ, responding to pressure from the structure under it, was pushing the CC team to take measures against some members of the *faction*. The suspected individuals that the IZ wanted to get rid of knew many members of the EPRP, and some of them had threatened to disclose the names they knew. The CC members demanded evidence and resisted the pressure from the IZ. Unable to furnish tangible evidence, the Addis Abeba IZ continued voicing its dissent. As we will see below, history was to prove the IZ's concern and intuitions correct.

The discussion generated by the publication of the "Intra Party Struggle" encouraged some members to come out publicly and express their earnest doubts, reservations and questions regarding the policies of the EPRP. In order to alleviate the problems, members of the leadership and the IZ conducted a number of sessions with lower party and YL committees. Even though most of the issues raised during these discussions had to be addressed by the EPRP CC, others, such as the issue of the involvement of the Soviet Union in Ethiopian politics, the Ethio-Somali conflict, etc., could not be postponed. They needed immediate response.

As a result of the discussion, the tension that had been building within the EPRP eased at least for a while. The majority of the members still remained loyal to the EPRP, while those who had ulterior motives laid low. They disguised themselves and their views and bided their time. Those who were suspected of factional connections were maintained on the basis of single contacts, until it was proven that they posed no danger to the committee members they knew. So, by the beginning of June 1977, about ten months after the formation of the faction, the party and a significant part of the YL were able to halt internal factional activities from spreading.

While the EPRP was conducting discussions on the internal conditions of the party, the *faction* was also engaged in its own activities.

Lieutenant Abebe Jemma and the Faction

One of the victims of the *faction's* activities was Lt. Abebe Jemma, who, in May 1977 confiscated a number of automatic machine guns from the police force at the Civil Aviation Authority. Other EPRP members took about 164,000 birr from the Anbessa Transport company and all of them went underground.[17] They passed on the confiscated material to their contact person, assuming that it would reach the EPRP. The property never reached the EPRP. The names and pictures of two of them appeared in the *Addis Zemen* newspaper and they were added to the regime's "most wanted" list.

When Gezahegne Tesfaye, a member of the *faction* was later detained and interrogated by the regime, he disclosed that Abiyu Airsamo and Gezahegne Simme, a very close friend of Getachew Maru, had taken the arms.[18] Sometime later, it was found that the arms had gone to the factional group in the Shoa area. The whereabouts of Lieutenant Abebe was virtually unknown for a long time. About six months later, however, it was learned that the officer was in a remote village in Shoa. However, according to information obtained recently, Abebe was taken to Shoa to join the Berhane Meskel's group. Upon arrival there, Lt. Abebe protested about the actions taken. He also expressed dissatisfaction about the line entertained by the group. During his stay with the Berhane Meskel group, Abebe was disarmed and closely watched. In due course, however, Abebe managed to escape and he joined an armed rebel peasant group led by Mengiste Defar.[19]

May Day and the Faction

After the declaration of the war of annihilation in September 1976, the EPRP had abandoned its protest demonstrations in major celebrations and, instead, opted for smaller protest marches organized at the level of kebeles. As far as the EPRP was concerned, the May Day of 1977 was to pass as an uneventful day, after the two-man CC team decided not to take any part in the celebration. The ELAMA IZ voiced some concern over that decision and proposed to organize protest demonstrations of small groups at the level of the kebeles. ELAMA's decision was endorsed by the Addis Abeba IZ and preparations began.[20]

As a precautionary measure, the protest demonstrations were to take place on April 29, instead of May 1, at six o'clock in the evening. On April 29, three or four hours before the demonstrations were to take place, the security department of the EPRP's Addis Abeba IZ obtained a report indicating that the regime had acquired detailed information about the planned demonstrations - the date, the starting and finishing points, their specific locations and time, etc. Upon receiving the report, the IZ made frantic efforts to stop the whole process, succeeding, however, in contacting very few participants. The other participants of the demonstrations were out for the day.

On April 29, the regime sent hundreds of its well-armed security personnel both, in uniforms and in civilian clothes. In some places, minutes after the demonstrations began, camouflaged military personnel, in collaboration with Abyot Tebeka groups of the localities opened fire. Hundreds of youth were killed. Some families lost two or three of their beloved children in just one incident.

On the same evening that the massacre was conducted, hundreds of corpses were sent to the morgue at the Menelik Hospital. The next morning, EA went to the hospital looking for his younger brother who did not come home the night before. When he reached the hospital, EA saw piles of corpses thrown on the floor and on the tables of the morgue room. These were corpses of very young children, teenagers, adults and older people, females in Afro-style and others in traditional hair style, 'gungune', some were in pants and others in skirts. Most of the corpses were bullet-ridden and some of the faces were so disfigured that it was impossible to tell their identity. Some of the corpses had no limbs or arms while the breasts of other corpses were mutilated. EA saw fathers, mothers, brothers, relatives and friends turning corpses over, looking for their beloved ones. Those who were 'lucky' enough to find the corpse of their beloved ones covered them with their jackets, shawl, scarves... anything they laid their hands on, and waited for funeral boxes. The Funeral Home by the Menelik Hospital and some of the major Funeral Homes of the city had soon ran out of caskets.

Those who found the remains of their beloved ones had to pay a ransom of 250 birr in exchange. The news spread and when a large number of people arrived at the Hospital, visiting the morgue was prohibited. Moreover, the embarrassed Derge arrested the doctor in charge of the Hospital.[21]

In its "Critical Assessment", MEISON denied having prior knowledge of the assault on demonstrators and argued that the actions taken by government security personnel were in self-defense.

> When the MEISON and other members of the POMOA were making preparations to celebrate the event (May Day)...a large number of youth demonstrators engulfed the kebeles. Among the participants in the demonstration were squad members of the EPRP. Mingled with the demonstrators, the squad members opened fire and threw grenades at kebele officials....Alarmed by the sudden offensive actions, *Abyot Tebeka* members fired back and killed many youth.[22]

Twelve years after the incident, MEISON would still argue that the *Abyot Tebeka* members took "defensive" actions. But how would one explain the fact that machine guns were used against the demonstrators? By mid-

1977, it was no secret that *Abyot Tebeka* members were not provided with automatic machine guns, even though that had been their demand.

The killings were a severe blow for the EPRP.[23] After this incident, it was evident that secrecy, an asset and trademark of the EPRP, had been compromised. It also became absolutely clear that it was now impossible to conduct any form of peaceful protest. That being said, both the CC team and the Addis Abeba IZ failed to foresee the adverse effect of EPRP's internal problem on preparing demonstrations.

Members of the Faction in the Movie Theaters

Some underground EPRP members hid themselves or used to pass their leisure time in movie theaters. Because of the radically inclined movies that it ran, the Ras Cinema Hall in Mercato had large audience. At the end of May 1977, government security officers commenced visiting movie theaters. In the midst of shows, they would line up the spectators and demand to see their ID cards. Along with the security officers, there came camouflaged informants, who pointed fingers at some of the spectators. Some EPRP members fell prey. Those who had frequented the movie halls as their refuge had to find alternatives.

Besides suspected EPRP members, a large number of other movie goers were rounded up and sent to the commercial farms run by the regime. Of some fifty youth who were sent to the commercial farm at Dubti, in the Afar region, about forty escaped and went to Somalia where a similar scenario awaited them. They languished in Somali prisons for about ten years. Most of them were released in 1989, as part of the Red Cross repatriation program.[24]

Other Factional Activities

In the Shoa province, particularly in the town of Debre Berhan and vicinity, some EPRP members who had joined the faction informed on their comrades and brought havoc upon the entire EPRP structure. Many EPRP members were arrested. Similar actions were taken in other areas. A case in point is an EPRP sub-zone committee of zone one in Addis Abeba that was to hold a meeting at a bar in the Sebategna area. Three members had arrived on time and were waiting for two others. During those days, if a member was late for more than five or ten minutes, it was assumed that he had been arrested or something had gone wrong. It had then become standard to wait no longer than ten minutes. The three sub-zone committee members waited for about ten minutes. They were about to leave when several security officers, who had been sitting by a corner approached them and told them to remain seated. AB, pretending to comply, pulled out his gun and shot two of the officers. All of the EPRP members ran for their lives. AB was hit in the back but was able to escape. AB had undergone similar ordeals four times and had escaped from all of them, although he had repeatedly been shot at and wounded. He was a veteran labor leader and one of the founding members of ELAMA. At a later investigation, it was established that one of the members who did not show up at the meeting, being also a member of the *faction,* had tipped the regime about the meeting.

Members of the *faction* also disclosed a number of other seemingly inconsequential but important means of communication between EPRP members. They informed the regime about locations, tea-rooms and bars which were frequented by EPRP or YL members. They taught the regime what the EPRP called a "mechanism" -- a system used to introduce two members to each other without involving a third party.[25]

Liquidation from Within - Party Zone Two

Besides the role that the *faction* members played, the "mass confession", the terror and the search and destroy campaigns, the EPRP faced other crisis. A large number of members of an important zone of the Addis Abeba area, known as zone two fell in the hands of the government. The zone covered the southwestern part of Addis Abeba where there are many government institutions, factories, hospitals, schools, etc. The peculiar characteristic of this zone was that many of the EPRP members were little known to the Derge or to the public. By special instruction of the Addis Abeba IZ, many of the members of the zone kept a very low profile. Many of them were degree-holding professionals in the Ministry of Justice, Highway Authority, Commercial Bank, Tikure Anbessa Hospital, etc., and some were in important posts in the Ministry of Interior. Some held important positions in printing companies, such as, the Artistic.

Zone two members began to mysteriously disappear and their whereabouts were unknown for quite a while. Sometime later, the EPRP leadership found that they had been arrested. Regarding the incidents as isolated, the Addis Abeba IZ did not conduct a special investigation. Soon the number of arrested members reached an alarming figure of about thirty. Among those arrested and executed were long time activists Fassika Amare of the Artistic Printing Press, Mekasha Solomon and Tsegaye Sebhatu, a lawyer and a judge, at the Ministry of Justice.[26]

After learning about the alarming number of EPRP members who had been arrested, the CC team intervened and analyzed the peculiar nature of their arrests. It was concluded that the pattern of arrest was totally different from previous arrests. Both the Addis Abeba IZ and the CC members concluded that zone two was infiltrated and that a systematic annihilation effort was underway.

After reaching that conclusion, the entire zone two structure was made nonfunctional. All organizational activities were suspended and contact between the members and the various levels of the zone two structure was halted until further notice. In the meantime, the zones in the adjacent areas took over some of the political and propaganda activities of the zone.

Sometime later, another provisional zonal committee composed of members from the other zones was formed and took over the activities of the zone. The provisional zonal committee was also given additional guidelines. After screening the entire structure, those committees that were regarded as free of infiltration were incorporated into the newly formed structure. Until conditions improved, the Addis Abeba IZ collaborated with the provisional zonal committee in its day to day activities. Following the reconstitution process, the zone began functioning, though it still was very weak and disorganized.

Sealing off the structure from further danger, the Addis Abeba IZ investigated the arrests and concluded that one cause was the collaboration of a former EPRP zonal committee (zone two) member with the Derge. Getachew Negatu, who had been arrested by the regime sometime earlier, disclosed under torture whatever information he had about the zone. Even though he might not have known the personnel of the regional committees, Getachew had some knowledge of committees in the various institutions. Sometime later, it became known that another EPRP member had played a major role in providing the regime names of EPRP members. The informant, who was incarcerated for about ten years, was a member of the zone two structure.

Liquidation from Within - ELAMA Zone Two

Over a period of several months, some members of an ELAMA zone committee (zone two) in Addis Abeba, Alemayehu Tilahun, Achameleh Kebede[27] and at least eight others disappeared without any trace. The zone operated in the Old Airport, the Mexico Square, the Nefas Silk areas and among important unions, such as, the Anbessa Transport Authority. While the disappearance of these members remained unexplained, the problem within zone two of the ELAMA structure came to the attention of the EPRP through a YL branch committee in the Old Airport area. The YL obtained its information from an ELAMA regional committee of the same area, which bypassed its legal channel believing it to be insecure. The ELAMA regional committee reached that conclusion after losing three or four members who had been assigned to represent it at the next higher level in the hierarchy, the sub-zonal committee. In order to solve the problem, the ELAMA IZ made a number of decisions, but none of them seemed to be executed. Finally, the ELAMA IZ conducted an investigation and concluded that someone who had access to both the regional and sub-zonal committees was behind the foul play. T was assigned to follow up and restructure the zone. He was a long time worker activist, a member of both the ELAMA IZ and its CC. In a preliminary encounter with a member of the ELAMA zone two committee, T concluded that the problem in the zone was the result of organizational incompetence. However, that feeling did not last long. Initially, T could only meet the secretary of the zone, however, he insisted upon meeting the other members of zone two committee. After procrastinating the case for quite a while, contact person Solomon Tekle gave in. He called a meeting of the ELAMA zonal committee and made an arrangement to take T to the place.

As a precaution, members were accustomed to pre-inspect meeting sites. Accordingly, T arrived about half an hour ahead of time and observed from a distance. He saw two individuals standing close together and seemingly waiting for something or someone. Solomon did not show up and T left. According to a later report, members of the zone committee asked Solomon why T did not show up. One of the zonal committee members recalled Solomon saying that he had been arrested. The members of the zone committee did not question his statement.

Anticipating danger, EPRP members used to arrange two or three contingent rendezvous, in case the first plan did not work out. Accordingly, on the second or third day, the members went and checked for their comrades at the prearranged site. Likewise, both T and Solomon showed up at the prearranged location and they set another appointment. Both the first and second meetings were to be held in very dangerous places, one by the Tele bar and the other by the Besse Company in Addis Abeba, where escape would be difficult.

As usual, T arrived early and inspected the area. A few minutes later, he saw a vehicle carrying three individuals. It was parked by the entrance to the bar. The three people left the vehicle and stood by the entrance. T saw Solomon and the other committee members enter the bar, so he went through a side entrance and warned the others about the three people outside. Before T reached the meeting place, Solomon had already informed members of the zonal committee that T had been arrested and therefore would not be coming. However, when T sneaked in through a back door, Solomon became very nervous. Without showing any sign of suspicion, T dispersed the meeting and set up another one. The three people standing by the door saw the ELAMA members leave the bar and were unable to identify T, who was well disguised. As they talked among themselves, the ELAMA members left the area.

Following this encounter, a member of the zonal committee expressed to T her reservations about Solomon and wondered how he could know in advance about the arrest of members. As a precautionary measure, she was advised to stay away from him.

In his preliminary investigation, T learned that Solomon had dissolved all the committees below the sub-zone and he himself contacted the basic committees, that is, committees at the level of institutions and factories. Furthermore, it was conjectured that in his eagerness to reach to the highest echelon, Solomon had entrapped members of higher committees. Solomon's haste to move fast alerted the ELAMA leadership. The ELAMA IZ, suspecting that Solomon was behind the foul play, observed the areas where he was residing and moving around and his relative daringness in conducting meetings in areas frequented by the regime's security personnel. It was concluded that his behavior had drastically changed from the first days when he went underground. The case was passed on to the Addis Abeba party IZ, which decided on his arrest for further investigation.

At a preset time, Solomon Tekle was told that he was to be detained. He made a violent effort to escape, but was overpowered. In the presence of three or four EPRP members, he offered to disclose everything he knew and begged for clemency. At the trial, however, Solomon refused to collaborate, remaining adamant and refusing to admit to any of the charges, demanding evidence and witnesses. The IZ, which had tangible information and had gathered additional circumstantial evidence, passed a sentence on Solomon and the problems in the zone halted, but it was too late to bring back those invaluable members who had been victimized.

The Addis Abeba IZ Fell in Danger

The Addis Abeba IZ and particularly the secretary Germatchew Lemma had anticipated danger. In the first week of June 1977, that committee was to be the target of the regime when most of the houses used by the committee were raided. A number of these houses were used as meeting places, residences, or served both purposes. Some of them were known to some former EPRP members who later had become members of the *faction*. Because of the involvement of former East German and Cuban intelligence, the Ethiopian regime's surveillance capacity had become very sophisticated. Using the information provided by the Anjas as the starting point and combining various espionage techniques, the regime was able to identify almost all of the houses that the IZ used. Vehicles used only two or three times were also identified by the regime.

Hours before the raid, the EPRP CC team found that the regime was using telephone tapping techniques to follow up EPRP activities. One of the CC members, on the phone with Germatchew, was about to hang up when he - heard a conversation on the line between two wiretappers.

Leading EPRP activists discussed the incident and decided to abandon some of the houses that had telephone lines. IZ members were also advised to do so. However, they checked their security networks and found no clue to a government raid on that day. Though alerted about the danger, some IZ members, including Germatchew, decided not to abandon the house where they were staying. On this same day, Getachew Maru who overpowered an EPRP guard and tried to escape imperiled his life. By the decision of the EPRP CC, Getachew had been detained since March 1977. For a period of three months or so, Getachew had been insisting that his case come to a conclusion. The Addis Abeba IZ which had no prison of its own had also been insisting that it was difficult to handle the prisoner. The last action of Getachew Maru precipitated a crisis and the Addis Abeba IZ refused to handle him any more. A hard working and long time activist, Getachew was one of the founding members of the Abyot group and a leading member of the EPRP. He was an effective organizer and one of the leaders of the younger generation of radical activists. Getachew was also one of the founding members of the *faction* within the EPRP.

A few hours after the discovery of the telephone tapping, the military regime's special security force raided thirteen EPRP houses within a few hours. One of these houses was the EPRP Addis Abeba IZ headquarters where Germatchew used to reside. Around eight o'clock in the evening, two *Abyot Tebeka* members came to the house. They asked the residents to turn on the lights of the veranda. Germatchew and "Asfaw", another IZ member, left the house and went to their vehicle. On the street, they encountered a large group of security officers preparing to raid the house. When they saw Germatchew and his colleague, the security officers tried to question them. Without hesitation, Germatchew pulled out his gun and began shooting. The gunfight lasted for more than half an hour. The EPRP members abandoned their vehicle and escaped. The security officers then raided the house. At least eleven EPRP members were inside the house and all of them managed to escape.

Germatchew and "Asfaw" ran for their lives. When they reached the Mercato area, it was past ten o'clock at night. They made an arrangement with the owner of a van and passed the night in the vehicle. The next morning, Germatchew went to another house where the IZ held meetings and found that the house was among those to be raided. Before he moved to another location, Germatchew made a phone call to one of the houses that the IZ used, but the line was busy. Apparently, it had been disconnected. He and "Asfaw" then headed to the house, located in the Kazanchis area. That house too had been raided and security officers were hiding in the compound and waiting for preys. When "Asfaw" peeped through the crack of the gate and saw officers in the compound, he alerted Germatchew and both of them tried to run away. Germatchew, who had sustained injuries to his ankle during his student days, was unable to escape. He pulled out his gun to defend himself, but was killed on the spot. Before he fell victm, Germatchew was making preparations to leave for Djibouti. The preparation included obtaining a military uniform.

The sudden death of Germatchew was a major blow to the EPRP. Germatchew was one of the leading members of the EPRP. His contribution to the struggle had been important, particularly when the organization found itself in deep crises. Germatchew was a respected figure among workers, who adored and admired him for his dedication to their cause. He was a founding member of the underground labor organization, ELAMA. Germatchew had served the EPRP as a member of the IZ and the urban armed wing. He had a few years of military training at the Harer Military Academy, before he joined the Law Faculty at the Addis Abeba University. Germatchew was a loving and caring human being.

Late that night, government security forces knocked on the door of a house used by EPRP members in the Kidist Mariam area and demanded admittance. The EPRP unit opened fire and, in the ensuing confusion, the members were able to escape. One of them was naked and he ended up in the gorge by the Ras Mekonnen bridge.

A few days after the raid on houses used by EPRP, an assessment of the damage was made. A special instruction prohibiting telephone use was passed on to all EPRP members in the Addis Abeba area. EPRP members had to resort to more primitive methods of communication, contacting each other physically in order to pass on simple messages. This policy averted the danger of telephone taps, but it meant that EPRP members would be out in the streets more.

Also, arrested during these operations were members totally unknown to the public. They did not belong to the EPRP structure proper. Some of them held important government posts. Some were in the Ministry of Internal Affairs. Two of them were from the Central Investigation Department. Contact with these officials was maintained through the Addis Abeba IZ security committee chairperson, Jarso. According to information provided by an arrested EPRP member of zone three committee and another EPRP member, the Derge security department had pictures that showed Jarso meeting EPRP members at various times and locations. That information was disclosed during interrogation sessions.[28]

A few days after these raids, it was known that a KGB team that specialized in telephone tapping technique had arrived in Ethiopia. It was also learned that a special "counter insurgency" committee made up of Ethiopians, Soviets, East Germans and Cubans had been formed.

In its few years in power, the Derge had restructured its intelligence network quite a few times. During the reign of Emperor Haile Selassie, the arcane Special Branch of the Police Force was the main institution responsible for charges related to activities of dissidents. Other offices included the Security Department and the office known as the Cabinet which also was in charge of dissident activities abroad. In 1974/75, the Special Branch was renamed and it was placed under the direct control of the intelligence department of the Derge headed by Colonel Tesfaye Wolde Selassie.[29] The officer in charge of the former Special Branch was Colonel Tekle Mikael Armede who was placed under arrest following the Derge's fall in 1991. The Derge was not content with the activities of the former Special Branch and consequently, another investigation committee was formed. As was indicated above, during the climax of the Red Terror, that committee, also known as the "counter-insurgence" committee was headed by Captain/Major Berhanu Kebede. Other members of the committee were Colonel Leulseged Fikre Mariam, Colonel Mulugeta Eshete and Major Alemayehu Asfaw. The committee was directly responsible to Mengistu. In July 1977, the former Special Branch and the newly formed investigation committee were combined to form what was known as the Central Revolutionary Investigation Department. It was headed by Colonel Legesse Belayneh. A few years later, it was renamed as the Central Investigation Department.

Not long after the formation of the Special Security (counter-insurgence) force mentioned above, three or four of its members were gunned down by

EPRP urban units, for reasons totally unrelated to the activities of the committee. At that time, the EPRP had no knowledge of the formation of the Special Security force. The decision to neutralize the individuals was made by EPRP zones that took the actions after considering the atrocities that the individuals had committed at the kebele level. One of the surviving members of the committee, Colonel Leulseged Fikre Mariam, became terribly frightened that he demanded permission to leave the country and accordingly was sent abroad.

The Addis Abeba IZ, which had been insisting on measures against the factional members all along, became the immediate target and the EPRP lost the inspiring leader, Germatchew Lemma. The remaining IZ members became understandably furious about the loss of their comrade, thinking that it had been due to delay in moving against the members of the *faction*. *After consulting the zones under their jurisdiction, the Addis Abeba IZ ignored the two-man CC team and unilaterally decided to take measures against suspected members of the faction. From mid-June 1977 on, the war declared by the faction was thus reciprocated.*

EPRP members who had lingering doubts about the *faction* realized that at least some members of the faction had been collaborating with the regime, thereby endangering the EPRP and its members. At about the time when the EPRP began retaliating, some of the Anjas, particularly those that had belonged to the EPRP or YL defense units, joined the regime and were organized into government assassination squads. They were armed and well financed and were given vehicles to roam the city, hunting down EPRP members, their former friends, brothers, sisters and comrades. A few months later, during the peak of the "Red Terror," some of these individuals were deployed at kebele prisons, where they served as guides in the "mass confession" and torture of those arrested.

EPRP members who were unknown even to the party leadership fell victim as a result of the cooperation of the Anja's with the regime. At the beginning of July 1977, the entire clandestine structure of the EPRP in the Central Intelligence Department (CID) was compromised. The names of some of the officers was released to the Derge by Gezahegne Sime, a very close friend of Getachew Maru. Many employees of the CID were arrested and some went underground. The CID was one of the most important security branches of the regime. It was also one of the most important sources of security information for the EPRP. Since the early days of the revolutionary movement, the EPRP had focused on the CID and had recruited numerous employees. In due course, EPRP members in the CID provided the organization names of suspects that the regime wanted to arrest, they supplied information of houses to be raided. Those officers that were placed in influential government posts facilitated the release of hundreds of prisoners. Some of these officers took some part in the urban military activities of the EPRP.

Partly because of EPRP's influence and infiltration, by mid 1977, the

CID had lost its efficiency as far as the Derge was concerned. This situation was perhaps a factor in Mengistu's decision to form the "Special Counter-insurgence" committee. Among those EPRP members and sympathizers were, Gonderit, a civilian at the CID, Lieutenant Tafa Daba, Main Police Headquarters; Lieutenant Wase Aman, Special Branch; Lt. Aklog Negatu, Special Investigation; Lieutenant Wonde Wossen, Special Security; Lt. Tamene Galore, Special Investigation; and Lt. Mohammed Ali. Most of these officers were exectued by the Derge. Most of the above officers attended the Police Academy in Holeta following their suspension from the former Haile Selassie University.

Among these officers, Lieutenant Tamene Galore (code name Tulema), who was one of the most wanted individuals went underground and was sent to a small town in Shoa. Both Tamene and the local EPRP party committee were given codes that would help them establish contact. Tamene went to the meeting sites for three or four consecutive days and it appeared that members of the local party committee were not showing up. When the repeated effort to introduce the two parties failed, a member of the Secretariat in Addis Abeba had to go to the small town in Shoa to accomplish the assignment. Upon arrival there, he found out that both parties had been going to the meeting places. Furthermore, he ascertained that members of the local party committee had seen Tamene at the appointment sites. The problem, however, was that members of the local party could not consider Tamene as an EPRP member because of his stocky physical appearance. Tamene was heavy-built and at that time he could be in his early thirties. Despite these initial difficulties, Tamene reached the EPRA. He was a hard-working individual who kept his sense of humor even under difficult conditions. Sometime in mid-1978, Tamene fell down a deep gorge in Tselemt and passed away.

Differing Perspective

It is important to mention that the faction was not a homogeneous group, but an eclectic one that came together for a variety of reasons. Leading members of this group, among them Berhane Meskel, could have their own interpretation of events and cause of discontent. Berhane Meskel's first dissatisfaction with the CC of the EPRP was manifested in mid-1975 when the leadership suspended the death penalty that he and other members of the EPRA had passed on former members of the EPRA who defected to the Derge. Berhane Meskel insisted that the death sentence be carried out.[30]

At a CC meeting held in mid-1975, Berhane Meskel protested on the proposed ammendment to abolish the post of the Secretary General. Berhane Meskel expressed his differing view when the CC discussed EPRP's constitution in preparation towards the Extended Conference which was held in August 1975. Berhane Meskel was the Secretary General of the party. The Extended Conference did abolish the post of the Secretary General of the party and replaced it with a post to be known as the secretary of the CC. At the

First Plenum of the EPRP CC held immediately after the Extended Conference, Tesfaye Debessai was elected as the secretary of the EPRP CC. Furthermore, an election was conducted on this same meeting and a new PB that did not include Berhane Meskel was formed. Until this time, Berhane Meskel was a member of the PB of the EPRP.

Since April 1976, Berhane Meskel began expressing open dissatisfaction on how the PB conducted its activities. Berhane Meskel's discontent became more pronounced following the EPRP CC meeting held in April 1976 which discussed the Derge's call for the formation of a front. Berhane Meskel strongly advocated forging an alliance with the Derge.[31]

Furthermore, Berhane Meskel along with Getachew Maru expressed differences at EPRP CC meetings held in August and September 1976. Both meetings discussed a PB report regarding the prevalent political condition of the country. In the report, the PB had suggested to take action onMengistu Haile Mariam. Even though no other paper was presented at both of these meetings, both Berhane Meskel and Getachew Maru opposed the idea of taking action on Mengistu Haile Mariam.[32] Even after the EPRP CC reached at a decision on the PB's proposal, both Berhane Meskel and Getachew Maru continued agitating against the decision. Both CC members who were accused of conducting agitation outside their designated party structures, were charged of violating the EPRP's constitution. Even though they retained party membership, the Third EPRP CC Plenum held in Novemebr 1976 expeled both CC members from the EPRP CC.

Sometime in the first months of 1977, it became known that Berhane Meskel and Getachew Maru had already formed a clandestine group within the EPRP. An article supposedly written by Berhane Meskel did not deny about the existence of such a group, but offered an altogether different view of its role. In the first place, Berhane Meskel and his group did not regard themselves as factional activists, but members of a process they labeled as "the Rectification Movement". The group professed that the EPRP had to undergo a rectification movement in order to follow "the mass line". In mid-1977, some members of the *faction* allied themselves with the Derge. In his article, Berhane Meskel dismissed the story about the alliance of the group with the Derge as false.[33]

Berhane Meskel did not admit that members of his group had taken part in the repression against the EPRP. Rather, in his article Berhane Meskel stated that the EPRP had executed many innocent members of the organization, whose only guilt was entertaining a line differing from that of the "clique". This was in reference to the EPRP PB which had ceased to function by March 1977. The article further stated that some members of the breakaway group had been forced to go underground and that some had been arrested by the Derge. Berhane Meskel's article stated that the followers of the "mass line" had begun to publish an internal paper called "*Red Star*". The publication was short lived, however. Members of the *faction* put out some leaflets and in some of them, they expressed opposition to the urban military actions of the EPRP.

In the article, Berhane Meskel condemned, "certain traitor individuals and groups who, using the name of the group (his group) published articles." He then asserted, "the movement will not be held accountable for those articles."[34]

Berhane Meskel, who had moved with his group to the Merhabete area in March 1977, probably could not have taken a direct role in factional activities in the Addis Abeba area. Particularly after the EPRP severed the link between the urban-based members of the *faction* and those in the rural area, it seemed that he had no direct control over his group. The factional activity he had initiated in January 1976 might have gone out of control.

For a number of months, the Berhane Meskel group which did not exceed twenty-five, traversed the Menz and Geshe area in Shoa. The group established contacts with peasant armed bands of the area. Among the relatively known peasant groups were those led by Biruke and Mengeste Defar. It is not known whether Berhane Meskel's group had any military engagement with the regime. However, a few months later, some active members of the Berhane Meskel group gave themselves up to the Derge. It is believed that the Derge had infiltrated the group.[35] Finally, the entire group was surrounded by government forces and was forced to surrender. Berhane Meskel stayed in prison until he was executed some months later.[36]

Berhane Meskel was a veteran leader of the Ethiopian student movement, and his contribution to the movement was immense. Furthermore, Berhane Meskel's role was of critical importance in founding the EPLO/EPRP, from 1970-1972. Berhane Meskel's popularity had helped bring the radicals together. Berhane Meskel was one of the leading figures of the nucleus of the EPRA. He had the lion's share in drafting some of the major documents of the EPLO. He was an eloquent orator.

EPRA and the Urban EPRP Structure Lost Communication

By the beginning of 1977, the EPRA had units both in the Tigrai and the Begemidir provinces and effort was made to initiate armed struggle in the Sidamo, Shoa and Harer areas. Besides their strategic military significance, the ostensible purpose of initiating armed activities in these areas was to use them as retreat areas for members from the urban areas. As a matter of fact, it was to the EPRA held territories in Begemidir and Tigrai that EPRP members who were on the wanted list of the regime were sent. After the decision of the Second Plenum of the EPRP CC in August 1976, the number of members joining the EPRA had increased.

Three categories of members were sent to the EPRA. The first included those who were on the wanted list of the government. In the second category fell members who for personal reasons demanded that they be sent to the army. The third group included vulnerable members or sympathizers who, if arrested and tortured, would cause serious problems for the EPRP.

By mid-1977, only a small fraction of those who had to leave the urban centers had been sent to the EPRA. There still remained a large number who were under government surveillance, but were unable to leave the urban areas. Some of them were retained by their committees. During those days, the various levels of the EPRP and YL structures, including some of the leading committees, tried to keep the ablest and the most dedicated members in their structures. Most of these members, selfless in their commitment to the struggle, accepted the demands and remained in the structures, even though they knew the danger. When the urban EPRP organization was attacked, it was these dedicated activists that paid the heaviest price. The loss of this dedicated group made the EPRP more vulnerable to internal problems. In the ongoing struggle against the Derge, the EPRP lost many of those members who had laid the foundation of the organization.

While EPRP members were being sent to the EPRA a few at a time, on a regular basis, startling information reached the Addis Abeba YL leadership from the EPRP clandestine structure in the Ledeta Military Police headquarters. The information came from a former member of the zone one party committee of Addis Abeba who had been arrested in Tigrai and imprisoned at the Military Police headquarters in Addis Abeba.

The prison cells of the Military Police (MP) were located in the center of the camp, surrounded by two layers of security personnel. If any message escaped the notice of the first group of guards, it still had to pass through the second layer of officers. The former zonal committee member, however, was able to relay the information through EPRP's organizational network in the Military Police, which at the time was active in both layers of the military camp. As a former member of zone one party committee, the detained member had some prior knowledge of the existence of the EPRP structure in the Military Police.

The EPRP detainee revealed that from the beginning of May 1977 to the middle of the month, fourteen to eighteen EPRP members, en route to Tigrai, had been arrested at the exact spot where they were supposed to meet their contact person from the EPRP Tigrai zonal committee. The security forces in Tigrai had detailed information on the individuals they were to arrest. They also knew the spot, the day, and the time to meet them. Moreover, they knew where the password was hidden. Usually, the password was sewn inside the collar of a coat or a shirt, or in the upper parts of pants. There were cases where EPRP members who had arrived in one of the Tigrai towns could not find anyone to escort them to the EPRA, and had been arrested. The former zone one committee member also informed the EPRP of the names of those detained and his opinion about the events that led to the arrest.

After this information reached the urban leadership of the EPRP, no more members were sent through that route. Investigation proved the main source of the information for the Derge security branch to be a member of the EPRP leadership in Tigrai. He was suspected of TPLF links. Furthermore, the TPLF had acknowledged that it did not like the large influx of EPRP members to the Tigrai area.[37] During this period, the TPLF was in conflict with the EPRA. The informant in the EPRP Tigrai structure inflicted incalculable damage upon the EPRP. The EPRP was unable to use the Tigrai route and from mid-May 1977 on, it was nearly impossible to send members to the EPRA in Tigrai. Since the danger in the cities had reached such unprecedented proportions, large numbers of members were anxious to leave and join the EPRA. In September 1977, the YL demanded passage for more than a thousand of its members.

When it was confirmed that the Tigrai route had been permanently severed, an alternative route was designed. An arrangement was made between the Wello EPRP party structure and the CC team in Addis Abeba to send exposed EPRP members to the Wello province. According to the agreement, when a group arrived in Wello, the zonal committee would send it to the rural area along the Wello-Tigrai border, where it would be met by the EPRA. In preparation for this mission, in October/November 1977, two well-armed EPRA contingents were sent to the Wello area to raid the town of Sekota. When the presence of EPRA units in the rural areas of northern Wello was known, peasants evacuated leaving the EPRA units without food. Before the EPRA contingents reached Sekota, Derge mobilized the peasantry, fortified the town and opened a surprise attack on the EPRA units as the contingents rested in a gorge, a "*moot meret*" (militarily speaking a dangerous terrain).[38] In military terminology, "*moot meret*" is a terrain where a force can neither defend itself nor retreat, but could easily be attacked. Because of the failure of this operation, the plan to escort EPRP members from the Wello area to Tigrai could not work as designed. Thus, thousands of EPRP members and sympathizers still remained trapped in the urban areas.

Furthermore, the crisis that befell the EPRP structure in Southern Wello exacerbated communication problems. Those EPRP members with access and possibilities left for Djibouti or Somalia. Some arrived in Sudan. Some Eritrean EPRP members left for the EPLF or ELF controlled areas. Many EPRP members camouflaged themselves as peasants and stayed in rural areas. Some became employed as maids and guards. During this period, leaving the urban areas became so difficult that some members of the EPRP leadership and leading activists, including CC members had to use public transportation to rural areas, which exposed them to obvious danger. Colonel Emiru Wonde, Administrator of the Begemidir province, came to Addis Abeba on government related activities. There, he was forced to go underground and it was decided that he should quickly leave the city. Disguised as a priest, the Colonel had to walk several hundred miles from Addis Abeba to the EPRA held territory in Begemidir.

The author of this book, who was on the most wanted list of the regime, had to take public transportation on his way to Gonder. Wearing a Muslim cap and dressed like a merchant, he boarded a bus along with A., another EPRP member. The two EPRP members took different seats. The bus was full to capacity and there were some Muslims seated in one corner of the bus.

When the bus stopped for lunch at Goha Tsion, a small town on the border of Shoa/Gojjam provinces, the author went into one of the small hotels to eat. As he was about to be seated for lunch, one of the Muslim passengers entered the hotel looking for soft drink and reminded the author that it was a Christian hotel. The author, born in a Christian family, exclaimed "Bismilahi" (equivalent to "Oh! My God") and left the hotel. The author did not know the man, neither did he see him on the bus. The author left the hotel, walked some distance, and took off his Muslim cap before he entered the next Christian hotel, where he ate his lunch.

The bus resumed its long journey and on the next day, some miles from Fenote Selam, a small town in the Gojjam province, in the midst of nowhere, the engine of the bus stalled. Until help arrived, the passengers scattered in all directions. Hours elapsed and they became hungry. The Muslims, who were carrying their meals, invited their "co-religionist", the author of this book, to join them for lunch. To the dismay of A., the other EPRP member, who was from a Muslim family, the author was provided with lunch while he had to go hungry.

After lunch, one of the Muslim passengers asked the author to pray with him. The author, who was not quite familiar with the rituals accompanying Muslim prayer, was caught in a fix. As a 'Muslim', it was expected of him to pray at least twice a day. However, if he ventured to do the prayer along with his new "friend", he would betray his ignorance of the rituals. To avoid the embarrassment, he told his new Muslim "friend" that he did not pray while traveling.

The bus was fixed and continued its journey. Before it reached its destination, Gonder, the bus was stopped by some *Abyot Tebeka* members at a small town called Maksegnit. The *Abyot Tebeka* members checked the identity of all those who were aboard the bus and found two irregular ID cards. One of them belonged to a militiaman who had been to Jijjiga, while the second was that of the author. The *Abyot Tebeka* members held back the militia member and the author, and allowed the bus to leave. They wanted to call Addis Abeba to check the identities of the two.

Aboard the bus, A. gathered sympathy and support from among the passengers. The driver sympathized with the author, whom he thought to be a simple Muslim merchant (a "miskeen"), and refused to continue his journey. The entire Muslim group in the bus, both male and female, came to the defense of the author, swearing that he was a "miskeen" who could harm no one.

The *Abyot Tebeka* members asked the author about the irregular file numbers on the accompanying letter that he was carrying. During those days, besides an ID card, one had to obtain a letter from a kebele to travel to any part of the country. The author told them that he was an illiterate person and had no knowledge of what was written on the "ID" card. The militiaman, on the other hand, became engaged in a heated argument with the members of the *Abyot Tebeka*. He recounted his exploit in the Ethio-Somalia conflict. The

Abyot Tebeka members, offended by the behavior of the militiaman, detained him, but they released the "miskeen" Muslim merchant, a member of the EPRP CC. The Muslim group was jubilant as the bus pulled away.

A few days after the bus had reached Gonder, the author was strolling in one of the kebeles with a well known local EPRP member. He heard someone calling. It was his Muslim "friend" from the bus trip, rushing out of a small retail shop. The author saw him and stopped, but the 'Muslim' friend exclaimed "Aha!" when he spotted the author's companion, a known EPRP member. He did not wait to greet the author. He had found the clue to his lingering doubts.

After it was known that the Tigrai route was permanently severed, northern Shoa served as a temporary sanctuary. However, due to the crisis in that province, Shoa could be of use for only a few months. The last alternative was the Begemidir route. Between June and July 1977, a member of the Secretariat, G/T, and a member of the ELAMA IZ, code-named "EDU", repeatedly went to the Begemidir province to discuss the route.[39] A CC member had another discussion with members of the Begemidir zonal committee in October 1977. The committee agreed to take eight to ten members per week. That limit was later raised. From August 1977 to January 1978, eight to fifteen members were provided passage to the EPRA in Begemidir every week.

As the influx of members grew, the regional army leadership in Gonder sent a letter stating that it could accept no more members, as it had no arms for them and was unable to provide shelter to unarmed members.[40] One of the basic rules of a guerilla force is constant and swift movement in order to avoid danger. It was feared that the large number of unarmed group would affect the army's movements and jeopardize it. Despite the regional leadership's refusal to accept them, EPRP members continued to join the EPRA in small numbers. In the meantime, the Begemidir EPRA's situation improved after a major military operation at the end of 1977, in which a Derge battalion was routed at Maileham, a small town on the Gonder-Tigrai highway.

EPRP's Organizational Condition in 1977/1978

By the decision of the committee composed of the four member CC sub-secretariat and the two CC members, one of the two CC members remaining in urban areas, Samuel Alemayehu, left for Assimba around the end of August or the beginning of September 1977 and reached Tigrai in December, four months later. The above mentioned committee had been operational since mid-1977 and it was entrusted to oversee EPRP activities in different parts of the country.

Among the main purposes of Samuel's trip to Tigrai was to participate in the long awaited EPRP CC meeting and to send arms to the urban areas. Samuel was also expected to forward questions raised by the membership and get arms, particularly grenades, for the urban military units.

Aware of Samuel's delay in the Wello area, the last CC member left Addis Abeba for the Begemidir province at the end of October 1977, that is, about two months after Samuel Alemayehu left for Tigrai. Kiflu Tadesse's departure was related to the general plan of shifting the leadership center to the Gonder area. It was his intention to meet CC member Tselote, who was with the EPRA in Begemidir. He also hoped to find ways of getting some arms for the urban units. Another major aim of his trip was to find ways for the Begemidir IZ to escort more EPRP members to the EPRA. Although the departure of EPRP members from the urban areas to the EPRA held areas had increased, a large number of members still remained trapped.

As was indicated above, many members of the YL, ELAMA and other mass organizations had gone underground. Many had been demanding to leave their areas, but the EPRP was unable to meet their expectations. As the number of members going underground increased, shortage of shelter became more acute. Many members who had provided shelter had themselves gone underground or had become victims. Parents became more cautious as they learned of the collaboration of some former EPRP members with the regime. Even leading members of the organization could not find shelters and had to spend most of their time on the streets, in bars, cemeteries, public parks, etc.

Trust, the thread that held the EPRP together was fast disintegrating. Many had become suspicious and skeptical. Because of the violent repression, pessimism was replacing the optimism of a year or so earlier.

The urban defense structure of the EPRP was exposed to grave dangers and its members faced greater risk than other EPRP members. Despite the introduction of the political commissar system in the defense structure and efforts to conduct political discussions with the members, very little was achieved, as there was little or no time for political studies. Because of the need for centers where the units could keep their arms, conduct training and hold meetings, defense unit members were exposed to a fairly large number of EPRP members and they knew many houses. Due to shortage of arms and other difficulties, after September/October 1977, defense activity was significantly reduced when compared to the previous year.

With the severe repression and loss of leading members, the composition of the EPRP underwent a noticeable change. Many committees were filled with less experienced members. For example, two of the six Addis Abeba IZ members serving in that committee in mid-1977 had joined the struggle in 1974. By 1976, they were elected to the YL CC and then transferred to the EPRP zonal committees, which elected them to the Addis Abeba IZ.

Although weakened and crisis-ridden, the EPRP structure was still in place around the country until the last months of 1977. In Addis Abeba, the party and the YL IZ committees and zonal committees still functioned, and the Sidamo and Shoa IZs were operational. The Gojjam and Begemidir zonal committees and the party structures in Wello were functioning. The newly reorganized groups in Jimma, Harer and Arsi still existed. However, from the last weeks of November 1977 to January 1978, the EPRP underwent the most severe crisis in its history.

In Addis Abeba, IZ members Mekonnen Belay and Muhidin Mohammed began collaborating with the regime. In May 1977, Mekonnen Belay, who was in charge of the EPRP publishing enterprise, Kokeb Publishers, was nominated by the IZ to become a member of the newly formed zone two. The previous zonal committee had been dissolved for fear of infiltration.[41] Mekonnen played a crucial role in reorganizing the zone and establishing contacts with the scattered members. When Germatchew fell victim in June 1977, Mekonnen was elected to represent his zone in the Addis Abeba IZ. In September, Mekonnen was arrested and tortured at Higher 25 prison. He collaborated with the regime and informed on zonal committee and other members, including his close friends and even his girl friend.

Throughout his stay in prison, Mekonnen tried to provide information about the two important EPRP moles in the government, Dereje I and II.[42] Mekonnen knew them only by their code names and did not know in which institutions they were. He revealed their association with Kifle, an EPRP member and a veteran activist who had an important role in organizing the teachers' opposition. Kifle was a former member of the Addis Abeba EPRP IZ and had been sent to the Shoa area, where the repression was not as severe. He was one of those EPRP members that the organization wanted to preserve. Kifle was summoned to Addis Abeba to give guidance and orientation to the newly formed Addis Abeba IZ, which had been weakened by the loss of Germatchew. Kifle never contacted the EPRP; he disappeared the moment he arrived in Addis Abeba. Sometime later, it was learned that he had been arrested as soon as he arrived in Addis Abeba. Kifle knew the EPRP "moles" in the state structure. Even though he was severely tortured, Kifle never gave in. While the interrogation process and the effort to find the two "moles" were underway, the Derge decided to bring Mekonnen under its custody and demanded that Higher 25 transfer him. The Higher kebele refused to obey the order on the ground that it was about to land on an important piece of information. One morning, armored vehicles surrounded the kebele and Mekonnen was taken and executed.[43] It still remains a mystery who ordered Mekonnen's transfer and why he was executed while he was collaborating with the regime.

When the IZ secretary, Muhidin Mohammed, was arrested in January 1978, there was no CC member in the Addis Abeba area to take responsibility and make arrangements to overcome the crisis. Muhidin, who had joined the IZ the previous year, knew its strengths and vulnerabilities, its activities, code of operations, and more. He knew a fairly large number of members who worked with the IZ and members of EPRP affiliated organizations, such as the YL and ELAMA. He knew the whereabouts of money, arms and other valuables. In short, Muhidin had a wealth of information that was transformed into gold in the hands of the regime, which was desperately trying to bring about an end to the EPRP. Muhidin disclosed all that he knew and that last straw broke the back of the EPRP, which already was undergoing severe repression and internal crisis. Muhidin's public denunciation and castigation of the EPRP further demoralized members and sympathizers. However, despite his collaboration, the Derge did not spare his life.

In the first months of 1978 again, another major disaster befell zone three of Addis Abeba. With the help of an informant, the Derge was able to arrest the entire members of the committee that had congregated briefly in the Kazanchis area. The majority of them were legally functioning members; among them, Nolawi Abebe, a veteran activist.

Repeated efforts were made to reconstitute the IZ, but the situation was so difficult that the newly formed committees could hardly operate. Contact between the various levels of committees and members was broken. The absence of a strong central authority in the urban centers made the EPRP extremely vulnerable and the problems continued compounding. The zones in Addis Abeba were victimized one after another. Hundreds and thousands of members were left without leadership. Unable to regroup, some EPRP cells and individuals survived on their own for quite some time. Some joined the army at a later date. Many of them lost contact. In the meantime, the Derge intensified the repression and many more members were arrested, tortured and executed. Some members found themselves helpless and were forced to collaborate.

Furthermore, the total absence of defense activity allowed the regime and *Abyot Tebeka* officials to conduct their repression more intensively and without fear. It was during this period that the most massive arrests and killings were conducted.

The crisis that befell the Addis Abeba IZ, which served as the center, had a snowball effect on EPRP structures in other parts of Ethiopia. Some were cut off from the center and were left on their own. The YL, ELAMA and other mass organizations were seriously affected.

Repression continued in Begemidir well into 1978 and 1979. The Begemidir and Gojjam IZ, being close to EPRA-held territory, was able to send many of its members there. As the situation in the Gonder urban areas worsened, most organizational activities were shifted to the rural areas of that province (the case of the Begemidir and Gojjam IZ will be discussed in greater detail in the next chapter).

At the beginning of 1978, a major disaster befell the EPRP structure in Shoa. It is believed that an insider(s) had provided the Derge with information. EPRP members, houses, documents and arms fell into the hands of the government. This scenario was repeated in the southern part of the Wello province. With the help of informers, the military regime took swift and violent measures against the Wello zonal committee and many members were lost. Some of them left for the EPRA, while others went underground living among the peasantry. Many decided to renounce their past and join the "self-denunciation" campaign.

During this period, CC member Fikre Zergaw, who was assigned in the

Wello area, was arrested in Dubti and brought to Addis Abeba. He was trying to lay down an EPRP network extending from Dessie, the capital city of Wello, to Djibouti. The network was to aid EPRP members fleeing the repression in the cities.[44] Even though tortured, Fikre did not give in. Fikre Zergaw, who refused to collaborate and was defiant all throughout, was one of the legendary figures of the prison population. He was executed in the late seventies or early eighties. Fikre Zergaw was a graduate of the Addis Abeba University law school and the Economic Department of the University of Illinois, USA.

Sometime before Fikre's arrest, KM, another leading EPRP member was apprehended in Dubti. Initially, KM was able to hide his identity, however, when he reached Addis Abeba, Tesfaye Mekonnen and Shewandagne Belete, former colleagues at the Ministry of Land Reform identified him.[45] Tesfaye Mekonnen belonged to the MALRED group, while Shewandagne initially belonged to the WAZ League, but later changed allegiance, joined the Ethiopian Workers Party and became a leader of that group.

The Sidamo IZ

The Sidamo IZ, in charge of EPRP organizations in Sidamo, Gamu Goffa, Bale, Southern Shoa and Arsi, was one of the relatively well organized EPRP institutions. As was indicated in *The Generation*, Part I, the party committee in Sidamo was among the first EPRP structures to be laid down. Subsequently, EPRP and Youth League committees were formed in Bale and Gamu Goffa provinces. The Gamu Goffa zonal committee had its regional committees in the Gardula, Chencha, Felege Newaye and Gelebe and Hamer Bako awerajas. By 1976, the total EPRP membership of Gamu Goffa was estimated in the hundreds.[46] The majority of members were indigenous students or teachers. The party structure produced its own publications.

The Sidamo IZ functioned properly until the unexpected execution of committee secretary Melaku Marcos in March 1977.[47] Melaku's loss resulted in a very serious leadership crisis. In order to follow military activities in Sidamo, which included preparations for rural armed struggle, a three-man military commission was formed. It included Getachew Kumsa, Berhanu Ijjigu and A. All of them were veteran activists and qualified organizers. Berhanu and A. were from the Addis Abeba party structure. Besides the need to send them to a safer area, Berhanu Ijjigu was selected because of his knowledge of EPRP affairs in Sidamo and A. was one of the first EPRP members to take part in the leadership of the Urban Armed Wing. Besides his role in the Sidamo Military Commission, Berhanu Ijjigu became a member and the Secretary of the Sidamo IZ and functioned as a liaison between the two committees. A former Addis Abeba IZ member, "Asfaw" and another zonal committee member of the Addis Abeba area also joined the Sidamo IZ. Kept under this arrangement since mid-1977, the Sidamo IZ became self-sufficient.

Among the members of the Sidamo IZ was Agere Addisu, a veteran activist who, as a security precaution, was confined to a room in a row of townhouses. In order to avoid the attention of the neighbors, he talked only in whispers for such a long time that he could not recover his voice back for quite a while.

The new Sidamo IZ under the leadership of Berhanu undertook the renewal of the rectification process which had been discontinued because of the death of the secretary, Melaku Marcos. During the rectification process, it was found that one of the major shortcomings of the Sidamo IZ was in its work among the peasantry. It was decided to send as many members as possible to rural areas, especially to the Yirga Alem and Wellaieta areas, where the EPRP had already laid down some structure.

Major projects of the Sidamo Military Commission (MC) included training members for the urban military structure, and following up and executing decisions regarding the rural armed struggle. In line with this plan, after organizing and training members of the defense units, the Sidamo MC, assisted by an insider, arranged a bank operation in Shashemene.

A planned operation took place on a Saturday, in October 1977. The guard was overpowered but he was left untied with only one EPRP member on the look out. When he had the opportunity, the guard attacked the EPRP member and called the police. Despite the setback, the units tried to escape with a quarter of a million birr, but the police spread the news that Somali insurgents were in the area. The word reached the nearby market where thousands of peasants had congregated. The alerted peasants, some on foot and some on horseback, pursued the EPRP members and killed most of them. The government recovered a portion of the cash.

Another major setback befell the Sidamo IZ when Berhanu Ijjigu fell victim in the Negele area. The EPRP had a contact system known as the "mechanism" which was used to introduce only the concerned individuals, avoiding a third party. In one such incident, when three attempts resulted in failure, a member of the Sidamo leadership, Berhanu Ijjigu, went out to meet the individual. When he reached the area, he discovered that the meeting was arranged near the Negele army headquarters. As he waited for his contact, a military officer approached Berhanu and asked him who he was and what he was doing in the area.

At the time, the Ethiopian army was at a heightened alert, because of the Ethio-Somali conflict. Berhanu was slim, tall and had Somali-like features. When he realized the danger, Berhanu tried to escape, but he was shot and killed.

Berhanu was one of the founding members of the EPRP and had served the organization under different capacities. A veteran activist, he was one of the leaders of the teachers' movement. He was an expert in organization building and was of tremendous importance to the EPRP. His early death was a colossal disaster for the entire organization, especially the Sidamo IZ.

Another major project of the Sidamo IZ was launching a Southern Front of the EPRA, a decision that had been made by the EPRP CC in 1975. As was mentioned in Chapter II, the first attempt in 1976 resulted in failure and the Sidamo IZ prepared a report identifying the reasons for that failure. Melaku discussed the commencement of a second effort with the Military Commission of the EPRP CC at the beginning of 1977. According to Melaku Marcos's report, the 1976 effort had failed due to lack of qualified military and political leadership, an unsuitable choice of area in which to conduct armed struggle, poor political work among the people of the area and poor communication of the military units with the urban party structure. Furthermore, the Land Reform Proclamation of 1975 had an important bearing on peasant readiness to follow EPRP's lead.

After identifying the causes of the previous failure, preparation for the second attempt began. Bolloso wereda in the Wellaieta aweraja was chosen as a possible site to begin the second round of the armed struggle. That area was chosen for its good terrain and proximity to Gamu Goffa and the Kembatta areas. It was also an area where the EPRP had conducted some political work among the peasantry.

By mid-1977, six indigenous members who had been trained by the EPRA in Assimba arrived in Sidamo. Other indigenous members, including some from the Gamu Goffa area, such as Belatchew (code name) were still in training in Assimba. The EPRP leadership sent some arms, while the Sidamo IZ itself purchased a few more. It was concluded that the group had sufficient arms and ammunition to arm the first two platoons of about forty-five people, including the leadership. After the preparation was completed, the Sidamo MC and the IZ decided to send the units to Bolloso. In October 1977, one of the platoons was sent to the specific area where the armed struggle would begin. The second platoon was to follow, but was delayed. The plan called for the second unit to pick up their arms from a designated place in a rural area. For security reasons, the plan was amended. It was decided that the group should carry its arms straight from Soddo, the capital of Wellaieta.

On the night that the second group was to leave Soddo, exactly an hour before the departure of the group, the place where the platoon was to pick up its weapons was suddenly surrounded by government forces. As a result, all of the arms were seized and three EPRP members were captured. The platoon could not be dispatched to the countryside. Due to heightened government security efforts and the crisis in the Soddo area, some of the members of the army command were unable to go and join the first platoon. Moreover, leading EPRP members had to stay away from the area.

After this incident, the *Addis Zemen* newspaper reported, "about three thousand two-hundred birr... and a large quantity of ammunition for an M-1 rifle was found." The newspaper concluded: "This proves that the EPRP has contact with the CIA."[48] The newspaper also wrote that a large quantity of ammunition was also seized in Soddo in the jurisdiction of the Shamba Kilena peasants' association.

Communication was lost with the unit that had gone into the Bolloso rural area. A few weeks later, the platoon was conducting agitation when it was confronted by the government's peasants' militia and ordered to discontinue the campaign. When the platoon refused to heed the order, a militiaman attacked Zewdu Kebede. Members of the units then retreated and opened fire, killing three of the peasant militia.

The news spread in the Wellaieta *aweraja*. The administrator, Simon Galore, mobilized the peasants' militia, the peasants' associations, POMOA, and began a military campaign. Within a few days, the EPRP platoon, whose contact with the rest of the EPRP structure in Sidamo was severed, faced a massive military force in the Koisha area. In the battle that ensued, nine members of the platoon were killed. Three others were captured in the Kindo Hangala area, including Paulos Sorsa, an activist who had participated in the attempt on the life of Mengistu in 1976.

The preparation that had taken more than two years resulted in a major disaster. The involvement of the peasantry on the side of the Derge spurred more doubts about the course of the rural armed struggle and it had a tremendous impact on the EPRP. Besides, that failure was a major setback for EPRP's efforts to consolidate the rural armed struggle. As indicated in Chapter V, one of the reasons why a Southern EPRA Front had to be launched was to provide sanctuary for EPRP members, and the defeat left the urban organization exposed to danger.

The Sidamo IZ abandoned its preparation for an armed struggle and shifted its attention to political and organizational activities. The IZ moved its center from Soddo, where it had operated from for three years, to Shashemene. Despite the crisis in Soddo and the stepped-up repression in the other parts of Sidamo, the EPRP was able to survive in the area due to the Sidamo IZ's organizational activities in the countryside. However, in early 1978, a major disaster struck the IZ itself. The Sidamo IZ was conducting a meeting in a house regarded as safe, in Kuyera, in the northern part of the province, where the EPRP had no visible organizational activity. The house belonged to Doctor X, a surgeon who was a member of the Ethiopian military and an EPRP member as well. While the IZ was conducting its meeting, the house was surrounded by kebele and *Abyot Tebeka* members of the Awasa and Kuyera areas. The Awasa kebele members came to Kuyera looking for a brother of the Doctor, who was being sought for "anti-revolutionary" activities. Forcing their way into the house, the kebele officials found members of the most important organizational institution of the EPRP in the Sidamo province, the IZ. The committee members were arrested and most of them were executed. Among them was Agere Addisu.

After severe torture, the Doctor's life was spared because of his service to the Ethiopian military. He was one of the few surgeons, along with some Cubans, who had served during the Ethio-Somali conflict. It was believed that Cuban Doctors had pleaded for his life. As a prisoner, he was escorted to hospitals to perform operations.

The disaster that struck the Sidamo IZ took place at about the same time as that of the Addis Abeba IZ. Due to the absence of a leading institution, structures under the Sidamo IZ were left on their own. One of the members of the MC, Getachew Kumsa, survived for the moment, but was arrested while he was camouflaging himself as a businessman involved in the sale of sheep. In October 1985, that is, several years later, Getachew Kumsa, along with ten suspected EPRP members, Yohannes Germatchew, Mahdi Kemal, Zewdu H/Micheal, an artist, Sulieman Mohammed,Tewedros Asfaw, Getachew Assefa, Zerihun Banti, Yemane Berhan Berhane, Asnake Getachew and Teshale Wondimu were taken out of prison and executed.[49]

EPRP Activities in Harerghe

The first provisional zonal committee in Harerghe was formed in 1974. From that time onwards, EPRP organizing efforts showed results. In Dire Dewa and other places, EPRP structure was in place by 1975 and[50] organizational work was conducted among the workers of the Cement, Chandris, Cotton, Railway Station, Malaria Eradication Center and other places. An ELAMA structure was also laid down, as was that of the underground women's organization, in which the energetic and bright female activist Nebila Abdosh participated. Nebila was a victim of the Red Terror who refused to give in to the sexual whims of her prison tormentors.

The Harerghe IZ included the zonal committees in Harer, Dire Dewa, Jijjiga and Asebe Teferi. In 1977, the Harerghe EPRP structure recruited thousands of members into the YL and the mass organizations, and hundreds into the party. Muslims and Christians, and large numbers of Aderes, Oromos, Somalis, Tigrayans and Amharas took part in EPRP related activities. Besides the radical political agenda of the EPRP, its policy on the national issue was an important element in bringing the diverse groups closer together. The EPRP was a microcosm of the province.

As was indicated in Chapter II, the entire EPRP leadership of Dire Dewa was imprisoned in mid-1976. With the declaration of the war of annihilation in September 1976, the EPRP structure in Dire Dewa and Harer was hit hard, and yet another severe repression was conducted during the last months of 1976. Unlike the repression of mid-1976, which in the main was a mass arrest, the one that took place in the last months of 1976 was systematic and selective. The confession of a YL member to Derge intelligence at Kelade Amba made this effort very effective.[51] Using the information provided by the youth as a starting point, the Derge intelligence dismantled almost the entire local organization. Of the EPRP members imprisoned, ten were executed when the escape tunnel they were digging was discovered. Among those executed were Mekonnen, Mohammed Yusuf, Mohammed Taher and Sisay Tessema.

Many more were executed in mid-1977. Zewdu Kebede was one of about one hundred prisoners from Dire Dewa who were transported to the execution site. Zewdu Kebede and five other prisoners jumped from the truck; three escaped unharmed, including Zewdu. He had recognized the officer in charge of the operation as Major Samuel, who served at the military camp where Zewdu grew up. Zewdu went to the residence of the major and gunned him down and tried to escape. However, he was wounded in a shoot out with pursuing officers and captured. He was executed a few days later.

Since September 1976, the EPRP repeatedly tried to rebuild the local party structures, but the unrelenting repression made that task difficult. When the need to rebuild became ominously clear, the two-man CC team devised a method in March/April 1977. An orientation course was given to members of the Harer and Jimma provisional zonal committees, some of whom had escaped the repression in their areas and were in hiding in Addis Abeba. After the orientation, the members were sent back to their areas. Because of MEISON's departure from the political scene and the sudden disappearance of POMOA representative Abdulahi Yusuf, the form of repression was modified.

Following the return of some of the leading EPRP activists to Harerghe, the leadership focused on two major concerns: rebuilding the EPRP structure, and deploying an armed group in the hinterlands of the Webera awaraja.

Since the first month of 1977, the newly reconstituted EPRP Harer leadership tried to establish links with isolated committees and individuals and conducted propaganda activities. The leadership did indeed reconstitute the EPRP structure in Harerghe and the party resumed full scale activities. However, in mid-1977, a significant part of the Harerghe province was transformed into a war zone when WSLF and SALF forces overran the area.

The EPRP leadership in Harerghe had been instructed to resume the study of areas where an armed struggle might be commenced. That study had begun in 1976, but it had been disrupted when the repression was intensified in the middle of the year. With the idea of initiating an armed struggle, some EPRP members of the Harerghe area had been sent to the EPRA in Assimba for military training.

Following the reconstitution of the EPRP structure in Harerghe, the party formed an armed group that conducted propaganda work in the Webera awaraja of Harerghe until the Ethio-Somali conflict intensified. The armed group did not initiate military activities. Knowing that contact with the center could be lost, the armed group was made autonomous. It was also entrusted with contacting the WSLF and the Somali Obo organization. When the Ethio-Somali conflict intensified, the EPRP group was pushed further away from its initial areas and moved to the Habro awaraja, which borders the Arsi, Bale and Harerghe provinces and has a favorable terrain for guerrilla warfare. The armed group survived the ordeal until mid-1978 when its existence came to an abrupt end due to a defector.

The EPRP leadership in Harer infiltrated WSLF forces.[52] One of the reasons for the infiltration was to minimize the killings (mostly Christians) perpetrated by the WSLF. Furthermore, the EPRP leadership of the Harer zone formed a committee to remain behind the lines in case Harer fell under the control of the Somali regime. One of the main tasks of this committee was to stay behind and rally resistance against the aggression of the Somali regime. The committee to remain behind the line was composed of Adere and Oromo EPRP members. During those days, followers of the Christian religion and Amharic speakers were the main targets of the Somali regime.

The EPRP structure in Harer had a major setback during the first months of 1978 when a member of a YL zonal committee, Bizuworqe, changed allegiance and provided Derge intelligence with detailed information on EPRP activities in the urban areas. Bizuworqe also informed on EPRP members, Yohannes Demisse and Dawit Negussie who had infiltrated the Seded and the WAZ groups. Both of them had provided the EPRP with invaluable information, such as, names of members to be arrested, houses to be raided, etc.[53] During this period, eleven EPRP members were killed in a shootout. Included in this group were, Enquo Taye, a member of the Harer EPRP leadership, Wendewosen Lemma, a member of the defense committee, and teacher Solomon. They had been staying in Adele, a town about twenty five km from Harer. Government forces went there looking for a duplicating machine that had been "confiscated" from the Medhani Alem School in Harer.

After the massive repression in 1977/1978, a large number of EPRP members and sympathizers in Harer were placed under detention and forced to undergo a "rehabilitation" program. A few months later, the regime released a good number of them after concluding that they had joined the "revolutionary" camp. However, about fifty of them were rearrested on the grounds that they had links with the armed units in Habro and Chercher aweraja, they did not provide the Derge with names of key EPRP members, did not disclose organizational secrets and did not provide details about the EPRP rural structure. Besides, they were accused of infiltrating political groups allied with the Derge.

EPRP Activities in Keffa

To reconstitute the EPRP structure and revitalize its activities and to provide leadership, a number of leading activists, including Taher Abdu and nurse Tigist were sent to the Keffa province during the last months of 1976 and early 1977. Following the arrival of these members, a provisional leadership committee for the Keffa area was formed and it resumed operation, though at a reduced and subdued level when compared to the condition in 1975, that is, before it was severely repressed.

EPRP committees were reorganized in the Limu, Keffa, Bonga and Jimma awerajas and in a short time, the EPRP mobilized a large following. An obvious advantage of the EPRP in the Keffa province was that none of the other political groups had any meaningful following. Perhaps that was why the EPRP was able to infiltrate most of these groups, which in mid-1977 were involved in a fierce competition among themselves. The MALRED and the Seded were easy targets; both accepted EPRP members whom they believed had changed allegiance. Recruitment was initiated in the prisons and to counter Seded's recruitment drive, its rival Waz League tried to see that imprisoned EPRP members never left prisons.[54]

The EPRP had recruited teachers and students. The Teachers' Association in Jimma was very well organized, and[55] it was in the Teachers' Training Institution that an important part of the movement in Jimma began.

The EPRP leadership committee of Keffa which based its operations in the rural area, initiated an armed struggle in Gepa Gepa Sedeni, a mountainous area bordering the Keffa and Illubabor provinces. A group of about twenty armed EPRP activists began operations in the area, but soon found many of the requisite conditions for conducting armed struggle lacking. The leadership was told to abandon the idea.

In mid-1977, some members of the zonal committee were killed in a shootout with government security forces. Among the victims was the secretary of the zone, Taher Abdu, a veteran EPRP activist who had formerly belonged to the party structure in Chilalo, Arsi province.

Sometime after he reached the Keffa town of Gera, Taher Abdu operated disguised as a Sheikh. He communicated with Gezahegne Esatu, another member of the leadership in Keffa and a fugitive, through a security guard at the microwave station where Gezahegne was hiding. On a day when the guard was away, some officials came to the station on government related business. Gezahegne, who was inside the station, thought he was surrounded and, after an exchange of gunfire, managed to escape.

Unaware of the incident, the guard returned to the station and was arrested. After being tortured, he led security forces to the residence of the "Sheikh". Security forces found a religious person performing his prayer, and they left the house. Shortly, however, they realized who the praying man could be and returned. The "Sheikh" tried to escape. In the shoot out that ensued, Taher Abdu, the "Sheikh" and other leading EPRP activists were killed, including some peasants. The government could not identify the "Sheikh", but his corpse was displayed for over half a day at the Gera police station.

Youth League Activities

In mid-1977, the YL organization of the Addis Abeba branch published papers focusing on issues related to kebeles. Most of the publications were geared to a specific audience and addressed the problems of the kebele inhabitants. As the "voices" of the kebeles, the papers were so successful that an article in the *Addis Zemen* newspaper "warned" inhabitants to be wary of the EPRP which "changes its color like a chameleon."[56]

In mid-1977, the YL organization in Addis Abeba, in coordination with party structures formed "Pioneers' Organizations" (*Tadagi Wetatoch Maheber*) for children under fourteen, at the kebele level. With the help of local YL committees, the pioneer kebele groups produced their own publications and, by August 1977, there were more than twenty-five such publications, many of which were written by pioneer activists themselves. The regime did not know about the existence of the pioneer groups until they made themselves visible on the "Buhe" holiday, held each year in mid-August. "Buhe" is a religious holiday where groups of male youth go from house to house chanting special religious and traditional songs and receive gifts either in cash or in kind.

In many of the kebeles of Addis Abeba, the pioneers went from house to house in groups of seven to ten and conducted anti-government agitation instead of chanting the traditional religious songs. Some of the pioneer groups composed and recited their own lyrics, with strong political content. Some of them went as far as mentioning the EPRP in their chanting. Kebele and *Abyot Tebeka* officials who had not anticipated such activities, targeted some of the pioneers they thought to be the key figures. Beginning in August 1977, pioneers, who were as young as ten years old were hunted and arrested by kebele officials.

Other activities of the YL included the formation of small bands of musicians. YL artists composed revolutionary songs, including Assimba, *'Betegel Memot Hiewete'*, *'Alegezam'*, *'Aleferam'*, *'Enachenefalen'*.

Beginning in September 1977, the formation of government-sponsored kebele youth associations became a major concern of the YL organization. Many youth, mainly EPRP YL members had joined the youth's associations as a last hope of survival.

To discuss the condition of the YL, a Youth League CC meeting was called in September 1977. The meeting was attended by almost all of its members and an EPRP CC member. Aklilu Hiruy, the former Secretary of the YL was, by then, in detention. His younger brother Tito Hiruy was elected Secretary.

The meeting was held when some Ethiopian mothers had begun taking active part in the anti-Derge resistance and conducting demonstrations. The impact of the mother's involvement was witnessed at the YL meeting and in the youth's activities of the period.

Among the issues discussed at the meeting was the prevalent Ethiopian political situation, the condition of the YL, and the handling of the newly formed kebele youth associations. It was decided to move the standing committee of the YL to a rural area in the Begemidir province. In order to handle day to day tasks of the YL, a three-man secretariat operating from Addis Abeba was to be formed. It was to be enforced by sub-secretariats formed for each region. In line with the decisions of the Second Plenum of the EPRP of 1976, YL CC members were also assigned to zonal and inter-zonal committees in different parts of Ethiopia.

The YL CC meeting was abruptly interrupted when a squad member assigned to oversee the safety of the gathering reported that an armed person had entered the compound. Without digesting the information, a YL CC member in charge of supervising the meeting place concluded that the whole group was surrounded and instructed all of the members to disperse. In the midst of this confusion, a shot was heard. It was learned that Tito had mistakenly fired at an EPRP squad. Fortunately, no one was hurt.

The YL CC members scattered in all directions and ran away from the compound. The first group, which included the EPRP CC member, jumped over a fence and landed on a three-feet deep dung heap next to a cattle pen. They jumped over two more fences and reached a lighted corner where a maid was seated by a veranda washing dishes. It was late at night and the maid was singing. They approached her to ask where the main gate was. The lady stared at the group and was utterly speechless. Unable to get a reply, they took off and continued jumping over fences until they reached a street. The frightened maid also stood up and ran away.

Some of the YL CC members climbed over the roof tops of houses and jumped from one to another. A heavy weight member went through the roof of a small house and landed on the floor beside a mother and son eating dinner. Another member of this group was caught by the guards protecting the compound as he descended from the roof of a house. However, a squad member following him shot in the air and he was quickly released. When all was over, the only damages were some broken bones.

Over the next day or so, it was learned that the armed man who had entered the compound was a resident and a member of an *Abyot Tebeka* group that belonged to the Democratic Front committee of the EPRP. The YL CC liaison had been informed about the person, his arrival time, and that he would be armed. However, that information had slipped his mind.

Be that as it may, the YL CC indeed tried to shift its center to the Begemidir area. However, because of the loss of capable members, the YL leadership found it very difficult to implement its decisions. YL members who were assigned to the sub-secretariats, the propaganda and zonal committees, were victimized one after another. The tempo of the crisis and the rate at which dedicated members fell victim was so fast that the YL CC was unable to reorganize itself and move the leadership center elsewhere. The YL leadership felt obliged to stay in the Addis Abeba area until a competent leadership, viable liaison, and a smooth communication system was established.

A few weeks after the leadership meeting, Tito and other YL CC members were arrested at one of their rendezvous. That arrest further exacerbated the crisis and the remaining YL CC members had to shoulder additional tasks. By January 1978, most of them were imprisoned and later executed. Among those arrested were Sirak Teferra, Gezatchew, Gebeyehu, Alemayehu Egzeru and others.

The Derge forced some of the youth leaders to go public against the EPRP. That was another terrible blow to the EPRP in general and the YL in particular, and it had a snow-ball effect on the "denunciation" and "self-denunciation" *(agalte and tegalete)* campaign which was still underway.

Most members of the YL were former members and leaders of the Ethiopian high-school student movement. It was a selfless and dedicated group that provided leadership to the youth movement - a movement that gathered momentum after the student zemetcha in 1974.

The YL CC was a formidable force, upholding the people's cause and struggling for a democratic transformation of the Ethiopian society. It was a monolithic group, loyal to its beliefs. At the same time, it was an ingenious and challenging group whose contribution to the struggle and the EPRP was boundless. It was an idealist group, completely dedicated to its cause and the country's welfare. The members were among the most valiant and finest human beings that Ethiopia had ever produced.

EPRP's Political Activities Abroad

Among the main branches of the EPRP in 1974 were those in Europe and America. Between 1973 and 1976, a relatively large number of mature and politically capable members were summoned to return to Ethiopia. The main goals of the EPRP branches abroad were to conduct political and organizational activities among Ethiopians and to popularize the Ethiopian people's struggle among the international community.

Initially, the structure abroad consisted of the EPRP Foreign Committee (FC) at the top of the ladder. Below the FC were the Regional Committees (RC) in the USA, Europe, the Middle East and Africa. The name RC was designated in the early stages of organizational formation. A few years later, the Regional Committees were renamed as "zonal committees" and fell under the EPRP IZ abroad.

The Foreign Committee was headed by Iyasu Alemayehu, EPRP CC member. Leading activists of the FC were MT and Yosef Mersha. The EPRP FC was in charge of foreign relations and other political activities, including the publication of *Abyot* and other papers. It was entrusted with contacting governments and organizations on behalf of the EPRP.

Because of the absence of a Secretariat, the Derge's excessive repression and the immense work load, the EPRP CC paid little attention to EPRP activities abroad. Due to lack of other means of communication, contact was maintained through letters. Physical contact was made twice a year on the average and important information reached the FC slowly. Sometimes, the FC would get information through informal channels before the official version arrived.

Despite inadequate communication, most essential information and major party activities were conveyed to the FC. An effort was made to bring the party structure abroad into the internal activities of the EPRP, including the preparation for the First Extended Conference of 1975.[57] When the party inside the country conducted a rectification movement, the structure abroad was also informed about the process.

The first members of the leading committees of the structure abroad were appointed by the EPRP CC. All of them had been among the founding members of the organization. Members of the FC and other leading committees remained in their position for several years. Inside the country, that practice gradually changed after the convocation of the first Extended Conference of 1975, which adopted a new constitution with an electoral procedure. In the EPRP structure abroad, the practice mentioned above remained the same even after the adoption of the new constitution.[58]

The main social base of the EPRP structure abroad was the student population, which was a fraction of the Ethiopian citizenry abroad. The Ethiopian population abroad then consisted of students, a few immigrants and professionals. By 1974/75, the student movement had already split.[59] The majority of the student population supported the EPRP, while the minority became affiliated with MEISON. The student movement served as a forum where the EPRP could conduct both political and organizational activities especially at the annual student congresses.

As was indicated above, the EPRP structure abroad sent many members to the EPRA. Most of them were trained in the Middle East. One of these groups was trained in acupuncture, which was a medical staple of the EPRA. The FC conducted negotiations with governments and organizations, including China and the PLO, on behalf of the EPRP. EPRP delegates also attended meetings of left and radical groups and organizations in Europe, such as the Italian group known as A'Luta Continua and the political wing of the Irish Republican Army, Sinn-Fein, etc.[60]

The FC informed the public about events in Ethiopia. It also sent, through the ELF, the arms which had been obtained in the mid-1970s. In order to enhance the leadership of the EPRP abroad, the Extended Conference of 1975 had elected a member of the EPRP RC of America as an alternate member of the EPRP CC. However, because of the conflict within the structure abroad, the extent of which the EPRP CC was not aware of, that decision did not reach the elected person.[61]

Regional Committee in North America

The EPRP group in the USA was one of the four leading groupings that had formed the EPRP in 1972. Ever since the foundation of the EPRP, the group in the USA had remained an important structure from which EPRA members were recruited.[62]

The population of Ethiopians living abroad in the 1970s was not known, however, there were a good number, mostly students, who were from well to do families. The Ethiopian Students Union in North America (ESUNA) served as the center of activity. At its peak in 1977/78, ESUNA's registered membership was estimated at four to six hundred. It was a well-organized union with chapters in some major cities of North America. The EPRP structure, whose membership was only a fraction of the student population, was laid down in those areas where ESUNA was active. In the early 1970s, ESUNA had split into at least three factions. However, in the mid-1970s, one of the factions that supported the political line of the EPRP mustered support and dominated student activities, until another group split and formed what was known as the Up-ESUNA in the late 1970s. ESUNA had its own publications and study materials were prepared whenever situation demanded.

In 1975, the upper echelon of the EPRP leadership in North America was the Regional Committee and under it came the sub-regional committees for New York, Washington, D.C., Los Angeles, Canada, Boston, and other cities.

Major activities of the EPRP structure in North America included political study sessions, fund raising events, rallies and demonstrations supporting the EPRP and the struggle or exposing the repression of the military regime. The 1975 rally organized by ESUNA to commemorate EPRP's public declaration of its existence was attended by thousands of people.

Even though EPRP members in the USA had facilities to publish an internal party journal, that did not happen. Partly because of the relationship between the regional committee in the USA and the FC [to be discussed below], very little effort was made to conduct in-depth studies on issues related to Ethiopian economic, political and social conditions. According to one of the participants of the movement, this phenomenon could be attributed to Chinese influence, which focused on propaganda activities.[63] Unlike the rest of the Ethiopian radical generation of the mid-seventies, the radicals of ESUNA were strong supporters of Mao Tse Tung's thought and most of their readings were influenced by Chinese literature. The rest of the Ethiopian radical generation had distanced itself from the lines advocated by the Chinese and, since the early seventies, many had become critical of Chinese policies.

EPRP Committees in Europe, Middle East and Africa

Since the early 1970s, the EPLO/EPRP had established branches in a number of European countries: France, Holland, Germany, Italy, Hungary, the former Soviet Union, Yugoslavia and other European countries. The EPLO/EPRP structures in these countries played an important role in the formative stage of the organization. As was discussed in the first part of *The Generation*, when the organization shifted its center to Ethiopia, a large number of active members left for home and that departure had an adverse effect on EPRP's activities in Europe. Particularly noticeable was the effect of the departure of almost the entire membership of the Regional Committee in 1977. As part of the continuous drive for EPRA recruitment, some EPRP members were sent to the Middle East. At the completion of military training, all of them joined the EPRA.[64]

The EPRP in Eastern Europe had its own set of structures as well. Major activities of the EPRP structure abroad consisted of recruitment among the Ethiopian population and particularly among students, producing EPRP publications, conducting political agitation among Ethiopians, popularizing the Ethiopian struggle among the international community, etc. Except in Italy, where there were many migrant workers, students were the social base of the EPRP structure in Europe.

The entire membership of the EPRP and its YL in Europe (including Eastern Europe) probably did not exceed two hundred.[65] Criteria for party membership remained very strict even after the EPRP Extended Conference of 1975 passed regulations to ease recruitment.

By 1975, the student population in Europe was split, with the majority supporting the EPRP line. However, as the East European governments began supporting the Derge, they imposed restrictions on the activities of students. In due course, student unions came under the control of Derge partisans.

Since the early seventies, the EPLO/EPRP had laid down some structures in the middle-east and some countries in Africa, such as, Egypt, Sudan, Djibouti and Kenya. Even though the EPRP structure in these places was clandestine, it conducted political and organizational activities among the refugee population. Besides, some of these committees were engaged in providing assistance to the EPRA. These included gathering material and finance, providing shelter to wounded and sick EPRA fighters, getting engaged in low level business transactions, contacting governments and establishing relationship with Ethiopian opposition groups.

Problems of the EPRP Structure Abroad[66]

The EPRP structure abroad had some political, as well as, organizational problems. Problems related to questions of organization were reflected in the conflict of the FC, later the IZ, with the RCs, and the RCs with the structures under their jurisdiction. Initially, the problems within the RC in North America were related to differences on political positions and policies of the EPRP, while that of the structure in Europe was in the main organizational. Eventually, however, the political differences assumed organizational form and vice versa.

One of the first problems of the structure abroad was lack of a cohesive organizational committee where the various RCs could be represented. To be sure, the IZ was supposed to be composed of the secretaries of the various RCs. However, as the difference with the RC in North America escalated, since mid-1977, its representative ceased to take part in the activities of the committee.[67] As a result, the IZ existed only nominally for some time and did not conduct meetings as stipulated by the internal regulation.[68]

Political Differences and Organizational Problems

The EPRP structure abroad did not have its own internal journal until that problem was addressed during the rectification movement in 1979/80. It was argued that the absence of an internal journal was a major source for the problems within the organization.

The Regional Committee of North America was the first to raise reservations and differences on some political positions of the EPRP. One of the first of such difference was manifested when the RC in 1974 suggested that the EPRP characterize the system in the former Soviet Union as Social Imperialist.[69] The RC expressed reservations on EPRP's policy (or lack of policy) regarding the nature of the Soviet Union. Both at the First Congress of 1972 and the First Extended Conference of 1975, the EPRP accepted the thesis that the CPSU was a revisionist party. When the RC in North America continued insisting that the EPRP characterize the Soviet Union, the CC member in the FC responded:

> ...[F]oreign parties want us to take positions and this is especially true of ...pro-Chinese groups and parties...our party must move very cautiously and with an overall view of the revolutionary struggle . . . repeating of slogans of others will not help us.[70]

The RC in North America also expressed differences regarding the support that the EPRP gave to the Mozambique Popular Liberation Army (MPLA) led government of Angola.[71] One of the organizations that fought for the independence of Angola, MPLA, had the support of the USSR. As far as the EPRP RC in North America was concerned, MPLA was a puppet organization of the Soviet Union.[72]

In its suggestions for the rectification movement of 1975, the RC in North America opposed the amended article on land issue in the program of the EPRP. The EPRP program tacitly supported nationalization of land.[73] The RC still supported the "land to the tiller" program. The RC expressed reservations on the Provisional Peoples Government (PPG) slogan and demanded that it should not be part of the minimum program of the EPRP. The PPG was one of the issues widely studied and discussed.

The RC also expressed differences on questions of organization. As early as 1975, it proposed, "organizational work conducted among the workers was adequate enough that the EPRP should totally shift to the countryside."[74] The RC came up with this proposal when the EPRP was just beginning to conduct activities among the workers. By 1975, the EPRP had very few worker members.

The RC in North America differed on EPRP's response to the call for the formation of a front with the Derge. The Derge's call was made public in April 1976. The EPRP responded positively and attached some preconditions before resuming negotiation.[75] The RC on the other hand opposed that idea, arguing that the Derge was a fascist group.[76] The EPRP FC responded,

> [O]ur party has approached the question of the united front in a correct manner...beyond the positions of our party and that of the ultra-left (group)

which rejects the call for the front, we must ask the basic questions: Do we consider fascism established or not? Do we consider the regime a weak one that is being forced into concessions by the mass struggle?"[77]

At the beginning of 1977, leading ESUNA activists characterized the Derge as a national-bourgeois and a progressive force to be supported in the course of the National Democratic Revolution. However, before ESUNA activists pursued their new political thinking and direction to its logical conclusion, the Derge became a client of the Soviet Union, which ESUNA activists characterized as an enemy.

The RC also raised disagreements on the question of Eritrea. Around the same time that the EPRP came out in support of Eritrean independence,[78] ESUNA, most of the leadership of which were members of the EPRP RC, reached an opposite conclusion and declared its opposition to Eritrean independence. The article produced by the ESUNA (See Chapter VI) condemned the EPLF leader, Esayeyas Afeworki. That article contributed in souring relations between the EPLF and the EPRP.[79] The EPRP CC member in the FC put out an article elaborating and defending EPRP's position, arguing "[I], myself, believe in the independence of the Basque [Eritrea]. This will help create confidence among the masses, amongst progressives."[80]

The other major issues that the EPRP RC in North America addressed in 1977 was the question of urban armed action. The RC's differences became clearer when *Democracia* No. 11 discussed the issue publicly. The *Democracia* issue came out a year after the urban armed activities of the EPRP were officially launched and it expressed a line similar to that in the PB paper.[81] The RC in North America advocated that the EPRP follow a line like that of China and Vietnam, that is, "since Ethiopia is a semi-feudal and semi-colonial country," the strategy of the revolution should be "encircling the cities from the countryside." Even after the 1975 land proclamation, the RC in North America still believed that the relationship between the Derge and the peasants in the south was antagonistic.[82] The RC opposed the thesis that "it is possible to conduct an armed struggle in the urban areas and if an adequate preparation is made," [both in the urban and rural areas], "in the final analysis it is possible to conduct a popular uprising."[83] The RC was not, however, opposed "to conducting urban military activities as long as they were limited to temporary objectives, ...like raiding banks, assassinating agents and hated military officers."[84]

In line with the PB paper, the EPRP FC refuted the RC's position and asserted that the armed struggle had to be conducted both in the urban and rural areas.[85] The FC further elaborated the relationship between insurrection and the New Democratic revolution, stating "insurrection (which includes peoples revolt and uprisings) forms part of the people's war strategy and is not opposed to the path that the NDR follows."[86] A similar idea was expressed by Mulugeta Zena, the EPRP CC contact person from Ethiopia, to the group in America.[87] In the letter he wrote to the group in America, he stated:

when we discuss the situation in Addis Abeba, we can say that there is an insurrectionary situation....The existence of such a situation doesn't conflict with the strategy of a people's war. In the course of a protracted war, an insurrection is possible, both in the rural and urban areas.[88]

To prove his statements, he then quoted Le Duan, one of the Vietnamese leaders.

Along with differences on political issues, the EPRP structure abroad faced organizational problems as well. There was also concern over the handling of mass organizations and the role of EPRP members within them.

Another area of worry was handling of differences, that is, the internal democracy of the structure abroad. Quite often, members were asked to go out and defend EPRP's new policies at public gatherings, before they themselves were thoroughly convinced, or given adequate information about the issues. When the issue of Eritrean independence was presented at the 17th Congress of ESUE, it was done before EPRP members themselves were convinced.[89] This problem was partly related to the absence of a forum through which members could express their views and pose questions. The leadership groups also failed to conduct discussions with members under their jurisdictions.[90]

The relationship between the party and the mass organizations was another area where the EPRP structure abroad had some problems. Often, ESUNA or ESUE were regarded as the offshoot of the EPRP and that perception might have some repercussion. Some members regarded ESUNA as their political party.[91] The student organizations, particularly ESUNA, had set exacting discipline and moral standards that many Ethiopians found difficult to live up to. At times, students that did not espouse the line advocated by the majority were intimidated.

Many of the problems within the EPRP structure abroad were revealed during the second RM that was conducted around 1979/80. At the end of the RM, the Coordinating Committee enumerated some of the problems and errors. Among these was the violation of one of the guiding principles of the EPRP, democratic centralism. The principle, which was supposed to work from top to bottom and vice versa, had been exercised only from top to bottom. There were bad practices of handling criticism and self-criticism sessions; reports were not properly handled; study sessions were poorly attended; and recruitment was not conducted according to the regulations of the EPRP. Some important information, such as the case of the *faction*, was withheld from the members.[92] There were other serious and unhealthy practices, including the expulsion of party members for raising serious reservations and differences on the lines that the EPRP espoused. The unhealthy practice was committed by the EPRP structure in North America and[93] that fact revealed that the EPRP FC had no other mechanism to control and check the structure under it.[94] Probably because of lack of knowledge of their rights, members did not appeal those violations to higher bodies.[95]

Members who expressed dissatisfaction or differences of opinion were regarded with suspicion. This was the fate of some EPRA members who had gone to the Sudan for medical treatment. They soon found out that party life inside the country was very much different from what they experienced in the Sudan.[96] The way the fighters were handled by the area party structure was worrisome. Report after report reached the leadership inside the country.

Even though not as serious as that of the EPRP group in North America, the EPRP branch in Europe was not immune from problems. From its early days in 1976, the EPRP RC in Europe sent criticisms, recommendations, its views on different issues, etc., to the FC through its contact person, MT. The RC said that it did not get response to its demands and questions and it was not sure whether its proposals were reaching the appropriate leadership committees. The RC also believed that MT was high-handed and authoritarian. Somewhat similar criticisms were made by the previous RC and other EPRP members as well.

One of the contentious issues of the EPRP group in Europe was *Abyot*, the organ of the FC. The former EPRP RC of Europe, which had expressed its disappointment with some of the journal's articles, had demanded that an Editorial Board be formed to include some members of the RC. That RC had also demanded that publication of the journal be suspended until the recommendations were implemented. To the dismay of the RC, the journal continued to be published.[97]

Another issue between the EPRP RC in Europe and the FC was the way that the FC handled affairs in North America. As was indicated elsewhere, the two committees, that is, the FC and the RC in North America, were in open conflict for some time. As the crisis intensified, the RC in Europe intervened and demanded, "2. the problem has to be resolved only through negotiation, therefore, a meeting should be called and attended by the FC and the EPRP RCs of North America and Europe."[98] Furthermore, the RC in Europe demanded that the RC in North America should take part in the production of *Abyot*. Members of the FC and the RCs met and tried to mend the situation, but to no avail.

As the inter-organizational crisis began to appear insoluble, the RC in Europe sent one of its members to the group in North America to discuss issues. The FC condemned that move and argued that the RC committee was conspiring and it had violated the EPRP Constitution, which did not allow horizontal relationships.[99] At the meeting of June 9-11, 1978, the dissident Regional Committee dismissed its secretary, MT, and confined him to his cell. Moreover, the RC held the FC responsible for all the ills of the structure in Europe and decided that the FC should not be involved in its activities.[100] Furthermore, the RC decided to call a congress of EPRP and YL members and issued a circular to that effect.[101]

The meeting, attended by twenty-four EPRP and YL members, was held in Berlin from August 3-8, 1978. The meeting endorsed many of the views entertained by the EPRP RC in Europe. According to the circular of the FC, the purpose of the meeting was "to rally members on an anti-EPRP platform and conduct similar activities at the student congress,"[102] which was to be held sometime during the same period.

A gathering of Ethiopian student unions in Europe was held in Berlin from August 11-18, 1978. This was different from previous gatherings in that none of the usual ceremonies were conducted. EPRP posters, songs, etc., were conspicuously absent. During this period, the leadership of the student union was controlled by supporters of the dissident EPRP RC in Europe. Issues of the agenda included the dangers of Trotskyism, Social Imperialism, the New Democratic Revolution, etc. In an intense discussion, dissident activists grouped around the RC argued that the FC was entertaining the Trotskyite line. Earlier on, the RC in Europe had stated, "[T]he FC has created and is creating a great danger to our struggle. We had sent criticisms regarding the way the FC handled organizational issues, on its ideology and political lines, however, it did not provide a reply."[103]

The students' gathering accused the EPRP of failing to characterize the Soviet Union as Social Imperialist and of adopting a political line contrary to the Maoist doctrines of the New Democratic Revolution, etc.[104] The dissidents expressed opposition to the urban military activity of the EPRP. They also accused the EPRP of making efforts to take power peacefully when it should have initiated armed struggles as early as 1972.[105] Supporters of the EPRP responded with a defense of its political lines. At length, a compromise was reached and the student union was saved from a split, at least temporarily. However, the process of disintegration continued.

The response of the FC was swift. It terminated the party membership of the entire RC in Europe and passed a circular condemning them. In the circular, the FC accused them of failing to fulfill their responsibilities, of participating in anti-EPRP activities, following improper recruitment guidelines, allying themselves with anti-EPRP groups in North America, publishing an unauthorized internal party paper, etc.[106] The FC then made efforts to form a parallel structure, bypassing the RC. Some members were approached to form the new RC. However, according to one of those members, the new RC did not hold a meeting for quite some time.[107] When situations went out of hand, the dissident EPRP RC of Europe demanded that members come up with ideas for resolving the crisis.[108]

As indicated above, the conflict between the FC and the RC of North America first emerged when the RC opposed some EPRP polices. Consequently, the FC became engaged in a continuous struggle with the RC in America. The RC in North America insisted that the EPRP accept its positions and it continued raising the same issues even after the 1975 EPRP Conference had decided on some of them - such as, the nature of the Soviet Union.[109]

The friction between the FC and the RC in North America remained unresolved. At the beginning of 1977, the EPRP RC in America refused to distribute *Abyot*, the publication of the FC. The RC did this on the ground that *Abyot* espoused views that it consistently opposed. Besides, the RC also failed to distribute one issue of *Democracia*. The RC itself was accused of censoring letters from EPRP members.[110] These and other issues were raised in the FC meeting of October 1977. A compromise agreement was reached: the RC of North America would distribute *Abyot* only if it carried news about Ethiopia.[111]

When tension between the FC and the RC in North America mounted, the RC somehow contacted the leadership in Ethiopia and notified that it was not receiving information. In April 1977, the EPRP urban leadership group in Ethiopia established direct contact with the RC in the USA and provided the needed information and party publications.

As the relationship between the FC and the RC in North America deteriorated, the FC demanded a chance to reach EPRP members. However, the RC in North America would not allow that. According to the FC, the RC in North America insulated EPRP members from higher echelons of the party and conducted organizational activities outside the structure. By this time, the RC was voicing its dissent through ESUNA.[112] The conflict between the EPRP FC and the RC in America had been kept secret until it was revealed in *Abyot*. When the Pandora box was opened, it created confusion among members. Besides, the public confrontation unleashed by the FC surprised the EPRP RC in America, which felt that it was being ambushed.[113]

The EPRP CC was aware of some of the problems in the structure abroad, but the gravity was not understood until August 1979, when the crisis had reached a point of no return. The report of the EPRP RC of America, dated April 1978, was presented to the EPRP CC in May 1979. The EPRP RC in North America claimed that it had sent its proposals in writing as early as July 1976.[114] Even though it was aware of the differences with the RC in North America and had expressed its views on some of the questions,[115] the Foreign Committee denied receiving any such report on that date.[116] In the same report, the FC criticized the RC of dogmatism. Most of the lines and policies advocated by ESUNA were considered Maoist.

In mid-1977, the EPRP RC in North America devised means of splitting from the EPRP and wanted to do it without the knowledge of the FC and EPRP rank and file members. In preparation toward the split, members of the EPRP RC in North America prepared a study guide which explained the relationship between ESUNA and the EPRP, emphasizing ESUNA's independence.[117]

In due course, the internal EPRP controversy became public. At the same time, the RC continued building a network separate from the EPRP and sent one of its followers to the Sudan to establish relations with dissident EPRP members. By this time, the RC in North America had already established contact with dissident EPRP members in Europe when two members of the former EPRP RC of Europe came to the USA on a secret mission. Another member of the RC North America, YT, who opposed the political direction of the dissident movement, is believed to have established a direct link with members of the FC and had begun a campaign against the

RC in North America. He also made efforts to rally supporters. In the controversy that ensued, he and six other EPRP members were expelled from ESUNA. In due course, the number of expelled members reached about twenty.

When the 25th Congress of ESUNA was in session during this period, the FC made efforts to reorganize the EPRP structure, bypassing the RC.[118] The FC was able to rally few EPRP members to its side. While the anti-EPRP campaign was still underway, the seeds of further fragmentation were sown within the ranks of ESUNA. Disintegration continued and splinter groups were formed on issues of peripheral importance to Ethiopia, such as, the Chinese and Albanian line of interpreting global contradictions.

Notes to Chapter 8

1. Regarding the conflict with the TPLF, see details in Chapter IX. See also Ethio-Somali Conflict, Chapter IV.

2. See details, Chapter IV.

3. See details, Chapter IX.

4. See details, Chapter IX.

5. See details, Chapter IV.

6. Kiflu Tadesse, The Generation, Part I, Independent Publishers, 1993, page 142.

7. See details Chapter IV.

8. See details, Chapter IX.

9. Authors memorandum, EPRP CC meetings in Gedarif, Sudan, 1979.

10. Author's recollection from the discussion he had with one of the delegates.

11. See details, Chapter IX.

12. EPRP Document, Intra-party Struggle, page 3.

13. Ibid., page 4.

14. Ibid., page 4.

15. Ibid., page 5.

16. Ibid., page 5.

17. Addis Zemen, May 24, 1977.

18. Interview, Y., 1989. Y. was an EPRP infiltrator of MEISON.

19. When the peasant group dispersed, Abebe secretly left for Awasa where he made an arrangement to go to Kenya.

20. It was argued in the MEISON's Critical Assessment that the decision to conduct the May Day demonstration was made by the EPRP leadership. The decision was made by the ELAMA IZ and it was endorsed by the party IZ.

21. Discussion with EA, 1995.

22. MEISON's Critical Assessment, page 20.

23. In an unrelated incident, in the Sidamo province, in the Shashemene area, one of the most notorious killers in the Derge, Major Ali Mussa, executed twenty-six people on May Day of 1977.

24. KT, Interview, 1993. KT was one of the prisoners in Somalia.

25. This is one instance of how the "mechanism" worked. Two members that were to be introduced to each other were given certain distinct identification codes and both parties were informed about the kinds of arrangements to be used. At the designated appointment place, one of them would be waiting for his new acquaintance leaning on a wall, standing only on one foot, with an unlighted cigarette in his mouth and rubbing his left eye. The second one, with one side of his pants rolled up, a stick in his hand and his eye-glasses on his forehead, would approach the first one and ask him what time it was. When the first one responds saying, "I am wearing a rolex watch", the "mechanism" is considered complete and the two will proceed with their tasks. In order to arrange a mechanism, a combination of special clothing, out of the ordinary actions, special movements of the hands or legs, objects that had to be carried in the hands, etc., were used.

26. Some of the prisoners were released some years later.

27. Before he was gunned down at a pre-set appointment, at the Old Airport area, residents of that locality had heard someone exclaiming, "how can you do that to me, you of all people can do that to me". That person was Achameleh who had an appointment on that day at the Old Airport.

28. Jarso had personal acquaintance with some Somalis residing in Addis Abeba. When it was known that he was under surveillance, Jarso was asked to leave for the EPRA. However, he chose to leave the country on his own; a few months later, he arrived in the Sudan.

29. Other members of the Derge Intelligence department included Colonel Teka Tulu, Major Kassahun Tafesse and Colonel Hiruy Haile Selassie. The last one was executed during the Mengistu coup of February 1977. The first two were placed under arrest following the fall of the Derge in 1991.

30. Kiflu Tadesse, op. cit., page 235.

31. Ibid., Chapter II.

32. Ibid., Chapter IV.

33. Berhane Meskel Redda, The Mass Line, page 3.

34. Ibid., page 3.

35. Interview, Melaku (code name), 1996. According to Melaku, the infiltrator was Gesesse, a member of the Derge's special brigade. Gesesse presumably

EPRP Organizational Activities 359

'deserted' the Ethiopian army and went to the bushes, in the hinterlands of Menz and Geshe. Gesesse, a native of the Menz and Geshe area, carried with him communication equipments. After establishing himself as a rebel, Gesesse contacted the Berhane Meskel group. It is believed that Gesesse informed the Derge about the activities of the Berhane group.

36. According to some political detainees who were in prison with Berhane Meskel, he had provided detailed report of EPRP's activities to the military regime.

37. The Assessment of the Ten Years Struggle of the Communist Group within the TPLF, July 1985, page 111.

38. Interview, Debebe, 1993.

39. "EDU's" well-fed appearance helped him get away after an encounter with Derge security officers. "EDU" went to the bar to meet a fellow member. The Derge security officers saw him enter and leave, but did not follow him or arrest him. They might have thought he was a wealthy businessman and they did not even bother to check his ID card.

40. During a personal discussion, a member of the regional command, AD, had attested this fact to the author.

41. See details on page 319.

42. Interview, Y. 1988.

43. Interview, Y. 1988.

44. KM, Interview, 1994.

45. KM, Interview, 1994.

46. Interview, Belatchew, 1989. Belatchew (code name) was a former EPRP member of the Gamu Goffa area. He had been sent to Assimba for military training and he was expected to return to his area following the training.

47. See Chapter V.

48. <u>Addis Zemen</u>, November 16, 1977, page 8.

49. Amnesty International report, May 30, 1991, page 57.

50. Interview GM, a member of the EPRP leadership in Harer. The process of forming the regional YL leadership was completed by December 1975. Among the first members of the YL leadership in Dire Dewa, only two survived the "Red Terror". Seleshi Zewde, Negussie Zenebe and Meneyeleshewa Woubishet perished in the process.

51. AKB, Interview, November 1994. Most of the information regarding the activities in Harer is provided by AKB and GM, both of them members of the EPRP leadership in Harer.

52. According to AKB, a member of the EPRP Harer zonal committee, EPRP members were able to win over the sympathy of Colonel Ezzedin, the commander of one of the battalions. (The first battalions of WSLF to arrive in Harer were known as Ahmed Gura (Gragne) and Abdelkadir Jilla)

53. Bizuworqe was detained by EPRDF following the downfall of the Derge. It was reported that he committed suicide while he was under investigation.

54. Ali, Interview, 1994. Ali was a member of the EPRP regional committee in Agaro and an infiltrator of the Waz League.

55. Kiflu Tadesse, op. cit., page 225.

56. Addis Zemen, July 18, 1977, page 8.

57. Report of the EPRP Regional Committee in North America, page 5.

58. Report on the Rectification Movement of the EPRP IZ abroad, page 5 and Compilation of the Coordinator of the Rectification Movement, page 13. The RM was concluded in April, 1980.

59. Kiflu Tadesse, op.cit., 1993, Chapter III.

60. Interview with a member of the EPRP RC in Europe, 1994.

61. Kiflu Tadesse, op.cit., page 243. ". . Solomon's inclusion created a problem with the Central Committee member in charge of foreign affairs, Iyasu Alemayehu, who did not agree. He was upset because he had not been consulted about the case. As a result, he never informed Solomon [about the decision],. ."

62. Ibid., Chapter III and V.

63. Interview, member of the EPRP RC in America.

64. Among those who were recruited for military training were, T. D/T and Y. from Germany, AH from Hungary, Gemetchu and A. From the Soviet Union, G. former USUAA officer and others. Some of them obtained their training at the EPRA.

65. Interview, M., December 1994.

66. As was indicated in the Preface, the part regarding the activities abroad is based mainly on the outcome of the Rectification Movement conducted in 1979/80. Since the outcome of the RM was part of EPRP's history, it has served as the basis to write EPRP's activities abroad. Furthermore, the report

on the RM sheds light on some of the main problems and difficulties of the organization. The author had sifted through a large collection of documents and had tried to summarize his findings.

67. Circular of RC in Europe to EPRP members, page 3. (Document 5)

68. From an article put out by the EPRP RC in Europe, No.1, page 3.

69. Report of the EPRP RC in the USA, 1978, page 4.

70. Rectification Note's - K's View, page 9. K stands for the EPRP CC member in the FC.

71. See details Chapter I.
A special English language edition of Democracia condemned the military regime for taking no position on the issue of Angola. Angola, which was about to become independent, was the main issue of the OAU meeting held in January 1975. Members of the African organization were divided on the support they gave to the various Angolan organizations struggling for independence. The special issue of Democracia, titled "Position of No Position", was distributed in the OAU meeting hall by reporters who belonged to the EPRP. The Democracia issue carried the decision of the EPRP CC supporting the Soviet backed MPLA government and criticized the military regime for remaining neutral on the grounds that it was the host country for the conference. (Addis Zemen, January 15, 1975)

72. Report of the EPRP Regional Committee in North America, page 6.

73. Kiflu Tadesse, op. cit., Chapter VIII.

74. Ibid., page 6.

75 See details, Chapter II.

76. Report of the EPRP Foreign Committee, page 11.

77. Rectification Notes - K's View, page 3, August 1977.

78. See details in Chapter V.

79. See details in Chapter VI.

80. Our Position on the Basque Struggle, page 3. An unsigned article of the FC, responding to the RC in the USA.

81. See details Chapter V.

82. Report sent to the EPRP CC from the RC in America.

83. 'PB Paper', page 21.

84. Report by Ismail, code name for the EPRP RC in America, to the EPRP Central Committee, page 18. (FC report to EPRP members, page 9)

85. Report by the EPRP Foreign Committee, page 3.

86. Ibid., page 7.

87. The CC contact person to Mulugeta Zena was Samuel Alemayehu.

88. Letter of Mulugeta Zena to the EPRP RC in America.

89. Compilation of the RM, page 11.

90. Report of the RM in Europe, page 7.

91. Report to the RC of America, by a cell known as Alemayehu, pages 10 and 12.

92. Ibid., page 11.

93. Report of the Rectification Committee, page 1.

94. Inside the country, members of EPRP higher institutions, including CC members, used to conduct sessions with members of lower structures.

95. Report of the RM, page 5.

96. Compilation of the RM, pages 16 and 17.

97. Interview, M., 1994. M. Was a member of the EPRP RC in Europe.

98. Circular of the EPRP RC in Europe, page 6.

99. Circular of the FC, page 8.

100. Circular of the EPRP RC in Europe, page 3.

101. Ibid., page 10.

102. Circular of the FC, page 12.

103. Circular, EPRP RC in Europe.

104. Report on the 18th Congress of ESUE, pages 3-10.

105. Ibid., page 10.

106. Hand written circular of the EPRP CC member in the FC, pages 6-10.

107. Interview, GTG, June 1994. GTG was a veteran member of the EPRP.

108. Circular of the EPRP Regional Committee, page 3.

109. Report of RC of America, pages 9-11.
110. Compilation of the RM, page 11.
111. Ibid., page 11.
112. Report of the FC, page 10.
113. Compilation of the RM, pages 17 and 18.
114. Regional Committee Report, page 13.
115. Report of the Foreign Committee, page 11.
116. Foreign IZ, Rectification Movement Report, page 2.
117. Report of the RC in America, page 18.
118. In the midst of this confusion and turmoil, ESUNA members conducted a fund raising event and collected nearly two hundred thousand dollars.

9

The Ethiopian People's Revolutionary Army (EPRA)

The guerillas were not a shadow army, ...The fact that they were so few forced them to greater sacrifices. The first was pain. Forced marches with thirty kilos of supplies on your back and your weapon in your hand--the sacred weapon that could not get wet or be struck, that could not be set down for an instant, walking, crouching, up, down, single file, not speaking, no food, no water, until all the muscles in your body were long-drawn-out wail....Climbing and more climbing, pain and more pain. And the silence....(Eva Luna, Isabel Allende,1988)

At the beginning of 1977, the EPRA group in Assimba had fewer than eighty automatic rifles including kalashinkovs, a large number of manual rifles and two heavy duty mortars. It had no ammunition except those the fighters carried on their backs. Three company-sized contingents were formed in September 1976 and the new development was considered a leap forward.

At the beginning of 1977, the EPRA in Tigrai consisted of two hundred to two hundred fifty fighters, organized in contingents of sixty and seventy. (The size of the army would change drastically by the third month of 1977.) The majority of the members were students who had taken part in the zemetcha of 1975. Fifteen to twenty percent of these were peasants from the Assimba area and individuals with strong peasant backgrounds.

The EPRA consisted of companies, agitation and propaganda departments, "Ta'alim" (the training center), clinics, intelligence units, militia committees; and mass organization committees that handled the political, administrative and organizational activities among the people.

The Life of a Guerrilla Army

The EPRA, which in the main was composed of urban-raised intellectuals and youth, had to overcome a number of hurdles before it was able to adjust to the new environment. As an infant guerilla army, it was subjected to a number of hardships to which many of its members were not accustomed. It encountered the harsh realities of rural life, that is, no means of transportation, inadequate medical care, and a total absence of urban related supplies.

EPRA members were given a few months of political and military training when they arrived at the base area. Until the first months of 1977, training lasted only for a couple of weeks. It was in the training camp that members came to terms with the hard realities of guerilla life. They also became acquainted with the rules by which a military organization was run. Initially, the fighters were oriented about the constitution of the EPRA. Then, they were introduced to the daily routine, military training, criticism and self-criticism sessions, food preparation and sentry duty (wardiya). The training camp had its own command and political leadership. For the most part, the command committee at the training center consisted of members who had formerly belonged to the Ethiopian army or the Airborne.

The basic military institution was known as the "ganta", platoon, and was organized in groups of about twenty. The "ganta" is equivalent to a platoon. Quite often, the entire EPRA forces, including the departments and leadership committees were organized in "ganta" format. The "ganta" command and party committees took part in many of the daily activities of the unit, including "wardiya", that is, sentry. The "ganta" consisted of three categories of members, party, YL and EPRA members. Party members were organized in clandestine cells, under the cover of committees.

The "ganta" spent a certain part of its day among the peasantry, conducting political education in order to raise their awareness, to get their support, and to facilitate recruitment of peasant fighters. Whenever possible, the mass organization committee of the EPRA or the EPRP structure of the area made efforts to conduct literacy campaign.

"Ganta" members conducted political discussion sessions on a regular basis and departments prepared reading materials. The Mass Organization and the Militia Committees were entrusted with conducting political agitation among the peasantry. The Militia Committee was also responsible for recruiting peasant militia.

Women's Committees were formed at various levels of the EPRP structure. The main task of these committees was to address issues about women both within the EPRA and among the people. The meeting that initiated the organization of women within the army was held in Assifat, Tigrai, from July 29 to August 1, 1977.

Fulfilling the daily needs of the "ganta" took a good part of the day, and all of its members, including the leadership, took active part to make ends meet. The expenses of the "ganta" were budgeted. In Tigrai, a "ganta" of about twenty people was budgeted for about two hundred fifty birr a month, that is, about twelve birr per fighter per month. The budget covered the daily food ration, mostly ground cereal, oil and salt, soap, stationary and cigarettes for those who smoked. In order to feed itself, the "ganta" either bought its own food or went to villages and asked the inhabitants to voluntarily collect food. Quite often, "ganta" members prepared their own food and one of the most popular "recipe" of the "ganta" was known as "*boj-boj*". This was a mixture of any edible item that the "ganta" lay its hands on.

The "ganta" had to travel for at least five hours every day. "Ganta" members woke up very early in the morning and walked for a few hours before taking a long break. The "ganta" might take a short break known as "*abruk*" depending on the security condition of the area. Depending on the topography, the "ganta" could cover a distance of four to six miles per hour. For military, economic and political reasons, a "ganta" could not stay in one area for more than half a day, but had to move from place to place constantly. By doing so, it distributed the economic burden broadly among the peasantry. Areas that had little to provide were avoided. For lack of supplies, many were the times that the "ganta" had to go hungry and most of its members were malnourished. In the Begemidir area, "gantas" were allowed to slaughter an ox every few months, particularly before a military operation. Besides, "gantas" who operated in the Simien highland, could afford buying one sheep for only five birr and selling the skin back for two or three birr. Because of the cold weather, sheep skin is valuable. EPRA members in Tigrai did not have the "privilege" of killing oxen, even though they could once in a while kill goats.

The "ganta" might stay the night where it had dinner if security conditions permitted. Often times, as a matter of precaution, the "ganta" would stay with the peasants until late at night and leave the area unnoticed to pass the night some distance from the village.

In line with the Chinese and Vietnamese experience, the EPRP had classified territories into two major categories, "white" and "red" areas. The "white" areas were those where the regime had its infrastructure and the people were subjected to its control. "Red" areas were those where peasants had stopped paying taxes to the regime and had identified themselves with the EPRP. Some of these areas were administered by committees elected by the peasants themselves. The committees were charged with administrative tasks and judicial power. Peasants living in the so called "red" areas took active part in the activities of the EPRP/EPRA, including military operations. In some cases, it was in these "red" areas that the EPRP/EPRA had its mini-base, where the clinics, training camps, etc., were found.

A company conducted criticism and self-criticism sessions every fifteen days. The entire membership was subjected to that process, which focused on the way the contingent operated, its movements, and the weaknesses and strength of its individual members. When possible, "ganta" discussions were conducted almost every night. At times, sessions were conducted to tell stories and jokes. Whenever circumstances allowed, theatrical plays were performed and the "ganta" members took part in cultural dances and songs.

Besides the gun and the rounds of ammunition, the average "ganta" member carried a sheet and a small piece of cloth called "*koushuke*" that he or she slept on. The "*koushuke*" was also used to carry "*kolo*", that is, roasted cereals, beans, etc. Many were the times that the *"ganta"* member was fed on *"kolo"* alone.

The "ganta" member slept on bare ground. Excep newcomers, very few complained about the discomfort. Depending on the size of the "ganta", two or three members were allowed to sleep together in order to share their sheets and for the sake of the warmth. Men and women slept together. If it rained, either the sheets or the "koushukes" were stretched and used as tents. Quite often, rain did not bother "ganta" members.

Malaria, typhus and relapsing fever were common. On the average, two members of a "ganta" would fall sick per day. Lice and bugs, the common "friends" of the guerilla, transmitted diseases. The "ganta" member would wash their bodies whenever water was available. Many were the times that the "ganta", which spent a number of hours walking and sweating, could not bathe for a period of fifteen days or even a month.

Both women and men fighters endured these hardships. Women fighters were also engaged in combat activities and many were as strong as the men. Some excelled at military operations, such as Delai (code name) who was assigned as commander of a contingent. Women fighters faced more problems than the men. Because of hygenic and other reasons, the menstruation period of many of them became irregular; in some cases it came quite frequently. In order to compensate for the loss of iron, some women fighters were fed on cattle liver whenever this was available.

The EPRA had no uniform and its members wore whatever was available. A typical member of the army had only one set of pants, a shirt and sandals. The clothes were stitched so many times that, at times, it was difficult to tell the original texture of the cloth. The members were provided with clothing whenever available, obtained either through a raid or from the urban party structures.

The EPRA had its own clinic where members and peasants were treated. The clinics were staffed by medical doctors, pharmacists, qualified health officers and nurses. Given the Ethiopian condition and the number of EPRP/EPRA members, the EPRA had a relatively high number of professional medical personnel. The medical group had conducted some major surgeries. Severe cases were sent to the Sudan. Medicine was obtained by the party structures in the urban areas, through members working in medical establishments.

Acupuncture was a common treatment both among the members and the peasantry. It was introduced by EPRA members who had been trained by Chinese medical groups in South Yemen who in turn trained others. Acupuncture had worked miracles among peasants: some who had come to the clinics on stretchers were on their feet in a matter of days and walked home. Peasants who had become impotent were able to regain their manhood. In 1979, a peasant in the Chilga district, western Begemidir, complained of impotency and was given acupuncture treatment for two or three days. On the fourth day, he told EPRA members that he did not need the treatment anymore; he 'already had checked out that his organ had begun functioning.'

Besides difficulties due to the internal political and military deficiencies of the EPRP/EPRA, the "ganta" faced a number of other problems. One of these was peasant attitude in Tigrai and on the western part of the Begemidir. Because of the lineage systems in these provinces, land was not a major issue. The peasant had a small plot that he tilled. Lack of proper administration and basic health facilities were the major concerns of the people. Peasant indifference to the struggle was a source of discontentment for the "ganta" member, who believed that he or she was sacrificing his or her life for the cause of the peasantry. The hardships that the "ganta" member faced were additional issues of concern.

Sex was another area of concern for the members of both the army and the party structure. The army categorically forbade sexual encounters among its members and with peasants as well. The minimum penalty for an attempted rape was dismissal. Depending on circumstances, rape could incur death penalty and consensual sex, dismissal. Sex was forbidden because the EPRA was not in a position to care for the offspring of such unions. Besides, there were few female fighters, an average of three or four to a "ganta". EPRA members understood the consequences of sexual interaction and many abided by the rules and regulations of the army. The EPRA took special precautions in regard to relationship between its members and peasant women. This was done to avoid the political crisis that could result from sexual encounters between EPRA members and peasant women. The peasant does not compromise in his religion, women, and land.

Even though men and women slept together, in the first few years, sex related "offenses" in the EPRA were almost non-existent, even though there were some "offenders". For political and other considerations, sex related infractions were leniently handled, but habitual offenders were expelled. When the internal political crisis of the EPRA grew acute, sex related offenses became major concerns of the army.

Unlike the EPRA, there was no law prohibiting sexual encounters in the EPRP party structure, and that was resented by some EPRA fighters. In a party rectification movement sometime after mid-1979, sex was discussed under the title "Sex and Revolution". The guideline sent by the EPRP CC had not included such a topic.

To control birth, the Begemidir IZ set up its own abortion clinic in the western part of the province. In an organization where the majority of the members were peasants with families and houses, problems related to sex might have not been as serious as they were in the EPRP.

An EPRA member had respect for places of worship. When passing by a church, members of the "ganta" took off their hats and performed the ordinary rituals. In a locality where the majority were followers of the Christian religion, Muslim names, such as, Ibrahim, Idris, etc., were changed to Abraham and Indrias and likewise in Muslim areas. Even though many

EPRA members did not fast, they made sure that fact was not known to the peasants. However, when it became more and more difficult to conceal infidelity, the EPRA in northwestern Begemidir was exempted from religious observances by the Monastery in Waldeba.

One of the main engagements of the "ganta" was military activity. Quite often, such activities were decided by the General Command or regional command committees. Before the "ganta" was deployed for an operation, a thorough study would presumably be conducted, looking at the type of operation, the numbers and military equipment of the enemy, the specific location where enemy forces were congregated. The "ganta" would then be assigned a specific task and given a defined location.

After an operation, particularly of an aborted or an unsuccessful one, a weary fighter sometimes had to carry a wounded comrade to safety on his or her shoulders over a distance of miles, through a treacherous and difficult terrain. In some cases, the retreating fighters encountered peasant resistance and had to fight their way out. As part of the moral obligation of the EPRA and for security considerations, a corpse of a fighter had to be removed from the battle scene and buried elsewhere.

An aborted or an unsuccessful operation was followed by chaos. The chain of command was severed and organized retreat would become impossible. As a result, there were several instances when fighters were left on their own. In the Tselemt area, an EPRA fighter was presumed dead and buried, but he walked back to EPRA held territory sometime later.

Military Operations

As was indicated elsewhere, the EPRA was inactive from March until September 1975.[1] One of the first operations conducted in January 1976 was dictated by EPRA's financial needs. The raided locality was a small town called Sabba, in the Tigrai province, wherein the guerillas entered along with a caravan of merchants and camels. Some money and arms were seized. Captives were released after a political education session. The operation took about two hours.[2]

In March 1976, a successful fifteen minute operation was conducted in Wukro, Tigrai, to obtain production facilities.

In April 1976, EPRA members walked nine hours a day for about ten days to conduct an operation in Adi Awe'ala, Shire district, to confiscate arms intended for the "Raza" Project. Thirty-five weapons were obtained.

In May 1976, EPRA units ambushed a peasant detachment that was to take part in the "Raza Project". About six hundred peasants were captured and released after a three day political session on the motives of the "Raza Project". The EPRA obtained hundreds of arms and thousands of rounds of ammunition.

At the end of May 1976, EPRA began collaborating with the ELF in military operations designed to counter the Derge's "Raza" operation.[3]

In May 1976, EPRA units, with the goal of dismantling government infrastructures and also obtaining arms, attacked police stations in five Tigrai wereda towns. A few weapons and some medicine were obtained. EPRA units also conducted some propaganda work. They entered Samre after seven of the members hijacked a Land-Rover just at the outskirts of the town. The seven member team overpowered the police force. The entire town was brought under control after the arrival of the rest of the EPRA force.

In June 1976, EPRA units ambushed a Derge convoy that was on its way to Adi Awlie from its military camp in Adigrat, and inflicted some casualties.

In July 1976, the EPLF, in collaboration with the EPRA, put a Derge force out of action at Intitcho, a small town in Tigrai.

In August 1976, in Tigrai, the EPRA collaborated with the EPLF and successfully ambushed a Derge convoy. In the same month again, the EPRA collaborated with the EPLF to conduct an operation in the town of Adigrat, in hopes of obtaining medicine. Indeed, a large quantity of medicine and perhaps thirty typewriters and duplicating machines were confiscated. However, the EPLF took away almost all of the booty. When the EPRA leadership demanded a fair share, tension grew between the two organizations.

In September 1976, at Bizet in Tigrai, EPRA units along with EPLF forces ambushed a Derge convoy on its way to Eritrea. Arms and military equipment were obtained.

In October 1976, the EPRA conducted another operation in Samre, Tigrai and confiscated some arms from the police and the employees of the Ministry of Internal Affairs. Suspected Derge intelligence agents were arrested and disarmed. Two POMOA members accused of instigating violence were executed. The following day, the EPRA confronted the Nebelbal reinforcing column that came from Mekele. The Nebelbal force suffered casualties, and the EPRP was able to acquire some grenades and other weapons.

In November 1976, some damage was inflicted on a Nebelbal force moving toward Assimba, the base area of the EPRA. The confrontation took place at a place called Adi Awlie.

Sometime in December 1976, a Nebelbal force opened a surprise attack on EPRA units in Adi Gereged, in the Enderta awerja. The Derge's contingents suffered some casualties, and the EPRA pulled out of the ambush without serious damage.

Both in Tigrai and Begemidir, EPRP forces severely punished bandits who they believed were causing problems to the peasantry. The mere presence of the EPRA in these areas deterred the activities of the bandits. Begemidir peasants recited lyrics dedicated to the EPRA and eulogizing it for protecting them from bandits and letting their herds graze freely. One of them runs, "*Eihease Aleme, Eihease Aleme, Duur aderetch laame*", meaning, because of the EPRA, my cow can pass the night outdoor.

Before March 1977, the EPRA conducted some operations, but these did not meet with the needs and demands of the organization. Consequently, serious reservations began to be expressed about the activities of the EPRA and dissidence began building.

To be sure, complaints were made in some of the EPRP CC meetings, particularly, in those of August 1976 and February 1977.[4] EPRA leading activists were criticized for lack of dynamism, inability to lead the army, inability to deploy the force under their structure, and dependency on the urban structure for the needs of the army, including, arms, finance, medicine and other necessary items. This was a concern raised by some CC members, with Fikre Zergaw in the lead. He had been to the EPRA and was very critical of the EPRA leadership. It was the assumption of many EPRP leading members that EPRA's leading group was of the same caliber and experience as that which had taken over the EPRP leadership in urban areas. However, it has to be recognized that urban political activity and rural armed struggles were very different. In order to enhance EPRA's military standing, the February 1977 EPRP CC meeting decided to conduct a rectification movement within the EPRA.

In the EPRP CC itself, there was a second voice that indeed recognized the weaknesses and shortcomings of the EPRA, but was more conciliatory and understanding of the problems in the EPRA. Proponents of this voice attributed EPRA's problems more to lack of arms, and the time it required for a member from the urban areas to adjust to a totally different environment and form of struggle, requiring psychological preparation and physical fitness. The physical readiness of some of the members of the EPRA for military action was an area of concern. The cautious military approach of EPRA's leading activists was also attributed to the setback in Wello in 1976, when more than a third of the entire EPRA group was wiped out. Zeru was among those who expressed this viewpoint. Until this time, there was no clear policy indicating the phases and stages of EPRA's military strategy and tactics.

The third voice was that of leading EPRA activists themselves. They were aware of some of the problems within the EPRA, but they attributed their failure to the EPRP CC, which they felt had abandoned them altogether. This was in reference to the period between March - September 1975 when contact was lost between the EPRP CC and the army. Besides, they believed that the CC did not give them enough political and military guidance, did not provide them with enough information and attention, and did not send capable members. Some even had lingering doubts that the EPRP CC considered them followers of Berhane Meskel.[5]

Rejecting the complaints, the EPRP CC enumerated the assistance it provided the EPRA. The CC believed that communications with the EPRA had been conducted on a fairly regular basis given the constraints of the EPRP.

The fourth voice was that of rank and file EPRA members, particularly those who had joined the army around the beginning of 1977. From the third month of 1977 until their arrival was halted by the Derge in May, hundreds of new members arrived at the EPRA base areas; the army grew by a factor of four or five. Moreover, EPRA's ethnic composition was changed following the arrival of a large number of members from the various national groups of the country. By the third month of 1977, the EPRA had eight fully armed combatant units of about seventy people each. The membership of the Mass Organization Committees covering three awerajas of Tigrai, the various departments and the intelligence committees expanded to more than three hundred. The EPRA in Assimba, which had not numbered more than three hundred a few months earlier, had more than a thousand combatants by the beginning of 1977. This did not include the units in Begemidir, which also had added members to their ranks. So, by March 1977, the EPRA in Tigrai and Begemidir had more than fifteen hundred fighters. However, as the number of fighters increased steeply, no adjustment was made in the EPRA leadership structure. Not only did the size of the EPRA leadership remain the same, but also three members of the leadership left for Eritrea. So, for a period of months, when the EPRA was larger than ever, the entire army was placed under the command of an individual, Gera.

The EPRA was so popular that members of the EPRP saw it as the ultimate form of organization which would enable them to build a just society, vent their frustration and anger, and fulfill their personal dreams as well. The EPRA was their ultimate institution through which they would avenge their fallen comrades. As far as they were concerned, the EPRA was a flawless organization and Assimba, the base area, was something resembling a worldly heaven. Particularly among youth activists, there was a wide notion that the EPRA base area had a well organized and equipped infrastructure. The military might of the EPRA was highly exaggerated. When the words 'EPRA' and Assimba were raised, they sent exhilaration through the spines of many. Lyrics were written and songs were composed eulogizing the EPRA and its base area Assimba.

For some of the new arrivals, their expectation about the EPRA base area and the reality did not match. Upon arrival, they discovered that Assimba was just one of those rugged Ethiopian mountains and the EPRA was a miniscule army that had to face innumerable hurdles. The group was also disappointed when it encountered mid-level EPRA leaders who had been in the army almost since the beginning and were not ideologically sophisticated. The newly arrived group still judged a leader's capacity in terms of his/her degree of political astuteness and clarity, rather than ones military capabilities. This attitude was a reflection of the differing views regarding the struggle in the urban and rural areas. The first question which some of the newly arrived members asked themselves was whether the "mediocre" mid-level leaders were to be their leaders. Even then, the newly arrived groups were ready to face the vicissitudes of army life. However, since many of them were part of the political structures in the urban areas, to unquestioningly obey military orders was something they had to get used to. Some of them believed that there was no democracy within the EPRA and began demanding for changes in the constitution of the army. A small incident that took place at the training center, "*Ta'alim*", can explain the state of mind of some of the newly arrived group. After the training day was over, the trainees were assigned an area to pass the night, in the open air. Not long after, it began to rain heavily. Soon, the group asked the leadership if it could move to a drier location. The "Ta'alim" leadership responded negatively and the group was forced to stay put despite torrential rain. Obeying orders and enduring hardships was part of the training process. Many of the members of the group were so agitated that they rioted at the criticism and self-criticism session that was held the next day. The same scenario repeated itself the next day. This time, when rain began pouring, the group left its assigned place without the approval of the leadership. In reaction to the disobedience, members of the leadership of the training center refused to provide training.[6]

Along with the difficulties of army life and other problems, serious reservations and doubts were raised regarding the way the General Command of the EPRA handled army affairs. One of the most insidious and serious reservations was how prisoners were handled, including suspected EPRP members. The EPRA had a small contingent known as Ganta 44 which handled prisoners. In order to extricate information from prisoners suspected of spying for the government, physical torture was used. The case of Ganta 44 became an issue of campaign against the leadership. Disgruntled army members, particularly those who were held responsible for the debacle in Ebenat and Arbaya conducted effective campaign against the army leadership. For many of the newcomers who had high esteem for the EPRA and an idealistic approach to the type of society they wanted to build, the way prisoners were handled was disillusioning. Some of those that were placed under detention were released when the Rectification Movement was initiated.

Another important issue raised during this period was EPRA's relative inactivity. Army members demanded to be more active and engage the Derge militarily.

This fourth "voice" was the major force in bringing about structural change within the EPRA.

During the first months of 1977, nearly two-hundred thousand birr, hundreds of automatic machine guns and ammunition arrived. The money was obtained from a bank raid in Addis Abeba and the arms were sent by the foreign committee of the EPRP. The EPRA, which had only about eighty machine guns a couple of months before, was able to carry hundreds of the latest versions of the Bulgarian kalashinkovs, which were famous for their double handles. The EPRA also acquired some Soviet made fifty-mm machine guns. These acquisitions were important elements in launching the rectification movement. Furthermore, the arrival of a large number of CC members expedited the process. During the first months of 1977, Zeru Kehishen, Tselote Hiskias, Fikre Zergaw, Iyasu Alemayehu, AB and ZB arrived in Assimba. This brought the number of the EPRP CC members to eight including Tsegaye Gebre Medhin and MGE, and such numbers were unprecedented in EPRA's brief history.

The Rectification Movement

When the rectification movement began in May 1977, the majority of the participants were long-time political activists, intellectuals, the vibrant youth and veteran labor leaders who had joined the army quite recently. Many of them had little or no military experience. In due course, the various dissident "voices" mentioned elsewhere began to converge. Already, in the first months of 1977, gossip and rumor had become part of the day to day life of the EPRA and some members of the Command became the topics. In the midst of this crisis, one of the companies compiled a report regarding the weaknesses and problems of the EPRA, and that paper, along with others, served as the basis for the Rectification Movement (RM).[7]

As things were about to get out of hand, an EPRP Central Committee group known as the "Delegates" was formed. The committee visited units, conducted discussions and tried to identify the sources of the problems. The "Delegates" were new comers with little or no exposure to conditions in the EPRA. None of them had taken EPRA's military training.

In the midst of this crisis, the large shipment of arms, mentioned elsewhere, arrived. Almost the entire EPRA force had to go to ELF-held territory in Eritrea to pick up the arms.

After making an assessment of the situation in the EPRA, the "Delegates" published their first "Manifesto" regarding the state of affairs in the EPRA. A number of points were cited as the possible causes for EPRA's problems. Some of the main reasons for the weaknesses of the EPRA, according to the "Manifesto" were: 'bureaucratic' work patterns rather than democratic, 'commandism' rather than the conscious participation of EPRA members, and a low level of political education within the EPRA."[8] The "Manifesto" also severely criticized the EPRA leadership for excessive dependence on arms, that is, "[W]hen it could do a lot with the arms it had, the EPRA leadership had hindered its activities by simply waiting for a large arms supply." The "Manifesto" also criticized the EPRA for its excessive dependence on the party structure for its needs. "The EPRA did not address its shortcomings and weaknesses, arguing that it would have solved its problems if the party had sent more money, ...if the EPLF had supplied fifty more kalashinkovs, ..."[9] The "Manifesto" criticized the EPRA for conducting inadequate political agitation among the people.[10] Other problems mentioned in the "Manifesto" were the absence of a party structure in the army, serious flaws of the EPRA Constitution, which was too strict and rigid.[11] The "Manifesto" also sharply criticized the General Command for its dictatorial tendencies. The "Manifesto" which focused on the EPRA leadership, served as the guiding document to conduct the RM which began in May 1977. A number of articles intended to generate discussion were prepared and circulated among the various units.

The "Delegates" called a meeting of the members of the Command and asked their opinion regarding the "Manifesto". Some of the members of the Command expressed strong differences regarding the points raised in the "Manifesto". When they found that their views were unacceptable, they demanded to present them to the fighters.[12]

The Rectification Movement (RM) began at the Assimba base area, among the various EPRA departments. It then extended to the various contingents, the combat units. Some of these sessions were attended by members of the "Delegates".

While the RM was underway, the Command lost control over the army and its links to the units were severely impeded. Some EPRA members derisively characterized the Command as a "white army" command, and all of its moves were regarded with suspicion. Rumors spread that the Command had arrested members of the "Delegates". In the midst of this crisis, the Command planned a raid on Wukro, a small town in Tigrai and an important center through which EPRP members transited from the urban areas. Sometime earlier, some EPRP members moving from the urban areas had been arrested and executed upon arrival in Wukro.

The main purpose of the Wukro operation was to cleanse the area of POMOA members who had perpetrated the violence in the area. The first attempt could not take place as scheduled. On the second try, the raid ended in a fiasco. Poor communication, leadership inability, inadequate information, unclear mission, and the critical and suspicious attitudes of the fighters were cited as the main reasons for the failure.

This and other problems prompted the CC "Delegates" to produce a second "Manifesto" sharply critical of the state of affairs in the army. The second "Manifesto" stated that lawlessness, defiance of orders, insubordination to commanders, unauthorized movement from one quarter to another had become rampant. The article criticized the attitude of the fighters and declared that the RM had to continue without disrupting the normal activities of the EPRA. The Command was commended for its cooperative attitude. When the crisis spread and it became difficult to control the army, some members of the EPRA leadership offered to resign.

The rank and file fighters regarded the second "Manifesto" as revisionist and in contradiction to the first one, which had sharply criticized the Command. As of this moment, some fighters began feeling more pessimistic about the course of the RM. The seeds of discontent continued to spread.

Despite these ups and downs, the RM went ahead as planned, emphasizing structural adjustments. The RM introduced major changes in the structure of the EPRA.[13] Alterations and amendments were made in a draft Constitution prepared by the Constitution Drafting Committee, composed of members of the various contingents and departments.[14] Reports on the Draft Constitution and the various proposals raised by EPRA members were compiled by a democratically elected coordinating committee. The committee then sent its report to the CC members who finalized the draft.[15]

The major documents governing the EPRA was finally produced. These documents included the amended EPRA's Constitution of seventy-five clauses, the EPRA By-laws of one hundred seven articles, and the internal regulations of the EPRA, of one hundred thirteen articles.

EPRA Documents - The Constitution

EPRA's Constitution was the result of the RM. Part I, Chapter II of the document discussed the basic principles by which the EPRA would be governed: democratic centralism, collective leadership, criticism and self-criticism and discipline. Chapter III discussed membership and recruitment. Part II, Chapter I covered the rights of the members and stipulated, "a member of the army could not be detained, searched and arrested without a warrant".[16] "Even if a member of the army was found guilty, he would not be subjected to inhuman treatment. It was unlawful to threaten, call names and beat a member."[17] The member had the right to know the charges that he was accused of and he had the right to present his own defense and take part in the litigation process. Finally, he had the right of appeals.[18] The Constitution recognized marriages that had occurred before joining the EPRA.[19] These were important clauses in light of the prevailing condition in the EPRA before the RM.

Part II, Chapter II discussed the duties of the EPRA member: he or she was obliged to respect the Constitution and regulation of the army, protect its secrets and defend it from enemy spies.[20] The member was required to respect the equality of the members of the army.[21] Regarding rumor, the constitution stipulated that, "[A]member was not allowed to criticize the condition of the army and the party, the weakness, mistakes and shortcomings of the leadership or members, outside his designated group or legal meetings."[22] The member was obliged to respect the human and democratic rights of the people. He had to respect their language, culture and belief.[23] *The member was forbidden to take any action or conduct any agitation that would create suspicion, hatred and mistrust among tribes, peoples, nationalities, nations and religions.*[24]

In Part III, the Constitution categorically asserted the hegemony of the EPRP over the EPRA. It was stipulated that the final decision making body was the EPRP CC, which would lead the EPRA through its military commission. In order to lead the various echelons of the army, two distinct hierarchies were formed at each level: the command (military) and party (political) committees, operating side by side. The General Leadership Committees (the title General Command was changed) were in charge of the military affairs of the EPRA. The party committees were to provide EPRP leadership (party hegemonies), and spread the ideology of the party within the army. Moreover, every echelon of the EPRA leadership would have a commander and vice commander, a commissar and a vice-commissar.

Under the new arrangement, a member of the party committee, the commissar most often, became a member of the command committee. Consequently, the new structural arrangement changed the composition of the military command, imbuing it with a heavy presence of the party structure at every level of the army echelon. In both command and party committees, some of the members of the leadership were appointed by the next higher leadership committees, while some were elected to the party committees either by the general EPRA membership or party members. Presumably, this was done to curb commandism. According to the new arrangement, the General Leadership Committee had at least nine members, two of whom were elected by members of the army and one by members of the EPRP in the army. The vice-commissar and the rest of the members would be selected by the EPRP CC. The General Leadership Committee would serve for two years.[25]

The major changes that the new constitution introduced were the formation of party committees at the various levels of the army structure. The "ganta" party committee was the basic institutional EPRP committee in the EPRA. Under the "ganta" party committees came clandestinely regrouped party cells. Cell membership was not made public. At the level of a company, the party committee consisted of the political commissar, the vice commissar and the political commissars of the three "gantas". The main functions of the party committees were to assure political leadership of the EPRP over the EPRA, to conduct political education, to recruit party members from among the ranks of the army structure, which consisted of party and non-party members.

The new constitution reduced the overriding power of the Commander. Any major decision was to be the collective responsibility of the General Leadership Committee, in which the Commander had only one vote.[26] He was also required to implement the decisions made by the General Leadership Committee. If the party committee or the commissar believed that a decision regarding an operation was contrary to EPRP's political line, they had the right to veto that decision. At the same time, if the Commander believed that a certain military activity would bring about danger, he also had the right to veto it.[27] Even though there were provisions regarding the limits of the power of the Commander, in practice, efforts were made to reach at a consensus before action was taken.

Included in EPRA's Constitution were the duties and functions of the Auditors Committee. The amended EPRA Constitution stressed protection of the rights of individual members. With this in mind, institutions, such as, the Committee for the Protection of the Rights of the members, known by its Amharic acronym (AMAACO), Military Tribunal, etc., were formed. According to the constitution, the main purpose of the AMAACO was to protect the democratic rights of the members.[28] Constitutionally, the AMAACO was independent of the EPRA leadership and was responsible only to the EPRP CC.[29] There were three AMAACO members. One was appointed by the EPRP CC, one was elected by the general members of the army, and the third was elected by party members in the army.³⁰ According to the Constitution, the AMAACO was duplicated at the company level; the three platoons of the company (Haayel), elected three members to form the committee.³¹ The AMAACO committees had the right of access to any organizational document or information.³² A member of the army could be arrested only in the presence of a member of the AMAACO.

The reformed Military Tribunal, which was an outcome of the RM, was composed of five members, three of whom were elected by the general membership of the army and two by party members. The Military Tribunal was independent of any committee [including the leadership] and could not be brought to justice for its decisions.³³ Death penalty on a member passed by the Military Tribunal had to be approved by two-third of the army leadership and had to be signed.³⁴ If a death penalty was passed on a party member, executive authority rested with the EPRP CC.³⁵ By law, the accused had the right to defend himself by finding a lawyer from among the army members.³⁶

The new Constitution also asserted that the member can be part of the struggle only if he chose to do so and he had the right to resign from the EPRA,³⁷ a right which was uncommon in other military groups of Ethiopia.³⁸

EPRA by-laws

Describing the motives for introducing the Code, the preamble stated,

> [T]he main purpose of such a Code was to avoid patterns of work that were chaotic and unjust, and to protect the rights of suspects and the accused....Unless proven guilty, no one is considered a criminal . . . Besides, it would be the duty of the plaintiff to provide evidences for the charges that he had initiated.³⁹

The by-laws stipulated six types of disciplinary actions, ranging from a simple warning to capital punishment, to be applied if the charge was related to stealing, hiding and selling EPRA's arms.⁴⁰ Disclosing the secrets of the EPRA/EPRP or organizations affiliated to the EPRP would result in severe punishment and perhaps capital punishment.⁴¹ Spying against the EPRP or collaborating with a spy would result in a punishment that might include death.⁴²

The Constitution categorically stated that a severe penalty would be imposed if anyone formed a group that "was not known and recognized by the leadership" or if he was involved in "forming a faction or taking part in one", except those allowed by the Constitution or the leadership. Depending on the severity of the violation and the danger that the action caused, death penalty could be imposed.⁴³ If a member came across such a group, he was obliged to report the case to the relevant authorities.⁴⁴ Any effort made to create discord between the EPRP and the EPRA or to organize a strike would result in suspension or capital punishment.⁴⁵

Mistreatment of a prisoner was an offense that would result in suspension.[46] Rape was one of the crimes that would incur the death penalty.[47] Severe penalties would be imposed on EPRA members who forced the people to collect food,[48] and imposed forced labor, [49]mistreated the people. [50] According to the Code, unlawful search was not permitted. Prevention of the freedom of movement of the people, curtailing their democratic rights, etc., would result in suspension.[51]

The structural changes and the Constitutional Amendments introduced during the RM were heartily accepted by the majority of the fighters. The changes were part of the solution to some of the lingering doubts and problems that the EPRA faced.

Following the introduction of the structural changes, the next task of the RM was to appoint and elect individuals to leadership positions. With this in mind, suggestions were demanded from the various sections of the army and a number of nominees were forwarded to the "Delegates". Among the names that were sent to the "Delegates", those with the highest approval rating by the members were selected as members of the leadership. The CC delegates appointed additional members to the General Leadership and General Party Committees. The EPRA's Constitution had a provision that allowed the EPRP CC to appoint individuals to the leadership.

The newly formed General Leadership Committee consisted of, DS, GM, Yirga Tessema (Mezmur), HWG (Indrias), Colonel Alemayehu Asfaw, AA, (Robba), Tsegaye Gebre Medhin, MGE and Lemlem. The General Party Committee consisted of, Gebre Egziabher Haile Mikael (Gayeem), TD/T. (Admassu), B. (Amde), GB (Desalegne), MGE (Tsehaye), M.(Gideon). Of the five members of the previous Command, which was the target of the RM, two were not included in the new leadership group. AA was reelected by the members themselves, while MGE and Tsegaye, who also were EPRP CC members, were retained. Of the fourteen members of the newly formed army leadership, only three were from the previous Command.

Of the total army leadership, five were Tigrigna speakers, five Amharic speakers, two spoke Oromiffa and two Gurage. Seven had bachelors and masters' degrees and an additional five had attended universities. One had completed high-school. Colonel Alemayehu Asfaw was a graduate of a Military Academy. The majority were veteran activists of the student movement, with ages ranging from the early twenties to the early forties. There was only one female member.

Of the entire EPRA leadership, only four had military experience of more than two years. Some had not taken part in military operations before they were placed in the leadership. Some had not even joined a "ganta". The complaint expressed immediately following the formation of the EPRA leadership was that, some of those elected had not even worn out the first fatigues that they brought when they joined the EPRA. This was in reference to those who came from Europe and who had uniforms when they joined the army.

Finally, the entire EPRA units were reshuffled in the process known as "*Teqelit*". During this period, it was disclosed that the EPRA was preparing to launch armed struggles in Wello, Harer, Sidamo and Shoa. Members were summoned and asked where they would prefer to go and struggle.[52]

The Rectification Movement in the EPRA lasted for about three and a half months. In Tigrai, it was over by the third week of August 1977, while in Begemidir, it began late and was over by mid-January 1978.

As indicated above, when the RM began, there were four different "voices" that either converged or collided to create the resultant new EPRA. The RM had different effects on the various groups that voiced their dissatisfaction. However, its effect was minimal on those who arrived after it was over. During the RM and after, EPRP members were still joining the EPRA.

As was explained above, when the second "Manifesto" was put out, some EPRA members had expressed some doubts. Not long after the RM was over and the names of the new leadership were made public, some members exhibited open dissatisfaction. The main focus of the dissatisfaction was the composition of the leadership. Some did not want any one of the former Command to take part in the new leadership. Some felt that the army leadership was composed of very close friends and associates of a CC member, the head of the "Delegates". Imagined or real, the new EPRA leadership was perceived of as composed of individuals who had close relationships amongst themselves. One of the members of the "Delegates", Fikre Zergaw, an alternate member of the EPRP CC, had expressed similar dissatisfaction about the composition of the army leadership to a rank and file member and a member of the EPRP CC.[53]

On the other hand, some members of the previous Command questioned the motive and purpose of the RM itself. Some of them wondered whether it was not intended to divert attention from the crisis that the EPRP itself was facing, particularly in the urban areas.[54] They concluded that the CC "Delegates" left the EPRA without any meaningful military leadership. They also believed that some members of the EPRA leadership were used as scapegoats for EPRP's crisis.

The dissatisfaction might have had personal aspects too. This way or that, resentment persisted even after the RM was over. For some inexplicable reasons, some still believed that the EPRA was controlled by the previous Command, even though only three of them were included in the new leadership.

Before the RM was concluded, the army leadership decided to launch an operation against the Derge force guarding the Microwave station near Adigrat. The army leadership claimed to have more than adequate information regarding Derge's troop disposition, the whereabouts of the Central Command, the number of military personnel, etc.[55] After conducting the necessary preparations, the army leadership led some EPRA contingents close to the location of the operation and explained the mission to them. The new EPRA Constitution had inserted a new provision which stated that the participants of an operation had to be informed beforehand about the mission they were to be involved in, and that there should be a discussion about it.

After deliberating on the issue, the fighters cancelled the operation on the ground that it was an adventurous move.[56] But another version has it that the operation was canceled after two members of the EPRA leadership, among them Colonel Alemayehu Asfaw, vetoed it arguing that the operation might result in the loss of many members.[57]

Whatever the source of dissatisfaction, from the first part of 1977 until the EPRA was forced to leave the Tigrai area in 1978, for a period of about a year, the EPRA group in Tigrai was not engaged in any major military activity. To be sure, EPRA forces ambushed Derge contingents in October 1977, in Ahezera, Dengelata, and Mederiba, all in Tigrai province.[58] In September 1977, EPRA units in Tigrai conducted an operation in a small town called Senkata and dismantled the government infrastructure there. In September again, EPRA units confiscated one hundred sacs of sugar in Maimegelta, Tigrai province. Sugar was one of the main sources of energy for the fighter. Whenever available, sugar would be carried by the units that were deployed for an operation. There were times when units would walk on for many more hours after feeding themselves on a handful of sugar. One of the major operations of the EPRA in Tigrai after the RM was in February 1978 when EPRA units controlled Wukro. In the battle to take over the town, many officers of the Nebelbal were killed.[59]

As stated above, the RM had introduced some structural changes and adjustments within the EPRA. The RM rectified some aspects of the political and organizational problems of the army by creating political institutions and asserting the role of the EPRP within the EPRA. That arrangement was considered an important step to enhance EPRA's activities.

The RM, however, did not address EPRA's military weaknesses. EPRA's strategies and tactics, its fighting ability, its military activities/inactivities, strength/shortcomings of the previous operations, major military achievements/errors of the EPRA, etc., were not addressed. Whether Assimba could still serve as a base area for the EPRA was not raised. By this time, it had become evident that relationship between the TPLF and the EPRA was growing worse. The RM also did not discuss the impact of the 1974 revolutionary movement, particularly the land reform proclamation on the course of the armed struggle. EPRP's broad policy regarding rural and urban armed struggle was not discussed. In May 1977 when the RM was initiated, the urban military activities of the EPRP was about nine months old. Besides, around the first months of 1977, the 'PB paper' which members of the CC were aware of, had reached the EPRA and was distributed to party members.[60]

It was evident that the RM created conditions for members to assert their rights, including participation in decisions to conduct operations. At the same time, the RM took away some power from the commanders. Some members of the Command even believed that the RM demilitarized the army and transformed it into some kind of a semi-military and semi-political institution.⁶¹ According to them, the RM created an undisciplined army that mistrusted its leaders. ⁶² Besides, members of the various levels of the army leadership refrained from making unpopular, yet important decisions, lest they be "lynched" and become targets of another RM.

As was indicated earlier, one focus of the new members who joined the EPRA in 1977 was the mid-level military leadership, which had been considered incapable. Most of the members of the mid-level leadership were very energetic, selfless and capable military leaders who thought that whatever they were doing was in the best interest of the EPRP/EPRA. Even though they were not the direct targets of the RM, members of the mid-level leadership were one of the sections that were negatively affected by the outcome of the RM. After the RM, almost none of them were promoted to leadership positions, even though they had been in the army for quite a while and had endured the tests of army life.⁶³ Some of them became disoriented and lost confidence in themselves and in the organization.

Furthermore, because of the new arrangement, which provided an important say to the party committees formed at every level of the EPRA hierarchy, the power of the mid-level command committee was weakened. Quite often, they were challenged by the newcomers, who had the ability to present coherent and sophisticated ideas. Besides, some of the mid-level leadership did not understand the whole purpose of the party structure in the army. As far as they were concerned, the EPRP party structure within the army was another form of an intelligence network. Thus, the problems within the EPRA lingered even after the RM was over. Dissidence was exhibited a few months later, albeit, in an altogether different form and forum (see details in the coming pages).

The "Manifesto" put out by the CC "Delegates" at the beginning of 1977 had criticized the EPRA for inactivity when "the party structure in urban areas had been subjected to severe search and destroy campaigns and many of its members were victimized."⁶⁴ That condition was not altered even after the conclusion of the RM. All through 1977, when the EPRP was emersed in one of its direst political crisis, caused by the internal problems of the organization and the exceedingly ruthless repression, the EPRA, more or less free of the dangers and crises that the urban structures were undergoing, was gripped in a crisis of its own. As a result, the EPRA, which became engaged in its own internal squabbles, was left on the periphery. When the military regime was doing every imaginable thing to destroy the EPRP, the crisis in the army placed the EPRA on the sideline when much was required of it.

The EPRP CC members in the EPRA were also bogged down in the crisis. As a result, the majority of CC members paid little or no attention to the activities of the EPRP in the various parts of the country and placed themselves on the sideline when the entire EPRP structure was enveloped by a severe crisis. Furthermore, the delay and postponement of the CC meeting left the entire EPRP structure without meaningful leadership.

The EPRP CC Group in Assimba

An EPRP CC meeting was long overdue. The previous meeting of the EPRP CC proper had taken place in February 1977, so there should have been a meeting in April/May 1977. However, such a meeting could not take place due to the absence of those CC members who remained in the Addis Abeba area. They were supposed to leave for the EPRA controlled areas, however, their departure was delayed due to lack of a leading body that would shoulder the enormous activities of the EPRP structures in the various parts of Ethiopia. While waiting for the convocation of a meeting, members of the CC who were in Assimba became involved in the rectification movement of the EPRA. In due course, however, those CC members who had come to the EPRA base area dispersed to their respective areas and some of those who stayed behind became engaged in EPRA related activities. Three of them were members of the EPRA leadership. Iyasu left for abroad and Fikre Zergaw to the Wello province. The other members of the CC became engaged in different activities and one of them was to reestablish relations with the ELF, which had remained more than cordial for quite some time. As was discussed in Chapter III, the ELF security chief had met and informed Tesfaye Debessai about his intention to hold a high level negotiation with the EPRP. That discussion took place in 1976 when Tesfaye was on his way to the EPRA after concluding negotiations with the EPLF. The gradual worsening of relations between the EPRP and the EPLF might have had an impact on the warming of relations between the EPRP and the ELF. The ELF had remained without a partner after the TPLF dissolved the TLF, one of the rebel groups in Tigrai, which had been in good standing with the ELF.

The EPRP CC, meeting in Addis Abeba in February 1977, had decided to negotiate with the ELF and had formed a delegation to be headed by Tesfaye. The EPRP CC was aware of the formation of a clandestine group within the ELF and it had decided to negotiate with the ELF itself rather than with the clandestine Labor Party. At the same time, the EPRP delegation was instructed to obtain more information about the newly formed Labor Party.

An EPRP delegation led by Zeru went to the ELF area in mid-1977. Members of the delegation included Zeru Kehishen, Iyasu Alemayehu, MGE, FGM and Gebre Egziabher Haile Mikael. The delegation, which had planned to negotiate with the ELF, reconsidered its position when it reached Akordat. It was advised to approach the Labor Party instead of the front leadership. It was argued that approaching the Labor Party would draw the attention of the ELF, which by then considered itself a government. Accordingly, the EPRP delegation informed the ELF that it was willing to negotiate with the Labor Party.[65]

The ELF leadership had to make some adjustments. EPRP delegates, who were given warm reception, had to wait for about a week.

When the negotiation resumed, the delegates of the Labor Party within the ELF, Azin Yassin, Tesfa Mariam, Totil Ibrahim and the Security Chief,

Melake Petros, attended the meeting. All of them were members of the PB of the ELF as well.

A wide range of issues were discussed, including recognition of the ELF as the sole representative of the Eritrean people, and recognition of Eritrea as an Ethiopian colony. The EPRP delegates expressed dissent on both issues. Regarding the first issue, they argued that it was upto the Eritrean people to determine who their representative was. The ELF/Labor Party leaders didn't insist. Concerning the second point, EPRP delegates expressed the organizations long-standing position on the Eritrean issue. The EPRP viewed the Eritrean issue as an internal Ethiopian problem that had to be resolved within the broad framework of the national question. There were differences on an EPRP proposal on the need for a proletarian party to successfully accomplish the New Democratic revolution and lay the basis for the socialist revolution.[66] There also were differences on the dangers of the Soviet Union's involvement in Ethiopian affairs. During this period, the Labor Party was cultivating a friendly relationship with the Soviets and it even advocated the theory known as the noncapitalist path of development - the Soviet Union's prescription that a developing country should follow.[67] Discussions continued on the question of Eritrean independence, military cooperation between the two organizations and about defectors who approached the organizations. The EPRP delegates also discussed the arms and ammunition that the ELF had failed to hand over to the EPRA. This was regarding the shipment sent by the EPRP Foreign Committee in the first months of 1977.

The discussion proceeded smoothly until the issue of recognizing the Labor Party was raised by the ELF delegates. They insisted that the EPRP recognize them as a left organization. Since the first months of 1977, dissidence within the ELF had been spreading. New groups had been formed, including those derogatively termed "Faluls", that is, anarchists.

Even though they had opted to negotiate with the Labor Party, the EPRP delegates insisted that they did not have a mandate to recognize them as a left organization, but would pass on the information to the EPRP CC. The EPRP delegates, having brought a problem upon themselves, were now in a very precarious situation. If they recognized the Labor Party, it would be a transgression of the mandate of the EPRP CC and if not, relations with the ELF, which were crucial for the EPRP, were to be strained. Unable to resolve the dilemma, the EPRP delegates informed their counterparts that they had no choice but to present the issue at the EPRP's next CC meeting. The ELF Labor Party delegates became annoyed and frustrated and the meeting ended without achieving a great deal.

The EPRA, whose relationship with the EPLF and TPLF was already strained, became more isolated after the negotiation with the ELF ended in a miscarriage. The new situation was very favorable for the TPLF.

The CC group in Assimba was enhanced by the arrival of Samuel Alemayehu in December 1977. However, a few months later, at the beginning of 1978, the EPRP faced another grave crisis when one of its active members,

Tselote Hiskias, passed away. According to the official statement of the EPRA, Tselote was killed by a very close friend and EPRA member, Belay Hassen who at this time was in a state of depression.[68] Colonel Alemayehu Asfaw was the first person to arrive at the scene where the incident took place and he saw Tselote gasping his last breath. Tselote was hit in his forehead with three bullets; fired from a very close range. Belay Hassen committed suicide shooting himself through his mouth. An inquiry committee composed of members of various departments, including the leadership and the clinic, was formed. On the day he was killed, Tselote came to where Belay was staying and asked him to go to a river to wash clothes. Tselote, a very warm and congenial individual, was making efforts to console and help Belay Hassen.

The death of Tselote Hiskias was another major setback to the EPRP and particularly the CC, when it needed the wisdom and experience of veteran activists who had founded and led the organization. Tselote, a veteran activist, was a very warm, straight-forward and knowledgeable leader. He was dedicated to the cause he believed in, to his friends and comrades. He was a caring and loving human being. Tselote was still mourning the unexpected death of his wife, Selamawit who had the same warm disposition as her husband. Her death was also mourned by many of her comrades.

Be that as it may, following the arrival of Samuel Alemayehu, CC activities were revitalized and discussions were held on the condition of the EPRP, on policy related and other issues of wider significance. Until this time, the CC group in Assimba had been engrossed in EPRA related activities.

In its first series of meetings, the CC group in Assimba discussed and took positions on two major issues. The first one was related to some major EPRP policies that were enacted since the formation of the organization. The CC group put out a statement interpreting, elaborating and clarifying those policies. The second issue was concerned with resolving the EPRP leadership crisis. The CC group decided to bring new blood into the CC by coopting new members.

Before resuming discussions on the issues raised above, voting CC members decided to exclude alternate members, that is, non-voting CC members. As a result, only Tsegaye Gebre Medhin, Samuel Alemayehu and Zeru Kehishen took part in the proceedings.[69] In the history of the EPRP, this was the first time that alternate members had been excluded from the proceedings of the EPRP CC.

With Samuel taking the lead, discussions were conducted on a number of existing and new political positions of the EPRP. Old policies of the struggle were elaborated and clarifications were made on some. Among others, the Eritrean question which had been categorized as a national one, was rephrased as an issue to be viewed within the broad framework of the national question. The PPG slogan, coined during the turbulent years of the 1974 revolutionary movement was characterized as a slogan to be raised as

part of the rural armed struggle.
The three-member EPRP CC group discussed EPRP's policies on urban armed activity. The issue regarding the possibility of a popular uprising, raised in a PB paper a year and a half earlier, was labeled as the work of "some" members and[70] that position was characterized as a deviation from the EPRP political line. This was in reference to the decision of the First EPRP Congress of 1972 which had characterized the struggle as one of a protracted people's war.
The second major issue that the three-man CC group decided to resolve was EPRP's leadership crisis. By this time, many of the eighteen EPRP CC members had become victims of the repression.[71] The CC was left with only half its capacity, and two members were abroad. It was feared that another crisis, whether due to the impending war with the TPLF or other unforeseen circumstances, would leave the EPRP without leadership.
The leadership crisis had become more severe because of factionalism and dissidence both in the rural and urban EPRP structures, the constant conflict of the EPRA with the TPLF, and the loss of many capable EPRP members. Resolution of EPRP's leadership crisis was one of the goals leading EPRP members agreed upon. However, how to resolve the problem was an unaddressed question.
To resolve the leadership crisis, the three-man CC group took the responsibility and coopted seven full-fledged CC members and three alternate CC members were made full-fledged members. In all, ten new CC members were coopted. Even though the alternate CC members were not included in the proceedings of the three-man CC group, some of them had been consulted to give opinions about those to be coopted. The seven coopted CC members were, GM, M., DS, AA, Yosef Mersha (BN), Mezgebnesh Abiyu and YA.
In its brief history, the EPRP CC was enlarged on two occasions. The first one was on the first Extended Conference of 1975 when seven members were coopted. The second one was on the second Plenum, in 1976, where almost all of the CC members took part. The Second Plenum coopted four new alternate members and one alternate member was raised to the status of full membership.
According to the EPRP constitution, the CC had the right to coopt only one/third of its number and following[72] the last co-optation in 1976, the EPRP CC could legally coopt only three more members. The constitution had no provision for filling vacant CC seats.
Be that as it may, following the co-optation of the CC members, a new PB was also *selected*. The previous PB, which was *elected* at the first Plenum of the EPRP CC, in 1975, conducted its last meeting in March 1977. To form the new PB, it was suggested that the newly coopted CC members should also take part in the deliberation. However, the three CC members decided to form the PB on their own and explain the matter at the next CC meeting. While *selecting* members of the PB, the three CC members decided that former PB members, such as, Zeru Kehishen and AW would be retained and

they *selected* Tsegaye Gebre Medhin and Samuel as additional PB members. DS and YA were selected as substitute PB members. They suspended Kiflu Tadesse from the PB and that decision remained undisclosed for over fifteen months.

During this process, Samuel made efforts to commit the three-man CC group to suspend Kiflu Tadesse from the leadership. However, the other two CC members decided to discuss the issue in the presence of the accused.[73] Unable to do the way he wanted, Samuel stepped up this campaign in a deeply personalized tone. The campaign was intensified after the co-optation of the new CC members.[74] It hinged on the "excesses" in urban armed action. Before the discussion on EPRP policies was wrapped up, Zeru Kehishen left for Eritrea and Tsegaye became engaged in the activities of the EPRA, which at this time was facing an internal crisis of its own. The task of finishing what the three CC members had began was left to Samuel and he finalized their discussion in March 1978, after the EPRA retreated and arrived in Eritrea.[75] The discussion came out under the title, "Some positions from the EPRP" and was distributed to the other CC and EPRP members.

After Zeru left, Samuel Alemayehu one more time presented Kiflu's case to the newly reconstituted EPRP CC. Even though most of the new CC members had no idea of what had taken place regarding urban armed activities and who had played what role, they all knew that Samuel had left the urban areas only a couple of months prior to Kiflu's departure. For lack of any other source of information, the CC members accepted his arguments, except a minority who maintained lingering doubts about the entire process. Consequently, Kiflu Tadesse was suspended from the EPRP CC altogether.

However, it was decided that Kiflu would not be notified about his suspension from the CC; it was decided to inform him that he was removed only from the PB. Should he demand a CC meeting, it was agreed to hold a mock one in order to ward off his suspicion. It was also decided that he would not be introduced to the newly coopted CC members; only those he already knew would attend the mock CC "meetings". Such mock CC meetings were conducted sometime later.

According to the Constitution and the tradition of the EPRP, even in the urban areas where security was tense, the defendant was given the right to attend the meetings where his case was discussed and verdict was reached at.[76]

Fikre Zergaw another member of the EPRP CC was removed from the leadership partly because of his association with EPRA members accused of factional activities. Fikre, who was convinced that the EPRA leadership was incompetent, was also accused of spreading accusations against some leading EPRP/EPRA members. Fikre did not attend the CC meeting and the verdict was passed in his absence.[77]

Following the co-optation, new assignments were made and Samuel Alemayehu was placed in many of the committees by the CC. He became a member of the PB and the Secretariat. He also became the chairperson of the newly formed, yet powerful committee known as the Politico-military department, which was directly in charge of the EPRA. He was assigned as the Foreign Committee contact man. He was in charge of the committee for urban affairs. He also became a member of the *Democracia* editorial board. When it was difficult to conduct meetings, it was Samuel who went around and discussed issues or passed on information to the other CC members.

Another engagement of the CC members in Tigrai was conducting negotiation with the TPLF.

The EPRP and the TPLF

The Tigrai People's Liberation Front (TPLF) was one of the groups that came into being during the early days of the 1974 movement. Prior to the formation of the TPLF, a number of other little known Tigrayan groups were formed under the guise of student and cultural centers. The first student organization of Tigrayan university students was formed in January 1966. Among the objectives of the group was to help high school students in Tigrai pass the high-school living examination.[78] In 1970, a group known as the Tigrai National Organization (TNO) was formed. This was a covert Tigrayan political group, the majority of whose members were university students. Some of the members of this group would later join the TPLF. In the summer of 1970, a cultural group known as the Tigray People's Cultural Organization (TPCO) was established. The overt purpose of this group was promoting Tigrai culture and folk dance, reviving Tigrayan history and Tigrigna. Founding members of this group were Abebe Tessema and Desta Bezabih. TPCO was somewhat active even during the Derge's regime and it was used as a vehicle to rally support for the nationalist cause. Another little known group that was formed in 1970 was the Tigrayan Socialist Youth League. Founding members of this group were Amare Tesfu, Abebe Tessema, Rezene Kidane and Giday Hagos. The ostensible aim of this group was spreading Marxism.

During the last months of 1974, a small, but a determined group of Tigrayans set out to initiate an armed struggle for the liberation of Tigrai against what they considered an Amhara rule. They "argued that a class struggle fought within an Ethiopia-wide front was not possible given the intensity of the national contradiction....They maintained that the resolution of these contradictions was a prerequisite to class emanication."[79] They were convinced that each nationality should fight for its own national liberation and consequently, they formed the Tigrai People's Liberation Front in February 1975.

The EPRP established relation with the group that formed the Tigrai People's Liberation Front in 1974 when Berhane Iyasu contacted Aregawi Berhe in Addis Abeba.[80] However, that contact was discontinued when the Tigrayan group left for Tigrai to initiate an armed struggle. The first official contact between the TPLF and the EPRA was made in January 1975 at Reissi

Adi, Eritrea, between Berhane Meskel Redda of the EPRA and Hailu Mengesha and Abbay Tsehaye of the TPLF.[81] Members of the TPLF approached the EPRA to request for arms.[82] Mainly due to shortage of arms, the EPRA was unable to satisfy TPLF's demands. A few months later, the two military groups began campaigning against each other. In the initial phase, TPLF members accused Berhane Meskel of labeling them as followers of Gessese Ayele, one of the founding members of the group and a member of the parliament during the Haile Selassie regime. Members of the EPRA believed that the TPLF was conducting a smear campaign against Berhane Meskel to minimize his influence. Berhane Meskel's mother was from the Adewa aweraja in Tigrai, as were most of the TPLF leaders.

The TPLF and the EPRA traversed the same area. Unlike the contacts with other organizations, EPRP's relationship with the TPLF was a necessity for the survival of both armed groups, who had differing political goals and conflicting objectives. The base area of the EPRA was the Agame aweraja in northern Tigrai, close to the Eritrean border; while the TPLF had laid down its infrastructure in the western part of Tigrai, in the Shire Awaraja. The TPLF was trained and armed by the EPLF and " . . . the first group of about thirty Tigrai youth went for training with the EPLF to Eritrea in January" and April 1975. At its Congress on February 18, 1976, the TPLF elected a seven-man leadership.[83]

Following the launching of the armed struggle, the TPLF toured some awarajas of Tigrai and proclaimed that the "the second Weyanne revolution had began".[84] The first one being the Tigrai peasant uprising of the early 1940s. Following that uprising, Tigrayan peasants had been disarmed, except those in Shire, Tembien and some of the lowland areas.[85]

Sometime before the emergence of the TPLF, a military group known as the Tigrayan Liberation Front (TLF), trained by and affiliated with the ELF appeared in the Agame aweraja. Since 1971/72, the ELF and the EPLF had been on a war footing. The TLF ceased to exist when in the guise of a merger, the TPLF executed and arrested some of the leaders of the group.[86]

Despite initial antagonisms, relations between the EPRA and the TPLF were established in October 1975 and continued for two and a half years. During this period, nine meetings were held. The first few meetings were conducted by members of the EPRA leadership, Berhane Iyasu, MGE, Tsegaye Gebre Medhin and AA. Representing the TPLF, Wolde Selassie Nega, Abaye Tsehaye and Giday Zeratsion attended most of the meetings.

The first meeting took place in Ocotober 1975, a few months after Berhane Meskel had left for Addis Abeba. In this meeting, leading members of the EPRA presented an analysis of the Ethiopian situation, in which the class struggle was portrayed as the main feature of the politics of Ethiopia.[87] The TPLF, on the other hand, envisaged the national contradiction as the main feature of the conflict in the country. This assertion was spelled out in 1985, at the Congress conducted to assess the ten years of struggle of the communist force within the TPLF.[88] The TPLF publication, *Weyen*, stated,

Ethiopian unity rests on the subjugation of the oppressed nationality by the oppressor nationality. As a result, there is now a deep and sharp national antagonism with a precedence of national consciousness over class consciousness. This has implied that the oppressed classes of the oppressed and oppressor nationalities cannot fight side by side against their class enemy. Under these conditions, the interests of democracy and socialism demand that the oppressed nationalities carry a new democratic revolution independently, for the sake of the oppressed classes of the oppressor nationality. This should be the strategy for the NDR in Ethiopia."[89]

Differences on the analysis of the Ethiopian situation notwithstanding, the EPRA delegates presented a four-point proposal regarding relationship. The first point discussed the integration of the two groups. If that was difficult to implement, the second option was to form a united front. If no understanding could be reached on the second proposal, the third option was to sign an agreement of cooperation. If the third option did not work out, the last option was to make an arrangement of "peaceful coexistence" and avoid military confrontation.

The TPLF was reviewing its program and did not present a specific proposal. It objected the merger of the two groups arguing that the TPLF was not a party.[90] The TPLF could not accept the formation of a united front on the grounds that it could not be initiated only by one nationalist and one multinational organization. In the assessment it conducted in 1985, about ten years later, the TPLF admitted that the position was wrong, and it was due to narrow nationalist feelings.[91]

While the option of "peaceful coexistence" was under discussion, the TPLF suggested that the EPRA leave Tigrai. The TPLF advocated the formation of nationalist organizations as opposed to multinational ones, and conducting the struggle on a strict national and regional basis. The TPLF proposed that each nationalist organization limit itself to its respective territory: the Amharas to Amharic speaking areas, the Oromos to Wellega, etc. The EPRA delegates found TPLF's request to leave Tigrai quite unacceptable and the idea was rejected outright. They explained that, as a multinational organization, the EPRP/EPRA had the right to operate wherever it felt appropriate. The delegates believed that the EPRP had more Tigrayan members than the TPLF itself and had equal rights to operate in the Tigrai area, even if ethnic composition would be given credence. Among the EPRP delegates who conducted the negotiation were Berhane Iyasu and MGE, from the Tigrai region. Once again, in the assessment conducted in 1985, the TPLF admitted that their position was wrong.[92]

While the negotiation was underway, the EPRA delegates disclosed that they were negotiating on behalf of the EPRA and not the EPLO/EPRP. The TPLF delegates could not comprehend the new disclosure. They thought it was a ploy to mislead them.[93] TPLF leaders believed that the EPRP considered it belittling itself negotiating with a nationalist group.[94]

With no agreement, the negotiators scheduled another date. In the meantime, the TPLF opened a campaign against the EPRP. In November 1975, at a place called Hareza, a TPLF contingent asserted that it would drive "Amharas" out of the area. This referred to the EPRA.

The second meeting took place a month later, in November 1975, at Saasie. The differences separating the organizations remained the same, and TPLF delegates were offended when EPRA delegates identified them as a small group of nationalists rather than a democratic national movement. By this time, the TPLF consisted of "a little over a hundred youth, most of them former students."[95] The EPRA delegates' comment reflected the prevalent attitude of many activists toward a nationalist deviation. It was regarded as ill-conceived, in as much as all sectors of the country had risen in unison and coordination of forces was very important. The impasse unbroken, the discussion was postponed for another date. In the meantime, the negotiators agreed to publish the positions of the two organizations and invite the EPLF to attend the next meeting. However, the statement never came out.

After the second meeting, the TPLF concluded that the EPRP was a chauvinist organization.[96] A paper published much later reflected that view: "[F]rom the very beginning, it was reflected that the EPRP was a national chauvinist petty-bourgeois organization that is inimical to the Tigrayan people."[97] After the two meetings, the TPLF bided its time waiting for an opportunity to implement its beliefs to drive out the EPRA from Tigrai.[98] A similar idea was expressed in the report titled the Assessment of the Marxist-Leninist League of Tigrai, July 1985.[99]

The third meeting, attended by Tesfaye Debessai and two EPLF representatives, Iyoob and Baraakhi took place in February 1976 at Saasie. Once again no agreement could be reached on the issues raised above. However, it was agreed to form a Coordinating Committee composed of members of the two organizations. The main task of this committee was to oversee and resolve conflicts as they arose. Even though there was no break through in the relationship of the two organizations, in its response to the Derge's call for the formation of a front in April 1976, the EPRP regarded the TPLF as one of the forces that should be included in the political process.[100]

The relationship between the two armed groups continued to deteriorate, and recriminations were intensified. In August and September 1976, the TPLF officially published anti-EPRP articles in its publication *Weyen*. All Tigrayan EPRP members and those who collaborated with the organization were nicknamed "*kurkurat*", a Tigrayan word which, directly translated means "puppies", but in this case stood for "lackey" of the Amharas. The EPRP was dubbed "Abaye Ethiopia", a Tigrayan word for Greater Ethiopia. It implied chauvinism. On the other hand, EPRP/EPRA members undermined the TPLF. Many in the EPRP camp had very low regard of the TPLF mainly because of their lack of sophistication, clarity and articulation of ideas. They were considered as a bunch of high-school dropouts. In those areas where EPRA members conducted propaganda activities, they portrayed the TPLF as a narrow nationalist organization and it seemed that Tigryans in the Agame Aweraja liked such presentation. Once, a peasant remarked, "to me Ethiopia means a full *injera* (bread) and Tigrai only half an injera."[101]

When the TPLF leadership published its "1976 manifesto" declaring that it was fighting for Tigrayan independence, the relationship between the two groups deteriorated further. A recent publication by one of the founding members and a former leader of the TPLF, Aregawi Berhe, stated that the "Manifesto" declaring the independence of Tigrai was prepared by only three members of the leadership, Abaye Tsehaye, Melesse Zenawi and Wolde Selassie Nega.[102]

No rapport could be established between the EPRA and the TPLF. To complicate matters, the TPLF moved from its hinterland in the Sheraro awerja to the Agame awerja, the rear area of the EPRA.

Throughout the whole period, the two organizations remained unable to create a platform on which to cooperate or work together. The main obstacles during the initial phase of contact were the different opinions of the two groups regarding the struggle and TPLF's insistence that the EPRA should leave Tigrai and operate elsewhere.

As tension mounted, members of both organizations confronted each other using all kinds of pretexts. Name calling was the common form of expressing discontent, until the TPLF went a step ahead and began harassing peasant militia and supporters of the EPRA. Some of the peasants were flogged. Then the TPLF began killing peasants who supported the EPRA. Among the first to be killed was Kahsai, a peasant of the Adi Irob area in the Agame district.[103] Following this incident, the EPRA leadership passed a memo expressing its intention to take measures against the TPLF. However, EPRA members protested and the leadership backed off.

On political and economic matters in Tigrai, the EPRP and the TPLF had marginal programmatic differences. In Tigrai, land distribution was handled by traditional institutions, in the age-old peasant redistribution method. Elders were elected every few years and at the level of villages, they made sure that land distribution and redistribution were properly executed. So, the role of both the TPLF and the EPRA were reduced to seeing that customary laws were fairly practiced and complaints properly handled.

Because of their marginal ability to change the economic condition of the people, both the TPLF and the EPRA had to resort to political agitation to win over the support of the people. The EPRP focused on broad political reforms of the system, including the formation of a democratic government. The TPLF harped on the neglect of Tigrai by the central government and used Tigrayan nationalism to rally the peasantry. Aboye Gebrai, an elderly peasant of the Adi Irob area once remarked, "you are our sons and we love you, but all of you (the TPLF, the Derge and the EPRA) promise us a very good future. You promise us that you will build clinics and dig wells, etc.", and pointing to a nearby mountain he continued, "but whoever comes and goes these rugged mountains and barren valleys will be there forever."[104]

These realities brought the TPLF and the EPRA to a confrontation. Both groups operated in the same area and made efforts to win over the same population. Conflicts that arose between two villages or two individuals involved the two organizations, each supporting the other side. Both organizations would involve themselves in a conflict to win over a peasant association. Conflicts would also arise when recruiting peasant militia and TPLF members were enraged when many peasants continued to support the EPRA. The conflicts were not confined to the EPRA and the TPLF alone, but also the ELF, which operated in the Tigrai-Eritrean border. Conflicts might arise because of territorial claims or grazing land that the villages on the Eritrean and the Tigrayan side wanted to control. The different organizations came out supporting the different villages. There were cases where conflict arose when the ELF prohibited Tigrayans from crossing over to Eritrea and the EPRA opposed that decision.[105]

The conflict between the TPLF and the EPRP was not limited to the rural structures. There were conflicts between the two organizations in the Tigrai urban areas as well. The EPRP believed that TPLF had collaborated with POMOA representatives of Adigrat and Mekele and passed on the names of suspected EPRP members.[106] In mid-1977, the EPRP detained a member of the Adigrat POMOA who was accused of endangering the lives of EPRP members. Before action was taken, the TPLF disclosed that he was among its members and the individual was turned over to the TPLF.[107] During the last months of 1977, the EPRA accused the TPLF of executing a line-man, that is, an EPRP member assigned to escort members from the urban areas. When he was killed, the line-man was guiding some members who never reached the EPRA. It was believed that they were kidnapped by the TPLF. On the other hand, the TPLF believed that the EPRP committed similar acts against its members using EPRP's connections in POMOA.[108]

For a year and a half, tension mounted between the EPRA and TPLF and both groups formed attitudes about each other. As was indicated above, most of the TPLF leadership had concluded that all Ethiopian multinational organizations, including the EPRP, were chauvinistic.[109] On the other hand, EPRP and EPRA members considered the TPLF a narrow nationalist organization. Ironically, the TPLF itself came to a similar conclusion in its assessment ten years later which linked TPLF's mistakes to "narrow nationalist deviations". The assessment, however, made a distinction between a "narrow nationalist line" and a deviation.[110]

Because of the fast growth of the EPRP, many of its members, including the leadership, were complacent. Many felt that the political line of the EPRP was correct and that it was an invincible and infallible political force.

The TPLF was a little known organization. It was regarded as a small force that would be limited to the Tigrai area alone.[111]

When the next rounds of negotiations were resumed in 1977, some major political developments had taken place. The peaceful form of struggle had become untenable and the EPRP publicly declared the armed struggle as the main one. Consequently, the EPRA had become EPRP's main organization. The transition to the armed struggle as the main form had also made Tigrai an area where the EPRP concentrated its forces and activities. Furthermore, the relationship between the EPLF and the EPRP had deteriorated after the EPRP failed to accept the "colonial" theory.[112] On the other hand, the TPLF had recognized Eritrea as an Ethiopian colony.[113] Besides, the TPLF and the EPLF had signed an agreement of cooperation and a joint-communique was released to that effect.[114] Moreover, before the fourth meeting between the TPLF and the EPRA was resumed, the TPLF had dropped its first program which advocated an independent Tigrai.[115] That change took place in September 1976 when the TPLF produced its second program. However, as the report of the 1985 Assessment...admitted, "[W]hile trying to rectify the errors, [narrow nationalist deviations], their root causes and essence were not assessed. Because of this, total rectification of the errors from their basic core remained difficult to overcome."[116]

As stated previously, the TPLF had involved itself in an internecine war with the EDU and hundreds of fighters had been killed on both sides. Sometime before contact with the EPRP was resumed, the TPLF had abandoned part of the area it had held in the Shire *aweraja*.

The fourth meeting took place in Tsorena, Eritrea, in April 1977. It was attended by members of the EPRP CC and the leadership of the EPRA, among them: Fikre Zergaw, Iyasu Alemayehu, Zeru Kehishen, DS and Tsegaye Gebre Medhin. This was the first time that a large number of EPRP CC members attended such a meeting. The Coordinating Committee formed by the TPLF and the EPRA a year or so earlier had become dysfunctional. The major accomplishment of this meeting was to create another committee to oversee and resolve conflicts arising between the two organizations. An announcement of the formation of the committee was published.

The fifth meeting was held in Menechusieto, Eritrea, in May 1977. At this meeting, EPRP delegates expressed their desire for cooperation. The main concern, however, was to make sure that the deteriorating relationship between the two organizations did not explode into a war. The EPRP believed that a war with a nationalist organization would tarnish its image not only among Tigrayans, but other nationalists as well. Besides, the EPRP did not want to be trapped into an internecine war with a nationalist organization while it was in a severe crisis and had other tasks to accomplish. Furthermore, the TPLF had already changed its political program and had dropped the question of Tigrayan independence; it had exhibited some flexibility, be it in earnest or feigned.

Agreement was reached on the urgency of forming a front, and the organizations decided to open themselves up. The Coordinating Committee was empowered to write and distribute articles to EPRA and TPLF members. Furthermore, the Coordinating Committee was empowered to conduct discussions among TPLF and EPRA members. It was agreed that the work of the committee would not be impeded by the leadership of the organizations.

The Coordinating Committee was expected to submit proposals on the formation of a front to both leadership bodies, and was expected to take the lead in that endeavor. Despite these points of agreements, there remained some major differences between the TPLF and the EPRA. The TPLF recognized the EPRP as a Marxist Leninist (ML) organization,[117] but refused to admit that it was a vanguard party, as EPRP delegates maintained. In mid 1976, eight months before this meeting, the TPLF had characterized the EPRP "not as a proletarian party, but a petty-bourgeois democratic organization." [118] It was difficult to tell whether the TPLF had changed its views. Another difference emerged when the TPLF insisted upon being recognized as the sole representative of the Tigrai people.[119] The EPRP delegates refused to accept that notion on the grounds that it was up to the Tigrayan people to make that decision.

There was a major point of difference over participation in the front to be formed. The EPRP delegates suggested that parties, groups, national movements, mass organizations and professional organizations should take part in the front.[120] During this period, the EPRP had formed a number of mass and national organizations that had accepted its program and leadership. The TPLF rejected the idea and suggested that only the EPRP should join the front. The fifth meeting between the TPLF and EPRP adjourned, agreeing that the details of front formation would be worked out at the next meeting.

Notwithstanding the differences on some of the issues, the EPRP leadership believed that the new agreement was a major break-through in its relationship with the TPLF. After the meeting, some EPRP CC members blamed the deteriorating relationship between the two organizations on EPRA's leadership, which had conducted the previous negotiations. Some EPRP CC members felt that it was possible to establish a peaceful working relationship with the TPLF. The political effect of the new agreement between the TPLF and the EPRP was that it created a rift between the EPRP CC members and the EPRA leadership. Intentional or not, the TPLF was able to create a wedge between the leadership bodies of the EPRP and EPRA, and this had a devastating subsequent effect. The leadership of the EPRA, which maintained strong reservations about the TPLF, became withdrawn and passive.

In the first months of 1977, the TPLF, probably to escalate the simmering conflict within the EPRA, claimed that it had established contact with some dissenting EPRA members. In its report of the 1985 Assessment..., it stated, "the TPLF used to conduct repeated and detailed discussions with individuals (EPRP members) that had democratic inclinations."[121] It is difficult to establish whether such a contact had existed, how far it had gone, or whether it had assumed any organizational form. However, it would be far fetched to think that the TPLF had a significant ability to instigate and exacerbate the EPRA crisis. Besides, there was no rule or regulation restricting EPRA members from conducting discussion with a member of another organization.

After reaching an agreement with the TPLF, the actual front formation and the details of this process were beyond the legal prerogatives of the EPRP CC delegates who met with the TPLF. These matters required a CC meeting, which could not be convened due to the severe crisis that the EPRP was in since February 1977. The delay contributed to the deterioration of relations between the two organizations.

The Coordinating Committee resolved some issues. However, the euphoria of front formation did not last long. "Assimba", an EPRA publication, warned that preparation for the formation of a front required secession of hostilities. The paper reminded that both groups had to stop waging campaigns and counter-campaigns.[122] A few days after the agreement to form a front was concluded, a member of the EPRA militia was killed by the TPLF. The anti-EPRP campaign was stepped-up and tension continued running high. The EPRA, in a deep political problem (associated with the rectification movement), was consumed by internal problems.

In 1976/77, the TPLF was involved in a war with the EDU-Terenafit. Besides, the TPLF also faced an internal crisis due to fighters discontent. One of the first demands of the fighters was regional representation in the TPLF leadership. During this time, the great majority of the TPLF leadership were from Adewa, one of the *awerajas* in Tigrai. Furthermore, the fighters wanted "to discuss on issues regarding the internal structure of the TPLF and matters concerning TPLF's relationship with other democratic organizations, such as the EPRP."[123] There were complaints against the members of the leadership of nepotism, favoritism, partiality, undemocratic practices, etc. The summary execution of nine TPLF fighters who resigned from the organization and demanded safe passage was another issue that exacerbated the crisis. The majority of those killed were from Tembien and Inderta.[124]

As the internal TPLF crisis continued, a ten-man military council elected from all of the branches of the front was set up. The committee was known as the *Wetaderawi Baito*. Discussions that involved the entire membership of the TPLF were held. Shortcomings, errors and wrong tendencies were raised and discussed. As the discussion unfolded, the TPLF leadership became the main target of the movement.[125] The leadership grew apprehensive and arrested members of the *Wetaderawi Baito*. In short, the rectification movement which the TPLF leadership dubbed as *hinfishfish*, a subversive activity, was short-lived. Leading figures of the movement became the targets of repression and a witch hunt was conducted. Some of the members of the *Wetaderawi Baito* were executed. According to Hailu Mengesha, a former member of the TPLF leadership and a victim of the *hinfishfish*, over half of TPLF's membership either abandoned the struggle or fell victim of the witch hunt. Nepotism, favoritism and regionalism were considered as the main factors for the massive desertions.[126] Hundreds of fighters were killed and[127] when all was over, a determined and monolithic TPLF leadership emerged. Such was the condition within the TPLF leadership until two of the leading figures of the leadership, Aregawi Berhe and Giday Zeratsion, were forced to resign from the TPLF sometime in 1985.

Be that as it may, the sixth meeting of the EPRA and the TPLF was called to discuss the death of an EPRA peasant militia. That incident had caused an uproar among EPRA members. The TPLF also presented its complaints. Once again, it was agreed to ease the tension between the two organizations.

During that period, the EPRP CC delegates came up with a "tit-for-tat" policy, for every EPRA member killed, a TPLF member would also be killed, for every EPRA fighter arrested, a TPLF fighter would be arrested. A few days after the sixth meeting, a TPLF member was killed and another wounded. Consequently, tension between the two organizations ran high again. It seemed that the two groups were headed toward an all out confrontation. Physical abuse of peasant members and supporters, exchange of threats, name calling and recrimination became everyday occurrences.

The seventh meeting was held in September 1977. The TPLF had many complaints. No agreement could be reached and the next meeting was set for November.

The eighth meeting was held in Sebeya, in December 1977. Once again, an agreement was reached to revitalize the Coordinating Committee, which had been inoperative for quite some time. A joint statement was drafted. However, at the insistence of the TPLF, the statement came out in only fifty copies, to be distributed only among members of the two organizations. For some curious reason, the TPLF did not want the paper to be distributed among the militia and the peasantry.

The EPRA distributed the joint statement, the TPLF, however, failed to do so even among its members. Apparently, the TPLF did not want to give its members false hope. At the meeting, the EPRA/EPRP delegates asked the TPLF about the contact the group had allegedly established with the Derge. The TPLF did not provide any explanation, but responded that the issue could be raised at the meeting to be held sometime in 1978.

A few weeks after the new agreement, two EPRA members were killed by the TPLF. The TPLF called the ninth meeting and it was held on 26 February 1978. Zeru Kehishen, Gebre Egziabher Haile Mikael, Gedion, A. and the late Haile Abaye from the EPRP; Tewedros, Berhane Gebre Kirstos and others from the TPLF attended the meeting. The TPLF and the EPRA had deployed some contingents not far from the meeting place.

The main point of the agenda which the TPLF wanted to discuss was regarding an EPRA contingent which was assigned in the Klete Awelalo area. The contingent, which was led by Redaye, had been conducting effective political and social activities (including farming) among the peasantry. Delegates of the TPLF demanded that the contingent be removed from Klete Awelalo. EPRP delegates could not accept the demand, rather, they insisted that the TPLF respect the decision passed by the Coordinating Committee. The TPLF argued that unless EPRA contingents refrained from their hostile activities, it would find it difficult to follow the decision of the Coordinating

Committee. The meeting was concluded without achieving much and another meeting was set for April.

While the meeting was about to be concluded, a messenger arrived at the meeting place to inform about the death of a TPLF member. This was an action taken by the EPRA to retaliate for the death of the two EPRA members mentioned above. The incident took place in Aiga, which the TPLF claimed was one of its base areas [128] The EPRA believed that it was a listening post' of the TPLF situated right in the middle of the EPRA base area. The EPRA had earlier demanded that the TPLF close down the 'post'.

On February 27, a TPLF force in Sebeya, about six miles from Aiga, opened fire on an unexpecting EPRA force.[129] Because of the presence of other EPRA forces in the vicinity, the TPLF force was overpowered and it retreated from the Agame area. Then, the EPRA attacked a TPLF prison in Sebeya and released more than twenty TPLF members. The prisoners claimed that they had been arrested because they had demanded to resign from the TPLF.[130]

The TPLF claimed the incident at Aiga as the prelude to the war that errupted in March 1978.[131] As far as the EPRA was concerned, that incident was no different from similar clashes that had been going on for quite some time.

When the confrontation between the TPLF and the EPRA was known, the EPRA leadership in the Begemidir area was alerted. However, before it could mobilize to augment the units in Tigrai, a messenger arrived to inform that the EPRA leadership was in full control, having repulsed TPLF's attack in Sebya. EPRA units in Begemidir were asked to focus on the Derge's offensive in their area.

EPRA's retaliation on a TPLF post was regarded as a prelude to the coming war. The extension of the skirmish to the Sebeya area made a further confrontation likely.

Predicament of the EPRA in Tigrai

In the last months of 1977, there was discontent among some EPRA members and participation in the activities of the army was subdued.[132] There was widespread complaint and the campaign targeted newly arrived members from the urban areas. The inactivity of the EPRA was one of the main causes for the grievance. In the Tigrai area, the EPRA had been inactive since the RM, except for operations in November 1977 and February 1978.[133] Besides, doubt and frustration were expressed by EPRA members regarding the strategy and tactics of the army, the role of the urban armed struggle, the competence of the EPRA leadership, democracy in the army, the formation of a United Front, favoritism and nepotism, etc. Members asked whether the EPRP still had a leadership. There was a belief that most of the members of the leadership had already been victimized. Furthermore, left-over grievances from the RM were expressed more forcefully, including the campaign against the members of the former EPRA leadership.[134] Convocation of a Congress of the army was among the demands raised.

The newly elected EPRA leadership soon became engaged in an intense activity involving Company 500. It took the EPRA leadership more than two months to resolve some of the problems raised. A platoon of Company 47 wrote an article in the army publication emphasizing the relationship between new/old comers, members of the leadership and rank and file members, etc. It also criticized certain individuals in the EPRP/EPRA leadership for nepotism and "bureaucratic elitism". The article was highly polemical and created a charged atmosphere.

The EPRA leadership produced a harshly worded article responding to the charges and this aggravated the controversy. The army leadership insisted that the criticism be withdrawn, but to no avail. Some platoon members expressed their earnest feelings about problems within the EPRA in order to find some remedy. Once again rumors and gossip emanating particularly from the Militia Committee, the clinic and contingents around the base area spread around. The clinic, where many members passed time, served as the forum for such activities.

When conditions worsened, apprehension reigned among the leaders of the army and they began expressing fear of anti-organization elements. Rumors indicating that the EPRA had been infiltrated by TPLF collaborators, anjas and government spies spread. The havoc that factional activities wrecked on the urban structures of the EPRP had an important bearing on the attitude of both leadership and rank and file members. By this time, colossal damage had befallen the EPRP, and the leadership had already been sensitized to the effect of factional activities. The EPRA leadership expressed fear of such activities to the contingents that had returned from the Wello area during the last months of 1977.[135]

During the last months of 1977, the EPRP/EPRA leadership formed a committee to conduct political training. Upon completion of the course, some of the trainees were assigned to units in order to provide guidance on issues that were raised by the members. However, the political problems did not ease. On February 18, 1978, seminars were conducted for selected rank and file members and members of the leadership of various contingents. While these activities were underway, some members began questioning the motive of organizing such seminars. It was rumored that the leadership was intending to eliminate those who had dissenting views and the seminars were regarded as "confession" (*magaletcha*) sessions.

Following the emotional *expose* of Anja activities in urban areas and the damage they had inflicted on the EPRP, the political training session took an abrupt turn. An EPRA member stated that he was an Anja (factionalist) and disclosed some of the activities that he participated in. A number of others disclosed that they, though unaware, had taken part in the campaign. Some even revealed very minor points of dissatisfaction which they had expressed to others. They confessed before others told on them and some others were asked to expose who or what they knew about certain individuals. Following these revelations, the seminars assumed different directions as members were reproved or denounced themselves. This sent a shock wave among others who themselves might have expressed dissenting views on party policies at one time or another.

At the seminars, accusations were made against those who were suspected of spreading rumors and discontent. They were accused of establishing connections with the TPLF, breaching the legal channels and the laws of the army, and wantonly expressing their views on policy matters and political stands of the EPRP. At the closing of the seminars, a good number of members were detained and the participants demanded that they be punished. However, tempers cooled off and most of those arrested were reprimanded and released.

Those who had confessed or were suspected of instigating the problem were arrested. A Commission of Inquiry was formed and the case was passed on to the Military Tribunal for prosecution. Among the charges labelled against those arrested was trying to form an organization within the EPRA, conducting underground meetings, conspiring to overthrow the EPRA leadership, spying or contacting the enemy, etc. Among those arrested was Yirga Tessema (Mezmur), a member of the Army Leadership Committee. His name was mentioned by those, including Belay Hassen, who claimed that they had conducted meetings with him. Belay Hassen was a graduate of the Addis Abeba University and the manager of the Berhanena Selam Printing Press before he joined the EPRA.

Yirga Tessema was blamed for conducting a number of meetings in the Alitena area, Tigrai province, with some of the accused individuals. He had no structural linkage with the individuals. All throughout his stay under detention, Yirga Tessema denied the charges.[136] Among those that Belay Hassen exposed was DHM, a leading EPRA member. DHM and Belay Hassen were members of the finance committee and they passed most of their time together. During this time, DHM and Belay Hassen discussed about inefficiency and bureaucracy in the EPRA. DHM who attended the seminar, successfully defended himself and accused Belay Hassen of spreading false information and tarnishing the image of EPRA members.[137]

It was while the EPRA was engaged in this internal crisis and while morale was low that the TPLF, which was believed to have left the Agame area began getting ready for the final confrontation. Before the TPLF became engaged in the 1978 war with the EPRA, the EPRP believed that the TPLF had assessed a number of conditions.[138] There were some incidents where TPLF members joined the EPRA training center and defected after arming themselves.[139] Furthermore, the TPLF knew that the EPRA was undergoing another crisis, this time, an internal dissent. It also knew that EPRP's relationship with the ELF and the EPLF was fast deteriorating.[140] The TPLF was also aware that the EPRP was undergoing a severe repression in the urban centers and thousands of fighters were joining the EPRA.[141] As was indicated elsewhere, the TPLF had concluded an agreement with the EPLF.

To launch the confrontation, the TPLF alerted its peasants' militia and had its supply ready. Almost the entire TPLF force was reorganized to assure combat readiness. Smaller units were incorporated into larger formations in a process known as 'metatef'. When these and other information became known, they were passed on to the EPRA and the EPRP leadership. However, both institutions did not react fast and did not ready themselves for the impending war.[142] None of the EPRA contingents were told to be on the alert and the EPRA leadership was preoccupied with the internal problems of the army and was campaigning to bring the situation under control. Some of the units had traveled some distance away from the base area, thereby making communications very difficult. Even though the EPRA was using walkie-talkies, quite often, urgent messages were relayed through a system known as *"toff"*, messenger. The clinic was packed with wounded and sick members. Hundreds of thousands of bullets, some arms, important and compromising documents were not hidden. The battle conducted in Sebya, mentioned earlier, was regarded as an isolated incident and the general membership was not alerted about the impending imbroglio. As a result, the EPRA was caught unprepared when the TPLF launched its attack and took many of them off-guard.

On the other hand, the TPLF argued that the EPRP initiated the war. As far as the TPLF was concerned, EPRA's attack in Aiga and the skirmish in Sebya were considered as first signs of the impending war. According to the TPLF, the EPRP was losing grounds both in the urban and rural areas, finally becoming confined to the Erob area, in Tigrai. Therefore, the EPRA had to challenge the TPLF which it believed was a factor for EPRA's isolation.[143] The TPLF further argued that it was not to its interest to be engaged with the EPRA when it was immersed in an incessant war with the EDU.[144]

Be that as it may, after retreating from the Agame areas for a few days, a reinforced TPLF force returned and on March 13, 1978, it attacked an unsuspecting EPRA contingent (company 74), putting a third of it out of action. Company 74 was conducting routine activities and it was uninformed even about the Sebeya battle between the TPLF and the EPRA. Furthermore, TPLF forces attacked two EPRA contingents at a place called Midro, not far from Nebelet.[145] EPRA forces sustained heavy casualities and the remaining forces retreated. When TPLF's unexpected attack was known, retreating EPRA forces regrouped around the base area. TPLF forces continued advancing and on March 25, at Bizet, they opened an offensive on EPRA contingents. Fierce war ensued. Both the TPLF and the EPRA sustained heavy casualities and many of EPRA's irreplaceable military leaders fell victim. Besides TPLF's surprise attack, lack of sleep, malaria, hunger and low morale constituted additional problems for EPRA fighters.

EPRA forces retreated further and TPLF forces advanced on two fronts. On one of the fronts, very close to the base area, another battle took place. The battle went on for the whole day, at which point, the EPRA leadership decided to lure in the TPLF to a more favorable terrain and attack it when darkness fell. Before it could implement its tactics, the EPRA was surprised when a large force in uniform came from Tsorena in the direction of Eritrea and blocked the exit. It was not confirmed with absolute certainity, but many EPRA fighters and the leadership concluded that the EPLF was also taking part in the war. Their conclusion was based on the uniform that the group was wearing, the style of the warfare it conducted, fire-power and the highland Eritrean dialect the combatants spoke. During this period, both the TPLF and the EPRP had no uniforms.

The TPLF argued that the Eritrean fronts never supported resolving the conflict between the EPRA and the TPLF through violent means.[146] Moreover, the TPLF still claims that the EPLF did not take part in the war and the force that came by way of Tsorena was one of TPLF's forces that had just concluded another war with the EDU, in the Shire district. The TPLF and the EDU had conducted more than thirty-two battles, according to a book published recently.[147] In this book it was stated that the EPLF was involved in the battles conducted between the EDU and the TPLF. According to the book, the liaison of the TPLF with the EPLF was Muse Barakhi [148] who was the first military commander of the TPLF.

MGE, a founding member of the EPRA, had met Muse Barakhi when the nucleus of the EPRA was in Eritrea, in 1974. At that time, Muse was a member of the EPLF. When he knew that the EPRA force was about to go to Tigrai, Muse asked MGE whether he could join the EPRA. MGE informed him that he did not have the authority to decide on such matters and referred him to Berhane Meskel. MGE did not know how the discussion fared, but Muse was not included in the EPRA group. Few months later, MGE met Muse in a small town by the Tigryan/Eritrean border. Muse, who was wearing a suit told MGE that he had been to Addis Abeba to make an arrangement for the arrival of those Tigrayan activists who would later be leading members of the TPLF.[149] He himself joined the TPLF.

As was indicated elsewhere, the EPRA and EPRP leadership also suspected that the TPLF had concluded an agreement with the Derge. During the war with the EPRA, the TPLF was transporting fighters on one of the main highways of Tigrai, at times getting as close as five to seven miles from the Derge's military base in Adigrat. A 1978 *Abyot* issue stated,

> ...The concrete agreements reached are, 1. the TPLF accepts the regional autonomy plan of the Derge; 2. the Derge agrees to incorporate the TPLF in EMALEDEH and thus [the Derge] will stop any hostile armed actions against the TPLF....[150]

A similar report was made in *Northeast African Studies*. The paper stated that the talk between the Derge and the TPLF was held "in late 1977 and early 1978, in Axum."[151] The Derge member Nadew Zakarias held the talks, according to the paper. However, the paper argued that "there is no reason to think Nadew's talk made any progress or that any deals were made with the TPLF". The TPLF never admitted such a charge and it argued that it had been on a war footing with the Derge all throughout.[152]

The battle between the EPRA and the TPLF continued. In light of EPRA's strong resistance, the TPLF was about to call for a cease-fire.[153] However, before it did so, the EPRA provisional leadership decided on a general retreat to Eritrea, through Shemezana. The leadership reached that conclusion after a series of defeat. It believed that the EPRA was surrounded on all sides and felt that the EPLF was also taking part in the war.

At the end of the war, both the TPLF and the EPRA sustained heavy casualties. It was known that peasants had buried hundreds of corpses. The exact number of fallen EPRA members is not known, however, before the war, the EPRA in Tigrai was considered more than a thousand strong. When the entire EPRA force retreated to Eritrea, that number had dwindled to about five-hundred. There also were some EPRA prisoners of war (POW's) in the hands of the TPLF.[154] Not all were victims of the war, some had resigned from the army, some had defected and some wounded members were sent to the Sudan. For an infant army, such a big loss of members as well as capable military leaders was a tragedy, to say the least.

The Strategic Retreat

EPRA's defeat in the hands of the TPLF was a major set-back which left many unanswered questions. What were the major causes for EPRA's defeat? Popular support, moral, political or military? Why did the EPRP/EPRA fail to prepare itself for TPLF's attack? Does this have to do with the perception that EPRP/EPRA leadership and members had towards the TPLF? How was the TPLF perceived and regarded on the eve of the conflict? What were EPRA forces in Begemidir doing during this time? Was there any discussion to mobilize them and attack the TPLF from the rear? These and other questions still remain unanswered. Anyhow, sometime before the war with the TPLF was concluded, the EPRP leadership in Tigrai drafted a contingency plan in case of defeat. As a last resort to avert fatal blow in the hands of the TPLF, the leadership considered retreating to Eritrea, to the area held by the ELF. A delegation consisting Zeru Kehishen, DS and H. went to Eritrea to negotiate with the ELF for a safe passage of EPRA members.

Finally, with defeat eminent, the EPRA Provisional Command decided that the EPRA should retreat to Eritrea. As a result, in the second week of April 1978, almost a month after the war began, the retreating EPRA force reached Eritrea. A group of fifteen EPRA fighters crossed Tigrai and reached the Begemidir province. Moreover, decisions were made on the prosecution of those EPRA members who had been accused but not yet convicted of factional activities. While the war with the TPLF was going on, the Military Tribunal of the EPRA was still conducting the investigation. The Provisional Command instructed the Military Tribunal to speed up the process, however, the later was unable to do so. By this time, the TPLF was a few hours away from the place where the investigation was being conducted. In this process, the Military Tribunal released eight of the accused, but could not come to conclusion regarding the rest.[155] The Provisional Command which believed that it did not have the luxury of pursuing the due process of law abruptly halted it and decreed death penalty on fourteen of them. Not all were accused of factional activities, a few of them were accused of other violations. The decision was signed by all of the members of the Provisional Command, but one, Colonel Alemayehu Asfaw.

Under EPRA's Constitution, inflicting death penalty on party members was the prerogative of the EPRP CC, after pursuing the due process of law. The decision of the Provisional Command was approved by those CC members who were with the EPRA, justifying their action as dictated by circumstances. The measure taken on those who were accused of factional activities was made public to EPRA members following their arrival in Eritrea. The summary executions further exacerbated the crisis within the EPRA.[156]

When the EPRA retreated to Eritrea, the initial reaction of ELF fighters was confusion. After some delay, the entire EPRA force was allowed into their territory and disarmed, an agonizing moment for the members of the army. Many felt betrayed. Sometime later, the whole EPRA force was allowed to go to Barka, by the Gash River, a malaria-infested area in the western part of Eritrea. The entire group stayed there for more than five months.

Following EPRA's retreat from the Agame district, some youth of the area continued to express sympathy with the EPRP. Peasants of the Adi Irob area, after arming themselves with the weapons hidden by the EPRA, conducted successive battles with the TPLF. In retaliation, the TPLF hunted down and killed some strong supporters of the EPRA. In the midst of this crisis, the Derge scored another victory over the EPRA when it seized a cache of ammunition and mortars, courtesy of former EPRA members and other informers.

When it retreated to Eritrea, the intention of the EPRA was to cross over to the EPRA group in the Begemidir area. However, the ELF did not consent and this step delayed the group's departure, despite the EPRA leadership's repeated insistence on leaving the area. Without ELF's consent, it was difficult for an unarmed group to traverse a distance of hundreds of miles. The EPRA leadership believed that the ELF was creating difficulties so that the EPRA would either disperse or go to the Sudan.[157] Had it not been for the endurance and the remarkable commitment of the members, the EPRA would have been weakened and many would have abandoned the struggle altogether. Following the failure of the negotiation conducted in mid-1977, relations between the ELF and the EPRP had remained tense.

During its stay in ELF territory, the EPRA force was supplied with one or two sacks of sorghum per week. That supply could last them only a few days. The rest of the time, the fighters ate all kinds of wild shrubs; most of them were malnourished and sick from malaria. Besides, the EPRA group was subjected to a continuous aerial bombardment by the military regime.

With the shock of the execution of "dissidents" within the ranks of the EPRA still felt, and the defeat by the TPLF still reverberating, EPRA members became engaged in discussions related to political and military issues. The paper titled "Some political positions from the EPRP" was made available to party members in Eritrea. As was indicated earlier, this paper was prepared mainly by Samuel Alemayehu, and it stirred confusion and suspicion and doubts among EPRA members. One of the controversies initiated by the paper was the alleged role that "some" individuals played in the urban military activities of the EPRP. The paper had indicated that popular uprising was advocated only by "some" individuals.

The paper was criticized by EPRA members who were part of the struggle in the urban centers and who had discussed and given some kind of support to the urban military activities of the EPRP. Those EPRA members knew that the issue mentioned above had the support of a good number of leading EPRP members in the Addis Abeba area. Some demanded that the leadership criticize itself instead of shifting the blame onto individuals. To be sure, some EPRA members had voiced reservations in the last months of 1977, after the circulation of an article that embraced lines advanced by the 'PB paper'.[158]

All through the crisis, both in Tigrai and Eritrea, most EPRP members had remained loyal to their organization, even though they had raised questions and had expressed doubts on some policies of the organization. After "Some political positions from the EPRP" came out, it became the last straw and whatever confidence was left in the EPRP leadership, it wore away fast and its sincerity was questioned.

Sometime before the departure of the EPRA from Eritrea, a dispute arose between the ELF and EPRA leaderships when the ELF exhibited unwillingness to hand back arms taken from the EPRA. After an intense negotiation, the ELF gave back some of the arms, retaining the better ones, the latest version kalashinkovs.

After enduring hardship for more than five months, the EPRA finally left Eritrea for Begemidir. The ELF allowed the EPRA to leave when the Tekeze River was at peak level and crossing was very difficult. Despite the odds, EPRA members set out to meet the difficulties.

The Tekeze River was not the only obstacle. Welkait, the Begemidir side of the river bank was controlled by the EDU, and the EPRA feared a confrontation. The EPRA group from Tigrai moved carefully and the Begemidir EPRA sent some members to the Welkait area to assist. Besides, the Northwest EPRA Command conducted an agreement with the EDU.

After some scouting and preparation, the EPRA group began crossing the Tekeze River on September 19, 1978. Rafts were built for the occasion and EPRA members clung to them while crossing. Even though skilled swimmers accompanied the rafts, there were few who were swept away by the raging torrent. Crossing the Tekeze was one of the sensational events in the history of the EPRA.

During the journey, there was a moment when starving EPRA members sustained themselves on three camels washed up on the river bank of Gash. After that "feast", many of the malnourished fighters fell ill of dysentery and typhus.

Crossing the river took almost a week. Except two, the entire EPRA force along with their packed animals and arms arrived in the Begemidir base area on October 5, 1978 and were happily reunited with other EPRA units.

Political Significance of the Defeat of the EPRA

The defeat of EPRA meant that the only formidable military opposition to the military regime in Tigrai was the TPLF. That enabled the TPLF to recruit many Tigrayan followers and spread Tigrayan nationalism. It also allowed the TPLF to become an undisputed force in that area.

Above all, the defeat of the EPRA by the TPLF, that is, a multinationalist force, at the hands of a nationalist group was a setback to the multinational cause. *The defeat of the EPRA signaled the ascendancy of nationalist forces. The victory of the TPLF over the EPRA was one of the first steps that brought the TPLF to power in 1991.*

Notes to Chapter 9

1. The report on the military operations of the EPRA is obtained from the organ of the EPRA, <u>Assimba</u>, Special Edition, No. 8.

2. <u>Northern Front of the EPRA</u>.

3. See details in Chapter I.

4. See Chapters III and V.

5. Interview, MGE, April 1991. MGE was one of the founding members of the EPRA.

6. Interview, GB, a member of the training center, 1994.

7. Interview, AM, November 1994.

8. Manifesto of the EPRA RM, pages 5-6.

9. Ibid., page 7.

10. Ibid., page 8.

11. The EPRA Constitution was first amended in 1975.

12. AM, Interview, 1994.

13. EPRA Constitution, A. iii.

14. Ibid., page ii.

15. Ibid., page iv.

16. Ibid., page 10, A.16.

17. Ibid., A.17.

18. Ibid., A.18.

19. Ibid., A.24.

20. Ibid., A.29,31 and 33.

21. Ibid., A.34.

22. Ibid., A.36.

23. Ibid., A.38.

24. Ibid., A.39.

25. Ibid., page 32.
26. Ibid., A.56.1 and 2.
27. Ibid., A.56.2b.
28. Ibid., Chapter VI, Section 1, No.1.
29. Ibid., Nos. 6 and 7.
30. Ibid., No. 8a.
31. Ibid., No. 9.
32. Ibid., No. 12.
33. Ibid., Section VII, Nos. 3 and 4.
34. Ibid., Section VII, No. 7a.
35. Ibid., Section VII, No 7b.
36. Ibid., Section VII, No.8.
37. Ibid., Section II, No. 10.
38. As we are going to witness in Chapter X, when a large number of EPRA members resigned, their right was respected. However, in some of the regional commands, members who resigned were victimized.
39. EPRA Civil Code, page iv.
40. Ibid., A.20 and 21.
41. Ibid., A.35, 36 and 37.
42. Ibid., A.40 and 41.
43. Ibid., A.51.
44. Ibid., Section, III, No. 9.
45. Ibid., A.52.
46. Ibid., A.72.
47. Ibid., A.79.
48. Ibid., A.87.
49. Ibid., A.88.
50. Ibid., A.90.

51. Ibid., A.95.

52. Interview, Debebe (code name), 1993.

53. Interview, BN, 1988.

54. Interview, a member of the EPRA leadership, 1994.

55. Interview, MGE, 1991.

56. Interview, MGE, 1991.

57. Discussion with a member of the EPRA leadership, 1994.

58. <u>Red Army</u>, Volume I, Special Issue, No.1, page 6.

59. Ibid., page 7.

60. In February 1977, an EPRA party cell that Yared Tibebu took part had discussed and sent in its views regarding the issues addressed in the 'PB paper'.

61. Interview, MGE, 1991.

62. Interview, AM, 1994.

63. Interview, MGE, 1991.

64. Manifesto of the RM, page 6.

65. Interview, MGE, 1991. He was part of the delegation.

66. Report of the EPRP FC to EPRP and Youth League members, page 6.

67. Kiflu Tadesse, <u>The Generation</u>, Part I, Independent Publishers, 1993, Chapter III.

68. While Tselote was washing his clothes, it was reported that Belay picked up his rifle and aimed at Tselote. Two members of the army, DS and Tsegaye Gebre Medhin, who as a matter of coincidence were in the area, saw Belay's actions and fired at him.

69. Zeru could not recall this decision. He argues that alternate members were excluded in those sessions where cooptation of new CC members was deliberated.

70. See details in Chapter V.

71. See details page ???

72. See details Chapter II.

73. See details Note No. 77.

74. Interview, MGE, 1991.

75. Zeru, however, disclaims taking any part in the preparation of the paper. (Interview, Zeru, 1988), and Memoir of the 4th Plenum of the CC, 1979.

76. Getahun Sisay who was suspected of infiltration, was treated differently. He was not present when his case was decided, see details Chapter V.

77. See details about Fikre, Chapter VII. Zeru Kehishen argues that he did not take part in the decisions to suspend both Kiflu and Fikre Zergaw from the EPRP leadership.

78. The back ground information regarding the groups that emerged among Tigrayan activists was provided by Abebe Tessema, October 1997. Until he abandoned the organization in 1979, Abebe Tessema was a leading member of the TPLF.

79. Kiflu Tadesse, op. cit., page 140.

80. Kiflu Tadesse, op.cit., pages 140-141.

81. Interview, Hailu Mengesha, 1997. He was one of the founding members of the TPLF.

82. One of the senior leaders of the TPLF, Aregawi Berhe, argues that as early as this period, "the TPLF leadership had decided to contact all Ethiopian organizations and create a working relationship that could develop to forming a united front or even a merger." Aregawi Berhe, January 1996.

83. John Markakis, Nationalism and Class Conflict in the Horn of Africa, Cambridge University Press, 1987, page 253.

84. Ibid., page 253.

85. Kiflu Tadesse, op.cit., pages 11-12.

86. The 10th Year Assessment of the Communist Force within the TPLF, pg. 99.

87. Kiflu Tadesse, op. cit., Chapter III.

88. The 10th Year Assessment of the Communist Force within the TPLF, pg. 10.

89. TPLF publication, Weyen, No I, February 1976.

90. The EPRP and the Ethiopian Revolution, page 37, April 1980. (A TPLF publication)

91. The 10th Year Assessment of the Communist Force within the TPLF, pages 20, 53.

92. Ibid., pages 19-20. According to Giday Zeratsion, a former TPLF leader, "... the TPLF proposed that the EPRP operates in other parts of Ethiopia not because the EPRP had no legitimacy, but because of bad relationship. It was considered unwise to compete in the same area." Giday Zerasion, 1997.

93. Discussion with a former TPLF leader and a delegate to the negotiation, August 1990, Washington, D.C.

94. Aregawi Berhe, January 1996.

95. John Markakis, op.cit., page 253.

96. Discussion with a former TPLF leader, August 1990, Washington, D.C.

97. "The EPRP and the Ethiopian Revolution", April 1980. (A TPLF publication)

98. Discussion of GKY with Melese Zenawi, 1984, TPLF liberated area. GKY was a former EPRP member and Meles Zenawi is one of the leading members of the TPLF/EPRDF.

99. The 10th Year Assessment of the Communist Force within the TPLF, pages 19-20.

100. Democracia, Volume III, Special issue.

101. From a discussion with DHM, a leading EPRA member in Assimba.

102. From the article, Malilit Zelali, Aregawi Berhe, former TPLF leader, June 1988, page 5. According to Giday Zeratsion, there was no oppostion from the TPLF leadership.

103. Aregawi Berhe, former TPLF leader, argues that such crimes were individualy instigated.

104. Zeru Kehishen's recollection, 1988.

105. Interview, a member of the EPRA General Command, November 1994.

106. Report of the EPRP FC to EPRP and Youth League members, page 10.

107. Ibid., page 12.

108. Aregawi Berhe, January 1996.

109. The 10th Year Assessment of the Communist Force within the TPLF, page 18.

110. Ibid., page 25.

111. Author's memorandum of the Shinfa seminar, June 1980. A point of view expressed by many of the participants of the seminar. The seminar was

conducted for members of the R-2 army and party structure.

112. See details in Chapter II and V.
113. The 10th Year Assessment of the Communist Force within the TPLF, page 122.
114. Whither the Eritrean People's Struggle? 1986/87 (1979 Eth.), page 140. A TPLF publication assessing the struggle in Eritrea.
115. The 10th Year Assessment of the Communist Force within the TPLF, page 17.
116. Ibid., 22.
117. According to Giday Zeratsion, such a statement did not reflect TPLF's position. Members of the TPLF delegation, Abaye Tsehaye and Meles Zenawi were criticized for the concession.
118. The 10th Year Assessment of the Communist Force within the TPLF, page 106.
119. Report of the EPRP FC to EPRP and Youth League members, page 11.
120. Ibid., page 53.
121. Assessment of the Communist Force. . ., page 107.
122. Assimba, Volume II, No.8, page 3.
123. Abebe Tessema, October 1997.
124. Interview, Hailu Mengesha, October 1997.
125. From an article by Abebe Tessema, October 1997.
126. The 10th Year Assessment of the Communist Force within the TPLF, page 86.
127. Interview, Hailu Mengesha, October 1997.
128. The 10th Year Assessment of the Communist Force within the TPLF, page 111.
129. "It was the EPRA that took the initiative to attack the TPLF contingent," Giday Zeratsion, 1997.
130. Interview, MGE, 1991.
131. Yetegel Tiri, 2nd Year, No.4, page 14. (A TPLF publication)
132. Red Army, Volume I, No.3, page 10.

133. Ibid., page 10.

134. EPRP CC 4th Plenum Assessment, page 26.

135. Interview, Debebe, 1993.

136. A member of AAMACO.

137. From a discussion with DHM, a leading member of the EPRA in Assimba.

138. TPLF: Kedetu wede Matu, June 1985, page 5. (An EPRP publication)

139. Interview, MGE, April 1991.

140. Yetegil Tiri, TPLF publication, 2nd Year, No. 4, page 11.

141. The 10th Year Assessment of the Communist Force within the TPLF, page 111.

142. Interview, AM, November 1994. AM also argued that he and other members of the EPRA leadership had suggested that TPLF's infrastructure should be studied. According to AM, some members of the EPRA leadership warned about the imminence of a war with the TPLF.

143. The 10th Year Assessment of the Communist Force within the TPLF, page 111.

144. Giday Zerasion contends that he "personally had read some EPRP CC documents which contained the decision to wage war against the TPLF." According to Giday, the documents were captured during the war.

145. Interview, AH, January 1996.

146. Yetegil Tiri, 2nd Year, No. 4, 1985/86, page 11. Aregawi Berhe argues that the EPLF never took part in the fight between the EPRA and the TPLF. Aregawi Berhe, January 1996.

147. Amora, (The Bird), Giday Bahrishum, 1993 (1985 Eth), page 196.

148. Ibid., page 168.

149. Interview, MGE, 1991.

150. Abyot, Volume III, No. 5, 1978, pages 20-21.

151. Northeast African Studies, Research News and Notes, "The Lives and Times of the Derge", Pliny the middle-aged, page 23.

152. Yetegil Tiri, 2nd Year, No. 4, 1985/86, page 12.

153. Discussion with a member of the TPLF leadership, August, 1990.

154. In 1978, the TPLF wanted to organize the POWs into an organization known as the Ethiopian People's Democratic Movement. Among the members of the leadership of this group were some who still maintained their EPRP membership. These individuals disrupted TPLF's effort and the first attempt to form a support group failed. Interview, Tebebe, 1997.

155. Discussion with a member of the Military Tribunal.

156. See details Chapter X.

157. Interview, MGE, 1991.

158. The author of this article was Germatchew Lemma. He sent his article to the CC members in Assimba for a review. However, it was distributed among EPRA members.

10

Party and Military Activities in Begemidir

Following the severe crisis and the retreat from Tigrai, EPRP's remaining force congregated in the Begemidir province where the EPRA had been operating since 1975.[1] Consequently, the EPRP was limited to the activities of one province and forced to recruit members mainly from the Begemidir area.

The regrouping of almost all EPRP/EPRA forces in one area made the task of the Derge much easier. A few months after the arrival of the EPRA from Assimba to Begemidir, the Derge established one of its five military centers ("*gebre haile*") in the area.

Initially, the EPRA in Begemidir consisted of two units of twenty-three fighters each. However, as a result of the influx of members from the urban areas, by mid-1977 the fighters numbered in the hundreds. At the climax of the "Red Terror", a large number of youth, mostly from Gonder and the surrounding areas, flocked to EPRA-held territory, and the EPRA was able to deploy contingents in three regions.

In the early days, EPRA units in Begemidir did not have a base area. New comers joined a unit and were provided "on the job" training. The movement of the units was fast and unpredictable and their contact with the urban party structure and the EPRA leadership in Assimba was minimal.[2] Among the leading figures of the EPRA in Begemidir were the commander Jiggsa (code name), Iskender Demisse, Yeabiyo, Jara, Abdi, Engeda (code names), Aklog.

In July 1976, one of the first operations of the EPRA unit in Begemidir was staged at the wereda city Adi Selam. In December 1976, another small town, Sanka Ber, and a police station in Mai Tsemri were raided. These actions helped publicize the EPRA at least in the immediate surroundings. The local government mobilized peasants repeatedly to regain control of the towns and crush the EPRA, but it was unsuccessful. During their first encounter, EPRA fighters refrained from killing peasants. However, during a campaign in which the four districts of the Semien aweraja were mobilized against EPRA units, one peasant was killed and sixty were taken prisoners, including the wereda administrator who headed the military campaign. Those captured were fined and released. Following this campaign, the peasantry began cooperating with the EPRA. The EPRA also brought the Semien National Park under control in an operation geared to obtain field equipments and medicine.[3] Among the prisoners taken in this operation were an American, a German and an Australian.

A few months later, units of the Begemidir EPRA traveled hundreds of miles along with a contingent from the EPRA in Tigrai to Ebenat and Arbaya, small towns in the Libo awaraja, with the hope of obtaining some arms. One of the units successfully raided Ebenat but was surrounded by peasants as it retreated. Some leading members of the units were killed, including Iskendir Demisse, a major figure in the EPRA. The second group raided the little town of Arbaya. The plan was to conduct the operation under cover of darkness, but by the time the group reached the town, daylight had broken. The unit was forced to wait until nightfall. Despite warnings from some members of the leadership that it was unwise to conduct the operation because the element of surprise had been lost.[4] However, the units, went ahead with the operation. The alerted government forces counter attacked and EPRA's attempt failed. The retreat was hampered by pursuing peasants. One unit lost all, but four of its members.

The memory of the debacle of EPRA units in Wello (See Chapter II) along with the defeat in Ebenat and Arbaya slowed EPRA's expansion in Begemidir. Probably that fact could be the reason why the EPRA leadership in Begemidir did not even consider the Gonder zonal committee's demand in 1976 for the EPRA to move into the Libo awaraja. Following the set back in Ebenat and Arbaya, government supporters in some districts of Semien mobilized the people and created difficulties for the EPRA command in Begemidir. The EPRA was confined to a small corner of northeast Begemidir and was unable to expand. Consequently, the EPRA had to face the challenge of launching a military campaign against those chieftains who had local support.

In the last months of 1977, the EPRA launched military campaign for control of the Beyeda and Janamora districts in Semein. Many EPRP members traveling through these districts from Gonder had fallen victim to the regime due to peasant collaboration with the Derge. Beyeda is located on one of the highest mountains in Ethiopia, Ras Dejen. It is surrounded by deep gorges. There are only three narrow passages leading to the area and one of them must be negotiated by a ladder. In times of war, the inhabitants removed the ladder.

Four EPRA units were sent to occupy the wereda city, Dilyebza. It took fourteen hours to get there, and a large number of the fighters were affected by shortage of oxygen at that altitude. When they reached Dilyebza, the administrator and his staff had been alerted and they escaped. Staying in the surrounding area, they mobilized opposition against the EPRA. However, when the EPRA command began confiscating the cattle of those who had allied with the administrator, many of them laid down their arms and the EPRA was able to bring Dilyebza under control.

The campaign to take Deresge, the wereda city of Janamora, took place in November 1977. The day the operation was launched was a holiday commemorating *Tsion Mariam* (Mary of Tsion) and a large number of peasants had congregated in the town. Government officials rallied the people and opened an offensive. EPRA contingents, not wanting to open fire on the people, retreated. Government officials mobilized the people to pursue EPRA contingents. At length, the EPRA commander gave the order to fire and at least fifteen peasants were killed. An EPRA member, Dirar *(nom de guerre)*, was also killed. Mission unaccomplished, EPRA contingents left for Tselemt.

A few months later, the EPRA launched another campaign to bring Janamora under control. This time the campaign was concluded with the surrender of the local police force. However, some days later, the awaraja administrator in Debark, along with MEISON member Yoseyas, deployed a large force to dislodge the EPRA from the area. The government force was defeated. Even though the EPRA was able to control most of the Semien highlands by the first months of 1978, former supporters of the regime and their followers continued creating difficulties.

Despite this initial setback, the EPRA force in Begemidir survived to become one of the important bastions of the EPRA. This success was attributable to the military skills of the regional leadership, the activities of the local party structure, and the hospitable surrounding where they began operating. The negligible presence of the central government could be an additional factor.

Following the Rectification Movement discussed in Chapter 9, EPRA forces in Begemidir were regrouped under the northwest EPRA Leadership and Party Committees - replicas of the national General Leadership and Party Committees. The regional army had its own political and propaganda departments, mass organization committee, finance committee, women's committee and militia committee. The regional command in Begemidir established a mini-base in the Tselemt wereda.

Until mid-1978, the Begemidir regional command was limited to the Semien awaraja. Military activity was directed mainly against Derge convoys that traveled on the Tigrai/Gonder highway. Unlike the group in Tigrai, EPRA units in Begemidir were scarcely affected by the internal crisis of the army. A very large number of the members had arrived after the RM was over and some of the errors and weaknesses of the EPRA had been rectified.

In September 1977, EPRA units confiscated 423 sacs of sugar and also put Derge forces out of action at Chewber, Zarema and Enseye. The Derge's Nebelbal force suffered heavy casualties. In the same month, EPRA forces confiscated medical equipment and a large supply of medicine from the small towns of Amba Midri and Adi Arekai.[5] In April 1977, an operation was conducted in Adi Arekai, a small town on the Gonder-Tigrai highway. The police station was the focus of operation and some police officers were killed.

EPRA units conducted another operation in Adi Arekai in April 1977. Along with the EPRA units, close to four hundred peasants of the Wasia and

Berra took part in the operation which was successful. The peasants mobilized by Derge were disbanded and the government infrastructure was dismantled.

The EPRA in Begemidir ambushed the 217th Nebelebal regiment during the last months of 1977 and put a battalion out of action. The battle took place at Mayleham. Nearly one hundred and fifty officers were captured. Among those who voluntarily gave themselves up was a battalion commander, Major Getachew. A large number of rifles, mortars (of all sorts), machine guns and ammunition were obtained. Nearly five-hundred sacks of sugar were confiscated.[6] After these operations, EPRA units carried out no actions in Begemidir until mid-1978, when members fleeing the "Red Terror" joined the army in large number and the need for more arms became apparent.

In July 1978, the regional command of the Begemidir area organized an operation against a Derge contingent assigned to guard the Lima Limu escarpment on the Tigrai/Gonder highway. EPRA units had to walk for many hours to reach the small town of Deb Bahir, where government troops were camped. It was a rainy season and the flooding of Shemele Weha delayed troop movement. The need to move under cover of darkness further slowed the march. Some of the exhausted fighters were sent back. Some three dozen were selected to assault the military camp. After a few hours of military engagement, EPRA units demolished the Derge's camp. Some government troops were taken prisoners; some retreated. The victory, however, was accompanied by the loss of many invaluable EPRA members, and many were wounded. Only very few arms were obtained.

This operation marked a departure for the EPRA. Until this period, most of EPRA's operations were ambushes of military convoys. Conducting a raid, however, is a different form of engagement. Under the rules of guerrilla warfare, a three-to-one numerical advantage was a requisite for a raid. The enemy's moral and physical state had to be known and the element of surprise was important.

After the Deb Bahir operation, where a fairly large number of EPRA leading figures fell victim, some members left the army and opted to join the party structure. Reacting to the problem encountered in Deb Bahir, the northwest EPRA Command passed a regulation prohibiting members of the various levels of the army leadership from combat, unless the entire "ganta" or contingent became involved in the operation.

Another unsuccessful operation was conducted in August 1978. The target of the operation was a Derge battalion in Adi Arekai which was preparing a campaign against the EPRA. EPRA forces harassed the force for quite some time and conducted the operation. However, the operation was unsuccessful and the EPRA lost some members.

EPRP Structure in Begemidir

The EPLO/EPRP had a well set-up organizational and political infrastructure in Begemidir. In its few years of activities, the EPRP structure in Begemidir was able to popularize the EPRP among a large sector of the population. Furthermore, the EPRP structure in Begemidir was among those that conducted political activities among the peasantry and laid organizational networks as early as 1975. As a result of the intense political and organizational activities, the EPRP was able to rally a large group in Begemidir. In the struggle against the repressive policies of the Derge, thousands had fallen victim.

Even though EPRP structure was laid in 1974, it had its genesis in the radical circles that sprouted in Gonder in the early 1970's.[7] Most of the members of these groups were drawn from among the student population. Student militancy had been witnessed since the late sixties, when issues related to academic freedom and the program known as the "sector review" surfaced.[8] In the early stages of the student movement, the high-school student's council provided the leadership. Among the leading figures of this group were Zeweale, Mohammed Tahir, Setotaw Hassen, Luleseged Minsa, Berhane Asfaw and Mola Chekole.[9] (Setotaw became a leading activist of the EPRP. Currently, his whereabouts are unknown, but he was languishing in the prisons of the EPRDF in 1991).

The study circles formed during the early seventies decided to initiate an armed struggle. To effect that decision, a member of the left groups was sent to Metema to start a commercial farm and raise money. However, the direction pursued by the study circles changed when they were approached by Abyot members, Setotaw Hassen and Gezahegn Fekadu. The last one fell victim during the "Red Terror".

In June 1974, the Abyot group merged with the EPLO/EPRP. Sometime later, the groups in Gonder were also placed under the EPLO. The first zonal committee of the Begemidir province was formed in 1974 and the founding members of this committee were Mengistu Teferra, Berhane, MD, Kassahun Gebre Hiwot and Gezahegne Fekadu. ZB, who later joined the EPRP CC, served as the liaison with the EPRP leadership.

When Derge initiated the Zemetcha program in 1974, an opportunity was created to expand the EPLO/EPRP into other parts of Begemidir and Gojjam.[10] As a result, EPLO/EPRP structures were laid down in peasant villages. Committees of peasants were formed in Belessa and Tselemt as early as 1974-75. Among leading peasant EPRP members of the Tselemt area were Aba Takele and Aba Taferre of Adi Wosenae, Aba Abate, Aba Alemu and Aya Reta; Aya Agedew, Hedego Mulaw of Birra Waseya, Aya Desta of Dembelo and Aya Hailu, and YL members Abebe and Tsegaye. Some of these EPRP peasant members were taking part in the peasant sub-zone committee which was in charge of activities among the peasantry. By 1978, a good number of the peasants were members of the EPRP sub-zone committee in the Tselemt area, thus taking over party leadership. Aya Hailu was a commander of the peasants' militia group of the Tselemt area.

With the armed struggle in mind, recruiting members from selected areas, such as Armacheho, Chilga, Tselemt and Welkaite was emphasized. Besides, the zonal committee formed a military committee. Utilizing EPLO's influence in the ministry of Education, the Gonder zone managed to place zematch teachers in areas where it believed that the armed struggle would start. Toward the middle of 1975, some members were sent to Welkaite to lay down EPLO/EPRP structures. However, EDU's influence on the local population made it difficult to conduct effective clandestine activity.

The Gonder zonal committee had undergone structural rearrangements since its formation in 1974. In 1975, Gonder was delineated into four geographical zones and EPRP leadership committees were formed for each of the districts. When the structure expanded in the subsequent months, EPRP sub-zonal committees were formed in the Libo, Semien, Chilga, Armacheho and Debre-Tabor awerajas. At the same time, the structure in the Gonder city was downgraded to a sub-zone. The zonal committee had an influence on many of the legal mass organizations, including the Teachers Association, kebele youth organizations and some local trade unions. The Youth League branch in Gonder had laid down its structure with the help of the national YL leadership. When the YL held its Congress in 1976, the Gonder branch sent two representatives. The Women's Coordinating Committee held several gatherings focusing on the role of women in society and encouraging women to be involved in the revolutionary struggle. As a result, teachers, nurses, students, including elementary school students, maids and some members of the police force joined the women's organization.

The Gonder Teachers' Associations and many of its branch offices, such as those in Addis Zemen, Debark, Dabat, etc., were under the influence of the EPRP. The secretary of the teachers association, Melaku Tsegaye, was an EPRP member who by special assignment was hired as secretary to the administrator of the Begemidir province. His contribution to the struggle was invaluable.[11] The Gonder Teachers' Association handled some of the production needs of the local EPRP structure. Most publications were mimeographed at the headquarters of the Teachers' Association.

The Gonder zonal committee created what it called the "underground railroad" - a communications network used to conduit people, dispatch logistics, letters, messages, propaganda materials, etc. The network ran from Gonder to Tselemt, Chilga, Metema and other parts of the Begemidir. It was through this network that hundreds of EPRP members were sent to join the EPRA group in Begemidir. Native cadres helped in creating peasant support and provided shelters for those who needed them.

EPRP activities in the Gonder city turned for the better following the formation of legal soccer teams at the level of kebeles in 1976. With the soccer teams as a cover, the EPRP organized study circles and held discussions. As a result, the Gonder EPRP structure was able to rally a large youth following. On the other hand, security was weakened as EPRP members and sympathizers were introduced to each other.

Efforts were made to appoint EPRP members and sympathizers to some important government posts. Among those appointed were Fetawrari Ayele,[12] and Zeweale, administrators of the Chilga and Semien awerajas, respectively. When the EDU rampaged in some parts of the Semien aweraja, Zeweale armed peasants to resist EDU's advance.

Another restructuring process was undertaken in July/August 1976. The Begemidir and Gojjam Interzone (IZ) was formed; it was composed of representatives from the Gonder, Bahir Dar and Debre Markos zones. The first meeting of the IZ was held in Fenote Selam, Gojam. Mengistu Ketsela, secretary of the Gonder Zone, served as the Secretary of the IZ.[13] By this time, the Gonder zonal committee had formed a propaganda committee and a production facility in Weleka, about five kilometers from Gonder. The first publication of the Zone was *Arso Ader* (The Peasantry) which was initiated in 1975 to organize peasants against the "Raza Project" of the Derge.

The second publication was *Ametse* (Revolt), launched in protest against the mass killing of December 1976, when Derge soldiers opened fire on peaceful demonstrators. That massacre also prompted the Gonder zonal committee to initiate urban military activities. In its few months of existence, the defense structure of the Gonder zonal committee had conducted some military operations.

The Gonder zonal Committee opened a bookstore and a radio repair shop in July and September 1978, respectively. Both businesses were managed and supervised by Berhane Gebre Meskel, a zonal committee member. These business activities provided legitimate cover to Berhane, who frequently traveled from Gonder to Addis Abeba; until he fell into the hands of security forces, Berhane transported leaflets and other important documents, large sums of money, and machine guns from Addis Abeba to Gonder. He was executed in 1979. The radio repair shop, located near the bus station, served as an alternative meeting site in emergency situations and when members coming from Addis Abeba to join the EPRA lost their host contacts in transition.

The Gonder zonal committee was restructured several times before September 1977 when many of the committee members left the city or were relieved from their positions to do other organizational tasks. Berhane and Kassahun Gebre Hiwot left for the EPRA. Kassahun Gebre Hiwot was killed by the TPLF in 1978. Kassahun was taken as a POW and apparently, he tried to escape from detention.

From the first zonal committee, Berihun Dagnew and Solomon Kebede were sent to Bahir Dar and Debre Markos to share their experience in organizing and to consolidate the party structures in those cities. They were both imprisoned later in Debre Markos and executed in 1977. Other leading members of the zone were also killed.[14] The remaining zone members Mohabaw and Demas were joined by new zonal committee members M., Geremew (Secretary of the Teachers Union), Mesele Abuhay (who later was killed by the security forces while trying to escape from a raid), and Addisu (the current president of Kelel three, the Amhara region, and a member of the former EPDM).

By 1977, the "Red Terror" was in full swing in Begemidir. In many of the cities and small towns, it was difficult to carry on organizational activities. The repression weakened the urban party structure. The link with Gojjam became fragile and the leadership of the Gonder zonal committee decided to relocate to the rural areas where adequate structure was already laid down.[15] As a result of the shift, activities had to be revised. Furthermore, the IZ was restructured for the second time in 1978. The IZ consisted of the newly restructured Gonder zone, demarcated as East and West zones, and the Gojjam zone. Poor communication was the main reason for the new arrangement.

A propaganda committee known as Agit-prop and a Cadre School were formed. The Cadre School provided an opportunity for party members to exchange organizational experience and help them improve their political awareness. The Agit-prop began publishing *Gommora*, a journal that dealt with theoretical issues and revolutionary literature. One of the typewriters that the Agit-prop used belonged to individuals who had protested against the policies of the Imperial regime in 1973. A few individuals, led by Nega Newete, had organized a protest when they learnt that the Imperial regime was about to cede some territory of Armacheho, Begemidir province to the Sudan. The rebels began publishing leaflets, and those suspected of putting them out were placed under arrest.

In 1978, the EPRP structure in Gojam was dealt a severe blow when Yared, zonal committee member and the IZ representative, and Eshetu, a former sub-zone member of the Gonder zonal committee, were burnt to death in their hut by government security forces.

Despite intensive organizational and political activities, the EPRP was unable to mobilize an important segment of the society in Begemidir and Gojam. Furthermore, the emergence of the EDU had made it more difficult to rally the upper echelon of the society both in the rural and urban areas. Consequently, a new organization was needed.

The Ethiopian Patriotic Democratic Organization (EPDO)

The idea of forming a broad-based patriotic organization began to circulate in 1977 and among those that raised the issue was the Gonder zonal committee. The EPDO was formed in mid-1978, at Armacheho, in the western part of Begemidir. The founding members of the organization were Colonel IW, Colonel A., AA, Fetawrari Ayele, and other influential peasants of the area. Some of the leading members of the organization belonged to the EPRP.

The formation of such an organization was dictated by the existence of a large rural sector that the EPRP program did not rally behind - well to do peasants and the gentry of the Begemidir and Gojam provinces. Because of the lineage system, tradition and economic status, the group constituted the traditional leadership of the peasantry. Most members of these groups were disgruntled local "chieftains", such as, weroda administrators, "feresegnas" and cheka shums of the Haile Selassie regime.

Armacheho, the center where the organization sprouted, is an area known for its rebelliousness. Armacheho, Chilga, Welkaite, Tsegede, Gayent and Belesa, in the Begemidir province had been an important resistance center during the five years of Italian occupation.[16] The well-armed peasantry of Armacheho rallied behind the EDU in 1976/77.

At a large meeting of the Patriotic Organization, the peasants adopted a program and elected leaders. The leadership strongly believed that external assistance was necessary. Upon formation of the organization, it left for the Sudan, seeking western support. It had intended to form its own military group, however, due to financial problems and the crisis within the EPRP, it was unable to achieve its objectives.

Fetawrari Ayele, one of the founding members of the organization, had been a resistance fighter in the Chilga area during the Italian occupation in the 1930s. Sometime in 1977, he abandoned his post of administering the Chilga district and was forced to go underground. The Fetawrari, who was half Kemante, was one of the leaders of the Kemante people and he enjoyed wide respect among them. The Kemantes are a minority group settled in the vicinity of the Gonder city. Fetawrari Ayele was also one of the few people who had allied with the EPRP as early as 1975 and had helped it deploy cadres among the peasantry. He was well informed about the world and his surroundings. He was an astute peasant politician who accepted the socialist ideology. Because of his affiliation with the EPRP, he was on the government's wanted list.[17]

Begemidir- The Restructuring of the EPRA

The EPRA group in the Begemidir area was militarily active and successful. During its existence of about two years, it had conducted a number of military operations. As was indicated earlier, in November 1977, it ambushed and destroyed a whole battalion and armed itself. However, some of the operations it conducted were not successful and cost the lives of invaluable fighters.

Very much in line with the EPRA in Assimba, in 1977/78, EPRA members in Begemidir raised questions about the direction of the struggle and some of the policies of the EPRP. However, unlike the EPRA in Tigrai, the EPRA in Begemidir was not affected by the serious shortcomings of the RM. Despite some weaknesses, the EPRA in Begemidir remained an effective military institution. Furthermore, the EPRA of Begemidir had the whole area to itself without a serious rival to contend with. The peasants of some of the districts, particularly those of the eastern part of the province, were receptive and sympathetic to EPRA's call.

Before the Assimba EPRA group arrived in Begemidir, the entire military force in Begemidir was restructured into three regions, known as R-1, R-2 and R-3. Each of the regional armies had its own chain of both military and party leadership. The first Regional Command was in charge of the northeastern part of Begemidir, the Semien *awerqja*; the second Regional Command was in charge of the eastern and southwestern part of Begemidir, the Gonder and Chilga awerajas; the third was in charge of the southern part of the province, the Libo, Debre Tabor and Gayente *awerajas*. Until December 1978, the R-3 regional army was in charge of the Libo and a certain part of the Semien *awerajas*.

Upon its arrival in Begemidir from Tigrai, the EPRA General leadership and General Party Leadership took over the entire leadership of the EPRA. Furthermore, some members of these committees were assigned to take part in the regional commands. The Northwestern EPRA Command, which until this period was in charge of the EPRA in Begemidir, was dissolved and some of the members were assigned to the Regional Commands or other committees. Most of the members of the EPRA leadership that took over command were new both to the surroundings and to some of the units.

After the assumption of authority by the General Leadership Committee, a fourth Regional Command was formed for the Northwestern part of Begemidir, the Wegera *awerqja*.

Army of Region One

The newly restructured R-1 command was in charge of the areas that the EPRA had controlled for quite some time. As was indicated elsewhere, the first EPRA units arrived in the area in 1975. When the restructuring was undertaken in 1978, the army had grown in size and was in control of a large part of the Semien and Wegera awerajas. Some of the weredas were under the total control of the regional command; these places were known as "Red" areas. The EPRA administered the areas, except that it did not collect taxes. Peasant associations were in charge of the administration of their localities and the judiciary. To resolve issues, quite often, the peasants resorted to custom. Both the EPRP party structure and the Mass Organization Committee of the EPRA assisted the incipient peasant political power. The EPRA and the local party structure ran schools to eradicate illiteracy. There were clinics that served both the populace and EPRP members. Political agitation was conducted when conditions allowed, on holidays and Sundays.

Sometime before the arrival of the EPRA from Assimba, the military regime was preparing a military campaign against EPRA units in Begemidir. The military regime, which came out victorious in the war with the Somali regime, was making preparations to quell opposition in Eritrea and the northern part of Ethiopia. The decision to conduct operations that would contain and eventually wipe out the EPRA was made at a meeting in Gonder, in late 1978, attended by the Derge's defense committee. At least three brigades of the Seventh Division were deployed.

The military regime had adequate information regarding the crisis of the EPRA in Tigrai. In order to familiarize itself with conditions of the EPRA in Begemidir, the Derge laid down a set of intelligence networks, one of which was unearthed by the EPRA. The network, many of whose members were Felashas (Bete-Israel), extended from the Semien, the northern tip of Begemidir, to Tseda, a small town on the main Bahir Dar/Gonder highway. The existence of the network was known following the death of Tilahun (nicknamed "Mao"), after a Derge informant disclosed his whereabouts. Tilahun (a code name), an able organizer, was one of the most honest and invaluable EPRP members of the Gonder zone. Tilahun served as a "liner" and his main task was to escort EPRP members from the urban areas to a safe location in the countryside. Fulfilling this duty, Tilahun had saved hundreds of lives. He endured the greatest hardships, walking ten to twelve hours, almost every day.

Another intelligence network that the EPRA dismantled was centered in Dabat, a town on the main Tigrayan/Gonder highway. Among the intelligence officers sent to infiltrate the EPRA was a person who had served the Haile Selassie regime and had been involved in the assassination of Kebede Tessema, the leader of a little known organization called the Ethiopian Democratic Movement, sometime in the early sixties. When he was killed, the leader of the movement was residing in Sudan as a political refugee.

The Dabat-based intelligence network of Derge was successful. The officer mentioned above conducted a study of the EPRP network that extended from Dabat to the Semien rural areas and inflicted some damage upon the EPRP structure. Derge intelligence officers, camouflaged as nuns and priests, were also apprehended by EPRA units.

After gathering some information about the condition of the EPRA, the Derge opened an offensive against most of the former EPRA-held areas. Even though EPRA's military loss was minimal, the Derge's offensive was a major set back to the EPRP, triggering a chain reaction that eventually resulted in a major crisis. The Derge's offensive triggered discussion on some concepts regarding guerilla warfare that the Assimba group had been entertaining for quite a while. When the Assimba group arrived in the Begemidir area following six months of starvation, anxiety, depression and confusion, what awaited it was not peace and tranquility, but another wave of military campaigns. The Assimba group propounded views regarding the military activities and strategy of the EPRA. Some argued that the army should have "no rear or front", but that it should be absolutely mobile. When the Assimba group arrived in Begemidir, the Regional army had a mini-base in Tselemt. Providing some excuses, some members of some of the contingents refused to take part in the operations meant to halt the Derge's advance.[18]

Despite discussions on some military concepts, the discontent and confusion of the Assimba group continued spreading. It was contagious enough that some elements of the EPRA in Begemidir were affected. Rumors and gossip spread. Following the distribution of the paper titled "Some positions of the EPRP . . . " to the Begemidir party and EPRA groups, strong reservations and objections were voiced.[19] Delegates were sent in groups to explain issues to the units, but to no avail. Confidence in the leadership was waning and members were resentful.

The defeat of EPRA forces by TPLF still fresh in mind, many continued to demand replies on the issues that they had raised. Due to the absence of guidance and leadership, many asked if the EPRP had any center (leadership) at all. Many were eager to know what went wrong and how the struggle should proceed. Because of the momentum of the struggle and the special attachment and love that many had toward the EPRP, they waited to hear from the leadership. The reconstituted EPRP CC itself was awaiting the convocation of a plenum, so many of the questions remained unanswered.

Despite the confusion, in 1978/79, the regional army conducted some operations against Derge forces in Adigerad, Janamora, Islamge, etc.

Army of Region Two

In July 1978, two contingents of about one hundred-fifty fighters were sent to the western part of the Begemidir to found the second regional command of the EPRA. On their way to the region, EPRA fighters had to cross an area controlled by the Derge under cover of darkness. While crossing this territory, some EPRA members defected. The defectors disclosed the presence of EPRA fighters about fifty miles north of the city of Gonder, but they did not know the mission of the contingents.

Operating without precise information, the Derge mobilized the peasants of the surrounding area to defend Amba Giorgis, a small town on the Gondar/Tigrai highway. This mobilization of most of the male peasants of the area to defend Amba Giorgis made EPRA contingents movement less dangerous.[20]

The political work conducted among the peasantry in the western part of the Begemidir was minimal. The EDU had conducted some military actions in 1976 and 1977 and had recruited followers who strongly believed in the cause of that organization. Besides, the peasantry of western Begemidir was well armed and renowned for its rebelliousness and assertiveness. The peasantry in some parts of the western part of the Begemidir produces harvest only for the consumption of his immediate family. Besides farming, a good number of the peasants of this region spend their time hunting. Some are involved in trade and travel to Sudan frequently.

Peasant insubordination was one of the first problems faced by the western regional command (R-2). The peasantry of one of the weredas of this area, Dawa, was mobilized against EPRA contingents. In that conflict, some

EPRA fighters were killed. To avoid further bloodshed, EPRA units retreated from the area. It was believed that some of the leaders of the peasantry had established contact with the Derge. Peasant hostility was expressed in various ways. Some would not allow EPRA contingents to pass through their area. Some attempted to snatch weapons from EPRA fighters. Others refused to provide food.

Initially, EPRA contingents were cautious when dealing with peasant rebels and bandits. In one of the localities, Sahari, peasants organized in the form of guerilla units, roamed the areas. When peasant insubordination began transforming itself into an open military confrontation, the regional command undertook swift punitive measures and quieted down the situation. The leaders of the peasants' guerilla groups, some of whom were village bandits, were apprehended.

There were other difficulties that the contingents in R-2 faced. Land was not a major concern of the peasants. In the lowland areas of Begemidir, the rist (lineage) system was in effect. The ratio of arable to non-arable land per person was quite high and the EPRP could not use the land question to rally the peasantry. Lack of administration, that is, lawlessness and banditry and the total absence of health facilities were major concerns of the peasantry. EPRA could provide few health services.

The peasantry of the western part of Begemidir could easily be rallied for a military campaign, but peasant recruitment into the EPRA structure remained a difficult endeavor. Peasant eagerness for military action might be related to the militarization of the local culture, and the hope of booty. Most of the peasants are familiar with warfare and some are reputed for their marksmanship. Many were acquainted with some of the techniques of guerilla warfare, one of which was avoiding a headlong confrontation. If they felt that they were the underdogs, the peasants would not confront the enemy, but would continue harassing it, or "*meneznez*", according to the peasants' lexicon. In any warfare, a high ground, however small the height might be, is considered advantageous militarily, but the peasants operated from low ground ("*moot merete*").

The peasant of the western part of Begemidir is exceptionally superstitious. Before he engaged in military activity, he would check his "*Wefe*" or stars. Literally translated, "*Wefe*" stands for a bird; however, in the lexicon of the peasantry of western Begemidir, "*Wefe*" stands for an omen. Before traveling or engaging in battles or other activities, the peasant listens for the first sound upon leaving his hut. That sound could be of birds or donkeys. Depending on the type of bird singing or the direction where the braying of the donkey is coming from, the peasant might cancel his plans. There are birds that are reputed to be carriers of bad and good omen. Often, the peasant waits until he is able to listen to the singing of the bird reputed to be a carrier of good omen. The direction the sound of the donkey came from - left, right or straight ahead - was also important. The peasant would wait for days or weeks until he ascertains that the "*Wefe*" was not negative.

Be that as it may, the EPRA was a poorly dressed, poorly armed and a poorly-fed army. On the other hand, the peasantry of western Begemidir was better off than EPRA members in life style, dress and arms. Many peasants were armed with the latest versions of American and Soviet made automatic rifles, M-14s and kalashinkovs. Consequently, the EPRA could not attract peasant recruits. Furthermore, peasants commonly said that the EPRA had no "murte", or external support.[21] That fact also constituted another setback for EPRA's recruitment efforts. Also, some peasants held low opinion of EPRA members who had to grind and cook to feed themselves. According to the peasants' custom, grinding and cooking was a woman's job.

Obtaining food was a challenging task for the army. Quite often, EPRA members had to buy, grind and prepare their own food. Due to the absence of grinding mills, flour had to be ground manually, taking three to four hours almost every day. As EPRA members became malnourished, they became vulnerable to typhus and malaria. An EPRA comedian once sarcastically commented, "if our struggle faces adversities such as in Armacheho, it had to be over in two years like that of Cuba. However, if we have to struggle in places like Alefa Takusa, it is ok if the struggle continued for twenty or thirty years, like that of China."[22] Alefa Takusa is an area close to the Gojam border on the southern end of Begemidir and peasant attitude toward EPRA was much better than in Armacheho.

During two years of activities, the R-2 EPRA conducted operations in a large area of the western part of the province, including Quara, Quola Sereqo, and the Boh Boh areas, where the peasantry was more sympathetic to the EPRA. The regional leadership, consisting of the command and the party committee, had its center in a place known as Chako. It conducted military operations, most of them along the road leading from Gonder to Negade Bahir, on the Gonder-Metema-Sudan road. In mid-1979, EPRA forces demolished Derge contingents in Delgi, a small town on Lake Tana. The regional army conducted military operations against Derge forces in Seraba, Genbera, Sanja, Tsebari and others. The most decisive of these operations was in Armacheho conducted for twenty-two days against a Derge force that was mobilized for a mopping up operation. Derge force was mobilized to wipe out the EPRA and its followers and bring the area under control. However, the Derge sustained heavy casualties and was forced to retreat.

Army of Region Three

The Begemidir party structure had popularized the EPRP and its cause well enough that in 1976 a section of the peasantry in the Libo district demanded that the EPRA move to its area. When two contingents of about one hundred-fifty fighters moved to the Libo area in May 1978, not only were they welcome by the peasantry, but their activities were also facilitated. Within a few months, the EPRA was able to recruit peasant militia from among the

Libo peasantry. Among the most enlightened peasant EPRP members of the Libo district were Asmare Bereye, Taye Gola, Gebre Meskel Fente, Ferede Azeze, Dessie Dawit and Dessie Guben.

A few months after the deployment of EPRA units in the R-3 area, the Derge opened up a military campaign. In December 1978, three more units were added to the R-3 command, bringing the total to five. The EPRA militia committee recruited close to four hundred well-trained peasant militia within a few months. Furthermore, the local party structure armed and organized thousands of peasant detachments under an organization known as "Hizbawi Arbegna".

In December 1978, the R-3 command raided Addis Zemen, a small town not far from the highway linking Bahir Dar and Gonder. The operation was successful and its political repercussion was favorable to the EPRA. However, in February 1979, the Derge conducted a military campaign in those parts of the Libo awerja where the EPRA had some support. During its stay of three weeks, the Derge's military force created havoc among the peasantry by burning down peasant huts, confiscating cattle and disarming a great many peasants. After this military campaign, the peasants realized that the EPRA was unable to defend them from the Derge's onslaught. Both among the peasantry and EPRA members, frustration and doubt took foothold.

In early 1979, two government battalions conducted a mopping up operation at Guahella, on the northern side of the Libo *awerja*. EPRA forces tried to stop the Derge's offensive, but were unable to do so. Following the repeated campaigns of the Derge, many peasants changed allegiance, including those that the EPRA had trained and the party structure had armed, and they fought on the side of the Derge. Peasants are very astute about the prevailing balance of force.

The failure to withstand the Derge's offensive further fueled dissatisfaction among EPRA members and the local EPRP party organization. Some believed that the regional command was incapable of leading its forces to victory. Consequently, a number of political and organizational issues surfaced. Individuals who shared similar ideas began to coalesce.

While the crisis in the R-3 area was unfolding, a major military operation against the Derge force in Mai-tsemri, on the Tigrai/Gonder highway, was planned for April 1979. The Derge's military force in Mai-tsemri served as the center and the support group for other Derge forces deployed in the various localities of the Semien awerja.

The operation was coordinated by the R-1 command and included contingents from other regions. The R-3 command sent two units. In that operation, the Derge military force was not annihilated, but it sustained a heavy blow and evacuated the camp some months later. As a result of the operation, conditions became more favorable for the R-1 command, but EPRA casualties had also been heavy. More than twenty dedicated and able leaders fell.

When contingents from the different regions congregated for the sake of that operation, an opportunity was created for EPRA members to share opinion and discuss on a wide range of EPRP and EPRA related issues. One of these issues was the departure of the EPRA General Leadership in the last months of 1978 for the western part of the Begemidir province. That departure had exacerbated the crisis within the EPRA of western Begemidir. Many could not understand why the army leadership had to leave the area where the majority of the members of the army were present. They believed that the leadership should have stayed in the R-1 and R-3 areas to coordinate the struggle, instead of looking for a "sanctuary". What the members did not know was that the EPRA leadership, both the party and the military command, constituted a very significant part of the EPRP CC which was preparing for its Fourth Plenum to be held in western Begemidir. Of the total number of the CC, including those coopted at the end of 1977, close to fifty-percent were members of the army leadership.

Members of the various contingents also discussed the disintegration of the urban structure and the crisis within the EPRP, Soviet involvement and the stabilization of the Derge, the imminence of TPLF's threat and the dispersal of the contingents to the various regions and the weakening of the EPRA. These and other issues spread to the various regional groups, via the contingents that came for the Mai-tsemri operation.

In May/June 1979, the regional command of R-3 raided a Derge contingent that was camping in Damot. The operation was successful and it provided the EPRA some publicity when it was broadcast over the British Broadcasting Corporation.[23] In July 1979, the Derge conducted another military operation in those areas controlled by the R-3 command. One more time the Derge military contingent burnt peasant huts and confiscated their properties. As a result, peasants became more fearful of the Derge and distanced themselves from the EPRA. More and more EPRA members became apprehensive about the regional command's leadership. Some questioned whether it was necessary to raid the Derge contingent in Damot in the first place. They argued that the regional command had to consolidate its forces rather than make efforts to expand to other areas. Some members demanded that a rectification movement be initiated. In due course, interpersonal contacts flourished, thus undermining EPRA's command structure.

To avert the crisis and to win over the peasants, the regional command planned to raid the aweraja town of Ebenat in September 1979. Believing that it had made the necessary preparations, the regional command deployed some contingents. Only a few miles away from the scene of operation, the mission of the operation was explained. As explained elsewhere, the EPRA Constitution required that members who take part in an operation had to be informed about the mission. At the discussion, commanders of three of the contingents opposed the operation on the grounds that it would not be successful, that EPRA forces could not annihilate Derge contingents, etc. Among the leading figures who opposed the operation were Daud, Asmare and Mahidere (code names).[24]

The operation was canceled and the incident constituted as the watershed for the very existence of the army and party structure of R-3.

When it realized the gravity of the crisis, the regional command called a seminar. Sometime before the seminar took place, a leaflet was distributed exposing the effort to organize clandestine groups within the EPRA. The leaflet appealed that EPRA members had to save their organization from disintegration. Reacting to the leaflet, members of the leadership of one of the units distributed another leaflet saying that the regional command was accused of incompetence and lack of discipline.

At the seminar, there was an acrimonious wrangle over the procedure of how the meeting should be conducted. It also became evident that the group opposing the regional leadership had a large following. At the closing of the seminar, the two groups who had distributed the different leaflets were condemned for their illegal actions and placed under custody. The persons behind the first leaflet were Tesfaye, Feleke and Imiru (code names). The last person was a member of the regional party command. The second leaflet which expressed the views of the opposition, was put out by Daud, Mahidere and Asmare. This was the group that was accused of forming clandestine groups within the EPRA.

During this period, the commissar of the EPRA, Tsegaye Gebre Medhin and another member of the EPRA General Leadership, Tsehaye, arrived in R-3 and held discussions with the regional command, with those arrested and other leading EPRA members. Following the discussion, the detainees were released, but they were stripped of their party memberships and demoted from the posts they had held. To find out whether there was an attempt to form a clandestine group within the EPRA, it was decided that an enquiry committee be formed from among the regional commands. In a concession to the demands of the opposition, controversial members of the R-3 regional command were removed from their posts and a new leadership group was formed. The new provisional leadership for the R-3 command included Ayalew Kebede (Yared), Ayele (code name) and Tamrat Layene who was transferred from the R-1 command. When the EPRDF took over power in 1991, Tamrat became a prime minister. He then was made the Defense Minister and Deputy prime minister. In October 1996, he was accused of corruption and incompetence and was removed from all posts.

The removal of some members of the R-3 command tipped the balance in favor of the opposition and proved to be a peaceful transfer of power. From this time on, the opposition, which had formed clandestine groups determined the course of the struggle.

The inclusion of Ayalew Kebede as a member of the R-3 command strengthened the opposition.[25] Since he joined the EPRA in 1975/76, it was believed that Ayalew was involved in anti-EPRA leadership activities.[26] In 1977/78, suspected of factional activities within the EPRA in Assimba, Ayalew was arrested along with the so-called Anjas. He was released when the TPLF overran Assimba and was kept under watch. The leadership, however, was unable to establish a case against him.[27] Ayalew was removed from EPRA structures and "exiled" to a small locality under R-3. The place was frequented by many members of the army and the party, and Ayalew made efforts to impress them by being cooperative, diligent and tenacious. He also took part in literary activities. Ayalew's performance gained him such sympathy from the fighters that his subjection to "humiliation" became a factor in the discontent against the EPRA leadership.[28] This sympathy was manifested by his nomination to a post in the provisional leadership.

Once placed in the leadership, Ayalew maintained discreet contact with the opposition, both in the army and the party.[29] In due course, some members of the provisional regional command were won over to the side of the opposition. Others members of the provisional leadership sensed the direction of the wind and joined the opposition. Most of the members of the opposition might have been motivated by earnest concerns about the fate of the EPRP and the struggle. However, there were others who had harbored personal grievances. Some of these individuals had been implicated in the factional activities of the EPRA in Assimba. Besides, there were others who had been reprimanded for promulgating their own policies. In 1975/76, a small group of EPRA fighters unilaterally promulgated a sweeping land reform in the EPRA controlled areas of the Begemidir province. The EPRA upheld the traditional land tenure system, while attempting to redistribute land to landless peasants.

Army of Region Four

The R-4 army which consisted of three companies and a platoon, a'ganta', was assigned the northwestern part of Begemidir, the Wegera *awaraja*, in particular, the Welkaite area, the home base of the EDU. The Wegera aweraja is one of the most fertile regions of the Begemidir province. In this area class distinctions are vivid. Most of the highland areas of this region are inhabited by well to do peasants, while the majority of poor peasants live in the malaria-infected lowland area known as the Mezega along the Tekeze River.

The lowland area is home to the "Bet Baria" (the family of the Slaves). This is a group of former slaves whose history and origins are little known, but they now speak Tigrigna and Amharic and have adopted Christianity and other values of the Welkataye (people living in the Welkaite area).[30]

The "*Bet Baria*" were employed in the lowland areas, tending the farms of well to do peasants who resided in the highland areas. According to an estimate made in 1979/80,[31] their number was between one thousand five hundred to two thousand families. A large percentage of the *"Bet Baria"* were "possessed" by few well to do peasants earlier on. Dejazmatch Desta and his sons used to "possess" those residing in the "Mezega" of the Telelo area, Grazmatch Gebre Micheal, those in the "Mezega" area of Welkaite while

Kegnazmatch Gebru "possessed" the ones in the "Mezega" of Birkutan. While the "*Barias*" looked after the farms of the well to do peasants and landlords, the latter in turn provided protection. Fearing abduction, members of the "Bet Baria" had to confine themselves to their immediate surroundings. If they had to travel to the nearest market or go out fishing or hunting, they had to travel in groups. To fetch water from the nearest pool or water well the women had to walk in groups.

When the EPRA began military activities in the Welkaite area, a small number of the "*Bet Baria*" still remained under the possession of the local gentry. A large number were freed but evicted from the cultivable land. For some months, the EPRA focused on the "Bet Baria".

On its way to Welkaite, the R-4 EPRA group was deployed in the Tsegede *wereda* on the southeastern side of Welkaite, to open up a corridor between the regional commands in eastern and western Begemidir. EPRA's presence was welcome by many of the peasants had it not been for the proclamation that the R-4 EPRA leadership put out prohibiting gambling and banditry. It was stated that the army would take stern measures against bandits. One of the towns of the Tsegede wereda, Janora, was believed to be a center where stolen cattle and arms were sold or bartered. The peasants were armed with the latest versions of automatic machine guns.

Some days after the untimely proclamation, conflict ensued between EPRA units and the people, and the EPRA publicly declared that the proclamation was canceled. However, EPRA forces were attacked on several occasions. Four members of the army were killed. The EPRA finally chose to retreat rather than confront the peasants. The entire R-4 army, which included four contingents, retreated to Welkaite.

When the regional army arrived in Welkaite, the area was under control by the EDU, which the Northwest EPRA leadership had made efforts to neutralize. That effort continued and sometime before the arrival of the EPRA group in Welkaite, SD and another EPRA member were sent to the area to continue the dialogue with the EDU leadership. However, the EDU leadership did not come up with a unified position. While some members of the EDU leadership were in favor of cooperation, others were skeptical and did not like EPRA's presence in what they called their liberated area. Furthermore, some EPRP members had infiltrated the EDU in order to reach it's rank and file members and win them over. Despite these and other political activities, peasants in Welkaite attacked the EPRA a few times. Some lives were lost, however, EPRA units were more decisive this time and they were victorious. The peasants' attacks were triggered by the incidents in Tsegede and the fact that the EPRA had been forced to retreat from that area. Peasants regard a retreating army as an easy prey.

The EDU began cooperating with the EPRA after witnessing the Derge's repeated military campaigns. At this time, the EDU was also at war with the TPLF and this had been going on for months. As was indicated elsewhere, the TPLF, without an outlet to the outside world, had an interest in the Welkaite region which borders Sudan. The TPLF regarded Welkaite and other parts of the Wegera *aweraja* as administrative parts of the Tigrai province, and resettled its members and supporters in the "mezega", the lowland areas of Welkaite.

Although more unified and cohesive, the R-4 army still had difficulties. Some months after the arrival of the army in Welkaite, the regional command conducted a study and decided to raid the small Ethiopian border town of Kaftia in order to create a link with the outside world. Hours before the operation was to take place, the regional command informed the fighters about the mission. In the discussion that ensued, some members argued that the study was insufficient. The raid was canceled.

A few months after EPRA units began operating in Welkaite, the TPLF launched a military campaign against EPRA units. They attacked the mini-base area of the R-4 army where members of the various departments and sick fighters were congregated. Among the victims of this campaign was one of the early recruits of the EPRA, Jemilla (code name).

A few weeks after this attack, the TPLF deployed three battalions for an uninterrupted military campaign. In the first major battle at Sherilla, both the TPLF and the EPRA sustained heavy casualties. On the TPLF's side, it was estimated that hundreds of fighters were killed. Unable to withstand the TPLF's advance, EPRA forces retreated As the entire force was taking a break at a river side, not very far away from the scene of the battle, the TPLF attacked again. The EPRA troops were caught unprepared, some of them naked and washing themselves in the river. Losses were heavy. The survivors regrouped and retreated to the R-1 area of Tselemt.

After driving the EPRA away from the area, the TPLF brought the entire Welkaite region under its control.

The TPLF justified its attack upon the EPRA as a preemptive measure against the rapprochement of the ELF and the EPRP. *Yetegel Tirri*, a TPLF publication stated,

> ...[B]efore the battles in Welkaite took place, the ELF and the EPRP had concluded an agreement to drive out the TPLF from the lowland areas of Shire (an area adjacent to Eritrea)...so the offensive that the TPLF opened up on the EPRP cannot be considered as one instigated by the former [TPLF].[32]

As far as the EPRP was concerned, no decision had been made at the level of the EPRP CC that would affect the TPLF, and Shire was not the immediate area in which the EPRP wanted to expand. The TPLF opened up the military campaign sometime after the Fourth Plenum of the EPRP CC took place. At that time, the relationship between the EPRP and the ELF was still strained. The EPRP CC sent members Samuel Alemayehu and DS to the ELF to mend that strained relationship. A low level contact was initiated when the EPRA regional leadership in the Welkaite area concluded some areas of agreement with the ELF. The latter agreed to provide some arms.

Another major confrontation with the TPLF took place a few months later. During this time, the EPRA had retreated from Welkaite to Tselemt and some units had to cross over to the territory controlled by the ELF in Eritrea, in order to bring back the arms which the ELF had provided. The ELF and the TPLF were at war for quite some time. One of the areas of conflict was the small piece of land on the Tigrayan/Eritrean border.

When the fighting was over, EPRA forces, accompanied by a small ELF unit, began their journey back to Tselemt. They overpowered a TPLF platoon which they accidentally met in Welkaite. On the same day, a major battle erupted between the TPLF on the one side and the ELF and the EPRA on the other. It lasted for days, and all sides sustained heavy casualties. In the end, they all retreated. EPRA units were unable to cross over to Tselemt and they had to wait a few more weeks to do so.

EPRA forces of R-4 retreated to Tselemt, where they found a section of the R-1 army in open rebellion against the EPRA command. They also realized that the R-3 EPRA group had retreated and settled in TPLF-controlled territory in Tigrai.[33]

In the war with the TPLF, the EPRA lost many active fighters. When the Welkaite contingents retreated to Tselemt, all of EPRA's forces in eastern Begemidir lost contact with the outside world and their General Leadership in the western part of Begemidir. The Derge had deployed forces between the various Regional commands of the EPRA, and outlying towns in those areas were under the Derge's control.

Relationship Between Regional EPRA and Local EPRP

Since 1975, there had been two independent EPRP institutions in Begemidir -- the IZ, with a number of committees under it, and the regional EPRA. From the first months of 1977 until October 1978, both institutions operated independently and without a coordinating body to oversee their activities. This was the period when the majority of the surviving EPRP CC members were bogged down in the activities of the EPRA in Tigrai. Left on their own, the leadership of the Begemidir IZ and EPRA command in Begemidir sorted out differences as they arose.

The two structures cooperated on a wide range of common concerns. They exchanged intelligence information and activities of individuals considered hostile. Members of the party structure facilitated the arrival of the army by conducting political and organizational work in advance. Furthermore, they assisted in the day to day activities of the army. In some areas, members of the party structure took some part in military activities as well. On the other hand, the presence of an army group in a certain locality facilitated the activities of the party structure. The security problem that members of the party structure faced was alleviated. Despite these and other areas of cooperation, the two structures had to face a number of hurdles.

Differences between the Begemidir party IZ and the Regional EPRA arose over ill-defined or unclear programs of action among the peasantry, interference of one institution in the activities of the other, undefined spheres of action, conceptualization of the role of the party regarding the regional army, that is, the peasant army to be formed. There was no agreement on who should provide leadership to the peasants' associations and also to the local organizations formed in what were known as the "liberated" areas. The role of the party structure in regard to the peasants' militia was not defined either. The sub-zone party committee believed that the party rather than the EPRA control the militia and militia formation was regarded as a step toward peasant empowerment.[34] On the other hand, the EPRA regarded the peasants' militia as an extension of the EPRA. The militia was headed by the Militia Committee of the army. On this and other issues, there were no clear guidance and the friction between the two institutions persisted.

Interference of one structure in the activities of the other was another matter. Members of the party structure were expected to get their instructions from their party leadership. However, there were cases where party members (the cadres, as they were called) were given assignments by EPRA leaders. Local party leadership felt that the EPRA command undermined the independence of the party structure. They believed that the local EPRA leadership regarded the party structure as an appendage for providing information and gathering food. On the other hand, some members of the army believed that the leadership of the party structure was insecure and consequently, was suspicious of some of the activities of the army leadership. This was witnessed following the assignment of some members of the army to the party structure. Even though prior agreement was reached between the army and the party leadership to assign these members to the party structure, they were regarded with suspicion and their activities was hampered.[35]

Contradiction between the party and army group was exhibited during election of officers of a peasant association. Party members argued that the EPRA interfered in the election process. Believing the election to be its area of responsibility, the party had passed on an instruction on how it was to be conducted and who should run for office.

Inter-organizational interference occurred also sometime in 1976 when the party leadership decided to disperse some party members away from those areas where the army was operating. The army leadership objected the party's decision. Another incident took place in Dembelo, Tselemt, where the peasants' association discussed a case involving two peasants and passed decision. Members of the party committee alleged that a passing-by EPRA contingent reversed the decision. A week later, the army called a meeting of the Denbelo peasants to form a peasant association. The peasants argued that they already had one. The EPRA could not be persuaded and the meeting dispersed without resolving the issue. The peasants appealed to the local party committee which advised them to petition the party committee of the EPRA, which they did. The peasants presented persuasive arguments and the

EPRA leadership backed off.

The party structure had been requesting the army to provide it with members who were politically and organizationally mature. The army leadership provided those members and at the same time, demanded that they be placed on area leadership committees. However, the party structure regarded such a suggestion as an interference and an attempt to control the party. The party structure was engaged in establishing cooperatives. The army which believed in the untimeliness of establishing cooperatives stopped the process.

While friction was still underway, the army leadership in Begemidir received a number of serious complaints regarding the abuse of power and corruption of some party members. The alarmed army leadership organized seminars for the youth of Mai-tsemri and Adi-Arkai. Following the seminar in Mai-tsemri, the army detained two leaders of the youth's association and a member of the local party leadership. An investigation committee composed of members of the army and the party structure was formed to review the case.[36] In the investigation, no evidence was forthcoming to prove the allegations and the detainees were released a few days later. When all was over, the legality of the army's decision and the danger it posed was questioned and the incident left a lasting fissure between the two institutions.

Some of the problems mentioned above could be related to the historical emergence of the EPRA itself. In 1975, when the EPRA began operations in Tigrai, there was no EPRP party structure to speak of. Dictated by circumstances and probably copying from the experience of the EPLF, at that time a military institution, the EPRA had to assume the tasks of a party structure along with its military activities. Hence the need to form the Mass Organizations Committee. The main purpose of the formation of this committee was to conduct political and organizational activities among the peasantry.

In Begemidir, unlike Tigrai, there was a relatively well organized and independent party structure which had mobilized hundreds of its members among the peasantry. Following its arrival in Begemidir, the EPRA employed the experience acquired in Tigrai. Mass Organization Committees were formed and they were assigned to conduct political activities among the peasantry. The regional EPRA command did not adjust to new conditions, nor did it review its role in the new environment. The army and the party became engaged in similar activities, duplicating efforts and decision-making processes. Sometimes, contradictory decisions were made.

Besides inter-organizational conflicts, there were differing approaches regarding EPRA activities. The Gonder zonal committee had realized that organizational activities in the urban areas had become untenable and EPRA's slow advancement would not match the organizing effort of the party structure. The slow pace of the army and its limited areas of operation induced more resentment among party members.[37] Moreover, the Derge's repression threatened those areas where organizational work had been underway since 1975. As early as 1976, the party leadership in Begemidir insisted that the EPRA conduct operations in the Libo and Armacheho awerajas. Because of the setback for EPRA units in the Begemidir area at the beginning of 1976 and other factors, the EPRA failed to respond to the demands.[38]

The attitude of the peasantry toward the EPRP and the EPRA was another source of anxiety. The peasantry had affection for the party cadre, but more respect for the army and its members. The peasantry, only recently exposed to politics, appreciated military action, and the army was its symbol of resistance. The peasantry respected and feared authority and anyone who carried guns. The EPRA was held in awe, its activities glorified, its endurance of hardship and hunger was thought to be superhuman. There were widespread belief among the peasants that EPRA fighters were given special tablets to subdue their sexual feelings, or that they were bullet proof, etc. The cadre, toiling day in and day out among the peasantry, was liked but was not given the same attention as the member of the army. Those party members whose political awareness was relatively low did not prefer the role of a party operative. Furthermore, due to lack of political clarity, some members of the army derided party work.[39]

Peasant attitude towards authority can be illustrated by an incident encountered by the author of this book while traveling from Tselemt to the Libo district with the Commander of the EPRA, AA, former Begemidir province administrator Colonel Emiru Wonde and three other members of the army. All five were incognito. When they arrived at Zaklta in the Semien district, the Colonel, who had a special ability to communicate with peasants, initiated a discussion with the local folk.[40]

As they discussed peasant issues with the Colonel, the relaxed peasants readily expressed and shared their opinions until one of them whispered something to the others and the attitude of the peasants was changed instantly. They stopped talking and started listening, and respectfully pulled down their "*gabis*" (shawls), from their heads. (Pulling down ones shawl from the head is considered a sign of respect.) The peasants had recognized the former administrator of the Begemidir province, the Colonel.

Upon arrival of the group at Zaklta, a peasant leader had ordered that food be gathered and shelter for the night be arranged. A small cottage that belonged to a brothel owner was designated as the place where the EPRP/EPRA group would pass the night. However, after the identity of the Colonel was known, the EPRA/EPRP members were regarded as celebrities and they were given the best of hospitality. The previous arrangement regarding food gathering and finding shelter was changed. The head of the village, a Grazmatch, was informed about the arrival of the Colonel and the whole group was invited to his house for the night. Dinner was served at his house and the Grazmatch and his wife gave their bed to the guests - a sign of deep respect in Ethiopian culture.

Before dinner was served, the Grazmatch, perplexed by the egalitarian life style of the EPRP/EPRA, did not know whom to invite to the table. The EPRA's Constitution made no distinction between the leaders and the led. By law, all of its members had the same rights and privileges and for the most part led a communal life, sharing whatever was available. The Grazmatch asked the Colonel if the member who had malaria and was not well dressed had to be invited for dinner. He was referring to the commander of the EPRA, AA. The Colonel nearly burst out laughing, but controlled himself and passed on the question to the author of this book.

Be that as it may, the conflict between the party structure and the army command in Begemidir persisted. Upon arrival of members of the EPRP CC from Tigrai, the sub-zone committee in Tselemt was dissolved and the members were given other assignments. New members were assigned to the IZ and other sub-zone committees. The entire membership of the Cadre School under the IZ was changed and a new institution was created. Leading members of the IZ and the sub-zones were not consulted before the EPRP CC members took decisions..

The Fourth EPRP CC Plenum

The long awaited Fourth Plenum of the EPRP CC was held in June 1979, at Walenta in the Chilga District, Begemidir. According to the EPRP's Constitution, a Plenum had to be called every six months. The Third Plenum was held in November 1976 and the last ordinary CC meeting in February 1977. So, the Fourth Plenum was held two and a half years later.

The Fourth Plenum was the longest meeting in the history of the CC; it lasted about two months. The meeting was disrupted a couple of times by the Derge's offensive.

A few minutes before the Fourth Plenum began its deliberation, Kiflu Tadesse was summoned to the meeting place and informed that he had been suspended from the EPRP CC since March 1978 - for a period of about fifteen months - and that he now was reinstated. He was also told that new members had been coopted into the EPRP CC. Kiflu was confused and startled. He asked for an explanation of how and when he was suspended and why he was not allowed to take part in the decision-making process in which his fate was decided. The three-man CC delegation consisting of Tsegaye Gebre Medhin, Samuel Alemayehu and ZB declined to answer his questions and explained that everything would be discussed at the Plenum.

Kiflu had little time to reflect on what course of action to follow, as the startling news was received half-hour before the meeting began. It is still not clear whether the timing was deliberately planned.

When Kiflu was suspended from the leadership, there was a tacit understanding to keep him under surveillance. He later learned that his movements, the contacts he made and his whereabouts were closely watched. A number of EPRA members and close confidants of Samuel Alemayehu, who by this time was in charge of many of the activities of the EPRP CC, were assigned to follow Kiflu's activities. Among them was a member of the EPRA General Party Committee. Besides, Samuel had instructed the commander of the army, AA, to take measures if Kiflu made a wrong move.[41] An effort was also made to keep Kiflu close to the platoon which consisted of the members of the EPRP/EPRA leadership. Whenever the leadership wanted to conduct a meeting some pretext was created to exclude Kiflu.

Kiflu still thought that he was a member of the leadership and demanded meetings. Fake ones were arranged. Such "meetings" were conducted in December 1978 and February 1979. In those "meetings", the procedures of any ordinary CC meeting were followed; there were agenda items, chairpersons were elected and some people were assigned to take minutes. Everything seemed normal, except the uneasiness of some CC members who were not very enthusiastic about the whole process and the intrigues accompanying it. At the meetings, seemingly heated discussions were conducted and "decisions" that would never be implemented were made. Kiflu wholeheartedly participated in the meetings.

All through this period, an intense character assassination was underway with Kiflu portrayed as the person responsible for the demise of the EPRP structure in the urban areas. He was so vilified that few people ventured to be associated with him. In mid-1978, Kiflu handed over a sealed letter sent from Tigrai to the EPRP structure in Begemidir. The letter was from ZB, a member of the EPRP CC. While going through the minutes of the EPRP CC a year and a half later, Kiflu found out that the letter he had delivered to the zonal committee was about himself. It stated that the committee should distance itself from him.[42] Similar letters were sent to some members of the army leadership in Begemidir.[43]

In January 1979, six months before the Fourth Plenum was held, while Kiflu was under surveillance, a CC member provided him with some money and told him to leave for the Sudan. That CC member did not disclose the motives for the suggestion, but expressed some concern. Kiflu became suspicious and could not understand why he had to run away. He became more resolved to stay put and solve the problem that he encountered.

Among those who did not distance himself from Kiflu was Colonel Emiru Wonde. The two of them had developed a close working relationship since 1977. It was Kiflu who arranged the safe exit of the Colonel from Addis Abeba when the Derge tried to arrest him. When members of the CC realized the close relationship between Kiflu and the Colonel, two of its members, GM and ZB, were sent to inform the Colonel so that he would distance himself from Kiflu Tadesse. The Colonel Emiru Wonde rejected the suggestion and, to show his defiance, he invited Kiflu to go along with him for a tour of the Maheber Selassie monastery.

For over a year, Kiflu was left on his own. He was not given an assignment and was not provided a place to live or a budget to cover his expenses. As a matter of necessity, EPRA members led a collective life. To cook oneself a dinner, one had to gather logs, fetch water over a distance of a few miles and perhaps grind flour. In mid-1979, Kiflu made an arrangement to stay with the members of the Cadre School. However, a few days later, members of the Cadre School politely told him that he could not stay with them unless he obtained permission from the army leadership.

The cover ups and the intrigues that had been going on for over a year had a devastating effect on many of the EPRP CC members. A good number of the CC members had only been co-opted recently. As we shall see, some of them had no idea how the CC conducted its activities before 1977. Many of these CC members were the products of the Ethiopian students' movement, which could be accused of many failings, but not of intrigue and machinations.

When they encountered intrigue, many of the newly coopted CC members began to ask how the former EPRP CC had operated. Their confidence began to erode. The "former"EPRP CC ,in its existence of a few years, that is, until the first months of 1977, could be accused of some wrongdoings, but trust and confidence of the majority of its members in each other had been a great asset. To the extent conditions permitted, problems and differences had been handled above board and leadership was collective. Trust and confidence was the glue that held the clandestine organization together and led to the spectacular rise of the EPRP within a few years.

A few weeks before the Fourth Plenum took place, another meeting of six or seven CC members took place in the Sudan. The apparent aim of this meeting was to get as much information from one of the PB members, Zeru, who for health and other reasons was unable to travel and attend the Fourth Plenum. Some CC members argued that the meeting was some sort of an investigative process, deliberately designed so that the remaining PB members could not come together.[44]

Whatever the intention, the meeting in Sudan decided that the CC would keep its previous proceedings secret from Kiflu, even after his reinstatement. Even though he was told about his reinstatement to the CC, it was decided that he should obtain no information and should have no access to the documents and minutes of the meetings that took place for the entire period that he was suspended.[45]

The Fourth Plenum was attended by about fourteen CC members. Zeru Kehishen and AW who were abroad did not attend the meeting. Eight of the fourteen CC members never attended any CC meetings conducted before 1977, the very period the activities of which the Fourth Plenum was to assess and evaluate. Seven of these were newly coopted CC members. Only six members attended some CC meetings and of these, three CC members, ZB, Tsegaye Gebre Medhin and Iyasu Alemayehu had attended one or two meetings held before 1977; ZB and Tsegaye Gebre Medhin had attended one CC meeting each. ZB had attended the Third Plenum and Tsegaye the Second. Iyasu Alemayehu, who was a member of the Foreign Committee, had attended two CC meetings that were held before 1974. There were only three CC members who had attended most of the CC meetings held before March 1977. Two of them intimately knew the activities of the EPRP and the CC as well. They were Samuel Alemayehu and Kiflu Tadesse. Samuel became an alternate member in August 1975 and he had attended most of the CC meetings, except those that were conducted between October 1975 and March 1976. During this period Samuel was in prison. Kiflu had attended all CC and PB meetings that were held from April 1972 until March 1977. For the reasons mentioned above and others, Kiflu did not attend any of the CC activities for more than two years, from March 1977 until June 1979.

Both Kiflu and Samuel were regarded with suspicion by the rest of the CC members who attended the Fourth plenum, for entirely different reasons. The first one, Kiflu, had been accused of "left deviation" and he was a target of a smear campaign and character assassination. Samuel Alemayehu was the main figure behind the smear campaign. The rest of the CC members, in the absence of any other information to the contrary had complied and accepted at least some part of what was said. However, some of the newly coopted members remained skeptical all throughout and they had begun raising doubts particularly when YA, another CC member, who had some working relationship with Kiflu cast a different light into the matter.

On the other hand, Samuel Alemayehu had aroused the suspicion of other CC members because of the way he handled Kiflu's case. Besides, Samuel had appointed himself to most of the committees by the EPRP CC and many members of the leadership had begun resenting the concentration of immense power in the hands of a single individual.

The main issues of the agenda of the Fourth Plenum were: 1. the assessment of the few years of struggle of the EPRP, 2. analysis of the prevalent Ethiopian condition, 3. new political positions of the EPRP, 4. criticism and self-criticism session and 5. election of officers to the PB and other departments.

When the Plenum began deliberation two more agenda items were proposed. The first one was regarding the suspension of the CC member, while the second one was about the legality of the CC that was in session. Kiflu, who proposed the two points of the agenda refused to take part in the discussion unless he knew how he was suspended and reinstated in the CC. He demanded to know how a verdict was passed on him without his presence. An intense discussion ensued, but none of the CC members ventured to provide prompt response. After a relatively lengthy discussion, the newly coopted CC members pleaded that Kiflu withdraw his demand temporarily. It was explained that his case would be discussed as part of the assessment of the activities of the EPRP.

The second point raised was regarding the legality of the CC that was in session, seven of the members of which were coopted unconstitutionally. According to the EPRP's Constitution, the CC was entitled to co-opt only three more members until the convocation of the second Congress.[46] Discussion was conducted on the issue and the majority of the participants of the meeting defended the decision on the grounds that it was a necessary step taken in order to save the EPRP. A vote was cast and the participants voted in support of that decision, except Kiflu.⁴⁷ The same issue, the legality of the CC in session was raised in the course of the assessment of the activities of the EPRP, a month and a half after the Plenum had begun. A bizarre situation took place when by a majority vote, the Fourth Plenum decided that the co-optation was illegal. The newly coopted members who were part of the proceedings of the Fourth Plenum for about a month and a half were asked to resign. To be sure, sometime before the decision was made, some of these members, among them AA and GM had declared that they would resign. Furthermore, the Plenum decided that the discussions conducted and the decisions made for a month and a half were considered null and void. It was also decided that only former CC members had the right to conduct the assessment. After electing only three more CC members, the Plenum continued with its discussions. Some of the decisions adopted earlier on were accepted, while others were amended.

The Fourth Plenum was one of the most difficult meetings that was conducted under the atmosphere where there were widespread suspicion, tension and animosity among the participants. It was a meeting where even a minor issue aroused a prolonged and heated debate. It was a meeting in which the participants questioned each others motive. This was a meeting where the tension that had been building for quite a long period was let loose and the participants vented out their frustrations. Unlike the previous experience where the EPRP CC made decisions on the basis of consensus, the Fourth Plenum was a meeting where almost every point, even a minor one, was voted upon.

Despite the cleavage and tension, the Fourth Plenum made efforts to assess the few years of struggle of the EPRP. The activities of the various structures of the EPRP, including the leadership, were assessed and a number of decisions were made The different phases of the struggle, the various decisions of the EPRP leadership, the different policies that came out at different phases of the struggle were reviewed and assessed. Different sections of the leadership, particularly the PB was made accountable for many of the fallouts of the organizations.

The Plenum's decision came out in a forty-page document. Part One of the report discussed the activities of the EPRP from its formation in 1972 until August 1976. In this part, organizational activities of the EPRP and its Youth branch and the various political issues that the party raised were discussed.⁴⁸ The second part of the Fourth Plenum report started by repudiating the 1976 PB paper, both for its content and the manner that it was introduced to the members. The Plenum also prepared an article refuting the thesis presented in the PB paper. The PB paper had analyzed EPRP's rural and urban armed struggle *vis-a-vis* the broad strategy of the organization.⁴⁹ The Fourth Plenum squarely blamed the PB for the analysis contained in the paper.⁵⁰ By so doing, the Plenum exonerated the CC, thus shifting the blame of accountability. The article that came out under the title "Some positions..." and that was mentioned elsewhere, had attributed the errors only to some "members" of the leadership.[51] As was indicated in Chapter V, the PB paper was read not only by the entire CC members, but other leading members and committees of the EPRP. Besides, after the first version of the PB paper came out in October/November 1977, two CC meetings had taken place in Addis Abeba. The first one was the Third CC Plenum which took place in November and the second one was the February 1977 CC meeting.

In its deliberations, the Fourth Plenum supported the urban military activities of the EPRP.[52] However, the meeting criticized what it termed were major shortcomings of the policy regarding the urban activities of the EPRP. Among the points of criticism was lack of clarity regarding the relationship between urban and rural armed struggles, failure to clarify when and how the urban military activities should have been intensified, cooled down or withdrawn. Furthermore, the meeting severely criticized the PB for linking the issue of urban military activities to that of popular uprising.

In the second section of the Fourth Plenum report, activities of the EPRP Foreign Committee were assessed positively. The Fourth Plenum commended the FC for conducting satisfactory organizational, propaganda and public relation activities.[53] However, by mid-1979, the EPRP structure abroad was in deep crisis and the majority of its members had already abandoned the organization.[54] The Plenum also commended the activities of the FC for gathering material support for the EPRP.

The third section of the report discussed the different political issues that the EPRP raised in its few years of struggle and its relationship with different political groups of the country. It was in this section that the leadership clarified its position on issues that it characterized were new. The Fourth Plenum commended the activities that the EPRP had conducted to combat what it termed as "big-nation chauvinism" and it[55] endorsed the decision regarding the recognition of Eritrean independence, which the EPRP had accepted in 1977. However, the Plenum characterized the EPLF as an anti-democratic organization that was inimical to the Ethiopian people's struggle.[56] The meeting characterized the EPLF as an enemy organization and resolved that it would fight and rally against it.

The relationship of the EPRP with other domestic groups and organizations, foreign governments and international organizations were discussed in the third section of the Fourth Plenum report.

The fourth section of the report dealt with the activities of the EPRA. The meeting endorsed the attempts made to dispatch units and expand EPRA activities to the various parts of Ethiopia. At the same time, it pointed out what it believed were the causes for the debacle of the group that went to Wello. The root causes for conducting a RM and its shortcomings were also discussed. Lack of assessment of the various military operations was pointed out as one of the major errors of the EPRA leadership.[57] The report concluded that little effort was made to recruit peasants as members of the army. While discussing issues related to the EPRA, members of the army leadership who at the same time belonged to the EPRP CC expressed their strong reservations about the way that the CC handled the EPRA.[58]

The Fourth Plenum criticized the EPRP leadership for considering the TPLF as a democratic organization.[59] At the same time, the EPRA leadership was criticized for underestimating the military strength of the TPLF. Though unstated, it was believed that the above-mentioned two points were some of the major factors for the defeat of the EPRA in Tigrai.

A criticism and self-criticism session, which took about a week was also conducted, both collectively on the CC, the PB and on individual CC members. Those members who were more responsible for the errors that the CC and the PB made were criticized severely. Criticisms were conducted on the way the EPRP CC handled the case of its suspended member, Kiflu Tadesse. The Plenum recognized that the entire procedure adopted regarding the case would remain a blemish spot in the history of the EPRP. Samuel Alemayehu was singled out and bitterly criticized for his role and the way he handled the issue. He was also criticized for amassing power and was removed from most of the committees. There were some members who praised Samuel for the efforts he made to keep the organization together following EPRA's defeat in the hands of the TPLF.[60] A founding member of the EPRP, Samuel's role was also of pivotal importance in the early days of the organization. As a secretary of the first Addis Abeba IZ, Samuel laid down the foundation of the local structure. Samuel also had an important role in organizing the Ethiopian workers opposition. A victim of the Red Terror, Samuel was one of the few leading EPRP members who gallantly fought the Derge's relentless repression. He was one of the few leading EPRP members who provided leadership to the organization during its most difficult period, the Red Terror.

Following the criticism session, all former PB members were removed from their posts and Zeru, who the majority believed did not conduct self-criticism and was not collaborative, particularly at the meeting held in Khartoum, was dismissed from the EPRP.

The Fourth Plenum then discussed the prevalent Ethiopian situation and the tasks awaiting the EPRP. In conclusion, the Plenum formed a new PB and a Secretariat. A rectification movement in the party structure was initiated and leading committees of the various party structures were assigned to take the lead. It was also decided to call a congress sometime soon and preparation which included drafting of a new program and constitution was initiated. Though it was decided that a congress would be called, for reasons of security, the Plenum did not disclose that information to EPRP members. The withholding of this information from the members that were desperately awaiting for a congress had a very negative and devastating effect. Not long after the decisions of the Plenum was passed down to the members, demand for holding a congress continued coming. The newly elected PB then released the decision of the Plenum regarding the issue. However, EPRP/EPRA members failed to accept the truthfulness of the PB's statements. By then, many of the members had become very skeptical of the leadership and they regarded the PB's statement as a gimmick designed to defuse their protest.

The Fourth Plenum report was sent down to EPRP members, however, it did not inform them about the reconstitution of the CC and its new composition and the fact that most of those CC members who attended the meeting knew little or nothing regarding the activities of the former EPRP leadership. Besides, EPRP members were not informed that CC and former PB documents were not available. Most of these documents were buried and some were lost. Furthermore, EPRP members were not informed that most of the leading members and a large part of the EPRP CC proper did not spare themselves, but had become victims of the "Red Terror". The members were not informed that the original EPRP CC did not stay long enough to assess its failures and achievements in its entirety. They also were not informed about the assessments that the "former" EPRP CC conducted during the Second Plenum in August 1976.[61] The members were not informed about the internal struggle and the deep division within the leadership. The members were not informed that the last time the "former" EPRP CC conducted a meeting was in February 1977 and the PB in March of the same year.

Rank and File Revolt in the "Liberated" Areas

Not long after the Fourth Plenum report reached the members, a wide spread dissatisfaction began unraveling. Members who believed that the EPRP was an infallible organization were utterly disappointed when the Plenum admitted that the EPRP had committed some major mistakes. The Plenum had stated that some of the mistakes committed were costly and had resulted in the destruction of the structure and the fall of many of its members.

Furthermore, the members became more disappointed when they realized that the Plenum's report regarding the urban armed activities contradicted the policy statement that came out in "Some Positions from the EPRP...." That article had pointed fingers at "some" individuals. However, the Fourth Plenum shifted the blame and held the PB accountable. EPRP members became disappointed when the blame continued shifting and they felt that the leadership was looking for scapegoats for a decision collectively made. It was perceived that the Plenum shifted the blame when EPRP members failed to accept what was proposed in the paper, "Some Positions from the EPRP....". That paper was passed on to EPRP members in the name of the leadership and it was perceived as such, when in actual fact it was the work of one or two CC members, as was discussed elsewhere.

Some members felt that the EPRP CC was not telling them the truth and the conflicting statements that were put out in the name of the leadership caused a blow to the main fabric of the EPRP, trust and confidence in the leadership. Coupled with other misgivings and reservations, EPRP members became disappointed and, from heretofore, they began questioning every small nuances and decisions. Decisions of the leadership, however well intentioned, were regarded with suspicion.

In a clandestine organization, where who is who was unknown, the activities of an organization could only be judged by the policies it promotes and how it conducted the struggle. Trust and confidence don't come on their own. They have to be earned. They are the results of a prolonged political and organizational effort. Once confidence is gained, members usually tend to follow the leadership blind, but when they find out a breach of that unsigned contract, they feel betrayed and go a few years back to question each and every activity that they themselves and the organization had conducted.

The reaction to the decisions of the Fourth Plenum was multifarious. Many rejected the assessment contained in the report of the Plenum and continued demanding for a congress that they thought would mend the situation. Some members of the R-3 party and army structure nicknamed the report "*moot wekash*" (an accuser of the dead); the dead being those CC members who died in the course of the struggle. In three of the regions, some sort of a mutiny began taking shape.

The opposition against the leadership was further fueled when four leading activists, some of whom enjoyed some degree of popularity resigned from the EPRP. They were AA, the commander of the EPRA; GM , a member of the army General Leadership; DS a member of the army General Leadership and the EPRP CC; and Gedion, a member of the General Party Leadership. All of them had attended the Plenum until it decided that their co-optation was illegal and they were asked to resign from the CC. Three of them could easily mobilize a large following against the CC had they chosen that path. EPRP CC members were little known to the members. All four of the leading activists produced statements declaring their resignation. They resigned from the EPRP in a group and their action was imitated by others and from this event onwards, resignation was adopted as a form of protest and many more members abandoned the EPRP.[62]

Sometime before the "assessment" of the Fourth Plenum was produced, the Derge had come out triumphant in its drive against the Somali regime and Eritrean rebels and, as a result, the level of frustration and pessimism amongst EPRP members had increased. Some had begun doubting if a small army like the EPRA could ever withstand the "mighty" force of the Derge, which had Soviet backing. A publication put out by an EPRA group in the Tselemt area titled "*Buta*" had stated that it was a dream to defeat "an army that had covered the sky with jet fighter-planes and the ground with tanks." Some members raised doubts if it was wise to stand in opposition to the military regime in the first place.

Furthermore, the EPRA and the party structure in some parts of eastern (Kinfaz, Begela, Semien) and western Begemidir became frustrated when they realized the peasantry's lack of support. There were times when the peasantry, allied with the regime, opened up a campaign against the EPRA. In some of the areas, such activities were organized by peasants who had established links with the Derge. The EPRA imposed penalties on those who collaborated with the regime. Some of these peasants were apprehensive of EPRP cadres who lived among them. The peasants regarded the cadres as EPRP informants and labeled them as *"Kerekere"* cadres. *"Kerekere"* is a bird found in the northwestern Begemidir that would lead a peasant to a desert honey comb or a termite mound. Hoovering around the peasant, the bird keeps on making noise until the peasant heeds to its appeal. When he does, the bird flies a few distance and waits until the peasant catches up and it repeats the process until the peasant reaches where the honey comb or the termite mound was located. If he is lucky, the peasant goes for the honey, but the bird for sure goes for its preys, bees or termites.

Some EPRP members questioned the feasibility of the rural armed struggle when the economic aspect of the land issue had been partially resolved. One of the basic tenets of the EPRP, self-reliance, was questioned and many cast doubts if a small organization like the EPRP could at all survive without getting substantial help from outside. Though not explicitly stated, some were of the opinion that the EPRP established some kind of a relationship with the west, a policy that would bring about a major shift of alliance. For some EPRA fighters, rural life became more and more unbearable and some resigned from the army and joined the party structure, while others abandoned the struggle altogether.

Both overt and clandestine coordinating committees of the opposition were formed in R-1 and R-3 (Tselemt and Belessa) areas and an opposition against the EPRP CC began building. These committees continued regrouping members and one of their rallying point was opposition to the leadership. The R-3 opposition published a paper titled, "[T]he Belessa's difference - Bombard the headquarters [the EPRP CC]". The last phrase was coined by Mao tse-tung during the so called "Cultural Revolution" of the mid-sixties. Besides major political and organizational issues, a number of other minor shortcomings and weaknesses were raised and discussed in order to rally a large following. In this process, leading figures of the opposition approached and won over individuals that were placed in important committees, such as, the Intelligence Department. Among the leading personalities of the opposition in R-1 and R-3 were, Yaekob, Girma Asfaw, Daud, Mahedere, Gebre Selassie (Abdi), Yared Tebebu and others.

The opposition did not have concerted objectives and it was not a homogeneous group both in its outlook and final aim. It was an eclectic group that came together for quite different purposes, mainly because of its opposition to the leadership. There were individuals and groups who had an ultimate aim of correcting the mistakes of the EPRP and continue the struggle on a new ground at the same time. There were those who had harped grievances against the EPRP for a variety of reasons. Some of them had been implicated in the "factional" activities of the Assimba area and few of them were on a revenge mission. There also were a good number of members who wanted to give up the struggle, on the pretext that "socialism in the third world cannot work, or, fighting the Derge was like pushing the 'Terarbe' mountain".

Crisis in Region One

The opposition in R-1 conducted its activities overtly and opted for a mutinous path. In one of the meetings where leaders of the various departments around the base area took part, the opposition demanded for the resignation of the EPRA General Leadership and the convocation of a party congress. Consequently, in May 1980, some members of the army leadership resigned. A seminar for the members of the various departments who could number about two hundred was called. At the seminar, the resignation of the members of the army leadership was disclosed and the need to form a Provisional EPRA leadership discussed. A three-man committee whose function was to rally support and coordinate activities in the various regions was formed. Members of this committee were Yared Tebebu, Girma Asfaw and Mesfin (code name). The decisions passed by the seminar were supported by Kokeb and Tekeze contingents. Sometime before the activities of the opposition took place, a section of the EPRA in R-1 consisting of two combat units of about one hundred fifty fighters was sent to the ELF, Eritrea, to pick up arms. During this same period, an EPRP CC delegation headed by Samuel Alemayehu had also arrived at the ELF base area.

The activities of the opposition in R-1 were relayed to the leadership and to those EPRA combat units that had arrived at the ELF base area. In the discussion that EPRA units in Eritrea conducted, the participants who did not opt for a mutinous path, but preferred resolving issues peacefully and legally, expressed opposition to the form of struggle pursued by the opposition. Furthermore, they concluded that the decisions enacted by the opposition, which was just a section of the R-1 army, was not all-inclusive. By this time, the EPRA had four regional commands and the EPRA leadership was accountable to all four of them.

A meeting of those members who returned from Eritrea was called upon their arrival in Tselemt to inform them about the new development. In the discussion that ensued, members of the two contingents expressed their disagreement to the moves undertaken by the opposition and, as a result, two rival groups, each of which mustered large followings and a comparable fire power came into being.

Soon after, a seminar of all members of R-1 was called. It was supposed to be held at Dil Yibza. As a result of the emergence of the two rival groups, an intense and explosive condition that would eventually lead to an armed confrontation was created. Regarding the problems within the EPRP, both groups had marginal differences. Indeed, many of those that later were labeled as "loyalists" shared some of the views entertained by the opposition. Despite their reservations about the decisions of the Fourth Plenum and the serious problems within the EPRP, the "loyalists" had opted to wait for the convocation of a congress.

An intense struggle ensued and the opposition accused its contenders as "loyalists" of the various echelons of the leadership, including the EPRP CC.

The latter, however, accused their "protagonists" as irresponsible "liquidationists" ("*betagne*"). The contradiction between the two groups grew so acute that armed confrontation became inevitable. The "loyalists" expressed resoluteness and as a result, the opposition disintegrated. From R-1, hundreds of EPRA members defected to the Derge controlled towns. Some of the contingents contacted government forces located in nearby areas before they gave themselves up. As a result, EPRA/EPRP force in Tselemt was dealt a heavy blow both in terms of manpower and armament. Even after the major crisis was over, the defection and resignation continued for quite some time.

Few contingents, determined to stay together, irrespective of the odds, rallied the scattered force to their side. They were led by the Regional Command of the Tselemt area. Among the leading figures of this group were EPRP CC members Tsegaye Gebre Medhin and Yosef Mersha, some members of the EPRA regional and General Party Committee, Yishaq Debre Tsion, Bekere, Gebre Egziabher Haile Mikael (Gayem) and Geleb Dafla.[63] Finally, it was this EPRA/EPRP group that survived the ordeal and was able to hold the scattered forces close together.

Problems of Region Three

It was indicated elsewhere that the R-3 army and party structure had been gripped by a crisis long before the Fourth Plenum report reached there. In that process, members of the EPRA General Leadership had removed some members of the regional command and had formed a provisional leadership. However, even after the change of leadership, the crisis in R-3 could not be contained and contingents refused to take part in military operations. Organizational discipline was violated, the authority of EPRP leadership was undermined, contingents refused to fight and obey orders, lawlessness, particularly among members of the army prevailed. The unruly behavior of the fighters spilled over and began affecting peasants too. Sex, which was a taboo and an illegal act punishable by expulsion, became a frequent phenomenon for certain individuals. In a matter of few weeks, some fighters came out as couples, some even became "married". Many fighters could be seen hanging around in small towns, most of the time drinking. In many of the regions, including the R-3, the EPRA ceased to function as an effective military organization.

In the midst of this crisis, in April 1980, a contingent from the R-3 was sent to take part in an operation against the TPLF. Sometime around this period, the TPLF had begun attacking the EPRA forces in R-4, in Welkaite.[64] After their arrival in Tselemt, about twenty-two fighters refused to take part in the operation and returned to the R-3 area after breaking away from their contingent. The "rebel" group maintained an independent existence for quite some time and no retaliatory action was taken against it. That sign became an additional factor to defy authority.

While the R-3 regional army and party structures were bogged down by local issues, the report of the Fourth Plenum reached the area and served as a fuel to exasperate the crisis.[65] Local issues were substituted by issues that were related to the policies and activities of the EPRP and EPRA. It was argued that the EPRP was not a proletarian party, but a petit-bourgeois group. Some members made efforts to trace back EPRP's problems to its foundation in the early seventies. Student journals abroad that printed critical articles about some policies of the EPRP began circulating among members.[66] Unlike R-1, the opposition in R-3 was conducting its activities clandestinely and committees were formed to that effect. Furthermore, the opposition within the EPRA and the local party structure had established clandestine links and made effort to coordinate activities. Leading figures of the opposition visited the various contingents and began discussing the need to form another organization and thus the condition for the formation of the Ethiopian People's Democratic Movement was laid down.

Around the same period that apathy reigned in R-3, there was crisis in R-1 as well. The opposition in R-1 had formed a coordinating committee and two members of this committee arrived in R-3 to inform the new development and coordinate activities. The delegates from R-1 contacted the various contingents and in the midst of this confusion, the breakaway "rebel" group, that was mentioned above, probably by the decision of the clandestine leadership arrested eleven EPRA members, including the entire leadership of the previous regional command of R-3 and some members it believed were unrepentant "loyalists". Among those arrested were Fassika Belete; a member of the General Party Leadership, WG, a member of the party sub-zonal committee, Haile Abaye, Berhe, Mekuria, Emiru, Tesfaye, Feleke, Yasin, (code names) and some others. Members of the regional command who controlled EPRA finance of the region were accused of desertion.

While the opposition was intending to form an inquiry committee and a tribunal, the Derge, which had up to date information regarding the condition of the regional army opened up a military campaign. As a result, Pandora's box was opened and an exodus that resulted in the total dispersal of the regional party and army structure began. Around the end of May and the beginning of June 1980 a colossal catastrophe befell the EPRP. Close to eight hundred EPRA/EPRP members left to the nearest Derge controlled towns and gave themselves up. They took away whatever property they had, including arms and handed them over to the regime. After a few weeks of debriefing, they were given an amnesty and sent to different parts of Ethiopia.

One of the members of the leadership, Emiru, who had been detained by the opposition escaped and gave himself up to a Derge force located in one of the nearby towns. Like the other EPRP members who had given themselves up, Emiru was treated leniently until a letter reached one of the Derge cadres of the locality. In that letter, Emiru was portrayed as a loyal member of the EPRP and that he did not defect voluntarily.

When they realized the degree of the crisis that the regional EPRA (R-3) faced, leading figures of the opposition decided for a strategic retreat. Their initial intention was to retreat to Tselemt, to R-1, however, as was indicated elsewhere, the opposition there had been weakened and the "loyalists" had gained the upper hand. Following a discussion held in the lowlands of the Semien, Sahela, EPRA/EPRP members were given the choices of joining EPRP forces in Tselemt, giving themselves up to the Derge or joining the opposition.

Those who had resolved to form the new organization decided to send a delegation to the TPLF to obtain safe sanctuary. It is not ascertained whether some individuals had been in contact with the TPLF all throughout. However, neither the TPLF nor its peasant followers, known as "*weyannes*", whom the retreating EPRP members initially met, were surprised about the turn of events. They also did not treat them as an enemy group, despite TPLF's and EPRP's longstanding hostility. More surprising was the TPLF did not disarm the group for quite sometime.[67]

One of the first TPLF leaders to contact the group was Gebru Asrat, the current governor of Tigrai and other leading members, such as, Weldesellasie Nega who conducted discussion with the group. Following the negotiation, the group was allowed to stay in the TPLF controlled territory and it was provided with some assistance. Some of them left for the Sudan. However, about five and a half months later, those who remained behind, thirty seven of them, formed the Ethiopian People's Democratic Movement (EPDM), in November 1980. Leading members of this group were Yared Tibebu, Tamrat Layene, Bereket Simon, (Amberber - code name), Daud (code name), Mahedere (code name), Gebre Selassie, Ayalew Kebede (Yared), Dejen (code name), Kobelew (code name) and others.

When the EPRP structure in the Belessa area became dismantled, some leading peasant activists were left on their own. These were peasants who had been involved in the struggle since 1975 and had given up their farms for the sake of the struggle. A group of these peasants, among whom were Ferede Assega, Dessie Dawit and Negussu Seteargew went to the Tselemt area to join the EPRA.[68] However, the R-1 EPRA was in crisis and the peasant group returned to Belessa and when the Derge controlled their area, most of them asked for amnesty. Some of these peasants began collaborating with the Derge and few of them became frustrated and abandoned the struggle altogether.

Some of the peasants could not stay under the Derge's rule for a long time and when some founding members of the EPDM sent them a letter to join the group, about fifty of these peasant activists joined it.[69]

When EPRA fighters gave themselves up to Derge forces or left for the Sudan, some of the peasants who rallied behind the EPRA felt betrayed. Out of desperation, some of them, such as, those in the Tselemt and Welkaite areas, engaged themselves in retaliatory actions. Some of them established secret contact with the Derge and to prove their change of allegiance, they informed on EPRP activities and the whereabouts of its contingents. In some cases, they handed over members of the EPRP to the Derge and unsuspecting EPRP cadres fell victim.

Among the preys who fell victim were SD and Solomon. SD, who was stationed in Welkaite, was a member of the EPRA Intelligence Committee. SD and Solomon, who were unaware of the state of mind of the peasants went to the Tselemt area for an assignment. They then contacted a group of peasants and passed the night together. The next day, they decided to take a bath in a river and five peasants volunteered to accompany them. When they reached the river, SD and Solomon, along with three of the peasants, undressed and went into the water. A few moments later, two of the peasants, who did not undress, approached the EPRP members and told them to hold their hands up.

Their hands tied up, SD and Solomon were then pulled out of the river and were placed under detention. Three other EPRA members who had already resigned and were on their way to the Sudan were also apprehended. However, the peasants let this group leave and took Solomon and SD to a nearest forest to execute them, but on that day, conditions were not conducive to do so. They then took them back to a house and let them pass the night there. When left alone, the detainees helped each other untie their hands and awaited for the worst. Early in the morning, the door was opened and the two detainees were summoned to come out.

Outside of the huts, the five peasants were waiting for them, lined up on two sides. As soon as he left the hut, Solomon hit one of the peasants on the eyes with an iron rod that he had found in the cottage and ran for his life. The peasants who expected tied up prisoners became alarmed and ran after Solomon and eventually, they caught and killed him. SD, who was able to hide himself amidst a corn field, was able to escape and he gave himself up at one of the nearest Derge controlled towns. Government officials treated him leniently until those peasants arrived the next day and informed about his status within the EPRP. The peasants also disclosed the event that took place the previous day and explained that he was forced to give his hands up. That revelation changed the way SD was handled and he became incarcerated in a Debark prison for about eleven months. Dabarek is a small town on the main Gonder/Tigrai highway.

SD was assigned to a ward that was congested and dimly lit. There were more than fifty prisoners in the ward. Throughout his stay in the prison, SD was chained to a sixty-five-year-old prisoner, who due to a severe kidney failure had to use the "bath facility", a barrel cut in half, every half-hour or so. The barrel was placed in the ward itself and whenever the man had to use it, he had to wake up SD and both of them had to cross over the bodies of sleeping inmates, thereby falling and getting up several times, before they returned to their place.

What a prisoner encountered the moment he landed in a prison was shaving off of his hair. In the Debark prison, the blade had been so much over used that the "barber" had to push hard, thereby cutting the skin and some blood vessels of the head in the meantime. To get better treatment, the 'barber' had to be bribed. The prisoner had to forfeit his breakfast. In that prison, inmates were allowed to leave their ward only twice a day and the interrogation was conducted late in the night and many of the internees never returned. Some passed out in the process of the interrogation and some were executed.[70]

SD was tortured so severely that his nerves under his feet were destroyed. He lost one kidney and the other one became seriously affected. By the order of Major Melaku Teferra, all political prisoners in the Debark prison were moved to Gonder. To counteract the activities of his rival, Sergeant Gebre Hiwot Gebre Egziabher, Major Melaku Teferra became more lenient and placed the prisoners under semi-detention. With the help of some acquaintances, SD escaped and left for Welkaite where he arranged safe passage to the Sudan.

Sergeant Gebre Hiwot Gebre Egziabher, the Administrator of the Semien aweraja, was in charge of the interrogation process in Debark. He was an army truck driver before he joined the mini-Derge in Eritrea. Mini-Derges were military committees that were formed during the 1974 revolutionary movement. In 1975, he joined a group of officers that traveled to different provinces to explain the Derge's aims and objectives.

For some very curious reasons, the Sergeant used to go beyond the call of duty to liquidate the EPRP. He had led and conducted a number of campaigns against the EPRA. Nicknamed the "lion of the north", Sergeant Gebre Hiwet was the main architect of the "Red Terror" in Dabat, Debark and other small towns.

Sergeant Gebre Hiwot, who posed a threat to Major Melaku Teferra, the administrator and the Derge representative of the Begemidir area, passed away in a very mysterious "plane crash". He was buried in Addis Abeba at the St. Yosef cemetery, at the special burial cite dedicated to "revolutionaries". A few months later, the corpse of the Sergeant was removed from the cemetery. It was believed that the Sergeant was implicated as a TPLF member following the arrest of hundreds of Tigrayans in Gonder sometime in the 1980s.

Region Two Army - Challenges

Following the disclosure of the decisions of the Fourth Plenum, discontent was openly manifested among members of the regional army and party structure of southwestern Begemidir. As some sort of a midway solution and also to avert the crisis, the EPRP leadership organized a seminar.

To conduct the seminar, a delegation that consisted of Kiflu Tadesse, NM, FGM, TM and GB was formed. When the delegation reached the area where the majority of the fighters were found, it discovered that members were resigning in large numbers and they were leaving for the Sudan. It also realized that the regional army command was not making efforts to stop the tide. According to later day discussions, it was known that some leading members of the regional command tacitly encouraged that process.[71] When the arrival of the delegation was known, a malicious rumor about the plans and intentions of the delegation was spread and the resignation continued.

The delegates made a final preparation to begin the seminar. However, they were informed that the military condition of the area was not conducive to do so. Sometime earlier the Derge had begun a military campaign against the R-2 EPRA and it had made conditions very difficult. Besides, some peasants that were allied with the Derge were causing some trouble. In order to bring the condition under control, the regional command organized an operation targeting some of the peasants that had allied with the Derge. For some odd reasons, that operation ended in failure, thereby boosting the moral of anti-EPRA peasants.

After realizing the difficulty of conducting a seminar in a hostile surrounding, the delegates and the regional command held a joint meeting and decided to conduct the seminar in a safe environment where military confrontation either with the Derge or with hostile peasants was minimal. Quara, a location that was considered free of Derge's influence was selected as the next possible site.

All throughout this period, major activities and decisions of the delegates were relayed to the members of the PB who were located in Armacheho, hundreds of miles away from where the delegates were found. Anticipating further fragmentation, the delegates sent messages to the members of the PB. One of the messages was the need regarding the strategic retreat of EPRA forces in R-1 and R-3 to the western part of the Begemidir province.[72] The radio message was, "possibly members of the army and party structure (R-2) will retreat to Sudan. The impact of the retreat on the other regions is obvious. Concentration of forces is a must. Pull forces from East [that is R-1, and R-3] before the rainy season starts. [Before the rivers become over-flooded and curtail movement]...." Members of the PB responded by saying that they were not mandated to initiate a strategic retreat. They believed that that decision was the prerogative of a congress. As indicated in the previous pages, by the time the above quoted message was relayed, both R-1 and R-3 were undergoing a severe crisis. After the entire R-2 EPRA/EPRP force reached Quara, it was realized that it would be difficult to defend itself in the event of a Derge offensive. Quara is located on a plateau and, during this period, the fighting spirit of many of the EPRA members was low. Finally, it was decided to conduct the seminar in an inhabited area, by the Sudanese border, close to the Shinfa river. That area was considered ideal not only in terms of its safety, but also to obtain grain and other supplies from the Sudan. The entire EPRP/EPRA force crossed over to the Sudanese side of the border and the next day, the Shinfa river overflooded.

Before the seminar began, the delegates initiated discussion and dialogue with members of the different units and an agreement was reached to conduct the seminar, provided that it was given to all of the EPRA/EPRP members at the same time. The delegates were instructed to conduct separate seminars for party members, YL and EPRA members. The party and the YL had their own separate clandestine structures within the EPRA. Furthermore, the identity of the members of these structures was a closely guarded secret.

Soon after the seminar began, the participants raised many sensitive and serious questions. Among the main questions raised were regarding the relationship between the PB and the CC. As was indicated above, many EPRP/EPRA were of the opinion that the Fourth Plenum of the CC had vindicated itself and put most of the blame on the shoulder of the PB. The participants of the seminar asked if the PB was present at the Fourth Plenum to defend itself, if it presented its rebuttal, what the relationship between the PB and the CC was, whether members of the CC did not see what was known as the PB paper, and what the opinion of "comrade x" was regarding his dismissal (this was in reference to Zeru Kehishen who was dismissed from the party). Close to fifty critical questions were asked and the participants of the seminar insisted that the delegates provide adequate replies.[73] Many of the issues raised were beyond the mandate of the delegates and the participants were told that their questions would be answered at the coming congress. The participants, who had thought that they would find adequate responses to their lingering doubts became disappointed and the crisis exasperated. When they realized the level of the crisis, the majority of the members of the delegates who had no knowledge about the questions raised demanded that Kiflu respond to them. When Kiflu insisted that he was unable to do so, some members of the delegation raised serious reservations and stated that they might be forced to resign from the delegation.

Even though he was not mandated to do so, Kiflu informed the delegates that he would discuss with them the conditions within the EPRP leadership. Besides, he notified the delegates that his interpretation and understanding of events within the leadership might be incongruous to the comprehension of the other members of the leadership. He then disclosed to them that the PB did not exist and that it had ceased to function as such as of March 1977. He disclosed the fact that he had been under some kind of "house arrest" for quite some time. In short, he informed them about the reality within the leadership, the details of which were discussed elsewhere. He then told them that if he had to disclose to the participants of the seminar what he knew, he would tell what he believed was the truth. The delegates became very annoyed and startled about the disclosure and they noted the adverse effects of such a revelation and advised Kiflu to keep the information to himself.

Many of the questions forwarded by the participants of the seminar remained unanswered, however, discussion on other issues was resumed, but the resignation process which had began earlier lingered and the fighting spirit of the members continued deteriorating. In the midst of this crisis, a number of small groups centered around some individuals emerged. Army discipline was undermined. Like the members of the army in the other regions, the basic codes of the EPRA were violated.

When the seminar seemed unable to improve the situation, the delegates went beyond their mandate and reviewed the program of the seminar. They took it upon themselves to call a regional conference and presented that idea at a joint meeting with the regional command of the R-2 army. They believed that calling a regional conference would partially solve the problems facing the entire group and avert the disintegration process. A heated discussion ensued when the regional command of the army vehemently opposed the idea on the grounds that EPRA units had already lost their fighting spirit. The regional command suggested that the entire force had to retreat to the Sudan. In the course of the discussion, three members of the delegates were won over to the side of the regional command and the idea of calling a regional conference was dropped. Kiflu then suggested that some EPRA units stay in the R-2 area until members of the other regions retreated to the west and the entire EPRP/EPRA force congregated. Abandoning the entire western side of the Begemidir, the area where the R-2 army was deployed, would leave the units in the eastern side no corridor in case of an emergency, he argued. That idea was also rejected citing lack of combat readiness of the EPRA units in R-2 as the excuse. Finally, the delegates, the regional command and the party sub-zonal committee proposed that the entire force should retreat to the Sudan where they would conduct a regional conference. That proposal was handed over to members of the newly formed PB, who by that time (along with other contingents) had come to the area where the seminar was underway. Members of the PB ratified the proposal and disclosed it to the regional army command. Furthermore, they agreed to make preparations for a regional conference to be held in the Sudan.

Unlike conditions in other regions where chaos and confusion reigned before dispersal, the R-2 group acted more responsibly when it endorsed the strategic retreat and moved to the Sudan in an organized manner. It decided to bury all the arms in a safe place, for future use. For lack of a better alternative, the regional army command was given the responsibility of burying the arms and EPRA/EPRP forces of R-2 arrived in the Sudan in June 1980.

After arriving in the Sudan, partly because of necessity, the majority of the fighters resided in groups and continued collaborating with the newly formed "Crisis Committee", which was composed of activists that the rank and file members had some confidence in. One of the main tasks of the committee was to handle the political crisis within the EPRA/EPRP and act as a liaison between the EPRP leadership and the members whose links had been hampered.

Splinter group formation had begun earlier on and when discipline continued getting loose and the thread that had been holding the members close together began breaking, and an absolute lack of confidence in the leadership reigned, loosely clustered groups emerged. These were groups of like-minded individuals who in some form or another wanted to continue the struggle.

In order to resolve the crisis, six of the EPRP CC members held an uninterrupted meeting that took more than two months. One of the first issues that the EPRP CC group raised was related to the formation of the splinter groups mentioned above, and two diametrically opposed views were expressed. The majority of those who attended the CC meeting bitterly opposed such a phenomenon on the ground that it contradicted one of the basic principles of the EPRP, democratic centralism. They argued that the basic rules and regulations of the EPRP had to be respected. On the other hand, Kiflu argued that political reality had to be grasped. For him the issue was not to enforce EPRP's regulations, but to take accommodative steps that would help bring an end to the process of fragmentation. According to him, the level of the crisis in the EPRP had gone so deep that the party could survive only if it was able to exhibit more tolerance and harp less on rules and regulations, such as, respect for democratic centralism. The EPRP should allow and assist the newly formed groups so that they still could stay in the struggle, in some form or another[74] and eventually gain their confidence. It should be remembered that this was a period when a large number of fighters had abandoned and were still abandoning the struggle altogether.

Instead of addressing the issue in a broader context, the EPRP CC members wanted to know who were forming the factions and they continued interrogating Kiflu Tadesse. Some of them thought that he was involved in the activities of the splinter groups. When Kiflu Tadesse insisted that the CC focus on the broader issue of how to resolve the crisis, the case led to a further misunderstanding and the CC meeting was temporarily halted. Kiflu, who did not belong to any of the groups, raised the issue in order to design a different approach to resolve the crisis, but was condemned for disloyalty.[75]

Furthermore, there were differences on whether the EPRP could still claim that it was a proletarian party or not. Taking note of the degree of crisis the EPRP was in, the condition of the labor movement and other factors, Kiflu argued that the EPRP had to transform itself into a left-inclined political movement. The rest of the CC members adamantly opposed such a notion. There were differences on the nature of the contradiction of the Ethiopian society, on how and where to continue the armed struggle, on the condition of the EPRP itself, etc. On almost all of the issues, there were sharp differences with the majority of the EPRP CC members on one side and, most of the time, Kiflu Tadesse on the other.

About a month and a half after the CC meeting started, Iyasu Alemayehu began attending it. Iyasu had been invited and repeatedly asked to disrupt other engagements and attend the CC meeting. However, members of the Foreign Committee informed the EPRP CC that Iyasu was away for a mission and was unable to come. One of the main reasons why Iyasu had to attend the CC meeting was to determine the financial status of the EPRP in order to attend to the needs of hundreds of members who by this period were undergoing very difficult times. During this period, whatever finance the

EPRP Activities in Begemidir 461

EPRP had was in the hands of the FC that was chaired by Iyasu Alemayehu. Even though the CC was informed that Iyasu Alemayehu was away on a mission, sometime later it was learned that he had been staying in Gedarif, a Sudanese city, where the CC was conducting its meeting. Without the knowledge of the EPRP CC, he was conducting secret communication with his brother, Samuel Alemayehu, who also informed Iyasu Alemayehu about the discussions and the developments within the CC. Zenabu, code named Ali and other EPRP members served as intermediaries between the two brothers.[76] Following Iyasu's attendance, the atmosphere of the discussion changed. Some of the issues discussed earlier were revised.

With the participation of Iyasu, one of the main points of discussion of the CC was what ought to be done in order to alleviate the financial condition of EPRP/EPRA members. These included the sick members that had arrived in the Sudan and were languishing in the refugee camps, helping themselves on United Nations handouts. The majority of the EPRP CC members reached a conclusion that most of those who had retreated to the Sudan were not ready to struggle and the EPRP had to invest its finance on those who were in the field and that the organization had no additional fund to help others. Furthermore, the promise to call a regional conference of members of R-2 was rescinded when the majority of the CC members decided that the only conference to be held was for the groups inside the country. It was also stated that any willing person could go inside the country and attend it. The CC's decision was contrary to the understanding of the entire membership of the EPRP/EPRA who earlier had been informed by members of the PB that a regional conference of the R-2 area would be held.

The above mentioned decision of the CC was supported by all (five CC members), except two, Kiflu Tadesse and AB. Kiflu Tadesse who supported the convocation of a regional conference of the R-2 resigned from the CC and produced a ten page statement under the heading "Who Constitutes the EPRP?" - the few leaders who controlled EPRP's finances or its members whose only asset was their will to struggle? In the statement, Kiflu Tadesse explained why he had to take that step. Kiflu also explicitly stated that he did not resign from the EPRP.[77] He then made the above mentioned CC decision public and informed R-2 members that the regional conference they were waiting for would not be called. A few days later the EPRP CC put out a statement on the resignation of Kiflu Tadesse.

Three more CC members resigned from the EPRP a few months later. By this time, Iyasu Alemayehu's and Samuel Alemayehu's secret communication had been known.

When the CC's decision regarding the cancellation of the conference for R-2 was known, most of the members of the EPRP, having no confidence in the leadership and uncertain of the outcome of the conference to be held inside the country, could not accept the decision. They still insisted that a conference for R-2 members be called. The CC group then distributed about ten Sudanese pounds to each member and curtailed whatever financial support it was providing, labeling these members "liquidationists". In one stroke, hundreds of activists were deprived of their EPRP membership. Even though it was true that a great majority of these members had expressed their lack of confidence in the leadership, they remained loyal to the EPRP till they learned about the final decision of the leadership. Hundreds of fighters patiently awaited for a resolution of the crisis. These members did not resign from the EPRP, *rather, they were purged* by five or six CC members. The only "fault" of these members was that they forcefully demanded for the convocation of a congress or a conference in which to air their grievances and fix the problems within the EPRP. Many of them found it difficult to comprehend why they were labeled "liquidationists".

Irrespective of the decision of the CC group, members who had regrouped around the Regional Command of R-2 had planned to convene their own regional conference. Before they could take that step, some members of the EPRP CC made attempts to forcibly possess the arms hidden by members of the R-2 as they retreated. They had unanimously entrusted the Regional Command to be the guardian of the arms. In the complication that ensued the possession of the arms, the Sudanese government was informed about the secret location where the arms were buried and became the beneficiary. That incident produced more frustration and complicated the predicament of members of R-2. The loss of the hidden arms accelerated the dispersal of the R-2.

The disappointment and frustration of EPRP members was deep. In the absence of an alternative in the Sudan, some gave themselves up to the Ethiopian regime. Others gave up the struggle altogether. Those who were left on their own and had no financial resources had to find livelihood as maids, construction workers, vendors, peddlers, etc.

The American State Department hastily came up with the plan known as "refuge resettlement". During this time, a pro-West political group and an off-shoot of the EDU, known as the Ethiopian Peoples Democratic Alliance, was making efforts to get organized.

Hundreds of former fighters and activists, many out of necessity, decided to be resettled in America. The hasty departure of some of the leading figures of the EPRA/EPRP further demoralized rank and file members.

By 1980, a large number of EPRP members in Begemidir abandoned the struggle and very few remained behind. They retreated to the ELF held territory in Eritrea and conducted a meeting. Soon afterwards, that force traveled to the western part of Begemidir and this group was able to preserve EPRP's name. To do that, it had to face all kinds of adversities, including peasant insubordination.

Notes to Chapter X

1. See details in Chapter II.

2. Interview, AM, November 1994.

3. Activities of the Northern Front of the EPRA, pages 3-4.

4. Interview, May 1994, Berhane, one of the leading members of the army.

5. Activities of the Northern Front of the EPRA, page 6.

6. Abyot, Volume III, No.1, January 1978.

7. Among the prominent groups were the Left Wingers and the Socialist Students Union of Gonder. There also was a third group with a traditional leaning. The Student Council election conducted during this period was marred by the struggle between the left-oriented groups and the traditionalists. The left-inclined groups emerged triumphant when Mensur Suleiman (Sumalew) was elected as the president of the student body during the 1972-73 student election.

8. Kiflu Tadesse, The Generation, Part I, Independent Publishers, 1993, page 109.

9. The details of the activities of the Begemidir zonal committee were provided by Mohabaw and Berhane, leading activists of the zonal committee.

10. Even when the Zemetcha program was officially called off, some EPRP members were asked to stay behind and continue party building.

11. Melaku Tsegaye was killed by the Derge in 1977. When it was known that the administrator, Colonel Emiru Wende and Melaku were to be arrested, the EPRP passed on the information to the concerned individuals.

12. See details, page 423.

13. Mengistu Ketsela was arrested in Addis Abeba while he had gone there to report to the EPRP leadership about EDU's military movement in Welkaite and Humera and the need to deploy an EPRA force before the area fell under the control of EDU. Mengistu's whereabouts still remain unknown.

14. Melaku Tsegaye was assigned to work with the Administrator, Colonel Emiru Wende. Berhane Gebre Meskel was relieved from the Zone Committee because of his frequent travel and busy schedule with the book store.

15. In mid-1977, the secretary of the IZ, Demas, was arrested. However, his position within the EPRP structure was not known to the security branch of the government and consequently, he was released a few months later.

16. Alberto Sbacchi, Ethiopia under Mussolini, Zed Publishers, 1985, pages 201-202.

17. When EDU's fighters tried to tear down EPRP's banner at the compound of the Fetawrari, one of his Kemante followers and relatives took it upon himself to defend his "uncles flag". Fetawrari Ayele died in the Sudan in the early 1980's. When he died, he was in his mid-sixties and a political refugee.

18. While two contingents of the Begemidir EPRA were deployed to dislodge the Derge from the locality known as Adi Wessene, contingents known as 47 and 18 refused to take part in that operation.

19. See details in Chapter IX.

20. Part of the discussion regarding the two contingents that crossed over to the western part of the Begemidir was provided by Girma T. and Debebe, participants of the expedition and leading members of the EPRA group.

21. "Murte" stands for buttock in Begemidir and for the male organ in the central part of Ethiopia.

22. The comedian is nicknamed Shaleka.

23. In that area, the Chinese government was involved in the construction of roads.

24. All of them were to be the founding members of the Ethiopian People's Democratic Movement.

25. He is the younger brother of Kassa Kebede, a prominent member of the Mengistu regime.

26. Discussion with Esatu, 1990.

27. Ayalew had confided to a member of the army that his activities would be discreet.

28. Interview, MA, 1994, a leading member of the EPRP party structure in the Libo aweraja.

29. A member of the General Party Command of the EPRA believes that Ayalew passed over to the opposition all of the discussions conducted at the meeting of the regional leadership. Interview, Fassika Belete, May 1994.

30. Even though their language is Tigrigna, the Welkataye sing in the Amharic language, and their songs are similar to those in the Begemidir province.

31. Report prepared in 1983 by Muzei, an EPRP member who had been assigned to the area.

EPRP Activities in Begemidir 465

32. TPLF publication, Yetegele Tirri, Second Year, No.4, pages 16 and 18.

33. See details pages 449-452.

34. Interview, Mohabaw, May 1995.

35. Interview, MZ, February 1997. MZ was one of the members of the army assigned to work in the party structure of the Tselemt area. When he found out that the difference could not be resolved, he resigned from the party structure.

36. Interview, Mohabaw, May 1995.

37. Interview, Mohabaw, May 1995.

38. See details, Chapter II.

39. Friction took place within the party structure. Such tension arose following the assignment of responsibilities to newly arrived veteran and experienced activists, some of whom questioned the ability of the mid-level local party leadership. In due course, the newcomers also raised ethical issues. Usually, friction was triggered by differences on questions of organization and politics. Some leading members of the Begemidir party structure became very cautious and suspicious of outsiders, including those who had already been placed in the party structures. As a result, there was conflict between the local party leadership and some of the veteran activists assigned in the local party structure. This condition was prevalent in the party structure of the Belessa area where the conflict reached a crisis level by 1979.

40. Communicating with peasants was one of the challenges that most EPRP members faced and very few were successful. Besides the difference of the spoken language in the rural and urban areas, drawing peasants attention was a challenge by itself. The peasantry is not used to abstraction and general themes. If one wants to deal with peasants, he had to raise issues that are dear to them and has to converse in a manner that would be intelligible. This issue brings to memory of an incident that took place in Bellessa, the Begemidir province. A female EPRP cadre gathered some peasants and conducted an agitation. When the meeting was over, one of the peasants remarked, "did you see how she spoke? She speaks like a radio anchorperson." This meant that she was speaking fast and the peasant did not comprehend what she was talking about. Most peasants do not understand what is announced over the radio and some provide their own interpretation of what they had heard.

41. Discussion with AA, July 1994.

42. From the Memoirs of the author, EPRP CC group meeting, Khartoum, April 1978.

43. The author learnt about these letters in August 1994.

44. Authors memorandum, GM, June 1980.

45. Minute of Khartoum CC meeting, April 1979.

46. See details in Chapter II.

47. Memoir of the author, 4th EPRP CC Plenum, 1979.

48. EPRP CC 4th Plenum Assessment, pages 2-7.

49. See details, Chapter V.

50. EPRP 4th Plenum Assessment, page 9.

51. In the second section of the report, the Plenum recognized that some of the issues raised in the article mentioned above were new and had to be discussed by the Central Committee.

52. EPRP Fourth Plenum, page 11.

53. Ibid., page 17.

54. See details Chapter VII.

55. EPRP Fourth Plenum Assessment, 1979, page 21.

56. Ibid., page 22.

57. Ibid., page 28.

58. Their arguments were in line with those expressed in the section that deals with the RM.

59. Ibid., page 28.

60. Tsegaye Gebre Medhin was among those who praised Samuel Alemayehu.

61. See details, Chapter II.

62. The author of this book had a prolonged discussion of three days with one of those who resigned, GM, sometime before he left for the Sudan. GM expressed pessimism regarding the direction and the outcome of the struggle and strongly believed that the EPRP was controlled by a dictatorial clique. The author did not share his pessimism regarding the struggle and explained that the dictatorial clique within the EPRP CC had been disgraced following the discussions that took place at the Fourth Plenum. GM could not accept that explanation and warned the author that he might be victimized sooner or later.

63. Some of these were among leading EPRP figures that were either imprisoned or killed by the EPRDF in 1991.

64. See details page ????

65. Aware of the consequences, a member of the regional command did not pass the Fourth Plenum report to the various contingents. However, the members obtained a copy from the local party structure. Interview, Fassika Belete, June 1994.

66. Interview, MA, 1994. MA was one of the leading members of the party structure of the area.

67. MA, Interview, 1994.

68. From a letter of one of the peasants, GMF.

69. According to GMF's letter, mentioned above, many of these peasants abandoned the EPDM sometime later.

71. Interview, SD, 1989.

71. From a discussion with a member of the regional command, GT, Sudan, 1980.

72. From the authors Memoir of the Shinfa meeting.

73. Memoirs of the Shinfa Seminar. The author had recorded and kept the questions that were raised during the seminar in Shinfa.

74. From the CC, statement on the resignation of Taye, September 19, 1980, page 7.

75. Ibid., pages 5-6.

76. Interview, Ali, 1987. He served as the liaison between the two brothers.

77. Taye's statement, "Who Constitutes the EPRP?", 1980.

Epilogue

As demonstrated in the *Generation* Part I and in this book as well, a significant section of the Ethiopian people resisted the installation of the military dictatorship in 1974. All throughout this period, political education raised the political awareness of the people, exposed the nature of the military regime and laid the basis for its eventual demise in the early 1990's. The struggle of the late 1970's was the dress rehearsal for the early 1990's. The two periods are linked in terms of the form of struggle, major political issues, major figures, etc. To be sure, the later period of the Derge's rule was characterized by further polarization of the society and the intensification of the conflict. Moreover, it was characterized by the gradual weakening of the multinational cause and the gradual spread of nationalism.

After the offensive of 1977, Eritrean rebel organizations controlled all Eritrean cities except Massawa and Asmera. After its success on the Somali front, the Derge opened an offensive and recaptured all those cities, save Nakfa in the Sahel. In January-February 1979, the regime attacked the EPLF in the Sahel, but without success. The offensive was renewed in March and July 1979, and "[T]he year 1979 witnessed the defection of Eritrean fighters to Ethiopia in greater number."[1]

At the beginning of 1980, the EPLF counter attacked and halted the regime's preparation for another offensive. Government forces were forced to regroup in Afabet.

In the first months of 1980, a section of the ELF leadership established relationship with the Soviet Union "which led to talks in Moscow between ELF delegates and leaders of the CPSU."[2] The EPLF on the other hand was condemning the Soviet Union for "masterminding" the military regime's offensives.[3] Violent strife between the rival Eritrean fronts began. This internecine struggle continued for a year and ended in ELF's defeat when attacked by the EPLF and the TPLF which played the main role.[4]

Many were killed in the battles and hundreds and thousands of ELF fighters abandoned the struggle and left for the Sudan and the Middle East. The ELF itself was forced to regroup along the Sudanese border. Some of the members of the ELF surrendered to the military regime.

> By August 1981, the surviving ELF units retreated to the Sudan where they were surrounded and disarmed by the Sudanese army. Some guerrillas refused to disarm and re-entered Eritrea under the leadership of Abdullah Idris, the ELF military chief. In March 1982, Abdullah arrested

Ahmed Nassir and other leaders and installed himself at the head of the front. Others denounced this move as a Beni Amer coup and, within months, a number of splinter groups emerged claiming to represent the ELF.[5]

The collapse of the regime's offensive led to a change in military tactics in 1980 and 1981. "The army became more selective in its targets. It abandoned the scorched earth policy ...."[6] The "Red Star" Multifaceted Revolutionary Campaign was launched in January 1982, projected as a military campaign combined with a large-scale rehabilitation and economic development programme.[7]

The "Red Star" offensive deployed a force more than 120,000 strong. The entire cabinet of the military regime was moved to Eritrea. The military regime made one more effort to overrun Nakfa, but could not do so. Six months after its initiation, the "Red Star" campaign floundered. It was discontinued in June 1982. "Every hope we had of ending the conflict was dashed at Nakfa. Instead of the final victory, it became a symbol of misplaced priorities."[8]

Bealu Girma, who covered the campaign as a journalist, wrote a book about the stark reality of Eritrea and the prospect of victory. The book was titled *Oromaye*, meaning 'It is Over'. The book was withdrawn from the market days after publication and the author disappeared a few months later.

The total number of casualties in the Eritrean war between 1975 and 1983 was estimated at 90,000 Ethiopian soldiers and 9,000 guerrillas killed or wounded. The total of civilian casualties was in the hundreds of thousands.[9]

After the defeat of the EDU and the EPRP in Tigrai in 1977/1978, the TPLF was the only military force opposed to the military regime's rule in that province. In February 1979, the TPLF held an "Organizational Congress' which adopted a programme and elected a CC and a Politburo.

Sometime in the mid-1980s, the TPLF adopted a military strategy that allowed the organization not to be confined to the Tigrai province alone. In this endeavour, the formation of the EPDM in the early 1980s was of great importance. Furthermore, the TPLF itself underwent some changes. In 1985, a group professing Marxism-Leninism emerged from among the TPLF and declared that it was the vanguard leading the front. The formation of this grouping brought about a major change in the composition of the TPLF leadership. Some founding and leading TPLF members, among whom were Aregawi Berhe and Giday Zeratsion, were pushed aside and eventually forced to resign from the organization.

From the early 1980s, the TPLF and EPDM conducted military operations in Wello and 'the TPLF and EPDM are able to hit the whole length of the Dessie-Mequele road.'[10] During this stage of cooperation, EPDM's role could only be auxiliary.

The Ethiopian army launched an unsuccessful offensive in Shire in August 1980, and tried again in February 1983. The renewed offensive lasted for about three months, after which the military regime controlled Sheraro, the stronghold and base area of the TPLF. In February 1985, the regime opened a three month long assault in Tembien, Central Tigrai, and in western Tigrai. Again, the military regime launched a huge offensive in August 1985. It lasted until October.

In March 1983, the TPLF overran Bati in Wello. TPLF and EPDM forces controlled Lalibella in April. Seqota in Wag district was occupied. In September, TPLF and EPDM forces overran Wuchale, Jarre and Haik, small towns located close to Dessie In August 1984, TPLF attacked Mille in eastern Wello. In October, Lalibella was recaptured. Sometime during the mid-eighties, the TPLF conducted an operation that freed hundreds of detainees from a prison in Mekele.

In 1979/80, a small group of EPRA members conducted a seminar in Eritrea in an area controlled by the ELF. Soon after, the entire group moved to western Gonder, however, a tragic incident triggered the departure of the group to southwestern Gonder, by the Gojjam province. This was related to the execution of Betwoded Adane Mekonnen, Abebe Jenber and other peasants. Bitwoded Adane Mekonnen was one the most respected elders of Begemidir. He was a leader of the anti-fascist resistance during the Italian invasion of the 1930s and a member of the EDU. Abebe Jenber was a member of the EPRP and a leading peasant figure of the Armacheho area. He was the brother of Major Zeleke Jenber, the father figure and leader of Armacheho peasants. Bitwoded Adane Mekonnen and Abebe were executed by four EPRA defecters who were on their way home to Tselemt after deserting the EPRA. Bitwoded Adane Mekonnen and his group were heading to Tsegede and they were taking a short break when they met their assailants. Upon arrival in Tselemt, it is believed that the four individuals had given themselves up to the TPLF. During this period, that is, in the early 1980s, Tselemt was under TPLF's control.

The peasants in Armacheho believed that the EPRP was behind the killings and moblised forces to push the EPRA out of the area. In the conflict that ensued, lives were lost. Among those killed was Major Zeleke, the brother of Abebe.

Following this incident, the EPRA had to leave the Armacheho area and after 1983, the EPRP extended its activities in northern Gojjam and was active in the area until the early 1990s. In 1984, the EPRP held its Second Congress in Quara.

Government forces launched repeated offensives in hopes of dislodging the EPRA from the area. The EPRA was able to win the sympathy of the inhabitants partially due to,

> [T]he establishment of the large Metekel settlement complex in late 1984" which "led to the displacement of the local Gumuz. The Gumuz of this area rely on shifting cultivation and gathering wild foods from the forest. The government declared that any arable land currently cultivated and forests were 'unused', and designated them resettlement areas.[11]

Besides the Gumuz, the Agew was another national group of the area affected by the resettlement program. It was projected that 250,000 people would be resettled. By 1986, 92,000 people from Wello, Shoa, Gonder and Gojjam were resettled. The resettlement project, known as the Beles project was further complicated by the involvement of an Italian contractor. The EPRA captured three Italians in 1987 and 1988 and that incident produced publicity for the EPRA.[12]

On the southern and southeastern part of Ethiopia, the tension that erupted in 1977 had eased following the defeat of the Somali regime in 1978. However, there were low scale guerrilla activities in Harer, Bale, Sidamo and Arsi provinces. The military regime conducted consecutive offensives lasting more than three years.

The OLF, one of the groups conducting low scale military operations in the eastern part of Ethiopia, was allowed to open an office in Mogadishu in 1979. "Siad Barre's regime insisted that the OLF come to terms with SALF, and a series of fruitless discussion ensued between the two ... with the failure of the talks, SALF pressed the Somali regime to expel the OLF (from Somalia), which was done in 1982."[13]

OLF opened an office in Khartoum in 1978 and established contact with the EPLF. "The EPLF offered to train OLF members, and the first group of ten went to the Sahel in the middle of 1979. A second group of about twenty followed in 1980. When they returned, some of them were sent to set up a base in the Qelem and Asosa district, a remote border region inhabited by small non-Oromo tribes."[14]

Discontent among segments of the Oromos in Ethiopia was further exacerbated by the arrest of about 400 Oromos in February 1980. Branches of the Mekane Yesus church were closed, church property was confiscated, and a large number of pastors were arrested between May and December 1981.

Ziad Barre regime's role in the Ethio-Somali conflict of 1977/78 had far-reaching consequences for the Somali regime and for the very existence of the Somali state. After the debacle of the Somali army, contradictions that had been submerged came to surface. Officers of the Somali army staged an unsuccessful coup. Some of the coup leaders were eliminated while others fled the country and organized the Somali Salvation Front. The name of that organization was changed to Somali Salvation Democratic Front (SSDF) when former members of the Somali Revolutionary Socialist party joined. The group then received the support of the military regime of Ethiopia and was allowed to use the broadcasting facilities of Ethiopia. "The SSDF appealed to the population of certain parts of the south, especially to the Mijertin, a Darod clan that had been politically prominent during the parliamentary period [that is, before 1969]. The Mijertin had lost ground after the October Revolution to the triple clan alliance referred to as MOD, comprising the Marehan, Ogaden and Dulbahante."[15]

An equally important development was the formation in late 1978 of the Somali National Movement, precipitated by abuses of the WSLF against the population of northern Somalia. The inter-clan conflict continued.

> In the beginning of 1980, the execution of several senior officers accused of collaboration with the opposition abroad was followed by a serious army mutiny in the north, which resulted in more executions and triggered another flight of dissidents abroad. This time, they came mostly from the north and with kindred spirits and kinsmen abroad formed another militant opposition group, the Somali National Movement (SNM). Representing mainly the Isaaq clan family, the SNM eschewed ideological posturing, but also accepted Ethiopia's invitation to set up bases across the border to fight Ziad Barre's regime.[16]

The SNM became active and along with the Ethiopian military regime's operations, it eventually hampered WSLF's activities in Ethiopian territory.

> ...[W]hen the SNM offered them a chance to gain an advantage through collaboration with the Ethiopians, the Isaaq did not hesitate to grasp it. In doing so, they found themselves fighting on the side of the traditional enemy against the nationalist drive to unite the Somali homeland. Relying on SNM and Ethiopian support, they strengthened their presence in the Haud and interfered with Ogaden trade and transport to Hargeisa . . . Addis Abeba's task was greatly simplified as Isaaq nomads and SNM guerillas hunted WSLF members with far greater efficiency than the Ethiopian regime.[17]

As a result of the uninterrupted offense and the role played by Somali dissident groups, both large scale assualt and low level guerilla activities had come to a halt in the eastern, southern and southeastern parts of Ethiopia by 1984, and the major drive to resettle the population in shelters began. It was also during this period that the villagization program was initiated (see below).

In the late 1970s, the military regime conducted one of its successful campaigns -- eradication of illiteracy. The first two rounds of campaign in 1979-80 established 35,000 literacy centers and recruited 241,000 instructors.[18] By the end of the 12th round in 1985, 16, 941,075 people had been enrolled for courses, of whom 12,037,542 had passed the end-of-course examination, and 10,070,102 had been enrolled in post-literacy programmes.[19] The campaign had been conducted in fifteen 'nationality languages'. The campaign obliged all able-bodied citizens to enroll. A very large number of maids, housewives, etc., had a chance to attend schools. A very small percentage of this group was able to pursue higher education. The literacy campaign, which also enrolled mothers, was a realm where the discipline of modern education and Ethiopian tradition were in conflict. It remained difficult to enforce the discipline of a student among the elderly participants of the campaign. It was a common phenomena for the teachers to wait until the mothers were over with the chorus of their greetings which usually took sometime. It also was a common phenomena for a mother to come to class late and discuss why she was late, of course interrupting the normal activities of the class.

Be that as it may, the military regime, having defeated Ziad Barre's regime, dealt a blow to the Eritrean rebels and the EPRP, continued to expand and build its military might. In his May Day speech of 1981, Mengistu Haile Mariam announced a plan for national military service. In May 1983, a decree was issued obliging all Ethiopians between the ages of eighteen to thirty to six month's of military training and two years of service.[20]

Conscription began in May 1984 and continued until the demise of the military regime in 1991. During this period, hundreds of thousands of Ethiopians were rounded up from the rural market areas or were handed over to the military regime by peasant associations. Workers were picked up from their workplaces and teen-agers were rounded up from the streets and the kebeles. The military regime's conscription included underaged children. Kebeles and Peasant Associations (PA's) were assigned conscription quotas.

Thousands of conscripts perished or were disabled. Due to the massive conscription of peasants, the number of farm hands decreased substantially, thus decreasing production and contributing to the famine of the mid-1980s. The 1984 Military Service Proclamation polarized the society and generated intense hatred to the military regime. Some parents were able to send their children abroad. Those who could not afford to do so employed bribery and other means to avoid conscription. Some parents eluded registration of their newly born babies, lest they be summoned for military service when they reach fourteen. As the "Red Terror" of the 1970s laid bare the uncouth nature of the regime, so did the conscription of the 1980s. The conscription was one of the ugliest features of the war of the 1980s and this unpopular policy contributed to the demise of the regime.

Conscription was not limited to the military regime, but was practiced by the insurgent movements as well. A U.S. State Department report noted,

> [N]otably the EPLF and TPLF have practiced forced conscription, imprisonment without recourse, violence against civilian populations, torture, and extrajudicial killing. Women have fallen victim to rape and abuse by government and rebel soldiers, as both sides loot and pillage.[21]

According to an insider, in the mid-1980s, the TPLF was overwhelmed by peasants who voluntarily joined the organization.[22]

Villagization was another policy of the military regime that had an important bearing on political developments of the 1980s. Villagization emerged in the late 1970s when the military regime adopted a multifaceted approach to counter the activities of insurgent movements. The approach included forcible settlement of a large percentage of the rural population into protected villages and wrecking assets outside of those villages, supporting groups that were opposed to the WSLF and the Somali regime, etc.

When the Ethio-Somali war was over in 1978, the number of displaced persons exceeded half a million, almost 200,000 in Relief and Rehabilitation Center (RRC) shelters in Harer, 66,000 in Bale and 20,000 in Sidamo. By October, the number had risen to 350,000 in Bale; by 1979, it was 586,000.[23] The resettlement process was not smooth, "[M]any families became separated, and because registration had been neglected it was extremely difficult to get them back together again."[24]

In certain areas, the resettlement program was replaced by villagization, a scheme with broader social, economic and political implications. According to Mengistu, villagization would promote social production, alter a peasant's life and his thinking, and ultimately lay the foundation for socialism.[25] Villagization was implemented in Bale between 1979 and 1982. By 1981, in Bale, the number reached 750,000 clustered in 280 villages.[26] In southern Bale, villagizing of 130,000 semi-nomads began in 1981 and was completed in the mid 1980s. In Harer, an all out villagization began in October 1984.[27] By mid-May 1985, the number of persons villagized reached 150,000 in the Harer province.[28] In Sidamo, 40,000 were villagized in 1979, and a further 190,000 gathered in shelters. In Arba Gugu, district of Arsi, villagization was implemented in 1982.[29] In 1985, a National Coordinating Committee for Villagization was set up at every level.[30]

Other areas selected for resettlement in the mid-1980s were Keffa, Gambella in Illubabor and Pawe in Gojjam. Shekacho in Illubabor resisted the villagization and killed few police officers. In retaliation, the regime bombarded the area and killed hundreds of people.

Over a quarter of a million people went to western Welega, swelling the number already sent there in the earlier phase. Nearly 150,000 people were settled south of Gambela in Illubabor, and just more than 100,000 around Pawe in western Gojjam. In addition, 78,000 went to Keffa, and much smaller numbers to Shoa and western Gonder. It is believed that more than 50,000 died during the resettlement.[31] Besides the problems associated with the process itself, the resettlement created tension between the newcomers and the indigenous people.[32]

In May/June 1980, a UN team visited Ethiopia and recommended that "the government's resettlement should be given all possible support."[33]

By September 1986, Mengistu was able to report that 976,084 new houses had been built, and 4,587,187 people moved into these houses.[34] By September 1987, the total had climbed to more than 1,300,000 houses for more than eight million people, representing an estimated 22% of the rural population.[35]

Villagization was partly used by the military regime in controlling the rural population. It afforded the military regime the tools to control not only dissent, but also production and recruitment for military training. Villagization facilitated the activities of the Agricultural Marketing Corporation to purchase produce from peasants at controlled prices, thereby weakening peasant incentive to produce more. During this period, producer cooperatives known as *malba*, *welba* and *weland* were under formation. By June 1984, 1489 producers' cooperatives were formed, farming 313,085 hectares. They built villages for their members, and up to June 1984, 232 of the cooperatives had done so.[36]

In March 1990, after some years of experiment, Mengistu abandoned the villagization program and the sites were deserted instantaneously. Hundreds of thousands of lives had been lost and the country's money had been squandered. Ethiopia had been a large laboratory for experiments, such as, conscription, nationalization, wars and now, villagization.

All universities were closed for over two months in 1985 and students and teachers were deployed to the resettlement areas to assist with settling the people. In frustration, many students did not return to the University; some of these, as well as a number of university teachers left the country.

> Villagization entailed radical deforestation, which ravaged the ecosystem. Unless concerted efforts were taken to arrest the accelerating rate of deforestation and soil erosion [in the settlement areas], there would be a major imbalance in the ecosystem in eight years. The magnitude of this imbalance and degradation would be similar to that of the famine-affected areas of the northern highlands of Ethiopia.[37]

So, stated a committee formed by the Council of Ministers. According to another official of the military regime,

> Resettlement and villagization... have displaced more than six million people.... Resentment, distrust, fear, and support for rebel groups are the main achievements of these programs. ...Our forests, which play a key role in combating desertification are now smaller than ever and a new famine cannot be far away.[38]

To be sure, in mid-1985, there was large scale famine in Tigray, Wello, Eritrea and some parts of Gonder.

> The famine that struck the plateau in the early 1980s was ten times worse than the visitation of ten years earlier. Unlike the earlier disaster, it did not strike suddenly or catch the regime by surprise. It had a gradual development that began in the late 1970s in the same blighted region of the north before the people had a chance to recover from the last famine. Pastoralists had no time to rebuild their herds and peasants were short of oxen. Wello had the first short fall of rain in 1977. Eastern Tigrai, Gonder and Northern Shoa followed, and millions of people were declared at risk by the Ethiopian RRC in 1979. When the rains again failed in Eastern Tigrai and Wello in 1981 and 1982, famine commenced in that region.[39]

Besides the above-mentioned reasons, the famine was the outcome of government policy and indifference, male conscription, the flight of peasants to towns, civil war, environmental changes, drought, etc. An outbreak of cholera during the famine exacerbated the problem. Mengistu ascribed the famine to the ignoble activities of merchants.[40]

In 1985, hundreds of thousands of Tigrai peasants arrived in Sudan. According to the RRC, the overall number displaced during 1984/85 was 6,098,000. In 1983, assistance amounted to $361 million, $417 million in 1984 and $784 million in 1985.[41] The world community responded generously, particularly after renown artists conducted a concert to raise funds. However, how to get the aid to the affected population and areas became an issue of dispute. By mid-1980, a significant portion of the famine-stricken area was under the control of the rebel groups in Tigrai and Eritrea. Finally, it was arranged to deliver the aid both through government facilities and rebel forces. Both the regime and the rebel groups used the aid as a means to obtain support. From October 1984 onwards, the presence of Western non-governmental agencies in Ethiopia became a reality and they established better relationships with rebel organizations.

With the spread of famine, the conventional relationship of government and guerrilla armies to the people changed. Instead of the troops relying on the people for food, the people flocked to feeding centers controlled either by the regime or the rebel groups. Joining the rebel groups was also facilitated and thousands were recruited.

The famine established Ethiopia as a country where children starved. The country's name became synonymous with famine and whatever prestige the regime had was eroded. It became evident that the earlier reforms had not altered the Ethiopian situation. The extravagant celebration of the military regime's 10th year anniversary further exposed the callousness of the regime.

Another important development of the 1980s was the formation of the state party. As was indicated in Chapter VI, all of the groups that comprised POMOA were disbanded and it was declared that the state party would be composed of individuals rather than groups. Individual recruitment followed and by December 1979, the commission that would organize the party was formed. It was known as the Commission to Organize the Workers Party of Ethiopia, (COPWE). The core group of COPWE remained former members of the Seded and the chairperson was Mengistu Haile Mariam. The First Congress of COPWE was held in 1980 and the second in 1983. Party building from above was accelerated and a large group of military officers, technocrats and government officials were recruited. COPWE was transformed into the Workers Party of Ethiopia (WPE) in 1984, during the 10th anniversary of the military regime. As of this moment, the WPE became the supreme and only organization destined to 'lead' the country. Following the formation of the party, the People's Democratic Republic of Ethiopia (PDRE) was proclaimed. The formation of the PDRE heralded the transfer of power from the PMAC.

Other important instruments of asserting power were the mass organizations, such as the women, youth, kebele and workers, which were restructured and placed under the control of the WPE. They served as media through which the WPE reached and controlled the people. At the same time, they were used as espionage networks of the regime.

The intense struggle of the various groups to bring the kebeles under control was discussed in the previous chapters. In the 1980s, the status of the kebeles as subservient institutions of the regime was established. The Proclamation of April 1981 formally placed urban dwellers' associations under the central leadership of COPWE. [42] In the 1980s, organizing "*kinet*" (artistic) groups was a major activity of the kebeles and the WPE-controlled youth organizations. These groups of youngsters regularly took part in traditional dances and folk songs. Even though the role of the 'kinet' groups in promoting traditional songs and dances could not be discounted, it must be mentioned that the formation of those groups enabled the military regime to subdue the youth's dissent and create political apathy.

State control was also apparent in retail and wholesale trade. The Addis Abeba Basic Commodities Supply Corporation, formed in April 1980, distributed grain to the kebeles through Keftenyas.[43] Consequently, kebele shops provided about two-thirds of the staple grain needs.[44] Similar arrangements were made in the rural areas, where the Agricultural Marketing Corporation (AMC) and other government agencies bought products at controlled prices, especially from the state farms which accounted for 3.4% of total grain production and provided about 35% of AMC grain purchases.[45] The AMC transported agricultural inputs to towns and maintained a national grain reserve.[46]

As stated elsewhere, government-sponsored labor organization had been formed in the late 1970s. The military regime had been unable to control the leadership of the AEWTU and a reorganization to control AEWTU began in the first quarter of 1982. By this time, membership of the national trade union had increased by about a hundred thousand. In 1976-77 total membership was 204,101, by 1983-84, it jumped to 313,434.[47] Elections were held for regional, provincial and finally for national offices. A National Congress was held in June 1982. The legal edifice of the AEWTU was revised following the proclamation of the Trade Union's Organization Proclamation in May 1982.[48] The name was changed to Ethiopian Trade Union (ETU) in 1986.

Most of the members of the ETU leadership at the regional and industrial level were made either full or alternate members of the CC of the WPE. That arrangement effectively brought the labor movement under the direct auspices of the WPE. ETU was used as an arm of the military regime. In preparation toward the establishment of the PDRE, the ETU held a Congress in 1986.

The All Ethiopian Peasants' Association was formed in December 1977 and reorganized in May 1982. Its name was changed to Ethiopian Peasants' Association (EPA) in 1986.[49] Most of the branch and national leadership of EPA were recruited as members of the WPE. The EPA was an important instrument in the hands of the military regime, expediting conscription, villagization, etc. Besides, the EPA had an important role in extracting money from the peasantry.

All farmers were required to pay agricultural income tax (20 birr), a PA membership fee (minimum five birr), surtax (approximately 25 birr), plus levies for road-building, school-construction, literacy and other campaigns. Members of the Womens' Association paid a 3-birr annual membership fee, and all households contributed at least 3 birr to the Youth Association. School fees ranged from 2 birr to 15 birr. All peasants were levied to pay the RRC, usually 20-25 birr.[50]

In the 1980s, the regime formed the "Working Peoples' Control Committees" at factories, ministries, and other institutions, to investigate malpractice and complaints and to control employees as well. By this time, the economic role of the state had increased manifold. Government domestic revenues had been rising at an average rate of 17% a year in cash terms over the six financial years from 1974-75 to 1979-80[51] and the state sector accounted for some 95% of industrial output and capital.[52] In 1982-83, revenues from houses nationalized in mid-1975 was 19.85 of the total. Other sources of revenue included business tax, 259.7 million birr, export duties, almost entirely on coffee, 157.8 million birr, alcoholic drinks excise tax, 125.8 million birr.[53]

In February 1986, with the economic crisis deepening, the military regime issued a proclamation allowing individuals to build, own, and mortgage houses, and even to sublet accommodations under an arrangement called 'co-dwelling.[54]

Despite the increasing economic role of the government, unemployment rates continued to rise. The number of graduates from higher institutions multiplied, but the country's economy could not absorb even its educated citizens. Between 1973-74 and 1983-84, the total number of students increased from 811,114 to 3,076, 948.[55] 40, 907 students took the Ethiopian School Leaving Certificate examination in 1985, up from 13, 698 in the late 1970s.[56] To ameliorate the situation, the military regime assigned many of the graduates to government institutions and factories. The number of civilian employees financed from the central government budget rose from 109,322 to 167,860, at an annual rate of increase of 9.5% in the five years period before 1983.[57]

Since the late 1970s, the Soviets had been the main suppliers of arms to the military regime. As of the late 1980s and early 90s, Ethiopian military debt amounted to 3-4 billion. There was a large number of Soviet military advisors and the USSR established a naval facility in the Dahlac Islands.[58] Despite their involvement in the military sphere, the Soviets failed to aid the Ethiopian economy. To be sure, "The Soviets do, however, supply all of Ethiopia's petroleum requirements, except for small amounts of specialized oils at a discount [rate] of 10% below the world market price."[59] Furthermore, since 1978, Ethiopia had been participating as an observer in the Soviet-controlled Council for Mutual Economic Assistance. Ethiopia gradually came to be entitled to assistance, which it received in the 1980s.

Under an agreement signed in April 1979, Cuba was involved in the production of sugar in Ethiopia. In 1980, an agreement was signed between the former German Democratic Republic (GDR), Czechoslovakia, and the Ethiopian regime, to build a large textile mill in Komboltcha, Wello province. The Czechoslovakian government had also been involved in manufacturing rubber and canvas shoes since 1965, and had a tanning factory in Mojjo, Shoa province. The Bulgarians had a role in organizing the state farms subsequent to the Land Reform Proclamation in 1975. In 1978, a Soviet-Ethiopian navigation agreement was signed. In February of the same year, an agreement was signed with the GDR to modernize the port of Aseb. The project was finished a few years later. In October of the same year, a Protocol was signed by the GDR and the Ethiopian Commission for Economic, Scientific and Technical Cooperation, "to draw up projects for developing Ethiopia's agriculture, transport, communications, and mining."[60] In September 1980, an agreement was signed with the GDR to build the Mugher Cement factory. The Nazret tractor assembly plant and Melka Wakena hydroelectric power station were among the projects built by the Soviet bloc.[61] The North Korean government signed an agreement with the Ethiopian regime in May 1977. The North Koreans supported the Mengistu regime in a number of ways, particularly in the military field.

The involvement of East European countries in the Ethiopian economy did not bring significant economic gains. The large military shipments had to be paid for in kind, so some of Ethiopia's exports had to be utilized for that purpose. Despite the rhetoric of self-reliance, Ethiopia's "[F]oreign assistance increased from an annual average of 76.7 million birr between 1970-1971 and 1973-74, to one of 247.3 million birr between 1974-75 and 1980-81 - a 222 per cent increase." [62] Despite Ethiopia's relationship with East European countries, Ethiopian exports to Western Europe, North America and Japan in 1984 accounted for 68.4 % of the total, while imports from the same sources came to 61.9 %.

When in the mid-1980s the Soviet Union and other East European countries were caught in deep crises, they had to extricate themselves from military commitments. Wary of Mengistu's appetite for military assistance and Ethiopia's repeated military disasters and famines, the USSR declared that arms deliveries would be cut off with the expiration of existing agreements in March 1991.

After the failed military campaign of 1982, the military fortunes of the regime continued to decline. War weary soldiers, stranded for years in the foxholes of Afabet and Nakfa, expressed resentment and dissatisfaction with the government's military strategy. There was serious conflict between the political appointees (cadres) and the command leadership of the various contingents. In the late 1980s, a large number of officers were removed from their posts or demoted by Mengistu. Others, including Brigadier General Tariku Ayene, commander of Nadew division, were executed. It is believed that the General was of the opinion that the only way to end the Eritrean conflict was through negotiation. The execution of Brigadier General Tariku

Ayene and other officers was one of the last disasters that Mengistu Haile Mariam inflicted on the Ethiopian Army in Eritrea. The army never recovered from that last disaster.

With morale already low, "On March 17-19, 1988, the EPLF overwhelmed the Ethiopian army's northern command at Afabet. More than 15,000 soldiers were killed, wounded, captured or dispersed, together with a vast quantity of arms and ammunition, including 50 tanks."[63]

In April 1988, the EPLF and the TPLF signed a defence pact. Since the mid-1980s, the relationship of the two organizations remained strained due to differences over military and political issues.

After the above mentioned victory of the EPLF at Afabet, the TPLF quickly succeeded in overpowering many garrisons in Tigrai, including Enda Selassie, Axum, Adwa, Adigrat, Wukro and Maichew. Government forces were forced to evacuate from other posts. Soon, government forces counter-attacked and won back Wukro, Adigrat, Adwa and Axum, and then attacked western Tigrai, taking Selekleka and Enda Selassie in early July 1988. The TPLF in its turn regrouped its forces and opened an offensive in Shire and northern Gonder and by the end of July, the Ethiopian army was defeated.

By the end of the 1980s, the military regime's days were numbered. A group of senior officers attempted to stage a coup d'etat on May 16, 1989. The stated objectives of the coup plotters included a negotiated settlement of the wars, and political and economic liberalization. Some of the plotters had established relations with the EPLF and had contacted the POWs under EPLF's custody. The EPLF was favorably inclined toward the coup, but the EPRDF opposed it, fearing that the reforms proposed by the coup plotters might ease the crisis.

The plot called for hijacking Mengistu's air plane on the way to East Germany. However, Mengist's intelligence department discovered the plot and his security forces struck first, precipitating an attempt by the plotters to seize power before they were fully prepared.[64]

On May 18, 176 army officers were detained. Many of them were executed sometime later. The army lost some of its ablest officers. It now seemed that peaceful resolution of the crisis was not to be. Mengistu once again came out on top, but the coup attempt had a reverberating effect. Crisis, despair, impotence and helplessness reigned among the armed forces and a large section of the Ethiopian people. Many concluded that the last hope for peaceful resolution of the Ethiopian crisis was gone. Pessimism and defeatism were rampant. An extremely favorable condition was created for the nationalist forces and it became evident that they had taken the upper hand in their struggle against the military regime.

The demise of the Mengistu regime was now certain. However, the existence of Ethiopia itself was at stake. The people were torn between the specter of the country's disintegration and deep hatred toward the military regime. Furthermore, the trauma of the "Red Terror" and other forms of repression had a crippling effect on the people. Few dared to get organized and present themselves as alternative forces. Apathy, indifference and confusion prevailed.

Nationalist forces in Tigrai seized the situation and their first step was to form the umbrella organization known as the Ethiopian Peoples Revolutionary Democratic Front in January 1989. Initially, the front included the TPLF and EPDM. However, in due course, it was declared that two other groups had joined it. The first one was an Oromo group regrouped around the Oromo Peoples Democratic Organization (OPDO) while the second one was composed of former officers of the Ethiopian army. It is believed that most of the members of these organzations were POWs. The formation of the EPRDF provided the TPLF political justification to conduct military operations in non-Tigrean areas and soon after EPRDF marched hundreds of miles to southern Ethiopia to territories where it had not set foot before.

In the first month of 1989, the TPLF opened an offensive in northern Gonder and western Tigrai. The following month, the TPLF/EPLF force captured Selekleka and then Enda Selassie. The fronts claimed that 26,000 soldiers were put out of action. Government forces evacuated Humera (on the Sudan border) and Adigrat, and on February 27-28, the provincial capital, Mekele, was abandoned leaving the government with only an outpost at Maichew.[65]

EPRDF forces captured Maichew and Korem in September and in October, they controlled Woldiya. In November, they deployed forces in Northern Shoa. In late December, EPRDF forces captured Debre Tabor in Southern Gonder, but were driven out by government forces a month later. After losing Debre Tabor, EPRDF forces prepared for a massive drive into Southern Ethiopia.

While trying to bring Gojjam and Gonder under control, EPRDF forces came in conflict with the EPRP which had been operating in the areas mentioned above for over a decade. Conditions turned critical when TPLF forces took over Metema, a small town at the Sudanese border. In a statement released by the EPRP FC it was stated, "... TPLF's incursion into the Metema area is the final stage in TPLF's long prepared war against the EPRP.[66] A few months later, skirmishes began between the two forces and between February - March 1991, the EPRP accused the EPRDF of 'declaring war' against it, of imprisoning EPRP supporters in the towns it occupied, of shooting unarmed demonstrators, and taking away infrastructure from the resettlement sites. The EPRDF on its side accused the EPRP of aggression, ambushes and of mining roads. On April 18, 1991, after the EPRDF occupied Dangla, there was a battle between the two forces.

In May, fighting continued between the EPRP and EPRDF in western Gojjam. The Sudan government withdrew its support to the EPRP and closed its border. The EPRP sustained heavy losses. A large number of EPRA fighters were captured by EPRDF forces. Among the captured leaders were the veteran activist, poet and writer Tsegaye Gebre Medhin, Yishaq Debre Tsion and Setotaw Hassen. Long-time activists Haile Abaye and Geleb

Dafela were killed. Furthermore, EPRDF forces abducted EPRP activists from Sudanese cities. After a few days of seminar and a denunciation ritual, thousands of EPRA members were set free. The whereabouts of EPRP leading figures mentioned above is still unknown.

On the northern front, the military activity continued and on February 8, 1990, the EPLF captured Massawa. However, the military regime bombarded and destroyed the port facilities.

On February 23, 1991, the EPRDF launched the campaign 'Operation Tewedros'. The Ethiopian army was in no condition to put up a strong resistance and within fifteen days the EPRDF brought Gonder and Gojjam under control. The government attempted to counterattack, but the EPRDF launched Operation *'Dula Billisuma Welkita'* (Equality and Freedom campaign) into Wellega. They captured Nekempte, the capital of Wellega, on April 1, and then advanced southward and eastward toward Addis Abeba. Subsequently, the EPRDF occupied Fincha, the site of the hydroelectric power station which serves Addis Abeba.

On May 15, the EPRDF launched "Operation Wallelign" on the Wello front. Dessie and Komboltcha were captured the following day. The final week of the war consisted of a slow EPRDF advance on Addis Abeba itself. EPRDF/EPLF forces surrounded the city, capturing the Air-Force base at Debre Zeit.

The Mengistu regime was in deep crisis. A government headed by the newly elected prime minister, Tesfaye Dinka, was formed. On the third week of May, Mengistu Haile Mariam fled to Zimbabwe and that incident exasperated the crisis further. Hopelessness reigned, the newly formed government was unable to contain the massive surrender of soldiers. The effort to salvage the regime faltered.

The EPLF, TPLF and OLF forces attended a meeting in London sponsored by the Secretary of the American State Department, Herman Cohen. The newly elected Ethiopian Prime Minister and his government was invited for the occasion, however, other multi-national organizations were not allowed to take part in the meeting. On May 21, the EPRDF captured Addis Abeba and on May 24, the EPLF took over Asmera and the grounds for the formation of an independent Eritrea was laid down.

Ethiopia as a unitary state disintegrated and the worst fear of the Ethiopian radical *generation* came true. In the late 1960s when the *Generation* began the onerous task of transforming its society, one of its main objectives was to save the country from fragmentation and disintegration. Poverty, joblessness, landlessness, lack of democracy, national oppression, etc., constituted the Achilles hills of the society. Besides the economic problems of the country, the problem of nationalities had began to haunt the consciousness of Ethiopians who wanted to resolve issues *along the class line* and consequently, supported the abolition of the absolute monarchy.[67] Such support was mixed with the apprehension for the burdensome legacy of national divisions and inequalities that the successors would inherit. It was understood that the nationality issue had to be dealt with in any agenda pertaining to Ethiopia's political future. It was believed that a proposed resolution of national contradictions was an indispensable prerequisite for mass participation in the future struggle. Without such an understanding, it was argued, there was clear danger that popular participation would be drawn to ethnic movements and separatist objectives. In addition, national contradictions had to be addressed because they were a structural feature of the situation in Ethiopia, and any design for the resolution of the country's problems had to be based on an objective evaluation of that situation. It was believed that it also was imperative for the struggle to gain the support of the oppressed nationalities and this could not be expected unless grievances were acknowledged and national equality respected. Such was the predicament just before the 1974 movement emerged.

A year or so after the 1974 revolutionary movement, land reform was proclaimed. By addressing the economic aspect of the national question, the land Reform Proclamation of 1975 significantly reduced the danger of disintegration, especially in southern Ethiopia. However, issues regarding democratic rights and the national question constituted major factors for the rift between multinational organizations, the military regime and nationalist forces. All three forces brought forth their proposed solutions. Multinational organizations, such as the EPRP contended that the national issue was one of the major worries of Ethiopia, and unless a solution was provided, it would place the country into serious danger. Unless a solution was sought, the various nationalist forces would muster followers and become factors for the country's fragmentation, they argued. Multinational forces argued that national equality had to be respected and that the national issue had to be resolved peacefully and democratically.

The military regime, on the other hand, failed to appreciate the importance of the national question. It failed to promulgate laws on fundamental democratic and human right issues. Furthermore, in line with the imperial regime, the military regime regarded the rebel forces as pawns of foreign powers ready to dismantle the country. The military regime and its supporters opted to resolve the problem militarily.

The third force, nationalist forces, were not concerned about issues regarding the overall affairs of Ethiopia. Eritrean rebel groups advocated Eritrean independence. Tigrayan nationalist were concerned about Tigrai. Oromo nationalists had resolved to struggle against what they labeled as Abyssinian colonialism, etc. *As a result, a three-sided struggle emerged in the early 1970s*: between the EPRP and the military regime; between the military regime and nationalists organizations, such as the Eritrean fronts and the TPLF; and between nationalist forces and multinational organizations.

Members of the *Generation* went out to the streets of Ethiopia demanding 'national equality', 'cessation of hostilities', 'resolution of the national problem peacefully and democratically', etc. To resolve the problems by force, they believed, would be detrimental to the country and its people. On the other hand, the military regime was determined to conclude the national issue through the use of force; and proposals for peaceful and democratic resolutions of the issue were regarded as diversionary and pernicious to the country. On this and other issues, the line was drawn between the regime and multinational forces, with the EPRP in the lead. The intense struggle that ensued finally led to the process known as the "Red Terror".

Determined nationalist forces were not ready to accept the alternative presented by multinational forces, that is, formation of a multinational Ethiopia based on national equality. This programme was seen by the nationalists as an impediment to their goal of independent and separate states. They were concerned that the alternative presented by multinational forces might erode their social base. As far as the nationalist forces were concerned, multinationalism was a variant of the *chauvinist* creed, as dangerous as that of the alternatives of the military regime, hence the bitter animosity. EPRP and other multinational forces were castigated as enemies, and, a large number of adherents to the multinational cause fell prey to the WSLF, TPLF and EPLF forces.[68]

In the course of the three-sided struggle, multinational forces were sandwiched between the intense repression of the military regime and the suppression and armed confrontation of nationalist forces. The voice of the multinational groups of the country was muted and the stage was left to the nationalists and the military regime, both of which had resolved to reach at a solution militarily.

By repressing multi-nationalist organizations, the military regime and nationalist forces deprived Ethiopia of a force that could have assisted in resolving the national issue and halting the fragmentation of the country. By repressing multinational forces, the military regime suppressed a strong Pan-Ethiopianist voice. The military regime weakened a force that would have served as a pillar to the multinational cause of Ethiopia, the very foundation of the country.

The setback that the multinational cause encountered signaled a dificult time for Ethiopia. The multinational political agenda was weakened thereby allowing the ethnic-based politics to take the upper hand. That setback opened the way for nationalist forces to launch a massive recruitment drive. During the repression, when it seemed that no alternative was left, thousands flocked to the nationalist organizations. Emboldened by their military success, the nationalist forces posed as the only alternative force, and their ideology was quickly emulated by like-minded aspirants.

Notes to Epilogue

1. Tesfa Tsion Medhane, <u>Eritrea, Dynamics of a National Question</u>, 1986, page 110.

2. Ibid., page 110.

3. Ibid., page 110, quoted from <u>The Guardian</u>, December 13, 1978.

4. Ibid., page 117. As was indicated elsewhere, among the causes for the conflict between the ELF and the TPLF was a territory that was found along the Tigrai/Eritrean border.

5. John Markakis, <u>National and Class Conflict in the Horn of Africa</u>, page 248. By 1990, the number of groups that splintered from the ELF was over five.

6. Dawit Wolde Giorgis, <u>Red Tears</u>, Red Sea Publishers, 1989, page 99.

7. <u>Ethiopian Herald</u>, January 26, 1982.

8. Dawit Wolde Giorgis, op. cit., page 109.

9. Ibid., page 113.

10. Africa Confidential, 24.19, September 21, 1983, page 4.

11. Dessalegne Rahmato, 'Settlement and Resettlement in Metekel, Western Ethiopia,' Africa (Roma), 43, 1988, pages 14-34.

12. Ethiopia - PAWE - Tana - Beles: Ethiopian "Hell" or Italian "Paradise"?, Published by the SPIC of the EPRP, page 9.

13. John Markakis, op. cit., page 263.

14. Ibid., page 264.

15. Ibid., page 233.

16. John Markakis, op. cit., page 233.

17. Ibid., pages 233-234.

18. <u>Ethiopian Herald</u>, September 12, 1980.

19. National Literacy Campaign Coordinating Committee, 14th Round Program.

20. National Military Service Proclamation, Negarit Gazetta, May 4, 1983.

21. US Department of State, "Country Reports on Human Rights Practices for 1990", p.118.

22. Interview, Yared Tibebu, February 1997.

23. RRC, The Challenges of Drought: Ethiopia's Decade of Struggle in Relief and Rehabilitation, Addis Abeba, 1985, pages 135.

24. Dawit Wolde Giorgis, op. cit., page 297.

25. President Mengistu Haile Mariam, Report to the Central Committee of the WPE, April 14, 1986.

26. UN Coordinating Committee for Relief and Rehabilitation and RRC of Ethiopia, "Short- term Relief and Rehabilitation Needs in Ethiopia," March 1981, page 13.

27. Ibid. page 13.

28. Ethiopian Herald, May 16, 1985.

29. RRC, 1985, pages 136-7.

30. Ministry of Agriculture, Villagization Guidelines.

31. The Sunday Times, November 3, 1985: Ethiopia's Bitter Medicine.

32. Dawit Wolde Giorgis, op. cit., page 305.

33. Evil Days, 30 Years of War and Famine in Ethiopia, Human Rights watch, page 92.

34. Mengistu Haile Mariam, 'Revolution Day Speech, 1986.'

35. Mengistu Haile Mariam, 'Address to the Inaugural Meeting of the National Shengo', September 1987.

36. Christopher Clapham, op. cit., page 173.

37. Evil Days, op. cit., page 229.

38. Dawit Wolde Giorgis, op. cit., page 308.

39. John Markakis, op. cit., page 268.

40. Ethiopian Herald, May 3, 1985.

41. Evil Days, op. cit., page 178, Figures quoted from Organization for Economic Cooperation and Development, "Geographical Distribution of Financial Flows to Developing Countries," 1984-1986.

42. Ethiopian Herald, May 8, 1981.

43. Ibid., March 23, 1980; May 3, 1980.

44. ILO, Socialism from the Grassroots, page 244.

45. Ibid., page 80.

46. Negarit Gazetta, November 20, 1976.

47. Christopher Clapham, op.cit., page 137.

48. Negarit Gazetta, May 24, 1982.

49. Negarit Gazetta, September 17, 1977; Peasant Associations Consolidation Proclamation, Negarit Gazetta, May 24, 1982.

50. Evil Days, op. cit., page 161.

51. Christopher Clapham, op. cit., page 106

52. Ibid., page 149, quoted from ONCCP, Ten Years Perspective Plan, page 97.

53. Ibid., page 125.

54. The Construction and Use of Urban Houses Proclamation, Negarit Gazetta, February 17, 1986.

55. Ethiopian Statistical Abstract, 1982, 1984.

56. ILO, op. cit., page 358.

57. Christopher Clapham, op.cit., page ?????

58. Holliday and Molyneux, The Ethiopian Revolution, Verso Editions and NLB, 1981, page 180

59. David A. Koran, Ethiopia: The United States and the Soviet Union, Southern Illinois University Press, 1986, page 92.

60. Georgi Galpirin, Ethiopia: Population Resources Economy, Progress Publishers, 1981, page 243.

61. Ethiopian Herald, January 30, 1985 and March 29, 1985.

62. Christopher Clapham, op. cit., page 121, quoted from ONCCP Ten Years Perspective Plan, page 317.

63. Evil Days, op. cit., page 237.

64. Africa Confidential, 30.11, May 26, 1989.

65. Evil Days, op. cit., page 266.

66. Press Release by EPRP FC, March 13, 1990.

67. This paragraph is based on the book by Kiflu Tadesse, *The Generation*, Independent Publishers, 1993, page 51.

68. See details in Chapters VI and IX.

Postscript

I am not certain whether it is appropriate to take a few pages off of a book that deals with the history of a generation to convey one's inner feelings regarding certain issues. I am also not sure whether such a practice is wrong or right. Nevertheless, I hope the reader would understand if I give myself a chance to express some personal thoughts. As I had indicated in the Preface, I had made an extra effort to stay neutral in dealing with issues that were related to the EPRP and its protagonists. I also had refrained from providing my role and contributions in the struggle. In this section, I have taken the liberty to unfathom just a few thoughts.

In the Ethiopian setting, writing a book is an exacting endeavor. Even though knowledgeable, very few Ethiopians venture to share their ideas and experience by putting out books. When I set out to write the first Sequel of the *Generation*, I did not know what to expect. In the years that followed, I received mixed signals from various quarters - both encouraging and discouraging ones.

As was indicated elsewhere, I cannot claim that this work provides a complete picture of the struggle. However, the information furnished would assist in conducting an assessment of the struggle. I believe that those who are interested in the study of Ethiopian history, and in particular the political history of the last twenty-five years or so, are provided with some ingredients to initiate their study. I believe that it is incumbent upon us to provide a balanced and reasonable solution that currently afflicts Ethiopia, hence the need for a serious assessment and analysis of the struggle.

Writing a book requires erudition, perseverance, dedication, discipline and purpose. In my case, one of the driving forces that enabled me to endure the vicissitudes of writing a book was guilt - *survivors* guilt. I wrote this book partly to express my indebtedness to the struggle and its martyrs. It was a vindication to those selfless, fearless and idealist young activists who gave up everything only to see a better future for their country.

While writing this book, I had to re-live and endure the agonizing period of the struggle. At times, I had to place myself in the 1970s to communicate, discuss and sometimes argue with some of the fallen comrades. I had to confirm and ascertain the correctness of certain incidents or facts. I regard that the fallen comrades are the custodians of our history. Those of us who survived the ordeal have changed with time. Some of us have even renounced our past, of course, exonerating ourselves from the fallouts of the struggle. I strongly believed in EPRP's cause. I was convinced that it was and still is just to struggle for social, economic and political justice. I believed that it was and still is honorable to struggle for equality and redistribution of wealth. I deemed that it was and still is right to stand up and voice one's dissent against a dictatorial regime. I had concluded that it was and still is just to struggle for the sovereignty of one's country. I thought it was and is right and honorable to struggle for the integrity of Ethiopia and the rights of its citizens (collective or individual).

The EPRP had paid an enormous sacrifice as a result of the complex political conditions the country was in, the barbarous nature of the regime and the unprecedented repression unleashed throughout the country. Some organizational and political errors that the EPRP committed were additional factors for EPRP's demise. Although no struggle takes place without sacrifice, the loss of a large number of activists had its ramifications.

In the brief space I have here, I cannot provide a detailed assessment, analysis or account of what went wrong and how. Hopefully, in due time, I may be able to provide an assessment.

Assessment can be made either on the entire course of the revolutionary movement, or on specific incidents pertaining to the struggle. Among other issues, the relationship between class and ethnic struggle, conflict resolution, economic vs. political struggle, armed vs. political struggle, the role of a leadership in a clandestine organization, democracy and underdevelopment, socialism in a third world country, etc., could serve as starting points of research.

As an active and leading activist of the struggle, I express my heart-felt apology for failing to deliver what was expected of me. To those who lost their beloved ones, particularly to the Ethiopian mothers, I convey my deepest sympathy. I will also like to make clear that it is us, the EPRP members, who are aggrieved most due to the loss of our comrades.

With certainty I can say that the great majority of leading EPRP members, particularly those who fell victim and paid the ultimate sacrifice had no other ulterior motive except standing up for their countrymen. EPRP's leading activists had no hidden agenda except struggling for what they believed was just - the well being of the Ethiopian poor. True to their cause, they stood in the forefront of the struggle and absorbed the heat. They did not lurk from their responsibilities and many of them fell victim.

The carnage on the Ethiopian generation of activists of the 1970s had left a devastating effect on many of us - the survivors. I am convinced that Ethiopia still mourns the death of its brightest and selfless children. In that mindless butchery, it is not only the EPRP that lost its most dedicated members, we all have lost - Ethiopia has lost its best sons and daughters. For sure, I have lost my best comrades and friends; comrades that I relied upon for their judgement, wisdom and advice. They were one of the main sources of inspiration to my activity. Particularly during the dark days of the Red Terror, to have those comrades on my side was an ultimate comfort. When these comrades fell victim one after another, part of my soul left along with them and I still have not recovered from the trauma. I still walk around with a soul that has a deep hole. A wounded soul, so to say.

Those fallen comrades, at least some of them, are my regular visitors, of course, in my dreams. I always see them with vibrant smile on their faces. They have not aged. Neither have they changed their clothes. They still seem to be enthusiastic and energetic. There is a time gap between us. We are in different time zones. I believe that they still are in the 1970s, in the midst of the intense struggle. Perseverant as they were, they still won't let me forget them. Their occasional visit haunts me and keeps reminding me that I had a mission to accomplish - writing their history.

I am one of the few leading EPRP members that survived the Red Terror. I have passed through the different stages of the repression. I was there when the Derge's 'bloodless revolution' was instantly transformed into a blood bath that devoured tens of thousands of Ethiopians. I was there when the hoodlums of the 'revolution' terrorized the citizens and everyone lived in fear and agony. I was there when kids of fifteen and sixteen years of age were slaughtered in the streets of Addis Abeba. Throughout this time, I was not a passive by-stander. As a member of the EPRP, I have taken an active part to stop the Derge's atrocities and massacre. I was among those whose chance of survival was almost nil and had overcome innumerable accidents that would have cost my life. During my stay in Addis Abeba and Shoa, I have experienced and passed through almost all of the major search and destroy campaigns. Besides, I escaped from six deadly encounters. On one of them, I was able to escape even though I was wounded following an exchange of gunfire.

For over a year and a half the EPRP operated under the barrel of a gun. It functioned under the close surveillance of armed government *vigilante*s. You could find these squads in government institutions, kebeles, schools, etc. You felt that each and every gun was pointed at you and, at times, unaware, reacted when you saw members of one of these squads pass by. As an underground activist, you felt that the armed squads had identified who you are, an EPRP member, a criminal of the first degree. You were under siege and operated thus.

This brings in mind Feoder Dostoyevsky, one of the greatest Russian writers of the nineteenth century. Early in his writing career, Dostoyevsky was accused of plotting to overthrow the Czar and he was exiled to Siberia. Dostoyevsky was then taken to a spot where he was to be killed by a firing squad. Dostoyevsky's eyes were wrapped up and what he repeatedly heard was the clicking sound of rifles. All of a sudden, an order was given to halt the firing. The commander exclaimed that he saw a man on a horse back carrying a white flag. The man on the horse back was coming towards them and they waited for him. Upon arrival, the man disclosed that he was carrying an amnesty from the Czar and Dostoyevsky's life was saved. The entire episode was a travesty and a pre-arranged event. However, it left a deep scar on Dostoyevsky that in his later works you find one of the characters asking what a man could feel a few seconds before he could be shot at. Likewise, what does a person feel when he/she operates under a gun pointed at him/her? What is the psychology of a person who expects his death just any second? What is the feeling of an individual who doesn't know what awaits him at one of the street corners? What is the feeling of a person who had heard about the death of his best comrade, friend, brother or sister a few hours ago? What is the state of mind of such a person?

A large number of the surviving generation of Ethiopian activists of the 1970 live with deep scars in their hearts. Those scars did not heal - mine didn't. Years after the event, we still visualize those 'hoodlums' of the revolution. We recreate them in our mind as if the event happened a few days back.

I went underground in September 1975. My 'crime' was taking an active part in the labor movement. To be sure, I was one of the organizers of the labor opposition and one of the coordinators of the September 1975 labor strike. During this time, over five-hundred labor activists were arrested. Me and another EPRP member, Germatchew Lemma, who were forewarned by our organization about the Derge's move, went underground. The Derge conducted an intensive manhunt to apprehend us. Germatchew Lemma, who was confined to his apartment, was killed in June 1977, about twenty one months after he went underground. I remained an underground activist for over twenty five months. All throughout this time, I conducted my organizational assignments diligently and few were the times that I had to be confined to my living quarter. Most of the time, I was out on the street corners of Addis Abeba to accomplish my daily organization routines.

It is difficult to provide a detailed account of my twenty-five months of underground life in such a short space, suffice it to mention that it was a very traumatic experience. As an underground activist, I had no defined place to live. When available, the organization provided shelter. However, quite often, I spent my time wherever I could. For lack of shelter and to minimize mobility, I spent most of my time in the busy quarters of the big market place, *Mercato*, strolling around or sitting by a corner and waiting until my next organizational appointment. There were times when I had to pose as a street vendor, lest I could not be recognized. Many were the times that I spent my time in cemeteries. Such places were free from government vigilantes. In my twenty-five or so months of underground life, I had encountered a number of incidents and accidents. I encountered people that I knew before who became petrified when they accidentally met me. These people knew that I was on the most wanted list of the government and quite often, they did not know how to handle the situation. In one of those incidents when I stopped a cab, the driver happened to be someone I knew. Although I was camouflaged, he recognized me. He did not know how to handle the situation. He wanted to give me a ride, but was frightened to carry a government fugitive in his vehicle in the midst of an intensive repression campaign. During this time, all citizens were warned to inform or turn over suspects. Before he could make up his mind, I jumped into the vehicle and sat besides him. All through out the trip, I kept quiet and he never uttered a word. He did not even turn around to look at me. He pretended that I was not there. Although it was a short journey, it seemed that it took ages. At my destination, when I tried to pay the fare, still gazing in front of him and without looking at me, the cab driver refused to take it and advised me to be careful.

Finally, it is my desire that this book will be of some importance for the coming generation. It will learn from our strengths and weaknesses, experiences and vulnerabilities and successes and failures. It is my wish that the coming generation will inherit our idealism, love for one's country and people. It is my wish that the coming generation inherits our passion and selflessness to one's cause. I strongly believe that all of us have to stand up and struggle for justice and fairness so that the massacre of the 1970s, the Red Terror, shall not be repeated.

Glossary of Amharic words

Abeyotawi Ethiopia	Revolutionary Ethiopia
Abeyotawi Seded	Revolutionary Flame
Abeyotawi Wetat	Revolutionary youth
Abruk	Short break
Abyot Tebeka	Revolutionary guard
Agalte and tegalete	"Denounce" and "self-denounce"
AMAACO	Committee formed to ascertain members rights
Anja	Faction
Aweraja	Local administration next to province
Betagne	Liquidationists
Birr	Ethiopian currency ($1.00=2.07 birr, until 1991)
Campaign	Zemetcha
Democracy yale gedeb	Unrestricted democracy
Democracy begedeb	Restricted democracy
Ethiopia Tikdem	Ethiopia first
Ferenje	Foreigner
Gabi	Shawl
Ganta	Platoon
Gohe	Dawn
Hailee	Company
Henfishfish	Subversive activity
Hizbawi Arbegna	Patriotic Force
Kebele	Urban dwellers associations
Kefetegna	Higher urban dwellers associations
Koushuke	Small piece of cloth
Labader	The Proletariat
Malba, Welba, Weland	Producers Cooperatives
Moot merete	Flat (dangerous) terrain
Nebelbal force	Raging Fire
Netsa Irmja	Unrestricted (punitive) action
Taalim	Training center
Teff	Cereal
Tenesh	Rise Up
Teqelit	Reshuffle
Tewahedo	Ethiopian Orthodox religion
WAZ League	Labor League
Wefe	Omen
Wereda	Local administration next to aweraja
Wetaderawi Baito	Military council
Yekatit	February also means the 'revolution'
Yewuyeyit Medrek	Discussion "clubs"

Bibliography

Published official sources

Ethiopian government

Addis Zemen, January 15, Feb. 27, 1975.
Addis Zemen, Feb. 6, 20, March 9, 20, 25, April 4, 9, 21, May 18, 27, 30, June 4, 10, 16, July 19, 23, 27, September 10, 16, 26, October 22, December 19, 30, 1976.
Addis Zemen, January 16, 31, Feb. 1, 12, 21, 27, March 10, 12, 15, 19, 22, 31, May 1, 10, 21, 25, 28, 29, June 12, July 12, 14, 18, 24, 27, 30, September 12, October 20, 24, November 6, 16, 18, December 24, 1977.
Addis Zemen, August 28, 1979.
Derge Statement, November 13, 1977.
Ethiopian Herald, 9 Nov. 1975, 12 September 1980, 8 May 1981, 26 January, 1982, 16 May 1985, 30 January 1985, 29 March 1985.
May Day POMOA representative speech, 1977.
Mengistu Haile Mariam, 'Address to the Inaugural Meeting of the Shengo', 15 September 1987.
Mengistu Haile Mariam, Ist COPWE Congress report, 16 June 1980.
Mengistu Haile Mariam, Report to the Central Committee of the WPE, April 14, 1986.
Mengistu Haile Mariam, 'Revolution Day Speech, 1986.'
Ministry of Agriculture, Villagization Guidelines. 1985.
National Democratic Revolution program, April 1976.
National Literacy Campaign Coordinating committee, 14th Round Program.
Negarit Gazetta
- Public Ownership and Control of Rural Lands Proclamation, No.31 of 1975, N/G 34/26, 29 April 1975.
- Peasant Associations Organization and Consolidation Proclamation, No. 71 of 1975, N/G 35/15, 14 December 1975.
- Declaration of State of Emergency Proclamation, No. 55 of 1975, N/G 35/4, 30 September 1975.
- Labor Proclamation, No. 64 of 1975, NG 35/11, 6 December 1975.
- National Revolutionary Development Campaign Decree.
- Agricultural Marketing Corporation Establishment Proclamation, No. 105 of 1976, NG 36/7, 20 November 1976.

-Provisional Organization of Mass Organization Affairs, Organization and Operation Improvement Proclamation, No. 119 of 1977, NG 36/22, 14 July, 1977.
- All-Ethiopian Peasant Association Establishment Proclamation, No. 130 of 1977, NG 37/1,17 September 1977.
- Peasant Associations Consolidation Proclamation, No.130 of 1977, NG 37/1, 24 May 1982.
- National Military Service Proclamation, No. 238 of 1983, NG 42/9, 4 May 1983.
- The Construction and Use of Urban Houses Proclamation, No 291 of 1986, NG 45/3, 17 February 1986.
Negat, Part II, Video tape prepared by the EPRDF in 1991.
Negat, Volume I, taped from Ethiopian TV, 1991.
RRC, The Challenges of Drought: Ethiopia's Decade of Struggle in Relief and Rehabilitation, Addis Abeba, 1985, p.135.

Other Sources

CELU Resolution, September 1968, Teglatchen, No.2, October 1975 (Eth. Cal. 1968).
Report presented at the AEWTU Congress of May 1978.

EPRP Publications

Underground publications

Abeyotawi Wetat, Vol. I, Nos .4, 10, 1975/76.
Democracia, Volume I, No. 6, 1974/75
Democracia, Volume II, Special Edition, January 1976 Special Edtition, Nos. 2,13, 19, 22, 23, 29, 30, 1975/76.
Democracia, Volume III, August Special Edition, Nos. 2, 3, 4, 5, 6, 7, 9, 11, 12,20, 1976/77.
Democracia, Volume IV, Nos. 1, 2, 4, 7, 8, 10, 1977/78.
ELAMA, Minimum Program, January 1976.
EPRP by-laws, August 1975.
EPRP Constitution, August 1975.
EPRP program, August 1975.
EPRP CC 4th Plenum Assessment, July 1979.
EPRP/EPLF Communique, 1976.
EPRP Politburo Document, January 1977.
Ethiopian People's Revolutionary YL Constitution, September 1976.
From the CC, A statement on the resignation of Taye, September 19, 1980.
Intra-party Struggle, April/May 1977.
Labader, Nos. 10, 12, 20, 26, 1975/76.
Modern Revisionism and Social-Imperialism, Introduction, May/June 1977.
Preamble of EPRP program, August 1975.

Report by Seifu, 1977.
Taye's statement, "Who constitutes the EPRP?", 1980.
The Mass Line, Berhane Meskel Redda, October 1979.
The Bolshevik Youth, Volume I, No. 1, April/May 1977, Volume IV, No. 7.
TPLF: Kedetu Wede Matu, June 1985.
Voice of ELAMA, August, December 10, 19, 1976.

EPRA publications

Activities of the Northern Front of the EPRA.
Assimba, Special Edition, No. 8., 1977.
Assimba, Volume II, No.8.
Manifesto of the EPRA Rectification Movement, April 1977.
Red Army, Volume I, No.3.
Red Army, Volume I, Special Issue, No.1. March 1978.

FC publications

(Most of the documents listed below were not dated. Probably most of them came out in 1977/78)
Abyot, Volume III, No.1, January 1978.
Abyot, Volume II, No.5.
Abyot, Volume VIII, No. 2.
Abyot, Volume III, No.5, September-November, 1978.
Circular of the EPRP Regional Committee.
Circular, EPRP RC in Europe.
Circular of RC in Europe to EPRP members.
Circular of the EPRP RC in Europe.
Circular of the EPRP RC in Europe.
Circular of the FC.
Compilation of the Rectification Movement (abroad), 1979/80
FC report to EPRP members.
Foreign IZ, Rectification Movement Report.
From an article put out by the EPRP RC in Europe, No.1.
Hand written circular of the CC member in the FC.
Letter of Mulugeta Zena to the EPRP RC in America, April 1977.
Our Position on the Basque Struggle. An unsigned article of the FC, responding to the RC in the USA.
Rectification Notes - K's View, August 1977.
Regional Committee Report.
Report of the Rectification Committee.
Report of the EPRP Foreign Committee.
Report of the EPRP RC in the USA, 1978.
Report to the RC of America, by a cell known as Alemayehu.
Report of the EPRP Regional Committee in the USA.
Report on the 18th Congress of Ethiopian Students Union in Europe.
Report of the RM in Europe.
Report sent to the EPRP CC from the RC in America.

Report of RC of America.
Report of the FC.
Report by Ismail, code name for the EPRP RC in America, to the EPRP Central Committee.
Report of the Foreign Committee.
Report of the EPRP Foreign Committee to EPRP and Youth League members, March 1977.
Report of the RC in America.
Report prepared in 1983 by an EPRP member who had been assigned in the area.

Other Publications: Opposition Movements

Combat, Volume V, No.2, October, 1976.
EFLNA publication, Liberation, Volume IV, No. 5.
EPRP and the Ethiopian Revolution, April 1980. TPLF publication.
Malilit Zelali, Aregawi Berhe, June 1988.
MEISON's Critical Assessment, 1981.
Sefiw Hizbe Dimtse, Nos. 31, 32, 33, 34, 35, 40, 50, 1975/76/77.
The EPRP and the Ethiopian Revolution, April, 1980. TPLF Publication.
The Assessment of the Ten Years Struggle of the of the Communist Group within the TPLF, July 1985.
Vanguard, EPLF Publication, August 1977.
Voice of Unity, Volume II, No. 5.
Voice of the Air force, December 27, 1975.
WAZ League, Volume I, No. II.
Weyenne, No I, February 1976.TPLF publication.
Whither the Eritrean People's Struggle? 1986/87. TPLF publication.
Yetegil Tiri, TPLF publication, 2nd Year, No.4, 1986.

International Organizations and United Nations Agencies

Amnesty International, 31 March, 1978.
Amnesty International, 30 May, 1991.
Amnesty International Index, AFR/25/04/79.
Economic memorandum in Ethiopia, World Bank, September 23, 1977.
Economic Memorandum in Ethiopia, World Bank, April 22, 1977.
United Nations Coordinating Committee for Relief and Rehabilitation and RRC of Ethiopia, "Short-term Relief and United Nations, Rehabilitation Needs in Ethiopia," March 1981.
International Labor Organization, Socialism from the Grassroots, Vol. I report 397, 1982.
US Department of State, "Country Reports on Human Rights Practices for 1990".

Books, Articles and Published Papers

Abera Yemane Ab, The Defeat of the Ethiopian Revolution and the Role

of the Soviet Union, Proceedings of the 2nd International Conference on the Horn of Africa.
Abeyotawi Ethiopia, Year I, No. 10, September 1976.
Addis Fana, April, May 8, 1977.
Africa South of the Sahara, 1978-79, Europa Publications, 1978.
Africa Confidential, 24.19, September 21, 1983.
Africa Confidential, 30.11, May 26, 1989.
Andargatchew Tiruneh, The Ethiopian Revolution, Cambridge University Press, 1993.
Babile Tola, To Kill a Generation, The Red Terror in Ethiopia, Washington D.C., 1989.
Brietzke, H.P., Law, Development and the Ethiopian Revolution, Bucknell University Press, 1982.
Clapham, C., Transformation and continuity in revolutionary Ethiopia, Cambridge University Press, 1988.
Dawit Wolde Giorgis, Red Tears, The Red See Press Inc., 1989.
Dessalegne Rahmato, Settlement and Resettlement in Metekel, Western Ethiopia,' Africa (Roma), 43, 1988.
Document prepared for the reform movement in the Derge, Addis Fana, June 1977.
Ethiopian Statistical Abstract, 1982, 1984.
Evil Days, 30 Years of War and Famine in Ethiopia, An African Watch Report, 1991.
Galprin, G., Ethiopia: Population Resources Economy, Moscow, Progress Publishers, 1981.
Giday Bahrisume, Amora, 1993 (1985 Eth).
Gilkes, P., The Dying Lion: Feudalism and Modernization in Ethiopia, St. Martin's Press, New York, 1975.
Hall, M. Ann, The Ethiopian Revolution: Group Interaction and Civil - military relations, (dissertation), George Washington University, 1977.
Halliday, F., Molyneux, M. The Ethiopian Revolution, London, Verso Editions, 1981.
Ifoyeta, April, June, 1992.
Joiner, H., American Foreign Policy: The Kissinger Era, The Strode Publishers, 1977.
Kiflu Tadesse, The Generation, Part I, Independent Publishers, 1993.
Koran, D. Ethiopia: The United States and the Soviet Union, Southern Illinois University Press, 1986.
London, Guardian, 6 July 1977.
Markakis, J., National and Class Conflict in the Horn, Cambridge University Press 1987.
Pliny the middle aged, The PMAC, Origins and Structure, North-East African Studies, No.1, 1979, Part II.
Pliny the middle-aged, "The Lives and Times of the Derge", Northeast African Studies, Research News and Notes.
Proceedings of the 5th International Conference on the Horn of Africa.

Proceedings of the 2nd International Conference on the Horn of Africa.
Sbacchi, A., Ethiopia under Mussolini, Zed Publishers, 1985.
Spencer, H. J., Ethiopia at Bay, Reference Publications Inc., 1984.
Tesfa Tsion Medhane, Eritrea, Dynamics of a National Question, 1986.
Tesfaye Mekonnen, Yederese Lebaletariku, Netherlands, October 1992 (1985 Eth. C.)
Voice of Unity, Volume II, No. 5.
'Ethiopia's Bitter Medicine', The Sunday Times, 3 November 1985 (1977).

Interviews, Correspondences and Others

Authors memoir of the Shinfa meeting, May/June 1980.
Authors memorandum, EPRP CC meetings in Gedarif, Sudan, 1979.
Authors memorandum, GM, June 1980.
Author's Recollections of Tesfaye's Testimony at the 2nd EPRP CC Plenum.
Commentary, Aregawi Berhe, January 1996.
Discussion with a member of the regional command, GT, Sudan, 1980.
Discussion with B. 1984, Sudan. B. was a leading military figure of the EPRA who later became a member of the regional command in Welkaite.
From a letter of one of the peasants, GMF.
From a letter sent to TT in 1977.

Interviews,
-AH, January 1996.
-AKB and GM, January 1995.
-Ali, November, 1987.
-Ali (Agaro), 1994.
-AM, November 1994.
-Berhane, May 1994. Berhane was one of the leading members of the army.
-Berhanu Nega, 1988.
-Colonel Alemayehu Asfaw, March 1997
-Corporal F. August 1990.
-Debebe and Girma T., 1993.
-Demelash, 1988.
-Fassika Belete, member of the Party Command, May 1994.
-TF, 1990.
-GB, 1994.
-Gezahegne Teferra, 1989.
-GKY, GA, 1989, 1990.
-GTG, June 1994.
-Kassu Kuma, 1990.
-KM, 1994.
-KT, 1993.
-M. 1994.
-MA, 1994. He was one of the leading members of the party

structure in the R-3
-Major General Nega Tegegne, April 1984, Sudan.
-Melaku, September 1996.
-MGE, April 1991.
-Mohabaw, 1995.
-SD, 1990.
-T. 1991.
-Tedla Fantaye 1994.
-Tebebe, September 1997
-Y. 1989.
-Yared Tibebu, February 1997.
-Zeru Kehishen, 1988.
-Memoirs of the author, EPRP CC group meeting, Khartoum, April 1979.
-Memorandum, Kiflu Tadesse and Zeru Kehishen, 1988, Amsterdam, Holland. Minute of Khartoum CC meeting, April 1979.

Index

Aba Abate 421
Aba Alemu 90, 421
Aba Takele 90, 421
Abate Achule 283
Abaye Tsehaye 390, 393
Abdi Abadir 3
Abdi Abdulahi 270
Abdulahi Idris 469
Abdulahi Yusuf 56, 102, 240, 285, 341
Abebe Fentaye 16
Abebe Jemma, Lieutenant 316
Abebe Seyoum, Fetawrari 243
Abebe Tessema 389
Aberra Lemma 276
Abeyotawi Seded 109
Abiyu Airsamo 79, 141, 143, 184, 275, 295, 313, 316
Aboye Gebrai 393
Abyotawi Seyef 247
Achameleh Kebede 193, 320
Addis Abeba branch
    POMOA office of 194
Addis Abeba EPRP IZ
    security network of 202
Addis Abeba IZ xlii, 21, 22, 36, 38, 40, 43, 123, 124, 141, 152, 295, 319, 320, 322, 325, 333-336
Adenew Gerito 281
AEWTU
    vice-president of 274
Afar Liberation Front 13, 45
Afeworque 136
African Communist Parties 227
Agedu Seweneh 280
Agere Addisu 310, 336, 339
Ahmed Nassir 470
Akale Worke H. Wolde 297
Aklilu Cabinet xl
Aklilu H. Wolde 297
Aklilu Hiruy 87, 275, 344

Aklog Negatu, Lieutenant 326
Alem Bekagne 287, 288, 290, 291
Alemayehu Asfaw, Colonel xxxvi, 104, 105, 380, 382, 386, 405
Alemayehu Asfaw, Major 324
Alemayehu Ayalew 136
Alemayehu Egzeru 87, 294, 345
Alemayehu Haile, Lieutenant 104, 106, 109, 164, 168, 194
Alemayehu Tessema 16
Alemayehu Tilahun 144, 198, 320
Alemu Abebe 54, 69, 239, 244, 271, 274, 285
Ali Hussien 18, 26, 144
Ali Musa, Major 2
All Ethiopian Workers Trade Union 147
Aman Andom, General xli, xlv
Amare Tesfu 389
American military base 7
American State Department 462
Amha Abebe, Captain 28, 76, 107, 150, 169, 194, 202-204
Andargatchew Aseged 54, 71, 147
Angola
    Mozambique Popular
    Liberation
    Army
    government of 350
Ansar Movement 226, 227
Arega, Captain 270
Aregawi Berhe xxxvi, 389, 393, 397, 470
Asefa Medhane 54
Asfaw Demisse 26
Asmare Bereye 431
Asmerom, Grazematch 16
Asnake Getachew 340
Asrat Desta, Colonel 168
Assefa Endeshaw 37-39

Assefa Gebre Mariam 182, 279
Atnafu Abate, Major 5, 164, 165, 169, 201, 247
Aya Agedew 421
Aya Desta 421
Aya Hailu 421
Aya Reta 421
Ayalew Kebede 433, 454
    POMOA representative 85
Ayalew Mandefro 285
Ayneshet Teferi 165, 168
Azin Yassin 384
Bale uprising of 1960s 44
Baro Tumsa 239
Basazenew Bayissa 286
Bealu Girma 470
Beedemariam, Engineer 17
Beewketu Kassa, Lieutenant 104, 106
Begashaw Atalaye, Corporal 109
Belay Hassen 386, 401
Belayneh G/Mariam 292, 294, 295, 297, 298, 300
Belissuma
    publication 37
Bellissuma group 43
Bereket Taeme 258
Berhane Asfaw 421
Berhane Gebre Kirstos 398
Berhane Gebre Meskel 423
Berhane Iyasu 91-93, 150, 177, 389-391
Berhane Meskel 31, 40, 63, 64, 80, 81, 88, 122, 125, 137, 138, 140, 146, 173, 177, 179-184, 196, 206, 207, 244, 257, 316, 326-328, 372, 390, 403
Berhane, Colonel 277
Berhanu Bayeh, Colonel 226
Berhanu Ijjigu 28, 122, 142, 143, 310, 336, 337
Berhanu Kebede, Captain 245, 324
Berhanu Zerihun 189
Berihun Dagnew 423
Berihun Mariye 198-200
Betsuamlak, Major 76, 77, 250
Bitwoded Adane Mekonnen 471
Boga Abajobir 3
British Broadcasting Corporation 432
Castro, Fidel 166, 220, 226, 228, 248
CC of WPE 478
CELU
    congress of xliv, 20
    leadership of l, 14-16, 24
    provisional leadership of xlix
    strike of 18, 32
CELU leadership 144
Central Intelligence Agency 229
Central Intelligence Department 325
Central Investigation Department 42, 43, 287, 324
Central Revolutionary Investigation Department 324
Charlie Johns xxxvi
Chinese government 188, 310-312
CID 276, 289, 291, 292, 294, 296, 300, 325
    prison population of 288
Cohen, Herman 483
Communist Party
    Chinese experience of 1920s 311
Communist Party of China 311
Communist Party of Soviet Union 76, 166
    paternalist approach of 170
Confederation of Ethiopian Labor Union xliii
Congress of Ethiopian Teachers Association 2
COPWE
    congress of 477
Czechoslovakian government 480
Dagnatchew Ayele 202-204
Damte, P.O 76
Daniel Asfaw, Colonel 103, 108, 165, 168
Daniel Mengesha 3
Daniel Tadesse 67, 69, 110, 238, 240, 243
Daro Negash 23, 26, 197
Dawit Negussie 342
Dawit Yacob 270
Degu Haile Selassie 136
Dejazmatch Desta 434

Index

Demeke Harege Weyene 3, 4, 149
Demisse Berhane 277
Democratic Republic of Ethiopia
    People s 477
Denbi Dissasa 102
Derge
    atrocities of 493
    congress of 163
    Dabat-based intelligence
        of 427
    intelligence department
        of 324
    intelligence of 294, 340,
        342, 371
    internal crisis of 107,
        172, 173, 204,
        222
    reform movement of 146
    security department of 40
Derge
    internal crisis 208
    social base 174
Derge security department 324
Dessie Dawit 431, 454
Dessie Guben 431
Desta Bezabih 389
Desta Tadesse 69, 243
Dinku, Lieutenant 245
Duan, Le 352
East-German government 228
EDU's activities 90
ELAMA
    Addis Abeba IZ of 101
    congress of 23, 27
    constitution of 27
    Harer zonal committee of
        101
    leadership 101
    military structure of 152
    program of 23
ELAMA IZ 316
ELAMA Leadership 321
ELF
    defeat of 469
    labor party of 385
    security chief of 384
ELF leadership 384, 469
Elias Nur 286
Elias W/Mariam 142
Emiru Gebcherasha 281
Emiru Wonde, Colonel 136, 330,
    440, 442
Endale Gossaye 286
Endalkatchew Mekonnen xl
EPLF

    first congress of 253
    infilteration of 258
EPLF forces 485
EPLF leadership 117, 121
EPLO
    political task of xlii
    first congress of xxxix, lii
    leadership of xlii, xliii,
        xlvi, li
    program of xliii, xlviii
    relationship of xlv
EPRA
    constitution of 366, 375,
        378, 382, 405,
        432, 441
    expansion of 418
    financial status of 460
    historical emergence of
        439
    history of 407
    intelligence committee of
        455
    military achievements
        /errors of 382
    military affairs of 377
    military approach of 372
    Northwest command of
        406, 426
    political crisis of 369
    provisional command
        451
    provisional leadership of
        404
    retreat of 404
    southern front of 337
EPRA command 437
EPRA General leadership 451, 452
EPRA General Party Committee
    442
EPRA leadership 33, 88, 89, 105,
        124, 371-373,
        375-378,
        380-382, 384,
        388, 390, 393,
        396, 399-402,
        405, 417-419,
        426, 432, 434,
        435, 438, 439,
        446, 447, 451
EPRA, Constitution 380
EPRDF forces 482, 483
EPRDF government 157, 281, 301
EPRP

land program of 350
offensive-defensive
    activities of
    181
appraisal of 118
Begemidir IZ of 333,
    369, 437
Begemidir zonal
    committee of
    8, 84, 332
Chinese relation of 311
constitution of 119, 124,
    143, 177, 179,
    206, 308, 353,
    387, 441, 444
constitution of 122, 178,
    179
corpse of 279
crimes of 114
death of a large number
    of 274
death of CC of 273
declaration of 1, 89
economic sabotage 134
extended conference of
    xxxii, li, 2, 11,
    19, 56, 64,
    204, 346, 347,
    349, 350, 354,
    387
first congress of 64, 175,
    311, 350, 387
Foreign committee of
    253, 346, 350,
    385, 446
foreign relations of 310
fourth plenum of CC of
    312, 441, 443,
    445, 449, 456
Gamu Goffa zonal
    committee of
    336
Gojjam IZ of 123
Gojjam zonal committee
    of 201
Gonder zonal committee
    of 422-424
Gonder zonal committee
    of 418
Harer zonal committee of
    39
Harerghe IZ of 340

Harerghe leadership
    committee of
    341
history of xxx, xxxiii,
    141, 158, 447
infiltration of MEISON
    of 75
Jimma zonal committee
    of 341
Keffa leadership
    committee of
    343
leadership crisis 386
militarization of 152
political activities abroad
    of 346
problems of 307
program of xxxii, lii, 11,
    34, 37, 42, 56,
    73, 82, 176,
    191, 232, 251,
    257, 424
public declaration of lii,
    29, 348
publishing house of 314,
    334
RC of America of 347,
    353, 355
RC of Europe of
    353-355
sacrifices of 492
second plenum of 208,
    252, 328
second Plenum of CC of
    82, 119
security department of
    77, 115
September 1976 CC
    meeting of 139
Shoa IZ of 333
Shoa structure of 313
Shoa zonal committee of
    184
Sidamo IZ of 310, 336
Sidamo IZ of 336-340
Sidamo zonal committee
    of 92, 123
social base of 349
structure of Jimma area of
    3
third plenum of 327
third plenum of CC of
    176

Index 511

Tigrai zonal committee of 329
urban activities of 406
urban defense structure of 333
urban military actions of 327
urban military activities of 149, 382
Wello zonal committee of 38, 39, 335
zonal committee in Eritrea 76, 254, 256, 258
EPRP
foreign committee 233
Harer zonal committee of 231
political position of 234
zonal committee of 231
EPRP CC 4, 18, 31, 32, 34, 38-42, 61, 63, 64, 73-75, 78-81, 83, 86, 89, 92, 118, 120, 121, 123, 124, 138, 143, 150, 152, 154, 177, 178, 180-182, 186-188, 198, 202, 204-208, 252, 257, 294, 312, 315, 322, 332, 337, 344, 346, 347, 351, 355, 369, 372, 374, 377-381, 383-388, 395, 396, 405, 428, 432, 436, 437, 441-452, 460-462
security department of 40
EPRP CC sub-secretariat 44
EPRP CC team 282, 322
EPRP central committee 41
EPRP leadership 37-39, 41, 43, 58, 74, 75, 80, 81, 84, 88, 91, 107, 108, 115, 119, 123, 133, 134, 136, 138, 148, 166, 171, 181, 184, 188, 196, 207, 237, 257, 307, 309, 313, 319, 329, 330, 338, 341, 372, 377, 396, 402-404, 421, 445, 448, 452, 456, 458, 459
EPRP leadership of Harer zone 341
EPRP PB 21, 33, 37, 38, 59, 62, 145
EPRP zonal committee 257
EPRP, Fourth Plenum of CC 436
EPRP/EPLF communiqué 186
EPRP/EPRA
financial condition of 461
military deficiencies of 369
Ergete Medebew 111, 286
Eritrean Liberation Front 134
Esayeyas Afeworki 120, 252, 351
Eshetu Ararso 56, 243
Eshetu Chole 54
ESUNA
congress of 356
ESUNA's registered membership 347
Ethio Somali conflict 472
Ethio-Somali conflict 217, 221, 222, 225, 227-229, 232-237, 285, 307-309, 314, 315, 331, 337, 339, 341
Ethio-Somali war 475
Ethio-Soviet relationship 69
Ethio-US relationship 218
Ethiopia
economic condition of 217, 223
famine-affected areas of northern highlands of 476
Italian occupation of 274
territorial integrity of 63
Ethiopian Communist Party 37
Ethiopian Democratic Union 9, 115-

Ethiopian National Liberation Front 64
Ethiopian Peasant Association 223, 478
Ethiopian Students Union
 anti-EPLF activities of 117
Ethiopian Teachers Association li, 54, 60, 65
 congress of 14
Ethiopian Trade Union 478
Ethiopian Workers Party 56, 244, 245, 336
 politburo of 244
Ethiopian Workers Revolutionary Union 3, 22
Ethiopian Writers Association 276
Fanta Belay, General 105
Fassika Belete 453
Fayeza Mohammed 276
Fekadu 112
Fekre Merid 54
Fekre Selassie Wege Deresse, Captain 109
Feoder Dostoyevsky 493
Ferede Assega 454
Ferede Azeze 431
Fesseha Gedda, Captain 294
Fetawrari Ayele 423, 425
Fikre Merid 157
Fikre Zergaw 123, 124, 188, 207, 309, 335, 336, 372, 374, 381, 384, 388, 395
Fikru Hiruy 276
Fikru of Ethiopian Airlines 19
Fikru Yosef 300
First Communist Party of Ethiopia xxxix
Gebeyaw Temesgen, Lieutenant 285
Gebeyehu 345
Gebre Egziabher Haile Mikael 254, 380, 384, 398, 452
Gebre Hiwot Gebre Egziabher, Sergeant 456
Gebre Kirstos Tewatcha 16
Gebre Meskel Fente 431
Gebre Michael 18
Gebre Selassie 77, 450, 454
Gebru Asrat 454
Gedlu Abebe 286
Geleb Dafla 452
 defeat of 482
General Leadership Committee 378, 380
General Party Committee 380, 452
General Party Leadership 453
Gerazmatch Gebre Micheal 434
Germa Ayele, Corporal 109
Germatchew Lemma 18, 42, 143, 150, 198, 322, 323, 325, 334, 494
Gessese Ayele 390
Gessese Hailu 16
Getachew Agede, Major 245
Getachew Amare 144
Getachew Assefa 180, 181, 294, 340
Getachew Begashaw xxxvi
Getachew Indayelalu 136
Getachew Kumsa 310, 336, 340
Getachew Maru 37-39, 43, 62, 86, 125, 137, 138, 140, 156, 171, 173, 177-181, 183, 207, 316, 322, 325, 327
Getachew Nadew, General 9
Getachew Negatu 320
Getachew Shibeshi, Major 3, 4, 18, 109, 149, 154, 169
Getachew, Major 420
Getachew, Master Technician 245
Getahun Sisay 37, 38, 40
Gezahegne Esatu 343
Gezahegne Fekadu 421
Gezahegne Gonderew 87
Gezahegne Simme 316, 325
Gezahegne Teferra 26, 288, 290
Gezahegne Tesfaye 316
Gezahegne Werke, Corporal 109
Gezatchew 345
Gezatchew Teferra 87
Giday Hagos 389
Giday Zeratsion xxxvi, 390, 397, 470
Girma Asfaw 450, 451
Girma Berhane 277
Girma Kebede 197
Girma Woldesenbet 18
Girma, Lieutenant 102
Gojjam Interzone 423
Gojjam IZ 335
Gonder zonal committee 439

Index

Gonderit 326
Government
    US 227
Grmai Tesfa Giorgis xxxvi
Gulilat G/Mariam 245
Gurage National Democratic Movement 79
Gutta Sernessa 285
Haddiya underground mass organization 79
Haile Abaye 19, 398, 453, 482
Haile Belay, Corporal 168
Haile Fida 44, 54, 71, 130, 199, 242, 243
Haile Mariam Woldu 254
Haile Selassie
    government of 56
Haile Selassie regime 11, 226, 390, 425, 427
Haile Selassie, Emperor xli, 227, 287, 324
Haile Wolde 79
Hailu Gerbaba 56, 70, 243
Haji Aba Foggi 2
Haji Kutta 37, 44, 231, 232
Hassen Abadir 3
Hebistu 105
Hedego Mulaw 421
Hiruy Haile Selassie, Colonel 164, 165, 168
Hitler, Adolf 229
Hussien, Ali 26
Intelligence
    Cuban 322
    Yemeni 253
International Communist Movement xxxix, 170, 314
Irish Republican Army
    political wing of 347
Iskender Demisse 90, 417
Italian Socialist Party 312
Iyasu Alemayehu 207, 346, 374, 384, 395, 443, 460, 461
Iyasu Mengesha, General 116
Iyob Berhe 118
Jafar Nimieri 116
Jafar Nimieri, General 221, 226
Kampuchian Khmer Rouge 312
Kassa Kebede 433
Kassahun G/Hiwot 421, 423
Kassai, Captain 76
Kassu Kumma xxxvi, 289, 296, 299, 300

Kebbebe G/Tsadik 3
Kebede Mengesha 56, 102, 194, 243
Kebede Tessema
    assassination of 427
Kebede Worku, Major General 10
Kebede Woubishet 45
Kedir Mohammed 42, 56, 243
Kefeyalew Adigeh, Major 270
Kegnazmatch Gebru
    Mezega area of Welkaite 434
Kelbessa Bekema 286
Kifle Alemu 136
Kiflu Tadesse xxxvi, 16, 18, 19, 23, 31, 63, 177, 195, 198, 207, 307, 333, 388, 441, 442, 444, 447, 456, 460, 461
Kiflu Teferra 115, 119, 142, 178, 202, 204, 207
Kiros Alemayehu, Major 9
Labor Code l, 19, 20, 23, 25, 65, 73
Labor movement
    Ethiopian xliv, l, 23
Lambert, member of Communist Party of former East Germany 166
Land reform proclamation xlviii, li, 4, 6, 10, 12, 79, 151, 158, 311, 338, 480, 484
Legesse Asfaw, Sergeant 109, 239, 241, 275
Legesse Belayneh, Colonel 324
Lemissa, Major 2
Leulseged Fikre Mariam, Colonel 153, 285, 324, 325
Libyan regime 226
Lij Michael Imru
    government of xli
Luleseged Minsa 421
Mahdi Kemal 340
Mahdi, Al 226
Marcos Hagos 18, 144
Mariye Teferi 18
Markakis, John 248
Marx, Karl 206

Marxist-Leninist Revolutionary League 77
May Peace Initiative 6
Meheret Wolde Amlak 276
MEISON
    alliance of 42
    appointment of 104
    departure of 341
    dispersal of 242
    effort of 243
    home base of 70
    influence of 201
    leadership 242
    leadership of li
    line of 57
    of the Addis Abeba area 77
    squad of 276
    Youth IZ of 76
MEISON
    over-concentration of power of 240
Mekasha Solomon 319
Mekedem Haile 136
Mekonnen Bayesa 310
Mekonnen Belay 277, 334
Mekonnen Jotte 69, 182
Mekonnen Seyoum, Major 153
Mekonnen Teklu 282
Mekonnen Wessenu, Kegnazmatch 10
Mekre Haile Selassie, Captain 250
Mekuria Tegegne 275
Melake Petros 385
Melaku Marcos 123, 142, 196, 336-338
Melaku Teferra, Major 136, 456
Melesse Zenawi 393
Mellese Ayalew 45, 54
Mengesha Seyoum, Ras 116
Mengiste Defar 328
Mengistu Gemetchu, Corporal 109
Mengistu Haile Mariam, Colonel xlv, 42, 55, 72, 102, 103, 105, 114, 129, 148, 153, 154, 163, 201, 204, 237, 239, 245, 270, 299, 300, 311, 326, 327, 474, 477, 481, 483
    coup of 194, 225
    dominance of 246
    rule of xxix
Mengistu Haile Mariam, Colonel
    coup of 165, 166, 168, 185
    crimes of 167
    dominance of 201
    rule of 169
Mengistu Ketsela 423
Mengistu regime 481, 483
Mengistu Teferra 421
Mengistu/POMOA alliance 108, 109, 111, 129, 131-134, 136-138, 144-146, 158, 163-168, 173, 189, 201
Mengistu/POMOA clique 107
Mensur Suleiman 421
Merid, Lieutenant 106, 150, 153
Mesele Abuhay 423
Mesfin Araya xxxvi
Mesfin Kassu 54, 156
Mesfin Tadesse xxxvi
Mezgebnesh Abiyu 142, 387
Military Service Proclamation 474
Mirah, Ali 45
Moges Berhane 277
Moges Wolde Mikael, Captain 104, 107, 109, 115, 137, 138, 155, 164, 165, 168, 310, 311
Moges Yemane 16
Mohammed Ali Samater, General 218
Mohammed Ali, Lieutenant 326
Mohammed Taher 340
Mohammed Tahir 421
Mohammed Yusuf 340
Mola Chekole 421
Monarchy
    abolition of absolute 483
Moomar, Qadaffi 226
Morton, William Hastings 63, 196
Muhidin Mohammed 334
Mulu Deneke 136
Mulugeta Eshete, Colonel 285, 324
Mulugeta Semu 286
Mulugeta Siltan 135
Mulugeta Zena 202, 204, 351
Muse Barakhi 403
Nadew Zakarias, Major 403

Index 515

Nadew Zekarias, Major 294
National Democratic Revolution Program 9, 54, 61, 63, 111, 113, 116, 190, 221
National Democratic Revolution Program of 45
National Revolutionary Campaign Council 245, 246
National Revolutionary Development Campaign 220
Nebila Abdosh 340
Nega Ayele 196
Nega Haile Mikael 298
Nega Tegegne, General 116
Negash Mussa 136
Negash Zergaw, Captain 76, 77, 250
Negash, Captain 245
Negash, Commander 245
Negede Gobeze 27, 54, 71, 92, 147, 200, 244
Negist Adane 27, 54, 243
Negussu Seteargew 454
Nolawi Abebe 335
North Korean government 480
Nuredin Mohammed 44, 79, 199, 277, 310
OLF forces 483
Organization of African Unity 220, 226
Organization Proclamation Trade Union s 478
Oromo Liberation Front 64
Oromo Peoples Liberation Organization 44
Osman Mohammed 32, 151, 292-294, 296, 297
Palestinian Liberation Organization xxxix
Paulos Sorsa 339
People's Organizing Political Committee 53
Peoples Revolt 37
Poe, Edgar Alan xxxi
POMOA
    Addis Abeba branch of 102
    Asmera branch of 76
    collaboration of 4
    formation of 4
    four main targets 65
    Harer branch of 56, 102
    incursion of 148
    involvement of 69
    political support of 103
    power of 68
POMOA's demise 238
Proclamation No 2/1975 112
Proclamation No 71 79
Proclamation No. 104 110, 111
Proclamation No. 71 10
Proclamation of April 1981 478
Proclamation of Ethiopian Socialism 53
Ras Mesfin Sileshi 26
Raza project 3, 6-9, 64, 90, 117, 229, 248, 370, 423
Rectification Movement 374, 376, 381, 419
Red Flag 38, 39, 41
Red Terror xxxii, 56, 129-131, 157, 193, 236, 247, 269-271, 276, 280-282, 284, 286, 288, 289, 291, 300, 301, 324, 325, 340, 417, 420, 424, 448, 474, 481, 485, 492, 493, 495
    MEISON of atrocities of 131
Rezene Kidane 389
Rousseau, Jean Jacques 206
Salvador Allende government 168
Samuel Alemayehu 18, 123, 124, 179, 207, 307, 311, 332, 385, 386, 388, 406, 436, 441, 444, 447, 451, 461
Samuel Bekele 18
Samuel, Major 341
Saudi Arabia government 116
Seleshi, Lieutenant 104-106
Semu Negus 39
Sennay Likke 27, 36, 37, 39, 40, 54, 68, 103,

109, 139, 168, 202, 239, 294
Setotaw Hassen 421, 482
Seyoum Demisse, Lieutenant 42
Seyoum Tsegaye 276
Seyoum, Major 244
Shewandagne Belete 202, 336
Shiferaw Tessema 26
Shitaye, Colonel 39, 202, 245, 294
Simet Birru 136
Simon Galore 339
Sirak Teferra 87, 345
Sirewe Mengiste 245
Sisay Habte, Captain 103, 130
Sisay Habte, Major 9, 218
Sisay Tessema 340
Sisay, Major 251, 256
Solomon Kebede 423
Solomon Tekle 322
Solomon, Sergeant 277
Somali Abo Liberation Front 217
Somali army 45
Somali government 44, 114
Somali National Movement 473
Somali Obo organizations 341
Somali regime 44, 63, 216-218, 220, 222, 225, 226, 230-235, 237, 248, 307, 341, 342, 426, 449, 472, 474
  invasion of 221
  territorial claims of 226
Somali Republic
  seditious propaganda of
  formed 216
Somali Revolutionary Socialist 472
Somali Salvation Democratic Front 472
Somali Salvation Front 282
Somalia
  Ziad Barre regime of 220
Somalia government 188
Soviet involvement 432
Soviet Union
  military expenditure 228
  military involvement of 222
  treaty of friendship of 226
Soviet Union, involvement 385
Stalin, Joseph 227
Sudan
  Nimeri regime of 227

Sudan government 482
Sudanese government 462
Sulieman Mohammed 340
T'am Yalew Eshete 25, 26
Tadele Mengesha 244
Tadesse Bogale 270
Tadesse Kidane Mariam 18
Tafa Daba, Lieutenant 326
Taher Abdu 342, 343
Takele, Lieutenant 251, 255
Tamene Galore, Lieutenant 326
Tamrat Layene 433, 454
Tariku Ayene, Birgadier General 480
Taye Gola 431
Taye Tola 105
Teachers Association
  Gonder of 422
Tebebe 202, 203
Tedla Fentaye 18, 26
Teferi Bente, General xlv, 104, 109, 164, 165, 167-169
Teferi Berhane 91
Teferi Mengistu 280
Teferra, Captain 168
Teffera Wonde 69
Tegegne Bedane 275
Teka Amare 142
Teka Tulu, Colonel 103, 109, 154, 157
Tekle Mikael Armede, Colonel 324
Temesgen Madebo 148
Tenagne 281
Terefe Wolde Tsadik 69, 243
Tesfa Mariam 384
Tesfaye Abebe 28
Tesfaye Debessai 31, 33, 34, 40, 62, 71, 88, 89, 91, 108, 118-122, 143, 150, 154, 172, 177, 181, 187, 188, 195, 198-200, 205, 207, 236, 384, 392
Tesfaye Gebre Kidan, General 107
Tesfaye Mekonnen 239, 336
Tesfaye Robele 270
Tesfaye Tadesse 158, 285
Tesfaye Tadesse; minister 133
Tesfaye Wolde Selassie, Colonel 324
Tesfaye, Chief 286

Teshager Berhane 19
Teshale Wondimu 340
Teshome Baye, Sergeant 285, 289, 292, 297, 300
Teshome, Major 158, 285
Tessema Deressa 19, 144
Tewedros Asfaw 340
Tewedros Bekele 148, 158
Tewefelos, Patriarch 10
Tezera 136
Tigrai People's Liberation Front 64, 389
Tigrayan Liberation Front 390
Tilahun
    death of 427
Tilaye Teshome 286
Tito Hiruy 87, 276
Totil Ibrahim 384
TPLF leadership 393
TPLF-controlled territory 437
Transport Workers Union 16
Tse tung
    Mao 170
Tse Tung, Mao 348
Tsegaye Alemayehu 144
Tsegaye Gebre Medhin 207, 253, 374, 380, 386, 388, 390, 395, 433, 441, 443, 452, 482
Tsegaye Sebhatu 319
Tsehai Inkosellasie, Dejazmatch 10
Tselote Hiskias 172, 177, 181, 207, 374, 386
Union of Ethiopian Marxist-Leninist Organizations 239
Union of Gas Stations 16
United Nations handouts 461
United Nations Secretary General 271
Urban Housing Proclamation 13, 66, 67
Urban Land Proclamation 1
Vance, Cyrus 221
Wakko Guttu 45
Wase Aman, Lieutenant 326
Waz League 77, 112, 167, 202, 238-240, 244, 245, 250, 294, 336, 343
Weldesellasie Nega 454
Wendemagne 105
Wendewosen Lemma 342

Wendirad Bekele
    zematch 2
Western Somalia Liberation Front 216, 217, 220
Wolde Medhin Abraha, Sergeant Major 28, 107, 169
Wolde Meskel, Major 245
Wolde Selassie Nega 390, 393
Wonde Wossen, Lieutenant 326
Wondewossen Seyoum 3
Wondifraw 19
Workers Party of Ethiopia 25, 109, 477
Working Peoples Control Committees 479
Worku Agelo 281
World Lutheran Church 189
Woubishet family 276
Woubishet Retta 91, 92, 135
Yared Tebebu xxxvi, 450, 451
Yaregal Demisse 26
Yayehyirad Kitaw 69
Yemane Araya 57
Yemane Berhan Berhane 340
Yemane, Captain 76
Yemen government 69
Yeshi Wolde Mariam 280
Yetbarek Hiskias 135, 157, 177
Yilma Tiruneh 144
Yirefu Bedane 16, 19
Yirga Tessema 380, 401
Yishaq Debre Tsion 452, 482
YL CC 275, 344-346
Yohannes Berhane 28, 63, 86, 142, 171, 178, 185, 196, 197, 207
Yohannes Demisse 342
Yohannes Germatchew 340
Yohannes Meseker, Captain 168
Yohannes Sultan 3
Yonas Admassu 54
Yosef Adane 32, 80, 135, 150, 207
Yosef Mersha 346, 387, 452
Youth Leage structures 251
Youth League
    cc meeting 344
    central committee of 87
    first congress 87
    first congress of 86
    higher committees 83
    membership of 81
    provisional leadership of

85
Youth League CC 172, 180
Youth League structures xlvi, 41, 64, 70, 172, 187, 195, 234, 312, 313
Yugoslav aid 217
Yusuf, Said 282
Zeleke Jenber 471
Zenebe Sineshaw 16
Zerea Beruk 135
Zerea Beruk Sori 270
Zerihun Banti 340
Zeru Kehishen xxxiii, xxxvi, 33, 45, 63, 88, 89, 143, 206, 207, 374, 384, 386-388, 395, 398, 404, 458
Zewdu H/Micheal 340
Zewdu Kebede 339, 340
Zeweale 423
Ziad Barre 217, 221, 473
Ziad Barre regime 231, 245
Ziad Barre regime's 472